The Wise Master Builder

The Wise Master Builder

Platonic Geometry in Plans
of
Medieval Abbeys and Cathedrals

Nigel Hiscock

Routledge
Taylor & Francis Group

LONDON AND NEW YORK

First published 2000 by Ashgate Publishing

Reissued 2018 by Routledge
2 Park Square, Milton Park, Abingdon, Oxon OX14 4RN
711 Third Avenue, New York, NY 10017, USA

Routledge is an imprint of the Taylor & Francis Group, an informa business

Publisher's Note
The publisher has gone to great lengths to ensure the quality of this reprint but points out that some imperfections in the original copies may be apparent.

Disclaimer
The publisher has made every effort to trace copyright holders and welcomes correspondence from those they have been unable to contact.

A Library of Congress record exists under LC control number: 99010786

ISBN 13: 978-1-138-71582-0 (hbk)
ISBN 13: 978-1-138-71581-3 (pbk)
ISBN 13: 978-1-315-19735-7 (ebk)

According to the grace . . . given unto me as a wise master builder . . . I have laid the foundation. And another buildeth on it . . . .

Clement, *Stromateis* V.4, paraphrasing I Corinthians 3.10

Contents

Preface

When Clement of Alexandria paraphrased Paul's Epistle to the Corinthians, he was contributing to a tradition of belief that was to be perpetuated for well over a thousand years. The recurring elements of this belief were that it was the grace of God that provided the necessary wisdom for the master builder to lay the foundation for others to build upon.

Yet it was no ordinary, practical wisdom that was being referred to here but divine wisdom. Nor was the foundation that of any ordinary building, it was the foundation of the created universe itself. And of all the metaphors which might have been chosen, the act of creation is not described as the work of a thinker, bringing it about for example by the power of thought, or a commander, or a miracle-worker, or a sower, as might have been the case. It is portrayed specifically and repeatedly as the work of a master builder.

Later in the same work, Clement reminds his readers of Solomon's statement that it was Wisdom as artificer that framed the temple. In the following century, the fourth, Basil the Great likened God's creation to the foundation of a house through the gift of wisdom, piety and order. Less than a century later, in the West, Augustine extended the idea to the Church when he promised that 'the master-builder himself . . . is going to show us a house built . . . of those who have been chosen. And that house will thereafter dread no downfall . . . .' That the identification of the Creator as the divine architect was extended to his mortal colleagues is borne out by Isidore of Seville writing in the seventh century that 'architects are masons who arrange [matters] in the foundations. Whence even the Apostle says of himself, "I lay the foundation like a wise architect" . . . .' And within a generation of the rebuilding of St Martin's Abbey at Tours at the turn of the millennium, it was recorded that its sacristan Heriveus, 'with the Holy Spirit teaching him . . . described to the masons how to lay the foundation of a work without equal . . . .' Architecturally, the groundwork of a building finishes at the plinth, which is levelled off as a base for the superstructure to be raised by the team of builders. At the other end of the middle ages, a German architect by the name of Lechler wrote to his son describing how stonemasons could devise and construct their work provided they already had the groundplan. Thus from Paul's letter to the citizens of Corinth to Lechler's instruction in the sixteenth century is the idea perpetuated of the wise master builder laying the foundation for others to follow.

Manuscript paintings depicting the act of creation were already common by the thirteenth century and show the divine Creator as the architect of the universe, wielding his dividers to bring about order from chaos through the application of mathematical laws. By this time, architects were becoming identifiable from ordinary masons and other tradesmen and their names begin to survive. This is the result of them quite literally inscribing their buildings. Yet of all the locations used for displaying their names, many chose the pavement and the plinth. At Reims Cathedral, Jean of Orbais, Jean-le-Loup, Gaucher of Reims and Bernard of Soissons had their names incorporated in the labyrinth of its nave pavement, whilst the name of Jean of Chelles is inscribed across the plinth of the south transept of Notre Dame in Paris and those of Robert of Luzarches, Thomas of Cormont and his son Regnault appear on the pavement labyrinth at Amiens Cathedral. Since other locations would have been just as visible to the public, had mere self-publicity been their aim, it is as if special importance were being attached to signing the groundwork of their own creations.

Danger is ever-present, of course, in confusing interpretation with intention. Yet this picture of the wise master builder was a result, not the starting-point, of an investigation into the design of early medieval abbeys and cathedrals which eventually became a doctoral thesis. In essence, the question this posed was, as far as the middle ages were concerned, did Wisdom ever frame the temple? If so, how and what form might this have taken? It is a description of this investigation and its conclusions, many of them surprising, that are the subject of this book.

List of Figures and Plates

Figures in text

Plates

104 St Maclou, Rouen: mathematical proof, steps 7-9.
105 St Maclou, Rouen: all alignments.
106 60° rectangle containing square and 36° rectangle.
107 Smithfield Market, London: attempted alignments; part plan after Sterling (1986).

Grateful acknowledgement is given to various individuals and organisations for kindly granting permission to reproduce illustrative material as follows:
James Addiss and Stephen Murray – fig. 2a; William MacDonald and Yale University Press – fig. 4; Carolyn Malone –fig. 8; Royal Archaeological Institute – fig. 10; Abaris Books Inc. – figs 11, 13, 14, 16, 17, pl. 17; Georg Olms Verlag – fig. 12; Southern Illinois University Press and the Society of Architectural Historians – figs 15, 18; John Wiley and Sons Limited – fig. 24; Stiftsbibliothek, St Gall – pl. 1; Bodleian Library, Oxford – pl. 2; Bibliothèque Nationale, Paris – pls 3, 16; Kestner Museum, Hanover – pl. 4; Österreichische Nationalbibliothek, Vienna – jacket image, pl. 5; Domschatzkammer, Aachen – pl. 6; Musée Condé, Chantilly – pl. 8; British Museum – pls 7, 13; Archivio Capitolare, Modena – pl. 12; C. H. Beck Verlag – pl. 14; W. W. Norton and Co. Inc. – pl. 18; Ministère de la Culture et de la Communication, Paris – pls 21, 43–6, 51–6; Hanns Josef Schäfer – pls 22–26; Gebr. Mann Verlag – pls 27–34; Entreprise Georges Lanfry – pls 47–50; Yves Boiret – pls 85–90; Service Départemental de l'Architecture d'Eure-et-Loir, Chartres – pls 91–5; Linda Neagley – pls 96–105; Department of Building and Services, Corporation of London – pl. 107.

The following figures and plates are by the author:
figs 1, 2b and c, 3, 25–28, plates 9–11, 15, 20, 35–42, 106.

Every effort has been made to trace the copyright holders for figs 5–7, 19 and 22. For these and any others inadvertently missed, the publishers will be pleased to add an acknowledgement in any future editions.

Acknowledgements

One of the attractions of the early medieval period is the apparent integrity of thought of its inhabitants. Consequently one of the challenges in studying it, so as to try to understand it better, is to bring together various fields of study which in modern enquiry have become separated into different specialized subjects. Coming to this project with little more than the training of an architect, I have therefore been unusually and gratefully dependent upon the patient advice of many kind people as my investigations delved into the history of antiquity, the early middle ages, philosophy, mathematics, religion and art as well as architecture.

I am most grateful both to Eric Fernie, then at the University of Edinburgh, for his support in formally establishing this study as a research degree project as well as for his thought-provoking advice and to Roland Newman of Oxford Brookes University for his probing questions and constant quest for rigour. Likewise, I am indebted to my examiners, Paul Crossley of the Courtauld Institute and Mike Jenks of Oxford Brookes University, not only for a fair yet searching examination of my thesis, but also for their advice in developing it for publication. My thanks are also due to Edward Chaney whose astute eye directly led to the thesis being placed for publication and especially to the Getty Grant Foundation for making the publication possible.

I have also benefited from the interest and support of colleagues in the School of Architecture of Oxford Brookes University, not least in granting me the sabbatical that made this study possible and which in large part was blissfully spent in the Bodleian Library here in Oxford.

I have particularly fond memories of the Faculty and students of the Washington–Alexandria Architecture Consortium outside Washington DC where I enjoyed the stimulus, peace and freedom to work first on the thesis and then on this book while teaching there on no fewer than three occasions.

Several authorities in specialist fields have graciously given their time in reading and commenting on various sections of the text, including Cyril Barrett of Campion Hall, Howard Colvin of St John's College, Alexander Murray of University College and Bryan Ward-Perkins of Trinity College in the University of Oxford; the late John Harvey was always a helpfully stern critic as well as a generous correspondent; and I am equally grateful to David Fowler of Warwick University for reading and corresponding so frequently on Greek mathematics, to the late Edward Ironmonger who, in the early stages of this study, was most generous with his time and his library and to Allan Whitcombe, whose passing is so greatly lamented and who with characteristic and tenacious good humour explained the mathematical proofs of everything I sent his way.

In addition to this, various people have made invaluable observations in response to papers I have given at conferences during the preparation of this study, including Ludwig Falkenstein and Dietrich Lohrmann of the Historisches Institut in Aachen, Stephen Murray of Columbia University, Warren Sanderson of Concordia University, Harald Witthöft of Siegen University and Charles Stegeman of Haverford and Paris.

Since it was necessary that this enquiry remain rooted in the feasible with regard to the working practices of masons, it was helpful to be able to inspect the tracing-houses at York Minster and Wells Cathedral, which was made possible by John Toy and John Shillingford respectively, the more so since I was equipped with papers and drawings kindly provided by John Harvey. In addition to this, the conversations I was fortunate to have with John David, setter-out mason at York, and Stan Day, retired mason in Oxford, also proved most useful.

Not all of the discoveries would have been made nor building plans acquired without the help of a battery of translators and interpreters who variously provided straight translations and textual searches, doggedly discussed obstinate passages of medieval Latin or persevered in making telephone calls to continental Europe in search of the architects in charge of the buildings examined so as to obtain their drawings. For all this, I am grateful to Frank Bernstein, Richard Burgess, Margaret Curran, Catherine Gay, Bernadette Kiernan, Peggy Smith, Hubert Stadler, Anna Stefouli, Robin Stieber, Caroline Williams and Heather Yesson. It will become clear that I have also depended heavily on Michael Masi's translation of *De arithmetica* by Boethius and, for their kind permission to reproduce extended extracts from this, my gratitude goes to Editions Rodopi of Amsterdam.

For providing the drawings, often following lengthy deliberations as to relative reliability, I am indebted to Hélène Gauthier of the Ministère de la Culture in Paris for the plans of Bernay Abbey and St Stephen's Abbey in Caen; to Yves Boiret, also of Paris, for the plan of St Sernin in Toulouse; to Bernard Collette of Fontainebleau for a wealth of material on St Bénigne, Dijon; to Hans Josef Schäfer of Cologne for his drawings of the abbey of St Pantaleon; to Hans-Günter Kirklies of Hildesheim for data and advice about plans of the abbey of St Michael; to Y. Flamand of Chartres for the plan of the cathedral; to Eric Fernie once again for his plan and data of St Peter's Old Basilica in Rome; to James Morganstern of Ohio State University for his advice concerning the plan of Jumièges Abbey; to Linda Neagley of Rice University, Houston for her plans and data of St Maclou in Rouen; and to Douglas Finch of the Corporation of London for plans of Smithfield Market. Several of these people and others were equally helpful in furnishing me with drawings which appeared in the thesis but not in this book.

Once secured, each plan had to be accurately photographed for the geometric investigation and for this the fullest possible credit is due to Peter Bailey and Paul Reuter of Berkshire Reprographics in Reading, to Rob Woodward of the School of Planning at Oxford Brookes University and latterly to Leo Clarke of Original Repro in Eynsham.

Finally, I would like to thank two people to whom I owe a debt probably too great ever to be repaid fully. The first is Roland Newman again for all the years of support, both moral and material, for my research interests long before supervising my thesis. The second, above all, is my wife Vi, not only for her tireless work in processing and proofing the text but especially for sharing the whole journey.

PART ONE

Introduction

Introduction

Abbeys and cathedrals increasingly provide the focus for many of the disciplines to be found in the field of medieval studies. Research continues to expand existing knowledge and understanding of the foundations, life and work of these institutions and the ideas and techniques underlying building construction, sculpture, stained glass, painting and the associated artefacts of metal workshops and scriptoria, as well as the composition and performance of sacred music and the liturgy. Yet it remains the case that little is known for certain about how master masons actually devised the layouts of their vast structures in the first place.

Countless theories have been put forward as to how this may have been achieved, including one in which the present study partly originated.[1] This consisted of an application of a geometric system to cathedral plans, accompanied by an attempted historical justification for the symbolical use of such a system, and is similar in approach to many other design theories. However, it is an approach that has also attracted strong objections, firstly because it is claimed there is no evidence that masons used geometry in expression of theological or philosophical beliefs or that their education even equipped them to do so. Secondly, the methods of demonstrating particular design theories by overlaying plans with geometric constructions are criticized for an inherent likelihood of inaccuracy or of an ability to prove almost anything provided sufficient lines are drawn over the plan in question. Instead, a counter-claim is made that, whilst geometry was used by medieval masons, it was a purely practical procedure devoid of any symbolic intent, despite the fact that other aspects of religious art and architecture clearly do express religious beliefs. A variant of this counter-claim is that geometry may have been used in architectural planning in such a way that could correspond to sets of numerical ratios for conversion into dimensions.

At present, it appears that both positions are still being perpetuated, each in the conviction of its own validity, with work on each proceeding independently of the other and with little effective discourse taking place between the two. This may be partly explained by a possible difference in outlook in that, whilst a common objection to some design theories has quite justifiably been a lack of historical rigour, the purely academic approach sometimes appears to have difficulty in understanding design as an activity that is both visual and expressive. The starting-point of this investigation, therefore, is to evaluate and draw upon both positions in the hope of encouraging discourse and extending current thinking on the design of medieval abbey and cathedral churches.

Existing theories

Design theories posited as the basis of medieval religious architecture date back at least to the late eighteenth century, coinciding with the revival of interest in Gothic architecture among German Romantics.[2] Numerous nineteenth-century studies were included in a survey by Gwilt[3] and they have continued to proliferate, with competing theories dividing protagonists and antagonists into various camps. The purpose of this summary, however, is not to chart the course of this debate but to classify the different types of theory and, in so doing, try to ensure that this investigation benefits from the valuable work done by others. Accordingly, the main types of theory may be identified as numerological, metrological and geometrical, either separately or in combination.

Numerological

There is abundant authority for attaching meanings to numbers. Ancient civilizations commonly did so, Pythagorean number theory was transmitted successively through various transformations and there is ample biblical authority besides.[4] The specification and dimensions of Noah's Ark, Moses' Tabernacle and Solomon's Temple[5] are quoted in detail, according to Augustine and Bede, with symbolic intent. Likewise the recurrence of 7 in the Revelation of St John is mystical, not accidental.[6]

Because the letters of the Greek and Hebrew alphabets also functioned as numerals, an elaboration of number theory arose in the form of *gematria*, in which the individual digits of numbers were taken as the initials of sacred phrases.[7] This has also been applied to architectural investigations.[8] For example, certain modules construed in the layout of Chartres Cathedral, when expressed in Roman feet, have been advanced as referring to Mary, 112 feet for instance standing for *Maria Mater Dei*. However, interpretations using *gematria* were questioned even at the time it was practised among Gnostics in the second century. Irenaeus wrote:

> It is therefore more certain and less hazardous to await the fulfillment of the prophecy than to be making surmises, and casting about for any names that may present themselves, inasmuch as many names can be found possessing the number mentioned; and the same question will after all remain unsolved.
>
> *Adversus Haereses* V.30, in Hopper 64–5

In his seminal study, Krautheimer set number symbolism, supported by textual authority, beside architectural symbolism such as is evident in round and cruciform plans. Moreover, by demonstrating a correlation between the occurrence of the number 8, its recorded associations with re-birth and the octagonal geometry of baptisteries, numerology can also be seen as extending into geometric expressionism. Yet Krautheimer stops short of claiming a systematic connection, seeing instead only 'uncertain connotation dimly visible' and different interpretations sometimes made by later observers.[9] A more recent study has applied his ideas to Anglo-Saxon architecture, suggesting similar correlations for certain religious buildings with function, dedication, number theory and, once again, shape as seen in round and cruciform layouts.[10] Beseler, on the other hand, claims a mixture of Platonic and sacramental meaning for certain numbers posited for St Michael's Abbey at Hildesheim. He argues that because arithmetic is anterior to geometry and because the irrational numbers produced by geometry would have been problematic in setting out a building, it was number that was significant, geometry being relegated to a purely practical position.[11]

Metrological

Akin to this is the suggestion that dimensions were so devised that they occur in numbers that are themselves significant.[12] For example, Horn sets the dimension of 40 feet, as stated on the ninth-century parchment *Plan of St Gall*, alongside the 40 years of the Hebrews in the desert and the days spent by Moses on Sinai and by Christ in the wilderness.[13]

An opposing view is that buildings were organized solely according to the units of measure used,[14] although identifying which measures these might have been is rarely easy. With so many cities in Europe possessing their own yardsticks, each often stipulating differing values for the same unit of measure, and with evidence of royal feet and local feet in use simultaneously,[15] serious problems continue to be posed for studies in medieval building metrology. On the one hand, the identification of specific units of measure is often accompanied by uncertainty or imprecision as to their particular values for the locality, or their documented use in building construction at the time and place in question[16] while, on the other hand, analysis of the buildings often resolves itself into units of measure similarly without independent corroboration as to their likely use at that time and place.[17] The consequent lack of direct connection between design and dimension undoubtedly explains why medieval drawings were produced not only to unidentified scales but, almost without exception, without dimensions. Thus any design could be built anywhere provided an appropriate unit of measure could be assigned to it. There was simply no advantage in designing to any one particular scale. Consequently, with few exceptions, a proportional method of design, derived from geometric figures or numerical ratios, has generally been accepted as a logical probability.[18]

Geometrical

It does not necessarily follow, however, that the use of certain measures in setting out a building also determined the way in which it was designed. In times of prolonged stability and centralization in which a standard system of measures existed, monuments might well have been designed with these measures in mind, yet countless studies have shown how the buildings of antiquity in particular also embody specific geometric proportions.[19]

As for the medieval period, some studies have attempted to show how several different systems can appear concentrated in the layout of a single monument such as Cluny, St Peter's Basilica in Rome and Chartres.[20] Conant goes so far as to suggest that certain tolerances were permitted in Cluny's dimensions so as to accommodate several systems overlaying each other.[21] In addition to these studies, some highly imaginative and individualistic theories have also been advanced[22] which have nevertheless been criticized for being insufficiently realistic.[23]

Square schematism and $\sqrt{2}$

The single figure most commonly advanced is the square, whether employed in a rectilinear grid,[24] or set diagonally,[25] or in the system of quadrature in which squares are progressively inscribed and rotated within each other.[26] To these are to be added proportions directly derived from the square and its diagonal, as 1 : $\sqrt{2}$,[27] and from the double square and its diagonal, as 1 : $\sqrt{5}$.[28] In most cases, the system is put forward as being a purely practical procedure, requiring only compasses and straight-edge to generate a geometric scheme, or a peg, cord and set-square to lay out on site, without any expressive intent necessarily being claimed for it or any explanation as to why one system and not another might have been chosen.[29]

Designing to grids of squares, or *ad quadratum*, is almost certainly supported by the *Plan of St Gall* already mentioned (pl. 1) and is definitely attested by the plan of a Cistercian church in the thirteenth-century *Sketchbook of Villard de Honnecourt* (fig. 17), for its caption actually states that it is made of squares. As perhaps an extension of this, square compartmentation has been posited as a system in which squares are used as a repeating module. These generally take the form of discrete compartments, each bounded by its wall or archway.[30] One example cited is St Michael at Hildesheim once again,[31] although this has been refuted along with other examples.[32]

Most attention, however, has been concentrated on the occurrence of the square and its diagonal in plan design, namely the ratio 1 : $\sqrt{2}$. The argument in favour of this has a history spanning several generations, during which time it has acquired authority through the support of leading scholars and has amassed a great body of evidence in support of it. The attractiveness of the proposition lies in the fact that medieval masons definitely used geometry as a practical procedure and are commonly shown holding squares and compasses. Furthermore, their work did involve the geometry of the square, as indicated above, and so nothing could be more simple or convenient than choosing to proportion their work according to the side and diagonal of the square as well.[33]

The proposition is supported by documentary evidence provided by Vitruvius, who makes specific reference to the $1 : \sqrt{2}$ rectangle in planning, also by the survival of tables of numerical approximations to $\sqrt{2}$ together with the related procedure of quadrature which can be found in the *Sketchbook* of Villard de Honnecourt already mentioned and the late medieval handbooks of German master masons. Architectural evidence is provided by a great weight of building analysis which shows close approximations to various $\sqrt{2}$ permutations in Romanesque and Gothic architecture, all of which has resulted in the $1 : \sqrt{2}$ rectangle being hailed as 'the true measure' that was preferred in medieval design, 'the standard Gothic rectangle', 'overwhelmingly more popular' than other proportions because it 'arises naturally in the design process'.[34] Resulting from this, it is now stated as historical fact that medieval architects actually used $\sqrt{2}$ to generate the design of their buildings.[35]

The evidence cited in Vitruvius concerns the planning of a house, in which the side and diagonal of a square is prescribed for its atrium.[36] Two other proportions are advanced as well, namely 3 : 5 and 2 : 3, yet he does not explain why these ratios are preferred, or why one should be chosen instead of the others. Were there to be no more justification than this, it would be difficult to understand why large numbers of medieval abbey and cathedral plans should have been based on the atrium of a Roman house and why upon $\sqrt{2}$ and not the other proportions.

Other sources cited from late antiquity point to numerical tables of $\sqrt{2}$ approximations which could have enabled architects to convert an otherwise incommensurable ratio into dimensions.[37] Such a table, occurring in a second-century treatise by Theon of Smyrna, includes the ratio 12 : 17. Whilst,

$$1 : \sqrt{2} :: 1 : 1.414... \qquad 12 : 17 :: 1 : 1.416...$$

This same ratio can also be found in the *Metrica* of Heron, written in the first century BC, and has been inferred from a series of perch measures of 10, 12, 15 and 17 feet in the *Pauca de mensuris* which has been attributed to the ninth century and repeats tables of measures from the *Etymologiae* of Isidore of Seville.[38] Any assumed use of tables for this purpose, however, needs to address the question as to why a ratio, the use of which is justified as a simple draughting expedient, should be important enough to be produced instead by an arithmetical process? If it were to arrive at numerical ratios which could be translated into dimensions that reproduced this proportion, what was special about this proportion in the first place?

The assumption that medieval architects knew and used such tables is not in any case essential to the argument since Vitruvius has already been shown to specify numerical ratios for his houses, whilst elsewhere he states that the length of temples should be twice their breadth and the proportion of fora should be two parts to three.[39] Villard's *Sketchbook* also provides graphic equivalents of ratios where diagrams for cutting and setting stone or determining the splay of a window reveal are calibrated into certain numbers of parts. One shows how to set out the inclination of a spire using a template in the ratio of 1 : 8 (fig. 11).[40] The use of numerical ratios, therefore, is well attested and is important in that it opens up the possibility of an infinite range of proportions.

Vitruvius and Villard are also cited as sources for quadrature and thence $\sqrt{2}$.[41] The $\sqrt{2}$ ratio is inherent in this procedure because the sides of each rotated square equal half the diagonal of the larger square enclosing it (fig. 1a). The principle underlies Vitruvius's paraphrase of Plato's method for doubling a square of a given area (fig. 1c)[42] and appears again as a diagram in Villard's *Sketchbook* (figs 1d, 14). Above it, an architectural application is shown in which a cloister is planned so that its garden is half the area of the enclosing square (fig. 1e). Whether or not this is evidence that the square root of two, or even an understanding of square roots, existed in the mason's mind as a concept is debatable to say the least, particularly when medieval masons appear to have had scant mathematical theory.[43] Since it is generally accepted that theirs was an empirical tradition, the manipulation of squares involved in these exercises could just as easily have resolved itself into a matter of counting similar triangles, just as ancient Greeks understood the theory of figurate numbers by counting pebbles.[44] Vitruvius says as much when he describes Plato's method for doubling a square (fig. 1b):

> . . . let a diagonal line be drawn from angle to angle in the [lesser] square . . . so that two triangles of equal magnitude . . . are described. On the length of the diagonal let a square be described with equal sides. Therefore two triangles . . . will be drawn upon the diagonal in the lesser square; four triangles of the same magnitude . . . will be described in the larger square . . .
>
> *De architectura* IX.Pref.5

The corresponding drawing in Villard's *Sketchbook* certainly seems to illustrate the principle as if by counting triangles without needing to know the theory of root numbers (fig. 1c). Similarly, the marks on the cloister drawing clearly suggest that all its draughtsman needed to know was that the side of the inner square is half the diagonal of the outer square. Whereas similar consideration needs to be given to the grids overlaying his sketches of people, Villard's plan of one of the towers at Laon could be based on quadrature (fig. 12), which would place it alongside the late medieval German handbooks of Roriczer and Schmuttermayer. These set out the method for elevating pinnacles and finials by taking heights proportionally from plans which consist of squares rotated within each other (fig. 15). Following these, Lechler uses quadrature to generate other constructional details for templates. Fol. 42v shows how to derive the proportions and profiles of two mullions from one module, in this case the thickness of a wall.[45] Yet in attempting to associate quadrature with

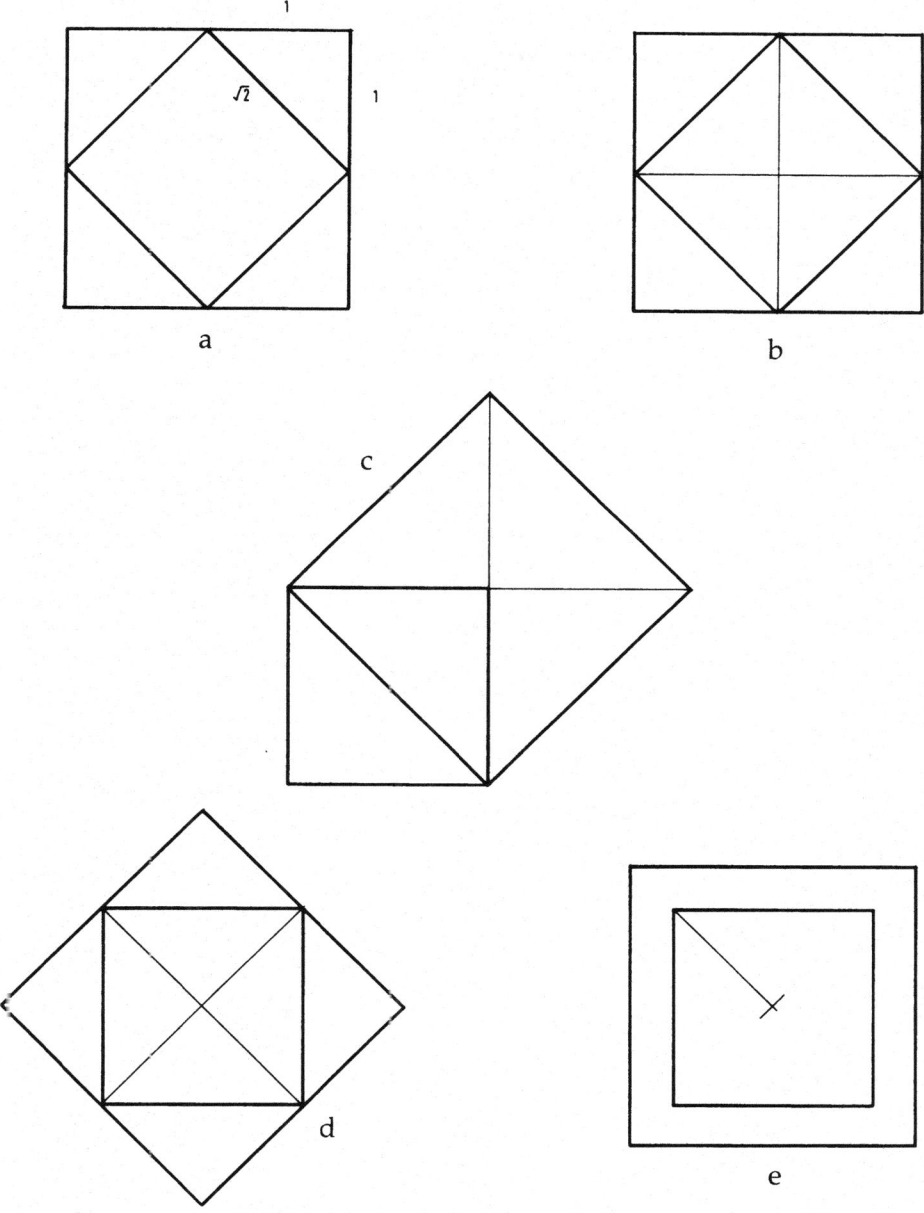

Fig. 1, a and b: Quadrature and √2, c: Doubling a square, after Plato and Vitruvius, d: Quadrature, after Villard de Honnecourt, e: Cloister plan, after Villard.

claims for $\sqrt{2}$, a difficulty needs to be faced in that the figures which quadrature produces are other squares, not $1 : \sqrt{2}$ rectangles.

The connection that is claimed for $\sqrt{2}$ through quadrature to plan design again rests partly on the cloister and tower plans in Villard's *Sketchbook*, yet this too may be debatable. There seems to be evidence for example that the use of quadrature for the individual elements of a building, such as these, might be distinct from the process of plan design, a possibility which will be explored later.[46]

On the other hand, a direct connection between the $1 : \sqrt{2}$ ratio and plan design has been advanced for Cluny III on the basis of a twelfth-century miniature of a dream. This shows Gunzo, a monk visiting Cluny, watching St Peter and St Paul setting out a new and larger basilica with rough diagonals of rope which St Stephen pays out to them (pl. 16). Since this reportedly led to the construction of Cluny III, one study has attempted to explain the proportions of its plan in terms of a line of squares rotated on their diagonal, a method which elsewhere is described as 'the generator of the dynamic and directional system underlying Gothic designs'.[47] Yet the scheme put forward only fits the plan if the width is taken to the centres of internal wall-shafts, the length to external column plinths and if the two end squares are reduced by one foot.[48] It also needs to be borne in mind that this system of extending rotated squares in a line does not in itself produce $1 : \sqrt{2}$ rectangles either and that the ropes in Gunzo's dream could be defining the diagonals of other rectangles than squares.

Turning to the architectural evidence, numerous building studies have succeeded in showing close approximations to $\sqrt{2}$ proportioning in the sections and plans of buildings dating back to ancient Greece and forward through early Christian Rome to Romanesque and Gothic Europe.[49] From such a weight of documentation, it is perhaps surprising to find that the case may not seem quite as clear-cut as might at first be thought, with some claims appearing more persuasive than others and with certain problems presenting themselves in the way evidence is accumulated. For example, the existence of $\sqrt{2}$ relations between different buildings in different cities might well be coincidental, rather than intentional, as might those between buildings drawn on a parchment plan and its uneven edges.[50]

Evidence is also compiled by including various permutations of the basic $\sqrt{2}$ ratio, some of them decidedly complex. In perhaps the most influential work on the subject, instances of up to eight different permutations are cited.[51] Since such claims are generally admitted to be close approximations to the measured building, it can be shown that some are also close approximations to rectangles defined by the angles of other geometric figures, for example 60° for the equilateral or regular triangle, 36° and 54° for the pentagon. Thus the values for $\sqrt{2}$ and $1 \div \sqrt{2}$ come to within 2.6% of tangent 54° and 36° for the pentagon, whilst $1 + (1 \div \sqrt{2})$ comes to within 1.4% of $\sqrt{3}$ for the 60° triangle. Another permutation advanced, namely the ratio of the side of a square plus half its diagonal, or $1 + (\sqrt{2} \div 2)$, has been put forward for St Gall and more recently for Amiens Cathedral, yet this also comes to within 1.4% of $\sqrt{3}$ (fig.

2).[52] In other words, any approximation to these √2 ratios greater than 1.3% or 0.7% might be closer to the angles of the regular triangle and pentagon. This is not to say that simple variants of the side and diagonal of a square should be ruled out. The side and half-diagonal cited here for Amiens is but an extension of a construction for an octagon from a square which is likely to have been known to medieval masons. Nevertheless, the complexity of other permutations which are put forward does seem to confound the original justification for √2 as a simple geometric procedure. Instead the theory seems in danger of becoming elaborated into one so versatile as to account for proportions that can equally be explained by other geometric figures. The presence of so many different proportions in buildings as complex as medieval abbeys and cathedrals is after all hardly surprising. One study of Salisbury Cathedral has found not only simple √2 relations in its dimensions to virtual exactitude, but also the golden mean, √3 and √5, along with three different grids and two units of measure.[53] To paraphrase Irenaeus, with so many proportions and systems present, the identification of those which may actually have been used in the design is likely to remain unresolved.

Such questions, however, do not remove those instances where 1 : √2 proportions have clearly been shown to exist in buildings and they are certainly numerous. Many account for the main outlines of a plan such as nave length : total length, or transept projection : nave width, or for individual bay design. The ratio is found in numerical ratios approximating to 1 : √2 and in dimensions taken sometimes to wall-faces and sometimes to pier centres. Results can point to planning grids of axis lines, or to √2 relations within compartments and bays.[54] Bays can incorporate cross-arches on one of their sides, or on the other, or on both sides, even in the same study.[55] As with the demonstration of other design theories, measuring points can vary and discrepancies can be acknowledged between a proposed scheme and the plan.[56] Yet despite the continuing accumulation of such evidence, surprisingly few studies succeed in showing the system as a complete method of design from start to finish. What they reveal, however, is how many √2 relations do occur to near-exactitude.

To summarize, whilst proof of the use of numerical ratios and quadrature is irrefutable, direct support for the use of the side and diagonal of the square specifically in plan design comes from a single reference in Vitruvius and from a substantial body of building analysis. From this, there can be no doubt that √2 relations are to be found in medieval buildings but, since other proportions are to be found in these buildings as well, it does not follow that this was how they were designed. It also needs to be asked whether the sheer quantity of such evidence in itself, circumstantial though it may be, makes it conclusive. Or does not evidence still require corroboration for it to be regarded as proof? If so, it seems premature to state as historical fact that medieval architects planned their cathedrals in this way. One final question also remains. What reason would architects have had to choose √2, or any system, as a method of design? Although it is not the purpose of this book to offer a detailed critique of the case for and against √2, these questions will be pursued later

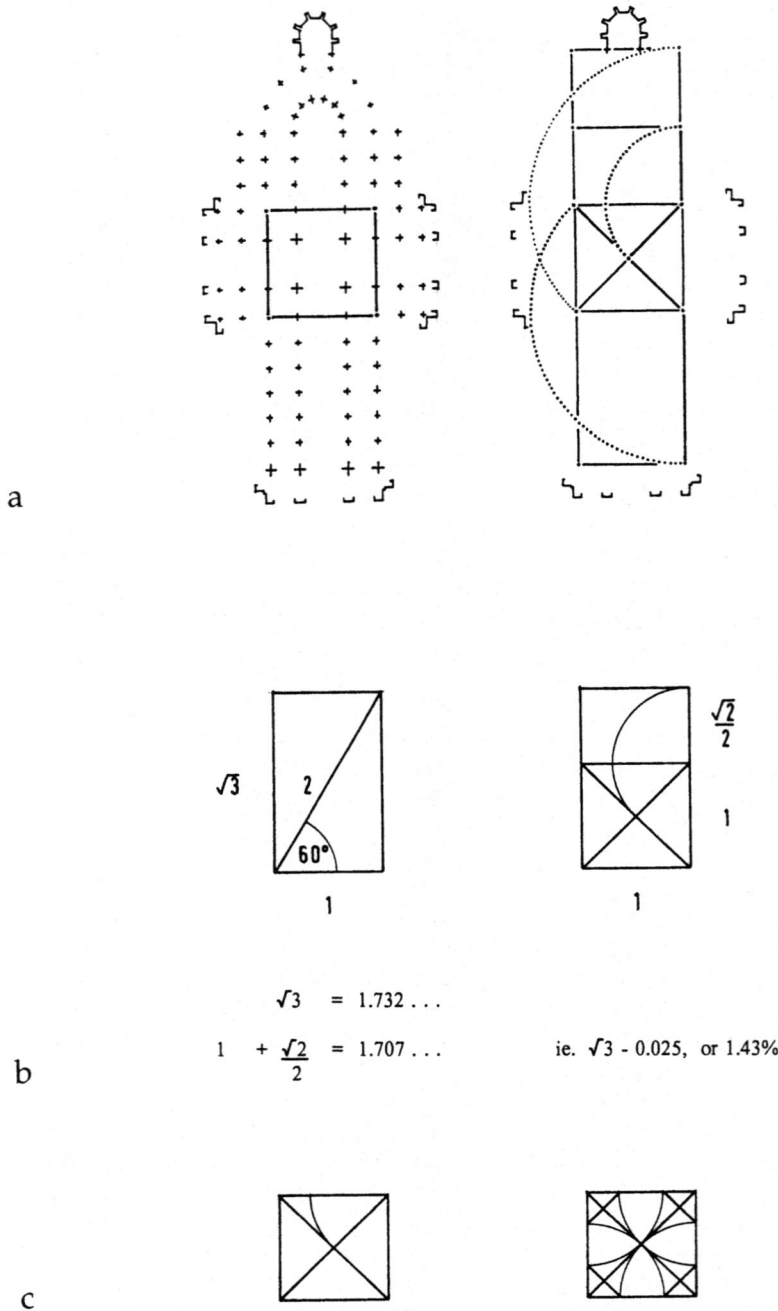

Fig. 2, a: The side and half diagonal of a square in Amiens Cathedral, after Murray and Addiss; b: approximations to √3; c: construction of an octagon from a square.

insofar as it seems relevant to the present study.

Platonic geometry

The question of meaning also arises in connection with the remaining category of geometric figures. These are the figures associated with Platonic geometry which have already been mentioned as approximating to permutations of $\sqrt{2}$, namely the regular triangle and the regular pentagon in addition to the square. Yet in noting the presence of all three in Gothic tracery, Gwilt suggests these were chosen simply because they are easy to draw.[57] The earliest studies dating back to the eighteenth century involved the square, the regular triangle and octagons. Late in the nineteenth century Dehio and von Drach took up the regular triangle although the latter only advanced it as a practical method for masons.[58] Claims have been made for plans being enclosed by the *vesica piscis*, which is the overlap of two equal circles through each other's centre, and which encloses two regular triangles, though any conscious programmatic intent has again been doubted.[59] Bechmann, in citing the common occurrence of equilateral arches and of vaulting bays composed of regular triangles point-to-point, also argues that though reference might have been made to symbolism to justify their use, the real reasons were practical.[60] The regular triangle and hexagon were considered as well as the square by Bucher, and by James in a somewhat different application.[61]

It may be seen, therefore, that not all of these authorities accept an intentional Platonic connection, although Frankl, who does, cites the square and the regular triangle but not the pentagon.[62] Lund put forward the double square and its diagonal for certain plans and the pentagon and pentagram for other plans and cross-sections. His association of the decagon with the plans of Greek temples is very close indeed to Moessel,[63] whose theory rests on the division of the circle into equal parts, mainly 5 and 10. This produces rectangles formed from diagonals at the angles of the pentagon and decagon. As it happens, virtually the same conclusions were reached by superimposing one pentagram inverted over another in the essay, already mentioned, which originally prompted the present study.[64] Nevertheless, for some reason, the pentagon has fared less well than other figures. Lesser rarely encountered it and both Lund and James consider it difficult to construct, despite the fact that Lund gives a construction known in the second century which involves just five moves starting with a square.[65] Very recently, however, the pentagon has made a reappearance in claims for the design of certain cathedral crossings and choirs.[66]

Decagons, as well as other polygons, were used in the design of chapter houses and choir chevets. In the latter, Gwilt noted a correspondence between the number of chapels or sides of the polygon and the number of bays in the nave, citing Amiens and Milan,[67] to which may be added Chartres, Reims and Bourges, possibly among others.[68]

From those supporting the symbolic connection between Platonic geometry and the design of medieval churches, Lund actually claims to have discovered its presence.[69] Although Krautheimer does not identify number symbolism as being either Pythagorean or Platonic in origin, it is nevertheless identifiable with Christian Platonism. Following his article and in the wake of Klibansky's Platonic studies,[70] Frankl also wholeheartedly upholds the link. Citing the cosmological significance of the regular polyhedra in Plato's *Timaeus*,[71] Frankl proclaims,

> . . . Plato sanctified the equilateral triangle and the square . . . The medieval esthetic, insofar as it was based on Plato, took over this identification . . . .[72]

Thus the architect of the Gothic cathedral used 'the two elementary triangles of the *Timaeus*' and although they were merely a practical expedient for the masons, they were chosen in respect to 'Plato's mythological and geometrical cosmology'.[73] The same theme was continued by von Simson, whose exposition is comprehensively Platonic and echoes Klibansky in pointing to the twelfth-century renaissance centred on Chartres and its Christian Platonism.[74] However, no proof of an actual connection has been advanced. One attempt to establish a link between scholars and architects was later refuted.[75] Beseler argues that there is no proof, Lund admits there is none for the use of the pentagon and, with von Simson's case more stated than demonstrated, Frankl leaves to others 'the necessary investigation of the buildings themselves'.[76] Treating the surviving monuments as a primary source in their own right is widely accepted,[77] more so it seems than the findings made from so doing. Yet other researchers, instead, have continued examining documentary sources and have generally concluded that no proof is to be found in them.

When it comes to doubting or denying a link with Platonist thought, it is striking how much uncertainty arises and how much the pervasiveness of Christian Platonism early in the middle ages is overlooked. Moessel grants the importance of Platonic geometry in medieval theory and practice, yet limits his theory to one originating as a 'technical system' of 'working geometry'.[78] Ackerman suggests that the choice of the square and regular triangle at Milan showed Platonic influence, yet feels that Gothic design 'is comparatively unconcerned with proportions'.[79] Frankl, having advocated Platonic geometry with such certainty, later proposes the system of quadrature as being the secret of the masons, a method purely practical, not aiming at 'mysterious calculations of beauty'.[80] Beseler speculates that the long axis at Hildesheim was determined by Platonic numbers yielding external measurements, with lateral dimensions being generated as internal measurements after conversion by an altogether different process and concept.[81] Research into medieval architectural drawings has also brought claims that there is no evidence of an overall system of proportional design nor one of symbolic significance;[82] yet what is presumably meant here is that there is no proof, for there certainly appears to be evidence, inconclusive though it may be. On the other hand, Bucher has produced much evidence for the use of quadrature as a practical operation by masons, yet in claiming it as being 'the geometric canon' he has some difficulties in reconciling the evidence with the theory.[83] He cites fol. 19v of Villard's *Sketchbook* in support of square schematism and quadrature, but ignores the previous page despite its display of all the figures of Platonic geometry.[84] However, he later seems to accept a Platonic interpretation, only to revert later still to a strictly practical reading of the evidence. In this he is supported by Shelby who, in a stream of studies related to masons' instruments, documents and treatises, consistently concludes that for medieval architects and masons the use of geometry was exclusively practical, though whether this conclusion is always fully supported by the evidence or by the argument may be open to question.[85] In his pronouncements, however, he could well have had Lund in mind, for Lund claims that:

It appears . . . that medieval church architecture is a direct continuation of the art of building classic temples, which in its turn expresses the perception of Greek philosophy concerning the harmony of the universe . . . Its proportioning was therefore established according to an irrational measure . . . as . . . appears in the pentagram, which for the Pythagoreans was the symbol of the harmonious system in the Cosmos . . . . It seems that these rules of religious architecture were a secret science in the Middle Ages . . . . through this secrecy, the rules became forgotten, and as a reflection of the ancient science there only existed in the following centuries the superstitious use of the pentagram . . . . It is this forgotten science which we have discovered . . . .[86]

Accordingly, the diagonal of the double square and its kinship with the golden section and the pentagon 'gave us the key to one riddle after another in medieval cathedral building art'.[87] To which, it might appear, Shelby replies:

To look for THE SECRET in some geometrical figure or formula, or some other even more esoteric idea, is to do a disservice to . . . medieval masons . . . .[88]

. . . the search . . . for the geometrical canons of mediaeval architecture is appropriate enough, so long as we keep clearly in mind the kind of geometry that was actually used by the masons. The nature of that geometry suggests that these canons, when recovered, will not be universal laws which will at last provide *the key* to mediaeval architecture . . . .[89]

Geometry applied to drawings

Regardless of the particular geometry being advanced, various objections are commonly raised as to the accuracy of methods used to demonstrate a particular application to drawings. Mazes of thick lines drawn over small-scale plans are unlikely to be convincing. Drawings of the plans themselves may not always be accurate representations of the actual plan of the building. The lines of a proposed geometric system may not always correspond with or intersect over significant points on a plan, or they may only do so inconsistently. This is also true of some studies relying on specific measures where some may be taken to wall or pier centres, others to inside or outside wall-faces. Some theories are potentially so versatile in their application as to be able perhaps to prove almost anything, whilst others that confine themselves to a single building beg the question of a more general applicability. Most pertinently, although many exercises may show a precise correlation between a particular system and the example tested at certain points in its layout, it is also important to demonstrate that the system can be reconstructed as a complete design method which could have been used systematically to set out an entire plan from start to finish. Finally, in the particular context of the middle ages, it may be fair to argue that a design theory is likely to be more convincing the more it can be shown to belong to its time and possess a cogent reason for being employed.

Conclusions

Arising from this preliminary survey, the following conclusions may be drawn.

- The use of geometry by medieval masons is generally accepted as historical fact.
- Its use is held to have been fundamentally symbolical by some authorities and purely practical by others.
- Various geometric proportions are present in medieval buildings, many being related to $\sqrt{2}$ and other root numbers, for which numerical ratios can produce close approximations.
- Among the geometric figures put forward are those commonly associated with Plato's cosmology although any intended symbolical expression is again disputed.
- Whereas historical justification for the symbolical use of Platonic geometry has been advanced in some of the literature, any positive connection between theory and practice has been assumed and remains to be proved.
- A systematic application of all three Platonic figures, demonstrating a complete design method from start to finish, appears to be rare, if not unknown.

- The validity of demonstrating applications of geometric systems graphically has been challenged on grounds of accuracy and plausibility.

Given the recurrence of Platonic geometry in the literature reviewed, it seems worth considering the three principal figures, the square, the regular triangle and the regular pentagon, to see if their use fits the historical context on the one hand and a sample of plans of medieval abbeys and cathedrals on the other. This will provide the basic structure for the study, in which this present introduction leads to an examination of the historical context, followed by a geometric investigation of the plans and the conclusions.

Scope and terms of reference

The purpose of this book, therefore, is to investigate whether the use of Platonic geometry in the planning of medieval abbeys and cathedrals would be consistent with the known historical context with regard to the beliefs held by the Church and the working methods used by master masons; and to investigate whether there is a correlation between the geometry as proposed and plans of medieval abbeys and cathedrals. It is intended to make the attempt in a way that takes account of various objections of methodology made in the literature.

Accordingly, it is beyond the scope of this book to examine and offer a detailed critique of other theories, notably those concerning $\sqrt{2}$, for this would require a separate study and they are not in any case necessarily to be seen in opposition. For this reason, it is regarded as important to understand how the evidence surrounding those claims for $\sqrt{2}$ may actually have related to the process of design and construction and might therefore relate to the proposition put forward here.

With so many assumptions now accepted as fact, it seems worthwhile to re-open the enquiry and engage once more in the debate about the symbolic content of medieval geometry and its possible role in medieval plan design. Given the differing positions taken with regard to the use of geometry and its Platonic content in the historiography of the question, a return to the sources is likely to prove useful, both from the middle ages and those that were available to the middle ages. Accordingly, these will be given precedence, leaving respective authors to speak for themselves as much as possible, rather than attempting to pursue the historiography of the matter. This approach has resulted in extensive quotation from medieval writings and earlier texts in English translation. To avoid making the study too cumbersome, the original Latin or Greek has generally been omitted except where a specific question of interpretation is crucial. Portions of text in translation have been italicised where this study has needed to draw particular attention to a part of a quotation.

As this book will in part be concerned with questions of arithmetic and geometry, the ambiguity of the term 'figure', which can mean either number or shape, will be avoided by restricting its intended meaning to geometric shape. Since it will be seen that the medieval study of arithmetic was chiefly concerned with the meaning of numbers, these are presented in the text as numerals where they are likely to have been in themselves significant and qualitative. Where other numbers appear to be merely quantitative and circumstantial, they are represented in the text as words. Regarding the definition of Platonic geometry, this is taken to mean that of which the regular polyhedra are composed, namely their associated plane figures of the square, the regular triangle and the regular pentagon. Consideration of the geometry of these figures will include not only their shapes but their proportions and angles as well. The equilateral triangle, being equiangular as well as equilateral, will normally be referred to as the regular triangle except where its equilateral characteristics alone are relevant. References to the pentagon and other polygons should normally be taken to mean those that are regular, unless otherwise stated. In the text of the geometric investigation, figures described as 36° rectangles and 60° rectangles refer to rectangles defined by diagonals set at those angles.

References to medieval abbeys and cathedrals should generally be understood to mean the churches of those foundations as they occur in the Latin West. Dates BC are indicated as such, otherwise AD should be assumed.

Method of approach

Part One comprises this *Introduction*, which has sketched in the background and scope of the study and continues here by setting out the method of approach.

Part Two investigates the *Historical context* and comprises Chapters 1–5. *Chapter 1* presents the case for examining the history of tenth-century Europe and continues by outlining the revival of the Holy Roman Empire under the Ottonian dynasty, including the revival in monasticism which accompanied it, together with its various reform movements and rebuilding programmes; and the revival in monastic learning, the liberal arts and writings from the classical and early Christian periods. *Chapter 2* presents a summary of classical and early Christian thought as transmitted to early medieval monasteries, which confirms the primary influence of Christian Platonism. Because it is contended here that insufficient weight has been given to this influence in much of the literature, an extended exposition is made of primary source material in translation together with evidence of its adoption in the tenth century. *Chapter 3* analyses the findings of the investigation so far, progressively focusing on received ideas concerning the status of geometry, architecture and symbolism and concludes with the development of the octagonal shrine as one example of a parallel between known metaphysical formulae and established architectural form. *Chapter 4* opens by presenting tenth-century evidence for the acceptance of the metaphysical beliefs outlined in Chapter 3, with examples of ninth- and tenth-century abbeys which illustrate how such beliefs might have been expressed. This is followed by an exploration of the architectural implications of the monastic revival. *Chapter 5* concludes Part Two with an investigation of medieval architectural practice which re-examines the documentary evidence for and against the expressive use of geometry in architectural design.

Part Three consists of the *Geometric investigation* and is set out in Chapters 6–8. *Chapter 6* outlines the terms of reference for the exercise, presenting arguments for and against the method chosen and lists a set of criteria for evaluating the test. It continues with the investigation itself in which the geometry is applied to the plans of abbeys and cathedrals dating from the fourth to the fifteenth centuries. An accompanying commentary summarizes the architectural history and findings of the geometrical test of each example, making cross-references to other examples investigated. *Chapter 7* analyses the similarities and differences between the various architectural groupings of examples and within each group. It also explores some actual and apparent coincidences between the different geometric figures and the possible inferences that can be drawn. *Chapter 8* discusses the possibility of the system being sufficiently versatile as to account for buildings that could not have been designed by it. It tests this by trying to apply the geometry to counter examples from the nineteenth century.

Part Four sets out the *Conclusions* and consists of Chapters 9 and 10. *Chapter 9* summarizes the findings of the study and extracts from these the main conclusions regarding the evidence provided by the historical record and by the investigation of the plans. It also shows how the system proposed could have been employed by medieval architects, with evidence that they might actually have done so, and concludes with a case study which outlines the whole process from design stage through to construction. *Chapter 10* examines the various inferences and implications that might flow from these conclusions, including the possible sources and subsequent history of such a system.

Notes

1 Finch.
2 Frankl 1945, 47–58.
3 Gwilt 1011–19.
4 Hopper, *passim*.
5 Genesis 6; Exodus 26; I Kings 6; 2 Chronicles 3, 4.
6 See pp. 104–5, also Bede.
7 Hopper 62–4.
8 Bannister; Michell 1973, 1975; James 107–8.

 9 Krautheimer 121–3, 131–7.
10 Gem.
11 Beseler and Roggenkamp 154f.
12 Conant 1963, 1971; Bannister; James.
13 Horn and Born, I.103.
14 Hecht; Beseler and Roggenkamp.
15 E.g. Murray 159–60.
16 See Hecht 285f, for example: in various medieval building contracts, estimates, instructions and accounts, references to foot measures occur without specifying which foot or value was meant because this would have been known to the parties concerned.
17 For an introduction to this problem, see Fernie 1978 (1): one notable attempt at a solution can be found in Moessel, while Hecht offers a detailed case study of Freiburg Minster, setting his own proposition against a comprehensive review of investigations of the monument by others.
18 Frankl 1945, 50; Kidson 1956, I.18–19, 41; Shelby 1964, 391; Bucher 1972, 37, 48–9; 1979, 10; Bechmann 1981, 199; Gimpel, 84, 95.
19 E.g. Lund; Moessel 1926.
20 Conant; Bannister; James.
21 Conant, 1963, 8.
22 E.g. Lesser; Morgan; Charpentier.
23 Branner 1958 (2), 34–5; Bucher 1968, 50n7; 1972, 42; Colvin 763; Shelby 1964, 392n25, 393n26; 1965, 247–8; Fernie 1993, 136n38.
24 Bucher 1968, 972; Horn and Born.
25 Conant 1963; Neagley; Davis.
26 Frankl 1960; Bucher 1968, 1972, 1979; Shelby 1976, 1977.
27 Kidson 1956; Conant 1963, 9, 45; Bucher 1968, 50–51; Fernie 1979, 1982, 1983; Murray and Addiss; Coldstream 34–8.
28 Lund; Cocke and Kidson 70, 72.
29 Kidson 1956; Frankl 1960; Bucher 1968, 1979; Harvey 1972; Shelby 1972, 1976, 1977; Fernie 1979, 1982, 1983; Coldstream; Neagley; Davis.
30 Bucher 1960, 94; 1972, 37; von Simson 14.
31 Bucher 1972, 37.
32 Fernie 1983, 17.
33 Kidson 1956, 37–9; Frankl 1945, 53–4, 70; Bucher 1972, 37; 1979, 10; Harvey 113; Shelby 1972, 420; 1976, 214; 1977, 74–5; Fernie 1979, 2f; 1982, 34f; 1983, 17f; Coldstream 34, 37.
34 von Simson 49; Bucher 1968, 50–51; Fernie 1990, 230; Wilson 172.
35 Coldstream 37–8; Wilson 172–3; Cocke and Kidson 62f.
36 Vitruvius VI.3.3.
37 Kidson 1990; Coldstream 38; Cocke and Kidson 92–3.
38 Kidson 1956, 112–25; 1990, 75–8.
39 Vitruvius III.IV.3, IV.IV.1, V.I.2.
40 Villard fols 20, 20v.
41 Bucher 1968, 40; Fernie 1990, 234.
42 Vitruvius IX. Pref. 4, 5; Plato, *Meno* 82f.
43 See pp. 182–4.
44 See p. 44.
45 Villard fols 19v, 9v; Roriczer, *Büchlein* and *Wimpergbüchlein*; Schmuttermayer, *Fialenbüchlein*; Lechler, *Unterweisung*.

46 See pp. 187–8.
47 Conant 1963, 7, 31; Bucher 1972, 43, 37.
48 Conant 1963, 7, 31.
49 Kidson 1956, 1.265–8, 2.30–42, 57–62, 78–9, 91–5, 102–66, 205–35.
50 Kidson 1956, 2.14, 135; Fernie 1978, 584–7.
51 Kidson 1956, 1.265–6, 2.60–170, 202.
52 Fernie 1978, 584; Murray and Addiss 64 fig. 24.

$\sqrt{2}$	= 1.414...	
tan 54°	= 1.376...	i.e. $\sqrt{2}$ - 0.038, or -2.6%
$1 \div \sqrt{2}$	= 0.707...	
tan 36°	= 0.726...	i.e. $(1 \div \sqrt{2}) + 0.019$, or +2.6%
$1 + (1 \div \sqrt{2})$	= 1.707...	
$\sqrt{3}$	= 1.732...	i.e. $1 + (1 \div \sqrt{2}) + 0.025$, or +1.4%
$1 + (\sqrt{2} \div 2)$	= 1.707...	
$\sqrt{3}$	= 1.732...	i.e. $1 + (\sqrt{2} \div 2) + 0.025$, or +1.4%

53 Cocke and Kidson 62–78.
54 E.g. Fernie 1983, 17; 1993, 92–4; Murray 1995; 1996, 40–1, pl. 45.
55 Fernie 1976, 77–8.
56 Fernie 1993, 92; Cocke and Kidson 70.
57 Gwilt 1039.
58 Frankl 1945, 48–58.
59 Gwilt 1911–16; see also pp. 154–6.
60 Bechmann 1981, 195–9.
61 Bucher 1972; James 93f.
62 Frankl 1945, 58–60.
63 Moessel 1926.
64 Finch.
65 Lesser 1957, 12; Lund 33, 130–31; James 116.
66 E.g. Wu; Shortell.
67 Gwilt 1006–7.
68 A possibility deserving of a separate study.
69 Lund xxi–xxii.
70 Krautheimer *passim*; Klibansky *passim*.
71 See pp. 45–8, *passim*.
72 Frankl 1945, 58.
73 Frankl 1945, 60.
74 von Simson 1962; see also Cowen 1979.
75 Panofsky; Shelby 1964, 389n9; see also Branner 1957.
76 Beseler and Roggenkamp 129; Lund 27; Frankl 1945, 51.
77 Hecht.
78 Moessel 1926, 5, 73; 1931, 139.
79 Ackerman 107, 105.
80 Frankl 1960, 54, 70.

81 Beseler and Roggenkamp 154f.
82 Branner 1958, 15f; Bucher 1979, 10.
83 Bucher 1968, 51, 53, 70; 1972, 38, 40; 1979; see also pp. 190–91.
84 Bucher 1972, 37, 49; 1979, 10.
85 Shelby 1964, 1965, 1970, 1971, 1972, 1976, 1977; see pp. 178, 182–90.
86 Lund xxi–xxii.
87 Lund 3.
88 Shelby 1976, 214.
89 Shelby 1972, 421, see also 1970, 24–5.

PART TWO

The Historical Context

Chapter 1

The Tenth Century

Despite the amount of attention that has centred on the twelfth century, a more fruitful period to examine could well be the tenth. During this century, a general recovery occurred under the Ottonian rulers which was accompanied by a monastic revival involving programmes of reform and rebuilding. Integral to this was a revival in learning which embraced secular as well as religious studies that were fundamentally Platonic in content, a fact borne out by some of the principal sources consulted in tenth-century monasteries. However, since the history of the tenth century is perhaps not generally as well known as that of the twelfth or thirteenth, it may be helpful to present rather more of its background than might be thought necessary for a later century.

One powerful reason for so much interest being shown in the twelfth century stems from the supremacy of the cathedral school at Chartres under its Platonist Chancellors Bernard, Gilbert and Thierry on the one hand,[1] and the seminal influence that its new Gothic cathedral was to have on the other, leading irresistibly to a link being assumed between the two.[2] Yet there may well be no evidence of such a connection by this time. As noted above, an attempt to demonstrate one for the following century[3] has not been accepted.[4] A possible reason for this is that the twelfth century marked the culmination, not the inception, of Christian Platonism, the study of which had initially been brought to Chartres by Fulbert in the tenth century.[5] And it was the tenth century which saw the widespread revival in learning led by Fulbert's teacher, Gerbert of Aurillac, later to become Pope Sylvester II.

Furthermore, plans of buildings from the next century, the eleventh, showed a strong correlation with the system of Platonic geometry that emerged from the investigation of this present study. Yet conversely, the evidence was more haphazard among earlier examples dating from before the millennium and, if the St Gall plan is at all significant, even more deficient in the Carolingian period. Quite independently, therefore, the tenth century suggests itself for examination.

The Ottonian Revival

Following the fragmentation of the Carolingian empire in the ninth century simultaneously with the depredations of Vikings all over Europe, the tenth century was reinvigorated by the new Saxon dynasty of Otto the Great and his son and grandson, Otto II and III, who between them ruled much of Europe from 936 to 1002. During this period the Holy Roman Empire was resurrected; a new ruling dynasty, which was to thrive for five hundred years in France, was founded when Otto's nephew, Hugh Capet,[6] was crowned king in 987; while in England a cultural revival continued under the heirs of Alfred the Great which also had strong European dimensions, granddaughters of Alfred, for instance, marrying Otto the Great and Hugh Capet.

After his election as the German king in 936 and notwithstanding periodic reverses, Otto the Great had by 962 brought the duchies of his German homeland under control and secured not only his eastern border, but Burgundy, Lombardy and most of Italy, as well as his own coronation as the new Holy Roman Emperor. In another ten years he gained control of the papacy and saw his own son Otto wedded to Princess Theophanou, niece of the Byzantine co-Emperor John.

The ten-year reign of Otto II, which commenced a year later, turned out to be the miniature of his father's, starting as it did with the need to pacify the German duchies again and ending with failed ambitions in southern Italy. On his premature death in 983, with his own son Otto III aged just three, his widow Theophanou and mother Adelaide ruled on the child's behalf until the fourteen-year-old took charge in 994.

Otto III appears to have been immensely proud of his Greek lineage, speaking Greek and, in emulation of his grandfather, sending his Greek tutor to Constantinople to seek a Byzantine bride for himself who, it was eventually agreed, would be a daughter of the co-Emperor Constantine.[7] The papacy was once again brought under control, Otto making his cousin the first German pope before, on his cousin's death in 999, appointing Gerbert in his place as Pope Sylvester II. Gerbert was already the young emperor's tutor and friend and in furtherance of their joint ambition to restore the prestige of nothing less than the Roman Empire itself, Otto's seal now read '*Renovatio imperii Romanorum*'. He revived titles and offices of the Roman and Byzantine Empires, referred to himself as Emperor Augustus of the Romans and set up an imperial court of his own on the Aventine hill.[8] Although Otto too was to die prematurely in 1002, just before his bride arrived in Italy, with Gerbert following him a year later, the momentum generated by the Ottonian revival continued to gather strength during the eleventh century first under Henry II, followed by the Salian emperors in Germany, the Capetian kings in France, the Normans in Normandy, England and southern Italy, and the Benedictine Order everywhere in Western Christendom.

Of particular relevance to this study is the importance given by the Ottonian rulers to gaining control of the Church and the papacy and the consequences this had for monastic growth. Following civil wars among the tribal duchies of Germany and between the German dukes and Otto the Great from 953, Otto took control of ecclesiastical appointments in order to use the Church as a counter-balance to ducal power. Thus his son William became archbishop of Mainz, his youngest brother Bruno archbishop of Cologne, then duke of Lorraine, whilst Trier's archbishop was also a kinsman.[9] Moreover, Otto promoted both William and Bruno as his joint chiefs of staff at court,[10] thereby concentrating both Church and State power in the same persons and placing them directly under his own royal control. Similarly, Otto II tried to extend his control over Italy with the aid of bishops and abbots who were loyal to him and his campaign against the Greeks and Saracens in southern Italy, unsuccessful though it was, stemmed partly from the cultivation of monasteries in the region which provided recruits for his army.[11]

Meanwhile, the papacy remained almost impossible to control, prey as it was to contending factions in Rome, but this did not prevent the Ottos from trying. When an imperilled Pope John XII asked for Otto I's aid, Otto gladly obliged whereupon John crowned him Holy Roman Emperor in 962, yet Otto made the papal territories swear an oath to him rather than to the pope. Although this caused the pope to defect, bringing Otto back to Rome to depose him the following year, the emperor used this occasion to alter the ninth-century *Sacramentum Romanorum* so that Romans henceforth were bound to secure a papal oath to the emperor's representatives prior to any papal consecration. This did little to stabilize the papacy, yet it did convert it, and therefore the Roman Church as well, into an imperial protectorate,[12] an act, however, which encouraged rather than deterred imperial appointees being deposed and even murdered by the Romans. It was after a spate of such events in 996 that Otto III arrived in Rome and chose his cousin's son Bruno as the new Pope Gregory V, whereupon Otto too was crowned Holy Roman Emperor.[13] When Gregory died three years later, the idea of the papacy as an imperial possession was perpetuated by Otto's own words,

> . . . we have elected for the love of St. Peter the Lord Silvester,
> our teacher, as we have by God's will ordered and created him
> pope . . . .

> *MGH. Dipl.* II.2, in Ullmann 113

The document in question was drawn up in 1001 and transferred various counties to Peter which the pope should 'have, hold and administer',[14] making clear that the pope was beholden to the emperor not only for his position but for his possessions too.[15] Before even being appointed as Pope Sylvester, however, Gerbert of Aurillac had been the abbot of Bobbio in Lombardy for eighteen years and the archbishop of Ravenna for two, positions which he had been using to further Ottonian policy in Italy by appointing Germans to Church lands. Indeed, once he was pope and in receipt of papal territories, he personally controlled lands on Otto's behalf stretching from Rome all the way up to the German border, enabling the emperor to travel between the two whenever he wished without ever having to set foot on territory that was Italian-held.[16]

Although Otto III had chosen to set up his court in Rome, he likewise surrounded himself with advisers who were not Italian. They were, however, all leading churchmen. Odilo was the illustrious abbot of Cluny, Bernward was Otto's former tutor and currently bishop of Hildesheim at Otto's instigation. Gerbert, it has already been seen, was both abbot and archbishop before being appointed pope by Otto and was currently his tutor too. One of Gerbert's former pupils, Heribert, was chancellor of Otto's government, abbot of Brogne and, in the same year Gerbert was made pope, became archbishop of Cologne.[17] Moreover, all these men were among the leading thinkers of the day and whilst Gerbert was the greatest teacher, the others proved to be tireless founders and builders of abbeys, with Odilo overseeing the completion of Cluny and many other monastic houses in France, Bernward directing the work of his own abbey at Hildesheim and Heribert building a new monastery at Deutz.[18] The significance for this study, which can hardly be over-stated, is that these historical personalities were among the leading churchmen and thinkers and were also monastic founders and builders, the relevance of which will become increasingly apparent. For the present, it is also important to recognise that, integral to Ottonian renewal, was a widespread revival in monasticism which also brought with it a revival in learning.

The revival in monasticism

During the previous century, the repeated attacks by Vikings across Europe, also by Saracens in the south and Magyars in the east, together with the violent break-up of the Carolingian Empire, had resulted in the near-extinction of Western monasticism. Communities were scattered, libraries destroyed, monasteries left to return to nature as burnt-out ruins. The Church lapsed into corruption and worldliness, with such monasteries as did survive often no better. Many had lay abbots whose families and retainers lived in; only monks and clerics had any letters and many of them understood little of what they read; public speaking was poor, ignorance and superstition rife.[19]

Yet as early as 909 a council of bishops met and decided to restore discipline to the churches and monasteries and this was followed by similar councils during the rest of the century. Emphasis was placed on the reintroduction of discipline which was to be informed by learning, making teaching a necessity and, by extension, the opening of monastic schools and the collecting of books. Though books were extremely precious at the time, no expense was spared in acquiring them and, once acquired, each was placed on the abbey altar in a special rite.[20]

With the monastic revival came reform, for the return to discipline meant a return to the Rule of St Benedict. This was variously implemented, since the founding, refounding or reforming of each house often arose from its own set of circumstances. Large reform movements certainly developed later as the product of concerted policy, but there were also many cases where local reform was led by individuals and bore an affinity rather than an allegiance to one of the main movements or later monastic orders. Consequently it is only possible to give a general outline of the principal trends, whilst many of the individuals, some of whom have already been identified here with the Ottonian revival, will provide crucial evidence later[21] in support of a possible programme of design for the abbeys they founded or re-founded.

In the very year after the first council met, in 910, the Benedictine abbey of Cluny was founded, its first abbot, Berno (910–27), insisting on the strictest observance of the Rule as modified by the ninth-century Synods at Aachen. This required more and more time being devoted to the elaborated liturgy of the *opus Dei* and to the teaching of novices.[22] Such was Cluny's success that, under the abbacy of Odo (927–42), it actually controlled seventeen other houses, on the death of Mayeul (948–94) thirty-seven and, on that of Odilo (994–1048), sixty-five.[23] In addition to these were many other monasteries in France, Italy and Spain that it reformed but which retained their independence.[24] During the abbacies of Mayeul and Odilo the reform was actively supported by Hugh Capet and his son Robert the Pious and before the end of the tenth century Cluny became answerable solely to the pope.[25]

Some of the first abbeys to be reformed by Cluny were, not surprisingly, older than Cluny and its intervention was not always welcome. Gerbert's own abbey at Aurillac had been founded at the beginning of the century and it was in 930 that Odo, who had earlier been its abbot, returned to reform it, only to be met with resistance by its monks. As soon as they acquiesced, Odo moved on to reform Fleury which was even older and where Benedict's remains, no less, were enshrined.[26] Despite Odo's reform, Fleury remained the more important of the two abbeys for some time, enjoying the status of sister-house with Cluny and its own independent sphere of reforming influence.[27]

One of the movements with which Fleury had relations originated in Lorraine at Gorze.[28] This was not the first centre of reform in Lorraine for one had already been established with the refounding in 914 of Brogne, where Heribert was to be abbot, and from which many other monasteries were to be reformed in Flanders and northern France.[29] Gorze however was similarly in need of reviving. Having been deserted, then sacked by the Magyars earlier in the century, its ruins were handed over in 933 by the local bishop of Metz to John of Vandières. He was joined by Einold, the archdeacon of Toul who became Gorze's superior, Anstaeus and Blidulf who were archdeacons of Metz, and several others. Heribert was later to receive his training there. Like Cluny, the Gorze reform also marked a return to the Rule of St Benedict as defined by the Aachen Synods, with emphasis placed on the *opus Dei* and a willingness to reform existing monasteries and found new ones.[30] The first new foundation was made as early as 935; in 941 the canons at St Arnulf in Metz were replaced by monks from Gorze, Anstaeus going there in 945 as abbot; and about five years later, monks were invited from Gorze by the pope to reform St Paul's Basilica outside Rome, so much had Gorze's reputation grown.[31] And just as Hugh and Robert Capet furthered reforms in France, so Otto the Great, his brother Bruno and son William personally advanced the Gorze reform, whence it spread from Lorraine into Flanders and Germany to the extent that German monasteries came to be reformed exclusively from Gorze. Despite the similarities between the Cluny and Gorze reforms, there were constitutional differences for, whilst Cluny evolved into the mother-house of a vast network of dependencies throughout England, France, northern Spain and Italy free from both secular and episcopal control, the monasteries of the Gorze reform remained within the diocesan structure of the empire, each under the control of the local bishop, their abbots even being liable for imperial service and the local magnates being entitled to send their children to its schools.[32]

By the time Dunstan was exiled from England in 955, arriving at St Peter's
Abbey in Ghent, not only was the abbey being reformed by Einold of Gorze
but fifty other houses had also undergone the Gorze reform as well. This
particular reform, together with Fleury, was also to influence the monastic
reform in England which Dunstan initiated with Ethelwold and Oswald on his
return.[33] A generation earlier Odo, not to be confused with the abbot of Cluny,
studied at Fleury before becoming archbishop of Canterbury in 934. Oswald,
who was his nephew, studied in his household, then at Fleury before being
recalled to England by Odo in 958, a year before the latter's death.[34] He was
succeeded by Dunstan as archbishop of Canterbury (960–88) on Dunstan's
return from exile in Ghent, Oswald being appointed bishop of Worcester the
same year, Ethelwold shortly after as bishop of Winchester (963–84) and
finally, whilst retaining the see at Worcester, Oswald also became archbishop
of York (972–92). On his return to England, Oswald had asked for some of
Fleury's monks to be sent to him and, having founded Ramsey Abbey in 969,
he eventually attracted Abbo, Fleury's renowned teacher, to come to Ramsey
as director of studies and generally assist in his reforms before returning home
to become Fleury's abbot. For his part, Ethelwold 'made many monasteries',
rebuilt others destroyed by Vikings and replaced secular clerics with monks.[35]
Probably in 973, King Edgar called a council in Winchester to regularize the
reform in England, by which time all three churchmen had reformed more
than thirty-five abbeys. The council, attended by monks from Fleury and
Ghent, led to Ethelwold's *Regularis Concordia*, an ordinance of new monastic
rules which acknowledges the help provided by the continental monks and
displays strong Gorzean influence.[36]

That monastic reform, even on a huge scale, was largely a matter of
individual enterprise, albeit with official support, is well attested by the career
of William of Volpiano. From his birth in Lombardy in 961, he was known
personally at the imperial court, his father having entered the service of Otto
the Great at the time Otto annexed the kingdom of Lombardy and Italy, and
at William's baptism Otto had given him the name of his own younger son
while his second wife, Adelaide, received him from the font. After studying
at various local schools and taking holy orders, he was brought by Mayeul to
Cluny around 985 where he continued his studies. Six years later, William
persuaded Odilo, who was to succeed Mayeul, also to take holy orders at
Cluny.[37] By this time, William had already presided over his own cell and had
embarked on a career of reforming other monasteries. One such request came
from Mayeul himself in 990, when William was sent with twelve monks to
reform the abbey of St Bénigne at Dijon in Burgundy. In the time it took him
to rebuild its crumbling buildings – the reconstructed church being
consecrated in 1018 – William had been invited to Normandy by its duke to
reform its monasteries, he had also created a new foundation at Fruttuaria in
his native Lombardy and, in a new twist to the reform movement, he had
been called in to reform monasteries in Lorraine of the Gorze reform,
including Gorze itself.

The consequences of these activities could hardly have been more
far-reaching or long-lasting and some of the architectural results have

provided examples for the geometric investigation of this study. In Burgundy, William's disciples built several churches including Vignory, a dependency of St Bénigne still standing.[38] In Normandy, having reformed Fécamp, a dependency was founded at Bernay, Le Bec was established, Jumièges and St Ouen at Rouen were reformed, as was St Germain in Paris, and his influence also carried to Le Mont St Michel and St Stephen's abbey in Caen. While remaining the abbot of Fécamp, he placed his own disciples in other houses – a brother from Fruttuaria as abbot of Le Mont St Michel, one from Dijon as prior of Fécamp then abbot of Jumièges and Le Mont St Michel, another as abbot of St Ouen, and John of Ravenna became first prior then abbot of Fécamp when William returned to Dijon in 1029. And just as the schools of the Gorze reform were open to children of the local aristocracy, so William founded dual schools at Fécamp and Dijon, the lay halves being open to all. William's reforms are also likely to have been carried to England. William the Conqueror was eventually to take Bernay's abbot Vitalis to Westminster, while Lanfranc, head of the abbey school at Le Bec and abbot of St Stephen's at Caen, became the first archbishop of Canterbury under the Normans and effectively chancellor of England.[39] The activities of William of Volpiano in Lombardy were no less influential. Having founded Fruttuaria, other new houses followed nearby, sometimes with William's kinsmen in charge. From here the Fruttuarian reform spread through northern Italy to monasteries in Switzerland, Austria and even Germany, numbering more than forty.[40] Finally in Lorraine, continuing turmoil in the region and worldliness in its Church late in the tenth century had weakened the effect of Gorze's earlier measures. Consequently, at the very time William was busy in Burgundy and Normandy in the earliest years of the new millennium, he was also asked by the bishop of Metz to reform St Arnulf in Metz, where Anstaeus had been abbot, then St Èvre in Toul in 1005 and in 1015 Gorze itself.[41] Here William brought in the prior of St Bénigne as Gorze's new prior with William himself ruling as abbot. Pupils of his also took charge of other houses in the district, giving him control of several monasteries there until his death in 1031.[42]

By the end of his life, William of Volpiano had founded or reformed numerous abbeys, dependencies and smaller cells totalling well in excess of forty and governing twelve hundred monks. He had personally ruled at various times, and often simultaneously, St Bénigne in Dijon, Fruttuaria in Lombardy, Fécamp in Normandy, St Germain in Paris, St Arnulf in Metz as well as Gorze and several others.[43] His influence had undoubtedly spread through Normandy to England, from Fruttuaria into northern Italy and Germany and from Metz and Gorze throughout Lorraine. Yet although he was a Cluniac by vocation and training and his reform was Cluniac in spirit, insisting as he did on strict communal observance and devotion to the liturgy and study, his many houses remained outside the institution of Cluny. Whilst they submitted to the Rule of St Benedict they did not submit to the rule of Cluny or its abbots, neither did they constitute a formal group among themselves, but followed instead their own separate destinies after his death.[44]

It can be seen, then, that a revival of Western monasticism began in the tenth century which was extremely active, widespread and accompanied by various reform movements. These, moreover, had their origins in the initiative of numerous individuals who were often well-connected and known to each other. Whilst the efforts of Odo, Mayeul and Odilo contributed to the evolution of Cluny as an international institution, other figures such as William of Volpiano could extend Cluny's customs far and wide while working outside its formal establishment. Whilst the reforms of Cluny, Gorze and Fleury can all be traced back to the provisions of the Aachen Synods and the Rule of St Benedict, they were nevertheless distinct from each other, though close contact existed between Fleury and the Gorze reform. Though the movement at Brogne was similar to Cluny's, neither affected the other.[45] Whilst Cluny's sphere of influence was centred on France, extending into Spain and Italy, Lorraine's occupied Flanders and Germany. The English reform, on the other hand, derived from Fleury and Gorze by way of Flanders. Yet the Norman Conquest caused it to be supplanted by customs that, whilst not officially Cluniac, were derived from William of Volpiano's reform in Normandy. Certainly Lanfranc's constitution for Canterbury was based on the customs of Cluny without Canterbury ever belonging to Cluny. And although William's reform in Lorraine may well have been partly Cluniac in content, it was adapted to local conditions and its monasteries remained under the control of the local bishops, just as they had following the earlier reform by Gorze.[46] Finally, although these different movements were diverse and extremely fluid, their common focus, apart from the communal life, was upon the liturgy and learning.

The revival in learning

At first sight, it might be reasonable to suppose that early medieval monasticism would devote itself to Christian doctrine rather than pagan philosophy. It has been stated for example that the Cluniac reform was 'directed against . . . the life of the mind', that abbots Odo and Odilo banned the classical poets whilst Mayeul tore profane pages from manuscripts at Cluny where he was librarian, condemning philosophy as madness. Similarly in Lorraine, John of Gorze considered himself to be without learning.[47] Yet it may be observed that throughout the hiatus in Europe following the age of Charlemagne, the dislocation in educated life had been dire but not total and a tradition in teaching had survived from the time Alcuin was Charlemagne's tutor and minister of education, of which John of Gorze was a beneficiary. This line had descended to Remi who taught in Paris, where one of his pupils was Odo, and he also restored the school at Reims. Hildebolde was another of his pupils who in turn moved to Lorraine where he taught John. At Toul, John learnt rhetoric and Church arithmetic and, on succeeding Einold as abbot of Gorze, revived education in monastic and cathedral schools throughout the dioceses of Metz, Liège and Gorze where, in his own abbey, he read the Church Fathers including Augustine's *De Trinitate*[48] and other works both sacred and secular.[49] As for his colleagues at Gorze, Einold had been versed in scripture and the humanities, Anstaeus in rhetoric, Bernacer in arithmetic whilst Blidulf was a grammarian and the best scholar in Metz. And when it came to be written by the abbot of St Arnulf, John's biography, *Vita Iohannis abbatis Gorziensis*, turned out to be one of the best *Lives* from the tenth century.[50]

It may also be fair to argue that Cluny's hostility was not to learning so much as to pagan writers and particularly Roman poets. When Odo entered Cluny he brought one hundred books with him, believing that piety needed the support of learning, and in Paris he had studied Aristotle. Yet a dream had warned him once of the dangers of reading Virgil. Even Mayeul's objection to philosophy did not deter him from becoming the librarian of Cluny which, together with other Cluniac houses, possessed works of Virgil, Ovid and Juvenal that were studied and copied there, with Homer, Virgil, Cicero and Horace all appearing in Cluniac writings. Neither did it prevent him from encouraging others to study and contribute their own writings.[51] It was accepted that, since a knowledge of Latin was a prerequisite for scholarly activity, not to mention all the business of the Church and State, Roman writers should be studied for their grammar, terminology and style so long as they were read with discretion. In so doing, however, an interest would naturally be awakened in some for the pagan world of antiquity which sometimes provoked a religious reaction.[52] Opinions were hardly more uniform in the tenth century than in any other age. When Gerbert's appointment as archbishop of Reims was disputed, the papal legate who had been sent to investigate declaimed,

> . . . the vicars of Peter and their disciples will not have for their teacher a Plato, a Virgil, a Terence or any other of that herd of philosophers.

> Leonis, *Ep.*, Gerbert 237–43, in Darlington 459

In other quarters, however, Gerbert's devotion to classical philosophy was openly applauded.

> Gerbert . . . was distinguished by learning and wisdom . . . he restored many of the learned studies of the ancient philosophers which is a remarkable attitude among the Latins after Boethius.

> *Annales Virdunenses* 8, Cantor I.803

It was a devotion, moreover, that appears to have been the rule, not the exception.

Perhaps the most compelling proof of this was the importance given to the study of the liberal arts. These had evolved since antiquity into the *trivium* of grammar, dialectic and rhetoric, and the *quadrivium* of arithmetic, music, geometry and astronomy. However, this was no mere curriculum of subjects to fill a school timetable but *ways* of perceiving truth and the view that was taken of it was Platonic, albeit as seen through Christian eyes.[53] The transmission of the liberal arts to the Latin middle ages occurred from the middle of the fourth century to late in the sixth when a succession of Latin authors advocated their pursuit through commentaries, encyclopedias and treatises on all or most of their subjects. Prominent among these was Chalcidius's commentary and part translation of Plato's *Timaeus*, Macrobius's *Commentarii in Ciceronis Somnium Scipionis* and Martianus Capella's *De nuptiis Philologiae et Mercurii*.[54] Augustine planned handbooks on all seven liberal arts and, although these were never accomplished, his writings nevertheless convey much of their content which, most important of all for this study, secured their acceptance by the Latin Church. Boethius wrote treatises on virtually all of the arts having advanced a logical order for their study, whereupon Cassiodorus effected their introduction into Benedictine monasticism with his *De institutione divinarum litterarum* and *De artibus ac discipliniis liberalium litterarum*.[55] In the early decades of the next century, Isidore of Seville incorporated Cassiodorus's curriculum into his own influential *Etymologiae sive origines*, the first three books of which amount to a compendium on the liberal arts for schools, which was shortly taken up by Bede.[56] And when in turn Alcuin joined Charlemagne's court in 782, immediately becoming master of the palace school and tutor to the entire royal family, charged with re-introducing learning into France, Charlemagne's biographer could state that:

> [Charlemagne] paid the greatest attention to the liberal arts . .
> When he was learning the rules of grammar he received tuition
> from Peter the Deacon of Pisa . . . but for all the other subjects
> he was taught by Alcuin . . . .
>
> Einhard, *Vita Caroli* III.25

At St Gall all seven of the liberal arts were taught and many *trivium* schoolbooks and manuscripts on all the *quadrivium* subjects are still preserved. Thus when the revival in learning in the tenth century brought with it secular studies in the liberal arts, this was very much a resumption, if not a continuance, of a tradition. It will be shown that they were taught by the leading teachers of the day at the most important schools,[57] with the result that copies and adaptations of Boethius's *quadrivium* treatises survive all over Europe in numbers too great to be catalogued here.[58] Moreover, this teaching was often accompanied by a regard for the classical learning in which the liberal arts were rooted. Bruno, the brother of Otto the Great, who was also held to be the leading scholar in Germany, introduced the liberal arts to Otto's court and attracted the best Greek and Latin scholars to his own school in Lorraine where he was proficient in Greek himself. Around the time of Theophanou's arrival from Byzantium as the bride of Otto II, more Greeks settled in Lorraine with several communities in and around Toul.[59] Otto III, it has already been noted, was half Greek and spoke Greek. In accepting his invitation to be his tutor, Gerbert replied,

> . . . I do not know what more evidence of the divine there can be than that a man, Greek by birth, Roman by empire, as if by hereditary right seeks to recapture for himself the treasures of Greek and Roman wisdom . . . .
>
> *Letter* 231, in Hill 33–4

Gerbert is particularly important to this study in showing how an education in the liberal arts was valued by the leading churchman and teacher of his day. Soon after he was sent as a boy to the local abbey school at Aurillac, the count of Barcelona, who was visiting the abbey in 967, agreed to take Gerbert back to Catalonia. It was at this time that Catalonia's vast Moorish neighbour led the civilization of Europe, with Cordoba the greatest city in the West. Whether or not Gerbert visited this city, he was to become the first European to introduce a version of Arabic numerals to the Christian West. At the time, however, he studied mathematics under the bishop of Vich and possibly at St Maria at Ripoll as well, which was a leading abbey school further up the Ter from Barcelona and Vich, where the liberal arts were also taught.[60] In 970 his bishop took him to Rome where Gerbert met the pope who introduced him to Otto the Great. Rather than accept Otto's invitation to teach the young Otto, however, Gerbert chose instead to complete his own studies in dialectic in Reims. Here he soon began teaching the other liberal arts and, on becoming the head of the cathedral school, he revised its curriculum by adopting Cassiodorus's plan for the liberal arts, as well as collecting Boethius's works whenever he could. The archbishop of Reims was Adalbero, the most powerful ecclesiastic in France, who had been brought up as a disciple of John of Gorze at his abbey.[61] Thus the two men formed a bridge between the Cluniac and Gorze reforms, with Gerbert becoming the archbishop's secretary and, when they secured the election in 987 of Hugh as the first Capetian king of France, Gerbert also became Hugh's principal secretary and tutor to his son Robert. Two years after Adalbero died in 989, Hugh also made Gerbert the new archbishop of Reims.[62] Yet life in the tenth century was still extremely turbulent and uncertain. After Otto II had created him abbot of Bobbio in 980, Gerbert became so unpopular with its monks that when Otto died in 983, Gerbert was forced to withdraw. During a war between the duke of Lorraine and Hugh, when the duke laid siege to Reims in 989, Gerbert found himself obliged to take charge of the city and the archbishopric before having to flee to another city. Seven years later, with his own position as archbishop in dispute he took his case to Rome, unsuccessfully, and when Hugh Capet died the same year, once again Gerbert was forced to flee, this time to Germany to enter the service of Otto III.[63]

The clamour of the times is all too apparent in his surviving correspondence yet so is the thriving and industrious life in the monasteries and Gerbert's own dogged commitment to teaching and book-collecting. Three or four times between 978 and 980 he wrote to a monk at Fleury to explain Boethius's *De arithmetica* and *De musica*, as well as the use of the abacus and the value of studying numbers.[64] Practical demonstrations of theory were important to his teaching. His use of Arabic numerals arose from improvements he made to the abacus and, to demonstrate the movement of the stars, he constructed a working model using a sphere and wires.[65] This resulted from his proposed division of philosophy and the *quadrivium* into theoretical and practical branches, following the Arab approach, an attempt, however, that was otherwise shunned by his contemporaries in the Latin West.[66] Indeed, later in the eleventh and twelfth centuries he was to be suspected in some quarters of wizardry for his dabbling in Arab science.[67] Nevertheless, at the time, his lessons were enthusiastically received by numerous pupils who went on to become abbots and bishops, founding new cathedral schools or joining existing ones in France, Flanders and Germany. Besides Robert who became king of France, may be mentioned Heribert who was archbishop of Cologne and Otto III's chancellor; Adelbald who was secretary to Otto III's successor, Henry II; Richer who wrote *Historiarum libri quatuor*, a history mainly of France inspired by and dedicated to Gerbert;[68] and Fulbert who took charge of the school at Chartres in 990, presiding as bishop from 1006 to 1028, and laying the foundations of the school's pre-eminence in the twelfth century as the centre for the study and teaching of Christian Platonism.[69]

Gerbert's letters are also much concerned with the collecting of books both specified and unspecified.[70] Of those named, the range is wide, covering works Christian and possibly Arabic;[71] Platonist, as in his request for Cicero's *Somnium Scipionis* and Macrobius's *Commentarii* on it;[72] as well as Roman history. The majority, however, relate to the subjects of the *quadrivium* and may be typified by extracts from two letters.[73] The first was written to Adalbero in 983 when Gerbert was still in residence at Bobbio:

> Procure the *Historia* of Julius Caesar from the Lord Adso, abbot of Montier-en-Der, to be copied again for us in order that you may have whichever are ours at Rheims, and may expect ones that we have discovered, namely eight volumes: Boethius *De astrologia*, also some beautiful figures of geometry, and others no less worthy of being admired . . .
>
> *Letter* 15, in Lattin 54

The *astrologia* is thought to be Boethius's *De astronomia*; the reference to geometry may have been to another of his discoveries in Bobbio's library, the *Codex Arcerianus*. This is a compilation of various extracts on geometry, mainly practical, by a group of Roman surveyors on which Gerbert partly based a treatise of his own.[74] However, when agents evidently found a copy later of Boethius's *De geometria*, he had this introduced to the curriculum.[75] Five years later and back in Reims, having been hounded out of Bobbio, Gerbert wrote secretively to a monk there:

You know with what zeal I am everywhere collecting copies of
books. You know also how many copyists there are here and
there in the cities and countryside of Italy. Act, therefore, and
without confiding in anyone, have copied for me at your
expense M. Manlius *De astrologia*, Victorius *De rhetorica*, and
Demosthenes *Optalmicus*.

Letter 138, in Lattin 168

Yet of all the authors both of interest to Gerbert and of importance to this
study,[76] it is Boethius for whom his regard – and that of Otto III – is clear
from Gerbert's own verses:

> . . . you Boethius Severinus . . . were equal in intelligence to the
> Greeks for the brilliance of your scholarship . . . Now the
> ornament of the Empire, Otto III, who gives great emphasis to
> the highest arts, has judged you worthy of his court and has
> perpetuated the monuments of your labor forever, suitably
> rewarding our noble talents.

Elogium Boethii 474-5, in Erdmann 99–100

> Now Otto comes, the power of Rome to raise.
> And to Boethius' name renews the praise.
> Thy picture in the Emperor's hall is hung.
> For ever now be thy merit sung.

Gerbert, *Epigramma* 294–5, in Southern 171

Attention has so far been concentrated on secular studies, partly in order
to dispel any doubts as to their presence in the monastery schools and partly
because it may be more readily taken for granted that monasteries also set
their monks to study scripture, Church history and canon law. A more
rounded picture of the contents of a monastic library, for instance, may be
gained from a poem of Alcuin's in which he lists many of the authors to be
found on the shelves at York where he was master of the school and librarian
before joining Charlemagne's court:

> There shalt thou find the volumes that contain
> All of the ancient fathers who remain;
> There all the Latin writers make their home
> With those that glorious Greece transferred to Rome,
> The Hebrews draw from their celestial stream,
> And Africa is bright with learning's beam.

Alcuin, *Versus de sanctis Eboracensis ecclesiae* 1535–61, in West 35

There follows a roll of over forty authors, among whom are Romans, both pre-Christian and early Christian, as well as fathers of the Greek Church, including Basil, although it is thought that at York these may have appeared in Latin,[77] hence the reference to writers of 'Greece transferred to Rome'. Among the authors of interest to this study, in addition to Basil, were to be found Ambrose, Victorinus and Augustine together with Boethius and Cassiodorus.[78] Nor is it surprising perhaps that in the very first lines of Alcuin's poem there should appear the doctors of the Latin Church, Jerome, Ambrose, Augustine and Gregory. Of these, Alcuin placed Augustine first and, in the transmission of Platonic thought, second only to Augustine was Boethius.[79]

Alcuin's list, however, should not be taken as typical. York's library was superior to any in Britain and to many in Europe at the time[80] and whatever may be true of the eighth century was certainly not necessarily true of the tenth. Nevertheless, the greatest monastic libraries of the tenth century regularly owned as many as five hundred books or more. At St Gall, which had been reformed by Gorze on Otto I's orders around 963, the library contained Augustine and Boethius as well as schoolbooks in the liberal arts; and it is hardly surprising to find the writings of Augustine recorded at Cluny among scriptures and the early fathers.[81]

But tenth-century letters also embraced the writing of new manuscripts. In addition to treatises on the subjects of the *quadrivium* by such as Gerbert and Abbo, are the *Histories*, for example, by Widukind on the Saxons, by Richer on the French late in the century and by Glaber, pupil and biographer of William of Volpiano, towards the middle of the eleventh.[82] Most, if not all, monasteries maintained their own annals, with Hildesheim producing several and John of Ravenna compiling St Bénigne's in the eleventh century,[83] to mention just two centres of interest to this study. Most leading figures were the subject of biographies. In addition to Otto I and Gerbert, whose lives are broadly recounted in the *Histories* of Widukind and Richer respectively, numerous individual *Lives* were written including one by John of Metz on John of Gorze, Gerard of Brogne's by an unknown author and Odo's by another John, whilst Odilo completed Mayeul's, Thangmar Bernward's and Glaber wrote William of Volpiano's.[84] Poems and plays also contributed to tenth-century literature, notably those of Hroswitha. Gandersheim, which she entered as a nun in the middle of the century, enjoyed close connections with the Ottonian court. It was founded by an ancestor of Otto I and its abbesses were generally drawn from Saxon royalty and its nuns and canonesses also of noble birth. Gerberga, who was abbess during Hroswitha's time was Otto's niece and was schooled at St Emmeram in Regensburg.[85] It was she who persuaded Hroswitha to compose her poem *Gesta Oddonis* which she dedicated to Otto and his son. For her own part, Hroswitha was probably related to the royal family and may have attended court at an early age. Several of her plays were possibly read at court and were copied in the eleventh and twelfth centuries. Among her output is a cycle of six, three of which enact the battles between flesh and spirit, the other three the sufferings of the early Church under the Romans. In one from each group, *Conversio Thaidis meretricis* and

Passio sanctarum virginum Fidei Spei et Karitatis respectively, the drama is unexpectedly suspended to admit a substantial discourse on the *quadrivium*, citing Boethius's sequence of subjects and summarizing material that appears in his treatise *De arithmetica*. Given Bernward's own connection with Otto's court and the location of Gandersheim within his own diocese, he is also likely to have been familiar with Hroswitha's writings.[86]

Another important part of the intellectual activity of monasteries in the tenth century was the dissemination of knowledge by the copying of texts, which was widespread and included Cluny, Corbie and St Gall, as well as St Bénigne where many copyists were maintained by William.[87] Ninth- and tenth-century copies of Boethian texts alone are recorded all over Europe, as noted above, including such influential centres as Bernward's abbey at Hildesheim, William's at Dijon as well as Cologne, St Gall, Paris and Tours among many others.[88]

The production of Gospels and other religious works was no less vigorous and reached the highest standards of design and technique. The Winchester School of illumination flourished under Ethelwold, with his *Regularis concordia* and *Benedictional* dating from between 971 and 984 and the *New Minster liber vitae* following early in the next century.[89] The *Aachen Gospel Book* was produced at Trier around 1000 and shows Otto III betwixt heaven and earth in glory.[90] These and other contemporary manuscripts will be examined later,[91] for it can be shown that much cosmological imagery is to be found among their miniatures, portrayed by a combination of geometric and architectural symbolism which, set beside the numerological interventions in Hroswitha's plays, provide further evidence not only of the Platonist basis of Christian thought at the time but a desire to express it.

Conclusion

The relevance of this part of the enquiry stems from two suggestions, both related to each other, that arose from the review of different theories in the Introduction. The first is that the application of geometry to architectural design was in expression of metaphysical beliefs and the second is that these were fundamentally Platonic in content.

A common objection to the first suggestion, it may be recalled, is that no connection between scholars and architects is known whereby the transmission of such ideas might have occurred.[92] In considering this objection, the tenth century may now perhaps be seen as a more profitable period to investigate than a later one, because it was during this century that Ottonian rule brought about a general revival in Western culture. Integral to this were both a reform in monasticism and a resurgence in learning, in which a pervasive element of Christian teaching was Platonist. This revival in monasticism, moreover, involved a network of leading individuals who were themselves educated and extremely active, generally known to each other and often operative at the highest levels of Church and State and so it is entirely possible that, in these individuals, the functions of scholar and architect may have at least sometimes occurred in one and the same person.

Before pursuing this possibility, now that a preliminary glimpse has already been gained into the nature of tenth-century thought by discovering what was read and collected in the monasteries and valued enough to be copied, it will perhaps be useful to investigate more fully the Platonic basis of these beliefs and how they came to be transmitted to the Latin West.

Notes

1 Klibansky 28, 75; Knowles 113, 132–3; Copleston 1972, 87–90.
2 von Simson *passim*; Cowen 13–15.
3 Panofsky.
4 Branner 1957; Shelby 1964, 389n9.
5 Copleston 1972, 64–5.
6 *Hist. Litt.* VI.304–5.
7 Brooke Z. 61; Lattin 377.
8 Brooke C. 171; Brooke Z. 61; Ullmann 113, 133.
9 Brooke Z. 43–4; Bergman 3–4.
10 Barraclough 1969, 83.
11 Brooke C. 167; Barraclough 1962, 59.
12 Ullmann 103–5.
13 Brooke Z. 59.
14 Schramm 141.
15 Ullmann 117.
16 Barraclough 1962, 60.
17 *Hist. Litt.* VI.43; Barraclough 1962, 60; Heer 43; Hill 56; Darlington 475.
18 Sackur II. 372–80; Beseler and Roggenkamp 114; Hallinger 105, 120.
19 *Hist. Litt.* VI.5, 6; Sackur II.369; *Hist. Litt.* VI. 4–10.
20 *Hist. Litt.* VI.18–20, 6.
21 See p. 158–66.
22 Brooke Z. 115; Sackur I.62; Brooke C. 242–4.
23 Hallinger 774.
24 Evans 4; Brooke Z. 116; Focillon 85.
25 *Hist. Litt.* VI.20–1; Brooke C, 246.
26 Sackur I.89–91; Darlington 457.
27 Sackur I.140; Klukas 95, 97; Fichtenau 15.
28 Klukas 97.
29 *Hist. Litt.* VI.20, 43; Sackur I.121–7.
30 *Hist. Litt.* VI.24–6; Sackur I.146, 150–53; Hallinger 51–3, 120; Brooke Z. 116; Klukas 97.
31 Hallinger 58, 67, 76.
32 Brooke Z. 116; Hallinger 55–8, 103, 744.
33 Hallinger 79; Klukas 82–3.
34 *Chronicon abbatiae Rameseiensis* I.6, 17, 18; ODCC 1015.
35 *Hist. Litt.* VI.36; *Chronicon abbatiae Rameseiensis* I.22; ODCC 1; *Anglo-Saxon Chronicles* 128.
36 Klukas 83–4, 91–2; Yorke 4–5.

37 Chevallier 5; Williams 523, 540.
38 Sackur II.390; see pp. 150, 218–19.
39 Sackur I.257–61; II.45–52; Chevallier 111, 150; Williams 535–7; Herval 40–42; Grodecki 26–7; Knowles 85, 98.
40 Sackur II.203–6; Williams 537.
41 Sackur II.118–25; Grodecki 25.
42 Sackur II.126–31; Hallinger 59, 68, 461, 463, 836–7.
43 Williams 535–6.
44 Grodecki 26, 28; France 502, 505.
45 Sackur, I.121, 140; Klukas 97.
46 Brooke Z. 117–18; Grodecki 26; France 506.
47 Focillon 89; Olleris 25; Sackur II.337, 358–9.
48 See p. 65.
49 *Hist. Litt.* VI.22, 25–6, 50, 65; Krem 233; Sackur I.46.
50 Olleris 20; *Hist. Litt.* VI.24, 27, 61; Hallinger 105.
51 *Hist. Litt.* VI.22, 44; Sackur I.46–7; II.328-30, 337; Chevallier 44.
52 *Hist. Litt.* VI.46, 49–50; Sackur II.330; Fichtenau 290, 292.
53 Chadwick 1981, 72-3.
54 See pp. 46–9, 62–4.
55 Martianus 127; West 18; see pp. 77–9.
56 Wagner 21; Huntsman 75; West 26, 30–1.
57 See p. 138.
58 Patch 4, 37–8; Ullman 267–9, 282–3; Masi 58–63.
59 *Hist. Litt.* VI.304; Dobson 146; Fichtenau 296; *Hist. Litt.* VI.29, 57.
60 Darlington 460; Brooke Z. 113–14; Cantor I.798; Darlington 462; Smith 75; Lattin 3; Focillon 92.
61 Heath 1921, I.365f; Darlington 463; Lattin 5, 9; Olleris 13.
62 Hill 31; Heer 39; Brooke Z. 105.
63 Brooke Z. 105; Lattin 7, 11–15.
64 Gerbert, *Letters* 3–7.
65 Smith II.75; Grant 14.
66 Richer, *Hist.* III.59,60; Lattin 155nl; see also Shelby 1972, 402–3.
67 Ball 138; Smith I. 195–6; Focillon 131.
68 Darlington 464, 473; Gow 14.
69 Knowles 94; Copleston 1972, 64–5.
70 Gerbert, *Letters* 14, 15, 25, 32, 33, 47, 88, 92, 118, 124, 132, 138, 175, 233.
71 Gerbert, *Letters* 25, 32.
72 Gerbert, *Letter* 92; see also pp. 62–4.
73 Gerbert, *Letters* 15, 138.
74 Lattin 54n4, 55n5; Heath 1921 I.365f.
75 Cantor I.811; Ball 136f.
76 See pp. 90–91.
77 West 36.
78 See pp. 56–9, 64–6, 77–9.
79 West 91; Klibansky 4, 23.
80 West 34.
81 Fichtenau 288; Hallinger 187; Patch 38; Sackur II.329.
82 Darlington 464; France 499–501.
83 Beseler and Roggenkamp 168; Sackur II.356.
84 *Hist. Litt.* VI.27, 61; Sackur II.341; Hill 48; France 499–500.

85 See pp. 145, 151.
86 Dronke 55–6, 75, 83, 294n11; Hroswitha/St John ix, xvi; Erdmann 97; Hroswitha/Tillyard 76-81; 106–8; Beseler and Roggenkamp 138; see p. 145.
87 Sackur II.329; *Hist. Litt.* VI.42; Patch 38; Chevallier 152.
88 Masi 37, 58f; Pingree 168; Ullman 267–9, 282–3; Masi 58–63.
89 Baker 268, pls.XXVI, XXVIII; White 1978, 65.
90 Holländer 128–45.
91 See pp. 153–7.
92 Shelby 1970, 14–15.

Chapter 2

Classical and Early Christian Sources

Platonic thought succeeded in being transmitted to the Latin middle ages to the extent that it was because it was largely compatible with Christian belief. It became, as a result, a pre-eminent influence early in the middle ages. Taking the form of Christian Platonism, its teaching of the significance of number and the maintenance of harmony through correct proportion was rational, detailed and definite. To confirm this, the principal sources of Christian Platonism, as far as the West is concerned, will be set out chronologically. Although its presence and influence are well enough attested, an extended exposition of the Platonic tradition is offered here because insufficient weight seems to be given to it in much of the literature that challenges a Platonic connection with architectural design.

Pythagoras and Plato

It might seem surprising that Pythagoras (c.569–500 BC) should have had any influence at all on Christian thought, still less a strong influence. Yet early Christianity, especially in Alexandria, was to embrace many of the ideas and methods of classical philosophy to the point where some of the tenets of the Pythagoreans would still be recognizable as almost Christian by modern believers. For instance, the doctrine of metempsychosis presupposes an after-life. The human body, living in a state of guilt and uncleanliness, is the temporal prison of the soul which requires purification as a preparation for the after-life.[1] It was due partly to this inherent compatibility, strengthened in time by its development by Plato and its subsequent adaptation by the early fathers of the Church, that Pythagoreanism came to make its contribution to early medieval thought, particularly with regard to the teaching of number and harmony.

Pythagoras's classes at Croton in southern Italy virtually constituted a secret sect, severely ascetic[2] and steeped in number theory. According to Aristotle,

> [Pythagoreans] reduce all things to numbers ... they construct the whole universe out of numbers ....
>
> *Metaphysica* 1036b, 1080b, in Fowler 302

They did so by interpreting numbers and assigning particular qualities to them. Accordingly,

1 =   mind, being, unity, the generator of numbers

2 =   opinion and, later, female

3 =   whole and, according to Aristotle, male

4 =   justice, as in the squaring of accounts, and the *tetract* (see below)

5 =   marriage, the first sum of female and male, even and odd

6 =   creation according to later tradition, i.e. the product of female and male

7 =   opportunity, right proportion, due measure; this came to be known as the mystical number of the Pythagoreans

8 =   friendship, love, according to later tradition

10 =   perfection, health, harmony. Presumably as the offspring of the decagon, the pentagram became the Pythagoreans' emblem signifying health.[3]

Fundamental to Pythagorean theory were the first 4 numbers because,

1 + 2 + 3 + 4 = 10, the number of perfection.

This was known as the *tetract* and, according to Aristotle, the Pythagoreans represented it as an arrangement of pebbles on the ground:

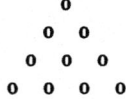

It was regarded as the essence of Pythagorean lore and the source of all things.[4] For example, by observing the fingering of a lyre, Pythagoreans discovered the musical intervals, which are composed of the first 4 numbers. Thus,

1 : 1 = unison

1 : 2 = diapason, or octave

2 : 3 = diapente, or a fifth

3 : 4 = diatessaron, or a fourth,

although only the diapente and diatessaron ratios were initially recognized by the Greeks.[5] The essential nature of the *tetract*, together with its incorporation of the musical ratios, is conveyed by Iamblichus as late as the fourth century:

What is the oracle of Delphi?
The tetractys; that is, the harmony in which the sirens sing.

De vita Pythagorica 85, in Burkert 187

The *tetract* was also understood by Speusippus, who was Plato's nephew and successor at his Academy, as containing the 4 elements of geometry:

1 = point
2 = line
3 = surface, the minimum number of sides for a plane being 3
4 = solid[6]

As an extension of this was the view that the universe embraced 4 elements which were each assigned one of the regular solids, although there is still some uncertainty as to how far the Pythagoreans developed this.[7] One explanation for such uncertainty may be the secrecy surrounding the sect, although this in itself may have been more apparent than real, arising perhaps from the oral tradition of teaching among Pythagoreans together with the difficulty outsiders may have had in grasping their doctrines. Nevertheless, about thirty years after Pythagoras died, Hippasus is said to have drowned at sea apparently for his impiety in revealing the fifth solid, the dodecahedron, as the sphere with the twelve pentagons and for claiming to have constructed it.[8] Not for another one hundred years, in about 370 BC, would the first Pythagorean treatise appear. This was produced by Philolaos who came from Croton.[9] Dealing with the elements, he wrote,

> . . . there are five bodies in the sphere, the fire, water, earth, and air in the sphere, and the vessel of the sphere itself making the fifth.

Stobaeus *Eclogarum* I, proem. 3, in Heath 1921, I.158

Plato (c.429–347BC) acquired a copy of this and was taught by another Pythagorean, Archytas. It was Archytas who developed the curriculum of arithmetic, geometry, music and astronomy. The Pythagorean content of this was brought from Italy by Plato who gave it special importance in his Academy[10] long before it became formalized as the *quadrivium* of the liberal arts. When Plato's work came to be revived later in Alexandria, early Christians were presented with a view of the universe and its creation in which the substance of the Deity issued in 3 persons consisting of God, the Creator and the Soul of the World,[11] where the Creator was benevolent and intelligent, the universe alive and the human soul immortal. It was a view understandably congenial to them.

Other integral themes recurring in Plato's Dialogues were the relationship between the world-soul of the universe and the individual soul of the human, together with the intelligible world of Forms as the unchanging model of the changing world as perceived by the senses.[12] And whilst the Pythagoreans had taught that all is number, inscribed over the portals of Plato's Academy in Athens was said to have been the injunction, 'Let no one who is not a geometer enter'.[13] Though arithmetic expresses whole numbers and fractions with precision, only geometry precisely defines such incommensurable ratios as π and ϕ. Thus geometry complements arithmetic. Yet when Plato distinguished between the sensible world and the intelligible, he did so in *Philebus* by alluding to the abstract forms of geometry:

> I do not mean by beauty of form such beauty as that of animals or pictures, which the many would suppose to be my meaning; but, says the argument, understand me to mean straight lines and circles, and the plane or solid figures which are formed out of them by turning-lathes and rulers and measurers of angles; for these I affirm to be not only relatively beautiful, like other things, but they are eternally and absolutely beautiful . . . .
>
> *Philebus* 51C

The Dialogue in which Plato brought all these ideas together is *Timaeus*. In its own day, its teachings were regarded as Pythagorean in origin and it would be difficult to exaggerate its influence upon medieval thought. Besides countless commentaries on it, which were written throughout late antiquity down to twelfth-century France and beyond, and the numerous works it inspired and informed over the same period, every medieval library of any account sought to possess a copy in its Latin translation.[14] In it God creates order out of chaos, the identification of order with his creation being so fundamental that *cosmos*, the Greek word for order, has become a synonym for the universe.[15] The manifestation of order is harmony which is achieved through the use of correct proportion. When Plato describes the elements of creation, he says,

> . . . from such constituents, four in number, the body of the universe was brought into being, coming into concord by means of proportion . . . .
>
> *Timaeus* 32C, Cornford 1937

> And for shape he gave it that which is fitting and akin to its nature. For the living creature that was to embrace all living creatures within itself, the fitting shape would be the figure that is in itself all the figures there are; accordingly, he turned its shape rounded and spherical; equidistant every way from the centre to extremity – a figure the most perfect and uniform of all . . . .
>
> *Timaeus* 33B, Cornford 1937

Relating the macrocosm of the universe to the human microcosm, a theme which runs throughout this Dialogue,[16] he says:

> Copying the round shape of the universe, they confined the two divine revolutions in a spherical body – the head, as we now call it – which is the divinest part of us and lord over all

the rest. To this the gods gave the whole body, when they had
assembled it, for its service . . . .

Timaeus 44D, Cornford 1937

Music is but another manifestation of the divine scheme, displaying the
same harmony of intelligible order.

Music . . . is given for the sake of harmony; and harmony,
whose motions are akin to the revolutions of the soul within
us, has been given by the Muses to him whose commerce with
them is guided by intelligence, not for the sake of irrational
pleasure, but as an ally against the inward discord . . . .

Timaeus 47D, Cornford 1937

Plato has been credited with being the first to associate all the regular
geometric solids with the elements and the universe.[17] The atmospheric
elements of fire, air and water are signified respectively by the tetrahedron,
octahedron and icosahedron. Earth is represented by a cube. The relationships
are logical for, just as each of the atmospheric elements can transform itself
into one of the others, the polyhedra of all three are derived from similar
triangles, namely the equilateral or regular triangle. This, being composed of
two scalene triangles, corresponds to the instability of its three elements.
Earth, on the other hand, is different and is therefore based on a different
triangle, namely the right-angled isosceles triangle which, being composed of
two similar isosceles triangles, represents the stability of earth. Thus,

fire	= tetrahedron	= 4 regular triangles	
		each from 2 scalene triangles	= unstable
air	= octahedron	= 8 regular triangles	
		each from 2 scalene triangles	= unstable
water	= icosahedron	= 20 regular triangles	
		each from 2 scalene triangles	= unstable
earth	= cube	= 12 × 90° isosceles triangles	
		each from 2 isosceles triangles	= stable

Having been so precise in his description of the elements and their solids,
Plato is strangely reticent when it comes to assigning to the universe the fifth
and last regular solid, the dodecahedron:

There still remained one construction, the fifth; and the god
used it for the whole [universe], making a pattern of animal
figures [constellations] thereon.

Timaeus 55C, Cornford 1937

There can be little doubt, however, that Plato was clear in his own mind. His friend and pupil at the Academy, Theaetetus, had already completed the theoretical construction and classification of all 5 regular solids each within a sphere[18] and these were eventually incorporated into Euclid's *Elementa*.[19] And in *Phaedo*, Plato has Socrates likening the Earth to a ball made of 12 pieces of leather.[20] Since the dodecahedron consists of 12 pentagons, Plato appears to be imagining a flexible dodecahedron expanding into a sphere, thereby signifying the universe.

Just as the solids of the 4 elements are composed of basic triangles, so is the dodecahedron. In this case, it is another isosceles triangle, that in which the base angles are double the apex angle, 72° and 36°, and it takes 5 of them to complete a pentagon. The connection between this triangle and the construction of the pentagon is thought to have been discovered by the Pythagoreans[21] whose emblem, after all, was the pentagram. This triangle also constitutes one-tenth of a decagon, a matter of significance given the Pythagorean connotation of 10 with perfection. However, this figure is particularly important in that its hypoteneuse and base are in extreme and mean ratio. In other words, they occur in the proportion in which the lesser is to the greater as the greater is to the whole, possibly known by the Greeks as 'the section' and much later as the golden section. Consequently, it has become commonly termed the golden triangle. According to Proclus, Eudoxus credited Plato with originating a 'number of theorems . . . regarding the section'.[22]

This being the case, Plato's evasiveness in *Timaeus* about 'the fifth construction' and its association with the universe requires explanation. One possible reason could be a concern for secrecy. He was later quoted as saying:

> We must speak in enigmas; that should the tablet come by any mischance . . . either by sea or land, he who reads it may remain ignorant . . . The greatest safeguard is not to write, but learn; for it is utterly impossible that what is written will not vanish.
>
> Clement, *Stromateis* V.10

One evident example of Plato speaking in enigmas, among countless others, occurs in his *Republic*:

> For the divine creature there is a period embraced by a perfect number; while for the human there is a geometrical number determining the better or worse quality of the births.
>
> *Republic* XXIX.546, Cornford 1941

Clearly much is meant here although it is left unexplained. This, therefore, must imply the existence of supplementary knowledge and the acceptance of informed interpretation as being a necessity. From other references to 'the divine creature' which Plato makes, this has been taken to mean the visible universe, the 'perfect number' probably the duration of the great year, and 'better or worse . . . births' the commonplace distinction between seven- and nine-month pregnancies.[23] Thus in this single extract, Plato appears to be binding together the universe, time and human birth.

Another explanation for his evasiveness could be that he considered the universe, as he might consider infinity and the ultimate Deity, to be simply inexpressible. He explores this idea in another of his Dialogues:

> Then the one has no name, nor is there any description or knowledge or perception or opinion of it. . . . And it is neither named or described nor thought of nor known, nor does any existing thing perceive it.
>
> *Parmenides* 142A

Evidently some of Plato's own followers preferred clarity because they explicitly attached the fifth solid to the fifth element which, instead of being the universe itself, was identified as ether, the substance believed to fill the universe. Hence the fifth element was quite literally ethereal.[24] By the time Aetius was writing around the turn of the second century the entire doctrine, despite being attributed to Pythagoras, appeared settled:

> Pythagoras, seeing that there are five solid figures, which are also called the mathematical figures, says that the earth arose from the cube, fire from the pyramid, air from the octahedron, water from the icosahedron, and the sphere of the universe from the dodecahedron.
>
> Aetius II.6.5, in Heath 1921, I.158–9

It needs to be pointed out, however, that Chalcidius's Latin translation of and commentary on *Timaeus*, which was available to early medieval scholars, stops short of Plato's treatment of the elements and their solids and there is no evidence of another version of it being consulted or produced in the middle ages until the fifteenth century. Yet parts of *Timaeus* were also translated by Cicero and passages appear in Macrobius's *Commentarii in Ciceronis Somnium Scipionis*. In addition to several other commentaries referring to *Timaeus* that have survived from the eleventh century onwards, there also exists the possibility of lost texts that might now have become unknown. For instance, the *Summarium librorum Platonis* is a thirteenth-century Latin manuscript that is part of a synopsis of all Plato's works. It is thought to be a copy of an early Carolingian codex from Corbie Abbey in France based on a Latin translation of a Greek text dating from the second century.[25] Above all, however, it was through the works of the Latin encyclopedists, followed by Augustine and Boethius, that Plato's concepts succeeded in reaching the medieval West.

In addition to this, a mathematical treatment of the geometry occurring in Plato's cosmology is also included in the *Elementa* of Euclid (fl. c.300 BC). Whilst Book IV is considered Pythagorean in content, propositions 10 and 11 deal respectively with the construction of the golden triangle and from it the regular pentagon. Book VI defines extreme and mean ratio and proposition 30 gives its construction. Book XIII, which is attributed to Theaetetus, sets out various properties of the pentagon and the decagon in relation to the golden section as well as the inscription of each of the regular polyhedra within a sphere. In addition to texts of the *Elementa* in Greek and a few commentaries, it is thought possible that, long before it was translated into Latin from Arabic in the twelfth century, other Latin translations may well have been available in the West. Of particular significance is that it was in the tenth century that Athelstan was said to have introduced the study of Euclid to England.[26]

The Greek Fathers

Clement, Origen and Plotinus

It was the cultural crucible of Alexandria that initiated early Christianity to Platonic thought. In the first century of the new era, the writings of Philo Judaeus, a Greek-speaking Jew, attempted the conciliation of the Hellenic and Judaic traditions of learning, a process continued by Clement (c.150–c.215) in the next century. As a Greek philosopher and convert to Christianity, Clement compared both traditions with each other and with the emergent teachings of Christianity. As a result, he was the first to appreciate how much the writings of Plato and the evangelists John and Paul had in common.[27] Recognized as the leading Christian scholar of his day and the foremost exponent of natural philosophy from the Christian point of view prior to Augustine, Clement was able to produce the synthesis of classical and Christian thought which gave birth to Christian Platonism.[28] This was developed by his most famous pupil, Origen, and provided the theological foundations for the writings in the East of the Cappadocian Fathers as well as for Augustine in the West.[29] Although it has to be admitted that Clement's own work might not have been read much in the middle ages, his teaching was nevertheless to reach the West through Cassian's adaptations in the fifth century which were soon to be consulted by Benedict himself.[30] Through Origen's writing, it was also to reach Ambrose in Greek and thence Augustine, along with translations by Rufinus, some of which were also known to Augustine.[31] The result of this was to be the permanent acceptance of Christian Platonism by the Latin Church. In these early centuries, it not only answered the pagan reaction of Porphyry and Julian, it also gave Christian faith its intellectual content [32] and, such was its enduring appeal, it was to reach its culmination in the cathedral school of Chartres nine hundred years after Clement died.

Clement's forum was the Didascaleon, or Catechetical School, in Alexandria of which he became head. It had only recently been opened by Pantaenus, also a Christian convert and a Pythagorean, with the purpose of promoting Christian studies for educated converts in opposition to the paganism of Alexandria's Museum and the esoteric cabalism of the Gnostics. Accordingly, the methods of classical philosophy were applied to a curriculum which included philosophy, mathematics and scripture. Education was the path to knowledge, or *gnosis*, which led to freedom. The union of knowledge with 'right reason' led to virtue just as the union between the human and divine spirit resulted in love.[33] Thus Plato's three-part division of rational, moral and natural philosophy found its place in Clement's school.

For the uneducated, a state of grace was still possible through the acceptance of faith[34] but from them, however, *gnosis* should be concealed:

> For Plato also thought it not lawful for 'the impure to touch the pure.' Thence the prophecies and oracles are spoken in enigmas, and the mysteries are not exhibited incontinently to all and sundry, but only after certain purifications and previous instructions.
>
> Clement, *Stromateis* V.4

> . . . even those myths in Plato . . . are to be expounded allegorically, not absolutely in all their expressions, but in those which express the general sense. And these we shall find indicated by symbols under the veil of allegory.
>
> *Stromateis* V.9

Clement found as much authority for obfuscation in the scriptures:

> But since this tradition is not published alone for him who perceives the magnificence of the word; it is requisite, therefore, to hide in a mystery the wisdom spoken, which the Son of God taught. . . . because, 'even now I fear,' as it is said, 'to cast the pearls before swine, lest they tread them underfoot, and turn and rend us' (Matthew vii.6). For it is difficult to exhibit the really pure and transparent words respecting the true light, to swinish and untrained hearers. For scarcely could anything which they could hear be more ludicrous than these to the multitude; nor any subjects on the other hand more admirable or more inspiring to those of noble nature.
>
> *Stromateis* I.12

In retrospect, such determined concealment of *gnosis* from the uninitiated might arguably be confused with the secret societies of the Gnostics themselves, particularly since Clement often refers to the followers of 'the true philosophy' as Gnostics. However, this would be a modern misperception, since Clement had simply decided to combat Gnosticism with his own invention of Christian Gnosticism. When he writes:

> Then [the Preaching of Peter, an apocryphal book] adds:
> 'Worship this God not as the Greeks,' – signifying plainly, that
> the excellent among the Greeks worshipped the same God as
> we, but that they had not learned by *perfect knowledge* that
> which was delivered by the Son.'
>
> *Stromateis* VI.5 [my italics]

Clement makes clear his regard for *gnosis* as 'perfect knowledge', as opposed to the arcane superstitions of the Gnostics.[35]

Clement's three main works constitute a progression in which the acquiring of *gnosis* leads to an understanding of *Logos*, the Word. *Protreptikos* exhorts the reader to renounce paganism; *Paedagogus* instructs him in Christian ethics; whilst the major part is *Stromateis*, a miscellany of essays devoted to a higher knowledge of God and his creation. In these works he repeatedly refers to and quotes from *Timaeus* and other Dialogues as well as scripture. Of the *Protreptikos* and *Paedagogus*, a tenth-century manuscript has been noted in the Bibliothèque Nationale in Paris together with an eleventh-century manuscript of *Stromateis* in the Laurentian Library in Florence.[36]

The origins of philosophy are succinctly stated by Clement:

> From Pythagoras Plato derived the immortality of the soul; and
> he from the Egyptians.
>
> *Stromateis* VI.2

However, the composition of the universe and the nature of the 4 elements had, even since Aetius, become somewhat muddled. Although he writes:

> And indeed the most elementary instruction of children
> embraces the interpretation of the four elements . . . .
>
> *Stromateis* V.8

> And Athamas the Pythagorean having said, 'Thus was
> produced the beginning of the universe; and there are four
> roots – fire, water, air, earth: for from these is the origination
> of what is produced'. . . .
>
> *Stromateis* VI.2

he continues,

> Empedocles of Agrigentum wrote:
> 'The four roots of all things first do thou hear –
> Fire, water, earth, and ether's boundless height:
> For of these all that was, is, shall be, comes.'
>
> *Stromateis* VI.2

Nevertheless, despite an apparent confusion between ether and air here, Clement himself seemed clear enough in his previous chapter when he repeated the colours associated with the 4 elements – blue for air, purple for water, scarlet for fire and linen for earth.[37] Interestingly, this reveals that the atmospheric elements are chromatically – as well as physically and geometrically – related to each other and distinct from the element earth. For just as fire can cause water to evaporate into air and cooling can cause water to condense in air, so the purple of water is a synthesis of the red and blue of fire and air and their geometric solids are also relations of each other in that they are each enclosed by the regular triangle, quite distinct therefore from the colour and cube of earth. Plato's relation of the macrocosm of the universe to the microcosm of the human also seems preserved by Clement, particularly when it is remembered that the number 10 was equated with perfection.

> And the perfect inheritance belongs to those who attain to 'a perfect man,' according to the image of the Lord.
>
> And there is a ten in man himself.
>
> *Stromateis* VI.14, 16; see also V.6

In this passage, Clement then refers to the 5 senses and adds to them another 5, namely power of speech, power of reproduction, spirit received through creation, rule of the soul, rule of the Holy Spirit through faith.

Thus the Platonic Christian appears complete, the conjunction of the two traditions seeming to be effortless.

> If then we consider, virtue is, in power, one. But it is the case, that when exhibited in some things, it is called prudence, in others temperance, and in others manliness or righteousness. By the same analogy, while truth is one, in geometry there is truth of geometry; in music, that of music; and in the right philosophy, there will be Hellenic truth. But that is the only authentic truth, unassailable, in which we are instructed by the Son of God.
>
> *Stromateis* I.20

The synthesis of the two traditions was evidently derived at least partly from the belief that Plato himself had had sight of certain scriptures. Several of Clement's essays are devoted to the theme of Greeks borrowing from Hebrews, or of the two traditions at least coinciding.[38] Nevertheless they were still distinguishable:

> Rightly, then, to the Jews belonged the Law, and to the Greeks Philosophy, until the Advent . . . .
>
> *Stromateis* VI.17

That scripture associated the Law with 10 is evident above all in the Decalogue, or Ten Commandments. More than being a mere list of rules, however, the Commandments were regarded as an image of heaven[39] and, in this aspect, they are to be identified with the same Pythagorean number of perfection. As Clement writes:

> But law is the opinion which is good, and what is good is that which is true, and that which is true is that which finds 'true being,' and attains to it. . . . In accordance with which, namely good opinion, some have called law, right reason, which enjoins what is to be done and forbids what is not to be done. . . . That ten is a sacred number, it is superfluous to say now.

> *Stromateis* I.25, VI.16

Therefore just as the equation of the law with perfection appears safe so, it seems, can references to law and perfection be equated with 10.

It may also be seen that the meaning of number was as integral to Clement's universal view as it had been to those of Pythagoras and Plato, the sole distinction between them being that he acknowledged his authority to be biblical as well as Platonic.

> They say, then, that the character representing 300 is, as to shape, the type of the Lord's sign . . . Now the number 300 is 3 by 100. Ten is allowed to be the perfect number . . . .

> 'The days of men shall be,' it is said, '120 years' (Genesis 6.3). And the sum is made up of the numbers from 1 to 15 added together.
>
> *Stromateis* VI.11

Numbers were not endowed with specific significance arbitrarily. For example, because the Greek letter T served as the numeral for 300 and resembled a cross, 300 became regarded as the Lord's sign.[40] Yet numbers were also held to be expressions of the divine order because of the order to be found within them. If the *tetract* was given importance partly because the sum of the first 4 numbers is 10, then 120 was important partly because it is the sum of the first 15 numbers. Moreover, Clement continues:

> On another principle, 120 is a triangular number, and consists of the equality of the number 64, [which consists of eight of the odd numbers beginning with unity],[41] the addition of which in succession generates squares; and of the inequality of the number 56, consisting of seven of the even numbers beginning with 2, which produce the numbers that are not squares.

> *Stromateis* VI.11

In other words,

$$64 + 56 = (8 \times 8) + (7 \times 8) = 120$$

64 is composed thus:

$$1 + 3 = 4, + 5 = 9, + 7 = 16, + 9 = 25, + 11 = 36, + 13 = 49, + 15 = 64$$

where each sum is a square number which, when added to the next odd number in the series, produces the next square number in the series. As for the series of the first 7 even numbers adding up to 56, each sum, whilst being even, is not square.

$$2 + 4 + 6 + 8 + 10 + 12 + 14 = 56$$

$$2 + 4 = 6; \ 4 + 6 = 10; \ 6 + 3 = 14; \ 8 + 10 = 18; \ 10 + 12 = 22$$

Following this, Clement continues

> Again, according to another way of indicating, the number 120 consists of four numbers – of one triangular, 15; of another, a square, 25; of a third, a pentagon, 35; and of a fourth, a hexagon, 45. The 5 is taken according to the same ratio in each mode. For in triangular numbers, from the unity 5 comes 15; and in squares, 25; and of those in succession proportionally.

Stromateis VI.11

It can be seen that in this apparently numerical analysis, geometry is clearly implicit. In addition to the importance given to numbers when they relate rationally to each other, the relationship is perceived and expressed in geometric terms, with the concept of figurate numbers standing for square, triangular and polygonal arrangements of numbers, originally in the form of pebble figures. This, together with the inherent order to be found in numbers themselves was to be treated by the Latin encyclopedists and Augustine.

Clement's successor at the Didascaleon was his former pupil Origen (c.185–c.254) who went on to study philosophy under Ammonius Saccas. He in turn had abandoned an earlier conversion to Christianity and was a Neoplatonist.[42] One result of Origen's varied education was a certain flexibility in calling upon the authority of Plato, not invariably, but when it supported his own theological speculations. In a huge output of literature, these were largely a development of Clement's and organized into his famous treatise, *De principiis*, which enjoyed particular influence in both the West and the East. Before they caught the attention of Ambrose and others in Italy, Origen's ideas had spread to Cappadocia reaching the generation of Basil the Great and his brother Gregory of Nyssa and, although some of his ideas were soon to be condemned, his main thesis remained intact.[43]

Ammonius Saccas also taught Platonic philosophy in Alexandria to the Greek Egyptian Plotinus (c.205–70) whose principal contribution lies in incorporating Plato's thought with Aristotle's methods and in bringing to this his own theories concerning progressive planes of spiritual existence.[44] As the doctrine of emanation, this was to have a profound effect on mystical thinkers, setting him among the greatest of the Neoplatonists. Care, it should be said, needs to be taken in the understanding of Neoplatonism as a term, since it is comprehensive rather than specific, referring to various individual developments of Platonic thought, some of which are more Christian than Platonic, or more theological than philosophical, or more mystical than intellectual, or vice versa. Despite such distinctions, however, Neoplatonists at the time called themselves Platonists.[45] As for Plotinus, his importance for this study is that in 244 he moved to Rome, where he taught and eventually died, and it was in Italy that Augustine may well have read his essay *On Beauty* from his *Enneads* (I, vi).[46]

Basil and Gregory

Basil (c.329–79) read philosophy and rhetoric in the young capital of the Eastern Empire, Constantinople, before continuing his studies in Athens with, among others, Julian, the apostate emperor of the Byzantines. It was only later in life, in 364, that he was ordained priest and only seven years before his premature demise that he was consecrated metropolitan of his native Caesarea, whereupon he made his younger brother Gregory (c.335–c.95) bishop of Nyssa. Before his ordination, Basil had spent some time as a hermit studying Origen and when Gregory stayed at his brother's cell he too studied 'his master Origen' along with everything Basil had learned in Athens. On Basil's death, Gregory came into his own as a churchman and teacher to the extent that he became known as the 'Father of Fathers'. In 381 he was summoned by the Emperor Theodosius to the Second Oecumenical Council in Constantinople, as a result of which he was recognized as a principal interpreter of the emergent orthodoxy of the Eastern Church.[47]

Of chief interest to this study is Basil's *Hexaëmeron*, a series of sermons on the 6 days of Creation delivered morning and evening during Lent to a congregation of workmen. As he acknowledges,

> I know that many artisans, belonging to the mechanical trades, are crowding around me. A day's labour hardly suffices to maintain them; therefore I am compelled to abridge my discourse, so as not to keep them too long from their work.

Hexaëmeron III.1

Although the sermons are systematically arranged, the final homily which should have described the creation of man seems to end prematurely and was supplemented by Gregory's treatise *De hominis opificio*.[48] Such was the importance of *Hexaëmeron* that its teaching quickly spread to the West.

Ambrose produced an adaptation of it which was soon translated into Latin by Eustathius in about 440 and, whether or not this was the work of Basil's already noted on Alcuin's shelves at York, a vernacular abbreviation of *Hexaëmeron* was produced in Anglo-Saxon in 969 by Aelfric.[49] As has been remarked elsewhere, the circulation of shortened versions of texts can usually be taken as evidence that such texts had become standard reading.[50] In addition to manuscripts of several of Gregory's writings surviving from the tenth century onwards, including no less than three of *De hominis opificio* from the tenth century itself, this same work had already been translated into Latin by John Scotus in the previous century.[51]

At first sight Basil appears largely to repudiate classical philosophy as he recounts how one theory about the origin of the universe became supplanted by another.[52]

> Those who have written about the nature of the universe have discussed at length the shape of the earth . . . all these conjectures have been suggested by cosmographers, each one upsetting that of his predecessor. It will not lead me to give less importance to the creation of the universe, that the servant of God, Moses, is silent as to shapes . . . Shall I then prefer foolish wisdom to the oracles of the Holy Spirit? . . . It is this which those seem to me not to have understood, who, giving themselves up to the distorted meaning of allegory, have undertaken to give a majesty of their own invention to Scripture . . . .
>
> Some have said that heaven is composed of four elements . . . Others have rejected this system as improbable, and introduced into the world, to form the heavens, a fifth element after their own fashioning. There exists, they say, an aethereal body which is neither fire, air, earth, nor water, nor in one word any simple body . . . . But yet another speaker arises and disperses and destroys this theory to give predominance to an idea of his own invention. Do not let us undertake to follow them for fear of falling into like frivolities; let them refute each other, and, without disquieting ourselves about essence, let us say with Moses 'God created the heaven and the earth'. Let us glorify the supreme Artificer for all that was wisely and skillfully made . . . Because . . . the objects which on all sides attract our notice are so marvellous, that the most penetrating mind cannot attain to the knowledge of the least of the phenomenon of this world.
>
> *Hexaëmeron* IX.1, I.11

Basil seems intent here on keeping the minds of his workaday congregation upon simple devotion. He lived, after all, at the time of violent religious disputes such as those caused by Julian's apostasy and Valens's Arianism, and both needed to be answered by an insistence on orthodoxy, particularly concerning the Holy Trinity, rather than by raking over old arguments about classical cosmogony. In fact, it was Basil himself who has been credited with precipitating the end of the Arian dispute, to be ratified soon after his death at the Council of 381 in the presence of his brother.[53] Given the determination to hold the line on orthodoxy which this indicates, Basil is hardly likely to have encouraged cosmological speculation from his own pulpit, especially since he considered such matters to be above the heads of his artisan audience.[54] Certainly the tradition of teaching he inherited from Clement and Origen of knowledge being reserved for the educated, leaving faith to the uneducated, would seem to support this. Indeed, it will be shown that the early Church actually developed its liturgy in a way that protected its innermost secrets from the uninitiated.[55]

Ambiguity in this passage over the fifth essence being ether still seems unabated for, although Basil appears to dismiss it here, when dealing elsewhere with God's command, 'Let there be light', he refers to it as a matter of course.

> Up it sprang to the very aether and heaven. In an instant it lighted up the whole extent of the world . . . For the aether also is such a subtle substance and so transparent that it needs not the space of a moment for light to pass through it . . . With light the aether becomes more pleasing . . . .
>
> *Hexaëmeron* III.3

Here it is surely the fifth essence, being distinct from the elements and yet associated with heaven. Later in the same homily, the implication again must surely be that ether is the substance surrounding the 7 planets which therefore fills the universe.

> These circles, they say, carried away in a direction contrary to that of the world, and striking the aether, make sweet and harmonious sounds, unequalled by the sweetest melody . . . .
>
> *Hexaëmeron* III.3

That such matters may sometimes be implied is clear from his treatment of the elements:

> . . . 'In the beginning God made heaven and earth.'. . . Thus, although there is no mention of the elements, fire, water and air, imagine that they were all compounds together, and you will find water, air and fire, in the earth . . . Do not ask, then, for an enumeration of all the elements; guess, from what Holy Scripture indicates, all that is passed over in silence.
>
> *Hexaëmeron* I.7

The underlying view here seems clearly to be Platonic as well as Christian, as it is when Basil deals with the divine order and the sensible and intelligible worlds.

> . . . 'In the beginning God created.' What a glorious order!

> It appears, indeed, that even before this world an order of things existed of which our mind can form an idea, but of which we can say nothing, because it is too lofty a subject for men who are but beginners and are still babies in knowledge. . . . The Creator and the Demiurge of the universe perfected His works in it, spiritual light for the happiness of all who love the Lord, intellectual and invisible natures, all the orderly arrangement of pure intelligences who are beyond the reach of our mind and of whom we cannot even discover the names.

> *Hexaëmeron* I.2, 5

> You will finally discover that the world . . . is really the school where reasonable souls exercise themselves, the training ground where they learn to know God; since by the sight of visible and sensible things the mind is led, as by a hand, to the contemplation of invisible things.

> *Hexaëmeron* I.6

This anagogical doctrine of the path that leads from the sensible to the intelligible, or from the material to the spiritual, was not only a logical corollary of Plato's world of Forms but, of importance to this study, it also justified religious art and architecture, as Suger was to write in explaining the design of his abbey of St Denis in the twelfth century.[56]

Gregory's completion of his brother's *Hexaëmeron* seems similarly Platonic.

> Now all is beautiful and good that is closely related to the First Good . . . If, then, . . . that which is truly good is one, and the mind itself also has its power of being beautiful and good, in so far as it is in the image of the good and beautiful, and the nature, which is sustained by the mind, has the like power, in so far as it is an image of the image, it is hereby shown that our material part holds together, and is upheld when it is controlled by nature; and on the other hand is dissolved and disorganized when it is separated from that which upholds and sustains it, and is dissevered from its conjunction with beauty and goodness.

> *De hominis opificio* XII.11

Although, like his brother, Gregory sometimes appears to refute a conventional Platonic doctrine, it reappears later albeit in slightly altered guise. For example, in referring to humans as a microcosm of the universe, he says,

> . . . how unworthy of the majesty of man are the fancies of some heathen writers, who magnify humanity as they supposed, by their comparison of it with this world! for they say that man is a little world, composed of the same elements with the universe.
>
> *De hominis opificio* XVI.1

Yet when he answers:

> In what then does the greatness of man consist, according to the doctrine of the Church? Not in his likeness to the created world, but in his being in the image of the nature of the Creator.
>
> *De hominis opificio* XVI.2

surely he is simply equating Creator and created with Origen's own distinction between the intelligible and sensible worlds.[57] His description of rational man certainly appears purely Platonic:

> Now since man is a rational animal, the instrument of his body must be made suitable for the use of reason . . . .
>
> *De hominis opificio* VIII.8; cf. Plato, *Timaeus* 44D

Likewise, in another treatise, Plato's world of Forms lies just beneath the surface as Gregory celebrates the liberal arts as the path to virtue. A virtuous man is one who,

> . . . has been led to the apprehension of a Master of the creation; he has taken the true Wisdom for his teacher, that Wisdom which the spectacle of the Universe suggests; and when he observed the beauty of this material sunlight he had grasped by analogy the beauty of the real sunlight . . . .
>
> Has a man who looks at such spectacles procured for himself only a slight power for the enjoyment of those delights beyond? Not to speak of the studies which sharpen the mind towards moral excellence, geometry, I mean, and astronomy, and the knowledge of the truth that the science of numbers gives, and every method that furnishes a proof of the unknown and a conviction of the known, and, before all these, the philosophy contained in the inspired Writings, which affords a complete purification to those who educate themselves thereby in the mysteries of God.
>
> *De infantibus praemature abreptis* 377–8

Once again it may be seen that the doctrines of Plato and Clement are conveyed in the importance given by Gregory to education and purification as preparations for the 'apprehension of a Master of the creation' and 'the spectacle of the Universe'. Part of this apprehension is to be gained in the understanding of numbers:

> ... number is nothing else than a combination of units growing into a multitude in a complete way ... accordingly, in order that we may be taught by Holy Scripture that nothing is unknown to God, it tells us that the multitude of the stars is numbered by Him, not that their numbering takes place as I have described, [for who is so simple as to think that God takes knowledge of things by odd and even, and that by putting units together He makes up the total of the collective quantity?] ... For to measure quantity by number is the part of those who want information. But He who knew all things before they were created needs not number as His informant. But when David says that He 'numbers the stars', it is evident that the Scripture descends to such language in accordance with our understanding, to teach us emblematically that the things which we know not are accurately known to God.

> *Contra Eunomium librum II* 293

The Latin Encyclopedists

In the foregoing sections, it has been shown that the passage of Platonic and Neoplatonic thought from Alexandria to Asia Minor and the Greek Fathers produced writings of sufficient importance that they were immediately to find their way to the West, reaching not only Ambrose in Milan but Rome as well, whence the teachings of Origen were to spread in the translations of Rufinus. In the meantime, however, Neoplatonism had already reached Rome with the arrival of Plotinus in 244.[58]

It was Plotinus's pupil, Porphyry (233–c.300), a leading Neoplatonist himself, who edited the work of his master and whose own writings included commentaries on *Timaeus* and apparently the *Elementa* as well. Writing in Greek though living in Rome, he was to be highly regarded by Augustine as a pagan philosopher,[59] though this was a tribute Augustine was to qualify because of Porphyry's anti-Christian stance, manifest for example in his treatise *Adversus Christianos*.[60]

Marius Victorinus, who taught rhetoric in Rome and became a Christian convert in the middle of the fourth century, translated writings of Plotinus and other Neoplatonists into Latin which may have numbered among the works of Victorinus recorded by Alcuin at York. He was in touch with

Simplicianus, the priest in Milan who prepared Ambrose for baptism the year before the latter became bishop of that city in 374.[61]

At about the time of Victorinus's conversion, Chalcidius was producing his celebrated *Timaeus* translation and commentary, copies of which, as already stated, were a necessary possession for all medieval libraries of note.[62] This was in spite of the text ending prematurely at a point [63] which immediately precedes Plato's treatment of the elements and the regular solids. Nevertheless, the work remained the most important of all Platonic sources for the Latin middle ages.[64]

This was followed by two more Platonic works of hardly less importance, namely the *Commentarii in Ciceronis Somnium Scipionis* of Macrobius and Martianus's *De nuptiis Philologiae et Mercurii*. Macrobius's *Commentarii*, second only to Chalcidius's, was written late in the fourth century or early in the fifth based on a lost commentary on *Timaeus* by Porphyry. Yet it is less a commentary than an encyclopedia of Neoplatonism illustrated with diagrams. Its starting-point is Plato's *Republic*, Cicero's original work also being entitled *De republica*, and it is with Scipio's Dream that he ends it as an obvious counterpart to Plato's Vision of Er.[65] Martianus's *De nuptiis* was approximately contemporary, being written between 410 and 439, and uses the allegorical marriage between Philology and Mercury as a setting for summarizing the seven liberal arts, in which each appears personified as a bridesmaid at the wedding.[66]

Whilst *Somnium Scipionis* is among the works most frequently referred to in early medieval manuscripts and is itself among the most common manuscripts from that time, so *De nuptiis* was perhaps the most widely used schoolbook, its popularity during the ninth and tenth centuries being matched by that of *Somnium Scipionis* possibly from early in the tenth. Their influence in transmitting Plato's cosmology was second only to Chalcidius partly as a result of expositions of number theory that deal not only with numerical relationships but with their powers as well, the attributes of the Pythagorean *decad* for example and the discovery of his musical ratios being relayed extensively in medieval literature.[67] This is not to say that the transmission was exact and unvarying since tradition was always open to interpretation and development. For example, Plato's and Clement's concept of 7 planets revolving around an eighth, which is Earth, becomes in *Somnium Scipionis* 7 planets revolving within an eighth which is an all-encompassing celestial sphere. This is composed of 5 zones.[68] Because justice is even-handed, to Clement it was represented by 4,[69] by Martianus 2 and by Macrobius 8.[70] 7, being a virgin number, is identified with Pallas Athene.[71] In *De nuptiis*, 9 is also a perfect number and signifies the Muses.[72] Nevertheless, it seems fair to say that these are additions to, not an undermining of, the basic precepts, for these remained those of Pythagoras and Plato as recognized by Martianus.

> Meanwhile the august company of the gods . . . acknowledged
> [Arithmetic] herself . . . to be in very truth the procreator of the
> gods. And the host of philosophers, too, who stood nearby – in
> particular, Pythagoras, with all his disciples, and Plato,

expounding the cryptic doctrines of his Timaeus – worshipped the lady with words of mystic praise . . . .

Martianus, *De nuptiis* 803

According to this whole tradition as transmitted, 1 is confirmed as the *monad* and the generator of numbers.[73] 2, being the first departure from unity, represents discord and is the female number because it lacks a middle term.[74] 3 is male because it possesses a middle term and is therefore the first number that is wholly odd. In other words, because,

$$1 + 1 + 1 = 3,$$

it is the first number comprising a mean and two extremes; it also stands for the triangle and the three divisions of the soul.[75] By the same reasoning, 4 is the first number wholly even because it is the first consisting of two means; it is the terminal number of the *tetract* as well as that of the geometric elements of point, line, plane and solid; it represents the quadrangle and the 4 elements and seasons.[76]

> The pentad comes next, the number assigned to the universe. This identification is reasonable, for after the four elements, the universe is a fifth body of a different nature.

Martianus, *De nuptiis* 735

To this Macrobius adds that 5,

> . . . alone embraces all things that are and seem to be.   I.6.19

Yet in conveying Plato's association of the macrocosm with the human microcosm, Martianus adds that 5 also stands for marriage, being the sum of the male and female numbers, as well as the sum of the human senses.[77] 6 is a perfect number because it is the sum of its parts. In other words,

$$1 \times 2 \times 3 = 1 + 2 + 3 = 6$$

Moreover, it is the product of the male and female numbers[78] and so signifies creation. Because 7 begets no numbers in the *decad*, it is virgin; as the sum of 3 + 4, it is the number by which the World-Soul is generated, according to *Timaeus*; and, the Moon being the seventh planet, it also relates to the phases of the Moon measured in 7-day periods and the lunar stages of each month.[79] 8 is the first cube and is perfect because it has 6 surfaces.[80]

> (10 is) the highest degree of perfection of all numbers . . . .

Macrobius, *Commentarii* I.6.76

> It contains within itself all numbers with their varied attributes
> and degrees of perfection . . . .
>
> Martianus, *De nuptiis* 742

Interestingly, it is important to note that Martianus has Geometry preceding Arithmetic at the wedding.[81] Her Book is the longest in the work and contains more geography than geometry, yet it does incorporate a ten-page summary of Euclid's *Elementa*. Here a classification of angles, planes and solids leads to a description of how solids are generated from planes. Having described the basic solids, among which are found the pyramid and cube, Martianus concludes with the 'noble' figures of the octahedron, dodecahedron and icosahedron.[82] Not surprisingly, geometric thinking finds its counterpart in arithmetic for, just as the sphere is recognized as containing all other figures, and in particular the regular solids, so 10 contains all numbers. And since geometric solids are recognized as being based upon plane figures, this would explain Macrobius's allusion to 5 embracing all things.[83] Because 5 is the first figurate number of the pentagon, which is the plane figure of the dodecahedron which signifies the universe, Macrobius seems clearly to be associating 5 directly with the macrocosm, as indeed does Martianus.[84]

Had Augustine written his text-books on the liberal arts,[85] he would undoubtedly have belonged to the encyclopedic tradition of his near-contemporaries Macrobius and Martianus. As it is, his importance for the present study is arguably even greater, not only for transmitting Platonic thought within a theological framework but also for securing thereby its acceptance by the Church. Consequently, his contribution will be considered next.

Augustine

Ambrose presumably had less need for Latinizers because of his own knowledge of Greek. It was partly this and his enthusiasm for Greek thought, both classical and Christian, and in particular the Platonists whom he regarded as the 'aristocrats of thought' that contributed to his standing as one of four Doctors of the Western Church.[86] In addition to adapting Basil's *Hexaëmeron*, he eagerly collected other Greek works, especially those of Origen, from whom he acquired his own understanding of allegory. Ambrose's contact with the Greek world evidently made his sermons the most progressive in the West[87] and it was into this environment that Augustine (354–430) arrived in 384.

Symmachus, the Prefect of Rome and one of the leading pagans of his day, had recommended Augustine for the post in rhetoric at the court of Milan. On his arrival from Rome, however, Augustine soon fell deeply under the influence of Ambrose and his sermons.[88] In just two turbulent years he had contemplated withdrawing from the world with a band of amateur philosophers; he had been introduced to various Neoplatonic writings in the translations of Victorinus, including probably the *Enneads* of Plotinus; then having turned to Simplicianus who particularly impressed him with the earlier conversion of Victorinus, Augustine underwent his own conversion; and, following a breakdown, he penned four Dialogues during his convalescence which marked his arrival as a Christian Platonist thinker, teacher and writer.[89]

It is of crucial importance to this study that his massive output, together with his command of classical and Christian thought and his ability to conduct an argument derived from personal reflection, ensured his place along with Gregory as the foremost authority for the Latin Church in the tenth century and either side of it.[90] Being comprehensive in span, his writings are concerned not only with purely theological interpretations of scripture and the Christian revelation but with Christian philosophy as well. In this he reveals the Platonic underpinning of his own thought, particularly that related to the universe, harmony and numbers, to the extent that he is credited with transmitting to the medieval Church the best account of Plato's teaching, thereby securing its acceptance by the Church.[91] Among the first of the early Dialogues was De ordine. Another Platonic work, De musica, was started a year later in 387 along with his treatise De quantitate animae. After an interval of ten years his Confessiones, compiled over a period of four years, also contains an exposition of Platonic metaphysics. This was overlapped by his treatise De Trinitate which was written between 399 and 419. During this time he commenced his greatest undertaking, De civitate Dei, a work of twenty-two volumes which was perhaps the most widely read of all books early in the middle ages apart from the Bible itself. It was written throughout the years 413 to 427, with what can be considered the Platonic volumes of the work, VII–XI, coming over two years from 415. Finally, as he was nearing the end of De civitate Dei, he issued his Retractationes in about 427.[92]

It needs to be borne in mind, however, that since Augustine's search for truth had already caused him several revisions, the views expressed in this huge collection of writings are neither uniform nor unchanging. For example, De ordine is a treatise dealing with the liberal arts as the path leading to comprehension of the universal order. It shows that their evolution was rational because it was orderly and it concludes with a generous tribute to Pythagoras. This and the predominance accorded the liberal arts were subsequently moderated, though by no means actually retracted, in his Retractiones.[93] De musica, on the other hand, constitutes a six-volume work on rhythm that was meant to be complemented by a further six on melody. The first five serve as an introduction to Book VI which places number and music in a cosmological scheme that is essentially Platonic and reflects material in Timaeus. The work as left by Augustine largely follows a Greek treatise on music written in the second century by Aristides Quintilianus.[94] However, the Platonic content of De musica and the early Dialogues which it followed was shortly to be put into perspective in Confessiones[95] as being but a preparation, albeit a necessary one, for understanding the Christian mysteries. This was a similar conclusion to Clement's, yet the importance of Platonism was hardly diminished thereby, for it is abundantly evident from his later De civitate Dei that the discipline of Platonic thought and the basic precepts of its natural philosophy remained indispensable for such an understanding.

However, this did not place Platonists beyond criticism, especially those who found the idea of the Incarnation of the Son of God profoundly distasteful. Augustine recalled Simplicianus recounting how one Platonist had maintained that the quotation, 'The Word was in the beginning of all things, and the Word was with God', should be displayed in gold in every church. This was sufficient, it was argued, and some could not accept the Christian sequel that 'The Word was made flesh'. Porphyry in particular was repelled by the suggestion that the Word, as Christ Incarnate, should appear as a body from a woman, bleed on the Cross and become resurrected.[96] This earned Augustine's dismissal:

> But god, the great teacher, became of no account in the eyes of the proud [Porphyry and the Platonists] simply because 'the Word became flesh . . . .'
>
> *De civitate Dei* X.29

> I read there that the Word, God, 'was born not of the flesh, but of God'. But, that 'the Word was made flesh and dwelt among us' – I did not read that there . . . that 'in due time He died for the ungodly' and 'that Thou didst not spare Thine Only-begotten Son, but didst deliver Him up for us all' – that is not there.
>
> *Confessiones* VII.9.14

That all gods should be worshipped, as urged by Plato, was also repudiated by Augustine together with the doctrine of metempsychosis. Porphyry was again criticized for upholding both these teachings along with Origen who, as recently as 400, had been criticized at a council in Alexandria for some of his views.[97]

Despite these differences, it can be seen that the two traditions remained essentially compatible. This was still partly explained by the belief that Plato may have learnt some scripture in Egypt,[98] a belief based on what was taken to be internal evidence as, for example, when Augustine compares *Timaeus* with Genesis:

> 'In the beginning God made heaven and earth. But the earth was invisible and unformed, and there was darkness over the abyss, and the spirit of God soared above the water (Genesis 1.1f)'. Now in the Timaeus, the book in which he writes about the creation of the world, Plato says that God in that work first brought together earth and fire (*Timaeus* 31B); and it is obvious that for Plato fire takes the place of the sky . . . Plato goes on to say that water and air were the two intermediaries whose interposition effected the junction of those two extremes

(*Timaeus* 32B). This is supposed to be his interpretation of the biblical statement: 'The spirit of God soared above the water.'

De civitate Dei VIII.11

And when God declared, 'I am He who is . . . (Exodus 3, 14)', it was the 'truth Plato vigorously maintained and diligently taught'. Augustine's own exegesis of Plato's moral philosophy acknowledged that, to Platonists, the highest good was to be found not in the mind or body, but in God, and that goodness, being equated with virtue, is only to be found through knowledge of God.[99]

> [Platonists] acknowledge a God who transcends any kind of soul, being the maker not only of this visible – heaven and earth, in the familiar phrase – but also of every soul whatsoever, a God who gives blessedness to the rational and intelligent soul – the class to which the human soul belongs – by giving it a share in his unchangeable and immaterial light.

De civitate Dei VIII.1

> Platonists assert that the true God is the author of the universe, the source of the light of truth, and the bestower of happiness.

De civitate Dei VIII.5

His synthesis of the two traditions appears as effortless as Clement's had been.

> The philosophy that is true . . . has no other function than to teach what is the First Principle of all things – Itself without beginning, – and how great an intellect dwells therein, and what has proceeded therefrom for our welfare, but without deterioration of any kind. Now, the venerated mysteries . . . teach that this First Principle is one God omnipotent, and that He is tripotent, Father and Son and Holy Spirit.

De ordine II.5.6

In his expositions of the cosmos, the elements, the liberal arts and the understanding of numbers, it may be seen that Augustine again very much continues the teaching of Clement.

> But what are the higher things . . . ? Where there is no time, because there is no change, and from where times are made and ordered and changed, initiating eternity as they do when the turn of the heavens comes back to the same state, and the heavenly bodies to the same place, and in days and months and years and centuries and other revolutions of the stars obey

> the laws of equality, unity and order. So terrestrial things are
> subject to celestial, and their time circuits join together in
> harmonious succession for a poem of the universe.

> *De musica* VI.11.29

In this is contained the original sense of universe as *unus versus*, namely one
that is turning.

> From him derives every mode of being, every species, every
> order, all measure, number and weight . . . he has not left them
> without a harmony of their constituent parts, a kind of peace.

> *De civitate Dei* V.11, paraphrasing *Wisdom* II.20

> . . . there is nothing . . . which is not brought into being by
> him, from whom comes all form, all shape, all order . . . .

> *De civitate Dei* XI.15

However, understanding the orderliness of the creation and what a
Christian's attitude towards it should be was naturally difficult, particularly
following the shock of the sack of Rome in 410 which prompted the writing
of *De civitate Dei*. In achieving such an understanding, Augustine evidently
differs somewhat from Clement for, whereas Clement excluded the
uneducated from the path to knowledge, Augustine seems prepared to include
anyone even at the risk of holding back the educated.

> If only the weak understanding of the ordinary man did not
> stubbornly resist the plain evidence of logic and truth! . . . The
> result is that we are forced very often to give an extended
> exposition of the obvious . . . .

> *De civitate Dei* II.1; see also VII. Pref.

> In all these branches of study, therefore, all things were being
> presented to reason as numerically proportioned . . . Then,
> reason gained much coinage and preconceived a great
> achievement; it ventured to prove the soul immortal. It treated
> diligently of all things. It came to feel that it possessed great
> power, and that it owed all its power to numerical proportions.
> Something wondrous urged it on. And it began to suspect that
> it itself was perhaps the very number by which all things are
> numbered, or if not, that this number was there whither it was
> striving to arrive . . . But, false images of the things which we
> number drift away from that most hidden something by which
> we ennumerate, snatch our attention to themselves, and

frequently make that hidden something slip away even when
it has been already in our grasp.

De ordine II.15.43

If a man does not yield to these images, and if he reduces to
simple, true and certain unity all the things that are scattered
far and wide throughout so many branches of study, then he
is most deserving of the attribute learned. Then, without being
rash, he can search after things divine . . . .

De ordine II.16.44

Open though this may be for anyone to attempt, Augustine both warns of the
difficulties that lie ahead and at the same time describes the milestones that
must be attained in order to succeed:

. . . no one ought to aspire to a knowledge of those matters
without that twofold science, so to speak – the science of right
reasoning and that of the power of numbers.

De ordine II.18.47

. . . only a rare class of men is capable of using [reason] as a
guide to the knowledge of God or of the soul; either of the soul
within us or of the world-soul.

De ordine II.11.30

If you have a care for order . . . you must return to those
verses, for instruction in the liberal arts . . . produces devotees
more alert and steadfast and better equipped for embracing
truth . . . .

De ordine I.8.24

But since all the liberal arts are learned partly for practical use
and partly for the knowledge and contemplation of things, to
attain the use of them is very difficult except for some very
gifted person who even from boyhood has earnestly and
constantly applied himself.

De ordine II.16.44

The Platonist scheme which was revealed through the study of the liberal arts
included, as already noted, the elements and Augustine's treatment of them
echoes the description he made slightly earlier[100] and shows how each element
relates to the others in a rational way.

The system by which Plato connects and disposes the four
elements in a symmetrical order interposes the two
intermediary elements of air and water between the two
extremes, fire, the most mobile element, and the motionless

earth, in such a way that water is as far above earth as air is
above water and fire above air.

De civitate Dei VIII.15

Elements and numbers are an indissoluble part and expression of the
universal order. Augustine also transmits the first 4 numbers of the
Pythagorean *tetract* as signifying the basic geometric concepts of point, line,
plane and solid,[101] as well as alluding to the 'corrationality' to be found within
the numbers themselves.

> Can these [trees and animals] be made of the elements and
> these elements not have been made of nothing? For which
> among them is more ordinary and lowly than earth. Yet first it
> has the general form of body where a unity and numbers and
> order are clearly shown to be.
>
> *De musica* VI.17.57

This he demonstrates by referring to the 4 elements of geometry in which 1,
a point, is extended to 2, a line, which in turn grows to 3, a plane, and 4, a
solid.

> From where, then, is the measure of this progression of one to
> four? And from where, too, the equality of the parts found in
> length, breadth, and height? . . . Where, I ask, do these things
> come from, if not from the highest and eternal rule of numbers,
> likeness, equality, and order? And if you abstract these things
> from earth, it will be nothing. And therefore God Almighty has
> made earth, and earth is made from nothing.
>
> *De musica* VI.17.57

At about the time he was writing this, he was similarly proving the soul
to be immaterial in his *De quantitate animae* by referring again to the basic
constituents of geometry. Drawing much on Plotinus as well as the Christian
revelation,[102] he reverses the development of point, line and figure back to the
point as the perfection of unity concluding as follows:

Augustine: Now, then, have you ever seen with the eyes of
            the body such a point, or such a line, or such width?
Evodius: No, never. These things are not bodily.
Augustine: But if . . . bodily things are seen with bodily eyes,
            it must be that the soul by means of which we see
            these incorporeal things is not a body,
            nor like a body . . . .

De quantitate animae 13

When dealing with the millennial theory, Augustine gives another demonstration of relating the theme of solid geometry to number.

> [John] may have intended the thousand years to stand for the whole period of this world's history, signifying the entirety of time by a perfect number. For, of course, the number 1,000 is the cube of 10, since 10 multiplied by 10 is 100, a square but plane figure; but to give height to the figure and make it solid 100 is again multiplied by 10, and we get 1,000. Moreover, it seems that 100 is sometimes used to stand for totality ... If this is so, how much more does 1,000 represent totality, being the square of 10 converted into a solid figure!

> *De civitate Dei* XX.7

At the time he wrote *De ordine*, Augustine already understood that numbers possessed both meaning and reason. For those in the 'search after things divine',

> ... whoever has grasped the meaning of simple and intelligible numbers will readily understand these matters.

> ... there is in reason nothing more excellent or dominant than numbers ... reason is nothing else than number ....

> *De ordine* II.16.44, 18.48

In his passage concerning the millennium, Augustine acknowledges 10 to be 'a perfect number' but it will be seen that it is no longer the only one. He also recognizes that it is to be identified with the law[103] and that it is the sum of the first 4 numbers. This is the conclusion of an exhaustive examination of their 'corrationality' (see above). In an extension of Macrobius's explanation of 3 and 4 as the first odd and even numbers,[104] Augustine concludes that, because something, to be whole, must consist of a beginning, a middle and an end, 3 is the first whole number, in that it has an indivisible middle.

$$3 = 1 + 1 + 1 \qquad \text{(see \textit{De musica} I.12.20)}$$

Yet, whilst to Macrobius and Martianus 4 is the first even number because it is the first possessing two extremes,[105] as,

$$4 = 2 + 2$$

to Augustine it is even because it has a divisible middle,

$$4 = 1 + 2 + 1 \qquad \text{(see \textit{De musica} I.12.21, 23)}$$

Accordingly, 'this great harmony is in the first 3 numbers' because,

$1 + 1 = 2$, and $1 + 2 = 3$, which is the next in the series, whereas,

$2 + 3 = 5$, which is not the next in the series.[106]

4 is admitted because,

$1 + 2 + 1 = 4$

Therefore, 'one, two, three, four is the most closely connected progression of numbers'[107] because,

3 follows 1 and 2, and is the sum of 1 and 2;

4 follows 1, 2 and 3 and consists of 1 and 3, and twice 2; in other words,

$1 + 3 = 2 \times 2 = 4$

Modest though this example is, such an agreement of extremes in a series with the mean, and of the mean with the extremes is called by the Greeks *analogia*, or proportion. This analysis was continued a decade or more later in *De Trinitate* when Augustine deals with 6 as a perfect number[108] because,

$1 + 2 + 3 = 6$

Yet it constitutes a different kind of arithmetical perfection from the perfection of 10 as the sum of the *tetract*.

At the same time, the Pythagorean powers attributed to numbers were also recognized by Augustine, albeit in Christian form. Thus *In Iohannis evangelicum*, 3 represents the Trinity and 4 the corners of the earth (see below). In *De Trinitate*, Augustine goes on to confirm the Pythagorean significance of 6 as Creation, being the product of 2 (female) and 3 (male). Thus, the Creation was accomplished in 6 days and man was created on the sixth day. Furthermore, 'six serves as a sort of symbol of time.'[109]

In extending the range of perfect numbers, Augustine points out, the 'number seven is also perfect', being the day of God's rest after the Creation.[110]

> There is a great deal that could be said about the perfection of the number seven . . . three is the first odd whole number, and four the first whole even number, and seven is made up of these two . . . For this reason the Holy Spirit is often referred to by this same number . . . .
>
> *De civitate Dei* XI.31

He thereby converts Macrobius's Platonic attribution of 7 to the World-soul[111] into its Christian counterpart.

8 is repeatedly identified with a new beginning and the journey to heaven, as in *De sermone Domini in monte*.[112]

> . . . 'Blessed are they who suffer persecution for justice' (*sic*) sake, for their's is the kingdom of heaven'. Perhaps this eighth maxim – which returns to the beginning, and designates the perfect man – is signified both by the circumcision on the eighth day in the Old Testament and by the Lord's Resurrection after the Sabbath [which is indeed both the eighth day and the first] . . . .

> *De sermone Domini* I.IV.12; see also *Epistolae* 55

Returning to 3 and 4 as root numbers,

> The mystical number remained, the number twelve, because through the entire world, that is, through the four cardinal points of the world, they were going to announce the Trinity. Thus three times four . . . .
> *In Iohannis evangelicum* 27.10.(4)

Again, 12,

> . . . is significant as being the number of the patriarchs and that of the apostles because it is the product of the two parts of seven – that is, three multiplied by four . . . .

> *De civitate Dei* XV.20; see also XX.5

It s surely an indication of Augustine's distinction in setting Platonic thought within a theological framework acceptable to the medieval Church that his *De civitate Dei* was being written at about the time Martianus was relaying in his *De nuptiis* the Platonic thought of late antiquity. In his turn, it will be shown that Boethius was to revert more to the encyclopedic tradition since his treatises on the liberal arts seem free from religious reference. Before considering them, however, it is proposed to extend this account to Dionysius and to his possible teacher Proclus, for in them is to be found further influence of Greek thought reaching the West which, in this case, presents a mystical development of Platonism and which goes beyond theology to matters of liturgy.

Proclus and Dionysius

A non-Christian Neoplatonist entirely of the Greek world, Proclus (c.410–85) was born in Constantinople and schooled in Alexandria and Athens. Here he learnt Neoplatonic philosophy from Plutarch and became head of the philosophy school for fifty years. His many commentaries on Plato's Dialogues, including one on *Timaeus*, drew on original works by Plato, Aristotle and possibly the Pythagoreans. These were supplemented by his own *Platonica theologica*, *Elementa theologica* and numerous hymns to the gods, counter-balanced by various scientific treatises on physics and astronomy and, most notably, *In primum Euclidis elementorum librum commentarii*. Prologue I of this explains the relationship between mathematics and philosophy whilst Prologue II sets out the geometry of Plato and Aristotle, followed by his Summary.[113] This is almost certainly based on an earlier history of Greek geometry[114] and contains what is probably a gloss perhaps by Proclus that, 'Pythagoras . . . it was who discovered . . . the structure of the cosmic figures',[115] meaning the 5 solids representing the 4 elements and the fifth essence. So important was their construction taken to be by Proclus that, erroneously it seems, he regarded this to be the purpose of Euclid's *Elementa*.[116] However, his importance for this study is both as a transmitter of Philolaos's account of Pythagorean doctrine, though not necessarily to the Latin West until late in the middle ages, and especially as the inspiration and possibly teacher of Dionysius.[117]

Known as Dionysius the Pseudo-Areopagite or the Pseudo-Dionysius on account of his masquerade as the Areopagite convert of Paul, Dionysius probably lived and wrote in Syria around 500. As with Clement's principal works, Dionysius's form a schematic sequence. His *De divinis nominibus* explains the biblical names and attributes of God; the *Mystica theologia* deals with the soul's ascent to God; *De coelesti hierarchia* Christianizes the divine orders of Proclus as the nine orders of angels interceding between God and mankind; and *De ecclesiastica hierarchia* gives liturgical details for baptism, communion and anointing, the consecration of clerics and monks and the rite for the dead.[118]

As problematic as Dionysius's own identity is that of his teacher whom he calls Hierotheus, a concoction surely rather than a name, perhaps to be translated as 'priest of God'. And yet in addition to Dionysius producing texts which evidently 'dressed up Proclus's philosophy in Christian draperies', he credits his teacher with being the author of *The elements of theology* and numerous hymns,[119] which Proclus was.

Both questions of attribution arose long after the Byzantine court in Constantinople had been visited and served by Gregory the Great. He was there for several years later in the sixth century and, being able to read Greek, is thought to have encountered Dionysius's writing, possibly bringing his complete works back with him to Rome. Such was their impact that Dionysius was accepted as a Doctor of the Church. Knowledge of his writings was revived in 827 when the Byzantine emperor sent a copy of them to the Holy Roman Emperor Louis the Pious, which within the next fifty years was translated twice and revised once. The second translation was completed by John Scotus in 862 for Charles the Bald, Louis' son and eventual successor, while John was head of the Laon palace school. This led not only to the revision of 875 but also to John's own great work, *De divisione naturae*, which attempts to unify Neoplatonic theory of emanation with Christian creation.[120]

Largely as a result of a connection mistakenly made with Dionysius's pseudonym, various versions of his writings were preserved at the abbey of St Denis and were to shape Suger's ideas in rebuilding the abbey in the twelfth century.

In spite of Dionysius's mystical proclivities, anyone reading him would nevertheless have found much Christian Platonist doctrine as might have been expounded by Clement or Augustine:

> . . . the things of God are revealed to each mind in proportion to its capacities; and the divine goodness is such that, out of concern for our salvation, it deals out the immeasurable and infinite in limited measures. . . .

> We now grasp these things in the best way we can, and as they come to us, wrapped in the sacred veils of that love toward humanity . . .

> . . . the Transcendentent (sic) is clothed in the terms of being, with shape and form or things which have neither, and numerous symbols are employed to convey the varied attributes of what is an imageless and supra-natural simplicity.

> *De divinis nominibus* 1.1, 1.4

> Everything looks to [the Good] for measure, eternity, number, order. It is the power which embraces the universe. It is the Cause of the universe and its end.
> . . . In itself and by itself [beauty] is the uniquely and the eternally beautiful . . . For beauty is the cause of harmony, of sympathy, of community . . . .
> [From] the Good and the Beautiful . . . come the small, the equal, and the great in nature, the measure and the proportion of all things . . . the unity underlying everything, the perfection of wholes.
> *De divinis nominibus* 4.4, 4.7, 4.10

> Every number preexists uniquely in the monad and the monad holds every number in itself singularly.

> *De divinis nominibus* 5.6

> The name 'One' means that God is uniquely all things through the transcendence of one unity and that he is the cause of all

> And if you take away the One, there will survive neither whole nor part nor anything else in creation. . . . For it is the source

and the cause, the number and the order of the one, of number,
and of all being . . . .

De divinis nominibus 13.2, 13.3

If echoes of Clement may be heard in these passages, so may his injunction
to secrecy, even recalling Clement's quotation of Matthew vii.6 concerning the
casting of pearls before swine.[121] In *De divinis nominibus* Dionysius warns,

> . . . let such things be kept away from the mockery and the
> laughter of the uninitiated. . . . you must guard these things in
> accordance with divine command and you must never speak
> nor divulge divine things to the uninitiated.

De divinis nominibus 1.7

Not only was symbolism ritualized as part of the liturgy, the uninitiated were
to be excluded from it. In describing the baptismal rite, for instance,

> . . . let us behold the divine symbols which have to do with the
> divine birth and let no-one who is uninitiated approach this
> spectacle.

De ecclesiastica hierarchia 2.1

For the 'mystery of the synaxis', for example,

> . . . the deacons begin the reading of the holy tablets, after
> which the catechumens leave the sacred precincts, followed by
> the possessed and the penitents . . . .

De ecclesiastica hierarchia 3.II

Later,

> . . . following the rules of order, it allows (catechumens) to
> enter into communion with that which will illuminate them
> and which will bring them to perfection.
>
> . . . [For the] holy sacraments bring about purification,
> illumination, and perfection.

De ecclesiastica hierarchia 3.III.6, 6.III.5

It does need to be stressed, however, that much uncertainty still surrounds
Proclus and Dionysius and, despite the evident influence of the one upon the
other and the impression made by Dionysius on Gregory the Great and the
late Carolingian Court, few claims can be made with any certainty for the
influence of Dionysius on tenth-century thought. Nevertheless, however much
or little he was read in translation in the West, it may be argued that
Dionysius's philosophy stands in its own right as endorsing the more
important tenets of Christian Platonism at the time and is further evidence of

its currency at least in the years leading up to the tenth century. Few such doubts, however, need be entertained about the provenance and influence of the work of Boethius.

Boethius and Cassiodorus

Perhaps a contemporary of Dionysius, Boethius (c.480–524) studied Greek and some of his writing evidently suggests a familiarity with Proclus's work. However, notwithstanding his Greek studies, Boethius was the son of a Roman consul serving under the Huns; he was the ward of a prefect of Rome, becoming a consul himself in 510, and finally rising under the Ostrogothic king Theodoric to become his chief executive and head of his palace at Ravenna.[122]

But for this public service Boethius might well have devoted his life to philosophy. As it was, his plans to translate Plato into Latin went unfulfilled, as largely did those to translate Aristotle. Nevertheless, in addition to various religious tracts, he did manage to write *De topicis differentiis* and *In Ciceronis topica* on rhetoric and dialectic,[123] as well as treatises on the *quadrivium* already mentioned,[124] before accomplishing his greatest work, *De consolatione philosophiae*, all of which ensured a place second only to Augustine as the foremost influence on Western thought and letters in the eleventh and twelfth centuries and as the main source of the Latin tradition of Plato. Boethius was also virtually the sole source for Aristotle prior to the thirteenth century and at least one of his works was to be found in every medieval library of substance.[125] He not only established the sequence of the mathematical subjects of the liberal arts as they were to be taught in the monastery schools, even coining the term *quadrivium* himself, but his books on those subjects were to become standard texts in the middle ages establishing him among the greatest teachers of the period.[126]

One agent in this, as already noted, was Cassiodorus (c.490–c.583) who, through his *De institutione divinarum litterarum* and *De artibus ac discipliniis liberalium litterarum*, stressed the importance of the liberal arts to Christian education.[127] Although there is some dispute as to whether or not he was a pupil of Boethius and a friend of Benedict of Nursia, he did found a monastery for his own retirement which became a model among Benedictines for its intellectual activity. It was as a result of this and of his own writings on the liberal arts that Boethius's curriculum came to be introduced into Benedictine monasticism.[128] In the next century and the ninth, Isidore and Alcuin were also to summarize mathematical material found in Boethius.

The first of Boethius's four mathematical works, *De institutione arithmetica*, is an adaptation of a Neopythagorean work of the second century and has survived. It deals with the theory of numbers and serves as an introduction to the second subject, *De institutione musica*. As such it remained a principal authority for scholars until the Italian Renaissance[129] with numerous texts wholly or partly surviving from the ninth century onwards. Many of these have been noted in centres that were important in the ninth and tenth centuries either for monastic reform or for architectural influence, or both. Twenty have been recorded from the ninth century including one at St Gall and two in Cologne; another twenty from the tenth century including another one at Cologne, with one each at Verdun and Bernward's Hildesheim; and twenty-six from the eleventh century including another at St Gall and one at Chartres.[130] In addition to this, it is noteworthy that an introduction to and summary of the work were being written late in the tenth century at St Bénigne in Dijon, presumably at or near the time William of Volpiano was engaged in rebuilding the abbey there and, at about the same time, Abbo of Fleury was also writing about it.[131]

Boethius's *De musica* was largely modelled on Ptolemy's *Harmonica* but the surviving text ends prematurely and contains only the first of three parts. At least one ninth-century manuscript of it from Corbie has been noted as well as another from early in the tenth century.[132] Continuing the tradition of Plato and Augustine, it treats music not in terms of the practicalities of music-making but as a means of perceiving the divine order. Quite understandably, therefore, its theories of harmony and melody derived from the musical ratios are said to have been put into practice most of all the arts by the Church and the treatise was read at St Gall and Chartres among other important centres.[133]

Boethius's *De institutione geometria* was consulted by Alcuin and Gerbert[134] but it has not survived. The treatises attributed to Boethius that have been transmitted under the title *Ars geometriae et arithmeticae*, although not his, are nevertheless partly derived from him. However, the authentic Boethian work is likely to have been in the Platonic tradition and to have contained passages from Euclid, including Book I and parts of Books III and IV.[135] Certainly Cassiodorus mentioned that Boethius had rendered Euclid into Latin.[136] And so detailed and exhaustive is his *De arithmetica*, and so pervasive its Platonic viewpoint, that it is reasonable to assume that his lost *De geometria* was equally so.

The surviving *Ars geometriae* also supports this contention. Although a compilation of various authors including Boethius, possibly emanating from Corbie once again, it was nevertheless attributed to Boethius in the middle ages. At least ten manuscripts have been noted from the ninth, tenth and eleventh centuries at such influential centres as Paris, Strasbourg and St Gall as well as Corbie, and usually in combination with other works including Boethius's *De arithmetica* and *De musica* and Augustine's *De musica*.[137] The first of its five books gives the propositions in shortened form from Books I–IV of Euclid's *Elementa* which, according to the text, are translations by Boethius. However, only an obscure rendering of them is given, sometimes with the relevant figure. Yet they do at least indicate some understanding of Euclid early in the middle ages and served perhaps, by way of this abbreviated paraphrase, as a teacher's prompt.[138]

Finally, Boethius's *De institutione astronomia* was also referred to by Gerbert, establishing its existence in the tenth century, but it too has since been lost.[139] However, on the evidence of Boethius's surviving texts and of other treatises on astronomy, it is again reasonable to assume a Platonic treatment, with the motion of the heavenly bodies being presented as the music of the spheres and a way of understanding the universal order.

Ironically, the misfortune which befell Boethius at once curtailed his scholastic endeavours and inspired the writing of his greatest work. As the result of a palace intrigue, he was imprisoned on a charge based apparently or false testimony and a year later put hideously to death. While in jail he wrote his *De consolatione philosophiae* in the form of a Platonic Dialogue, albeit combining prose with verse, in which Philosophy appears to Boethius as a woman. Despite the fact that it is not an explicitly Christian work, nearly four hundred medieval manuscripts have been noted, a large number dating from the ninth and tenth centuries when it was studied in various schools including, once again, St Gall. Moreover, before the tenth century, Remigius of Auxerre had already written a standard commentary on it and Alfred the Great had personally produced a paraphrase of it in Anglo-Saxon for the edification of his subjects, a tenth-century manuscript of which exists in the Cotton collection of the British Museum.[140]

Early in the tenth century the Christian credentials of *De consolatione philosophiae* were doubted by Bruno and Bovo of Corvey. Yet Boethius's handling of such questions as those concerning the Holy Trinity and the Incarnation in his earlier theological tracts must surely leave his own Christian status in very little doubt, as is testified by his canonization as St Severinus. The debate at Corvey centred on Book III.ix which is a distillation of *Timaeus* by Boethius, who evidently read it together with Proclus's commentary on it. Bovo, in comparing Boethius's poem with Macrobius's *Commentarii in Ciceronis Somnium Scipionis*, assigned to it a greater Platonic than Christian weight, though this did little to dim his enthusiasm for it.[141] The passage in question seeks to distinguish between true and false happiness.

'But since in the Timaeus my servant Plato was pleased to ask for divine help even over small matters, what do you think we ought to do now in order to be worthy of discovering the source of that supreme good?'

'We ought to pray to the Father of all things. To omit to do so would not be laying a proper foundation.'

'Right,' she said, and immediately began the following hymn.

'O Thou who dost by everlasting reason rule,
Creator of the planets and the sky, who time
From timelessness didst bring, unchanging Mover,
No cause drove Thee to mould unstable matter, but
The form benign of highest good within Thee set.

All things Thou bringest forth from Thy high archetype:
Thou, height of beauty, in Thy mind the beauteous world

Dost bear, and in that ideal likeness shaping it,
Dost order perfect parts a perfect whole to frame.

The elements by harmony Thou dost constrain,
That hot to cold and wet to dry are equal made,
That fire grow not too light, or earth too fraught with weight.
The bridge of threefold nature madest Thou soul, which spreads
Through nature's limbs harmonious and all things moves.

The soul once cut, in circles two its motion joins,
Goes round and to itself returns encircling mind,
And turns in pattern similar the firmament.

From causes like Thou bringst forth souls and lesser lives,
Which from above in chariots swift Thou dost disperse
Through sky and earth, and by Thy law benign they turn
And back to Thee they come through fire that brings them home.'

De consolatione philosophiae III.ix

Poetic though this is, it nevertheless contains the basic ingredients of Platonic cosmology, namely, the Father of all things who rules by reason, shaping an 'ideal likeness' of his 'high archetype' so that the 'perfect parts' are framed by a 'perfect whole', the perfection of which, as has been shown, was usually signified by 10. Also apparent are the 3-fold soul, the 4 elements that are constrained by divine harmony and the return of souls to the Father through his benign law which, it has been shown, may also be equated with 10.

As for the universal order that is perceptible in numbers, Boethius was quite definite in his *De arithmetica*. This was closely modelled on the *Introductionis arithmeticae libri duo*, a standard textbook for Neoplatonic studies in Athens and Alexandria which had been written by Nicomachus of Gerasa, a Neopythagorean, in the second century.[142] As Boethius says in the *Proemium*:

Those things which were discussed in a rather diffuse manner
by Nicomachus concerning numbers, I have put together with
moderate brevity; those things which demanded a greater care
of understanding, but are gone through quickly, I clarified with
a small additional explanation and I have even used formulae
and diagrams for greater clarity of matters.

De arithmetica, Proemium

It may be seen that Boethius's version consists of terms and definitions and the composition and relationships of numbers from first principles, demonstrating their inherent order. The account itself is systematic. Proceeding from unity, Book I deals with quantity on its own, then quantity in relation. This continues in Book II and is further developed through figurate numbers that are planar, to those that are solid. After two chapters of metaphysics, the remaining work is devoted to various forms of numerical proportion concluding, as his introduction to *De musica*, with various medial proportions including the harmonic.

As with his *De consolatione*, Boethius acknowledges his debt to *Timaeus* and, in so doing, he echoes Clement and Augustine concerning the intellectual demands that will be made on the student:

> . . . it is now time we related something very useful in Platonic disputation which is treated in that all encompassing work, the Timaeus, and which is by no means easy for anyone unless he is trained in a very discerning reason.
>
> *De arithmetica* II.46

The importance he gives to the elements and to number again conveys the Platonic tradition, as does his observation of the original concept of universe as the turning of one.

> Number was the principal exemplar in the mind of the Creator. From it was derived the multiplicity of the four elements, from it were derived the changes of the seasons, from it the movement of the stars and the turning of the heavens.
>
> *De arithmetica* I.2; cf. Augustine, *De musica* VI.11.29

> We are not ignorant of the fact that the four elements make up the world; as they say, material bodies are born from fire, air, earth, and water. But for these elements, again, there is a prior composition . . . .
>
> *De arithmetica* II.1

To apprehend the 'prior composition' or 'the first element of all things',[143] Boethius points out that,

> . . . hardly anyone has been able to reach the highest perfection of the disciplines of philosophy unless the nobility of such

wisdom was investigated by him in a certain four-part study, the quadrivium . . . .

There are various steps and certain dimensions of progressing by which the mind is able to ascend so that by means of the eye of the mind, which (as Plato says) is composed of many corporeal eyes and is of higher dignity than they, truth can be investigated and beheld. This eye, I say, submerged and surrounded by the corporal senses, is in turn illuminated by the disciplines of the quadrivium.

De arithmetica I.1

In explaining the primacy of arithmetic in the *quadrivium*, Boethius continues,

[Arithmetic] is prior to all not only because God the Creator of the massive structure of the world considered this first discipline as the exemplar of his own thought and established all things in accord with it; or that through numbers of an assigned order all things exhibiting the logic of their maker found concord; but arithmetic is said to be first for this reason, also, because whatever things are prior in nature, it is to these underlying elements that the posterior elements can be referred. . . . The same thing is seen to occur in geometry and arithmetic. If you take away numbers, in what will consist the triangle, quadrangle, or whatever else is treated in geometry? All of those things are in the domain of number. If you were to remove the triangle and the quadrangle and all of geometry, still 'three' and 'four' and the terminology of the other numbers would not perish. Again, when I name some geometrical form, in that term the numbers are implicit. But when I say numbers, I have not implied any geometrical form.

De arithmetica I.1

He then goes on to explain his ordering of the remaining two subjects of the *quadrivium*, music and astronomy.

An extended summary of his *De arithmetica* is given here so as to show how exhaustive and detailed the demonstrations of numerical order, harmony and proportion could be for anyone reading it in the tenth century. To begin with, Boethius reveals the order that exists in the simplest of numbers. Following Macrobius and Martianus rather than Augustine, he defines even and odd numbers as being divided into equal parts without and with unity in the middle.[144] Of the three forms of even number, those which are even by even can be arranged thus,

1,	2,	4,	8,	16,	32,	64,	128

in which,

			8	×	16				= 128
		4		×		32			= 128
	2			×			64		= 128
1				×				128	= 128

Similarly, if the series is curtailed at 64,

1,	2,	4,	8,	16,	32,	64

			8	×	8			= 64
		4		×	16			= 64
	2			×		32		= 64
1				×			64	= 64

About this Boethius says:

> This basic ordering of numbers has come about through careful consideration and through the great constancy of divinity . . . .

> *De arithmetica* I.9

An even number is overperfect when the sum of its divisors exceeds the number itself. For example, 12 is overperfect because,

$1 + 2 + 3 + 4 + 6 = 16$, which exceeds 12.

Underperfect numbers are the reverse. For example, 8 is an underperfect number because,

$1 + 2 + 4 = 7$, which is less than 8.

This is why numbers which are exactly the sum of their divisors are called perfect numbers, such as 6, where,

$1 + 2 + 3 = 6$ (see I.19; cf. Augustine, *De Trinitate* IV.4.7)

There is in these a great similarity to the virtues and vices. You
find the perfect numbers rarely, you may enumerate them more
easily and they are produced in a very regular order. But you
find (overperfect or underperfect) numbers to be many and
infinite and not disposed in any order, but arranged randomly
and illogically, not generated from a certain point. Within the
first ten numbers there is only one perfect number, 6; within the
first hundred, there is 28; within a thousand, 496; within ten
thousand, 8,128.

De arithmetica I.20

In asserting that number is 'the principal exemplar in the mind of the Creator'
and that the ordering of numbers occurred 'through the great constancy of
divinity',[145] Boethius is adopting the same stance as Clement and Augustine
before him. Yet his *De arithmetica*, being in effect a text-book designed to
introduce music theory, is more a mathematical, as distinct from metaphysical,
exposition of numbers than those of his two predecessors. The distinction is
not absolute, however, for he does cover much the same ground, as when he
echoes Augustine in relating the first 4 numbers to the geometric elements of
point, line, surface and solid.[146]

Moving from definitions of a point to linear numbers,[147] then to figurate
numbers, Boethius makes a similar observation to Plato:

Every figure is made of triangles . . . if from the middle to each
angle are drawn lines until so many triangles divide the figure
as that figure happens to have angles.

De arithmetica II.6; cf. Plato, *Timaeus* 53C

This is followed by a graphic depiction of triangular, square and polygonal
numbers, as originating in the arrangement of numbers of pebbles in
geometric shapes.[148] In so doing, Boethius illustrates their composition and
reveals how each series of figurate numbers is rationally ordered.

o o o

Triangular numbers are composed thus:

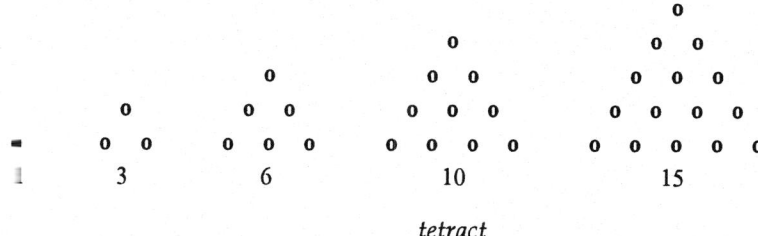

1	3	6	10	15

tetract

The series of triangular numbers is shown below with the number of intervals occurring between them arranged underneath. The third triangular number after unity, incidentally, illustrates the *tetract*, namely 3 sides of 4 units amounting to 10.

1, **2**, 3, 4, 5, 6, 7, 8, 9, **10**, 11, 12, 13, 14, **15**, 16, 17, 18, 19, 20, **21** – 28
     2   3   4   5   6

Square numbers occur like this:

4	9	16	25

Their series and the intervals between them read as follows:

1, **4**, 3, 4, 5, 6, 7, 8, **9**, 10, 11, 12, 13, 14, 15, **16**, 17, 18, 19, 20, 21, 22, 23, 24, **25**
   2   4   6   8

Pentagonal numbers follow in a similar fashion:

5	12	22	35

The series of pentagonal numbers and their intervals are as follows:

1, **2**, 3, 4, **5**, 6, 7, 8, 9, 10, 11, **12**, 13, 14, 15, 16, 17, 18, 19, 20, 21, **22** – **35**
    3   6   9   12

Other polygonal numbers are then shown not only to follow suit[149] but to be the sum of a triangular number and a number of the preceding polygon. In this way, square numbers are derived from the addition of two adjacent triangular numbers; pentagonal numbers are the sum of triangular and square numbers; hexagonal numbers from triangular and pentagonal numbers.

square   = triangle + triangle
4 = 1+3,   9 = 3+6,   16 = 6+10,   25 = 10+15

pentagon = triangle + square
5 = 1+4,   12 = 3+9,   22 = 6+16,   35 = 10+25

hexagon = triangle + pentagon
6 = 1+5,   15 = 3+12,   28 = 6+22,   45 = 10+35

If all these numbers were compared with respect to numbers of sides, that is the triangles to the tetragons, or the tetragons to the pentagons . . . without any doubt each will exceed the others in terms of triangles.

De arithmetica II.19

Not only does this illustrate Plato's theory whereby the polyhedra of the elements are all composed from triangles, it also explains why Boethius's polygons are equilateral and not regular. He is demonstrating an additive process involving triangles in which the pentagon is a square plus an equilateral triangle, and a hexagon a square plus two equilateral triangles. His interest lies not in angles but in shapes with equal sides.[150]

His treatment of solid bodies is similarly systematic though somewhat briefer.

Now for the creation of solid bodies the [figurate] numbers naturally provide surfaces for us.

De arithmetica II.23; cf. Martianus 721

With a triangle written and described, if we place single lines from the three angles, first standing straight then inclined so that they join at a vertex on one point in the middle, a pyramid is produced.

De arithmetica II.21

When the numbers of cubes are so extended that from any number of cubic quantity a side begins, and the extremity is terminated at the same point of height, then that number is called cyclical or spherical. Such are the multiplications which begin from five or six. Five times five, which makes 25, having progressed from 5, ends at the same 5. If you extend this five out again, its terminus will again come to 5. Five times 25 makes 125 and if you bring this number to five times more, it will be terminated in a five number. And this will always happen the same way, all the way to infinity. It would also be suitable to consider this process in the number six.

De arithmetica II.30

In associating 5 with the sphere, this not only recalls Macrobius's description of 5 embracing all things and Martianus's assignment of 5 to the universe,[151] it is interesting that this particular passage immediately precedes two chapters dealing with the metaphysics of the universe with their references to *Timaeus*.

Thus it is known to us, that just as it is in this matter, so in the world are things joined together. Either things are of the same immutable proper substance, as are God, the soul or the mind, or whatever is blessed with incorporality by its own nature, or they are of a variable and mutable nature, which we undoubtedly see is the case in corporeal things.

De arithmetica II.31

Turning to numerical proportion, Boethius says:

It is testified to and known among the ancients who have studied the learning of Pythagoras, or Plato, or Aristotle, that these are the three ways to knowledge: arithmetic, geometric, harmonic. After these relationships of proportions there are three others, which are conveyed to us without names but are called fourth, fifth, and sixth, and which are contrasted with the above. Then later thinkers, on account of the perfection of the number ten, which was pleasing to Pythagoras, added four other kinds, so that in these proportionalities they brought together a body of proportions ten in number.

De arithmetica II.41

Of the three principal proportions, the arithmetic displays an equal difference between its numbers and is therefore non-expanding, such as,

1, 2, 3, 4   (see *De arithmetica* II.43)

A geometric series will expand by an equal proportion, as in,

2, 4, 8, 16, or 1, 3, 9, 27   (see *De arithmetica* II.44)

The harmonic proportion,

. . . asks that just as there be extreme terms in a ratio to each other, so the difference of the larger to the smaller stands compared to the difference of the median to the final term.

De arithmetica II.48

For example,

3, 4, 6, or 2, 3, 6,

because,

$6 : 3 :: (6 - 4) : (4 - 3)$

and, $6 : 2 :: (6 - 3) : (3 - 2)$

The relationship between arithmetic, geometry and music was indissoluble. In his *De arithmetica* Boethius states:

> The same relationship which we remarked in geometry can be found in music.
>
> *De arithmetica* I.1

and in his *De musica*,

> . . . the ear is affected by sounds in quite the same way as the eye is by optical impressions . . . .
>
> *De musica* I.32, in von Simson 33

> Of those musical consonances which they call symphonies, you will find practically all the ratios of the harmonic medial proportion. For that symphony called diatessaron, which is the principal one, and, as it were, the one holding the force of a primal element, it is constituted in a *epitrita* ratio, as a four is to three . . . .
>
> *De arithmetica* II.48

In other words, of the harmonic proportion 3, 4, 6,

$3 : 6 = 1 : 2$ = diapason

$4 : 6 = 2 : 3$ = diapente

$3 : 4$ = diatessaron (see *De arithmetica* II.48)

As for geometric harmony:

> An harmonic median is called such because its proportionality is related to geometric harmony. They call a cube geometric harmony because it is so extended from longitude into latitude and it also grows into an accumulation of height so that starting out from equals and going to equals, it has developed so that it fits totally evenly in relation to itself. This type of medial proportion exists in all cubes which, it has been seen, is a

geometric harmony. Every cube has 12 sides, 8 angles, 6 surfaces. This order and disposition is [*sic*] harmonic.

De arithmetica II.49

For example, of the foregoing numbers of the cube,

6, 8, 12 = 2 × (3, 4, 6)	= harmonic proportion
6 : 8	= diatessaron
8 : 12	= diapente
6 : 12	= diapason (see *De arith.* II.49)

Boethius then incorporates the three principal types of proportion within the single concept of a median moving to any one of the three positions within the same fixed extremes. He exemplifies this as when:

. . . a musician raises the pitch by stretching, or lowers it by loosening, the string. Thus with two numbers given, we may introduce now the arithmetic, now the geometric, and now the harmonic medial proportion. Thus the right and proper name of the medial proportion may be given when, with the extremities remaining unchanged, the median may be seen to move to this or that number, and so be carried back and forth.

De arithmetica II.50

Thus, 10, 25, 40 = arithmetic median

10, 20, 40 = geometric median

10, 16, 40 = harmonic median (see *De arithmetica* II.50)

After completing his exposition of the remaining medial proportions which fulfill 'the perfection of the number ten',[152] Boethius concludes with 'the greatest and most perfect symphony shown in three intervals', which is,

6, 8, 9, 12 (see *De arithmetica* II.54)

and which is also cited by Clement and Martianus.[153] Firstly it can be shown that all 4 numbers are products of those of the *tetract*:

$6 = 1 \times 2 \times 3$

$8 = 1 \times 2 \times 4$

$9 = 1 \times 3 \times 3$

$12 = 1 \times 3 \times 4$

Therefore all 4 musical ratios inhere in the series.

$$8 : 6 :: 12 : 9 :: 4 : 3 \qquad \text{= diatessaron}$$

$$6 : 9 :: 8 : 12 :: 2 : 3 \qquad \text{= diapente}$$

$$6 : 12 :: 1 : 2 \qquad \text{= diapason}$$

$$8 : 9 \qquad \text{= one tone}$$

The series incorporates all three principal medial proportions. The arithmetic proportion is present in that,

$$6 + 3 = 9, + 3 = 12$$

The geometric proportion is expressed thus:

$$6 : 9 :: 8 : 12$$

$$2 : 3 :: 2 : 3$$

And the harmonic proportion occurs because,

$$12 : 6 :: (12 - 8) : (8 - 6)$$

$$2 : 1 :: 4 : 2$$

Furthermore, although not mentioned by Boethius, the series displays another instance of *analogia* since its extremes and means are in agreement, a fact pointed out by Isidore[154] for,

$$6 \times 12 = 8 \times 9 = 72$$

To summarize, Boethius followed Nicomachus in starting with unity and showing how number develops from simple numbers to figurate numbers, both planar and solid, before moving to numerical proportions, and how this development was logical because of the inherent order to be found in numbers. Boethius's 'greatest and most perfect symphony' is perhaps the best model of this, showing as it does how numerical ratio, musical harmony and geometric proportion are but manifestations of the same universal order, where every part is in proportion to the other parts and to the whole – the classical meaning of symmetry. And as this final example shows, it may be seen that the result of true symmetry is a symphony, for it follows that an 'agreement of sounds' must result from an 'agreement of measures'.

Conclusion

In the fact that Platonic thought was transmitted to the Latin West so comprehensively, perhaps something of its pervasiveness in contemporary literature can also be appreciated together with its concern with number, harmony and proportion. Besides the massive influence of Augustine and the Latin encyclopedists, evidence for the spread of Platonic thought to the Latin middle ages is diverse and attested, for example, by the transmission of Clement through Cassian, Origen by Rufinus and Ambrose, Plotinus by Victorinus to Augustine as well as Dionysius by Gregory and John Scotus. Proof of acceptance is given by the countless texts dating from the ninth, tenth and eleventh centuries in the form of copies or translations of, or commentaries on, original texts, as well as shortened versions of standard texts, with even popular editions in the vernacular, such as Alfred's interpretation of Boethius's *De consolatione philosophiae* and Aelfric's adaptation of Basil's *Hexaëmeron* which appeared in Anglo-Saxon in the ninth and tenth centuries respectively. Crucially, it is also supported by the fact that the *quadrivium* actually formed part of the curriculum in monastery schools, where treatises such as Boethius's *De arithmetica* were used as standard text-books.

Summarized most simply, it is beyond doubt that the *Timaeus* translation and commentary by Chalcidius conveyed Plato's cosmology to the West and to the early middle ages along with Macrobius's *Somnium Scipionis*; Martianus's *De nuptiis* transmitted a synopsis and curriculum of the liberal arts; Augustine secured the acceptance of Christian Platonism by the Latin Church, not least through his *De civitate Dei*; Boethius provided treatises on the liberal arts; and Cassiodorus's *De institutione* introduced the liberal arts to Benedictine monasticism. The fact that each of these manuscripts was also among the most widely collected, read, copied and adapted early in the middle ages seems conclusive.

The essence of these beliefs posited a universal order that was to be seen first and foremost in numbers; that these numbers, either singly or in series, were invested with special significance; that the authority for this was both Platonic and biblical. It is also noted that the path to apprehending the divine order, it was believed, lay through the mathematical subjects of the liberal arts, the *quadrivium* of arithmetic, music, geometry and astronomy; that these subjects revealed manifestations of the same divine order, which was both rational and harmonious; and that the harmony of the cosmos was maintained by the constituent parts of creation being in proportion to each other and to the whole.

Whilst it is recognized that this material in itself is no longer controversial, it has been presented here at length because, as already argued, full weight has not always been given to the reality and likely implications of Christian Platonism by the literature that challenges its connection with medieval religious architecture.

Notes

1   Parker 269.
2   Ball 19.
3   Boyer 57; Burkert 467, 474; Copleston 1966, 36; but see also Böckh 158; Heath 1921, I.161.
4   Burkert 72, 186; see pp. 70–72, 89–90, 106, 109.

5   Heath 1921, I.75–6; Copleston 1966, 33; Chadwick 1981, 88; Augustine, *De musica* 155.
6   Speusippus, *Theologumena arithmetices* 62.17–22 in Heath 1921, I.76; Burkert 23; Guthrie 38; see also Böckh 157.
7   Boyer 94, Smith II.295.
8   Ball 19–20; Heath 1921, I.66, 160.
9   Ball 20, Lasserre 20; see p. 74.
10 Lasserre 20; Kline 42; Boyer 91; Burkert 421–2.
11 Augustine, *De civitate Dei* 403n87.
12 Plato, *Timaeus* 9f.
13 Fowler 200.
14 Burkert 85; Klibansky 28.
15 Plato, *Timaeus* 8; Augustine, *De civitate Dei* VII.6.
16 Cornford 1937, 6.
17 Cornford 1937, 210.
18 Boyer 94; Cornford 1937, 210; *OCD* 1051.
19 Euclid, *Elementa* Bk.XIII.
20 Plato, *Phaedo* 110B, Cornford 1937, 219.
21 Heath 1956, II.97.
22 Boyer 55; Proclus, Summary 67,6 in Heath 1956, II.99.
23 Cornford 1941, 263n2,3; see pp. 106–7.
24 Philippus 981BC; Lasserre 81–2.
25 Klibansky 6–7, 51–2.
26 Burkert 450; Lasserre 73; Pingree 157; Smith I.187.
27 Casey 96.
28 Marlowe 251; Chadwick 1970, 180; Casey 96.
29 Osborn 123.
30 Casey 97; Chadwick and Oulton 38; *ODCC* 246.
31 Origen 27–9, 77n16.
32 Casey 59, 100; Dudden 113, 457, 459; Brown 84–6, 271; Chadwick 1970, 181; Marlowe 251.
33 Clement, *Stromateis* I.25; Marlowe 251.
34 Marlowe 252–3.
35 See also Copleston 1972, 20; Osborn 122.
36 Clement I.12–15; Tonnington 208.
37 Clement, *Stromateis* V.6.
38 E.g. I.25; II.5, 22; V.14; VI.2; V.4; VI.5.
39 Clement, *Stromateis* VI.16.
40 Ps-Barn. *Epistolae* 9.8.
41 Clause added by Hervetus to complete the sense, Clement, *Stromateis* 353n1.
42 Augustine, *De civitate Dei* 455n46; Marlowe 249.
43 Casey 100.
44 Marlowe 249; Knowles 30.
45 See Klibansky 36; Brown 91.
46 Augustine, *De civitate Dei* 316n32; Brown 95–6; see p. 64.
47 Gregory 1–8; Basil xi–xv.
48 Basil xliv; Gregory 87; Klibansky 24.
49 Klibansky 24; Basil 51; p. 37–8.
50 White 1981, 168.
51 Klibansky 24.

52 Basil, I.2.
53 *ODCC* 140.
54 See also Basil, I.5 below.
55 See pp. 76, 98.
56 Suger, *De administratione* XXVII, XXXIII.
57 Gregory 18.
58 Origen 27–9; see pp. 50, 55–6, 64.
59 *OCD* 635; Heath 1921, II.529; Augustine, *De civitate Dei* VII.25.
60 Brown 91–2; Augustine, *De civitate Dei* xxvi, 285n58; *OCD* 864; Heath 1921, II.529.
61 Brown 92–3; Augustine, *De civitate Dei* 417n117; see pp. 61–2, 64–5.
62 Klibansky 28.
63 Plato, *Timaeus* 53C.
64 Macrobius 10.
65 Macrobius 10, 13, 57; 11, 15, 81; Kren 230.
66 Martianus 15.
67 Macrobius 39-41, 47, 51, 60; Martianus 22; Wagner 19, Kren 230.
68 Macrobius I.5.15; I.6.18.
69 Clement, *Stromateis* VI.12.
70 Martianus 732; Macrobius I.5.17.
71 Macrobius I.6.11.
72 Martianus 741.
73 Macrobius I.6.7; Martianus 731.
74 Macrobius I.6.18; Martianus 732, 736.
75 Martianus 736, 733; Macrobius I.6.22, 23, 42.
76 Macrobius I.6.22, 23, 36, 41; Martianus 734.
77 Martianus 735.
78 Macrobius I.6.12; Martianus 736.
79 Plato, *Timaeus* 35B–C; Macrobius I.6.11, 34, 45–7, 54–5; Martianus 738.
80 Martianus 740; Macrobius I.6.15–16.
81 See p. 114.
82 Martianus 721–2.
83 Martianus 722, 742; 721; Macrobius I.6.19.
84 Martianus 735.
85 Martianus 127.
86 Ambrose, *Epistolarum Classis* 34.1, PL 16, 1119; Brown 84, 93; *ODCC* 43.
87 Dudden 113, 457, 459; Brown 84.
88 Augustine, *De civitate Dei* xi; Brown 84–6; *ODCC* 43.
89 Augustine, *Confessiones* 177n35; Brown 95; Copleston 1972, 28; Brown 105–110.
90 *Hist. Litt.* VI.76.
91 Chadwick 1981, 80; Klibansky 23.
92 Augustine, *Confessiones* VII; dates from Brown 74, 184, 282.
93 Augustine, *De ordine* II.12–15; 331n4.
94 Augustine, *De musica* 155–65.
95 Augustine, *Confessiones* VII.17–21.
96 Augustine, *De civitate Dei* X.29; X.28; Brown 102.
97 Augustine, *De civitate Dei* VIII.12; X. *passim*; XI.23, XXI.17, 455n46.
98 Augustine, *De civitate Dei* VIII.11.
99 Augustine, *De civitate Dei* VIII.11; VIII.8.
100 Augustine, *De civitate Dei* VIII.11, see above.

101 See p. 45.
102 Augustine, *De quantitate animae* 9.
103 Augustine, *De civitate Dei* XV.20.
104 Augustine, *De musica* I.12.26; I.6.22–3; see p. 63.
105 Macrobius I.6.23; Martianus 733.
106 Augustine, *De musica* I.12.22.
107 Augustine, *De musica* I.12.23.
108 Augustine, *De musica* I.12.24; *De Trinitate* IV.4.7.
109 Krautheimer 123; Augustine, *De Trinitate* IV.4.7, see pp. 48–9, 106–7.
110 Augustine, *De civitate Dei* XI.31; see also *Epistolae* 55.
111 Macrobius I.6.45–6.
112 Also Clement, *Stromateis* V.14; see pp. 107–9.
113 Ball 112; Heath 1921, II.529f; Pedoe 167; Proclus 1970, xviii–xx.
114 Gow 134.
115 Proclus, Summary 65.19; Fowler 297–8.
116 Pedoe 168; Proclus 1970, xxvi.
117 See pp. 115–16; Rosan 223.
118 *ODCC* 406; Rosan 223; Ps-Dionysius, *passim*.
119 Proclus 1963, xxvi; Ps-Dionysius, *De divinis nominibus* 3.2, 4.15.
120 Leclercq 26–7; *ODCC* 468.
121 Clement, *Stromateis* I.12; Ps-Dionysius, *De coelesti hierarchia* 2.5.
122 Patch 5, 118; see below; Boethius, *De consolatione philosophiae* 10, 11.
123 Camargo 98, 101; Stump 133.
124 See pp. 33–4.
125 Knowles 53; Klibansky 23–4; Patch 21.
126 Boethius, *De arithmetica* 13–14; Chadwick 1981, xii; Ball 132; Boyer 212; Patch 31.
127 Wagner 20.
128 Bennett 123–4; Lund 145; Leff 50; *OCD* 211; West 23f; PL 69, 70; see also p. 33.
129 Patch 36.
130 Boethius, *De arithmetica* 58–63.
131 White, A. 1981, 168; Smith I.190.
132 White, A. 1981, 164–5.
133 Chadwick 1981, 81, 85–7; White, A. 1981, 163; Boethius, *De arithmetica* 25–6; Patch 37–8.
134 Patch 37.
135 Chadwick 1981, 103–4: Boethius, *De arithmetica* 39n30; Ball 132–3.
136 Chadwick 1981, 103; Patch 2.
137 Ullman 267–83.
138 Ullman 271; *Ars geometriae* 389; see also Chasles 4.476 in Lund 144.
139 Chadwick 1981, 102; Lattin 54n4; Patch 4, 37.
140 Patch 12, 22, 27, 38, 50-51; Liebeschütz 588.
141 Liebeschütz 588–9; Patch 5, 27; Boethius, *De consolatione philosophiae* 18.
142 Chadwick 1981, 71.
143 Boethius, *De arithmetica* II.32, see above.
144 Boethius, *De arithmetica* I.3; cf. Augustine, *De musica* I.12.20–3.
145 Boethius, *De arithmetica* I.2, see above; I.9.
146 Boethius, *De arithmetica* II.4.
147 Boethius, *De arithmetica* II.4; II.5.

148 Burkert 72. The diagrams and numerical series are drawn from *De arithmetica*:
     for triangular numbers, II.7, 9, 16; for square numbers, II.10, 12, 16; for
     pentagonal numbers, II.13, 14, 16.
149 Boethius, *De arithmetica* II.15, 16.
150 See pp. 114–15.
151 Macrobius I.6.19; Martianus 735; see p. 63.
152 Boethius, *De arithmetica* II.41, see above.
153 Clement, *Stromateis* VI.11; Martianus 736.
154 Isidore, *Etymologiae* III.13.

Chapter 3

Metaphysical Belief
and
Architectural Metaphor

Since one likely implication of Christian Platonist thought is the influence it might be expected to have had on the design of religious architecture, it is now proposed to investigate this possibility. To this end, the writings available to the tenth century during the revival in monasticism and learning, as outlined in Chapter 1, will be examined for evidence which could point to such a connection, looking first at the practice of secrecy and use of allegory; then the study of philosophy and the liberal arts; the significance of number and proportion; the importance and use of geometry, architecture and symbolism; and concluding with a well-known example where a connection between geometry, architecture and symbolism appears to have existed.

Veiling the Truth

Many studies concerned with the design of sacred architecture in the middle ages have dealt with the question of trade secrecy among medieval masons, a topic which will also be taken up shortly here.[1] The point at issue is that if secrecy prevailed in the lodges, presumably extending to a lodge's design methods, this could explain the lack so far of conclusive evidence proving the existence of such design methods. Yet it is also important to note that in earlier centuries there was a deliberate policy at least on the part of Clement, Origen, Dionysius and others to veil truth from those who had not received 'certain purifications and previous instructions'.[2]

Clement's authority for this, as already noted, was once again both Platonic and biblical when he states that,

> . . . even those myths in Plato . . . are to be expounded allegorically . . . .
>
> *Stromateis* V.9

> Rightly, then, Plato, in the epistles, treating of God, says: 'We must speak in enigmas . . . .'
>
> *Stromateis* V.10

And quoting from the New Testament,

... even now I fear ... 'to cast the pearls before swine, lest
they tread them underfoot ....'

Stromateis I.12, quoting Matthew vii.6

For many reasons, then, the Scriptures hide the sense. First, that
we may become inquisitive, and be ever on the watch for the
discovery of the words of salvation. Then it was not suitable
for all to understand, so that they might not receive harm in
consequence of taking in another sense the things declared for
salvation by the Holy Spirit. Wherefore the holy mysteries of
the prophecies are veiled in parables – preserved for chosen
men, selected to knowledge in consequence of their faith; for
the style of the Scriptures is parabolic.

Stromateis VI.15

As if to bear this out, the contents of various chapters of Clement's *Stromateis*
are explicitly concerned with secrecy and mystery[3] and Clement continues his
exhortations throughout these chapters:

... we speak the wisdom of God hidden in a mystery ....

Stromateis V.4

... it is not wished that all things should be exposed
indiscriminately to all and sundry, or the benefits of wisdom
communicated to those who have not even in a dream been
purified in soul, [for it is not allowed to hand to every chance
comer what has been procured with such laborious efforts] ..

Stromateis V.9

It was doubtless in furtherance of this tradition that such exclusiveness was
actually formalized to the point where, according to Dionysius, the early
Church devised the liturgy so that its secrets remained protected during some
of its offices. As already seen, in describing baptism and communion, he
writes,

... let us behold the divine symbols which have to do with the
divine birth and let no-one who is uninitiated approach this
spectacle.

[And when] ... the deacons begin the reading of the holy
tablets ... the catechumens leave the sacred precincts, followed
by the possessed and the penitents ....

De ecclesiastica hierarchia 2.1, 3.II

To become initiated, on the other hand, was not easy and it was conceded that for the majority the apprehension of the divine scheme would necessarily remain a closed book. Basil speaks of,

> . . . too lofty a subject for men who are but beginners and are still babies in knowledge.
>
> *Hexaëmeron* I.5

Augustine acknowledges that,

> . . . only a rare class of men is capable of using [reason] as a guide to the knowledge of God . . . .
>
> *De ordine* II.11.30

As already noted, the way lay through a knowledge of the liberal arts, yet these are,

> . . . very difficult except for some very gifted person who even from boyhood has earnestly and constantly applied himself.
>
> *De ordine* II.16.44

Boethius concurs that it,

> . . . is by no means easy for anyone unless he is trained in a very discerning reason.
>
> *De arithmetica* II.46

However, despite Augustine's general appeal to,

> . . . livelier . . . intelligences . . . for the sake of others, not to think superfluous what for themselves they feel to be unnecessary. . . . [because] . . . we are forced very often to give an extended exposition of the obvious . . . .
>
> *De civitate Dei* VII Pref., II.1

he too could concede for example that,

> . . . although this mystery of the eighth day by which the Resurrection is symbolized was not concealed from the holy Patriarchs . . . it was locked up and hidden and taught only as the sabbath observance . . . .
>
> *Epistolae*, 55

Elsewhere he appears evasive when concluding a summary of the evolution of the liberal arts in *De ordine* with a passage about geometry and the power of reason. Just as he seems to be arriving at the number of reason itself, he suddenly veers away.

And it began to suspect that it itself was perhaps the very
number by which all things are numbered . . . But, false images
of the things which we number drift away from that most
hidden something . . . .

De ordine II.15.43

If a man does not yield to these images, and if he reduces to a
simple, true and certain unity all the things that are scattered
far and wide throughout so many branches of study, then he
is most deserving of the attribute learned. Then, without being
rash, he can search after things divine . . . .

De ordine II.16.44

This evasiveness is somewhat reminiscent of Plato when in *Timaeus*, having
described the 4 elements and their solids in considerable detail, he appears
almost to dismiss the final solid:

There still remained one construction, the fifth; and the god
used it for the whole, making a pattern of animal figures
thereon.

Timaeus 55C, Cornford 1937

The two possible explanations already referred to for such reticence are not
incompatible, the first being that Plato could be 'speaking in enigmas', the
second that he may have regarded it impossible to express the inexpressible,
as when he says in *Parmenides*:

Then the one has no name . . . .   *Parmenides* 142A

Or when Clement quotes him:

'For both is it a difficult task to discover the Father and Maker
of the universe; and having found Him, it is impossible to
declare Him to all. For this is by no means capable of
expression, like the other subjects of instruction', says the
truth-loving Plato.

Stromateis V.12

Such hesitancy naturally led to a certain amount of ambiguity and uncertainty.
Clement goes on to observe:

For doubting, in Timaeus, whether we ought to regard several
worlds as to be understood by many heavens, or this one, he
makes no distinction in the names, calling the world and

heaven by the same name. But the words of the statement are as follows: 'Whether, then, have we rightly spoken of one heaven, or of many and infinite? It were more correct to say one, if indeed it was created according to the model.'

Stromateis V.12, discussing *Timaeus* 55C, D

This again recalls the differences already noted over the nature of the fifth essence, as well as the numerological accretions of Macrobius and Martianus. Even Boethius, committed to precision though he was in *De arithmetica*, admits to the existence of ambiguity. In comparing the 10 types of medial proportion with the 10 predicaments, he writes:

So Plato, a very zealous student of Pythagoras, divided them according to the same argument, and Archytas the Pythagorean, before Aristotle, even though in some it may seem ambiguous, established those same ten predicaments . .

De arithmetica II.41

However, it may be seen that some ambiguity is more apparent than real. For example, it is a simple matter to distinguish between the various kinds of numerical perfection, as between 10 as the sum of the *tetract*, 6 as the sum of all its divisors or 7, being the sum of 3 and 4, and 12 being the product of 3 and 4. On the other hand, because 6 is also the product of 2 and 3, the female and male numbers, and is therefore associated with creation, as distinct from 5 which, being the sum of 2 and 3, is the number of marriage, Clement refers to 6 as the 'genital number', a term perhaps better translated as 'generative'. However, in the same passage he rather confusingly states that 6 'is called by the Pythagoreans marriage . . .'[4]

There would be a danger in all this, if taken to extremes, of playing the numbers game and hunting the symbol in scripture. It needs to be stressed therefore that, though some peripheral matters might sometimes be open to interpretation, the central notions of Christian Platonism were understood, albeit by the indoctrinated, and they only rarely gave rise to serious disagreement, such as concerned the theory of metempsychosis and of God as the Soul of the World.

It is debatable, of course, whether signs and symbols were intended to conceal the truth or reveal it. On the evidence, it seems that they were used as a key to understanding for those who were eligible and were left unexplained as an impediment to those who were not. A good example of this is perhaps Boethius's Book III poem ix of *De consolatione philosophiae* in which, as it has already been shown, it is possible to discern quite clearly even through 'the veil of allegory' all the principal particulars of the Platonic scheme. That this would have required 'certain previous instructions' is perhaps obvious, yet it does not follow that without those previous instructions the signs themselves do not exist in the text.

Philosophy and the Liberal Arts

Since it was held to be self-evident that God had endowed human beings with the capacity to reason,[5] the Christian acceptance of classical philosophy with respect to its methods and many of its fundamental conclusions was not an issue, any more than were the benefits of philosophy in any doubt. Clement had no difficulty in declaring that,

> . . . philosophy is the study of wisdom, and wisdom is the knowledge of things divine and human; and their causes.

Stromateis I.5

> Philosophy is not, then, the product of vice, since it makes men virtuous; and it follows, then, that it is the work of God, whose work it is solely to do good.

Stromateis VI.17

Likewise Augustine, since philosophers,

> . . . profess to be 'lovers of wisdom'. Now if wisdom is identical with God . . . then the true philosopher is the lover of God.

De civitate Dei VIII.1

After summarizing the history of Greek philosophy, Augustine notes that whilst Socrates may have been the first to develop moral philosophy, it was Plato who defined the 3 branches of natural, rational and moral philosophy, which Augustine later identifies as physics, logic and ethics respectively. This corresponds, moreover, with the 3 aspects of God as the cause of existence, the principle of reason and the rule of life[6] and,

> Platonists assert that the true God is the author of the universe, the source of the light of truth, and the bestower of happiness.

De civitate Dei VIII.5

Thus natural philosophy involves the study of the universe, its shapes, qualities and order, as well as the elements, bodies and all life as the creation of the One who is uncreated and immutable. Rational philosophy seeks God's illumination in distinguishing between the intelligible and sensible worlds as a way of acquiring knowledge. Moral philosophy teaches that virtue is only to be found through knowledge of God.[7]

The way to acquire knowledge was through the liberal arts which had already appeared as a curriculum in Plato's Academy.[8] It was expanded by Varro in the first century to incorporate grammar, dialectic, rhetoric, geometry, arithmetic, astronomy, music, medicine and architecture. By the time

Martianus wrote *De nuptiis*, the number of subjects had been reduced back to seven by the omission of medicine and architecture. This left a syllabus which fell rationally into a group of three subjects and one of four, for the first three, grammar, dialectic and rhetoric form the foundation for an education in the others.[9]

Without a working knowledge of Latin grammar, for example, little or no academic study was possible in the West. The principal schoolbooks for this were the fourth-century *De partibus orationis ars minor* and the *Ars grammatica* by Donatus, plus Priscian's *Institutiones grammaticae* from early in the sixth century, the survival of all three in hundreds of manuscripts and commentaries pointing to their influence throughout the medieval period.[10] Dialectic came next in the curriculum because it provides the means of assessing and interpreting the material and for this Boethius's *De topicis differentiis* and *In Ciceronis topica* dealt with the discovery and development of arguments.[11] After this, rhetoric trains the student to set out the argument formally and persuasively, for which Cicero's *De inventione* was the principal source together with the *Rhetorica ad Herennium* which was attributed to him.[12]

The student being thus equipped to read, understand and argue, there followed the four mathematical subjects and these were viewed as the means to higher knowledge whence the divine order of the intelligible world might be perceived. To Pythagoras they were 'steps', to Plato 'progressive steps', Nicomachus defined them as 'methods' and Boethius as the 'four ways', the *quadrivium*.[13]

Regarding the composition of the *quadrivium*, Martianus paired astronomy and music after geometry and arithmetic as being harmonic studies.[14] Boethius adopted a different order resulting from his own strict reasoning. Arithmetic comes first, being the 'root and mother' of the others. Music is then paired with arithmetic because both deal with multitudes. Whilst arithmetic demonstrates multitude on its own, music treats it in relation to other multitudes. Likewise, he groups geometry and astronomy together because both deal with magnitude, the first being static, the second being mobile.[15] In fact, Martianus also had a point because it can be seen that arithmetic and geometry are both pure subjects whilst music and astronomy are both applied. Nevertheless, such was the logical integrity of Boethius's sequence that it became adopted in the schools as the standard curriculum initially through the agency of Cassiodorus.[16]

Number and Proportion

Reason, number and proportion were inextricable facets of a single concept. As far as Augustine was concerned,

> ... reason is nothing else than number ....
>
> *De ordine* II.18.48

Now the Latin for both reason and ratio is *ratio*. Numerical ratios then are by definition rational. This transmitted to the Roman world and to the Latin middle ages the Greek concept of *logos*, or 'the Word', which also means both reason and ratio. When Augustine discusses 4 in relation to 1, 2, 3, he points out that 4 is both the sum of the extremes, 1 + 3, and the product of the mean, 2 × 2, and that an agreement such as this between extreme terms with their mean and vice versa is called *analogia*, or proportion, by the Greeks. And proportion is also, to him, by definition rational, the product of reason. Because the 4-step progression from point, line and plane to solid can be related to the 4 numbers of the *tetract*, both displaying as they do an equality of parts, Augustine calls this 'a corrationality (for so I have chosen to call proportion) . . .'[17] To Boethius, proportion and ratio were interchangeable terms.[18] Proportion, after all, consists in sets of ratios.

One point of importance for the present study is that the numerical and proportional relationships transmitted by thinkers from Pythagoras to Boethius had been discovered, not invented, by man. They were acknowledged as manifestations of mathematical laws already in existence.

> It appears, indeed, that even before this world an order of things existed of which our mind can form an idea . . . .
>
> Basil, *Hexaëmeron* I.5

The question this posed, as well as the answer to it, were obvious to Augustine:

> Where, I ask, do these things come from, if not from the highest and eternal rule of numbers, likeness, equality, and order? And if you abstract these things from earth, it will be nothing. And therefore God Almighty has made earth . . . .
>
> *De musica* VI.17.57

And to Boethius too:

> Number was the principal exemplar in the mind of the Creator.
>
> *De arithmetica* I.2

A second point of importance is that it was presumably as a result of this conclusion that qualities or powers were attributed to numbers. About the significance of this, Augustine was unequivocal:

> And now a word about the reasons for putting these numbers in the Sacred Scriptures . . . let no one be so foolish or so absurd as to contend that they have been put in the Scriptures

for no purpose at all, and that there are no mystical reasons why these numbers have been mentioned.

De Trinitate IV.4.10

. . . the theory of number is not to be lightly regarded, since it is made quite clear, in many passages of the holy Scriptures, how highly it is to be valued. It was not for nothing that it was said in praise of God, 'You have ordered all things in measure, number and weight.'

De civitate Dei XI.30, quoting Wisdom XI.20

This was repeated by Isidore of Seville in the seventh century.

The doctrine of numbers must not be despised. In many places . . . of the holy scriptures it shines forth, where they have a mysterious meaning. It is not in vain . . . that in the praises of God it is said 'Thou has made everything in measure, number and weight'. . . . Take away number in all things, and everything perishes.

Etymologiae III.4

Accordingly 1 is the First Principle and the generator of all numbers.[19] Geometrically,

. . . unity has the potential of a point, the beginning of interval and longitude . . . a point exists without magnitude or a body or dimension of an interval . . . .

Boethius, *De arithmetica* II.4

2 is the first interval, the first departure from unity and is the female number.[20]

3 as the first triangular number, is the first plane, the triangle being the irreducible of figures. 3 is also the first number to be wholly odd.[21] With the 3 divisions of philosophy corresponding to the 3 aspects of God, 3 also stands for the Trinity which, at least by the twelfth century, was being represented in Thierry's *Heptateuchon* by the regular triangle,[22] thereby geometrically expressing that,

. . . this great harmony is in the first three numbers.

Augustine, *De musica* I.12.22

4 is the first number that is wholly even. It is the first square number and the sum of the elements, the cardinal points of Earth and, once the New Testament was promulgated, the number of evangelists and gospels. Because it gives height to a plane, 4 extends the geometric elements of point, line and plane to solids. Because of its association with quadrangles,[23]

> . . . a figure of four equal lines . . . [reminds Augustine that] justice is identical with equity; and equity seems to derive its name from . . . equality . . . .
>
> *De quantitate animae* 9

In this he transmits the original Pythagorean meaning of 4. Finally, the 'corrationality' of the numbers of the *tetract* persuades Augustine that,

> . . . one, two, three, four is the most closely connected progression of numbers.
>
> *De musica* I.12.23

This, however, seems to have been extended to 5 because:

> If there are numbers 1, 2, 3, 4, one and four make 5, two and 3 of the middle part also make five . . . .
>
> Boethius, *De arithmetica* II.43

As Plato's 'fifth construction', 5 represents the universe that embraces all things, as well as the human microcosm with its 5 senses.[24] It also binds the first 4 categories of figurate numbers together into the sum of 120:

> . . . the number 120 consists of four numbers – of one triangular, 15; of another, a square, 25; of a third, a pentagon, 35; and of a fourth, a hexagon, 45. The 5 is taken according to the same ratio in each mode.
>
> Clement, *Stromateis* VI.11

6 is the first perfect number and, as the product of the female number 2 and the male number 3, stands for creation and thence as a 'symbol of time':[25]

> . . . this same number six is taken as the equivalent of a year in the building up of the Lord's body . . . For they said: 'Forty-six years has this temple been in building.' And forty-six times six makes two hundred and seventy-six. . . . [and] the perfection itself of the Lord's body is known to have been brought to birth in so many days . . . .
>
> Augustine, *De Trinitate* IV.4.9

This appears to have been foreshadowed by Plato:

> For the divine creature there is a period embraced by a perfect number; while for the human there is a geometrical number determining the better or worse quality of the births.
>
> *Republic* XXIX.546

Not only does 6 lie at the root of time, it also binds together 3, 4, 5 for,

$$3^3 \quad + \quad 4^3 \quad + \quad 5^3 \quad = \quad 5^3 \qquad\qquad = \quad 216$$

$$3 \quad \times \quad 4 \quad \times \quad 5 \quad = \quad 6 \times 10 \qquad = \quad 60$$

and, $216 + 60 \qquad\qquad\qquad = \quad 276 \quad = \quad 46 \times 6$

The significance of 216 and 276 partly lies in the distinction made in antiquity between seven- and nine-month pregnancies, in that they are the number of days in seven and nine months, a distinction apparently meant by Plato's 'better or worse . . . births'[26] and by Augustine recording the full gestation period for 'the Lord's body'. Although this may appear abstruse or even fanciful to the modern reader, it was not held to be so at the time, for 6 was evidently seen as the root of a series of relationships which bound together the creation of the universe with time, Christ's Nativity and human birth. This seems to have been understood in the tenth century when Hroswitha in one of her plays has Sapientia praise the Creator, who,

> . . . created the world out of nothing, and set everything in number, measure, and weight, and then, *in time and the age of man*, formulated a science which reveals fresh wonders the more we study it.
>
> *Passio sanctarum*, in Hroswitha/St John 140 [my italics]

7 was significant partly because,

> . . . three is the first odd whole number, and four is the first whole even number, and seven is made up of these two. . . . For this reason the Holy Spirit is often referred to by this same number . . . .
>
> Augustine, *De civitate Dei* XI.31

and because it also stood for God's rest on the seventh day of Creation.[27]

> And the Lord's day Plato prophetically speaks of in the tenth book of the Republic, in these words: 'And when the seven days have passed to each of them in the meadow, on the eighth day they are to set out and arrive in four days.' By the meadow is to be understood the fixed sphere . . . and the locality of the

pious; and by the seven days each motion of the seven planets, and the whole practical art which speeds to the end of rest. But after the wandering orbs the journey leads to heaven, that is, to the eighth motion and day. And he says, that souls are gone on the fourth day, pointing out the passage through the four elements. But the seventh day is recognized as sacred, not by the Hebrews alone, but also by the Greeks . . . .

> Clement, *Stromateis* V.14, quoting Plato, *Republic* X.616B

Here the association of 7 with sanctity, the Lord's rest and the 7 planets is clear enough, as is the reference to the 4 elements. 8 on the other hand seems to signify a new beginning:

'. . . on the eighth day they are to set out . . .' (on) the journey (that) leads to heaven, that is, to the eighth motion and day . . .'

It certainly signalled a new beginning to Augustine when he compared the renewal that comes from circumcision on the eighth day with that inaugurated by the Resurrection, for,

. . . what does the eighth day symbolize but Christ, who rose again after the completion of seven days, that is, after the Sabbath? . . . .

> *De civitate Dei* XVI.26; see also *De sermone Domini* I.IV.12

8 however also represents 'the fixed sphere', or the meadow in Clement's explanation of Plato's prophecy,[28] namely Earth itself, as Plato tried to describe.

You must conceive it to be of such a kind as this: as if in some great hollow swirl, carved throughout, there was such another, but lesser, within it . . . and in the same manner a third, and a fourth, and four others, for that the whirls were eight in all, as circles one within another . . . but that the whole of them, being eight, composed one harmony.

> *Republic* X.616C-E, in Basil 66n4; see also Crombie 14f

Clement evidently had this in mind in a further reference:

And they call eight a cube, counting the fixed sphere along with the seven revolving ones, by which is produced 'the great year'. . . .

> *Stromateis* VI.16

The additional connection here with the cube is in reference to 8 being the first cube number, namely 2^3. Because a cube is enclosed by 6 surfaces, it was regarded as perfect [29] and, by extension, Boethius demonstrates how it contains geometric harmony because:

> Every cube has 12 sides, 8 angles, 6 surfaces.
>
> *De arithmetica* II.49

As the sum of the *tetract*, 10 contains all numbers and represents both the highest degree of perfection and the law.[30] Because the *tetract* amounted to 10, 4 was regarded as a 'potential decad'.[31] Moreover, 10, as a triangular number, has 3 sides of 4 units and in an apparent reference to this, Lucian, writing in the second century, puts these words into the mouth of Pythagoras:

> . . . what thou thinkest four is ten, and a perfect triangle, and our oath.
>
> *Vitarum auctio* II.457, in Hopper 42

He thereby embraces within 10, numerical and geometric perfection, along with the Pythagoreans' sacred oath. Yet the unifying properties of 10 operated not only for distinct ideas and traditions but numerically as well, for both Clement and Augustine saw its value as a highly rational multiplier, qualifying them perhaps to be among the earliest champions of the decimal system.[32]

12 marks the passage of time, as when Clement expounds on Plato's *Republic*,[33]

> . . . on the eighth day they are to set out and arrive in four days, (on the) journey (that) leads to heaven . . . .
>
> *Stromateis* V.14

This makes 12 days in all. It is also,

> . . . significant as being the number of the patriarchs and of the apostles because it is the product of the two parts of seven - that is, three multiplied by four . . . .
>
> Augustine, *De civitate Dei* XV.20
> see also *In Iohannis evangelicum* 27.10(A)

> . . . 'you who have followed me will also sit on the twelve thrones as judges of the twelve tribes of Israel'. . . For the numbers three and four are parts of seven; and seven is a customary symbol of universality. And the product of three and four is twelve . . . .
>
> *De civitate Dei* XX.5

And when the angels mated with humans,

> . . . the Lord said: '. . . their days be a hundred and twenty
> years'. . . .
>
> De civitate Dei XV.23
> cf. Clement, Stromateis VI.11

Whilst not perhaps the most staggering event in the Bible, except for the
people concerned, 120 is numerically comprehensive being the product of:

2 × 60, **3** × 40, **4** × 30, **5** × 24, **6** × 20, 8 × 15, **10** × 12 and **12** × 10,

as well as the sum of the first 15 numbers.[34]

12 not only encompasses the geometric harmony of the cube, namely 6, 8, 12,
which incorporates the musical harmonies of diapason, diapente and
diatessaron, but also 'the greatest and most perfect symphony shown in three
intervals', namely 6, 8, 9, 12.[35] As noted above, this is entirely generated by the
numbers of the *tetract*, its extremes and means are in agreement with each
other, it incorporates all three principal medial proportions and, once again,
the three musical ratios of diapason, diapente and diatessaron, not to mention
the third figurate numbers of the triangle, the square and the pentagon as well
as the first cube. In addition to the relationships recorded by Boethius and
Isidore, Clement had put forward yet another:

> And the number 35 depends also on the arithmetic, geometric,
> and harmonic scale of doubles – 6, 8, 9, 12; the addition of
> which makes 35.
>
> Stromateis VI.11

As it happens, 35 is also the fifth of the pentagonal numbers with which 12
is again connected, for it follows the fourth pentagonal number, 22, after an
interval of 12, and the dodecahedron of the universe consists of 12 pentagons.

Returning to 12 and its association with time, it has been suggested that
the perfect number embracing the period of the universe in Plato's allegory is
probably the universal great year.[36] This was calculated as 36,000 solar years
of 360 days which, incidentally, concurs with the composition of the
dodecahedron. As Plutarch observed, this consists of 12 faces each of 30
elementary triangles making 360 in all.[37] If this interpretation is correct, the
great year may be expressed as,

$$(3 \times 4 \times 5)^2 \times 10 = (6 \times 10)^2 \times 10 = 36{,}000$$

thereby uniting 3, 4, 5 once again with the two foremost numbers of
perfection, 6 and 10. Put more simply, as has already been shown,

$$3 \times 4 \times 5 = 6 \times 10$$

The importance of 3, 4, 5 as a numerical series seems to be implied in a passage by Philo about the number of pillars inside the Tabernacle, a description which might otherwise be obscure:

> ... there will then be left that most holy number of fifty, being the power of a rectangular triangle, which is the foundation of the creation of the universe . . . .
>
> *De vita Mosis* III.3

Now the 'rectangular triangle' of Pythagoras has sides of 3, 4, 5 and,

$$3^2 + 4^2 + 5^2 = 50$$

It is thought that Pythagoras's theorem for a right-angled triangle was invested with more than just mathematical meaning by his followers and that the numerical series of 3, 4, 5 which it exemplifies was equally significant to them.[38] If Philo was implying, as he seems to be, that this series itself provided the foundation for the created universe, it could hardly be more important. Certainly, in consisting of the first figurate numbers of the triangle, the square and the pentagon, it represents the regular solids of the 4 elements and the universe. And if it is expressed as the equation of Pythagoras's theorem,

$$3^2 + 4^2 = 5^2$$

it also demonstrates how the atmospheric elements and earth, 3 and 4, are unified within the encompassing universe, 5 (fig. 3). This in itself might qualify it as being at least one of the secrets of the universe, about which much mirth is sometimes made. Yet it has already been shown that this same series displays a union with 6, the number of creation, and thence with time itself. It might be thought therefore, in comparison with such universal equations as these, its better known manifestation in Pythagoras's theorem is somehow of a lesser order. But in describing the angle which is not only upstanding to the plane of earth but alone is 'right', the series 3, 4, 5 provides a construct that is fundamental to the perception of the world and lies at the very root of geometry.

By demonstrating the connection between this series and its corresponding geometry with Plato's cosmology, as well as the fundamental importance of this connection, the pivotal point of the argument has been reached in justifying the geometric figures put forward in this study. In order to seek support for their application to religious architecture, it is now proposed to examine the connection between geometry, architecture and symbolism.

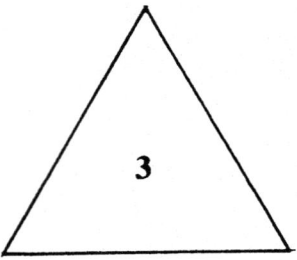

Fire, Air, Water

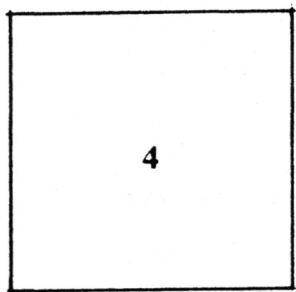

Earth

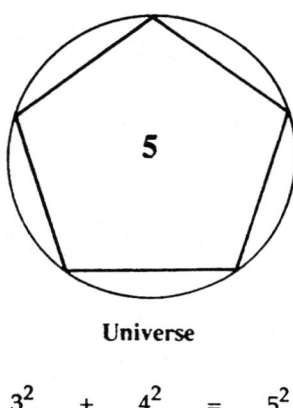

Universe

$$3^2 \quad + \quad 4^2 \quad = \quad 5^2$$

Fig.3 The elements, the Platonic figures and their figurate numbers.

Geometry, architecture and symbolism

Geometry

The subjects of the *quadrivium* had a practical as well as theoretical value for,

> . . . philosophy knows the world of thought and the world of sense – the former archetypal, and the latter the image of that which is called the model . . . .
>
> Clement, *Stromateis* V.14

However, according to Augustine, since,

> . . . all the liberal arts are learned partly for practical use and partly for the knowledge and contemplation of things, to attain the use of them is very difficult . . . .
>
> *De ordine* II.16.44

Nevertheless, it was evidently geometric theory that was held in special regard, offering as it did a glimpse of the intelligible world. In fact, although each subject of the *quadrivium* naturally enjoyed its own importance, particularly arithmetic which was anterior to all, geometry to Clement was pure essence.

> Prosecuting, then, the proportion of harmonies in music; and in arithmetic noting the increasing and decreasing of numbers, and their relations to one another, and how the most of things fall under some proportion of numbers; studying geometry, which is abstract essence, he perceives a continuous distance, and an immutable essence.
>
> *Stromateis* VI.10

This recalls Plato's allusion, already quoted:

> I do not mean by beauty of form such beauty as that of animals or pictures . . . but, says the argument, understand me to mean straight lines and circles, and the plane or solid figures which are formed out of them . . . for these I affirm to be not only relatively beautiful, like other things, but they are eternally and absolutely beautiful . . . .
>
> *Philebus* 51C

This is a thought closely echoed by Augustine:

> For there is a wide difference between knowing something in the cause of its creation, and knowing it as it is itself. Compare, for example, the conception of a straight line, or any figure as

truly apprehended by the mind, with the representation of it
drawn in the dust . . . .

De civitate Dei XI.29

Shortly before using the principles of geometry in his *De quantitate animae* to
demonstrate the perfection of unity and the immateriality of the soul, he
wrote:

> Scanning the earth and the heavens, [reason] realized that
> nothing please it but beauty; and in beauty, design; and in
> design, dimensions; and in dimensions, number. It asked itself
> whether any line or curve or any other form or shape in that
> realm was of such kind as intelligence comprehended. It found
> that they were far inferior, and that nothing which the eyes
> beheld could in any way be compared with what the mind
> discerned. These distinct and separate realities it also reduced
> to a branch of learning, and called it geometry.

De ordine II.15.42

Despite the anterior position of arithmetic, there is arguably an apparent
ascendency sometimes of geometry over arithmetic, in the recourse arithmetic
persistently has in expressing its relationships geometrically through figurate
numbers. In Martianus's *De nuptiis*, Geometry even precedes Arithmetic and,
at the conclusion of her exposition:

> When Geometry saw that these matters were accepted, she
> drew a straight line upon the abacus and asked: 'How does one
> go about constructing an equilateral triangle upon a given finite
> straight line?' When the learned company realized that she was
> intending to construct the first proposition of Euclid, they
> immediately began to break out in acclaim and applause of
> Euclid. . . . Through this performance of her's [Geometry] was
> acknowledged to be the most learned and generous of all the
> bridesmaids.

De nuptiis 724

Boethius's exposition has already shown how figures and their corresponding
figurate numbers are built up by the addition of the triangle to the preceding
figure.[39] The process commences with the triangle, being the plane that is
irreducible; then the square is obtained by adding another triangle to it; a
pentagon by adding another triangle to the square and so on.

Accordingly, the shapes need only be equilateral for this process to work.
As it happens, however, both the equilateral triangle and the square are also
regular figures, but not so the polygons. Because of the additive process
involved, Boethius's diagrams reveal that the pentagon for example is only a
square plus an equilateral triangle, which is what makes the complete figure

equilateral. To transform it into a regular pentagon requires the agency, in the form of the golden triangle, of φ, the ratio known much later as the golden section or divine proportion.

This additive process can equally be seen in terms of Platonic cosmology whereby equilateral triangles represent the three atmospheric elements, the square the earth, and the regular pentagon the plane figure of the dodecahedron of the universe. Yet the process above shows that, by merely combining the geometric figures of the 4 elements, only an equilateral pentagon is obtained. To create the regular pentagon of the universe requires the injection once again of the proportion later known as divine.

For evidence that geometry had actually been regarded as expressing divinity, at least in the Greek world, it is necessary to turn to *In primum Euclidis elementorum librum commentarii*, written by Proclus in the fifth century. In commenting on Euclid's Definitions in Book I concerning angles, triangles and rectangles, Proclus writes:

> The angle is a symbol and a likeness . . . of the coherence that obtains in the realm of divine things . . . For the angle functions as a bond between the several lines and planes . . . Of plane angles some represent the primary and unmixed unifying agencies, others those that contain the infinity of their own progressions; *some the unifying forces of the intelligible forms* . . .

> *In primum Euclidis*, Definition IX, 128–9

Because the right angle is,

> . . . always determinate and fixed in nature, not admitting of either growth or diminution . . . (the Pythagoreans) refer right angles to the immaculate essences in the divine orders . . . for what is upright, uninclined to evil, and inflexible accords with the character of those high gods . . . .

> *In primum Euclidis*, Definition X, 132

> The Pythagoreans assert that the triangle is the ultimate source of generation . . . Consequently the Timaeus says that the ideas of natural science, those used in the construction of the cosmic elements are triangles. . . . Rightly, then, Philolaus dedicates the angle of the triangle to the four gods Kronos, Hades, Ares and Dionysus, since he includes within their province the entire fourfold ordering of the cosmic elements derived from the heavens or from the four segments of the zodiacal circle. Kronos gives being to all the moist and cold essences, Ares engenders every fiery nature, Hades has control of all terrestrial life, and Dionysus supervises moist and warm generation . . .

> *In primum Euclidis*, Definitions XXIV–XXIX, 166–7

The Pythagoreans thought that [the square] more than any
other four-sided figure carries the image of the divine nature.
. . . Philolaus, moreover, in another of his reflections calls the
angle of the square the angle of Rhea, Demeter, and Hestia. For
since the square is the substance of earth and the element
nearest it, as we learn from the Timaeus . . . he rightly
dedicates the angle of the square to these life-giving divine
forces. For some call the earth Hestia or Demeter, and they say
that it partakes of all that Rhea is . . . They also liken the
square to the whole of virtue, since it has four right angles,
each of them perfect . . . We must not omit to observe that
Philolaus dedicates the angle of the triangle to four gods and
the angle of the square to three, showing their penetration of
one another and the communion of all in all, of odd numbers
in the even and of even in the odd. Hence a tetradic triad and
a triadic tetrad that partake of the generative and creative
goods maintain the whole order of generated things. The
number twelve, which is their product, ascends towards a
single monad, the sovereignty of Zeus. Philolaus says that the
angle of the dodecagon is the angle of Zeus, because Zeus
holds together in a single unity the whole duodecimal number.
In Plato likewise Zeus leads 'the twelve' and has absolute
dominion over all things.

In primum Euclidis, Definitions XXX–XXXIV, 173–4

As it happens, the references Proclus makes to 'the zodiacal circle' and the
dodecagon as representing Zeus appear to support Moessel's thesis that sacred
buildings from antiquity were planned in proportions derived from dividing
a circle into certain numbers of parts, including 12 in relation to the division
of time.[40] However, it needs to be stressed that Proclus is recounting beliefs
held much earlier by Philolaos and by other Pythagoreans and, though these
beliefs may well have informed temple design, Proclus does not say so. As
already noted, Proclus belongs to the Greek tradition rather than the Latin,
despite such influence as is evidently found in Boethius and John Scotus.[41]
Nevertheless, since this information was available, albeit in the Greek world
of the fifth century, the possibility at least exists that the tradition was known
elsewhere.

For example, akin to the connection Proclus makes between geometry and
divinity, it has also been shown that Augustine attached Platonic qualities to
geometry in his *De quantitate animae*. Whilst equality and the quadrangle
represent justice, the more equal the properties of a figure, the more perfect
it is; the point, as the perfection of unity, being the 'most excellent of all'.[42]
Since geometric symbolism can be attested late in antiquity, it needs to be
asked whether there is evidence of its expressive use in architectural design.

Architecture and symbolism

It is understandable that theoretical geometry should have had practical associations with draughtsmanship and architecture, which was itself formerly one of the liberal arts. Clement, acknowledging the practical applications of the liberal arts, writes,

> The same holds also of astronomy. . . . since also navigation and husbandry derive from this much benefit, as architecture and building from geometry.
>
> *Stromateis* VI.11

There must have been those who saw only a practical value in the *quadrivium*, for he goes on to correct them:

> But to those who object, What use is there in knowing the causes of the manner of the sun's motion, for example, and the rest of the heavenly bodies, or in having studied the theorems of geometry or logic, and each of the other branches of study? – for, these are of no service in the discharge of duties, and the Hellenic philosophy is human wisdom, for it is incapable of teaching the truth – the following remarks are to be made. . . they have not read what is said by Solomon; for, treating of the construction of the temple, he says expressly, 'And it was Wisdom as artificer that framed it; and Thy providence, Father, governs throughout'. And how irrational, to regard philosophy as inferior to architecture and shipbuilding!
>
> *Stromateis* VI.11

The reference here to Wisdom framing the construction of the Temple brings this study to the question as to whether or not, in the Christian era, it ever did. With temples to build, are there any indications that some may have been 'framed by Wisdom' through a tradition of design either inherited or initiated?

Both the Tabernacle and the Temple were regarded as universal symbols by writers as early as Philo and Josephus. Bede was to describe them as signifying the Church of Christ, the Tabernacle designating the present Church because it was constructed on the journey to the promised land, the Temple designating the future Church because it was erected once the promised land was reached.[43] Basing his description on biblical sources together with Cassiodorus and Josephus, to the extent even of having sight of a plan of the Temple, Bede's treatises amount to a detailed exposition of the numerology of both structures, as well as their fittings and furnishings, in terms of the numbers of items and dimensions.[44] Underlying these is a similarity in proportions between the two. The Court of the Tabernacle is 50 cubits by 100 cubits, a double square, inside which the Holy Place is 20 cubits by 10 cubits, another double square, preceding the Holy of Holies which measures 10 cubits by 10 cubits. The basic dimensions of the Temple are 20 cubits by 40 cubits for the Sanctuary, which opens into the Most Holy House of 20 cubits by 20 cubits. In other words, both structures consist of a square and a double square.

This proportion is partially confirmed by Vitruvius in his treatise *De architectura*, which was written in the first century BC. Of importance to this study is the survival of over fifty manuscripts of the work from the ninth century onwards, including a transcription of one bearing the signature of the first abbot of Bernward's newly completed abbey at Hildesheim.[45] However, evidence for the expressive use of geometry seems indefinite, as when he writes:

> Geometry provides many aids for architecture and first of all from right angles it teaches the use of compasses from which plans of buildings on their sites and the alignments of set-squares and the determinations of the horizontal and of plumb-lines are most easily achieved.

> *De architectura* I.I.4, 1989

This neither concludes that geometry was used in expression of metaphysical beliefs nor does it exclude the possibility either. For example, in Book III on planning temples, Vitruvius is aware that the 'ancients' and Plato regarded 10 as a perfect number, as mathematicians regarded 6. And he does state that the planning of temples requires the use of symmetry which arises from proportion after the fashion of the human body. After an analysis of human proportions and measures,[46] he says:

> Therefore if Nature has planned the human body so that the members correspond in their proportions to its complete configuration, the ancients seem to have had reason in determining that in the execution of their works they should observe an exact adjustment to the several members to the general pattern of the plan.

> *De architectura* III.I.4, 1931

It may be observed that none of this seems written with much assurance and when he actually itemizes various plans, no connection is made at all between number theory and temple design, in spite of the foregoing passage. Nevertheless, he does state that the overall proportion of a plan for a temple should be a double square, although he specifies 1 : 1¼ for the cell. A forum should be 2 : 3, a basilica between 1 : 2 and 1 : 3, whilst Greek theatres are designed from squares and Roman theatres from regular triangles.[47] No explanation or justification is given for the choice of these proportions or figures and when he continues Books III and IV with an account of the classical orders, which admittedly is exhaustively detailed, it seems very much a straight prescription of rules, again without any explanation or connection being made with his earlier observations about symmetry, proportions derived from anthropometrics, or number theory. This seems to leave an impression of there having been an ancient tradition of design which in itself expressed sacred beliefs[48] but which had already become a distant memory, with knowledge of its implementation possibly forgotten.

More definite indications seem to be offered by references made to wisdom and the laying of foundations. Building on a firm foundation is still a common enough metaphor and it appears in the most famous of Boethius's poems in *De consolatione philosophiae*:

> We ought to pray to the Father of all things. To omit to do so would not be laying a proper foundation.

> *De consolatione philosophiae* III.ix

This may imply no more than to provide a sound basis for an enterprise. Even if a specifically architectural connotation were intended, it might simply mean sound site-preparation and construction rather than anything esoteric about the plan. Nevertheless, the reference is repeatedly associated with wisdom and divine intention. Basil, again with the composition of his audience in mind, preaches:

> 'In the beginning God created'. . . we call 'beginning' the essential and first part from which a thing proceeds, such as the foundation of a house . . . it is in this sense that it is said, 'The fear of the Lord is the beginning of wisdom,' that is to say that piety is . . . the groundwork and foundation of perfection. . . . the creation of the heavens and of the earth were like the foundation and groundwork, and afterwards that an intelligent reason, as the word beginning indicates, presided in the order of visible things.

> *Hexaëmeron* I.5, 6

The Church and its teaching are invested with similar allegory:

> . . . 'according to the grace,' it is said, 'given to me as a wise master builder, I have laid the foundation. And another buildeth on it gold and silver, precious stones.'

> Clement, *Stromateis* V.4

> Certainly He is called 'the chief corner stone, in whom the whole building, fitly joined together, groweth into an holy temple of God,' according to the divine apostle.

> Clement, *Stromateis* VI.17

Later, Bede was to state that:

> The foundation of the temple is to be understood mystically
>
> De templo 4.1

Since architecture is habitually used as a metaphor for the divine creation and the Church, it follows that its foundation, as well as its superstructure, should conform to perfection. The whole context of Clement's earlier image of Wisdom framing the temple is, not that this is mere practical wisdom, but the Wisdom that comes from perceiving the intelligible world as revealed through the liberal arts which he had just enunciated. Basil shortly returns to the metaphor:

> Thus, then, to show that the world is a work of art displayed for the beholding of all people; to make them know Him who created it, Moses does not use another word. 'In the beginning,' he says 'God created.' He does not say 'God worked', 'God formed', but 'God created.'. . . Being good, He made it an useful work. Being wise, He made it everything that was most beautiful. Being powerful He made it very great. *Moses almost shows us the finger of the supreme artisan taking possession of the substance of the universe, forming the different parts in one perfect accord, and making a harmonious symphony result from the whole.*
>
> Hexaëmeron I.7 [my italics]

Here in this fourth-century text that was rendered into Anglo-Saxon in the tenth century is surely the precursor of images of the divine architect creating cosmos out of chaos so familiar in the twelfth and thirteenth centuries (pl. 5). In fact, an image of the Creator who 'ordered all things in measure, number and weight' appeared on a page of the *Eadui Gospel* which was produced at Canterbury shortly after the millennium, only a generation after Aelfric's Anglo-Saxon adaptation of the *Hexaëmeron* (pl. 4).[49]

In Basil's next sermon, architecture seems to represent the path to knowledge:

> . . . we have found such a depth of thought that we despair of penetrating further. If such is the forecourt of the sanctuary, if the portico of the temple is so grand and magnificent, if the splendour of its beauty thus dazzles the eyes of the soul, what will be the holy of holies? Who will dare to try to gain access to the innermost shrine? Who will look into its secrets? To gaze into it is indeed forbidden us, and language is powerless to express what the mind conceives.
>
> Hexaëmeron II.1

Forbidden though it may be, the temptation to penetrate further is almost palpable. There were secrets, according to this, capable of being apprehended by the mind but not language of being expressed. Now these architectural allusions which Basil makes are confined to the first two of his nine sermons, namely, those which deal with the very beginning of creation. In other words, when he thinks of the universe before anything else was created in it, he thinks in architectural terms of an abstract model. Is it likely therefore that the designing of sacred architecture itself did not reciprocate?

Further support for the concept of architecture as symbol comes with connections in Augustine's writing between geometry as abstract essence and architecture as symbolizing the divine creation. Having written that,

> . . . [reason] realized that nothing please it but beauty; and in beauty, design; and in design, dimensions; and in dimensions, number.
>
> *De ordine* II.15.42

Augustine elaborated upon this a few chapters later. Here an explicit analogy seems to be made once again to the Divine Creator forming cosmos from chaos.

> Out of several pieces of material lying around in scattered fashion [*chaos*] and then assembled into one design, I can make a house [*cosmos*]. If, indeed, I am the maker and it is made, then I am the more excellent, and the more excellent precisely because I am the maker [*Divine Creator*]. There is no doubt that I am on that account more excellent than a house. But, not on that account am I more excellent than a swallow or a small bee, for skillfully does the one build nests, and the other construct honey-combs. I am, however, more excellent than they because I am a rational creature.
>
> Now, if reason is found in calculated measurements, does it follow that the work of birds is not accurately and aptly measured? Nay, it is most accurately and aptly proportioned. Therefore, it is not by making well-measured things, but by grasping the nature of numbers, that I am the more excellent.
>
> *De ordine* II.19.49

In other words, it is not the mere construction, but what it actually means as expressed in terms of numbers and their proportions, that is important. He offers another example, relating 6, the number of creation and the first that is perfect, to the temple of the Lord's body:

> . . . this same number six is taken as the equivalent of a year in the building up of the Lord's body; for he spoke of it

frequently as the temple, and said that He would raise up in three days the temple destroyed by the Jews. For they said: 'Forty-six years has this temple been in building.' And forty-six times six makes two hundred and seventy-six. And . . . the perfection itself of the Lord's body is known to have been brought to birth in so many days.

De Trinitate IV.4.9

Augustine's allegorization seems even more explicit in *De civitate Dei* which, it should be remembered, was started years after he had returned to his native Africa and became the bishop of Hippo, for here was no desert hermit but an episcopal leader with his own church and his own diocese of churches to oversee.

> Whether we call it the 'House of God' or the 'Temple of God', or the 'City of God', it is the same thing.

> Indeed this house, the City of God, which is the holy Church, is now being built in the whole world after the captivity in which the demons held captive those men who, on believing in God, have become like 'living stones' of which the house is being built.

> Thus when God said . . . 'And I shall grant peace in that place,' the word 'place' is symbolic, and by it we are to understand the person whom it symbolizes. And so the re-building 'in that place' stands for the Church which was destined to be built by Christ; and the only acceptable meaning of the saying, 'I shall grant peace in this place' is, 'I shall grant peace in the place which this place symbolizes'. . . . Then, we may be sure, the master builder himself, who said, 'Many are called, but few are chosen,' is going to show us a house, built not of those who were called . . . but of those who have been chosen. And that house will thereafter dread no downfall . . . .

> *De civitate Dei* XV.9, VIII.24, XVIII.48

With 'the house' accepted as a symbol, the ceremonies held within it are also symbolic, a fact repeatedly emphasized by Dionysius:

> . . . let us behold the divine symbols which have to do with the divine birth.

> *De ecclesiastica hierarchia* 2.1

> . . . I have already clearly shown . . . that sacred symbols are actually the perceptible tokens of the conceptual things.
>
> *De ecclesiastica hierarchia* 2.III.2

> Join me in observing how appropriately the symbols convey the sacred.
>
> *De ecclesiastica hierarchia* 2.III.7

The various services, starting with baptism, which Dionysius describes in *De ecclesiastica hierarchia*, all stress the symbolism of the liturgy. As to the symbolism of 'the house' itself, it is possible that this was explained in another treatise of his, *The Symbolic Theology*. As mentioned earlier, although there is no evidence that this was ever written, Dionysius refers to it several times in his other writings:

> This was all dealt with in more detail by me in *The Symbolic Theology* when I was explicating the four elements.
>
> *De coelesti hierarchia* 15.6

> I am sending you the full text of my *Symbolic Theology*, where you will find explanations for the house of wisdom, the seven pillars . . . .
>
> *Epistola ad Titum* 1113B

The justification of symbolism is the encouragement of anagogy, as acknowledged by Christian writers from Clement onwards, including once again Dionysius.

> We use whatever appropriate symbols we can for the things of God. With these analogies we are raised upward toward the truth of the mind's vision, a truth which is simple and one.
>
> *De divinis nominibus* 1.4

> He revealed all this to us in the sacred pictures of the scriptures so that he might lift us in spirit up through the perceptible to the conceptual, from sacred shapes and symbols to the simple peaks of the hierarchies of heaven.
>
> *De coelesti hierarchia* 1.3

As a result:

> Theological tradition has a dual aspect, the ineffable and mysterious on the one hand, the open and more evident on the other. The one resorts to symbolism and involves initiation. The

other is philosophic and employs the method of demonstration
. . . This is why the sacred initiators of our tradition, together
with those of the tradition of the Law, resorted freely to
symbolism appropriate to God . . . .

Epistola ad Titum 1105D-1108A

If Moses' Tabernacle and Solomon's Temple were acknowledged symbols,
with their elaborate numerology underpinned by the proportions of the square
and double square, so was Noah's Ark. Yet, though it shares some similarities
with the Tabernacle and Temple regarding number symbolism, its proportions
differ and, whilst the Tabernacle and Temple signify the living Church, the
Ark appears to be an embodiment of salvation. Clement, in describing the
Tabernacle and the Ark, is quite specific in linking a sacred canon to
constructional design and in confirming the anagogical function of the
architecture:

And let the testimony of geometry be the tabernacle that was
constructed, and the ark that was fashioned, constructed in
most regular proportions, and through divine ideas, by the gift
of understanding, which leads us from things of the sense to .
. . the holy of holies. For the squares of wood indicate that the
square form, producing right angles, pervades all, and points
out security. And the length of the structure was three hundred
cubits, and the breadth fifty, and the height thirty . .
Now there are some who say that three hundred cubits are the
symbol of the Lord's sign; and fifty, of hope and of remission
given at Pentecost; and thirty . . . because the Lord preached in
His thirtieth year.

Stromateis VI.11

In describing the Tabernacle, Philo appeared to attribute 50 to the 3, 4, 5
right-angled triangle and thence to the foundation of the universe[50] and,
interestingly, particular emphasis seems to be placed in his and other
explanations of the Ark on the square form of its timbers:

Why does he make the ark of squared pieces of wood?
He does this in the first place, because the figure of a square.
. . . is steady and firm, consisting as it does of right angles.

Quaestiones in Genesim II.2

To Clement, the squares of wood, pervading all, point out security, an
observation that was to be echoed by Augustine (see below). Origen explains
the Ark's dimensions thus:

> ... the text speaks of the length and breadth and height of the
> ark and numbers are proposed in these dimensions indeed
> which have been consecrated by great mysteries.
>
> Three hundred is three one hundreds. Now . . . one
> hundred is shown to be full and perfect in everything and to
> contain the mystery of the whole rational creation. . . . It is
> stated as tripled in as much as it is . . . increased to perfection
> by the grace of the Trinity.
>
> The width has the number fifty which has been consecrated
> as the number of forgiveness and remission. For according to
> the law there was a remission in the fiftieth year.
>
> But the number thirty . . . contains a mystery like the
> number three hundred. For what a hundred multiplied by three
> makes there, ten multiplied by three makes here.

In Genesim homiliae II.5

In addition to assigning meaning to the overall dimensions of the Ark,
Clement analyses them thus:

> And the numbers introduced are six-fold, as three hundred is
> six times fifty; and ten-fold, as three hundred is ten times thirty

Stromateis VI.11

In that $300 = 6 \times 50 = 10 \times 30$, both the breadth and the height are divisors of
the length, giving the 'most regular proportions' and displaying therefore
analogia or true symmetry. 6, it has been shown, represents creation and is the
first perfect number. 10 is given particular prominence, representing both the
law and the Pythagorean quality of perfection, leading to the assertion that,

Noah was a *just* man and *perfect* in his generations. Genesis 6.9 [my italics]

This was pointed out by both Origen and Augustine in their explanations of
the Ark.[51] Thus it can be seen that both 6 and 10 are integral to the whole
scheme of the Ark for,

$$
\begin{array}{lrcl}
 & 300 & = & \mathbf{10} \times 30 \\
\text{or} & & & \mathbf{6} \times 50
\end{array}
$$

$$
\begin{array}{lrcl}
 & 50 & = & \mathbf{10} \times 5
\end{array}
$$

$$
\begin{array}{lrcl}
 & 30 & = & \mathbf{6} \times 5 \\
\text{or} & & & \mathbf{10} \times 3
\end{array}
$$

As it happens, both these numbers are also divisors in the plans of the
Tabernacle and Temple, measuring as they do 30×10 cubits and 60×20

cubits respectively. In his own exegesis of the Ark, Augustine, who had seen Origen's homily in Rufinus's translation,[52] practically paraphrases both Clement and Origen and, in so doing, casts it as a vessel of salvation.

> That Noah, with his family, is saved by water and wood, as the family of Christ is saved by baptism, as representing the suffering of the cross. That this ark is made of beams formed in a square . . . for a square stands firm on any side. That the length is six times the breadth, and ten times the height, like a human body, to show that Christ appeared in a human body. That the breadth reaches to fifty cubits . . . That it is three hundred cubits long, to make up six times fifty . . . That it is thirty cubits high, a tenth part of the length . . . Now the ten commandments are known to be the heart of the law; and so the length of the ark is ten times thirty.
>
> *Contra Faustum* XII.14; see Hopper 80, 81

It was an interpretation he maintained twenty years later when writing *De civitate Dei*:

> Without doubt this is a symbol of the City of God on pilgrimage in this world, of the Church which is saved through the wood [of the Cross].
>
> The actual measurements of the ark, its length, height and breadth, symbolize the human body . . . For the length of the human body from the top of the head to the sole of the foot is six times its breadth from side to side, and ten times its depth, measured on the side from back to belly . . . That was why the ark was made 300 cubits in length, fifty cubits in breadth, and thirty in height. . . . All the other details mentioned in the construction of the ark are symbols of realities found in the Church.
>
> *De civitate Dei* XV.26

In revealing that the Ark partly signifies the human body, which itself embodies the numbers 6 and 10 in its proportions, Augustine confirms not only what Vitruvius claimed but could not demonstrate,[53] but also the continuing Platonic and biblical concept of relating the human microcosm to the universal macrocosm. As Philo pointed out,

> . . . the ark itself appears to me to be very fitly compared to the human body . . . for whatever was alive and supported on the earth, the ark now bore within itself . . . and on that account God ordained it.
>
> *Quaestiones in Genesim* II.7

In addition to this, it can be seen that all three Christian writers reveal the Ark to be a symbol of salvation – the wooden vessel, the flood and Noah's escape all prefiguring Christian salvation. Whilst Clement points out the association of 300 with the Lord's sign of the Cross, to Origen Christ is 'the spiritual Noah', 'his ark . . . is . . . his Church'. According to Augustine, Noah's own salvation through water and wood foreshadows the Christian's salvation through baptism and Christ's sacrifice on the cross. Origen, in reference to the height of the Ark, points out that Christ was thirty at his baptism.[54]

Much nearer to the tenth century, Alcuin interpreted Noah's salvation not only with 8, noting there were 8 souls aboard the Ark, but with the re-birth of the human race after the flood.[55] This accords well with the meaning of 8 already shown as signifying re-birth – salvation and re-birth arguably being the two sides of the same coin.

It has already been noted that, in the case of early Christian baptisteries, one common architectural archetype exists which was also associated with salvation and which evolved into a form that is eight-sided.[56] It is now proposed to re-examine this in the context of related ideas and architecture from late in antiquity onwards so as to determine whether there is further evidence of a correlation between metaphysical formulae and architectural form.

The Octagonal Shrine[57]

In order to investigate the possibility of such a correlation, metaphysical ideas already presented are now summarized and set beside the architectural form of the octagonal shrine.[58]

The first cube number after unity is 8 and, as Boethius points out:

> Every cube has 12 sides, 8 angles, 6 surfaces.
>
> *De arithmetica* II.49

Because the cube has 6 surfaces, it was also regarded as perfect, 6 being the first perfect number. Consequently, it is also the number of creation.[59] In terms of Platonic solids, the cube represents earth which, by extension, may be identified with the square and the number 4.[60] 4 also stands for justice[61] and is the number of the elements and the gospels. Yet Plato regarded Earth as the fixed sphere around which the 7 planets were believed to circle.[62] Clement confirms that these connections with 8 were actually understood in the Christian era:

> And they call eight a cube, counting the fixed sphere along with the seven revolving ones.
>
> *Stromateis* VI.16

In an earlier passage, it may be recalled, Clement explains Plato's allegorization of the seventh day marking the Lord's rest and the idea that 8

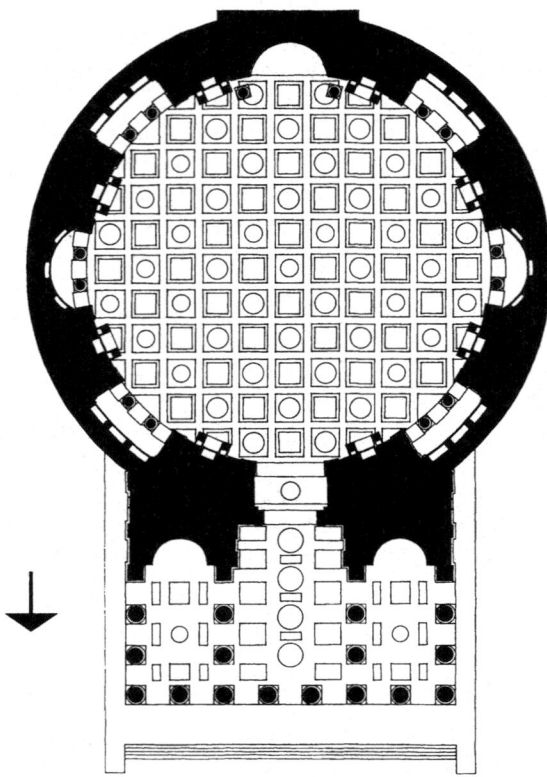

Fig. 4 Plan, the Pantheon, Rome, after MacDonald.

Fig. 5 Plan, Gregory of Nyssa's Church of All Martyrs, after Lethaby.

inaugurates the journey that leads to heaven. Further authority for this is lent by Augustine when he relates circumcision to the resurrection which both occur on the eighth day.[63] 7 is significant because it is the sum of 3 and 4 by which the Holy Spirit is known.[64] 12 represents time and the duration of the spiritual journey as well as being a mystical number and the sum of the apostles because it is the product of 3 and 4.[65]

In terms of architectural form, the Pantheon offers an exact correlation with some of the foregoing formulae (fig. 4). Despite continuing uncertainty as to its original function and dedication,[66] it was nevertheless known as the Pantheon, meaning *All the gods*, in Hadrian's day when the principal deities were identified with the 7 planets. These in turn were regarded, quite literally, as heavenly bodies, five of them even carrying their names as indeed they still do. It also remains the case that the interior of the rotunda is inscribed with 7 monumental niches in which each god could have been commemorated. Yet in Plato's eyes, there were 8 spheres in all if the fixed sphere of Earth is counted and, appropriately enough, the eighth side of the Pantheon, in accommodating the entrance from this world which is the fixed sphere, completes the eight-fold scheme with a layout that is eight-sided. As if to emphasize the point, 8 columns are arranged across the front of the portico too, with another two groups of four of a different colour standing either side of the entrance.

Closer inspection of the layout reveals that the internal niches are alternately squared and curved and that the entire building appears deliberately orientated. The niches therefore seem to be arranged in a hierarchy of 3 and 4, with the triad of curved niches facing the cardinal points and the tetrad of squared niches set diagonally across them. This might agree with the planetary system put forward by Plato. With Earth at the centre, the planets are disposed concentrically about it with the Moon first, then the Sun, Venus and Mercury, which complete their orbits in the same time and could therefore relate to the 4 squared niches. This would leave the triad of curved niches to the outer planets of Mars, Jupiter and Saturn. Alternatively, the layout could correlate with a later variation which was still attributed to the Pythagoreans.[67] Here the Sun is located between Venus, Mercury and the Moon towards the Earth and, away from it, Mars, Jupiter and Saturn. Thus the location of the Earth at the entrance would place the Sun opposite and due south, with the other planets parted either side of the axis between them and numbering 6, the number of creation. It needs to be stressed, however, that there is no positive evidence to support this conjecture, yet the basic correspondence between layout and numerology, Earth and entrance, 7 niches and the number of planets, all within a scheme that is 8-sided does seem compelling.

Be this as it may, octagonal geometry is also present in Roman baths and mausolea.[68] If the form may be thought incidental in baths such as Caracalla's around 215, it is surely quite deliberate in Diocletian's Mausoleum around 300. Moreover, the transposition from pagan Roman to early Christian shrine seems to be not only geometrical but functional too, with the octagonal bath and mausoleum yielding to the octagonal baptistery and martyrion.

Furthermore, both functions were linked by the idea of rebirth, as explained by Paul:

> Know ye not, that so many of us as were baptized into Jesus
> Christ were baptized into his death?
> Therefore we are buried with him by baptism into death: that
> like as Christ was raised up from the dead by the glory of the
> Father, even so we also should walk in newness of life.
>
> Romans VI.3,4

Since baptism was believed to bring about the re-birth of the heathen as a Christian, it is perhaps no surprise that from around 350 baptisteries seem increasingly to display octagonal geometry. Thus, once again, may be seen a layout enclosed by 7 sides, 7 being the sum of 3 and 4 and signifying the Holy Spirit, with the entrance in the eighth side representing entry from the sphere of Earth, and the sum of 8 the journey that leads to heaven. Even after adult baptism in large detached baptisteries gave way to infant baptism in fonts, fonts and their steps are usually eight-sided. Implicit also may be 12 as the product of 3 and 4, signifying the duration of the spiritual journey and the number of apostles. Dome mosaics of the apostles waiting around an empty throne, common in certain baptisteries, would seem to support this.

Martyrdom likewise was numerologically associated with 8 and re-birth, as Augustine confirms in explaining Christ's words on the mount.

> . . .'Blessed are they who suffer persecution for justice' (sic)
> sake, for theirs is the kingdom of heaven'. Perhaps this eighth
> maxim . . . is signified both by the circumcision on the eighth
> day in the Old Testament and by the Lord's Resurrection after
> the Sabbath [which is indeed both the eighth day and the first].
>
> De sermone Domini I.IV.12

An instance of an early martyrion is described in a letter Gregory of Nyssa wrote in the 380s, the text of which survives in an eleventh-century manuscript in the Laurentian Library in Florence.[69]

> The form of the chapel is a cross, which has its figure
> completed throughout, as you would expect, by four structures.
> The junctions of the buildings intercept one another, as we see
> everywhere in the cruciform pattern. But within the cross there
> lies a circle, divided by eight angles (I call the octagonal figure
> a circle in view of its circumference), in such wise that the two
> pairs of sides of the octagon which are diametrically opposed
> to one another, unite by means of arches the central circle to
> the adjoining blocks of the building; while the other four sides

of the octagon, which lie between the quadrilateral buildings, will not themselves be carried to meet the buildings, but upon each of them will be described a semicircle like a shell, terminating in an arch above: so that the arches will be eight in all, and by their means the quadrilateral and semicircular buildings will be connected, side by side, with the central structure. In the blocks of masonry formed by the angles there will be an equal number of pillars, at once for ornament and for strength, and these again will carry arches built of equal size to correspond with those within. And above these eight arches, with the symmetry of an upper range of windows, the octagonal building will be raised to the height of four cubits: the part rising from it will be a cone shaped like a top, as the vaulting narrows the figure of the roof from its full width to a pointed wedge. The dimensions below will be, – the width of each of the quadrilateral buildings, eight cubits, the length of them half as much again, the height as much as the proportion of the width allows. It will be as much in the semicircles also. The whole length between the piers extends in the same way to eight cubits, and the depth will be as much as will be given by the sweep of the compasses with the fixed point placed in the middle of the side and extending to the end. The height will be determined in this case too by the proportion to the width. And the thickness of the wall, an interval of three feet from inside these spaces, which are measured internally, will run round the whole building.

Epistolae, XVI

It may be seen that the proposed building is described in considerable detail as if already designed and it is visualized partly in terms of drawing and wholly in terms of geometric form to which key dimensions are assigned (fig. 5). The alternating arrangement of exedrae closely resembles the interior of the Pantheon, although the sequence of squared and curved chambers is reversed here. The reason for this seems evident from Gregory's description of the design as cruciform, with its squared arms rising above the diagonal apses. All the same, the numbers 3 and 4 may be clearly distinguished once again together with their association with the Holy Spirit. As in the Pantheon, the entrance in the eighth side could represent Earth, as well as 8 itself indicating the cube of the element earth. Yet in also signifying the soul's rebirth and the journey that leads to heaven, both 3 and the octagonal martyrion can be seen to stand for the spiritual journey of martyrs which starts at the scene of their martyrdom on Earth and leads to heaven. It is surely no coincidence therefore that the dedication of Gregory's church was to the Martyrs, nor that the only measures he specifies, apart from the wall thickness, happen to be 8 cubits and 4 and, by implication perhaps, their sum of 12. Neither may it be a coincidence that when the Christians took over the Pantheon in 608, their rededication of it was to Mary and All Martyrs.

To summarize, in addition to the Pantheon, development in octagonal shrines appears to extend from Roman baths and mausolea to early Christian baptisteries and martyria to which the soul's re-birth and journey to heaven are central to their liturgical functions. Thus while 8 is explicitly identified with salvation, baptisteries and martyria, which stand as specific models of salvation, are octagonal. It is argued here, therefore, that at least in this case, a common architectural form exists which appears to match known metaphysical formulae exactly, without departing from the strict representation of either.

Furthermore, there is evidence that architecture was designed in conscious expression of these beliefs. According to an inscription on the cathedral baptistery in Milan which was attributed to Ambrose:[70]

> He erected an eight-choired temple for use by the saints
> and an octagonal font is worthy of its number.
> This number proved fitting for the elevation of a housing of the
> holy baptism, which gave back to the people true deliverance,
> Raising them again in the light of Christ, who loosened the bonds
> of death, and (who) from their graves raised the lifeless . . . .[71]
>
> *Sylloge Laureshamensis III*, in Dölger 155

Whether it was Ambrose or not, the author of this could hardly make clearer the connection between number, geometry and architecture and the celebration of baptism and resurrection. Since this is documentary evidence of an intentional connection, was it a connection that was made only in cases where the use of geometry happens to be self-evident, or would it not also have been applied to other religious architecture where it is not so self-evident as in, for example, early Christian basilicas?[72]

Conclusion

Selected writings have been examined for evidence which may point to a connection between Christian Platonist thought and the design of religious architecture and it can be seen that the record of the Ambrosian inscription definitely supports the existence of a connection, so from the weight of circumstantial evidence as well, it may be reasonable to infer that one did exist.

The lack of conclusive proof, however, may well be explained in part by the deliberate policy of obscuring the truth and in this there is no reason to suppose that the Alexandrian Didascaleon was alone. Clement's *Stromateis* and other writings, available though they now are to the modern reader, are likely to have been for restricted use at the time.[73] Basil openly discourages his workaday congregation from enquiring into what he considers beyond their comprehension. Dionysius is repeatedly insistent on secrecy. Both Augustine and Boethius acknowledge that an understanding of the divine scheme is no doubt beyond the ordinary individual. However, Augustine at least tries to make the information more widely accessible, yet in doing so, he reveals that the material is largely represented as allegory. This is expounded to some extent in the texts, leaving the rest requiring exposition within the schools. Under these circumstances, it seems reasonable to suppose that any extensive documentary proof of geometry actually being used expressively in architecture is unlikely to be found.

The circumstantial evidence, however, is arguably very strong. Philosophy, both as a subject and the way in which it was taught, was thoroughly organized along strictly rational lines. Just as the three branches of philosophy were complementary, so the seven liberal arts were completely interdependent and rigorously systematized into a logical programme. Also, just as the view of the universe was one in which all its parts bore a rational relationship to each other and to the whole, so was the method of studying it, with each subject or discipline being inseparable from the others.

Leading the *quadrivium*, arithmetic taught that numbers and their ratios reveal a pre-existing order and express identified qualities. About this, and about the importance of this, there can be little doubt since all writers accept it as axiomatic and Augustine is completely insistent on it. The corollary of this is that numerical ratio, geometric proportion, musical harmony and the motion of the planets are but manifestations of the same divine order and were expounded to initiates in expressive celebration of it.

Geometry enjoyed a special place in the *quadrivium* as exemplifying abstract essence. Architecture was consistently used as a metaphor for the divine creation and the Church, models of which were repeatedly conceptualized in architectural terms. It might reasonably be expected therefore that this was reciprocated in the actual design of religious architecture, thereby also fulfilling the anagogical function of leading 'from things of the sense to . . . holy things'. If so, the necessary information was available in those texts that defined the allegorical meanings and specified the principal measures and proportions of such models as the Tabernacle, Temple and Ark. For architecture to have been so persistently perceived as a symbol must surely suggest that it was also conceived as a symbol.

There can be no doubt either that the rituals staged in sacred architecture were formulated symbolically. Particular numbers recur in the performance of the liturgy and were just as fundamental to it as the harmonies of the musical ratios, not to mention the numerological allegorizations revealed through readings from the scriptures. Given the physical expression of these branches of the *quadrivium*, and the utter integrity of belief in the universal scheme together with the imperative of maintaining all-embracing harmony, is it likely that geometry alone would not also have been used expressively in the architecture? And if it was used, is it likely that it would have been used for everything but the layout of the plan? The frequent associations made of foundation-laying with divinity and wisdom in the Platonic sense would suggest not.

In addition to the square and double square layouts of the Tabernacle and Temple, a clear example of a geometric basis to the design of religious architecture is found in octagonal baptisteries and martyria. Whilst the Milan baptistery inscription indicates that this amounted to deliberate architectural symbolism, it perforce stops short of general proof. Yet the exact match that is claimed here between Christian Platonist thought and architectural form, particularly in relation to the specific functions for which these buildings were raised, clearly suggests intended symbolism and the fact that this form persisted into Carolingian times and beyond is of particular importance to this study. As a corollary of this argument, if a connection between metaphysical belief and formal architectural expression did once exist in cases where the geometry is self-evident, would similar thinking not also have been applied to other cases as well?

Given an historical context pervaded by Christian Platonism in which the importance of number was paramount, any method of design applied to religious architecture might reasonably be expected to reflect this. From the complex relationships of numbers and their meanings reviewed so far, including those attributed to the Tabernacle and Temple, also 8 as signifying salvation, 6 and 10 representing creation, the human microcosm and the law as well as numerical perfection, underlying them all is the series 3, 4, 5, the various equations and meanings of which are now finally summarized.

3		= atmospheric elements, Holy Trinity
4		= earth, justice, elements, gospels
5		= human microcosm, universal macrocosm
$3 : 4$		= diatessaron, the principal harmony
$3 + 4$	$= 7$	= Holy Spirit
3×4	$= 12$	= time, apostles
$3^2 + 4^2 = 5^2$		= union of elements within universe Pythagoras's theorem
$3 + 4 + 5$	$= 12$	= time, apostles
$3^2 + 4^2 + 5^2$	$= 50$	= foundation of universe
$3 \times 4 \times 5^2$	$= 300$	= Lord's sign of the cross
$3^3 + 4^3 + 5^3$	$= 6^3$	= union of elements and universe within creation
$3 \times 4 \times 5$	$= 6 \times 10$	= union between Plato's cosmology and numbers of perfection, union of macrocosm and microcosm

Being also the first figurate numbers of the triangle, square and pentagon, the choice of these figures as the basis of the geometric investigation would appear to be justified.

Before proceeding, however, it may be profitable to return to the tenth century for two purposes. The first is to establish the degree of acceptance then of the beliefs outlined in this chapter with regard to number symbolism and geometry. The second is to investigate the building activities arising from the monastic revival and the working methods of medieval architects. This should help in determining whether there is further support for the actual use of geometry expressively, especially any involving the three geometric figures that are being advanced.

Notes

1 See pp. 186–7.
2 Clement, *Stromateis* V.4.
3 Clement, *Stromateis* I.12; V.4,5,9; VI.15.
4 Clement, *Stromateis* V.14.
5 See Chadwick 1970, 170.
6 Augustine, *De civitate Dei* VIII.3, 4; XI.25.
7 Augustine, *De civitate Dei* VIII.6, 7, 8.
8 Burkert 421–2; Martianus 90.
9 Chadwick 1981, xii; Evans, G. 38.
10 Huntsman 71–3.
11 Stump 130, 133.
12 Camargo 97, 99.
13 Chadwick 1981, 72–3.
14 Masi 13.
15 Boethius, *De arithmetica* II.4; I.1.
16 Chadwick 1981, 73; Boethius, *De arithmetica* 14.
17 Augustine, *De musica* 194n8; I.12.24; VI.17.57; see pp. 69–72.
18 Boethius, *De arithmetica* 11–12.
19 Augustine, *De ordine* II.5.16; Martianus 731.
20 Boethius, *De arithmetica* II.4; Macrobius I.6.18; Martianus 736.
21 Boethius, *De arithmetica* II.4, 6, 7, 9; Macrobius I.6.22.
22 Augustine, *De civitate Dei* VIII.4; *In Iohannis evangelicum* 27.10.(4); Boethius, *De arithmetica* 32–3.
23 Macrobius I.6.22, 24; Boethius, *De arithmetica* II.10, 12; Augustine, *In Iohannis evangelicum* 27.10(4); Boethius, *De arithmetica* II.4.
24 Plato, *Timaeus* 55C; Martianus 735; Macrobius I.6.19.
25 Augustine, *De Trinitate* IV.4.7.
26 Cornford 1941, 263n3.
27 Augustine, *De civitate Dei* XI.31.
28 Clement, *Stromateis* V.14, above.
29 Martianus 740.
30 Martianus 742; Macrobius I.6.76: Augustine, *De Trinitate* IV.4.10; Boethius, *De arithmetica* II.41; Augustine, *Contra Faustum* XII.14; *De civitate Dei* XV.20.
31 Philo, *De opificio mundi* 7 in Hopper 48.
32 Clement, *Stromateis* VI.11; Augustine, *De musica* I.12.19, *De civitate Dei.* XX.7.
33 Plato, *Republic* X.616B.
34 Clement, *Stromateis* VI.11.
35 Boethius, *De arithmetica* II.48, 49, 54; see pp. 89–90.
36 Plato, *Republic* XXIX.546; see pp. 48, 106–7 and above; Cornford 1941, 263n2, 3.
37 Heath 1956, II.98.
38 Burkert 429.
39 Proclus, *In primum Euclidis* I.5, 8; II.11, 13.
40 See pp. 13, 109–10.
41 See p. 74.
42 Augustine, *De quantitate animae* 8–11.

43 Bede, *De tabernaculo* xv–xvi, 45; *De templo* xiv–xvii, 5–6.
44 Exodus 24.12–30.21; I Kings 6, 7; II Chronicles 3, 4; Josephus, *Antiquitates* III.6; Bede, *De tabernaculo, De templo, passim*; also *Codex Grandior* and *Codex Amiatinus*, see Bede, *De templo* lii.
45 Frankl 1945, 57; Hallinger 123; see also p. 27.
46 Vitruvius III.I.5; III.I.6; III.I.1,5; III.I.2.
47 Vitruvius III.IV.3; IV.IV.1; V.I.2,4; V.VIII.2.
48 Vitruvius I.Pref; 1931 I.5n3; III.1.
49 Hanover, Kest. Mus. WM XXIᵃ, 36, fol.9ᵛ; White 1961/78, 65; Basil 1895, 51; see pp. 153–6.
50 See p. 111.
51 Origen, II.3; Augustine, *De civitate Dei* XV.26.
52 Origen, 77n16.
53 Vitruvius III.I.4; see above.
54 Clement, *Stromateis* VI.11; Origen II.5; see p. 54.
55 Alcuin, *Epistolae*, 259; see p. 146.
56 Krautheimer 123, 131–7; see p. 5.
57 A conflation of this section with the Aachen Chapel (pp. 146–8) has been published and appears in the Bibliography under Hiscock 1993.
58 Chapter 2, also pp. 103–13.
59 Martianus 736, 740; Augustine, *De civitate Dei* XI.30.
60 Plato, *Timaeus* 55E-56D; Augustine, *In Iohannis evangelicum* 27.10.(4).
61 Augustine, *De quantitate animae* 9.
62 Plato, *Timaeus* 38C, *Republic* 616C–E.
63 Clement, *Stromateis* V.14; Augustine, *De civitate Dei* XVI.26; *Epitolae* 55; *De sermone Domini* I.IV.12; see p. 108.
64 Augustine, *De civitate Dei* XI.31.
65 Clement, *Stromateis* VI.11, V.14; Augustine, *De civitate Dei* XV.20, XX.5; *In Iohannis evangelicum* 27.10 (4).
66 Godfrey 195–6, 199–204.
67 Plato, *Timaeus* 38; Burkert 300; 318.
68 Krautheimer 131–7.
69 Gregory, *Epistolae*, XVI; 31.
70 Krautheimer 137–8.
71 *Octachorum s(an)c(t)os templum surrexit in usus,*
    octagonus fons est numere dignus eo.
  Hoc numero decuit sacri baptismatis aulam
    surgere, quo populis vera salus rediit
  luce resurgentis Chr(ist)i, qui claustra resolvit
    mortis et e tumulis suscitat exanimes . . . in Dölger 153–87.
72 See St Peter's Old Basilica, pp. 215–17.
73 Casey 70.

Chapter 4

'The White Mantle of Churches'

In order to examine what evidence there may be for the acceptance in the tenth century of the beliefs outlined in the previous chapter, this chapter will follow the same sequence, starting with the question of secrecy, the study of philosophy and the liberal arts and the importance of number. Following this, evidence for the expressive use of geometry, citing architecture and other material evidence where possible, will lead to a review of the building activities of the monastic revival.

Summary

The convention of veiling the truth seen in earlier centuries seems to have been perpetuated in the tenth, for here again there is contemporary evidence which, moreover, is specifically related to the design of religious architecture. According to the chronicle of Mouzon Abbey, a visit was paid to it by Gerbert's patron, Archbishop Adalbero of Reims when,

> . . . he began to call upon the leaders of the church, making up some things for others, as if keeping something secret, and conversing about the site, the situation and the composition of the buildings.
>
> *Historia monasterii Mosomensis* II.4, 612

John of Ravenna provides another instance when he had the opportunity to explain William of Volpiano's design at Dijon; he was, after all, William's nephew and successor at Fécamp.[1] Yet, he actually writes that,

> The form and subtlety of this ingenious work is not vainly presented in words for all those who are less informed, since many things in it seem to have been made with a mystical significance.
>
> *Altera vita* 8–9

Even when material was made explicit, it has already been argued that although the texts may nowadays be openly available to all, many of them at the time will have been meant for a readership restricted to those who were initiates.[2] As far as the tenth century is concerned, such texts would doubtless have been studied within the confines of the monastery school and therefore under guidance, as earlier had been the case in the Academy of Athens and the Didascaleon of Alexandria, so that any difficulties with the material might have been resolved by the teacher expounding the text verbally. It was precisely to encourage such understanding that Charlemagne had written to his abbots urging the study of letters,

> . . . so that you may be able to penetrate with greater ease and certainty the mysteries of the Holy Scriptures. For as these contain images, tropes and similar figures, it is impossible to doubt that the reader will arrive far more readily at the spiritual sense according as he is the better instructed in learning.

> *Epistolae*, 3; *Beati Caroli Magni operum*, in Mullinger 97–9

Turning to the content of teaching, it has been shown that the revival in learning in the ninth and tenth centuries strengthened a continuing interest in the liberal arts. Among the hundred volumes of the classics that Gunzo was to bring out of Italy was that of Martianus on the seven liberal arts. These were taught for example at Lyons, Arras and Cambrai, and were introduced to Bamberg from Liège.[3]

It has also been shown that the curriculum had earlier been transmitted to the monastery schools by way of Martianus, Boethius and Cassiodorus. For the *trivium* subjects, the most important authorities early in the middle ages were Donatus and Priscian for grammar, Boethius for dialectic and Cicero for rhetoric. The *quadrivium* was taught from a multiplicity of sources, principal among whom was Boethius. This is not to say, however, that the curriculum was unvarying or that all seven arts were taught with monolithic uniformity. Boethius's treatise *De Trinitate* relayed an alternative Aristotelian division of science into physics, mathematics and theology whilst Gerbert's separation of philosophy into theoretical and practical branches combined politics and economics, with ethics subsumed within the latter. Rhetoric successively lost its place to grammar and then to dialectic, which enjoyed a general revival in the eleventh century largely due to Gerbert's endeavours.[4] Yet as a student, Gerbert had had to move to Reims to progress at dialectic; Abbo, on the other hand, found dialectic taught at Fleury along with grammar and arithmetic but had to go to Orléans for music, Reims for astronomy and Paris for other subjects.[5]

Nevertheless, although a little of the integrity of the liberal arts curriculum may have been lost in the intervening centuries, its revival by such as Bruno at Otto I's court, John and Anstaeus at Gorze, Abbo at Fleury and Gerbert at Reims evidently succeeded in shaping the education of a particularly notable generation of churchmen and monastic reformers in the late tenth and early eleventh centuries.[6] Consequently, just as the prevailing view of the universe was that it was rationally organized, so were the methods of studying it. The means were actually an integral part of the end.

So as to try to understand the pervasiveness of this world of thought, proper account needs to be taken of the terms used and of various changes in their meaning through time. Modern usage can amount to a dilution of an original acuity of definition whilst at the same time testifying to a continuing habit of thought. For example, modern English takes it for granted that a collection of monasteries subscribing to a particular *Rule* constitutes an *Order*. Yet behind this commonplace seems to lie the concept of universal order being achieved through observance of rule. By extension, law is observed by issuing and obeying commands and, because it is assumed that obeying the law maintains order, the giving and taking of commands has become synonymous with giving and taking orders. If something actually breaks down, it is out of order. On another count, it has already been noted that the Greek for order, *cosmos*, has come to mean 'universe', which in turn, more than simply being a collection of celestial bodies, actually signified 'one that turns'. Harmony was not just a pleasant combination of sounds; in Greek *harmonia* was the result of fitting together disparate elements that are otherwise potentially in conflict.[7] In modern English once again, if something is fitting, it is usually held simply to mean appropriate, yet it is only appropriate when it does actually fit the circumstances. It was this more precise sense that was presumably intended by Plato when he described the shaping of the universe:

> For the living creature that was to embrace all living creatures within itself, the fitting shape would be the figure that comprehends in itself all the figures there are.
>
> *Timaeus* 33B

Clement also seems to have intended this when he quotes Paul describing:

> He (that is) the chief corner stone; in whom the whole building, fitly joined together, groweth into an holy temple of God.
>
> *Stromateis* VI.17

An agreeable experience is usually synonymous with one that is pleasant, yet it is only pleasant because all the elements are in agreement with each other, everything fits and therefore harmony is the result. Both the Latin for art, *ars*, and the Greek for virtue, *arete*, are derived from the Indo-European *ar-* which again means 'fitting'.[8] The way in which such fitting together is achieved is by all the parts being in proportion to each other and to the whole which, as has already been pointed out, was the original Latin definition of symmetry and the Greek *analogia*. Thus the liberal arts are components which fit together to form a whole. Yet mathematics included the study of music, which had little to do with making nice tunes, except among professional entertainers, but was that imparted by the Muses to him who was 'guided by intelligence . . . as an ally against the inward discord'.[9] Arithmetic, likewise, had little to do with counting and calculation which were rather the Greek study of logistics or medieval algorism, but was concerned instead with the theory of number.[10] Something of the real importance of the order of numbers is still conveyed in English whenever something is dismissed because 'it does not count'. Something is also conveyed of the close identity of arithmetic with geometry and the concept of figurate numbers in the complete lack of ambiguity in the term 'number' compared with 'figure', which can equally mean number or shape. Continuing references to quintessence and matters that are essential, elementary and universal all seem to be signs of Platonic concepts surviving in modern thought and speech whether consciously or not. And yet it is only with the conscious recognition of the Platonic connotation of such terms that modern misperceptions and anachronistic attitudes towards early medieval thought are likely to be avoided.

Acceptance of the philosophy of Christian Platonism in the tenth century must be inferred by the wide circulation of the writings of the Latin encyclopedists and Augustine, in particular Chalcidius's version of *Timaeus*, Macrobius's *Somnium Scipionis*, Martianus's *De nuptiis*, Augustine's *De civitate Dei* alongside Boethius's liberal arts treatises and his *De consolatione philosophiae*. The likely implications of this can hardly be emphasized too strongly; nor can the significance of the adaptation into Anglo-Saxon of works such as *De consolatione* and Basil's *Hexaëmeron* in the ninth and tenth centuries.

Holy writ also enjoyed renewed importance in the tenth century, understandably so since both the Gorzean and Cluniac reforms marked a return to the *Rule* of St Benedict. Ethelwold ejected the secular clerics from his bishopric 'because they would not keep any monastic rule'.[11] Benedict's Rule related to divine law, the observance of which maintained divine order, and the law was contained in scripture. The perception of the two Testaments as being the old and new law appears to be supported by a colophon added to the Bible of William of Volpiano possibly around the 980s.

> Commands from either law this little book doth hold,
> And mystic actions too within its text unfold;
> Designed, with zeal to serve forever one whose name
> Is rightly 'St Benign', a martyr of great fame.
> An energetic man, named Abbot William bade
> From two books counterset these extracts to be made.

> MS Ham.82 fol.435r, Berlin; Vregille 86

This has been thought to refer to a work which set corresponding passages from the Old and New Testaments in parallel with each other, which the author characterizes as 'commands from either law'.[12] This appears remarkably close to an exercise conducted by Alcuin nearly two centuries earlier when he set out biblical meanings for all the numbers from 10 to 1, introducing it as,

> . . . the doctrine of numbers, or rather, the comparison which
> can be found between the ancient law and the authority of the
> New Testament . . . .
>
> *Epistolae*, 260

The conceptual connection between the two Testaments can be found illustrated in the Ottonian period in the *Gospels of Otto III*, produced in Trier around the millennium, in which Luke is portrayed in a *mandorla*. He sits beneath his own ox-symbol and bears aloft the prophets in a cosmic cloud, thereby symbolizing the unity of the Old and New Testaments.[13]

Another connection between the two Testaments is to be seen in the status accorded to Pentecost, as well as the significance it had for Benedictine communities and the meaning of number underlying Pentecost. In about 925, Odo of Cluny had written a seven-volume history, *Odonis abbatis Cluniacensis occupatio*, which treats the biblical account as a series of historical events from Creation to Resurrection. This is followed by the story of Pentecost which, bringing as it did the visitation of the Holy Spirit upon the Apostles, Odo interprets as the creation of the ideal Christian community, which in turn was represented in the monastic way of life.[14] Monastic communities regularly consisted of an abbot and 12 monks, at least as a minimum in the first instance, which was the number accompanying William when he took over the abbey of St Bénigne.[15] Since this work was written by one of Cluny's earliest and most influential abbots, it is likely to have been regarded virtually as a manifesto of Benedictine monasticism. At Auxerre and Trier, Pentecost was marked early in the tenth century by priests and people of the entire diocese converging on the cathedral carrying their parish crosses.[16] Following the Norman Conquest of England, which was actively supported by the Benedictines and resulted in the English Church establishment being largely supplanted by them, Pentecost was one of three important celebrations in the Church's calendar. The entry in *The Anglo-Saxon Chronicles* for 1087 records:

> At Easter [William bore his crown] in Winchester, at Pentecost
> at Westminster, and at Christmas at Gloucester; then there were
> with him all the powerful men all over England.
>
> *Anglo-Saxon Chronicles* 219

This, moreover, is but one of numerous such references.

It may also be seen that Pentecost represents another synthesis between the Old and New Law in that it commemorates the creation of the first Christian community on the fiftieth day after Passover which was when Moses had initially presented the law of the Old Testament, namely the Ten Commandments.[23] That the law was associated with 10 has already been noted. 50 days on the other hand, as Augustine points out, follows 7 weeks of 7 days and may therefore signify another instance of a new beginning.[17] Accordingly, Pentecost was associated with the Ark.

> Now there are some who say that three hundred cubits are the
> symbol of the Lord's sign; and fifty, of hope and of remission
> given at Pentecost; and thirty . . . because the Lord preached in
> His thirtieth year . . . .
>
> Clement, *Stromateis* VI.11

In addition to the number symbolism already cited for the Ark, it can be seen from its dimensions that it can be enclosed by 6 squares, each of 50 × 50 cubits, in which 6 was recognized as the first perfect number as well as the number of creation; the square stands for the element earth and justice; whilst 50 can be identified with Pentecost, the Law and, in Benedictine eyes, the inception of Christian monasticism.

Direct evidence of the acceptance of number theory in the tenth century is abundant, to the extent that it clearly appears to have been a habit of thought. For example, Hroswitha of Gandersheim interrupted two of her plays with discourses on metaphysics and numbers,[18] each moreover in a scenario seemingly designed to give them added point. In Scene III of *Passio sanctarum virginum Fidei Spei et Karitatis*, Sapientia discloses the ages of her daughters Charity, Hope and Faith as being 8, 10 and 12 years, prompting an exposition on number theory to Hadrian which appears to summarize Boethius's *De arithmetica* on numbers that are underperfect, overperfect and perfect, as well as evenly even and unevenly even. In Scene I of *Conversio Thaidis meretricis*, Paphnutius addresses his disciples on the elements, harmony and music, quoting the subjects of the *quadrivium* in Boethius's sequence. The universe consists of 4 elements which are contrary, yet agree due to the harmonious rule of the Creator's will. Thus Hroswitha acknowledges the Greek meaning of harmony already noted, which is achieved by the rule of the Creator through his universal laws. Similarly, three kinds of music are enumerated, each produced by the rule of proportion, with universal music occurring among the 7 planets and the heavenly sphere in the ratios of diatessaron, diapente, diapason and of one whole tone. It is, incidentally, of interest that a manuscript of her complete works dating from the turn of the millennium was kept at St Emmeram in Regensburg.[19]

At about the same time, Abbo wrote on the secret meaning of numbers in a work thought to be a commentary on Victorius's treatise *Argumentum calculandi* which itself extensively expounds number mysticism. Besides drawing frequently on Martianus, Macrobius, Chalcidius and Boethius, he also displays a knowledge of Isidore of Seville and, later, having travelled to England to assist Oswald, the abbot of Ramsey, he returned to the subject in his *Quaestiones grammaticales*.[20]

At the end of the century, in reply to Otto III's invitation to him to become his tutor, Gerbert wrote:

> For, unless you were not firmly convinced that the power of numbers contained both the origins of all things in itself and explained all from itself, you would not be hastening to a full and perfect knowledge of them with such zeal.

Letter 231, in Hill 33-4

Two years earlier, in an account of the trial of an ecclesiastical opponent, Gerbert had referred to the bishops at the Council of Nicaea:

As for the sacred and mystic Nicene Synod . . . St Ambrose says: 'Not by human effort nor by any arrangement did the 318 bishops convene at the council. But, as in their number, through the sign of His Passion and His Name, Lord Jesus proves that he was present at their council, for the cross is in the 300, the name Jesus is in the 10, and the 8 in the priests.'

Letter 201, in Lattin 245f, quoting Ambrose, *De fide* I.18,121

In complete contrast, an anonymous Irishman of the tenth century wrote *The Wish of Manchán of Liath*, evidently in longing for a life of contemplation in isolation, somewhere presumably in Ireland.

I wish, O son of the Living God, ancient eternal King,
for a secret hut in the wilderness that it may be my dwelling.

A very blue shallow well to be beside it, a clear pool
for washing away sins through the grace of the Holy Ghost.

A beautiful wood close by around it on every side,
for the nurture of many-voiced birds, to shelter and hide it.

Facing south for warmth, a little stream across its enclosure,
a choice ground with abundant bounties which would be good
for every plant.

A few sage disciples, I will tell their number,
humble and obedient, to pray to the King.

Four threes, three fours, fit for every need,
two sixes in the church, both south and north.

Six couples in addition to myself,
praying through the long ages to the King who moves the sun.

A lovely church decked with linen, a dwelling for God of
Heaven;
then, bright candles over the holy white Scriptures.

Celtic Miscellany, K. Jackson 280

One reason why the lines in question come as such a surprise perhaps is because the writer does not content himself with wishing simply for 12 acolytes. That he did not suggests a significance to 4 × 3, 3 × 4 and 6 × 2 which he recognized and wished to allude to without actually explaining.

In some sources the meaning of numbers is not only freely explained, but ingenuity was used in extending their meaning. Glaber opens his *Historiarum* by saying:

> Since we are to treat of events in the four quarters of the earth; it will be well to touch first upon the power of divine and abstract quaternity.
>
> *Historiarum* I.1, in Thorndike, I.674

He goes on to relate the 4 elements to the 4 Gospels in which Matthew represents earth because he deals with the Incarnation, Mark water because he emphasizes baptism, air is given to Luke's Gospel, being the most extensive, whilst John's, being the most spiritual, is equated with fire or ether. Likewise the 4 rivers of Paradise are identified with the 4 virtues.[21] However far-fetched this may seem to a modern reader, importance needs to be given to what was actually believed at the time and the importance of this passage lies in the continuing compatibility perceived between Platonist and biblical teaching.

'Measure, number and weight'

Perhaps the most compelling evidence of all for the tenth-century view of number theory also explains why it was given such prominence. It can be seen in a verse widely adopted from the *Book of Wisdom*[22] and cited by Augustine in *De civitate Dei*:

> . . . the theory of number is not to be lightly regarded, since it is made quite clear, in many passages of the holy Scriptures, how highly it is to be valued. It was not for nothing that it was said in praise of God, 'You have ordered all things in measure, number and weight.'
>
> *De civitate Dei* XI.30

Furthermore, it is a quotation which Augustine already appears to have paraphrased earlier when he writes:

> From him derives every mode of being, every species, every order, all measure, number and weight.
>
> *De civitate Dei* V.11

This was to be echoed less than a century later by Dionysius:

> Everything looks to [the Good] for measure, eternity, number, order.
>
> *De divinis nominibus* 4.4

And yet again in the seventh century when Isidore quoted the verse in his *Etymologiae*.[23]

That this verse also formed a corner-stone of tenth-century thought seems borne out by Abbo and Hroswitha. In his *Quaestiones grammaticales* noted above, which was written some time after 985, Abbo propounds the secret significance of numbers, but only cursorily, having included a lengthier treatment in his previous work which he describes as,

> . . . a little book on number, measure and weight which I once published, prompted by the prayers of my brothers, concerning the calculus of Victorius.
>
> *Quaestiones grammaticales*, in Cantor 795

This in itself does not amount to evidence that the belief was actually expressed. However, a clear exhortation to use the knowledge gained from the liberal arts in order to praise the Creator comes from Hroswitha in her two plays.

> And I would ask you – unto whose praise can the knowledge of the arts be more worthily or most justly turned than to the praise of Him Who made things capable of being known, and gave us the capacity to know them?
>
> The more a man realizes the wonderful way in which God has set all things in number and measure and weight, the more ardent his love.
>
> Hroswitha, *Conversio*, tr. St John 101

> It would be unprofitable if it did not lead us to appreciate the wisdom of our Creator, and the wondrous knowledge of the Author of the world, Who in the beginning created the world out of nothing, and set everything in number, measure and weight, and then, in time and the age of man, formulated a science which reveals fresh wonders the more we study it.
>
> Hroswitha, *Passio*, tr. St John 140

Added point is given to her second reference to Wisdom by putting it into the mouth of Sapientia, or Wisdom, herself. It has already been pointed out that Hroswitha's plays enjoyed a certain currency, being read possibly at court and copied in the following century. One manuscript of her complete works was kept at St Emmeram in Regensburg at the turn of the millennium when Bernward may also have come into contact with them, Gandersheim being in his own diocese.[24]

To be set alongside this apparently overt encouragement of metaphysical expressionism are four Benedictine abbey churches of the tenth century, namely Cluny Abbey II, St Bénigne in Dijon, St Emmeram in Regensburg and the New Minster in Winchester, the designs of which do appear to embody 'measure and number' in quantities metaphysically significant, and these are preceded by two celebrated examples from the previous century, the Aachen Chapel and St Gall.

The Aachen Chapel (fig. 6)[25]

In addition to the connection between metaphysical and geometric significance already advanced for the octagonal shrine, a further numerological correlation is suggested by the ordering of Charlemagne's Chapel at Aachen. Since Einhard recorded that Charlemagne,

> . . . took great pleasure in the books of Saint Augustine and especially in those which are called The City of God.

> *Vita Caroli* III.24

Charlemagne was presumably familiar with Augustine's passages about number theory and how highly it is to be valued, God having ordered all things according to measure, number and weight.[26] It seems very much in this spirit that he issued his proclamation to abbots, already noted, urging the study of letters so that an understanding of scriptural 'images, tropes and similar figures' will reveal their spiritual meaning. This was evidently drafted by Alcuin whose own letters contain references to number theory. As it happens, it was by way of interpreting the symbolism of the Ark that Alcuin compared 6 with 8, being perfect and underperfect numbers respectively. Six is a perfect number,[27]

> . . . because the most perfect Creator, who made all things very well, made in this number [of days] the creatures of the original world, to show that all things which He made are perfect in their kind. Now the number 8, if you divide it into factors given by itself, is found less than itself . . . and therefore the second family of this type begins to grow from the number 8. Namely: we read that there were eight souls in the Ark, from whom the multitude of the whole human race sprouted forth, to show that the second family is more imperfect than the first, which was created in the number 6.

> *Epistolae* 259; see also Cantor I.784

It was while Alcuin was still in Aachen that Charlemagne's Chapel was planned around 790. It is important to note that, despite this being an era of great basilica-building, such as Angilbert's at St Riquier, Baugulf's at Fulda, and Einhard's at Steinbach and Seligenstadt, for the Palace Chapel at Aachen the octagon was selected. Given Charlemagne's interest in Ravenna and the

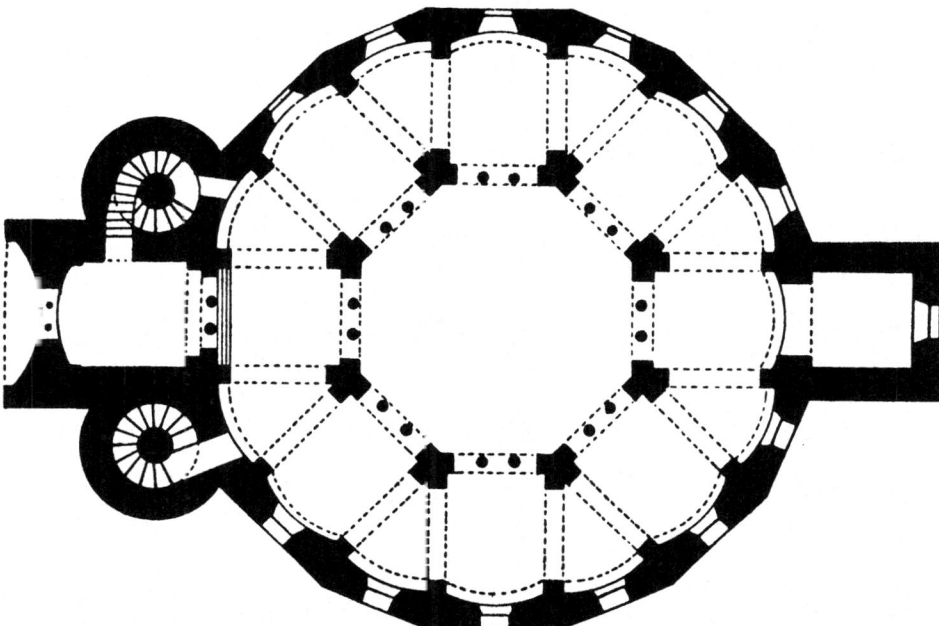

Fig. 6 The Aachen Chapel, plan of the upper gallery, after Hubsch.

career of Theodoric, there is good reason to suppose that his own project was inspired by the octagonal martyrion of St Vitalis in Ravenna as much as by the custom for palace chapels to be designed to centralized plans.

Thus the ground floor of the Aachen Chapel consists of an 8-sided enclosure surrounded by an ambulatory and wall that is 16-sided. This is interrupted to the west by the entrance and to the east by the sanctuary.

Above the ambulatory is a gallery that opens into the central space beneath the dome through 8 arches, each containing a screen of 4 pillars. A similar arch with 4 pillars opens into the westwork from the gallery above the entrance. In other words, whilst the number of pillars around the octagon is 32, the total number is 36. And so in addition to the layout already noted as familiar to baptisteries and martyria, each enclosed by 7 sides and entered through the eighth, and each therefore identifiable with the Holy Spirit and salvation, may also be seen here 6 squared as the sum of pillars, 8 being the number of sides defining the central space, 4 squared the sides enclosing the whole, and 8 × 4 the number of pillars around the octagon; 4 being identifiable with earth, the elements, justice and the gospels; 6 with the first perfect number and creation; and 8 with re-birth and salvation.

If such an interpretation may be thought fanciful, Charlemagne's Chapel happens to be dedicated in part to Christ specifically as Saviour and the inscription around the interior of its rotunda, which remains in place in a modern facsimile, opens thus:

As the living stones are bonded in a fabric of peace, *and all come together in matching numbers,* the work of the lord who has built the entire hall[28] shines forth brightly . . . .[29]

It is interesting to speculate how much Otto the Great might have been aware of this on the occasion of his coronation in the chapel.

St Gall (pl. 1)

It will be recalled that inscribed on the *Plan of St Gall* [30] is a set of dimensions that have been translated thus:

> From east to west the length [is] 200 feet.
> The width of the nave of the church [is] 40 feet.
> The width of each aisle [is] 20 feet.
> Measure twice six feet between the columns
> To have them arranged in this way is suitable.
> Between these columns [western Paradise] measure ten feet.
>
> Horn I.77

The plan is thought to have been copied in about 817 from an original drawing by Abbot Haito of Reichenau nearby and dedicated to Abbot Gozbert of St Gall for use in reconstructing his abbey. That the dimensions stated do not fit the plan as drawn has been explained as a possible correction in favour of a smaller structure following disagreements at the Aachen Synod of 816. The dimensions may be interpreted in various ways, yet, if allowance is made for the plan having been traced onto parchment from the original,[31] the church itself between the two main apses appears to consist of a grid of double squares, squares and half-squares of 40 feet.[32] This recalls Augustine's definition of,

> . . . the number most frequently employed in the Scriptures to make known the mystery of perfection in the four divisions of the world. For the number ten has a certain perfection, and when multiplied by four it makes forty.
>
> *De Trinitate* IV.4.10

It also recalls Glaber's 'divine and abstract quaternity' combined with the renewed interest among Benedictines in monastic rule and the Law, expressed as it was by 10. As a scheme of squares and double squares, it might also bear a relation to the Tabernacle and Temple.

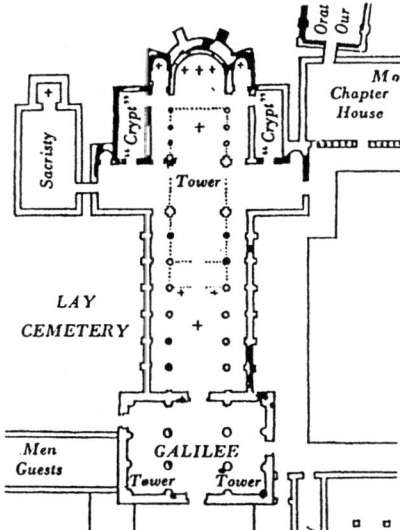

Fig. 7 Plan of Cluny II, after Conant.

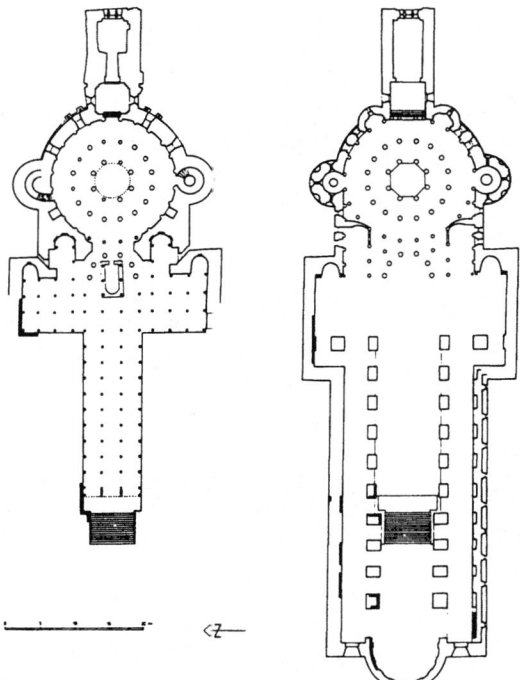

Fig. 8 Plan of St Bénigne, Dijon, after Monthel.

Cluny II (fig. 7)

The building of the second abbey church at Cluny took place between 948 and 981 during the abbacies of Mayeul and Odilo. One analysis of the plan, made from documentary and archaeological evidence, has led to a claim that the longitudinal dimensions occur in modules of 7 as measured in Carolingian feet, a claim that seems less than conclusive since the lateral dimensions vary from this. However, there were, it seems, 7 chapels including the main apse, 7 bays and 28 windows to the nave, with another 35 around the sanctuary, 7 being explicitly identified with the Holy Spirit and with the Lord's day of rest by Augustine.[33] Being multiplied by 4 and 5 respectively could also indicate Platonic significance in terms of the element earth for the nave, and the universe, or heaven, for the sanctuary.

St Bénigne, Dijon (fig. 8)

Shortly after 997, according to Glaber's *Vita sancti Guillelmi*, William of Volpiano started to rebuild 'the whole temple from its foundations', making it 'much longer and broader than it had been'.[34] Attached to the main apse of the rebuilt basilica was William's great rotunda, the crypt of which still survives, and to the east of that was an original chapel retained from the previous century.[35] Whilst the basilica was supported by 40 piers and was lit by 120 windows, again with connotations explained by Augustine, William's rotunda was arranged in 3 storeys beneath an *oculus*, its circular plan divided into 8 with an inner ring of 8 columns, an outer ring of 16, or 4 squared, with a further 4 to the west linking the rotunda to the basilica's main apse. In addition to the association of 4 and 8 with martyria and baptisteries already noted, the sum of columns here amounts to 28 which is a perfect number, the product of 7×4 and the sum of the first 7 numbers.[36] Whilst circular and octagonal shrines regularly served as baptisteries and martyria, at Dijon William's rotunda was both since its crypt, dedicated to John the Baptist, also housed the tomb of Benignus. Furthermore, the rotunda as a whole was dedicated to Mary and All Martyrs, as was the Pantheon. The dedication of the ground storey also fitted the geometry of the layout, with Mary's altar in the axial chapel being accompanied by those of the 12 apostles in the body of the rotunda. Finally, the upper storey was ringed by pillars numbering 36, which is not only the square of 6 as at Aachen but also the product of 12×3 and, not surprisingly, it was dedicated to the Holy Trinity.[37]

Whilst independent evidence may be lacking to support these interpretations, it seems reasonable to claim the internal evidence offered by the layouts of all four of these buildings and their correlation with known number theory and the correspondence at Aachen and Dijon with their dedications. One common objection to such interpretations, however, is that they do not in themselves prove that the architecture was originally conceived in that way, or any other way for that matter. Yet this may be the case at St Emmeram's Abbey in Regensburg and at the New Minster in Winchester.

St Emmeram, Regensburg

Abbot Ramwold's construction of the church's crypt in 976 was described by Arnold of Emmeram thus:

> Ramwold . . . commanded the erection of a crypt at St Emmeram. This building – very artfully ordered by the man of God – exhibited in threefold and even fourfold notion what was intended. And because the originator of this work loved the holy Trinity and held fast in the faith of the four Gospels he produced thus a kind of credible evidence. The columns, indeed which hold up this underground church compose wonderfully the duality of his twofold love, namely of God and the neighbour. Also the five altars – in which . . . relics are arranged . . . keep in mind foremost respect for the five Books of Moses, and they urge strongly ever to have fivefold circumspection regarding the five bodily senses. The sixth altar, however . . . announces the perfection of the 'sextuple', comprising everything.
>
> Arnold, Liber II.40; 568

Arnold was not only a monk at the abbey, he was describing Ramwold's crypt only sixty years after its construction[38] and if it might still be doubted that Arnold was conveying Ramwold's intentions, he does actually record that Ramwold ordered the crypt in threefold and fourfold manner *because* of his love of the Trinity and Gospels. As it happens, St Emmeram had by then acquired its copy of Hroswitha's works, including her discourses on number theory and her exhortations to praise the Creator for knowledge of it, which at least demonstrates a concordance of thought.

New Minster, Winchester

A few years after Ramwold's work, sometime in the 980s, King Ethelred built a tower at the New Minster in Winchester at the instigation of Abbot Ethelgar and this was recorded about forty years later in the Minster's *Liber vitae* as follows:

> When at last the long-desired growth of this marvellous tower had been completed . . . Aethelgar . . . longing to embark on the course of perfection with his own labours, skilfully distinguished the totality of the elegant fabric itself by the number of perfection which . . . is made up of the sum of its parts, is sufficient for the sacred mysteries and is most perfect by the rules of philosophy, that is, he distinguished it by the six *caelaturae*[39] of the stages . . . .
>
> Birch V.9–10, in Gem 15

Once again, not only is 6 recognized as a perfect number but a connection also seems to be made between 6 and the completion of creation, in the otherwise convoluted sequence of the king completing the tower and being followed by the abbot dividing it into 6 stages in order to point to its perfection.[40]

Both these accounts from Regensburg and Winchester followed within a generation or so of the projects they describe and so it is still possible that there could be a difference between interpretation and intention. But how likely is this, given the consistency of thought within the monastic world regarding number theory and the possibility of living memory bridging the gap between event and record? Yet if number were being expressed symbolically here, the question remains as to whether geometry was similarly employed.

Geometric expressionism

The knowledge and teaching of geometry in the tenth century is supported by the abundance of copies of Martianus's treatise *De nuptiis*. This contains abbreviated material from Books I, V, X and XI of Euclid's *Elementa*, including the classification of angles, planes and solids and the construction of solids from planes.[41] *De geometria* by Boethius was also extant and when Gerbert's agent found a copy of it, Gerbert introduced it into his teaching syllabus, supplementing his own *Geometria*. This was mainly practical, being based largely on the *Codex Arcerianus* of Roman land surveying.[42] Although Boethius's original work is thought to have included some information on surveying, it was also concerned with more theoretical material derived from Plato and Euclid.[43] The surviving *Ars geometriae et arithmeticae*, which was attributed to Boethius, includes paraphrases, however obscurely, of some of Euclid's Propositions, for example 389.8–9 and 10–11 correspond to IV.12 and 11 for circumscribing a regular pentagon about a given circle and vice versa.

The Platonic solids are dealt with in the *Elementa* of Euclid in Book XIII, which shows how each may be inscribed within a sphere. Knowledge of the regular polyhedra early in the middle ages appears substantiated by Isidore who states there are 5 geometric solids[44] and by Walter of Speyer who alludes to them, albeit enigmatically, in his poem *Vita et passio sancti Christophori martyris* written in 983. Here Walter describes his own education which was based on a curriculum evidently brought to Speyer from St Gall and which included the arithmetic, geometric and harmonic proportions and other material found in Boethius. Having dealt with plane figures, he moves on to the solids and says of Geometry:

> Then she has joined together surfaces setting down several in turn,
> Triangular, tetragonal and pentagonal,
> Vigorously about to bring the idea of the pyramid in the sphere below
> the heavens.
>
> *Vita et passio* I.173–8; see Cantor I.801–2, also Lund 146

Technical treatises, moreover, were commonly illustrated. An Italian copy of Chalcidius's version of *Timaeus*, dating from the first half of the tenth century, is not only distinguished by a very neat Latin script but is liberally illustrated with coloured diagrams constructed geometrically.[45] To this may be added a late tenth-century manuscript of the *Somnium Scipionis* by Macrobius which includes a diagram of the world composed of 4 elements (pl. 2).[46] In 983 Gerbert wrote to Adalbero from Bobbio that he had discovered in its library certain manuscripts including 'some beautiful figures of geometry'[47] and a codex survives at St Gall which is illustrated with various figures of plane and solid geometry.[48]

To return to Walter's poem, this is more than a narrow mathematical reference to Euclidean geometry. Images of cosmic geometry were not confined to the text-books of the *quadrivium*, for geometric figures had been used symbolically in religious art down the centuries to the tenth and beyond. Manuscript illumination, in particular, from the Irish and Anglo-Saxon monasteries of the seventh and eighth centuries and Carolingian houses of the ninth routinely embodied triangles, squares, rhomboids and circles allegorically in the presentation of scripture.[49] Foremost in this was St Martin's Abbey at Tours, to which Alcuin had retired as abbot. One of its scriptorium's greatest works, from about 845, was the *Vivian Bible* (pl. 3) in which Christ is depicted as Creator of the Cosmos, enthroned in majesty within two vertically overlapping circles and enclosed by a rhombus with circles at each apex. These carry busts of 4 prophets, with the 4 evangelists appearing in the 4 corners of the page.[50] It has been pointed out that this would have been a transposition from existing diagrams of the world, such as that in the Macrobius manuscript mentioned above, of a square resting upon one angle with the 4 cardinal points and 4 elements contained within the circles at the corners.[51] Glaber could well have had precisely this in mind when writing of 'divine and abstract quaternity'. Of further significance is the rhombus framing Christ in the *Vivian Bible*, for this actually consists of two regular triangles. Another page from this *Bible* portrays David as the cosmic musician within a *mandorla*, so called because of the almond shape of its two enclosing arcs.[52] One more example of this form appears surrounding Christ in Majesty in the *Sacramentary of Charles the Bald* dating from around 860. The influence of the Tours scriptorium, with its preoccupation with cosmic geometry, continued late into the tenth century, contributing to the wealth of symbolism in Ottonian manuscripts, to the extent that this period more than any other early in the middle ages, it has been said, attempted through its art to express the inexpressible.[53]

An illustration of this is provided by the *Eadui Gospel Book* in yet another possible allusion to the verse from *Wisdom*. Written shortly after 1000, it breaks new ground by appearing to illustrate the Creation according to measure, number and weight (pl. 4).[54] Until then it was usual for God to be depicted creating the universe impassively, as if by the force of his mind. The *Eadui* image, in showing the hand of God in the act of creation clasping a pair of scales and a second instrument, has therefore been regarded as an important innovation[55] and seems to answer the call, made at least by Hroswitha just a few decades earlier, for the Creation according to measure, number and weight actually to be celebrated. The picture is also remarkably close to Basil's words in his *Hexaëmeron* which, it may be remembered, was turned into Anglo-Saxon at about the time Hroswitha was writing, when he says:

> Moses almost shows us the finger of the supreme artisan taking possession of the substance of the universe, forming the different parts in one perfect accord . . . .
>
> *Hexaëmeron* I.7

The second instrument shown in God's hand has been variously described and dismissed as scissors, compasses and ordinary dividers.[56] However, it clearly appears to be a pair of proportional dividers complete with pivotal pin plainly in view. Although proportional dividers and compasses are said to have been unknown or little known until the end of the middle ages, they were known to the ancient world, a pair of such dividers for example surviving in a set of bronze instruments at Pompeii. Others that have been preserved, commonly set in the ratio of 1 : 2, have been regarded more as craft tools useful for doubling, halving and centring rather than as drawing instruments.[57] Yet it does seem that they were familiar to the *Eadui* illustrator at the turn of the millennium and, more important, not only was the verse from *Wisdom* now being visually expressed, apparently for the first time, but the manner of its depiction introduces, through the presence of the dividers,

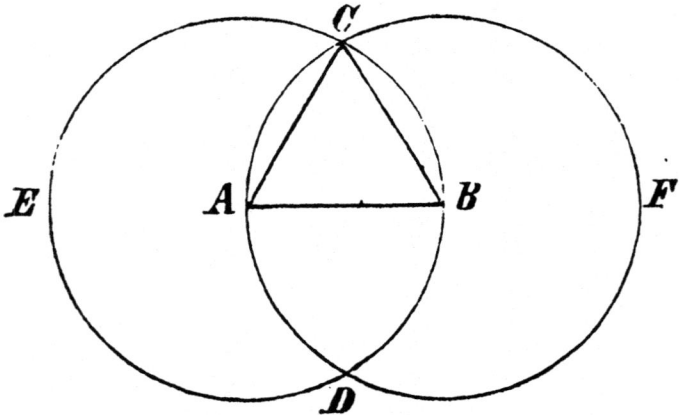

Fig. 9 The *vesica piscis*, *Ars geometriae et arithmeticae*, Friedlein edn.

the application of geometry and proportion, thus foreshadowing more familiar portrayals over the next two centuries (pl. 5). This, it has been suggested,[58] could have been in response to a knowledge of Proverbs:

> When he prepared the heavens, I was there:
> when he set a compass upon the face of the depth. . . .
> when he appointed the foundations of the earth . . .
> Then I was by him . . . .
>
> Proverbs VIII.27, 29, 30

That the *Eadui* illustration constitutes the visual representation of a metaphysical belief is perhaps self-evident. However, it may be argued that just as the teaching of such a doctrine in a monastery school may be indistinguishable from the portrayal of it in religious art, so its visual expression was similarly regarded as the illustration of a perceived fact. Another example occurs in the *Ars geometriae et arithmeticae* in which a diagram shows two equal circles overlapping each other with their circumferences passing through their respective centres. Inscribed within the overlap is the upper of two regular triangles which the construction encloses (fig. 9). Its purpose was undoubtedly understood as an illustration of several geometric axioms relating to the radii of equal circles, the regular triangles thereby produced being one-sixth of the hexagons inscribed within those circles. By ontological extension, it has been shown that 6 was not only recognized as the first perfect number, it was also identified with Creation, whilst the regular triangle formed the polyhedra of the atmospheric elements and came to symbolize the Holy Trinity. The *Vivian Bible* has already been seen to frame Christ within two regular triangles, whilst elsewhere he was similarly shown within a *mandorla*, a figure which gradually took the form of the overlap of two equal circles. Known as the *vesica piscis*, it had made an early appearance around 845 as the figure surrounding David in the *Vivian Bible*. By the Ottonian period, it has already been encountered enclosing Luke in the *Gospels of Otto III* and likewise frames Otto in his *Aachen Gospel Book* (pl. 6) which is thought to have been produced for him around the millennium in Trier.[59] As for the *Ars geometriae*, numerous copies of this either survive or are recorded from the ninth century onwards.[60] Thus with the *vesica piscis* appearing in both text-books and gospel-books, many of which must have been found in the same monastic libraries, it is argued here that the diagram in the *Ars geometriae* and the illumination in the *Aachen Gospel Book* are inseparable parts of the same teaching and reciprocate each other. The one expressed the other and the celebration of these beliefs, as urged by Hroswitha, was as essential as their demonstration in a textbook. As Isidore had put it in the seventh century:

> The sixfold [number] . . . which is perfect in its parts states the perfection of the world, indicating it by its number.
>
> *Etymologiae* III.4

Here, yet again, not only are the mathematics and the metaphysics seen in conjunction with each other but also the reality in the early medieval mind that 'the perfection of the world' was actually indicated by the number 6.

At about the time Otto III was presented with his *Aachen Gospel Book*, he donated the metal altar frontal for the Aachen Chapel.[60] On this, Christ is displayed in a *vesica piscis*,[61] thus forming the centrepiece of the entire architectural setting of the Chapel. Fresco painters also included the regular triangle in the geometry they applied to the composition of their work. By snapping cords across the wet plaster, the artist laid out his scheme, helpfully leaving in the process evidence of the particular geometry used. Around 890, for example, frescoes in the crypt of St Maximin in Trier were laid out in a system of triangles, one regular triangle fixing the positions of Mary, John and the head of Christ on the Cross.[62]

Contemporary with the *Eadui Gospels* was the work of the Winchester School, which followed a style of manuscript illumination which first appeared with the *New Minster Foundation Charter* of Edgar in 966. Among the pages of the *Charter* is a portrayal of Christ within a *vesica piscis*.[63] This particular figure, together with earlier Carolingian examples, is much more bulbous than the *vesica* in the *Ars geometriae* and therefore does not exactly contain two regular triangles. Shortly afterwards, however, the *Benedictional* of Ethelwold was produced and its Ascension scene does show Christ in what may be termed a regular *vesica* (pl. 7) and this was followed early in the next century by the *New Minster liber vitae* mentioned above,[64] the frontispiece of which again shows Christ in a regular *vesica*. The two Aachen examples, although not exact, are certainly close enough to appear to be clear attempts at the true figure and the marginal discrepancy involved could easily have arisen during the process of copying and manufacture, particularly when it is remembered that the altar frontal was formed of metal sheet that had to be beaten into shape.

It is of special significance for this study that the circle, the square and the *vesica piscis* were geometric figures of both mathematical and metaphysical importance and that they were used both didactically in textbooks and expressively in tenth-century religious art. That geometry would also have been used in architectural design might be suggested by the example of Ethelwold, in whose person is found concentrated the career of abbot and bishop, schoolman and scriptorium supervisor, as well as reformer and rebuilder of monasteries. On being made abbot of the derelict abbey of Abingdon around 955, he reformed it with monks from Glastonbury, where he had studied with Dunstan, and rebuilt it to a form described, curiously perhaps, in the abbey's chronicle:

> The chancel was round, the church itself was also round, having twice the length of the chancel. The tower was also round.
>
> *Chronicon monasterii de Abingdon* II.277–8

His appointment as bishop of Winchester in 963 was followed by reforms of other abbeys across the country accompanied by his own teaching of the liberal arts at his schools in Abingdon and Winchester. As already noted, by 975 the reforming council at Winchester had been held which led to the *Regularis Concordia*. Thus, at the time the geometry of the *vesica piscis* was being drawn in his *Benedictional*, a work for his own use written by his chaplain and supervised by Ethelwold himself, Ethelwold had long been practised in the rebuilding of monasteries and was described moreover as an architect.[65]

To invert an earlier argument, for architecture to have been conceived as a symbol surely implies that it was perceived as a symbol and there is evidence, once again in manuscript illumination, that in the ninth and tenth centuries architecture was indeed associated with the Kingdom of Heaven. In Carolingian manuscripts, most notably the *St Médard Gospels* of Charlemagne's own court school, architecture not only frames important scenes but provides their background as well.[66] The symbolic content of the architecture and its continuity into the Ottonian period are borne out by the *Registrum Gregorii* of about 983 from Trier in which the architecture of Gregory's picture appears to symbolize both a church and the Church and in which Otto is shown enthroned within a baldaquin. Whilst a group of 4 pillars such as this is equated by Bede and others with the strength and support of the 4 gospels and cardinal virtues, personifications of the 4 corners of Otto's kingdom do homage by offering spheres which represent the orb of his imperial authority (pl. 8). Ethelwold's *Benedictional* is also replete with architectural metaphor[67] and, some three decades later, Bernward shows that architectural content in religious art was not confined to manuscript illumination when for his bronze doors at Hildesheim the Nativity was portrayed against a background of idealized architecture. A century later, architecture was again chosen to illustrate how well ordered Paradise was in the Judgment scene over the portal of Ste Foy at Conques, one of many examples from the period (pl. 9).

There can be little doubt either that, once built, abbeys became the setting for ritual that was pre-eminently symbolic. Obedience to monastic rule covered every detail of a monk's life, his habit, the number of psalms to recite each day, his required behaviour for the *opus Dei*, in which every word and gesture of the liturgy was invested with underlying meaning. Typical of this was the liturgy for the dedication of churches, during which the bishop knocked three times on the door and, after being admitted, traced letters diagonally across the floor with his crozier. The blessing was then administered using water to represent baptized Christians, mixed with salt to symbolize Christian teaching and ashes signifying the Passion.[68] Is it likely, therefore, that the church being dedicated had not been similarly invested with symbolism in its design? The image of the Church, according to Clement, was to be,

> . . . constructed in most regular proportions . . . through divine
> ideas, by the gift of understanding, which leads us from things
> of sense to . . . holy things, and to the holy of holies.
>
> *Stromateis* VI.11

Therefore what was a church builder or founder in the tenth century to do
when confronted with such writings and others in his own monastery library
illuminated as they were with geometric and architectural symbolism? At the
very least, a strong incentive would be provided to use such a tradition of
design if one already existed, or to help to develop one if it did not, or to
revive one if one had fallen out of use. In order to explore this possibility, it
is now proposed to examine more closely the building activities caused by the
monastic revival of the tenth and early eleventh centuries.

Architecture and the monastic revival

> Shortly after the year 1000 it came about that churches were
> rebuilt practically throughout the world, and mainly in Italy
> and Gaul; and although most of them were very suitable,
> scarcely needing any alteration, all Christian peoples were
> seized with a great desire to outdo one another in
> magnificence. It was as if the world shook and cast off its old
> age, everywhere investing itself with the white mantle of
> churches.
>
> Glaber, *Historiarum* III.4, in Oursel 14

This celebrated passage comes from the *Historiarum* of Glaber which was
inspired by William of Volpiano and dedicated to Odilo of Cluny. Glaber
probably wrote it shortly before 1040 following a spell of about five years at
Cluny under Odilo, where he had written his *Vita sancti Guillelmi* and, before
that, about fifteen years under William at St Bénigne in Dijon, when William's
great abbey church reached completion.[69] Since the whole work covers the end
of the old millennium and the beginning of the new, it is perhaps
understandable that it should be preoccupied with what the new millennium
might bring. Glaber's view, it appears, was much influenced by such
apocalyptic predictions of the world coming to an end as made in Revelation
20.7 and his own description of Europe's brand new 'mantle of churches'
might therefore be interpreted as a celebration of relief that the world had not
come to an end after all. However, Glaber appears to have been not only
unruly in his behaviour, having been shown the door of more than one
monastery, but unreliable as a chronicler, for he places Vesuvius in Africa and
the great famines of 1003 and 1033, which occurred in his own lifetime, in the
year 1000. Whatever his own fears about the end of the world – and they were
shared by others, for Abbo had had to refute them twice in the 950s – they do
not seem to have been generally shared. The apocalyptic view was hardly

consistent with the forward momentum created by Europe's revival during the tenth century and no credence appears to have been given to it in any official utterance.[70] Through all of Gerbert's vicissitudes, for example, not a word is to be found in his letters that the year 1000 was expected to be any different from any other.[71] On the contrary, the optimism of the age may be typified by a letter he wrote in 987 for Adalbero to Mayeul of Cluny:

> The season changes, and the good land, long barren through no fault of its own, brings forth marvellous flowers and fruits. For, behold, the little cell of the blessed Martin revives the host of monks, long dead up to now.
>
> *Letter* 117, in Lattin 150

It was the monastic revival, then, that seems to have produced 'the white mantle of churches', the coincidence of which with the millennium possibly being explained by the progress of that revival. The monastic world at the beginning of the tenth century has been described as one of desolation, obsolescence and corruption. The renewal this provoked in turn produced reform and with both came rebuilding and new building right across Western Christendom. At first, construction was evidently hurried, with buildings thrown up to meet immediate needs, and therefore simple, even primitive, often either wooden or the result of quarrying other ruins, sometimes raised by unskilled hands, not always having been designed in the accepted sense and often destined to fall within decades to fire or storm. As the new millennium approached, the increased stability and relative prosperity brought by the tenth-century revival also brought a second wave of monastic building, usually replacing the earlier buildings on a larger scale, generally in stone and both planned and supervised by clerics who were sometimes acknowledged at the time as being builders and even architects.[72]

Cluny itself exemplifies this process. The first abbey church was started by Berno in 910 and completed by his successor Odo. Yet between 948 and 981, as already noted, Mayeul raised a second over or near the first to a design some 42 m long and 13 m high. It comprised an apsed choir and transepts, a crossing tower and nave probably with barrel-vaulted aisles, twin towers and narthex at the west end,[73] yet even this was to be replaced a century later by Hugh's massive structure. Similarly, the third basilica at Ripoll, where Gerbert probably studied, was started in 970, the year he was taken to Rome. Seven years later, the new building was consecrated, having been laid out with triple apses, double aisles and clerestoreys above its bold masonry arcades. In 1032, it was consecrated again following the addition of a narthex flanked by towers and a massive east transept with no fewer than 7 apses.[74] The rebuilding of St Remi at Reims that started in 1005 was on such a large scale that it had to be reduced, yet its central span still exceeded 14 m.[75] Still standing are two examples between Reims, where Gerbert was teaching, and Dijon, where William was soon to be at work. At about the time of Gerbert's reference to Adso in his letter to Adalbero in 983, Adso, who had studied at Gorze,[76] started rebuilding the derelict abbey at Montier-en-Der, the substantial nave of which remains and is 40 m long and 23 m high, aisled, arcaded, three-storeyed and originally incorporating a narthex (pl. 10). Similarly, the priory church nearby at Vignory, which dates from around 1030, preserves a nave that is also aisled and galleried. Even earlier than these is a church founded in 961 at Gernrode, in Otto's heartland of Saxony, not far from Hildesheim. This too is large, aisled, arcaded and three-storeyed (pl. 11). As the new millennium approached, a number of these were matched by other projects such as William's abbey at Dijon where rebuilding was planned around 997, St Martin's at Tours which Heriveus started replacing around 1003, and St Michael's at Hildesheim which Bernward commenced shortly after his return from Tours in 1007.[77]

Much has been written about the actual part likely to have been played by such individuals in their building work, as to whether they were simply founders of buildings raised anonymously by others, or whether they may have been the builders themselves, either actively or in the role perhaps of overseers, or whether any can be regarded as architects in the sense of supervising the erection of buildings to a pre-determined design.[78] Rather than continue the speculation here, it may be of advantage to review the historical record. For example, when Otto the Great's brother, Bruno, is said to have built impressive new churches in Cologne, this may mean no more than that he caused them to be built in his capacity as archbishop of that city. On the other hand, since he was personally responsible for reforming both Lorsch Abbey and St Pantaleon's in Cologne, which led to the rebuilding of the latter by his immediate successor and to his own burial there, he could have had much more of a direct hand in the work of its re-foundation before his death.[79]

Towards the end of the century, three of Otto III's and Gerbert's circle, Odilo, Heribert and Bernward, were all involved in building work.[80] As the abbot of Cluny, Odilo had charge of its expanding collection of monastic dependencies, resulting in many new churches being built. Judging by the architectural influence of Cluny II elsewhere, these may well have borne the same hall-marks.[81] Whatever Odilo's own function was precisely, this at least suggests that the hand of a designer may have been present. Heribert, who had been educated at Gorze, was not only Otto III's chancellor but archbishop of Cologne as well. In 1002 he founded St Mary's Abbey at Deutz in Otto's memory[82] and was recorded,

> . . . seeking out architects from foreign borders and imparting to them the science of all building.[83]

Lehmann-Brockhaus 1938 no.270, in Pevsner 556

Quite what status his architects enjoyed and, if they were architects, why they needed him to impart 'the science of all building' must remain open questions. This might be no more than a chronicler's flattery or it might mean that his role was as close as Bernward's appears to have been at Hildesheim. By the time Bernward became bishop at Otto's instigation in 993, he was already planning his abbey of St Michael. Six years after a visit to Rome in 1001, when he doubtless saw its principal basilicas, he travelled to St Denis's Abbey outside Paris, which had been reformed by Mayeul,[84] and to St Martin's Abbey at Tours, which was currently being rebuilt by Heriveus. Whether Bernward or anyone else in his party made notes on this tour, both the motive for making it and the possible transmission of architectural ideas, even from his earlier trip to Rome, to the singular layout of St Michael's Abbey may again suggest the presence of a designer or at least someone with an interest in architectural design. There appears to be no reason why this should not have been Bernward himself, since he was also famed as a metalworker, both in gold and in casting architectural bronze-work which, together with his presence throughout the abbey's construction, has led to at least one authority to conclude that he was also the architect.[85]

Thus far, however, the evidence may be regarded as equivocal. Even when Evraclus, who was bishop of Liège in the tenth century, was described as *sapiens architectus*, this was apparently a common compliment at the time for an eccliastic who was, say, 'a wise architect' of the Church's affairs.[86] However, such an interpretation would be less convincing were it to be applied to Hugh, a monk of Montier-en-Der towards the end of the tenth century who had trained in several arts and was employed in restoring the bishop's churches,[87] or to Bishop Argerich of Verdun who in the following century was 'a good architect and painter'.[88] Also in the eleventh century Benno, who became bishop of Osnabruck in 1068, operated in a manner that has been accepted as that of an architect. Earlier in his career he visited Jerusalem with Bishop William of Strasbourg who built several monasteries. He subsequently spent some years at Speyer when its cathedral was under construction before becoming head of the cathedral school at Hildesheim, provost of the cathedral and episcopal administrator. Prior to his consecration at Osnabruck, he moved to Goslar and an imperial appointment under Henry II, which was maintained by his successor, and then to Cologne. During this whole period Benno was active architecturally, his output including a number of forts for the emperor, as well as church and cathedral work in Hildesheim and Speyer and, finally, the church and monastery at Iburg where he died in 1088. Whether Benno was the architect for all these projects or whether he was assisted by someone who was, similarities of details in architectural design, otherwise untypical of the period, have been observed at all the locations mentioned here and at which Benno was certainly present at the time.[89] Moreover, his biographer, Norbert, states that Benno, 'an outstanding architect, an expert in masonry work, was the planner'[90] and hails the great talent he displayed at Speyer in *'architecturiae artis'*.[91]

The possible existence of bishop-architects may also be evident in tenth-century England. Following his stay at Fleury, Odo became archbishop of Canterbury in 934, whereupon he restored the cathedral and its buildings for which 'he directed the assembled craftsmen'.[92] Much the same description was made of his nephew Oswald. He also studied at Fleury after being brought up in Odo's household and, as bishop of Worcester, went on to found Ramsey Abbey in 969. Here he was also recorded giving instructions, this time to the eventual prior who,

. . . constructed the necessary *officinae*[93] with a beautiful design according to the method and plan shown to him beforehand by the holy man.[94]

Chronicon abbatiae Rameseiensis I.22.39,
in Lehmann-Brockhaus 1935, 38

A clue as to what this plan may have been appears to be disclosed in another account written only a generation after the event, which states that Oswald,

. . . began to initiate the foundations of the church. And since he had protected it by the sign of the revered cross, through which we believe ourselves to be saved, so also therefore he began to construct the buildings of that place in the fashion of a cross.[95]

Vita sancti Oswaldi, Rolls 71, 434, in Gem 13

In 960, Odo had been succeeded as archbishop of Canterbury by Dunstan on his return from exile at the Abbey of St Peter in Ghent which, it may be recalled, was currently being reformed by Einold of Gorze. Three years later, the *Anglo-Saxon Chronicles* record that:

King Edgar chose St Aethelwold for bishophood in Winchester, and St Dunstan, the archbishop of Canterbury, hallowed him. In the year after he was hallowed he made many monasteries, and drove out the secular clerics from the bishopric, because they would not keep any monastic rule, and appointed monks there.
Afterwards, he came to king Edgar and asked that he be given all the monasteries the heathen men had destroyed, because he wished to rebuild them; and the king gladly granted it.

Anglo-Saxon Chronicles 128

Ethelwold's earlier rebuilding of Abingdon Abbey has already been mentioned and for this he was described as '*magnus aedificator*'. Being the 'great builder' may not necessarily mean he was also the architect, but he did personally involve himself in the building works of his various foundations, including Abingdon where he was nearly killed by a falling timber. Once he was installed at Winchester, however, he was described as '*theoreticus architectus*'.[96] Bearing in mind his personal supervision of his own *Benedictional*, complete with its expressive use of geometry and extensive architectural symbolism, it would be difficult to believe that he would contrive such a use of geometry and symbolism in sacred literature and not in his sacred architecture. That he did devise religious architecture symbolically appears attested by his foundation of Thorney Abbey, where he 'constructed a church, tripartite in its unity, to the praise of the Trinity'[97] and since this occurs in the *Foundation*

Charter of about 973 rather than in a later account, it would appear to indicate the founder's own intention.

As already observed, another prolific individual of the period was William of Volpiano who built, rebuilt and reformed numerous abbeys simultaneously in Burgundy, Normandy, Lombardy and Lorraine, even bringing his own brand of the Cluniac reform to Gorze. Opinion, however, as to his actual function in all these works has also been divided between those who accept that he clearly operated as an architect and at least one who does not.[98] Accordingly, it may be profitable to return to two contemporary sources, namely Glaber and John of Ravenna, for not only were they both disciples of William, John was also his nephew and Glaber was a monk at William's Abbey of St Bénigne when its rebuilding was reaching completion. Both therefore would have been in a position to know precisely what William's role was at least in Dijon.

> . . . part of the church of the blessed martyr Benignus to which [William], at God's instigation, had originally been given as father, fell into ruin. When the stone-masons wished to restore it, the same section fell into a worse ruin. Perceiving this, this devotee of God recognized that it was a judgement given to him from heaven that it was appropriate to rebuild the whole temple from its foundations. Immediately with the great genius of his mind he began to embark upon wonderful preparations for rebuilding that church. And when he had finally begun to rebuild it on a marvellous site, much longer and broader than it had been . . . he arranged for it to be completed . . . .[99]

> Glaber, *Vita sancti Guillelmi* XV.710–11

> In the wonderful work on this basilica . . . the reverend abbot hired the master craftsmen and dictated the work itself . . . The form and subtlety of this ingenious work is not vainly presented in words for all those who are less informed, since many things in it seem to have been made with a mystical significance . . . .[100]

> John, *Altera vita* 8–9

There seems to be no reason to suppose that the record means anything other than it says. Mention of 'mystical significance' here in the design of St Bénigne may be compared with the description of work at Mouzon already noted, when Adalbero,

> . . . began to call upon the leaders of the church, making up some things for others, as if keeping something secret, and conversing about the site, the situation and the composition of the buildings.[101]

> *Historia monasterii Mosomensis* II.4, 612

To this may be added Heribert at Deutz,

> . . . seeking out architects from foreign borders and imparting
> to them the science of all building.

Lehmann-Brockhaus 1938, no.270,
in Pevsner 556; see above

Around the millennium, the Abbey of St Martin at Tours was being rebuilt by
its treasurer, Heriveus.

> Moreover, this man, full of God, conceived of the idea of
> raising this church, of which he had been admitted as guardian,
> with a structure of an overall larger and higher construction.
> Therefore, *with the Holy Spirit teaching him, he described to the
> masons how to lay the foundation of a work without equal* . . . .[102]

Glaber, *Historiarum* III.4 [my italics]

Given the consistent references to ecclesiastics actually directing building
works, imparting specialist knowledge to the masons, being regarded by their
contemporaries as architects, or at least operating as if they were architects
and, given the specific references made to particular projects sometimes by
writers personally acquainted with the people concerned, it is argued here that
such a concentration of examples cannot reasonably be discounted simply as
a chronicler's flattery. Perhaps the most illuminating reference of all is to
Anstaeus who studied the liberal arts and was among the first monks at Gorze
before becoming abbot of St Arnulf in Metz in 945.[103] Not only did he
construct buildings at Gorze to,

> . . . a very beautiful plan . . . a not undistinguished skill in
> architecture lurked in him so that whatever he had once
> designed, in all the symmetry and proportions of the buildings,
> could not easily be criticized in the judgment of anybody.[104]

Vita Iohannis 355–6, c. 67, 66

Bearing in mind the special definition of symmetry in the liberal arts, this
surely means that Anstaeus could design buildings so that the parts and the
whole were in proportion to each other.

Herein perhaps lies a clue as to the relationship these particular clerics
may have had to the building process (pl. 13). It has already been observed
that as churchmen they were also scholars whose education on the whole had
been theoretical, broad and at least sometimes practical too. However, there

is little or no suggestion that they actually took over any of the building construction themselves apart, that is, from Ethelwold. For Tours and Canterbury, separate reference is made to masons and craftsmen and at Deutz even to architects, as distinct from Heribert who was the archbishop. Likewise, to rebuild the Abbey of St Remi, its abbot brought together men recognized as being skilled in architecture.[105] Yet as patrons they were entitled to prescribe the work they wanted and as educated churchmen of the period this is likely to have comprised a programme that was symbolical as well as functional, there being, no doubt, no real difference in their eyes between the two. This would leave to the practical masters the tectonic details and erection of the building in accordance with the programme.[106] Thus the 'method and plan' of Oswald, the 'theory' of Ethelwold, the 'science' of Heribert, the 'mystical significance' of St Bénigne and William's 'genius of mind', Adalbero's 'secret', the 'beautiful plan' of Anstaeus and the 'symmetry and proportions' of his buildings, could all be references to schematic design as distinct from building construction. Thus if a connection were needed between beliefs held and beliefs expressed in architectural design, there might be little need to look further, for here may well be examples of the theologian and architectural programmer concentrated into one and the same person.

Intriguingly, several of these men were connected with Gorze. Anstaeus studied there from around 933, as did Adalbero and Heribert; Dunstan spent his exile in the 950s in a monastery that was being reformed by Einold of Gorze and then went on to teach Ethelwold; whilst William of Volpiano went to Gorze in 1015 to reform it, having previously reorganized Anstaeus's own Abbey of St Arnulf. This was at a time when William was already active in Normandy and St Bénigne was nearing completion.[107] Finally, his own reform of St Bénigne which commenced in 990 had been preceded by an abortive attempt in 982 by Abbot Adso of Montier-en-Der, the monastery which Adso was about to rebuild and where Hugh was also busy rebuilding churches (see above). For his own part, Adso had been a pupil at Gorze before directing the school of St Aper in Toul which was itself a Gorzean abbey.[108] Therefore, if any particular method of design did exist or was brought into existence, it may not be too fanciful to look to Gorze as a possible source and thence to the Cluniac reform, spearheaded by Odilo and William, which superseded it.

To return to Glaber's 'white mantle of churches', it might be reasonable to ask why these 'churches were rebuilt practically throughout the world' when 'most of them were very suitable, scarcely needing any alteration'.[110] The answer might simply be Cluniac bombast, for it was Glaber's stay at Cluny which apparently caused the revision and completion of Book III of his *Historiarum*,[110] or it might be a chronicler's desire to impress by exaggerating. Bearing in mind Glaber's own obsession with the millennium and his unreliability as a reporter outside his own ambit, this may not be too difficult to accept. On the other hand, it has already been noted that the first hurried constructions early in the century caused a second wave of more permanent and impressive building towards the turn of the eleventh century and so if a method of design, or various methods of design, as distinct from a method of construction, were to have been adopted for what was evidently a concerted programme of rebuilding and new building, then signs of this might be apparent in the architecture that resulted. Consequently, plans of reformed abbeys dating from around the millennium and associated with some of the personalities considered here will be included in the geometric investigation.

The documentary evidence already cited from tenth-century chronicles seems at least to permit the idea of some form of schematic design being passed by churchmen to builders and it may be reasonable to suppose that this is likely to have been born of the universal view of creation put forward in the liberal arts and manifest in the repeated belief that the Creator had so ordered the cosmos according to measure, number and weight. Whilst the evidence also appears to demonstrate that number, geometry and architecture were understood as expressing the divine order in writing, illumination, sculpture and liturgy, and that architecture in at least the instances of Regensburg, Winchester and Thorney was understood and probably organized numerologically in expression of that belief, this nevertheless falls short of proof that geometry was also used expressively in the design of religious architecture. Yet to be set beside this is the octagonal geometry of the chapel at Aachen and the importance of matching numbers that is actually proclaimed in its dedicatory inscription. To the tenth century belongs William's rotunda at Dijon, which can similarly be interpreted, as well as Oswald's cruciform church at Ramsey where the intentional symbolism of its layout was actually declared.

Beyond this are questions awaiting answers. For example, what was 'the science of all building' Heribert needed to impart to his architects at Deutz? Assuming Heriveus's builders at Tours would already have known the accepted procedure for laying foundations, being masons, what was the teaching of the Holy Spirit concerning the foundations that Heriveus felt it necessary to describe to them? According to the text, it was to accomplish 'a work without equal', one that was 'larger and higher' than the building it replaced. But was it simply to build it bigger that was the subject of divine instruction? If, as suggested by the text, it was the laying out of the foundation that was to make it without equal, then the teaching of the Holy Spirit could well have amounted to 'Wisdom framing the temple', as may also have been the case at St Bénigne, which William 'made with a mystical significance' that was 'more a result of divine inspiration'. Finally, since geometry as much as number was believed to reveal the divine order, would it have been confined to the pages issuing from William's scriptorium and witheld from the design of his abbey, or to the pages from Tours's famous scriptorium and not Heriveus's new abbey? Would the number theory and geometry taught by Ethelwold at his schools and displayed on the pages of his own *Benedictional* not also be deployed in the design of the abbeys for which he was simultaneously *theoreticus architectus*? In an age that believed in the total integrity of the created universe and in the Christians' mission to study it and express it, such would surely be expected.

Conclusion

This chapter has tried to show that documentary evidence from the tenth century confirms the general currency given to Christian Platonist beliefs, advancing in particular the significance and expression of number, and that this also extended to geometric expressionism. Furthermore, the record of building activities associated with the monastic revival appears to support the application of schematic design in religious architecture.

The principles of Christian Platonism were transmitted to the tenth century and adherence to them appears to have been extended by the Benedictines' own regard for the Law, Pentecost and the state of monastic order that came about through a return to the Rule of St Benedict. Continuing belief in the divine order stemmed from the notion, recurrently quoted and illustrated in contemporary literature, that God had created the universe according to measure, number and weight – which evidently subsumed geometry and proportion as well – for which the Creator should be praised. As the expression of these beliefs was actively encouraged, various churches of the period answer to the presence of number symbolism, intentionally, it seems, at least in the cases of Regensburg, Winchester and Thorney.

Evidence for the use of geometry, as well as number, is commonplace both didactically in textbooks and expressively in manuscript illumination, being inseparably illustrations of mathematics as fact and metaphysics as belief perceived as fact. Idealizations of architecture were commonly used to symbolize Paradise and the ritual that took place inside religious architecture was similarly symbolical. It is postulated therefore that it would be only consistent for geometry to have been used expressively in the planning of religious architecture as well.

In examining the monastic architecture of the period, there seems little doubt that Glaber's 'white mantle of churches' referred to a second wave of building and rebuilding in the monastic revival after the middle of the tenth century, which resulted in abbeys becoming larger and architecturally more complex. Work was often directed by abbots and bishops who were described at the time as architects or at least as experts in architecture and, whilst the building was doubtless left to builders, these churchmen are repeatedly recorded as imparting to them theoretical aspects of the design. In the light of this, the theologian and architectural programmer might well be found combined here in one and the same person, thereby enabling the expression of these beliefs to be made in the design of religious architecture. That this did involve not only number symbolism but also the expressive use of geometry seems certain in the case of Ramsey and reasonable to suppose at Dijon and elsewhere.

To conclude this part of the study, early medieval architectural practice will be examined for evidence of the actual, expressive use of geometry, in particular the square, the regular triangle and the pentagon.

Notes

1   Grodecki 28; Sackur II.51, 356.
2   See pp. 132–3.
3   *Hist. Litt.* VI.47, 44, 40, 30–1.
4   Fichtenau 298; McInerny 250; Lattin 155n1; Richer III.59, 60; Camargo 101; Knowles 93.
5   Darlington 463; Focillon 90; Fichtenau 294.
6   See pp. 27–8, 30–38.
7   Chadwick 1981, 82.
8   Augustine, *De civitate Dei* 160, 160n70.
9   Plato, *Timaeus* 47D, Cornford 1937; see p. 47.
10   Masi 11–12.
11   *Anglo-Saxon Chronicles* 128; see p. 162.
12   Vregille 87-9, 96.
13   Mun. Bay. Staats. Clun. 4453 fol. 139v; Holländer 139, 145.
14   Odo, VI in Hallinger 33–4.
15   Sackur I.261, see also Hallinger 464.
16   Fichtenau 55.
17   *ODCC* 1062; Augustine, *De sermone Domini* I.IV.12; Krautheimer 123.
18   See pp. 38–9.
19   Dronke 83, 294n11; Hroswitha/Tillyard 76–80, 101–8.
20   Cantor I.795–6.
21   Thorndike I.674–5.
22   *Wisdom* XI.20.
23   Isidore III.4; see p. 105.
24   See pp. 38–9.
25   A conflation of this section with the Octagonal Shrine (pp. 127–32) has been published and appears in the Bibliography under Hiscock 1993.
26   E.g. Augustine, *De civitate Dei* XI.30, 31, XV.20, XVI.26.
27   Alcuin, *Epistolae*, 3; Bullough 115.
28   In the context of Aachen's documentary sources, this is generally interpreted as 'church'.
29   Tr. H. Stadler, from site notes by author: *CUM LAPIDES VIVI PACIS COMPAGE LIGANTUR INQUE PARES NUMEROS OMNIA CONVENIUNT CLARET OPUS DOMINI TOTAM QUI CONSTRUIT AULAM.*
30   St Gall, Stiftsbibliothek MS.1092.
31   Horn and Born I.25, 81, 89.
32   Fernie 1978, 583; Horn and Born I.82, 103, 214 fig. 173.
33   Conant 1963, 2, 4; 1971, 83; Augustine, *De civitate Dei* XI.31; see pp. 72, 107.
34   Glaber, *Vita sancti Guillelmi* XV.
35   Flipo 13–24.
36   Martianus 738.
37   Chevallier 135–7; Malone 1996, 2–11.
38   *Die deutsche literatur* I.466–8.
39   In this context, possibly carved bands or string courses.
40   Gem 15.
41   Martianus 143–8; see pp. 62–4.
42   Cantor I.811; Ball 136f; Gow 206; Heath 1921, I.365f; Smith I.183; see p. 36.
43   Chadwick 1981, 104.

44   Isidore III.11.

45   Chalcidius, Bibl. Apost. Vat. Reg.lat. 1308, 21v, 22r.

46   Macrobius, Bodl. MS. Auct. T.227, fol. 12v; see see pp. 62–3.

47   Lattin 15; see p. 36.

48   Cod. Sang. 818.62.

49   Holländer 29, 76, 82.

50   *Vivian Bible*, Paris, Bibl. Nat. MS. lat.1; fol. 330b; Holländer 76 fig. 59.

51   Holländer 89.

52   *Vivian Bible*, fol. 215v; Holländer 84 fig. 67.

53   *Sacramentary of Charles the Bald*, Paris, Bibl. Nat. lat.1141 fol. 6; Holländer 84 fig. 72; 82, 133, 140.

54   *Eadui Gospels*, Hanover, Kest. Mus. WM.XXI^a, 36, fol. 9^v.

55   White 1978, 65; 1978, 239.

56   Panofsky 1923 67n3; White 1978, 65.

57   Hambly 19, 127–8; Moessel 1931, II.151; Stanley 112; see also Shelby 1965, 240.

58   White 1978, 65.

59   *Aachen Gospels*, Aachen, Dom. fol. 16r; Holländer 124.

60   Ullman 267, 270n1.

61   Focillon 31.

62   Sanderson 1996; see also Eichler 227, Hubert 88. I am especially grateful to Warren Sanderson for drawing my attention to this material.

63   Ohlgren 8.1; see also White 1978, 65; *New Minster Foundation Charter*, BM. Cotton MS Vespasian A.VIII fol. 2b; Baker 268, pl.XXV.

64   Ethelwold, *Benedictional*, BM. Add. MS.49598 fol. 64b; *New Minster liber vitae*, BM. Stowe MS.944 fol. 7.

65   Yorke 2–5, 7–8, 11; Thacker 54, 57; *Anglo-Saxon Chronicles* 131.

66   *St Médard Gospels*, Paris, Bibl. Nat. MS. lat.8850; Holländer 51, 82.

67   *Registrum Gregorii*, Trier, Stadtbibliothek; Holländer 137 fig. 108, 130; Chantilly, Mus. Condée; Holländer 137 fig. 109, 131; Bede, *De tabernaculo* 101, *De templo* 59, xlv–xlvi.

68   Fichtenau 252–4, 77, 211–12.

69   France 498–501.

70   Focillon 60-61, 65-8, 77-8; France 1988, 498–9; Williams 522; Sackur II.224; Knowles 79; Oursel 16.

71   Lattin 28–9.

72   Sackur II.369–71; Lehmann-Brockhaus 1935 12–15, 38–43.

73   See pp. 149–50; Sackur I.68, II.372–3; Conant 1963 2–4; 1971, 83.

74   Junyent 13–17.

75   *Historia dedicationis ecclesiae sancti Remigii*, in Harvey 56–7.

76   Lattin 15; see 2.1.3; Sackur II.391.

77   Chevallier 88; Glaber, *Historiarum* III.4; Beseler and Roggenkamp 113.

78   Lehmann-Brockhaus 1935 38–43; Pevsner 549–62; Salzman 4–16; Harvey 9f; du Colombier 61–71.

79   Dobson 146; Hallinger 99, 100, 180; see Bergmann 4–5.

80   See pp. 27–9.

81   Sackur II.375–81.

82   Darlington 473; Hallinger 105, 120.

83   . . . *architectos ab externis finibus exquirens et eis disciplinam totius structurae committens.*

84   Beseler and Roggenkamp 113; Focillon 82.

85   Beseler and Roggenkamp 113; Holländer 162.
86   *Vita Evracli*, MGH.S.XX.561, 10, in Lehmann-Brockhaus 1935, 43; Pevsner 554.
87   *Miraculi sancti Bercharii*, A.SS.II.855.22; in *Hist. Litt.* VI.67.
88   *. . . architector pictorque bonus . . . Life of Argerich*, Knoegel no.461 in Pevsner 554.
89   Pevsner 554–5; du Colombier 61f; Hindenburg 16–26.
90   *Architectus praecipuus caementariae operis solertissimus erat dispositor. . .* , *Vita Bennonis II*, MGH.S. Sep. Ed. 9 in Lehmann-Brockhaus 1938, nos.1364, 3005, and Pevsner 554–5.
91   *Vita Bennonis* 21 in Hindenberg 21.
92   *ODCC* 992; see 2.1.2; *. . . congregatis artificibus praecepit. . . Vita sancti Odonis* 11; PL 133, 940 in Lehman-Brockhaus 1935, 39.
93   Colloquialism for workshop of prayer; see Bucher 1979, 94.
94   *. . . officinas quoque necessarias iuxta modum et formam a sancto viri sibi praemonstratam pulchro schemate construxit.*
95   *. . . Coepit fundamenta initiari ecclesiae. Quoniam igitur reuerrendae crucis signo munierat, per quod nos credimus saluari, sicut et ipse ideo illius loci aedificia coepit construere in modum crucis. . .*
96   *Chronicon monasterii de Abingdon* II.259 in Salzman 6n1; *Historia I. Translationis sanctae Witburgae* A.SS.II.604.c.1 in Pevsner 553.
97   *. . . Ecclesia ad laudem trinitatis . . . in unitate tripartitam construens . . .* , Hart 167, in Gem 14.
98   Bougaud 277; Chevallier 88; Herval 31; Conant 1971 82; Grodecki 25.
99   *. . . pars ecclesiae beati martyris Benigni, cui, auctore Deo, primitus pater datus fuerat, ruinam corruens daret. Quam cum reformare cuperent artifices caementarii, graviorem pars eadem dedit ruinam. Quod cernens vir Deo devotus, intellexit divinitus sibi dari indicium quod totum a fundamentis renovari conveniret templum. Illicoque summo mentis ingenio coepit ipsius ecclesiae reformandae mirificum construere apparatum: quam denique cum coepisset reaedificare positione mirabili, valde longiore ac latiore quam fuerat . . . perficere disponebat.*
100 *. . . In cujus basilicae miro opere . . . reverendus abbas magistros conducendo et ipsum opus dictando.*
     . . . Cujus artificiosi operis forma et subtilitas non inaniter quibusque minus edoctis ostenditur per litteras, quoniam in eo multa videntur mystico sensu facta . . .
101 *. . . priores ecclesiae appelare coepit, alia pro aliis quasi dissimulando fingens, deque situ et statuae dificiis compositis confabulans.*
102 *. . . Sancto . . . Spiritu se docente, designavit latomis incomparabilis jactare fundamentum operis . . .*
103 *Hist. Litt.* VI.25–7; see pp. 29, 32.
104 *. . . pulcherimo schemate. . . architecturae non ignobilis ei pericia suberat, ut quicquid semel dispossuisset, in omnibus locorum et edificiorum sinmetriis vel commensurationibus non facile cuiusquam argui posset iudicio.*
105 *. . . qui architecturae periti ferebantur. . . Historia dedicationis ecclesiae sancti Remigii*, in Harvey 56–7.
106 Harvey, J., letter to author 16.2.1991; see also Shelby 1970, 17.
107 *Hist. Litt.* VI.25–6; Hallinger 105, 463; 9; Klukas 82–3; Grodecki 25; Sackur II.45–51.
108 Sackur II.391; Hallinger 88.
109 Glaber, *Historiarum* III.4; see above.
110 France 500–1; see also Focillon 158.

Chapter 5

Medieval Architectural Practice

Well before the end of the eleventh century, the function of master mason was already becoming differentiated from that of working mason to the point where the master mason had begun to operate and be recognized as a lay architect. To the instances at the turn of the century cited in the previous chapter, of Heribert 'seeking out architects from foreign borders' and Airard bringing together men skilled in architecture to rebuild St Remi, may be added the preparations for rebuilding Santiago de Compostela around 1071. This was achieved by a clerical committee which included the abbot and treasurer working with a building committee under Master Bernard who, with Robert had charge of about fifty masons.[1] Such an arrangement, incidentally, may have formalized the distinction posited above between clerical programmers and lay builders. In 1099, Lanfranc started rebuilding Modena Cathedral and around 1200 was portrayed beneath the words *Lanfranc architector* at the head of a group of onlookers while directing some disgruntled workmen digging foundations and laying bricks (pl. 12).[2] Later in the thirteenth century Nicolas of Biard confirmed that:

> In these great buildings it is the custom to have a chief master who only directs things by word, seldom or never lays hand to the work himself . . . .
>
> *Distinctiones*, in Mortet 1906, 268

By the middle decades of the thirteenth century, Villard de Honnecourt, despite uncertainty as to his occupation,[3] was at the very least a keen architectural enthusiast and had compiled a *Sketchbook* which has largely survived. So have various architectural drawings of Reims Cathedral and Strasbourg, each displaying surprising accuracy and refinement. By this time, architects' names were appearing on their buildings, with those of Jean of Orbais, Jean-le-Loup, Gaucher of Reims and Bernard of Soissons commemorated on the pavement labyrinth at Reims; similarly Robert of Luzarches, Thomas of Cormont and his son Regnault on that of Amiens; whilst Jean of Chelles's name is inscribed across the plinth of the south transept of Notre Dame in Paris; and Hugh Libergier's tombstone, which stood in St Nicaise in Reims before being removed to the cathedral, bears his portrait complete with the tools of his trade.[4] Finally, the *Paris Statutes* of 1268 laid down a constitution for its masons as a self-governing body, including regulations for a six-year apprenticeship, whilst eight years later the Strasbourg lodge was founded by Erwin of Steinbach, currently the cathedral architect, which similarly established itself as a self-governing body, becoming the master-lodge of all Germany a year later.[5]

For the status of architects to have become as established as this by the mid-thirteenth century, a process which could hardly have occurred overnight, it needs to be asked when it could have commenced. Beside the possibility of continuity from the Roman world, if the origins of the medieval architect lay at least partly with the cleric programmers and lay builders of the second half of the tenth century, then this would allow just over a century before Lanfranc started work at Modena, with another century and a half before the Paris lodge organized itself.

In order to determine the nature of architectural practice up to this time, given the size and relative sophistication of the aisled, arcaded and galleried abbey churches encountered so far, it will be assumed as a working hypothesis that such building will have needed to be thought out and possibly drawn out in advance for it to have been set out on site. Although other considerations would have had to be made in the erection thereafter, at least the setting out will have established location, orientation and the form and size of the building in the horizontal plane. If, as frequently put forward, heights were extrapolated from the plan, then much of the cross-section may also have been determined. This assumption is made in order to have a paradigm to set beside the historical record. Whilst it is not the only one possible, it is perhaps that most closely resembling the process of building design and construction as they are presently understood. Accordingly, the record will be examined in relation to plans, drawings, design, dimension and groundwork.

Plans

According to Vitruvius, whose treatise was available at the Abbey of St Peter in Ghent and at St Michael's at Hildesheim among other places:[6]

> It is from the plan of a temple that the effect of its design arises.
>
> *De architectura* III.II.1

> . . . the architect, when once he has formed his plan, has a definite idea how it will turn out in respect to grace, convenience, and propriety.
>
> *De architectura* VI.VIII.10

This seems to have been echoed in the seventh century by Isidore of Seville in his *Etymologiae*:

> . . . architects are masons who arrange [matters] in the foundations. Whence even the Apostle says of himself, 'I lay the foundation like a wise architect' . . . Buildings have three

parts: the plan, the construction and the aesthetic considerations. The plan is the description of the site or ground and of the foundation.

Etymologiae XIX.8–9

In the tenth century, work on Oswald's foundation at Ramsey Abbey was described thus:

Then having agreed on a plan they prepared during the whole of the winter that followed all that seemed needful for the future building . . . .

Chronicon abbatiae Rameseiensis I.22.40, in Harvey 228

The brother who was about to be prior,

. . . also constructed the necessary *officinae* with a beautiful design according to the method and plan shown to him beforehand by the holy man.

Chronicon abbatiae Rameseiensis I.22.39
in Lehmann-Brockhaus 1935, 38

Drawings

Reference to having plans for a building does not necessarily signify an architectural drawing, although something of the sort seems to be meant in some of these extracts. Neither is there a reason why such an implication should not have been intended since the practice of drawing plans is well attested either side of the period in question. Later in the same century in which Isidore was writing, Bishop Arculf returned from a pilgrimage to the Holy Land with a detailed description of his travels which Adamnan, who was the abbot of Iona, turned into *De locis sanctis*. Of all the methods Arculf could have chosen in order to convey some of the shrines he visited, the one he chose was to make sketch plans of them on wax tablets.[7] Equally, the *Plan of St Gall* not only demonstrates a proficient standard of draughtsmanship early in the ninth century but also a self-evident familiarity with plans as a medium of communication (pl. 1). In the first third of the thirteenth century, Villard included several plans and part-plans of churches in his *Sketchbook* whilst properly drawn layouts of the twelfth- and thirteenth-century sanctuaries at Notre Dame in Paris and Ste Croix at Orléans are thought to be later copies of contemporary originals.[8]

That more plans have not survived has been variously explained by the supposition that they might have been drawn on plaster or boards, or that there was no point in keeping them, or that the parchment on which they are otherwise presumed to have been drawn was later used in book-binding or melted down for glue.[9] Perhaps the most plausible explanation is that, since parchment was expensive, the same set of skins may have been successively re-used for the duration of a project, sometimes over a period of decades, by washing them in the parchment shop in preparation for the drawings needed in the next stage of the project. One thirteenth-century document of the Reims Cathedral chapter has been written over several different layers of architectural drawings of the cathedral, Sheet D displaying at least four levels and Sheet E three. Since the plan would presumably be the first drawing to be erased in such a process, this would not only account for the scarcity of plans but also the fact that the bulk of drawings which do survive relate to the later stages of construction, namely elevations of the facade and various details.[10]

The method of drawing apparent in these examples suggests the use of a straight-edge, perhaps a square, and a pair of dividers for pricking and indenting the parchment, followed by a ruling pen and compasses for inking in or, in the case of Villard's *Sketchbook*, lead pencil followed by ink a few years later.[11] The use of the square as a drawing instrument, however, cannot be taken for granted.[12] And yet for it to be shown that the procedures to be explored in the geometric investigation of this study were within the technical capability of medieval architects, it is important to try to establish the drawing instruments they were likely to have used, including the possible availability and type of set-square. Such references to it as exist are variously translated as 'square' or 'set-square'. Illustrations usually portray a square consisting simply of two unequal arms at right-angles which masons used on site to ensure stones were cut and set square. These are clearly masons' squares, those with tapering arms, it has been suggested, possibly being voussoir squares. It does not follow therefore that either was used for drawing other than on blocks of stone.[13] In at least two portrayals of thirteenth-century architects (pl. 13)[14] it is with this mason's square, not an architect's set-square, that they are depicted. The dividers shown are not to be mistaken either for the architect's small-scale draughting instrument, being instead the large dividers often held with a single or double stay that were used for describing arcs full-size on a tracing-floor and for making templates. Since medieval art necessarily constituted a picture language, an architect was perhaps identified by whatever was familiar to outsiders. If an ordinary monk or layman encountered an architect anywhere it was presumably on a building site where work on large ecclesiastical projects continued for generations and which people constantly traversed on their way into those parts of the church already open for use. It is less likely that they would have been familiar with the architect in the more secluded setting of his tracing-house, situated as it could be in the roof-space above a porch, as at Wells Cathedral, or above the chapter house vestibule, as at York Minster. Therefore it is perhaps understandable if he was pictured with the tools of his trade as master mason, rather than with the drawing instruments of his profession as architectural designer. Yet it cannot be doubted that drawing instruments were used, given the existence of drawings, though whether they included a set-square and whether it was L-shaped or triangular still remains open to question. It has been surmised, for instance, that the modern triangular set-square originated with the introduction of T-squares and drawing boards once paper in large sheets became commonly available after the fifteenth century.[15] A triangular set-square, on the other hand, can serve as either a drawing or a surveying instrument. Vitruvius includes the use of a square in setting out a building on site and alludes to Pythagoras in specifying a triangular set-square with sides of 3, 4 and 5 feet,[16] certainly too large for drawing yet just large enough perhaps for squaring on site. The foundations of Oswald's abbey at Ramsey were set out in the tenth century using a 'threefold triangle'.[17] Conversely, Isidore mentions a set-square 2'0" × 2'0" × 2'10"[18] which forms a 45° isosceles triangle, too small it would seem for site use yet it could have been employed for drawing either on parchment or on the tracing-floor. At the other end of the middle ages, in 1486, Mathes Roriczer published his *Büchlein von der Fialen Gerechtikait* which shows a method for constructing the elevation of a pinnacle from its plan. It also appears to restrict itself to the use of straight-edge and dividers, yet at one point the square is prescribed,[19] but without specifying whether or not it was triangular. However, about two years later Schmuttermayer published his own *Fialenbüchlein* in the Preface of which he salutes:

> This high art of building construction, which has its original true basis in the level, set-square, triangle, dividers, and straight-edge . . . .
>
> *Fialenbüchlein*, in Shelby 1977, 127

Here the 'triangle' can hardly be mistaken for either the triangular level that is sometimes illustrated or the mason's square because these are independently mentioned. However, it remains inconclusive whether this triangle was for squaring on site or drawing in the tracing-house and it cannot be assumed, in either case, that a practice in fifteenth-century Germany necessarily obtained in tenth- or eleventh-century France.

Nevertheless, since masonic practice from early in the middle ages depended on the constant making and using of various kinds of template, moulds and patterns, it would be consistent with such a tradition for templates to be made for drawing and used in the form of set-squares, capable therefore of reproducing selected geometric figures and proportions.[20] Once made, they could have been kept in the lodge and used from generation to generation as part of the working practice of the lodge. Something akin to this has been noted in the numerous instances of geometric decoration consisting of repeated golden triangles, for which a template would undoubtedly have been employed. Friezes displaying this pattern were common from antiquity to the Romanesque period, as has been shown at St Donato on Murano (pl. 14.[21] and can also be seen around one of the arcade piers at Vignory. Likewise, the 45°, 60° and Pythagorean triangles that are also inscribed around Vignory's piers and the net of 60° diagonals on the Norman tympanum of Winstone's south door in Gloucestershire would all have needed some sort of guide for making angles (pl. 15). The tracing-floor at Wells Cathedral may also point to

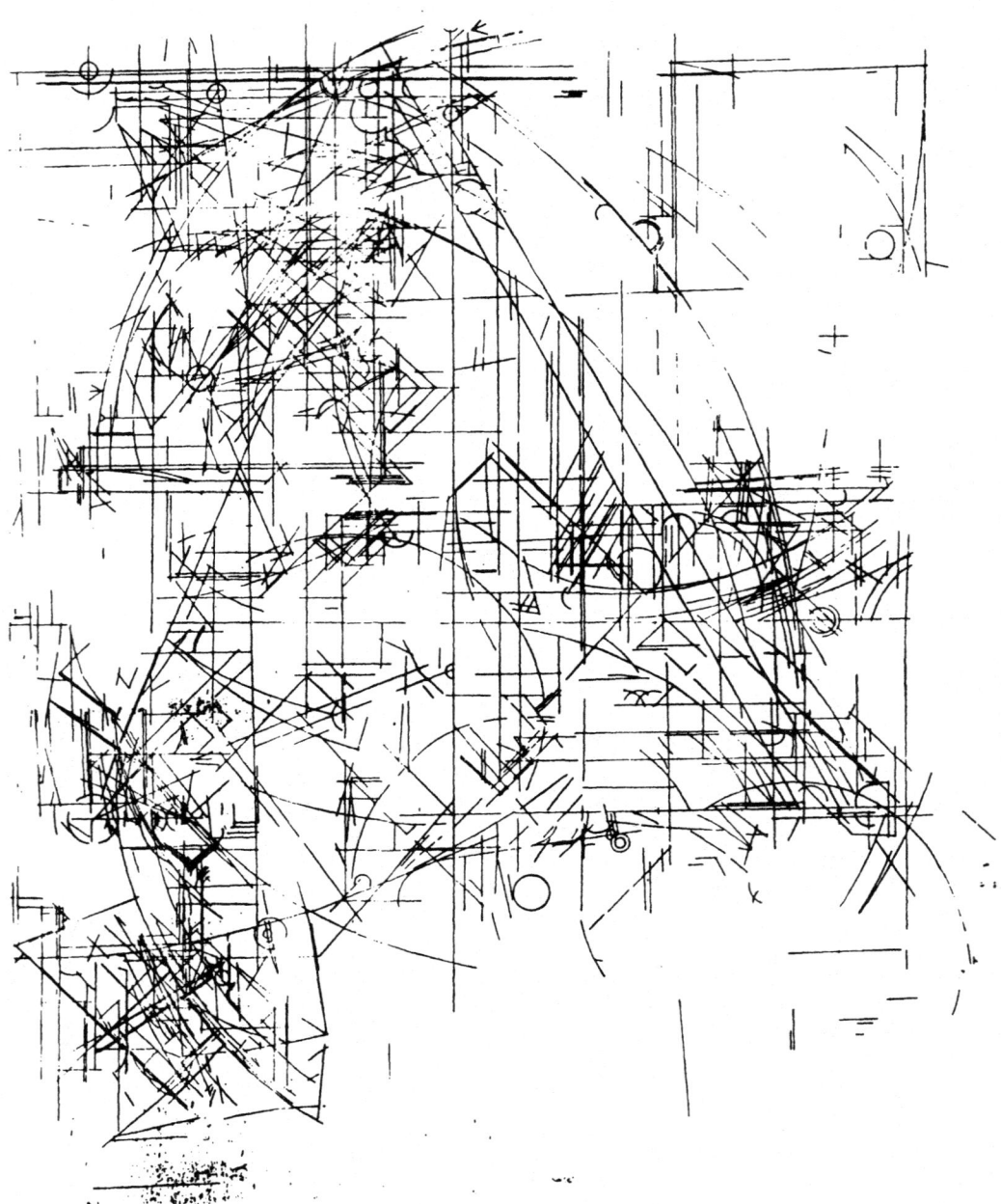

Fig. 10 Tracing-floor, Wells Cathedral, after Harvey (*Archaeological Journal*).

a similar possibility (fig. 10). Several lines have been inscribed in the plaster approximating to 45°, 22½°, even 60° to the main axis and to one or two subsidiary axes as well. Although any of these angles could have been described by compasses, the necessary arcs for doing so are no longer apparent. They could have faded with time, yet none of the existing marks has. Alternatively, set-squares could have been used to set out the angles.

To summarize, whilst the existence of straight-edges, dividers and compasses is self-evident from the drawings, the evidence for set-squares is more tenuous. Yet there do remain Isidore's triangular set-square and both Loriczer's and Schmuttermayer's squares of unspecified type, as well as the known use of templates. In addition to this, exercises in Villard's *Sketchbook* have already shown that angles were reproduced for masonry details by the device of calibration which, in effect, makes use of numerical ratios. It may be recalled that the inclination of a spire is set out in this way to a template calibrated 1 : 8 (fig. 11).

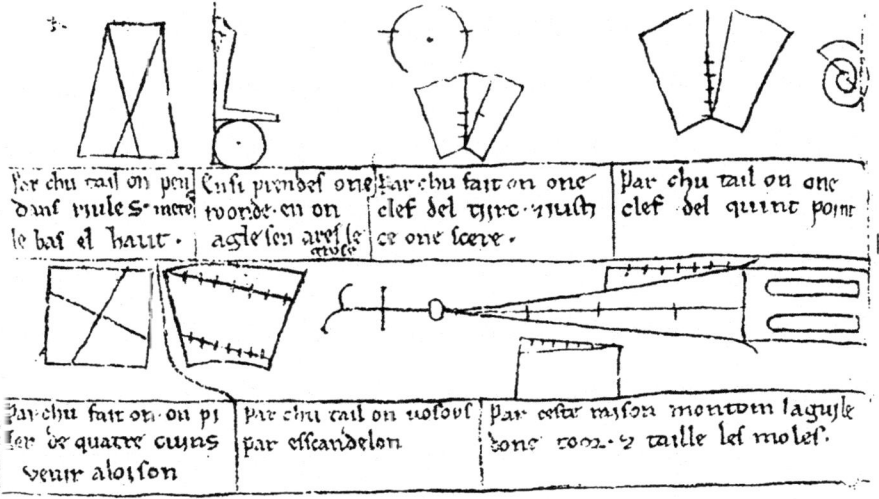

Fig. 11 Setting-out for spire by ratios, Villard de Honnecourt fol. 20v, after Bucher.

Design

What the drawing instruments and architectural drawings have in common with the craft tools and the making of templates is the employment of geometry. As Vitruvius wrote:

> Geometry provides many aids for architecture and first of all from right angles it teaches the use of compasses from which plans of buildings on their sites and the alignments of set-squares and the determinations of the horizontal and of plumb-lines are most easily achieved.
>
> *De architectura* I.I.4, 1989

In the introduction to his *Sketchbook*, Villard writes,

> . . . you will find in it the art of drawings which the principles and the discipline of geometry requires and teaches.
>
> *Sketchbook* fol. 1v, in Bucher 1979, 44–5

And later:

> On these pages are figures from the art of geometry. But to know them one must exercise great care, so that one may know the specific use of each.
>
> *Sketchbook* fol. 19v, in Bucher 1979, 116V38

As late as 1400 or thereabouts the *Constitutions of Masonry* declared,

> . . . Geometry is the science that all reasonable men live by . . Ye shall understand that among all the crafts of the world of man's craft masonry hath the most notability and most part of this science of Geometry . . .
> And this worthy clerk Euclid . . . was one of the first founders of Geometry . . . and he taught to them the craft of masonry and gave it the name of Geometry . . .
>
> Cooke MS. 127, 132–7, 445, 455–6, 507–10

One question this poses is what geometric principles were used and whether any particular methods of design were employed. As a corollary, was geometry employed simply as a practical expedient for setting out work, as numerous studies have suggested?[22] Or did its use also embrace the expression of the beliefs the architecture was erected to proclaim?[23]

The review of existing design theories which was outlined in the Introduction showed that, since many different proportions are present in medieval buildings, many different systems of design are theoretically possible. Yet in spite of the fact that each may be shown to work in particular instances, the same problem remains as that faced by interpretations relying on *gematria*. Numerous systems may present themselves, inasmuch as many can be found to be present in the architecture, therefore the question as to which might actually have been used will still remain unsolved. Given the weight attached to signification in the middle ages, a relevant test to apply might be one of justification. Why should one system or another have been used and how firm is the evidence for the use of any system? Following the sequence adopted in the Introduction, these questions will be discussed in relation to square schematism in its various forms, including square grids, squares set on their diagonal, $1 : \sqrt{2}$ rectangles and quadrature, before examining the evidence offered by the figures of Platonic geometry.

It has already been noted that the system of designing *ad quadratum*, using grids of squares, clearly underlies the basilica of the *Plan of St Gall* and is explicit in the sketch plan of a Cistercian church in Villard's *Sketchbook* (fig. 17). A causal connection to these plans might be found in the square schematism of the Tabernacle and the Temple, the more so since the medieval grids compose themselves into squares for aisles and double squares for main bays, a concomitant of which is also the $\sqrt{5}$ diagonal and its relation to the golden mean, though whether this was known at the time remains to be established. This is not to say, however, that only the square was used, as maintained in some studies, for this has led to certain difficulties. Villard's declaration that his plan of the Cistercian abbey is 'made up of squares' has had to be dismissed as a 'condescending remark'. The fourteenth-century debate over the design of Milan Cathedral, which considered Pythagoras's triangle and the regular triangle as well as the square, has similarly had to be dismissed as a 'comical exception'. And when part of a church layout is seen not to conform to a presupposed scheme of squares, its architect is credited with making 'controlled irregularities'... 'the firmer the rules became', despite a previous claim for a strictly practical discipline.[24] Against this, the use of geometric figures other than squares might well be justified by reference once again to Proclus. Even though he may not be a tenable authority for the tenth century, it may be recalled that his commentary on Euclid points to a tradition at least in the fifth century that associated divinity with certain angles and geometric figures.

The diagonals of ropes in the miniature of Gunzo's dream have also been encountered and invite explanation. The dream was experienced in the eleventh-century by Gunzo, a monk visiting Cluny, and was illustrated around 1180 in a manuscript from a Cluniac priory in Paris (pl. 16).[25] In the dream, saints Peter, Paul and Stephen appear to Gunzo, who is ill in bed, and urge him to tell Abbot Hugh that Cluny II has become too small for its complement of monks and must be enlarged.[26] Eventually Hugh complied, for within twenty years he built the massive edifice of Cluny III. In the portrayal of the dream, Stephen uncoils a rope for Peter and Paul to lay out in the form of diagonals across the building site. This has been interpreted in the study already mentioned as a layout of squares set diagonally in a line and the attempt was made to show how such an arrangement could account for the plan of Cluny III.[27] The fact that the geometry had to be adapted to fit the plan, however, does not in itself mean that abbeys were not designed in this way. On the other hand, it does not follow either that the ropes are meant to be defining squares set on their diagonal axis, or the diagonals of a grid of squares *ad quadratum*, or even the diagonals of rectangles other than squares. As it happens – and most importantly – the latter will appear to be suggested by the geometric investigation of the present study. Nevertheless, it also needs to be borne in mind that a technique for laying out a building on site is not necessarily the technique by which it was designed. One example of squares on the diagonal, however, does appear in a fifteenth-century drawing of a church plan in Nürnberg.[28] This shows a grid of squares with two of the bays rotated, which might possibly be a late medieval variation of designing *ad quadratum*.

Taking the preponderance of claims for $\sqrt{2}$ relations, it might seem inconceivable that the design of something as complex as a cathedral, which stood as a triumph of the human imagination and intellect and as an attempted model of the Christian universe, should be confined to the possibilities of the square and its diagonal, especially if this originated as no more than a simple draughting expedient. Yet the $1 : \sqrt{2}$ rectangle could actually have been used with the ratios $2 : 3$ and $3 : 5$ for no other reason than that they are set out in Vitruvius. Indeed, ratios such as these and others approximating to the golden mean are common in plans and have been found in the division of internal elevations, such as at Salisbury and Reims.[29] It is a justification that would need to rely on Vitruvius being regarded as a decisive authority for architectural design early in the middle ages which, in the light of the widespread survival of Vitruvian manuscripts, several in centres of architectural significance, may be perfectly possible but is beyond the scope of this study to pursue. On the other hand, the continuing concentration upon finding $\sqrt{2}$ relations in buildings has the effect of isolating them somewhat from other forms of square schematism and more effort seems to be used in adding to the existing weight of examples than in trying to explain why the side and diagonal of a square might have been used in the first place. Yet if $\sqrt{2}$ relations were to be considered as an adjunct of designing *ad quadratum*, further clues to its possible justification might be found at the following points in Vitruvius:

> The architect's greatest care must be that his buildings should have their design determined by the proportions of a fixed unit. When therefore account has been taken of the symmetries of the design and the dimensions have been worked out by calculation, it is then the business of his skill . . . to produce a proper balance by adjustment, adding or subtracting from the symmetry of the design . . . .
>
> *De architectura* VI.II.1

It is important to bear in mind the particular meaning of *symmetria* as an agreement of measures when considering its relationship to dimension and 'the fixed unit':

> Dimension is the taking of modules from the parts of the work; and the suitable effect of the whole work arising from the several subdivisions of the parts.

> . . . the difficult problems of symmetry are solved by geometrical rules and methods.
>
> *De architectura* I.II.2, I.4

According to this, an architect could have chosen a particular dimension and assigned it to his schematic design for laying out on site. There seems to be no reason why this should not sometimes have consisted of a grid of squares which could then be subdivided into parts by 'geometrical rules and methods', using rule and compass on a drawing, or a cord and pegs on site. This could explain the presence of such derivatives of the square as the double square, half square and side and diagonal of a square. It might also have been possible to convert by the very same process a grid which consisted of other proportions than squares, a possibility which will be explored shortly. In order to create the architectural details from the grid, the allied method of quadrature could have followed. It certainly did in the middle ages and could be implied again by Vitruvius.

> Symmetry also is the appropriate harmony arising out of the details of the work itself; the correspondence of each given detail among the separate details to the form of the design as a whole.
>
> *De architectura* I.II.4

Although Vitruvius does not identify the method of design he has in mind, this may seem a reasonable interpretation. Yet it still leaves the question of meaning unanswered. Elsewhere he states baldly,

> . . . especially in architecture are these two things found; that which signifies and that which is signified.
>
> *De architectura* I.I.1

To a medieval mind, designing *ad quadratum* could indeed have been signified by the Tabernacle and Temple, more so perhaps than by a Pythagorean or Platonic association with the square or the number 4. However, a simpler and more plausible explanation has been advanced elsewhere wherein dimensions and elements were arranged to occur in numbers which themselves were significant. Examples of this have already been noted in the occurrence of 40 in the *Plan of St Gall* and the recurrence of 7 at Cluny II.[30] This alone might have invested a grid of squares with theological or metaphysical validity.

Turning now to quadrature, the various claims that have been made for it are that it constitutes evidence of geometry being used as no more than a practical procedure; that it is the only design system for which there is documentary evidence; that it enjoyed the status of trade secrecy; and, there being no evidence of similar secrets relating to other systems, it must also have been the system used for plan design as well. Finally, should other secrets have existed, these are as likely to have been practical in nature too, rather than esoteric.

The evidence already cited as justifying quadrature as a purely practical procedure is to be found in Villard's *Sketchbook* and the late medieval handbooks of German masters.[31] Villard's *Sketchbook* reveals various versions. On fol. 19v, grids of squares and diagonals have been drawn, presumably as a mnemonic guide for the faces and figures of people, and the procedure may also be implicit in the plan of one of the towers at Laon Cathedral (figs 12, 13).[32] It is certainly present twice on fol. 20r, which may have been added by a second master sometime between 1250 and 1255 (fig. 14).[33] These drawings are thought to have been copied from a workshop manual and may exemplify the sort of elementary exercises an apprentice might be expected to learn. The construction in the fourth row, as already noted, although directed to the cutting of stone, is actually a geometric demonstration of Plato's formula for doubling a square, which was paraphrased by Vitruvius.[34] In the row of sketches above it, the architectural application of this is shown as a method for planning the cloister.

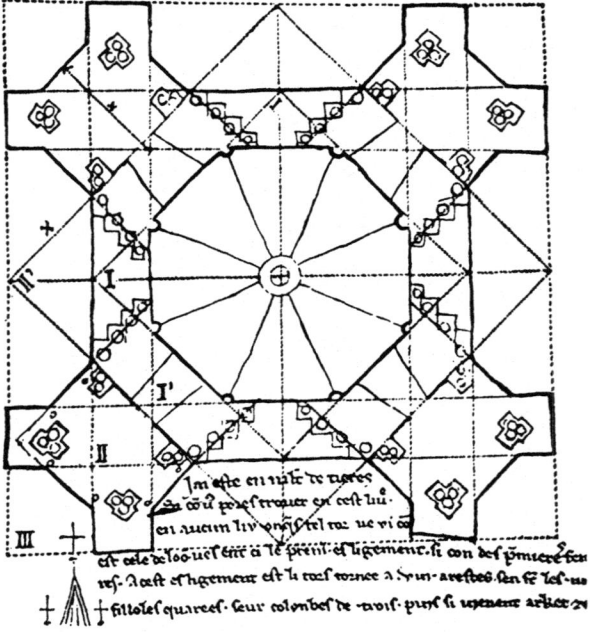

Fig. 12 Plan of Laon tower, Villard de Honnecourt fol. 9v, after Hecht.

Fig. 13 Quadrature and figure drawings, Villard de Honnecourt fol. 19v, after Bucher.

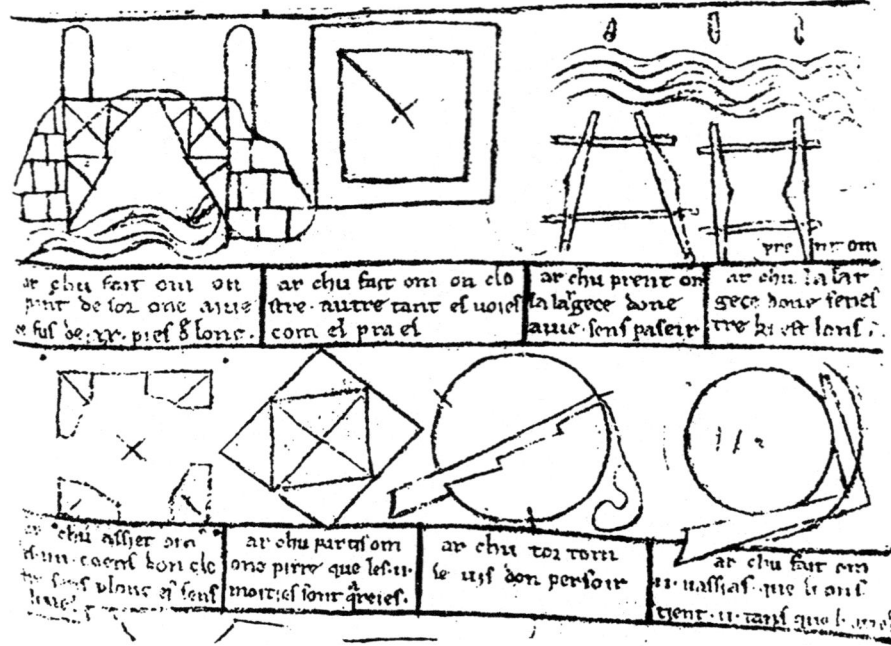

Fig. 14 Quadrature and cloister plan, Villard de Honnecourt fol. 20r, after Bucher.

The late medieval handbooks of Roriczer and Schmuttermayer already mentioned demonstrate how pinnacles and finials were elevated by extrapolating heights proportionately from their plans which consist of squares rotated within each other. To these are to be added Lechler's *Unterweisung* of 1516, which uses quadrature to generate the proportions and profiles of two mullions from a single module given, in this case, by the thickness of a wall (fig. 15).[35] There can be little doubt therefore that the technique was used by medieval architects and masons, though it may be open to interpretation as to whether it was purely practical in intent.

Negative evidence has been adduced from the absence of any other system than quadrature in these late German treatises.[36] By an unexplained coincidence, Roriczer's *Büchlein von der fialen* and Schmuttermayer's *Fialenbüchlein* both confine themselves to the design of pinnacles. That they were clearly meant to be elementary exercises for beginners is indicated, at least in Roriczer's book, by the implication that only a straight-edge and dividers were to be used. The only mention of a square, as already noted, is much later and incidental. Even where a set-square would logically be used, such as in the construction of 45° angles, it is avoided by explicitly restricting the learner to a 'straight-edge or ruler'.[37] It is clear that Roriczer had set himself the task of going back to first principles so as to demonstrate with an easy example what was possible with the minimum means, for he says,

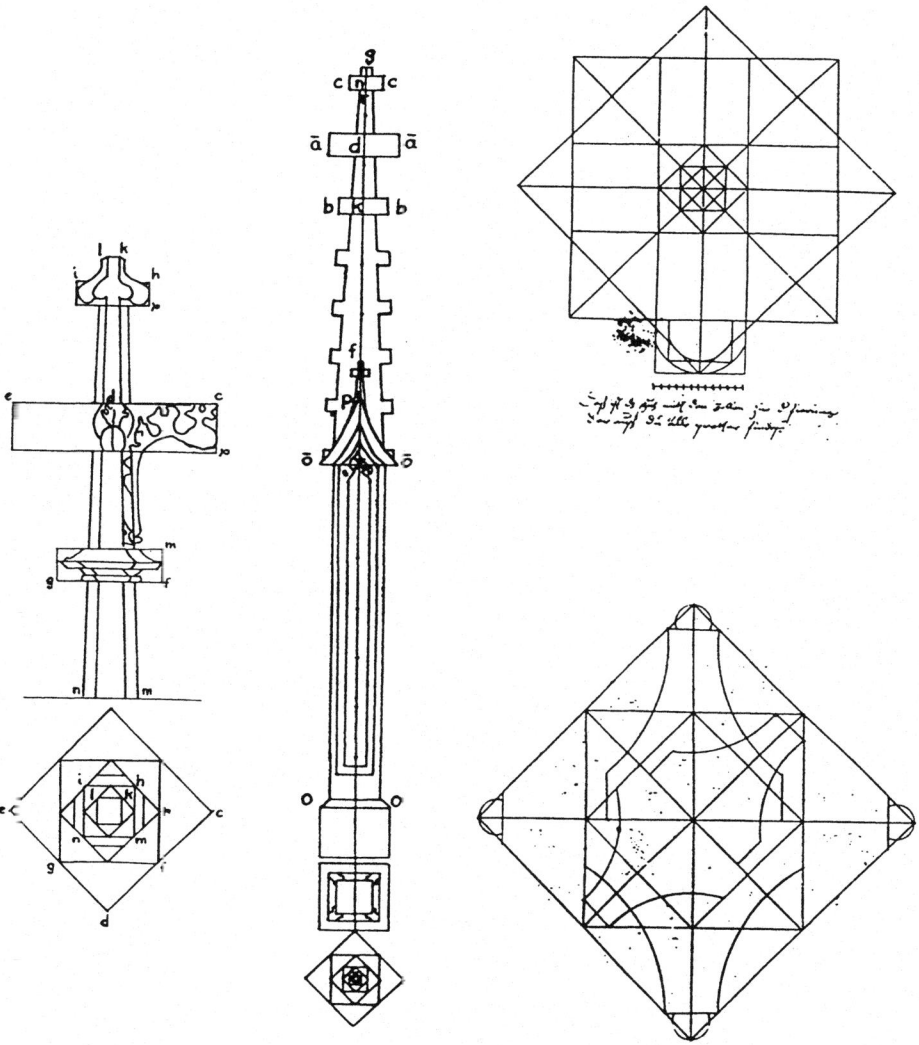

F g. 15 Quadrature: elevation of a finial after Roriczer, elevation of a pinnacle after
S hmuttermayer, profiles of mullions from wall module after Lechler.

> . . . for the first time, to explain the beginning of drawn-out
> stonework – how and in what measure it arises out of the
> fundamentals of geometry through manipulation of the
> dividers . . . .
>
> Büchlein von der fialen, in Shelby 1977, 83

This is an intention that again appears to have been overlooked. Surely it should signify little that primers for beginners contain none of the extra knowledge needed by a master.

One final argument that has been deployed against the use of geometry expressively has involved the question of trade secrecy. However, since it has been generally accepted that craft teaching was done verbally and by practical example within the lodge,[38] there would seem little point in searching for trade secrets in written documents in the first place and still less in implying that their absence suggests there were none. It does appear, however, that the taking of the elevation from the plan, presumably by quadrature, may have been one technique to be kept within the lodge. This was spelled out, it has been claimed, in the *Regensburg Ordinances* of 1459, on the strength of which it has been suggested that this was the only or principal secret of the medieval masons.[39] Since Roriczer and Schmuttermayer show the technique to have been that of quadrature, allegedly a purely practical procedure lacking any other meaning, the import of this is meant to be that no metaphysical significance attached to any use of geometry.[40]

It is a curiosity yet to be satisfactorily explained that Roriczer chose to publicize quadrature, or any procedure at all, since he was Regensburg's cathedral architect, producing his booklet on his own printing press in Regensburg twenty-seven years after his colleagues had passed these *Ordinances* in the same city. Moreover, this had been at a congress that his own father, then head of the Regensburg lodge, had arranged.[41] The answer might lie in the eventual abstention of the Regensburg masons from signing the *Ordinances*, choosing instead to subscribe to craft statutes of their own city which were instituted that same year. Views on secrecy could also have altered over such a lengthy period. With the advent of printing came the urge to publish, which was evidently the motive of Schmuttermayer and Dürer, both of whom wished to make masons' geometric methods available to all artists and craftsmen.[42] Not being masons themselves, they were presumably not bound by masons' rules or secrecy. The terms of the original *Ordinances* restricted the knowledge to all grades of masons except apprentices. It has been argued therefore that a secret shared by so many is really no secret at all, also that no mechanism appears in various masons' constitutions for ensuring secrets were kept. Without such a mechanism, it seems to be implied, there could be no secrets.[43] Yet it remains the case that the English *Constitutions of Masonry* around 1390 said of an apprentice:

> His master's counsel he keep and close,
> And his fellows by his good purpose.

The privaties of the chamber tell he no man,
Nor in the lodge whatsoever they have done.

Regius MS. 277–80

It also remains the case that secrecy was enjoined by the *Regensburg Ordinances* upon its members and, however and why this came to be breached by Roriczer, the injunction was repeated in later editions.[44] And as late as 1516, Lechler stipulated in his *Unterweisung* that,

> . . . you should not lay out this art for every man, not even for any stonemason who is not to practice the art, for this art belongs only to the artists who understand it and know how it should be used . . . .

Unterweisung fol. 49, 147–8, in Shelby 1971, 152

Exhortation to secrecy surely suggests the existence of secrets. Yet such secrets, it has also been ventured, are likely to have been just normal trade secrets, practical in nature rather than 'esoteric'. What is apparently meant by 'esoteric' is something with a 'symbolic or numerological meaning'.[45] This, however, seems to be anachronistic. Since, earlier in the middle ages, the divine creation was accepted as a fact, together with the imperative of maintaining harmony through the observance of correct proportion, the employment of any such system was likely to have been regarded by architects not as esoteric but pragmatic and required. It need only have involved certain procedures using, for example, compasses or one or two templates hanging on the wall of the tracing-house, the existence of which could have been common knowledge, whilst their exact application might have remained a 'mistery' until it was 'mastered' under the lodge master's instruction.[46]

This modern dichotomy between the practical and the expressive seems to go to the heart of the matter. To assume that quadrature, for instance, can only provide evidence of a purely practical use of geometry misses an important point: that the controlling idea behind the procedure is that all the parts should be related to each other and to the whole, whether the elevation of a pinnacle to its plan, or a profile of a mullion to its wall thickness, and this emphatically is a purely Platonic idea. The problem presented by quadrature is not its lack of expressive potential but that all the documentary evidence points to its use for generating architectural elements and details, such as a tower or a cloister, a pinnacle or a mullion, and not the whole layouts of buildings.

It is possible, for instance, that undue reliance has been placed on the cloister in Villard's *Sketchbook* in suggesting a connection between quadrature and the design of complete ecclesiastical plans. Its caption has been translated thus:

In such a way one makes the galleries and the garden of a
cloister.

Sketchbook fol. 20, Bucher 1979, 120

The marks on the drawing indicate that the draughtsman understood that the
side of the inner square equals half the diagonal of the outer square. In the
row below it is the demonstration of quadrature which shows that its inner
square is half the area of the enclosing square because it consists of half the
number of similar triangles and indirectly because its sides equal half the
diagonal of the enclosing square (fig. 14). None of this leads necessarily to a
conclusion that quadrature was used in general plan design. Furthermore, a
survey of cloisters shows that they can be square, oblong, or out of square and
have varying positions in relation to their churches, either to the south, or to
the north, adjoining an aisle or separated from it. In no sense are they integral
to the plan of the church in the way that a crossing or transept is, but are
instead variable and subordinate. In this sense, they are a secondary element,
albeit large, and therefore potentially subject to the same design procedures
as other elements.

As it happens, there is evidence in the material already cited, but which
again appears to have been overlooked elsewhere, that plan design may
actually have been distinct from the process of detailed design that employed
quadrature. To return to Lechler, he opens his *Unterweisung* by stating its
purpose:

> For I wish to give brief . . . report [concerning] some structures
> and stonework, with drawings and explanations, so that one
> may . . . understand the much better art which is useful for a
> stonemason and workman to know. Therefore I wish first . . .
> to show how you can [obtain] correct proportions from
> beginning to end with many structures *if you have their
> groundplan and dimensions.*

Unterweisung fol. 43, 133, in Shelby 1971, 147 [my italics]

This must surely indicate that the 'stonemason and workman' worked from
a pre-existing 'groundplan and dimensions', produced presumably by the
master mason or architect. Lechler then goes on to show how the 'stonemason
and workman' could work out the architectural details for the building, such
as the profiles of window mullions, given no more than the wall thickness and
the technique of quadrature. In other words, they need have no knowledge
whatsoever of any other part of the design method which the architect may
have used to produce the general layout, since quadrature was a procedure
which guaranteed 'correct proportions . . . if you have the groundplan and
dimensions'. According to this, it is possible that plan design and detailed
design were distinct phases of a design process that was, not surprisingly,
sequential.

Fig. 16 Use of the figures of Platonic geometry, Villard fol. 18v, after Bucher.

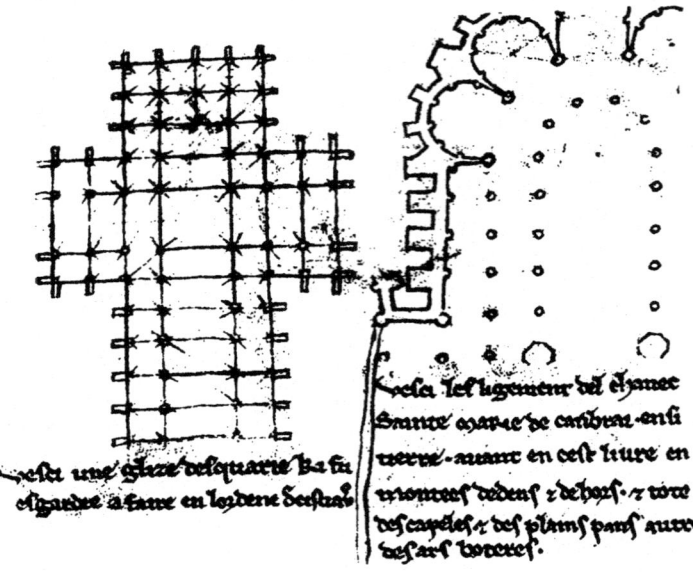

Fig. 17 Cistercian plan on a grid of squares, Villard fol. 14v, after Bucher.

The absence of any other method of design mentioned in apprentices'
manuals or written constitutions, which are in any case concerned with
secrecy, surely cannot be taken as evidence that none existed. Indeed, it may
only be necessary to return to Villard's *Sketchbook*. His initial intention seems
clearly to have been to record interesting novelties encountered on his travels.
In addition to sketches of architectural ideas, it includes classical statuary, wild
animals, gadgets and any other detail that caught his eye for future
reference.[47] Since there was little point in filling pages of expensive parchment
with the familiar, it should follow that anything that was familiar to him as
common practice would not by definition be found in the book in the first
place, not, that is, until the pages of exemplars were added later. Yet there
could well be internal evidence.

It has already been shown that, whilst two pages from his *Sketchbook* have
been cited in support of quadrature,[48] the two preceding pages have been
unaccountably overlooked although they include all three figures of Platonic
geometry, the square, the regular triangle and the pentagon in the form of the
pentagram, including one superimposed on an architectural elevation (fig. 16).
These figures seem clearly to be used once more as a mnemonic guide for
reproducing Villard's subjects in exactly the same way as his grids of squares
on the next page already mentioned.[49] In other words, whilst the evidence of
quadrature may point simply to the production of architectural elements and
details and as a mnemonic, Villard's other examples of applied geometry
consistently point to the Platonic figures. Accordingly, any familiarity on
Villard's part with a method of design involving the three Platonic figures

might well explain his inclusion of the Cistercian plan already mentioned, pointing out that it was 'made up of squares' (fig. 17).[50] Far from this being a 'condescending remark' therefore,[51] he could actually have been noting that the plan is made up *only* of squares. Indeed, Cistercian evidence suggests a return to designing *ad quadratum* at this time.

A possible connection has already been suggested between the square schematism of the Tabernacle and the Temple and designing *ad quadratum*. It has also been shown that, whilst the Tabernacle and Temple were regarded as models of the living Church, the Ark was specifically associated with the idea of salvation. Since these structures were acknowledged as symbols and exemplars and, given the existence of ninth-century copies of Bede's treatises *De tabernaculo* and *De templo* in monasteries such as St Gall, Regensburg, Fleury and Tours,[52] as well as Augustine's writings, it may not be too fanciful to suggest that distinct traditions of design could have arisen, possibly in parallel with each other or even overlaying each other as sometimes suggested in the literature.[53] Yet underlying the dimensions of all three models, it may be recalled, is the numerical series of 3, 4, 5 and their corresponding geometric figures, as displayed in Villard's *Sketchbook*.

Villard's routine use of the Platonic figures on these pages must surely indicate that he knew how to draw them, otherwise why choose them as a guide? The fact that he drew some inaccurately, such as the pentagram over the eagle (fig. 16),[54] may simply be the result of the sketches being hurried and

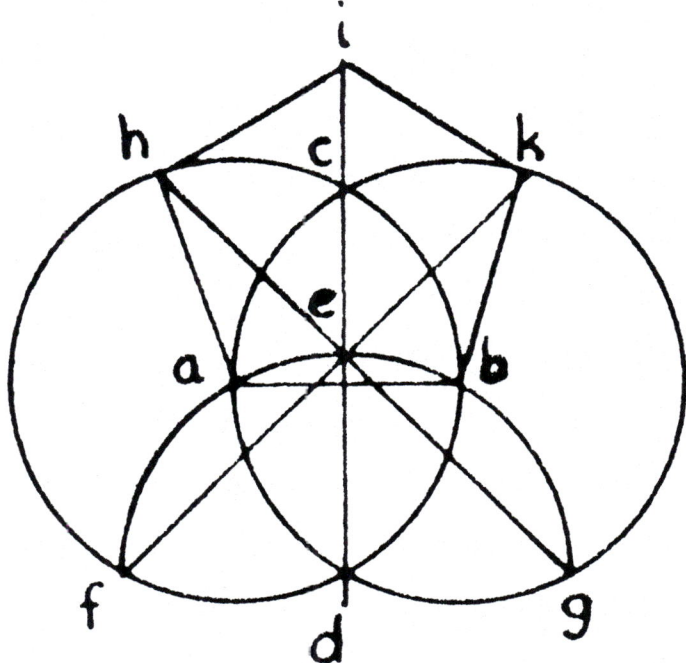

Fig. 18 Construction of a pentagon by Roriczer, after Shelby.

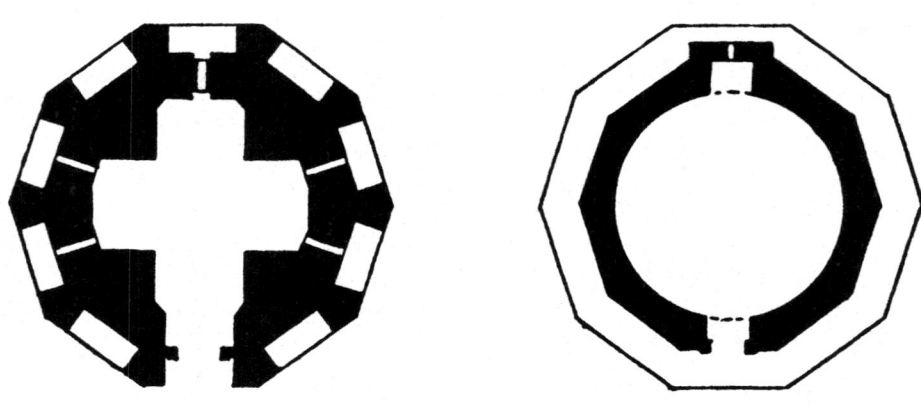

Fig. 19 Plan of Theodoric's Mausoleum, Ravenna, after d'Agincourt.

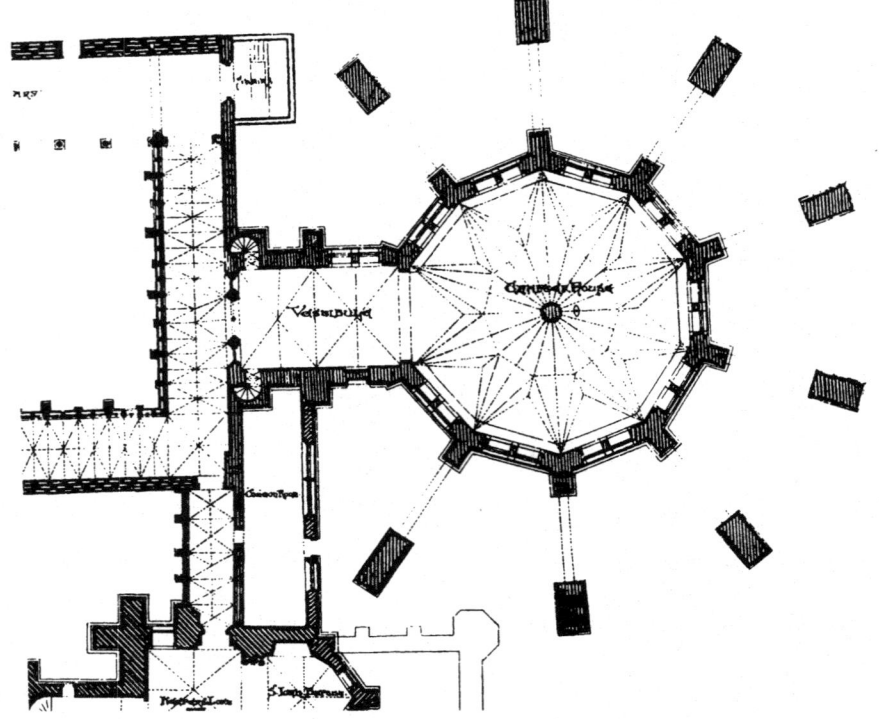

Fig. 20 Plan of Chapter House, Lincoln Cathedral, after Pite.

for his own reference. After all, his Cistercian plan, declaredly 'made up of squares', has been drawn with a crossing that is anything but square. Of the three figures in question, both the square and the regular triangle can easily be constructed with a straight-edge and compasses. For the hypothesis of this study to be sustainable, however, it must also have been possible to draw the angles of the pentagon, despite this allegedly being most difficult to accomplish.[55] In addition to the second-century method previously noted,[56] which can also be achieved with straight-edge and compasses, the possibility has been raised of various geometric treatises surviving into the early middle ages, including perhaps an early Latin translation of Euclid, whilst the *Ars geometriae* describes a method by adapting, however obscurely, Euclid's Propositions IV.12, 11.[57] Once this is understood, a straight-edge and compasses are again all that is needed. The use of the golden triangle as a template,[58] as posited above, is another possibility and offers a direct method of drawing a pentagon. There also remains the internal evidence of Villard's *Sketchbook*, especially fol. 18v. The system he might have used for drawing a pentagram in order to reproduce these three examples accurately must remain open, as must the question as to whether he may have used a template or set-square in the first place, and whether it was in the form of the relevant triangle. However, one of the exemplars added to his *Sketchbook* shows a purely empirical construction of a pentagon from right angles.[59] From the sixteenth century, the *Frankfurt Lodgebook* shows a pentagon which has been drawn inside a circle without any discernible means of constructing it (pl. 17).[60] Now with a golden triangle as a template, all four angles of the pentagon can be drawn, 36° and 72° with one long side horizontal, 18° and 54° if set vertically. With its base horizontal, one-tenth of a decagon can be drawn and thence a pentagon with its centre located for describing a circle. The centre of the Frankfurt example appears to have been located by the isosceles triangle, the angles of which should be 54° and 72°. Finally, the *Geometria deutsch*, which was based on an earlier booklet by Roriczer and published in about 1498, illustrates a construction for a pentagon from two overlapping circles and a *vesica piscis* (fig. 18). Although it is incorrect, two of its sides being 0.951 : 1 out, Roriczer at least believed it to be accurate.[61]

Although these possibilities may seem little more than tentative clues, it cannot be doubted that a method did exist and was used, for this is evident from the surviving architecture. The plans of Theodoric's sixth-century mausoleum in Ravenna and the thirteenth-century cathedral chapter house at Lincoln are both decagonal (figs 19, 20). The round chapter house at Worcester, dating from the early twelfth century, is also divided into ten, whilst the thirteenth-century chevet of Reims Cathedral appears to be derived from half a decagon.[62] As it happens, Reims is one of the places Villard visited during its construction, prompting him to sketch it extensively.

Dimension

Since no standard set of measures existed across Europe in the middle ages, it has been widely accepted that, whilst architectural drawings may have been drawn to scale, they were not drawn to a particular scale.[63] Plans could even be drawn to different scales on the same sheet, those of the sanctuaries of Notre Dame in Paris and Ste Croix in Orléans, mentioned above, being set out at about 1 : 108 and 1 : 105 respectively, often to suit the size of parchment.[64] It has also been observed that of about five thousand extant medieval drawings, only ten or so indicate any size for their building and some of these appear to have been later additions. Written contracts seem to have been the place where sizes were specified.[65] All the same, the plan as drawn did have to be converted into measurements for it to be set out on site and for this, as already noted, Vitruvius may offer a clue when he states that:

> Dimension is the taking of the modules from the parts of the work . . . .
>
> *De architectura* I.II.1.2

One study of the eleventh-century nave of Ely Cathedral appears to confirm this by showing that if the arcade wall thickness is taken as one unit, then the clear width of the aisle is three units and the nave six.[66] It needs to be stressed, however, that a mechanical technique for translating a plan into dimensions is not necessarily the means by which the plan was designed. Nonetheless, making the main wall thickness the basic module could hardly be simpler, especially since the architect had to know how thick to make his wall for any given height, a task which is listed in the *Regensburg Ordinances* of 1514 as one of the 'master-pieces' required of him to graduate.[67] Whatever did provide the module for a project, the method of conversion seems to have been kept as another trade secret. One article in the *Ordinances* of 1459 states that:

> . . . no workman, master, undermaster, or journeyman should instruct anyone on how to take the extrapolation device from the base plan.
>
> *Regensburg Ordinances*, Neuwirth cols. 207–8 in Shelby 1977, 48

In the following year, Article 15 of the *Tirol Hüttenbuch* stipulates that:

> If someone wants to devise a stone structure by means of measures or by the extrapolation device, and he does not know how to take them out of the basic figure [*grund*], and he has served no workman nor been through the lodge promotion process, then he should not take up the task in any way.
>
> *Regensburg Ordinances*, Neuwirth col. 203 in Shelby 1976, 211–2

In other words, the construction of the *grund* takes place first and from this a structure may be devised either 'by means of measures or by the extrapolation device'. Although the 'extrapolation device' has been interpreted as a reference to the technique of taking an elevation from the plan by quadrature,[68] there seems to be no reason why this should not equally be referring to obtaining the basic modular dimension from the plan. An earlier article of the *Regensburg Ordinances* refers to undertaking stonework 'with measure or *an* extrapolation device',[69] suggesting there was more than one. The analysis of Ely certainly seems to suggest that dimensions could be extrapolated proportionally from the schematic design and rounded up or down to the nearest whole unit of measure[70] and this will again be explored shortly. Yet not only would entire layouts be capable of being set out in this way, it has already been shown that the module could provide the geometric key for the architectural details as well through quadrature (fig. 15). Lechler describes the process:

> . . . take the wall thickness of the choir . . . then draw two squares through one another; therein you will find all templates in a larger square, just as you will find them drawn in this book. . . . Then divide the wall thickness of the choir into three parts; of these parts take one and divide the same part again into seven parts – that is the correct Old Mullion for all buildings.
>
> *Unterweisung* fol. 44, 135, in Shelby 1971, 147–8

However a chosen dimension was assigned to the plan, the use of yardsticks by architects is commonly portrayed, the best known example perhaps being the thirteenth-century tombstone of Hugh Libergier now in Reims Cathedral.[71]

Groundwork

Anyone consulting Vitruvius in the tenth century should have come across the passage already cited which deals with,

> . . . plans of buildings on their sites and the alignments of set-squares and the determinations of the horizontal and of plumb-lines.
>
> *De architectura* I.I.4, 1989

At Ramsey Abbey in 969, Oswald,

> . . . sought most keenly for masons who would know how to set out the foundations . . . with the straight line of the rule, the threefold triangle and the compasses.
>
> *Vita sancti Oswaldi* IV, in Harvey 107

In setting out the new work at the Abbey of St Denis in the 1140s, Suger's own account mentions the use of *geometricis et arithmetricis instrumentis*.[72] Later in the same century, Gerald of Wales described a dream:

> For I seemed to myself to behold the King's son, John, in a green plain, appearing as though he were about to found a church. . . . after the fashion of surveyors, he marked the turf making lines on all sides over the surface of the earth, visibly drawing the plan of a building . . . .
>
> *De rebus a se gestis*, in Butler 89; see also Knoop/Jones 30

It is perhaps obvious that in order to dig the foundations of a building, its plan has first to be marked out over the site. Yet for this reason, presumably, in addition to the practical knowledge needed to lay foundations which are sound, any special skill in devising the plan itself seems to have become invested in the groundwork as well.[73] Basil's words, for example, may be recalled:

> . . . the creation of the heavens and of the earth were like the foundation and the groundwork . . . .
>
> *Hexaëmeron* I.6

Similarly Clement's abbreviation of I Corinthians,[74] the full text of which says:

> According to the grace of God which is given unto me, as a wise masterbuilder, I have laid the foundation, and another buildeth thereon.
>
> I Corinthians III.10

This accords with actual building practice, since the plinth of a building is the top of the groundwork carried up and levelled off as a base for the main walls.[75] It also seems remarkably close to Lechler's description at the end of the middle ages of masons taking up the work once the groundplan and dimensions had been given, supposedly by the 'wise masterbuilder'. It has already been noted that several of the cleric-builders of the tenth century were described as possessing either architectural skill in planning and symmetry, architectural theory, science or 'something secret', including Heriveus who,

> . . . with the Holy Spirit teaching him . . . described to the masons how to lay the foundation of a work without equal . .
>
> Glaber, *Historiarum* III.4

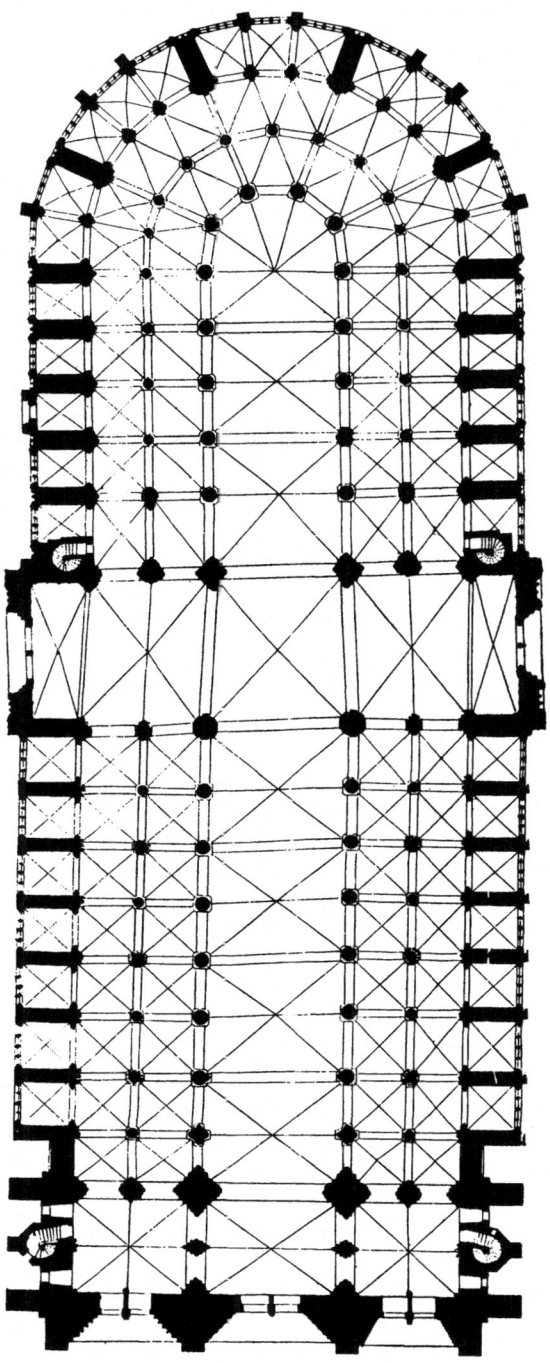

Fig. 21 Plan of Notre Dame, Paris, after Lecomte.

A second dream concerning groundwork has already been mentioned, namely Gunzo's in relation to Cluny. Setting aside interpretations of the miniature, the text of c.1115 at least throws light on the technique used.

> When Peter had finished speaking, he seemed to be holding surveyor's cords and to be measuring the length and the width. And he even showed him the nature of the basilica which was to be built, commanding him to keep most tenaciously in his mind the memory of both the dimensions and the form.
>
> Hildebert, *Vita sancti Hugonis*

For ropes to have been used in this way suggests that the initial setting-out for a building consisted of a pattern of lines forming some sort of planning grid. The *Plan of St Gall* (pl. 1)[76] is a diagram of single lines coinciding with the axes and sometimes cross-axes of arcade piers and setting-out lines of walls as well. Sketch plans in Villard's book, especially his Cistercian plan (fig. 17), suggest a planning grid, as do surviving drawings of Reims.[77] Lechler also discloses the method whereby the inside and outside wall-faces can be located in one of five different alignments relative to the grid-line (fig. 15). The grid-line itself may well have determined the position of the glass line of the windows within the overall wall thickness, something which has been suggested at Vézelay and Laon[78] and which will become apparent during the geometric investigation. This would be logical since it is the glass which marks the dividing line between the sanctified interior and temporal exterior.

The portrayal of Gunzo's dream also shows how inaccurate the method of setting out was likely to be. Ropes can be heavy and therefore difficult to keep taut and their length varies with their moisture content. The use of the large squares already encountered might seem helpful but not even Vitruvius's four-foot square could guarantee an accurate projection of an angle over long distances. In fact, all the evidence suggests that builders at least up to the thirteenth century had no accurate technique for setting out work, as many of the buildings testify. Irregularities were common in pier spacing, alignment and angles involving errors of 3% or more, sometimes much more. Neither are these defects only present in minor works in remote country districts. The main axis of Cluny III was bent twice, Canterbury's is misaligned twice and bent once, Laon's nave tapers by 3%, Bourges's by nearly 6% and the entire layouts of Vézelay and Notre Dame in Paris are little short of chaotic (fig. 21).[79] If an accurate method had existed at all, it would surely have been employed on projects as prestigious as these.

Errors could arise from one or more of the following causes: inaccurate drawing, unstable drawings, the extrapolation of dimensions, inaccurate setting-out, or inaccurate construction. Inaccurate drawing can occur either in draughting or geometric construction, or both. Several errors are apparent in the Reims palimpsest, with similar column-shafts differing in size, wrong pin-pricks being connected and someone's straight-edge slipping.[80] Even the draughtsmanship of the *Frankfurt Lodge Book*, dating though it does from the latter half of the sixteenth century, is generally inexact. Compounding this was an apparent lack of theoretical geometry, which also resulted in a drawing being inaccurate. For example, it may be recalled that Roriczer's constructions for the pentagon and heptagon are theoretically wrong.[81]

Unstable drawings will result when any design is drawn on organic material such as parchment, because it is liable to distortion through movement of the material, caused, as with ropes, by variations in moisture content. The *Plan of St Gall* has evidently shrunk 5–6% and still moves.[82] Moreover, such instability is not necessarily uniform.

The extrapolation of dimensions is another source of inaccuracy. Once a key dimension were assigned to one part of the design, as proposed above, mistakes could arise in arriving at the other dimensions. If this was done on a proportional basis, the likelihood of error would be greater the smaller the drawing. Yet the size of plans was probably limited by the sizes of parchment generally available. The planometric drawing of Christ Church Abbey in Canterbury, dating from around 1160, measures approximately 295 × 420 mm, a size considered to be large for a single sheet of parchment.[83] That a large sheet was chosen for this might be explained if its purpose was, as seems likely, not a routine working drawing for masons, but a presentation drawing. The same may be ventured for the *Plan of St Gall* which measures 780 × 1120 mm, yet this is a composite of five skins sewn together. Most of the church is drawn on the largest sheet which, at 388 × 584 mm, is still under A2 in size. The sheets of the Reims palimpsest are thought to have been about 450 × 660 mm before they were cut, whilst the original size of the leaves used in Villard's book were roughly 180 × 530 mm.[84] Since these sizes are under or not much over A2, had a complete plan of a typical abbey church been confined to one sheet, the scale of the drawing would have needed to be within the range of 1 : 100 to 1 : 200, which encompasses the scales calculated for St Gall, Notre Dame in Paris and Ste Croix, Orléans.[85] Accurately translating the layout from such a small-scale drawing to full-size on site would have been practically impossible.

Inaccurate setting out is also likely when, as the known site practices and the known results suggest, a precise method of setting out did not exist, at least early in the middle ages. In spite of his geometrical and arithmetical instruments, Suger's choir at St Denis is extremely irregular.

Inaccurate building will almost certainly result from laying the foundations of a large structure without modern aids. In addition to common human error, the operation involved manoeuvring large blocks of stone into position in the confined spaces of deep foundation trenches which must often have been difficult to keep drained. At Ramsey Abbey,

> . . . the foundations (were) dug more deeply on account of the wet neighbourhood all around, and by repeated blows of rams beaten down to provide a yet stronger basis for the load to be set upon them.

> *Chronicon abbatiae Rameseiensis* I.40, in Harvey 228

This was difficult enough where the foundations for walls were concerned, but the difficulties could only have increased when erecting piers in an arcade. Although these were built off continuous sleeper walls,[86] the effect of point loads being exerted on the foundations, combined with any changes in the subsoil down the length of a building, or the existence of foundations of earlier structures, could and often did cause differential settlement and this became perhaps the most common cause of structural failure in the middle ages. If this started to occur during the course of construction, constant adjustment must have been needed as the work went up and, with building campaigns usually ceasing each winter,[87] such differences must have been that much more noticeable when operations recommenced each spring. For all these reasons, therefore, a substantial discrepancy was possible between the design as meant and the design as built, which makes the attempted deduction of the intended design that much more difficult, a problem which will be faced in Part Three.

This brief outline of architectural and building practice between the mid-tenth and mid-thirteenth centuries has drawn on the documentary evidence of the period as much as possible. Where evidence has had to be taken from outside this period, it needs to be borne in mind that what may be true of one century, or even half-century, may not necessarily be true of another. However, much of this evidence does seem to demonstrate a continuing tradition in several practices. Plans were drawn at least from the seventh century onwards. Vitruvius's references to setting out on site and assigning dimensions to the layout are borne out by descriptions cited from the tenth, twelfth and even sixteenth centuries. And whilst Vitruvius's treatise continued to be available in the tenth century and well beyond, Roriczer and Schmuttermayer both stress in the fifteenth how they are passing on the techniques of the 'old-timers'.[88]

Conclusion

The documentary and architectural evidence of medieval architectural practice, as outlined in this chapter, suggests that arguments made against the expressive use of geometry are themselves open to question and some of them have apparently overlooked internal evidence that might point to an expressive tradition of design. Whilst the evidence suggests that the technique of quadrature was used to produce not complete layouts, but modules and profiles for architectural elements and details once the layout had been provided, Villard's inclusion of the Cistercian plan which was designed *ad quadratum* suggests that any design method he was familiar with was different. As far as his *Sketchbook* illustrates, such a system, whatever it may have been, could be and presumably was taken for granted. It would, after all, be unnecessary for him to duplicate the familiar. This being the case, it may be significant that, in addition to Villard's own employment of quadrature, his pages also display a routine familiarity with the three Platonic figures as proposed, the construction of which he also seems to take for granted. Slender though this evidence may be, it does seem to point to the use of Platonic geometry in architectural design and it does fit the historical facts. If it is to be argued that this does not prove a use of geometry that is expressive of beliefs, it would then need to be asked why these particular figures were chosen in the first place.

Finally, the evidence of medieval architectural practice suggests multiple opportunities for inaccuracy spanning from the drawing stage to construction. Therefore, in anticipation of the geometric investigation, any exploration of a particular layout will need to try to distinguish between what was meant and what was built. As Part Two has examined the documentary evidence, so Part Three will investigate the architectural evidence.

Notes

1 *Liber de miraculis sancti Jacobi* IV; in Harvey 34.
2 *Relatio translationis corporis sancti Geminiani*, Arch. Cap. di Mod., in Bertoni 86f; see also Pevsner 559.
3 See Barnes 1989.
4 Lethaby 178–81; Gimpel 41, 94; see also Shelby 1965, 240.
5 Harvey 137–8.
6 Vitruvius I.xix; Hallinger 123; see p. 118.
7 Adamnan I.2,3; PL 88 779–814; see also Rosenau 13.
8 Bucher 1979 *passim*; 1968, 58–9.
9 Gimpel 95; Harvey 102; see also Salzman 16; du Colombier 72f; Bechmann 1981, 229f.
10 Reims MS.G.661; Andrews 81; Branner 1958, 9–10, 18; du Colombier 79f.
11 Branner 1958, 15, 18; Bucher 1968, 52; 1979, 28.
12 See Hambly 105.
13 Branner 1957 (2) 65; see also Shelby 1965, 247; Bucher 1979, 118–20; Morgan 48f; Harvey 127.
14 *Alban*, Dublin, Trin. Coll. Lib. MS.177 fol. 59v.
15 Major, J., letter to author 6.1.1991.
16 Vitruvius I.I.4; IX. Pref. 6.
17 *Vita sancti Oswaldi* IV in Harvey 107.
18 Isidore XIX.18,I in Shelby 1965, 244–5.
19 Roriczer, *Büchlein* No. 18. fol. 9v. fig. 17, in Shelby 1977, 104–5.
20 Shelby 1971, 140–54; Harvey 127.
21 Moessel 1931 II.79 fig. 128.
22 Kidson 1956, I.39; Branner 1958, 15f; Morgan 17–19; Shelby 1964, 389n9; 1971, 153–4; 1972, 420; 1976, 214; 1977, 69; Bucher 1968, 50–51, 70–71; 1972, 37, 42; 1979, 10; Harvey 113–4; du Colombier 87–93; Bechmann 1981 198–9, 229–41; Gimpel 90.
23 Lund *passim*; Krautheimer 1971, 115–40; Frankl 1945, 57–60; Beseler and Roggenkamp *passim*; von Simsor *passim*; Conant 1963, *passim*; Bannister 20–22; James *passim*.
24 Bucher 1963, 51–3; 1972, 37–8.
25 See also Conant 1968.
26 Raynaldo, *Vita sancti Hugonis*, PL 159, 895–906.
27 Conant 1963 *passim*; see App.1.

28 Nürnberg, Germ. Nat. Mus. Hz.3818.333, in Bucher 1972, 38 fig. 3.
29 Cocke and Kidson 76; Kidson 1997.
30 Conant 1968 (2), 33–8; see also pp. 148–50.
31 Bucher 1972, *passim*; Shelby 1977, 71f; Coldstream 34–8.
32 Hecht 207f.
33 Branner 1957, 372, 375.
34 Plato, *Meno* 82f; Vitruvius IX. Pref. 5; II.199; Frankl 1945, 57–8.
35 Shelby 1971, 1977; see p. 8.
36 Shelby 1971, 152–4; 1972, 419–21; 1977, 71, 75.
37 Roriczer, *Büchlein* No. 8. fol. 4v. fig. 7 in Shelby 1977, 89.
38 Shelby 1964, 388; 1972, 398; 1977, 3; Harvey 87–91; White 1978, 330–36.
39 Frankl 1945, 46, 50.
40 Shelby 1972, 420; 1976, 214.
41 Shelby 1977, 22–3, 31–2, 37–8, 50–51.
42 Shelby 1977, 58.
43 Shelby 1976, 204–9; 214.
44 Shelby 1977, 49.
45 Gimpel 90, in support of Knoop and Jones 1949; Shelby 1976, 208; Bucher 1979,
     10.
46 Harvey 137.
47 Salzman 16, 18.
48 Bucher 1968, 40 figs 8, 9; Villard fols 19v, 20.
49 Villard fols 18v, 19; for an alternative interpretation, see Bechmann 1991 *passim*.
50 Bucher 1979, 95.
51 Bucher 1972, 38; see above.
52 Bede, *De tabernaculo* xxii.
53 Conant 1963; Bannister; James.
54 See also Villard fol. 19.
55 Lund 33; James 116; see p. 13.
56 Lund 130–31; see p. 13.
57 Pingree 157, see pp. 49–50, 152.
58 Moessel 1931, II.75–9.
59 Villard fol. 21, see Bechmann 1991, 146f.
60 See also Bucher 1979, WG103, 276.
61 Roriczer, *Geometria deutsch* 4. fol. 2, Shelby 1977, 37–40, 116–18.
62 Wu 155 fig. 34.
63 Frankl 1945, 49; Kidson 1956, I.18–9; Gimpel 84; Bucher 1972, 48–9; Bechmann
     1981, 199.
64 Strasbourg, Musée de l'Oeuvre, ND. 21rv; Bucher 1972, 49n38; 1968, 58–9.
65 Bucher 1979, 10.
66 Fernie 1979, 2–4; see also Shelby 1977, 71–2.
67 Harvey 149.
68 Frankl 1945, 46, 50; Shelby 1977, *passim*; see p. 186.
69 Shelby 1977, 47.
70 Fernie 1979 *passim*; Coldstream 37–8; see also Moessel 1926, I.19.
71 Lethaby 180 fig. 90; see also Binding 66–7.
72 Suger, *De consecratione* 4.
73 See pp. 119–20.
74 Clement, *Stromateis* V.4.
75 Lund 2.

75 Horn I.82, 90.
77 Gwilt 1008.
73 Kidson 1956, II.77, 104.
79 Conant 1963, 8; Borst 467f; Kidson 1956, II.103, 151, 157.
80 Reims MS.G.661, see p. 174; Branner 1958; see also 9–10, 18.
81 Bucher 1979, 196f; see Shelby 1977, 117–19.
82 Horn and Born I.35.
83 Cambridge, Trin. Coll. Lib. MS.R.17.1; Horn and Born I.72.
84 Horn and Born I.35; Branner 1958, 10; Bucher 1979, 28.
85 Horn and Born I.87; Bucher 1972, 49n38.
86 Andrews 63.
87 Gimpel 56–7.
88 Shelby 1977, 57–8, 83.

PART THREE

The Geometric Investigation

Chapter 6

Application of Geometry to Plans

Introduction

As arguments have been presented to show how the use of Platonic geometry in the design of abbeys and cathedrals would be consistent with early medieval thought, the next step is to see if the same geometry actually fits the plans of buildings from that period.

The drawing of geometric constructions over plans of medieval churches has been the chosen method for countless studies reaching back over three centuries and yet it is a method that has also attracted many objections, some so strong as to dismiss it altogether as a valid procedure. It is important therefore that these objections are taken seriously. Since they can be categorized as challenging both the reliability of drawings used for examination and the plausibility of geometric constructions superimposed over them, this chapter and its Appendices will discuss the question of measured drawings and will put forward procedures designed to achieve an acceptable degree of accuracy in selecting and reproducing them as well as in conducting and presenting the geometric exercises. Finally, it will propose criteria for evaluating the results of the tests.

An important distinction needs to be made between the original thesis and this book. Whereas the thesis included drawings of all the examples examined in it, their number has been reduced here. The unillustrated examples have been retained, however, for the purpose of cross-referencing.[1] For further convenience, the various considerations and provisions that were made to maximize the accuracy of the investigation are referred to here but set out in detail in Appendices 1 and 2.

Measurement and accuracy

In 1346, Dominicus de Clavasio explained in his *Practica geometriae*,[2]

> ... the difference between the geometric and lay measurer [is]
> that what the lay measurer knows ... by ... dashing around
> the sides of a field with his rods and cords, the geometric
> measurer will know by standing still by mental reflection alone
> or by drawing lines.
>
> *Practica geometriae* fol. 99r, in Busard 559–60

In the belief that, for investigations into medieval plan design, the geometer and the surveyor need each other, this present study examines the ground-plans of various early medieval abbeys and cathedrals by the application of geometry and then tests the results of a sample against measurements taken independently by others.

It is often held to be essential, however, that each building study should be supported by measurements taken from the building in question by the person studying it,[3] which raises the question of verification and the status of drawings as documentary evidence. This is discussed in Appendix 1, along with questions of accuracy relating to the drawings selected and to their reproduction, to the geometric test itself and to the method of presenting the results of the test.[3]

For the purposes of the geometric investigation, the geometry applied to the plans consisted of the sides of the regular triangle and the diagonals of the square and the pentagon. The sole assumption made was that plan design at least sometimes took the form of planning grids as suggested by the *Plan of St Gall* and the *Sketchbook* of Villard, with arcade piers located at grid intersections. Accordingly, pier centres were plotted to establish the beginnings of a grid (pl. 21) and this was extended laterally towards the aisle walls. By projecting diagonals from pier centres at the angles of the Platonic figures, possible axis-lines for the outer walls were drawn where diagonals intersected the lateral grid-lines. Once all possible connections were plotted, a complete setting-out procedure was sought, starting from a single base figure (pl. 51). Reconstructions are presented as separate steps, with the sides of the regular triangle shown in mauve, the diagonals of the square green, those of the pentagon blue and the resultant grid red. Each step is numbered and that part of the grid which it generates carries the same number. From the beginning, middle and end of the sample, St Peter's Old Basilica, Hildesheim Abbey and St Maclou in Rouen were tested against independent measured surveys. The percentages of accuracy presented in these cases are intended to show the closeness of the geometry proposed to the building as measured, not to suggest that medieval architects set out to achieve such degrees of accuracy, or were able to, or necessarily shared the modern concept of precision.

Criteria for evaluation[4]

The foregoing procedures were kept as systematic and as objective as possible. Any judgment that needed to be exercised was governed by criteria that were also formulated to assess the results of the investigation. These were designed to establish whether the geometric connections and grid that were revealed for each plan formed a coherent, systematic scheme that could be set out from one given length or figure, that followed the known or likely sequence of construction and showed a consistent relationship between geometry, grid and building. Finally, the results of each plan were examined both for similarities with other buildings or groups of buildings known to be generically related to it and for evidence of any evolution of the geometric system through time.

Selection of sample

From the initial sample of plans, results from twenty-seven are included in this book – one additional to the thesis – fourteen of which are illustrated here. Priority was given to buildings associated with some of the churchmen encountered in the earlier parts of this study as being leading figures in the various monastic reforms either side of the millennium. These include St Pantaleon in Cologne for its association with Bruno, Hildesheim for Bernward, Montier-en-Der for Adso, followed by St Bénigne, Vignory and examples in Normandy for the influence of William of Volpiano.

Although initial tests showed a correlation between the geometry and plans of Speyer Cathedral and Southwell Minster, these were omitted in the interest of conciseness. Despite a correlation similarly displayed by the cathedrals at Amiens, Lincoln and Salisbury, these were omitted partly for the same reason and also because it became apparent that the historical case could be concluded with the building of Chartres Cathedral at the end of the twelfth century. Had reliable drawings of Cluny II and III and Santiago de Compostela been available in time, they would have been included in the sample.

Of the twenty-five examples, St Bénigne was retained because of its historical importance but without a geometric test because it was not possible to obtain a reliable reconstruction of William's basilica. The *Plan of St Gall* yielded two cases for consideration, namely the plan as drawn and the plan as dimensioned on the manuscript. St Maclou in Rouen was added to the sample for reasons stated below. The total number of plans investigated therefore remained twenty-seven with one, St Gall, presenting two cases.

For the purposes of the investigation, discussions of individual buildings were arranged partly chronologically and partly geographically. Since the historical enquiry has focused on the tenth-century revival in monasticism, it was thought important to ascertain whether geometry might be applicable to plans earlier than this, although, strictly speaking, these lie outside the scope of this study. Accordingly, the *Plan of St Gall* and Cologne Cathedral were chosen, dating as they do from the early ninth century. From the tenth and early eleventh centuries, St Pantaleon at Cologne and St Michael at Hildesheim were included for their historical importance and they complete an early German sample. Also from the tenth and early eleventh centuries, the churches at Montier-en-Der and Vignory were added to St Bénigne for reasons already stated and as representing parallel development in France.

Because of William of Volpiano's connection with Normandy, the enquiry was extended to early Norman architecture with the abbeys at Bernay, Jumièges, Mont St Michel and St Stephen at Caen and, since Anglo-Norman cathedrals and abbeys have clear architectural antecedents in Normandy, a sample of them is also included, commencing with Winchester and ending with Durham. In between, three examples from the eastern counties were tested, Ely, Norwich and Peterborough, along with three from the Welsh borders, Gloucester, Tewkesbury and Hereford.

Contemporary with Anglo-Norman architecture was the development of pilgrim churches in France along roads leading to Santiago de Compostela. For this reason, the abbey churches at Conques, Fleury, Tours and Toulouse are also included, along with Nevers because of certain similarities it shares with the group. Chartres Cathedral is investigated because of the connection of its cathedral building, both Romanesque and Gothic, with the location of the school that was foremost in Christian Platonist teaching. Given the Platonic basis of the geometry proposed, it was thought important for Chartres, of all buildings, to be included in the test.

From the whole sample of buildings analysed here, the following have been selected for illustration. St Pantaleon in Cologne and St Michael at Hildesheim have been chosen as early German examples; St Peter's Old Basilica has been retained for reasons that are explained in the text; Bernay, Jumièges and Caen represent the early Norman group; Winchester, Ely, Norwich, Peterborough and Durham complete the Anglo-Norman sample; Toulouse is taken as representing the pilgrim churches; whilst Chartres is kept for the reasons outlined above. The summaries of the others are given here for the purpose of comparison. In addition to this, an investigation of St Maclou in Rouen concludes the sample partly out of curiosity – being a late medieval layout though still in Normandy – and partly because reliable measurements and drawings were available which could be used to check the geometry. This has also been the case for St Peter's Basilica and St Michael's Abbey in Hildesheim.

EARLY GERMAN

The St Gall Plan (pl. 1)

As the *Plan of St Gall* is a dimensioned drawing surviving from the ninth century, possibly arising from the Aachen Synods, being transmitted between abbots at the forefront of the Benedictine movement, it was included even though it dates from a century or more prior to the main focus of this study. The following dimensions are inscribed on the plan:

> From east to west the length [is] 200 feet.
> The width of the nave of the church [is] 40 feet.
> The width of each aisle [is] 20 feet.
> Measure twice six feet between the columns . . .
> Between these columns [western Paradise] measure ten feet.

> Horn I.77

Since the plan as drawn is a single-line diagram suggesting an axial grid, it is assumed that the dimensions are similarly intended to refer to a single-line grid. However, because the plan as drawn consists of square nave bays and double square aisle bays, the configuration of the plan as dimensioned must be different. It is not clear either from the inscription whether there were meant to be transepts or whether the 200-feet measurement was supposed to be taken between apse chords, or include the apses, or the greater apses enclosing them. For these reasons, this version of the plan has been set aside.

On the other hand, the plan as drawn can be set out from a single square, or equally from a grid of nine squares, in five operations. All three Platonic figures can be employed in the first three steps, which is also the case in nearly all the succeeding examples.

However, the inner west apse has not been located and there are slight mismatches with the north transept and aisle and with some intermediate piers. These might well be explained by the plan having been traced from an original onto five sheets of parchment which have been stitched together and which have moved by at least 5%. Thus although the geometric constructions represent a coherent scheme, they do depend on the north transept and aisle having been drawn inaccurately.

Cologne Cathedral[5]

Cologne Cathedral was included because of its status and its location in a leading city of the Carolingian Empire and because its construction between 800, or shortly after, and 870 spanned either side of the *Plan of St Gall*.

The plan can be set out from a single square over the west crossing, or equally from a grid of three squares coinciding with the western transept in five further operations, as at St Gall. All three Platonic figures are employed in the first three operations, again as at St Gall.

The projection of the west apse can be triangulated from 60° diagonals from the crossing piers via the transept faces, although these do not coincide with any pertinent part of the structure. One possible explanation for this could be that certain design procedures were important in generating the plan but not in erecting the building. The possibility of schematic constructions existing independently of building construction also arises in many other examples.

The nave can be set out from three rectangles formed by 60° diagonals, provided each module can be divided equally into three. In the sixteenth century, Serlio shows an exact method for achieving this which, by involving no more than the division of a square, could well have been known earlier in the middle ages (fig. 24).[6] The need to divide a given distance equally into three occurs in several more examples.

St Pantaleon, Cologne (pls 22–26)[7]

The Benedictine abbey of St Pantaleon had important imperial connections, since it was refounded by Bruno, the archbishop of Cologne and brother of

Otto the Great, in the 950s. Having ordered communal quarters to be built, at his death in 965 he bequeathed money for the church, which was eventually completed around 996 with further contributions from Otto II's widow Theophanou and her son Otto.

The plan of the upper church has been selected as representing the original structure before the aisles and arcades were added in the twelfth century. Initially, it was found that the entire layout could be set out from a single 36° rectangle between the east arms of the plan. However, since these are in the nature of *porticus*, the church having been designed without an east crossing, this has now been re-examined. In the light of this, it turns out that the layout can also be set out from the west, in common with other examples that also lack crossings and transepts. This has resulted in a far more coherent scheme for the westwork, which can be set out in five steps, the first three once again involving all three Platonic figures. Since the two stair turrets turn out to be eccentric to the grid proposed (4), secondary constructions would be needed to locate their true centres.

The rest of the layout can be completed in a further seven steps with subsidiary construction possibly required for the original main apse. It is striking how prevalent the occurrence of 60° diagonals is from which the whole of the nave and both *porticus* can be constructed, namely steps (6), (8), (9) and (10a). Step (10b) provides an alternative for locating grid-line (10) and, in so doing, reveals an instance of geometric harmony between the sides of the triangle and the diagonals of the pentagon. It will be noticed, however, that the grid-lines of the east and west sides of the *porticus*, (8) and (10), are located inconsistently in comparison with other wall-grids. Yet the easternmost grid-line (8) nevertheless bisects the external wall pilasters in the same manner as those to the west whilst step (10), which is constructed from it, coincides with the chord of the side apses.

St Michael, Hildesheim (pls 27–34)[8]

At the time Bernward was planning his abbey, he called the abbot of St Pantaleon and some of his monks to Hildesheim. It is therefore possible that he was advised by them and, as it happens, there are some similarities in the applied geometry. The best expertise would in any case have been made available for the venture, given Bernward's position as an intimate of Otto III. He had been Otto's tutor, travelling extensively with him before being elected bishop of Hildesheim at Otto's instigation in 993. While planning his abbey, he went to Rome in 1001 and in 1007 visited the abbeys of St Denis outside Paris and St Martin at Tours. Three years later he laid the foundation for his own Abbey of St Michael and consecrated it in 1022.[9]

Allowing for obvious irregularities in the construction, the main outline of the plan can be set out in nine operations, with a further three required to complete the apses. As at St Gall, Cologne Cathedral and St Pantaleon, the first three moves use all three of the Platonic figures. Step (1) consists of the 45° diagonals of a square defining the east crossing and therefore the transept lengths and main arcades. Step (2) employs the 36° diagonals of the pentagon to fix the centre-line of the side apse and axial pier terminating each aisle. Step (3) uses the 60° sides of the regular triangle to define the transept arcade and the aisle wall, approximating to its inner face. Steps (2) and (3) can then be repeated from the north arcade grid-line (1) to give the south apse axis and aisle wall in a procedure already seen at Caen.

With grid-lines (1), (2) and (3) established, step (4) consists of 45° diagonals from which the 36° diagonals of step (5) determine the chord of the main apse. To complete the eastern half of the basilica, step (6) employs 45° diagonals to delineate the major bay west of its crossing.

In order to set out the western half, step (7) consists of 45° diagonals to fix the major bay east of its crossing and, in so doing, completes the middle bay of the nave which, from the published measurements, is clearly not a square. This is followed by step (8) which is identical to the square bays that resulted from steps (1) and (6), thereby establishing the west crossing and transepts and the chord of the western apse.

Finally, step (9) employs 60° diagonals to determine the transept projections while diagonals of all three Platonic figures complete the profiles of the three apses.

As at Cologne, the nave compartments require division into three in order to set the column spacing for the arcades. As at St Pantaleon, 45° diagonals occur at both the east and west ends and long diagonals can be drawn at 60° from the transept corners. However, unlike St Pantaleon, there is an apparent geometric harmony between all three figures occurring over the main nave compartments adjacent to the east and west crossings (pl. 31). If each nave bay is defined by a square and one aisle bay by a 36° rectangle, the two appear unified by a 60° rectangle exactly. By calculation, this turns out to be the case to 99.65% accuracy, a margin of error imperceptible to the eye (pl. 106). The final plan shows these and other apparent alignments, with no fewer than seven of them converging on the crossing piers.

The plan was then subjected to a mathematical check by using trigonometry against a set of dimensions independently provided. The source chosen, on the recommendation of the architect currently in charge of the monument, was the measured survey by Roggenkamp.[10] Details of the calculations made to convert them to a planning grid of axis lines are set out in Appendix 3 (figs 26, 27).

Since general irregularities were revealed in the building, even between one structural compartment and the next, Roggenkamp's measurements were averaged as follows. Measurements for the square bays ranged between 944.5 cm to 988 cm, a variation of 4.4%, with an average of 964.625 cm. The aisle bays measure 689.5 cm to 698.5 cm, a variation of 1.29% with an average of 692.94 cm. The transept bays range between 379.5 cm and 399.5 cm, varying by 5.01% and averaging 390.37 cm.

After these averaged dimensions were assigned to the grid, the diagonal that was posited for each step of the geometric construction, together with the rectangle it defined, was extracted from the plan and shown with the averaged dimensions taken from the grid (pls 32–34). A second lateral length was then calculated from the longitudinal dimension by trigonometry using $\sqrt{3}$ for the regular triangle and tangent 36° and 54° for the pentagon. This mathematically correct number is shown in brackets below the averaged dimension and the difference between the two expressed as a percentage.

Step (1) was taken to result in a square of the dimensions as averaged. Step (2), using the diagonal of the pentagon, is accurate to 99.58%. Step (3), using the side of the regular triangle, is accurate to 99.21%. No dimensions from the survey allowed steps (4) or (5) to be checked. Step (6) was taken to generate one of the typical square bays. Step (7) produced a larger square accurate to 98.99%. Step (8) produced three more typical square bays. Step (9) uses the side of a regular triangle to an accuracy of 99.19%.

The overall range of accuracy therefore lies between 99.58% and 98.99%, which is a considerably smaller margin than the discrepancy in the dimensions themselves and would be imperceptible to the eye of anyone employing the draughting techniques available in the middle ages for setting out a drawing.

o o o

Although it cannot be claimed that this was the geometry that was actually used to design Bernward's abbey, the question nevertheless arises as to how a method as sophisticated as that which fits St Pantaleon and Hildesheim could even have been available at such a time. One clue might lie in Bernward's visit to Rome. The purpose of this was evidently to settle a legal dispute, but it was also common for founders of monasteries to visit Rome to receive papal privileges and other material assistance for their new foundations. Biscop returned to Northumbria from Rome in the seventh century equipped with relics, vestments and the chief singer of St Peter's and went on to dedicate his twin monasteries of Jarrow and Wearmouth to Rome's apostles, Peter and Paul. He also acquired masons from Gaul to build in the Roman manner.[11] Others returned from Rome equipped with copies of gospels and other manuscripts for use in their new foundations. William of Volpiano travelled to Rome in 996 immediately prior to his rebuilding of St Bénigne and returned from Italy with,

> . . . some men well accomplished in letters, others learned in
> the skill of diverse works . . . whose craft and talent were of
> the greatest benefit.
>
> *Altera vita 7*, in Williams 533

It has been said that William's rotunda at Dijon was copied from the apostle's crypt at St Peter's Basilica.[12] Bernward's bronze doors and column, otherwise lacking precedents outside Rome, are thought to have been inspired by those at St Sabina and Trajan's Basilica respectively. The unusual double-apsed termination of Trajan's Basilica seems clearly echoed by that in the *Plan of St*

Call. Baugulf's original layout for Fulda strongly resembles St Peter's Basilica. And it was St Peter's Basilica throughout the Carolingian and Ottonian periods that was so often the setting for imperial ceremonies, thereby establishing it as a familiar focal point for the Holy Roman Empire. Since the founders of abbeys habitually resorted to Rome for help in setting up their new foundations and would certainly have visited St Peter's in that capacity while they were there, they could have consulted its staff over a whole range of matters related to the work they would have to undertake on their return in order to realise their plans. Given some of the physical similairities outlined above that suggest Roman models, might not such advice have also included a method of design for sacred buildings, if one existed? It is for this reason therefore that the layout of St Peter's Basilica is included next in the investigation.

St Peter, Rome (pls 35–42)[13]

St Peter's Basilica was completed in 330, having been commissioned by Constantine adjacent to the legendary site of Peter's martyrdom in Nero's Circus. Dimensions to axis lines have been calculated from those advanced by Fernie[14] in order to arrive at a theoretical planning grid. Once this was established, walls and columns were added to it diagrammatically.

The entire layout can be set out in nine operations from a single square with the first three involving all three Platonic figures, as was the case with Hildesheim. The setting-out can be completed to within 99.95% (8) to 98.75% (4 accuracy over distances up to 129.92 m. At least six further alignments are possible, falling within 99.2% accuracy.

Nine out of sixteen operations align with the sixth column line from the *bema* wall, suggesting another instance of schematic construction being independent of building construction.

Steps (6) and (8) together with two of the additional alignments coincide with the north-west and south-west corners of the *bema* using all three Platonic figures to within 99.95% and 99.47% accuracy.

Step (7) is strikingly similar to (9) at Hildesheim except that the latter defines the outer corner of each transept. As at Cologne and Hildesheim, the column spacing (9) depends on the division of a repeated module into three.

Step (3) coincides with the outer walls to 99.31% accuracy. Its mid-point would also coincide with the intermediate colonnades were they equidistant from the outer walls and inner colonnades, but the dimensions suggest otherwise, resulting in 0.7% error with the theoretical dimension of 20.01 m (fig. 28). The discrepancy could well be explained by the fact that the positions of these three elements, namely the inner and outer colonnades and the outer wall, align with the earlier foundations of Nero's Circus upon which they appear to have been built (fig. 22).[15] Were this otherwise, there would have been nothing to prevent these intermediate colonnades being located at the mid-point, and this sole discrepancy in the drawings would disappear.

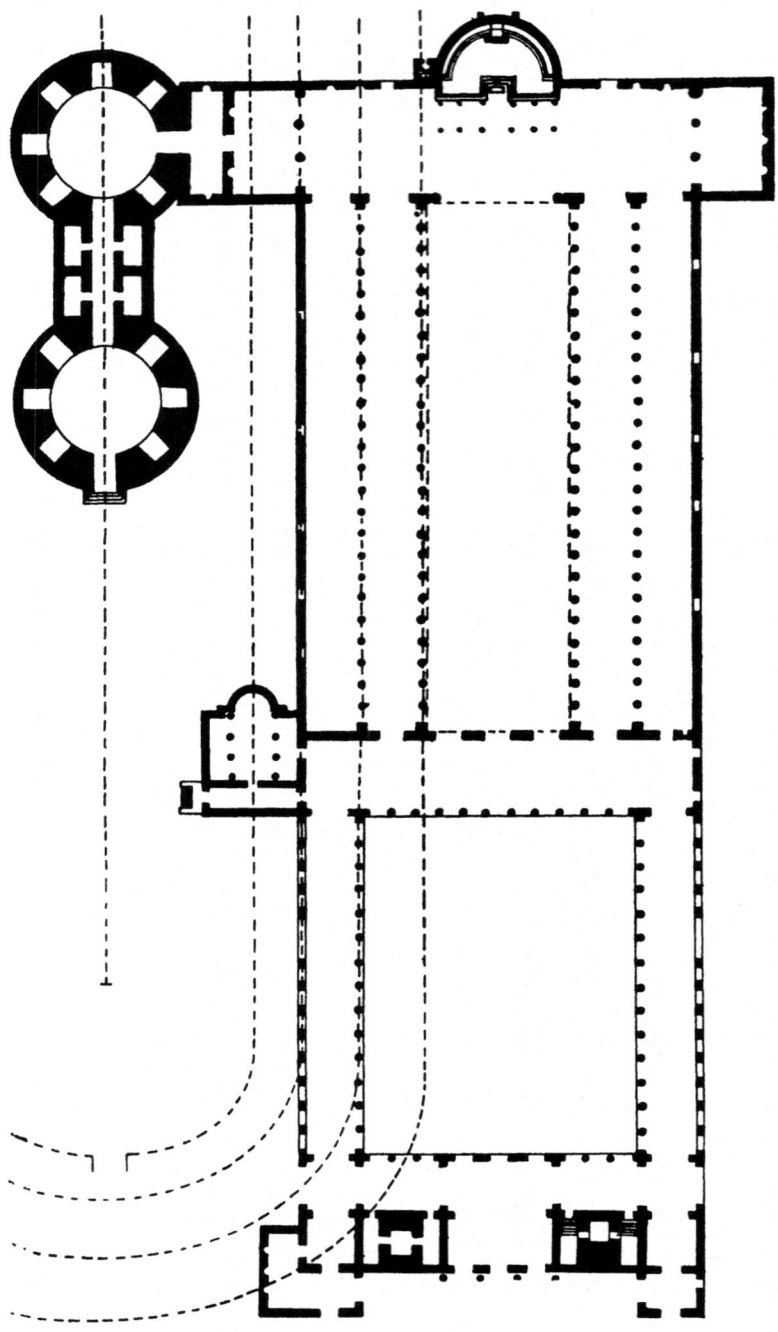

Fig. 22 Plan of St Peter's Old Basilica, Rome, after Hubsch.

The calculations that produced the range of accuracy cited for the setting-out were made in an exercise similar to that for Hildesheim (pls 40–42). The diagonal connection that was used in each step, together with the rectangle it defines, was extracted from the plan and shown with the dimensions derived from the source cited above (fig. 28). A second longitudinal distance was then calculated from the lateral dimension by trigonometry using $\sqrt{3}$ and tangent 35° as factors for the regular triangle and pentagon respectively. Again, this mathematically correct number is shown in brackets below the actual dimension and the difference between the two has then been expressed below it as a percentage.

Such fine degrees of accuracy as these might be thought remarkable for any method of design and might warrant an attempted explanation. Although it is beyond the scope of this study to trace the origin of any presumed system, the history of St Peter's Basilica points to a source in late antiquity. Unless a design method was especially devised for the first time specifically for Christian architecture and used from the outset, which admittedly is possible, a classical precedent is likely if one existed at all. As it happens, a Platonic connection seems to be implied in a letter Constantine wrote in 334, in which he states that:

> There is a need of as many architects as possible . . . who are about eighteen years old and have had a taste of the liberal arts.
>
> *Codex Theodosianus* XIII.4.1, in Mango 35

It would be interesting to know what Constantine meant by 'a taste of the liberal arts' and whether this would have embraced the *quadrivium* with its teaching on number and geometry. If so, it might imply a possible route by which Platonic thinking could have been transmitted to early Christian architecture. If a precedent for the design of St Peter's Basilica were to be sought, there are reasons for examining Trajan's Basilica, but this would require a separate study.

EARLY FRENCH

Sts Peter and Paul, Montier-en-Der[16]

Although the original seventh-century dedication of this abbey was also to Rome's two apostles, any further connection with Rome at the time of its refoundation in the tenth century cannot be asserted here, although one is at least possible. Rebuilding commenced under Adso in 983 with consecration by his successor following in 998. Of interest to this study is a possible connection with the Gorze reform because Adso had studied there and had subsequently led the school of the Gorzean abbey at Toul. In comparison with its German contemporary, St Pantaleon, the architecture of Montier is more elaborate, being aisled, arcaded and three-storeyed from the outset.

As with St Peter's Basilica in Rome, the plan of the original nave can be set out from a single square, with the first three steps involving each of the Platonic figures, and it can be completed in eight operations. It was discovered, however, that the setting-out here could only be started towards the west end, as was possible at St Pantaleon. On the other hand, two of the alignments appear to coincide exactly at the north-west and south-west corners of the structure, again as at St Peter's Basilica.

Alignments with three pier positions in the arcading are inexact, presumably because of the slight irregularity of their spacing. Finally, whilst one grid-line towards the west end coincides with three other alignments, it does not relate to a point of obvious significance in the present fabric. However, it does coincide with a conjectured bay division in the original westwork before it was remodelled,[17] a correlation that only became apparent after the geometric exercise was completed.

St Stephen, Vignory[18]

St Stephen's Priory has been included because it is situated not far from Montier-en-Der and it became a priory under St Bénigne. It follows Montier chronologically and is similarly complex for the period in being aisled, arcaded and three-storeyed. The nave dates from around 1032 when a college of canons was established here. The present choir was built in the 1050s, by which time the church had become a Benedictine priory.

The plan can be set out in ten operations from a single square at the west end followed by a 36° rectangle, both as at Montier; 45° diagonals also occur at the east end, again as at Montier, St Pantaleon and Hildesheim.

There is, however, a mismatch between the proposed geometry and the north aisle, as with St Gall. Whilst external factors could account for this, the rest of the structure does seem to answer to the geometry and constitute a possible method of design.

The only possibility of setting out the plan, however, was from the west end, which was the case at Montier and was also possible at St Pantaleon. This turned out to be unusual in comparison with subsequent examples and is likely to be explained by the fact that Vignory, Montier and St Pantaleon were all originally built without crossings and transepts. In later examples where crossings were part of the original design, it is from there that the setting-out can be started almost without exception.

The later chevet consists of half of a circle that is divided into fourteen, for which a method of division by seven would have been needed. This could have been accomplished either by trial and error on the ground using a rope and peg, or by using a rope marked into thirteen equal segments.[19] This can describe a 5, 4, 4 triangle, which approximates to a seventh part of a circle to within 99.67%. Whilst this does not conform to angles of the Platonic figures, the association of seven with the Holy Spirit would make such a division understandable.

It has already been shown that several capitals around Vignory's nave arcade are inscribed with a collection of triangles, including the regular and the Pythagorean approximately, as well as the 45° isosceles and the golden triangle exactly (pl. 15). This is not to assert that the same angles were necessarily used in the plan, although their presence in the plan was revealed by the investigation, but their display in the nave certainly suggests an interest in them and the builders would have needed templates cut to these angles in order to reproduce them.

St Bénigne, Dijon (fig. 8)

Following an unsuccessful attempt by Adso of Montier-en-Der to reform the abbey of St Bénigne in 982, Mayeul sent William of Volpiano to reimpose the reform in 990. At that time the church had fallen into neglect and the whereabouts of the relics of Benignus were forgotten. Attempts to repair the church brought about further collapse and it was following the rediscovery of the saint's tomb that William travelled to Italy in 996, visiting Rome and returning from Ravenna with various artisans to help in the rebuilding of the abbey. The foundation was laid in 1001 and the consecration followed in 1018.

Since none of William's abbey survives above ground, it cannot be stated with any certainty how closely, if at all, his basilica followed the earlier building. It is chronicled that, having razed it to the ground, he rebuilt it from the foundations, yet, at the same time, he made it longer and broader than before.[20] The Chapel of St Mary was retained beyond the east end and he inserted the rotunda between the apse at the east end and the chapel, above the saint's tomb, and the crypt has survived.

The conjectural plan of William's building has not been subjected to geometric analysis because it was not possible to secure an accurate reproduction of the original drawing. However, certain observations have already been made regarding the rotunda and tests of other churches connected with William are demonstrated in the next section.

EARLY NORMAN

Bernay Abbey (pls 43–46)[21]

A group of abbeys in Normandy was examined because they had variously been founded, reformed or influenced by William of Volpiano. William's connection with Normandy dates from the turn of the millennium when the Norman Duke Richard II appealed to him to reform Fécamp. On William's arrival in 1001, with the church already built, he oversaw the construction of other monastic buildings, sending to Dijon for masons.[22]

In 1013, Bernay was founded by the wife of Richard II as a cell of Fécamp.[23] Following her death, construction continued under William between 1025 and 1028 when he erected the nave arcades and surrounding walls,[24] with the crossing, choir and upper transepts being completed by Vitalis between 1060 and 1072. Although it survives incompletely, the original layout has been reconstructed[25] and is typical of Benedictine abbeys of the period in its parallel-apsed Latin cross, aisled choir and nave, with a tower formerly over the crossing.

Despite its early date, the plan appears generally regular, the transverse arch between the north choir aisle bays and the mismatch between the easterly ends of the nave and its aisles being two exceptions. Once these are allowed for, the layout can be set out in ten steps from a single square, the first three involving all the Platonic figures. Some additional constructions would be needed to fix the transept apses.

Step (1) consists of the 45° diagonals of a square defining the crossing and therefore the transept lengths and main arcades. Step (2) employs the 60° sides of the triangle to define the bay between the crossing and transept arm and therefore the aisle walls. Step (3) employs the 36° diagonals of the pentagon to complete the transepts.

With grid-lines (1), (2) and (3) established, step (4) consists of 36° diagonals which fix the choir bay east of the crossing and from this, step (5) uses 60° diagonals to fix the nave bay west of the crossing. It will be noticed, however, that this procedure relies on extending the grid beyond the limits of the church as built. This will be discussed shortly.

In order to complete the grid, the diagonals of the pentagon fix the chords of the easterly apses through steps (6) and (7) and their diameters with steps (8) and (9). Finally, the nave bays can be set out in repeating modules using 60° diagonals for the main bays, (10a), or 45° diagonals for the aisle bays, (10b).

The possibility of schematic construction being distinct from building construction is raised once more in the extension here of the transept grid to meet the line of the first choir and nave bays (4) and (5). This would offer the practical advantage to the designer of being able to select a transept scheme with bays on both sides of the main span, or on one side only, or not at all. Something similar to this has been suggested whereby a notional double-aisled scheme could be reduced to one that is single-aisled.[26] In marking out the bays on all four sides of the inner crossing, forming what may be termed a greater crossing, this also overcomes the modular problem that would otherwise arise in these bays because of the additional size of the crossing piers. Since crossing piers were usually intended to support a tower or lantern, they are nearly always much thicker than other arcade piers, therefore a repeating module that started at the crossing piers would cause the first arches to be narrower than those that followed. By defining a greater crossing, the grid avoids this difficulty. Conjectural though this may be, once a greater crossing was found at Bernay, it was seen to recur in at least twelve out of eighteen succeeding examples, and it was from the greater crossing that the rest of each layout was generated. Of incidental interest to this is Gervase's twelfth-century description of Canterbury Cathedral, which the Normans started rebuilding around 1070 only half a century or so after the completion of Bernay:

> The tower, raised upon great pillars, is placed in the midst of the church, like the centre in the middle of a circle.

> Gervase, *Chronica Gervasii*, in Willis 37

Turning to the rest of the layout, it can be seen that, whilst the choir, choir aisles and apses can be set out using only 36° diagonals, namely steps (4), (6), (7), (8) and (9), the nave requires only the repetition of 45° diagonals for its aisle bays (10b), or 60° diagonals for its main bays (10a), thus resembling St Pantaleon. The fact that they can apparently be combined to produce the same result provides one further instance of geometric harmony and, that the five bays west of the inner crossing can also be enclosed by a 36° rectangle, as shown on the final drawing, provides yet another.

Since the overall width of the choir is noticeably less than that of the nave, grid-line (2) occupies a different position relative to their respective wall thicknesses, which is perfectly possible according to the procedure shown by Lechler. Alternatively, a separate outer grid for the choir from the nave would allow a similar relationship for setting out the walls to be maintained and is an arrangement that becomes apparent in some later examples.

Jumièges Abbey (pls 47–50)[27]

William of Volpiano also reformed Jumièges Abbey, installing as abbot in 1017 Theoderic from Dijon who, in addition, had charge of Bernay and later Mont St Michel.[28] Construction of the church followed under the abbacy of Robert II which commenced in 1037, with work reaching the nave in 1052 and the consecration taking place in 1067 under an archbishop of Rouen who was another disciple of William. The plan bears certain similarities with Hildesheim, which was consecrated in 1022, both in its bold apsidal ambulatory and in a nave compartmented into major bays marked by piers alternating with pillars, though single here rather than paired as at Hildesheim. Jumièges also has much in common with Bernay.

Although the nave is slightly wider than the choir, the discrepancy in alignment along the south arcade is greater than to the north. Several pillars also appear to be misplaced, including one in the south transept and three in the nave. Allowing for this, the layout can be set out in ten moves from a single square, the first three of which once again involve each of the Platonic figures as well as suggesting a greater crossing. This consists of a square inner crossing as at Bernay, but within a larger square (1).

Again as with step (2) at Bernay, 60° rectangular bays intervene between the inner crossing and the projecting transepts (3). The division of the colonnaded apse and ambulatory approximates to a rotated dodecagon.

The nave is thought to have been compartmented by heavy diaphragm arches spanning it and carried on the large alternating piers. Since this structural subdivision closely repeats that set up by the crossing, the modular problems discussed in the previous section do not arise to the same extent. Nevertheless, a greater crossing has still been suggested by the first three steps and, although the first pair of pillars west of the inner crossing lie noticeably west of grid-line (1), the rest of the nave can be set out from this line through step (8) with apparent exactitude, with the exception of one other pillar.

As it turns out, the nave can be completed by repeating either the square aisle bays (8) as at Bernay, or continuing the 18° diagonals (2) as at Vignory. Although step (10) shows a construction for the west porch, it will be seen that three sides of the 36° rectangle approximate to its inner wall-faces whilst the westerly line coincides with the axis of its entrance.

In addition to the setting-out sequence, thirteen other alignments were found to be possible and they are all shown on the final drawing.

Mont St Michel[29]

Having reformed Fécamp, William of Volpiano was given control of Mont St Michel by Duke Richard II, whereupon he installed Theoderic as abbot in 1024, adding to his positions at Bernay and Jumièges. Theoderic was succeeded after an interval by Suppo, another disciple of William, who retired in 1048.[30]

It was during this time that the original choir was erected followed by the nave sometime during the abbacy of Ralph between 1055 and 1085. The choir was replaced in the fifteenth century; three end bays of the nave have been removed and, in the nineteenth century, the superstructure of the crossing was remodelled.[31] Despite these alterations, the layout remains a more accomplished version of Bernay's, still a Latin cross with apsidal transepts and aisled nave, but with more refined arcading and less irregularity, except for the south aisle being wider than the north and a north transept that has been adapted to the topography of the Mount.

The original layout of transepts, crossing and nave can be set out in seven operations starting from a single square, the first three involving each of the Platonic figures. In these first three steps, all three figures appear to coincide with each other, with a 60° rectangle overlaying the initial square and pairs of 36° bays between the crossing and transepts. Upon calculation, this turns out to be the case to within 99.65% accuracy and is a variant of the example already encountered at Hildesheim.

In the occurrence of the three figures in the first three steps, and in the inner crossing being square, Mont St Michel resembles Bernay and Jumièges. Although a greater crossing is also suggested here, it is the result, not the generator, of the setting-out procedure advanced for this plan, unlike its two predecessors. In common with step (5) at Jumièges, an identical 45° triangle from the transepts locates the apse centre and the rotated dodecagon of the apse colonnade, whilst in common with step (10a) at Bernay, the nave bays here also correspond to 60°rectangles.

The construction results in every part of the structure being geometrically connected with another at least twice and, in the case of one pair of nave piers, seven times.

St Stephen, Caen (pls 51–56)[32]

This was an especially important project, being founded by Duke William in his newly-designated capital. Its first abbot, Lanfranc, came from Le Bec, a foundation of William of Volpiano. Like its founder, Lanfranc was a Lombard. It is of particular interest to this study that he had earlier abandoned a career as a lawyer in Lombardy in order to study grammar and dialectic, first at Tours and then at Le Bec, which he then made important for the teaching of the liberal arts, becoming regarded as the greatest master of them in the West.[33] After the Conquest, Lanfranc became the king's first archbishop of Canterbury and effectively his chancellor during the Conqueror's long absences from England.

Building at St Stephen's Abbey began between 1063 and 1066 with the consecration taking place in 1077. Its layout is a further variant of Bernay's, lacking apse projections to the choir aisles whilst adding galleries across the transepts, as well as twin towers at the west end as at Jumièges. The compartmentation of the nave also recalls Jumièges with its large bays and main piers alternating with intermediate piers, their differentiation here, however, being much subtler. Given the ducal status of the abbey's foundation and the primacy of Lanfranc in England, it is perhaps not surprising that this abbey was to exert considerable architectural influence in Norman England.

Excepting the thirteenth-century choir, the Norman layout can be set out in twelve steps starting with a single square, the first three once again employing all three Platonic figures in common with Bernay, Jumièges and Mont St Michel, as well as most of the other preceding examples. As with Hildesheim, these first three operations occur to one side of the layout and can therefore be duplicated for the other side. Steps (4) and (5) establish the distance between the two. As at Bernay and Jumièges, a construction for the greater crossing can be produced from which the rest of the layout may be generated, though here a further instance of geometric harmony is revealed such as has already been seen at Hildesheim. This occurs between steps (1), (3) and the 36° rectangle that is the difference between the two (pl. 56) and which is accurate to 99.65% (pl. 105).

The sequence has resulted in a grid which restores the original Norman choir and apse, whilst the south transept apse is preserved in the existing structure and can be set out with step (9). The north transept apse could be restored with a similar construction.

The nave aisle bays correspond to squares in common with Bernay and Jumièges. The large nave bays are also square, though the third and fourth piers west of the crossing are slightly displaced. Otherwise, the structure as built appears to be remarkably regular in comparison with earlier examples. Again in common with Jumièges, long diagonals connect with the angles of the transepts from piers in the nave, at 60° for Jumièges and 60° (8a) and 36° (8b) here. It may also be seen that they intersect at the centres of each spiral stair, or vice, in the angles of the transepts, a correlation which is repeated with step (10) for the vices in the west towers and will be encountered elsewhere. The correspondence of 36° rectangles with the layout of the west end also recalls both Jumièges and Mont St Michel.

ANGLO-NORMAN

William's conquest of England brought not only the Norman expropriation of the Saxon kingdom but also a Benedictine reform of the English Church. This was effected by the Conqueror, aided by Lanfranc, and involved appointing ecclesiastics from Normandy and northern France, generally from houses reformed or founded by William of Volpiano. Thus following Lanfranc's move from Caen to Canterbury, his nephew Paul, a monk of Caen, became abbot of St Alban's while Ernulf, who had studied under Lanfranc at Le Bec, joined him in Canterbury as schoolmaster, then prior, assisting him in reorganising the English Church, before moving to Peterborough as abbot. Also from Le Bec, first Arnost then Gundulf became bishops of Rochester, Remigius left Fécamp to become bishop of Dorchester before moving with its see to Lincoln. Herbert, formerly prior of Fécamp and then abbot of Ramsey, was consecrated bishop of Norwich. Vitalis, abbot of Bernay, took over Westminster, Serlo moved from Mont St Michel to be abbot of Gloucester. Thomas, canon and treasurer of Bayeux, became archbishop of York, William of St Calais, also from Bayeux and St Vincent in Maine, was appointed bishop of Durham, Maurice left Le Mans for the see of London, while the Conqueror's kinsman Walkelin had been a canon of Rouen before William appointed him bishop of Winchester. Sweeping though these changes appear to be, however, William, Lanfranc and his successor Anselm took their time to effect them in order to minimise the upsetting of English sensibilities. Yet it remains the case that, among the new appointments from houses connected to William of Volpiano: four came from Fécamp, four from Le Bec, five from Jumièges, three each from Mont St Michel and Caen and one each from Bernay and St Ouen in Rouen. By the time the Conqueror died, eleven out of fifteen bishops in England were Norman.[34]

In common with earlier reforms, learning and building went hand in hand. As already noted, Lanfranc's pupils had hailed him as the greatest of masters teaching the liberal arts, whilst Ernulf, who had studied under him and joined him as schoolmaster at Canterbury, was distinguished both as a theologian and as a builder. Similarly, Gundulf was to build Rochester Castle and

Herbert accompanied the construction of his new cathedral at Norwich with the establishment of a library and school there, ensuring in the process that the curriculum included all the subjects of the liberal arts. In addition to Herbert and Ernulf, Remigius and Thomas were also noted for supporting scholars, while Walkelin, formerly a canon of Rouen, came to Winchester as an experienced builder and administrator.[35]

The significance of this for the present investigation is that, once again, men of learning, schooled in the liberal arts, are found operating both as patrons – and therefore presumably as architectural programmers – and as builders at the same time. Moreover, this was a programme of rebuilding that was vast, concurrent and to a large extent inter-related, as in virtually every case the surviving Saxon architecture was swept away. Among the first churches to be rebuilt were Canterbury Cathedral starting in 1070, which reproduced the layout of St Stephen's in Caen, St Alban's in 1077 which followed the Trinity Abbey at Caen, and Winchester where rebuilding commenced in 1079, its choir being in use by 1093.

Winchester Cathedral (pls 57–60)[36]

The present state of Winchester Cathedral displays subsequent alterations from every phase of medieval architecture, yet the Norman crypt, transepts and crossing survive intact along with the pier positions in the nave, notwithstanding their late Gothic remodelling. Thus with the exceptions of an original west transept and tower that were later removed and the apsidal choir that was superseded at the east end, the crypt and the present structure west of the presbytery still preserve the original layout. Besides an apsidal choir and ambulatory similar to Jumièges, Winchester represents a considerable enlargement of earlier Norman models, for its greater crossing is fully developed into transepts with arcades on all three sides while the nave is longer than ever, terminating originally with the west transept and tower. Yet it will be seen, by applying the proposed geometry to the layout, that Winchester also bears striking similarities with each of the antecedents already examined.

For the purposes of the test, the position of the foundations of the Norman west end have been restored to the plan. In the transepts, it will be noticed that the aisle responds and transverse arches of the north-west, north-east and south-east piers are offset from the axis of the gallery arcades which extend across the ends of the transepts. The south wall of the south transept is also thicker than that of the north transept and therefore its relation to the grid is different. These variations apart, the layout can be set out in eleven operations starting with a single square, the first three yet again involving each of the Platonic figures. Whilst the initial square (1) defines the greater crossing and each 60° rectangle of step (3) incorporates the greater crossing and one transept, each transept can also be set out by adding a 36° rectangle to the square, as shown on the final drawing. This provides an example of geometric harmony equivalent to Mont St Michel and identical to Hildesheim and Caen to 99.65% accuracy (pl. 106).

The square aisle bays in the nave repeat those in step (10a) at Bernay. The 60° bay between the inner crossing and transept (5) also occurred as step (2) at Bernay. Here, however, it accounts for the axis of the first pair of piers in the transepts which lie beyond the main line of the outer walls (1). This is exactly the arrangement seen in step (3) at Jumièges. The square greater crossing (1), the 36° rectangle for the transept, the large double-bay subdivision of the nave and the square aisle bays also repeat the scheme for Jumièges.

The occurrence of 60° diagonals over the crossing and transepts resembles Mont St Michel. The large foursquare nave bays and square aisle bays are found at St Stephen's Abbey at Caen (7) together with the long 60° and 36° diagonals between the western angles of the transepts and piers in the nave, as in steps (8a, b) at Caen. They are shown on the final drawing here.

o o o

In order to arrive at a sample drawn from the principal abbeys and cathedrals of Norman England, a group of three was selected from the eastern counties, namely Ely, Norwich and Peterborough, and another along the Welsh Marches, at Gloucester, Tewkesbury and Hereford. Each group constitutes a chronological sequence where work started within a decade or two and continued concurrently for several decades. Whilst architectural similarities within each group are very strong, the differences between the two groups are equally marked. In addition therefore to determining whether a correlation exists between the proposed geometry and their plans, it should be of interest to see if such differences and similarities are also reflected in the geometric findings. To complete the sample, Durham Cathedral has been chosen because it forms no obvious part of any geographical or other grouping and yet it stands undeniably as the most advanced of all Romanesque structures.

Ely Cathedral (pls 61–67)[37]

The rebuilding of Ely, initially as an abbey, commenced shortly after William the Conqueror appointed Simeon as abbot in 1081. On his death in 1093, the abbacy was kept vacant for a while, delaying the construction, so that the nave was not to be completed until 1120 and the west transept not until 1189.

Simeon was not only the brother of Walkelin, the bishop of Winchester, he had also been Winchester's prior when construction on the new cathedral began in 1079. Thus it is hardly surprising that, with his move to Ely as abbot only two years later to start construction here, the layouts of Winchester and Ely as originally designed should resemble each other so much in features unusual elsewhere. In addition to the Latin cross with apsidal choir, crossing tower and long nave common to Norman England in general, both Winchester and Ely have transepts with arcades and side bays on both their east and west sides, the easterly doubtless accommodating chapels, whilst the unusual western transept and axial tower, later removed at Winchester, foreshadowed that which survives at Ely, despite a northern arm left incomplete. Further similarities emerged from the geometric exercise and are noted below. In comparison with antecedents in Normandy, the scale of Ely's internal elevation, with gallery arches virtually as large as the main arcades, particularly recalls St Stephen in Caen, with which it also shares geometric similarities. For the purposes of the test, Ely's crossing piers, which were removed after the collapse of the Norman tower, have been reinstated and the grid has been completed with the unbuilt northern arm of the west transept.

The plan can be set out in eighteen operations, with subsidiary constructions needed to complete the west transept apses and porch. The first three steps once more involve each of the Platonic figures, though here the first comprises the 36° rectangle (1), which could equally have been the case at Caen with step (2), and Winchester with step (2), and is identical to step (4) at Bernay as well as Winchester. The overlapping of this same rectangle with its counterpart (4) recalls those at Caen, except that their long axes are at right angles. Also identical to step (3) at Winchester, is the 60° rectangle that delineates Ely's transepts, as in step (3). The 60° bays shown in the transept side bays on the final drawing also recall those at the transept ends at Winchester and the coincidence of grid-intersections with vices in both transepts repeats similar occurrences at Caen. Beside these detailed similarities, these exercises have all produced a greater crossing at Bernay, Jumièges, Caen, Winchester and Ely from which the rest of their layouts can be completed.

In the transepts and Gothic choir at Ely, the pier spacing is irregular, as is the case at Winchester. A grid for the original apse has been shown together with the easternmost bay (7, 8), whilst the remaining bays of the original Norman choir up to the greater crossing might have been fixed either by the intersections of the 45° and 60° diagonals that are shown on the final drawing, or by dividing the distance between grid-lines (8) and (1) equally into three, as in previous examples. The unequal division of bays in the north transept has been accounted for by the geometry and has been repeated for the south transept, although its south wall and internal bays lie to the north of the grid. One reason for this could have been an adjustment made necessary in order to fit in conventual buildings to the south along the eastern side of the cloister. Finally, the former pillars supporting the galleries across the ends of the transepts have been located by a combination of steps (5) and (6).

One respect in which Ely differs from Bernay, Jumièges, Caen and Winchester, the naves of which consist of repeated modules, is that the nave piers at Ely are unequally spaced to a marked extent. Of its thirteen bays, only two dimensions occur twice and even these are not adjacent to each other.[38]

Nevertheless, apart from bays 5 and 6 from the inner crossing which align slightly east of the grid, all the other bays can be fixed using Platonic geometry, which accounts for the unusually large number of operations in this example. The 36° and 60° diagonals from the transept angles at Caen and Winchester which intersect with the nave grid, also occur at Ely along with the 45° diagonal, thus combining the three basic figures. It may be difficult to accept, however, that a nave apparently requiring just a simple repetition of bays, as in other examples, could have been set out by such complicated means. On the other hand, it is just as difficult to understand how the repetition of a single bay length, using the same yardstick, could have been got so consistently wrong, if repetition were the intention. All that can be stated is that a correlation with the geometry appears to exist.

The similarity between the west transepts at Ely and Winchester is also reflected in geometric connections with their respective naves, including the square end bays of Ely's aisles (17) and Winchester's (6); Ely's 36° diagonals (15) and Winchester's (10); and Winchester's 60° diagonals resembling Ely's (16).

The combination of these setting-out procedures with other alignments, some of which could equally have been used in constructing the grid, are also shown (pl. 66). At first sight, it might be objected that the more lines that are drawn over a plan, the more can appear to be proved.[39] It is argued here, however, that there is nothing indiscriminate or random about these results. Instead, a coherent scheme is revealed which is confined to the three geometric figures as hypothesized and which can be used as a method for laying out the complete plan systematically. Moreover, in addition to accounting for the enigmatic spacing of piers – apart from the two marginal exceptions already noted – all choir, transept and nave aisles end in square bays with a double 60° bay next to them (pls 67a, b). The row of square bays running north to south, west of the inner crossing (2), is matched by similar bays at the west end of the nave, to the east of the crossing and across the choir. One large 36° rectangle at the west end (15) is matched by another identical to it extending westwards from the choir (10) (pl. 67c). The 60° diagonals extending into the nave from the west transept are duplicated by an identical construction extending from the main crossing into the nave, both constructions reaching either side of the middle bay of thirteen in the nave (pl. 67d). In addition to this, it has already been shown that the outline of the choir and transepts can also be defined by 60° rectangles overlapping each other (pl. 67e). The master mason's purpose in accomplishing such complexity and order, should a system like this have been employed, might have been to demonstrate that the more the parts of a sacred edifice could be connected with each other by Platonic geometry, the more they were in harmony with each other and with the whole, as well as with the system believed to underlie the created universe. At Ely, with the exception of the two transept columns already mentioned, every part of the structure is connected in this way up to six times.

Norwich Cathedral (pls 68–72)[40]

Bishop Herbert, who laid the foundation of his new cathedral in 1096, had been a student at, then prior of, Fécamp, the abbey initially reformed by William of Volpiano and of which William remained abbot until his death in 1031. As already noted, with construction of the new cathedral under way at Norwich, Herbert also founded a library and school which taught, among other subjects, the complete programme of liberal arts. After only five years, in 1101, Herbert's cathedral was dedicated and, on his death in 1119, it seems the eastern arm and four nave bays stood complete. The rest of the church was finished around the middle of the century during the episcopacy of Herbert's successor Eborard, with the tower following around 1170.

The plan of the cathedral is most distinctive, yet it may still be described as combining the aisleless apsidal transepts of Jumièges, a choir apse and ambulatory as formerly at Winchester – though given unusual tangential chapels – plus the long nave of Winchester and Ely and an internal elevation very like Ely's in scale and proportion, though the gallery arches at Norwich are left completely open as at St Stephen in Caen.

The plan can be set out in seventeen operations with further constructions needed to complete the chevet chapels. The first three steps, starting with a single square, once again employ each of the Platonic figures and are identical to their counterparts at Winchester. They also lead to a grid for a greater crossing, although the transepts here lack side bays. Be this as it may, it can be seen that the rest of the plan can be set out from it.

Detailed examination of the various geometric constructions possible at Norwich shows a striking correspondence with those at Ely and Winchester – and even further back to Jumièges and Bernay – both in terms of identical constructions and of others bearing a close resemblance. Just as the similarities between Winchester and Ely are likely to be explained by Simeon, Walkelin's brother, moving from Winchester to Ely as construction started there, so similarities between Norwich and Winchester might well be explained by Walkelin's participation in the preparations for the building campaign at Norwich. As it was recorded:

> I gave bishop Herbert all those lands – which have been seen and defined by, and around which went bishop Walkelin and Ralph the chaplain and Roger Bigod – that he may build his church and quarters for himself and his monks . . . .

> *Registrum primum* fol. 1v 28–31[41]

Whether or not Walkelin's survey actually extended to the cathedral's layout, Herbert did look to Winchester for his own monastic rules.[42]

Turning to the layout, steps (1), (2) and (3) are identical to (1), (3) and (2) at Winchester. Step (8) at Norwich can also be found at Winchester, whilst step (5) in both buildings forms similar bays between their inner and greater crossings; step (7) at Norwich also finds a close relation at Winchester.

Furthermore, since steps (1), (2) and (8) can be found at Winchester, so can the embodiment of the same geometric harmony (pl. 106).

The strong likeness between the interiors of Norwich and Ely is also matched by much of the geometry. The 36° rectangles (3) and (4) are the same as (1) and (4) at Ely, where their overlap is also determined by the square but in a different way. Step (2) at Norwich is identical to (3) at Ely, whilst steps (10) and especially (14) at Norwich resemble (9) at Ely.

Relating this to previous examples in Normandy, it will be recalled that Jumièges appears to have the same square greater crossing as at Norwich. Step (3) at Norwich is identical to (4) at Bernay and there is a clear resemblance between the diagonal constructions (8) and (5) at Norwich and Bernay respectively, as well as (10) and (8). Similarly, step (8) at Norwich has its counterpart in (7) at Jumièges.

It should be pointed out, however, that grid-line (4) misses the north–south axis of the east crossing piers if this is defined by the twin attached shafts facing the aisles. This is not inevitable given the complex outline of the piers together with their extension along the east–west axis, for the placement of the aisle shafts could have been produced by a secondary procedure. All that can be stated is that, despite this, step (4) does connect with fourteen other constructions and has its counterpart at Ely. Similarly, grid-line (11) lies to the east of the likely axis of its piers, but no other part of the layout is dependent on this procedure. Beyond it, the choir apse requires division of a semi-circle by five.

It is noticeable in the nave that the geometric scheme differs either side of the fourth bay west of the inner crossing along grid-line (15). Whilst the first bay is defined by the greater crossing and the remaining bays by the raking diagonals of steps (14) and (15), the rest of the nave simply consists of a repeating module of 36° rectangles (16), each depending on the division of bays into three. Such a division has already been encountered at Cologne, Hildesheim, Rome, Jumièges and possibly the original choir at Ely, for which the method later demonstrated by Serlio exists as a possible source (fig. 24). Now the dividing line between the two systems exactly coincides with a change in construction, which is thought to have occurred at the fourth bay, between Herbert's death and Eborard's appointment some two years later. Moreover, this used to be visible in the details of the main arcades, in that the first four arches originally lacked billet mouldings in contrast to the rest of the nave.[43] It needs to be stressed that the existence in the literature of this change in design only came to light after it had been revealed by the geometry during the present investigation.

The occurrence of the repeating modules in the nave recalls those at Bernay, Jumièges, Caen and Winchester, just as the coincidence of the westernmost corners of the grid with the centres of stair vices was also found at Caen and Ely.

The final drawing (pl. 72) shows these and other alignments. As at Ely, and with the exception of some intermediate piers, each part of the plan is connected to others up to six times. Moreover, diagonals appear to share a common intersection in the first and third bays of each transept, an occurrence that will be seen in succeeding examples.

One study already published of Norwich Cathedral has shown several instances of the $1 : \sqrt{2}$ ratio of the side and diagonal of the square to virtual exactitude. According to measurements advanced in the study, the diagonal of the cloister equals the length of the nave. If this length becomes the side of a larger square, its diagonal approximates to the internal length up to the chord of the apse, provided an addition is made for the thickness of the west transept wall. In a separate operation, by dividing the nave aisles into their fourteen bays and assuming them to be square, the diagonal of the square equals the width of the aisle plus the thickness of the arcade wall, whilst the width of the nave between the arcades is twice the width of the aisles.[44] In other words, the cloister can provide the major module for lengths but not widths, aisle bays provide a minor module for widths but not lengths and longitudinal subdivision is made by a different procedure not necessarily geometrical. It would be interesting to see therefore if a connection can be advanced linking these three separate procedures into a single design method that is both consistent and complete, for this might enable some useful comparisons to be made.

For example, excepting the possible anomaly of the east crossing piers, the scheme for Norwich that has been demonstrated in this book appears to reveal a system that is coherent and comprehensive both within itself and in relation to other buildings that are historically connected and generically related. These include not only Ely and Winchester but Jumièges and Bernay as well.

Alternatively, it is noticeable that whilst the $\sqrt{2}$ system for Norwich was found in dimensions taken between walls, the Platonic method investigated here produces a planning grid of single lines, suggesting the intriguing possibility that the two systems need not be mutually exclusive. For instance, might not a procedure for laying out squares and the sides and diagonals of squares have sometimes provided an empirical method for converting a grid – whether designed *ad quadratum* or not – to a plan complete with its wall thicknesses? Once a grid was laid out on site, it might not be completely beyond the bounds of possibility that a method of conversion existed for extrapolating the plan from the grid by using pegs and cords and by swinging arcs, perhaps over the shorter distances of aisle bays, to establish bay sizes and wall thicknesses. Although this is beyond the scope of this present study to pursue, it might explain the occurrence of compartmentation in squares, double squares and side–and–diagonal ratios that is generally only evident in dimensions taken between walls.

Peterborough Cathedral (pls 73–78)[45]

To complete this regional group of buildings, Peterborough Cathedral was tested to ascertain whether the Platonic system proposed in this study could also be applied here and whether further similarities might be present with other buildings in the group.

Before Ernulf arrived at Peterborough in 1107 as its new abbot, he had been prior of Canterbury, overseeing construction of its choir and having initially come from Le Bec to run the cathedral school for Lanfranc. As a result, he brought to Peterborough a reputation of a notable scholar, a leading reformer and a renowned builder.

Leaving the Saxon church standing temporarily, he started laying out the new monastery by building the dormitory and chapter house, as well as the refectory which he began before being succeeded in 1114 by John. Following a serious fire, John laid the foundations of the new church in 1118 which, it has been argued, is likely to have followed the layout established by Ernulf. Originally the church was to have had bays to the east and west of its transepts, like Ely, and a nave of nine bays terminating with a twin-towered facade. In the event, the westerly bays of the transepts were abandoned and the nave was subsequently extended to the present west front. Under abbot Martin, who also issued from Le Bec, construction continued, with the choir being completed in 1140. His successor William finished the transepts and three stories of the tower by 1175 and, within another twenty years, the nave had reached the original west front.[46]

Being built between 1118 and 1194, construction overlapped the campaign at Ely by seventy years and Norwich by over fifty. Whilst showing the refinement of later Norman building, its plan is nevertheless similar to Ely's except for having the single side bays to its transepts. Thus all three transept conditions that can be generated from a greater crossing are met in this group, with Ely's double arcades, Peterborough's single arcade and Norwich lacking arcades and side bays altogether.

The plan can be set out in thirteen operations, the first comprising a line of three 36° rectangles, whilst the next two steps involve the other two Platonic figures. The second 36° rectangle exactly repeats those at Norwich and Ely. The transept arms are defined by the 60° diagonals of step (2) in a procedure similar to Bernay's 54° diagonals in step (3). The 45° diagonals of step (3) are found repeated in step (7). The division of the apse results from rotating an octagon. As with Ely, the eastern half of the nave can be set out from diagonals extending from various points of the transepts, steps (8 to 11), whilst the original west end can be constructed from a combination of 54° and 45° diagonals, steps (12) and (13), in an arrangement which is an exact replica of steps (16) and (17) at Norwich. And just as the final constructions there intersected on or very near the stair vices in the west front, so the intersections of steps (3) and (4) appear to coincide exactly with the transept vices here.

Compelling though these relationships are, it does need to be pointed out that some piers appear to be offset from the resulting grid by a small margin, notably the first pair east of the crossing. Others result from step (8) and include the southerly pier in the south transept and two northerly piers in the north transept. No explanation was found for this except that the grid-lines for the outermost piers of both transepts align with the wall-shafts on the west wall and that the next pier in the north transept has its counterpart in the south transept, which appears exactly aligned not only with its grid-line but with its wall-shaft as well and is the meeting point of no fewer than seven geometric connections. Marginal misplacement might seem the likeliest explanation. Finally, the last drawing shows the full range of connections possible, including five converging on each transept vice, two sets of intersections in space, as at Norwich, and up to seven alignments converging on a single point.

To summarize the similarities revealed in the geometry found at Peterborough, the overlap of 54° rectangles (1) and (4) is identical to (1) and (4) at Ely and at Norwich. Step (1) is the same as (2) at Winchester and similar to (16) at Norwich. The combination of (12) and (13) is identical to (16) and (17) at Norwich, (11) is also the same as (11) at Ely. Steps (3) and (9) resemble (2) and (12) at Ely. There are other similarities in geometric construction, though different angles may be involved, such as step (9) with (11) at Ely, steps (5) and (8) with (5) and (7) at Jumièges and step (2) with (3) at Bernay. Given such a series of geometric inter-relationships, it seems justifiable to suggest that, should a geometric tradition of design have actually existed, it would be reasonable to expect its hallmarks to resemble the sort of characteristics found among this group of buildings.

o o o

Gloucester Cathedral[47]

The rebuilding of St Peter's Abbey in Gloucester, later the cathedral, was begun in 1089 by Serlo. He was a chaplain of William the Conqueror and appointed by him as the first abbot of the new Norman foundation. The consecration took place in 1100.

Serlo had been a canon at Avranches and a monk at Mont St Michel, to which the plan of Gloucester bears a general resemblance, both being a Latin cross with aisleless transepts with apses and crossing tower. However, more specific similarities in the geometry became apparent in the test and are summarized below. Conversely, the differences in design from the eastern group of cathedrals could hardly be more striking. Although Gloucester is a close contemporary of Ely, its nave is much shorter and lined with tall, repetitive, cylindrical piers beneath a gallery low enough to register as a horizontal, arcaded frieze. This is in complete contrast to the long nave of tall bays at Ely defined by alternating piers and gallery arches virtually as high as the main arcades below them. Nevertheless, some similarities in the geometry are also apparent and are noted below.

With the exception of its four chapels, Gloucester's layout can be set out in ten operations starting with a 36° rectangle, the first three involving each of the Platonic figures. Despite the lack of transept arcades, a greater crossing is again suggested.

Since the chevet displays several irregularities, it was not possible to show a correlation with any one geometric system. The transept chapels are also geometrically irregular. Notwithstanding these problems, the overlapping of 36° rectangles to define the greater crossing bears a resemblance to Ely, Norwich and Peterborough. A 60° rectangle west of the inner crossing is also to be found at Norwich (5), as well as north and south of the inner crossing at Bernay (2), Jumièges (3) and Winchester (5).

In common with Mont St Michel, however, are 45° diagonals from the transept ends to the nave aisles and arcades. The 60° diagonals in the nave and between transepts and nave are also identical to Mont St Michel and 36° rectangles occurring side by side east of Gloucester's nave were also found at the west end of Mont St Michel. The diagonals of a 36° rectangle towards the west end of the nave appear to share the same intersection with a pair of 60° diagonals, recalling similar coincidences later at Norwich and Peterborough.

Tewkesbury Abbey[48]

The Norman foundation was laid in 1092 by Abbot Giraldus and the building was completed and consecrated in 1121. The strong resemblance already noted between Ely and Norwich is fully matched by similarities between the interiors of Tewkesbury and Gloucester. With work commencing at Tewkesbury just three years after the start at Gloucester, both are distinguished by plain cylindrical piers, main arcades surmounted by low arcaded galleries, aisleless transepts with apses, and a crossing arrangement unusual elsewhere. In place of the usual crossing piers, those at Tewkesbury and Gloucester are elongated along the east–west axis. The greater precision, however, lies with Tewkesbury in the ordering of the crossing and transepts and especially in its surviving semi-circular apse in comparison with the mis-shapen geometry at Gloucester. Nevertheless, the piers of the south choir arcade at Tewkesbury are slightly displaced to the north whilst the pair behind the high altar, if they were meant to complete a semi-hexagon, are also misaligned.

Bearing in mind such strong visible similarities between Tewkesbury and Gloucester, it needs to be remembered that the abbot of Gloucester had studied at Mont St Michel where its church had only recently been completed. It may be of interest therefore that similarities were also seen in the geometry of the layouts of all three buildings – Mont St Michel, Gloucester and Tewkesbury – which again are unusual elsewhere.

The layout of Tewkesbury can be set out in sixteen operations starting with a single square, exactly as at Mont St Michel. On the other hand, neither a greater crossing nor a projection of one out to the transepts was needed here to generate the rest of the layout. Instead a 60° rectangle appeared to fix the first nave bay and incorporates the first transept bays in resemblance to Mont St Michel.

A fundamental difference between the geometry of Tewkesbury and that of Gloucester and all preceding examples is the absence of pentagonal constructions from the early stages of the procedure. Indeed, the geometry of the different Platonic figures occurs here zonally, with the square prevalent over the crossing and transepts, the pentagon over the nave, and with triangular alignments extending over the whole layout.

In common with Gloucester, the aisle grid-line lies on or near the glass-line of the windows. The nave piers are irregularly spaced and require diagonals from the crossing and transepts to fix them, as at Ely.

Against the singular characteristics of Tewkesbury's geometry, the combination of the square and 60° rectangle over the crossing is very similar to that of Mont St Michel. The bays between the crossing and transept also have their counterpart at Mont St Michel. The sharing of a common intersection by diagonals towards the end of the nave bears a strong resemblance to Gloucester. The long 60° diagonals from the transepts to the end of the nave are identical to Gloucester and similar to Mont St Michel; also at the west end, two 36° rectangles are identical to those in the same position at Mont St Michel.

Hereford Cathedral[49]

Completing this group, the Norman cathedral at Hereford is thought to have been founded by Bishop Reynelm, with construction commencing around 1110 and consecration following some time between 1142 and 1148. The consecration of Gloucester had already taken place a decade before work began at Hereford whilst Tewkesbury was more than half built. Thus Hereford bears a somewhat similar chronological relationship to its two predecessors as its contemporary Peterborough bears to Norwich and Ely. Also in common with Peterborough, a greater refinement in execution is nevertheless accompanied by similarities with its local predecessors both in the visible design and in the geometry produced by the test. In particular, the characteristic crossing, aisleless transepts and cylindrical piers of Gloucester and Tewkesbury are all present at Hereford, though its north transept was subsequently rebuilt and its south transept has no apse. The nave was originally one bay longer, terminating in a large west portal as indicated on the plan, and excavations have revealed three apses at the east end.

The plan can be set out in eleven steps starting with a single square as at Tewkesbury. The first three operations involve all three Platonic figures as at Gloucester and elsewhere. The choir, being slightly wider than the nave, has arcades offset from those in the nave. Because the north transept was subsequently rebuilt, its geometric construction was not incorporated in the setting-out. If the fourteenth-century nave aisle walls follow the line of the Norman structure, their grid-line once again would be close to the glass-line, as at Gloucester and Tewkesbury.

Any one of four procedures can be used to set out the nave arcade, incorporating once again all three Platonic figures, and the correlation of twin aisle bays with 60° rectangles is identical to Tewkesbury. Finally, the long 60° diagonals connecting the transept with the west end of the nave are also found at Tewkesbury, Gloucester and Peterborough.

o o o

Durham Cathedral (pls 79–84)[50]

In 1093, the Norman cathedral was founded by Durham's bishop, William of St Calais, formerly of the chapter at Bayeux and then abbot of St Vincent in Maine. By 1104 the choir, which was originally parallel-apsed, was complete, along with the crossing and south transept. The north transept stood up to gallery level and, to buttress the eastern arm, the first double bay of the nave arcade and a single bay of the gallery above it were also built. By 1128, the rest of the nave stood ready for its vault, which was in place just five years later. The building was finished in 1140 except for the upper towers. Thus by the time construction started, Winchester's choir was already in use and work had been in progress at Ely and Gloucester for twelve and four years respectively. Tewkesbury, 1092–1121, is a close contemporary and so is Norwich, 1096–c.1150, which shortly followed Durham. Later still were Hereford, c.1110–c.1145, and Peterborough, 1118–c.1198.

Although far from being the last Norman foundation to be built, Durham remains the most advanced of all Romanesque structures because it was vaulted from the start; the surviving vaults are fully ribbed cross-vaults, the nave vault even being pointed and the quadrant arches at gallery level may be the precursors of the flying buttress, although this has been disputed.[51] Yet the building design was progressively modified as construction proceeded from east to west. The original choir vault proved unstable and was later replaced. As a result, the north transept was initially given a wooden roof and was only vaulted after reverting to the original plan. The transept vaults are semi-circular, those in the nave are pointed. The transverse arches across the choir and transept galleries are semi-circular, the nave's are quadrants. The round intermediate pillars in the choir and transepts have shafts attached to them on the aisle side, those in the nave are left without. The arcade arches in the choir, transepts and first two bays of the nave are plain, those in the rest of the nave are carved.

The particular relevance of the fact that changes were progressively made to the design is that this may also have some bearing on the spacing of the nave piers, because they are by no means regular. If Billings's dimensions of 1842 are converted to give the centre-lines of each pier in metric (fig. 23), the spacings from the crossing to the west end are:

$$\underline{7.194} + \underline{7.127} + \underline{7.127} \ + \underline{7.807} + \underline{7.756} + \underline{7.769} \ + \underline{8.034} \ + \underline{8.582}$$

Allowing for discrepancies of less than 1% which may reasonably be attributed to building errors, it can be seen that the first three bays appear to be set at one interval, the next three at another, whilst the two end bays are each different. In other words, the nave consists of two groups of three bays each with their own spacing, followed by a different bay between the porch and towers and ending with the base storey of the towers. It has already been noted, however, that the change between the plain and carved arches occurs

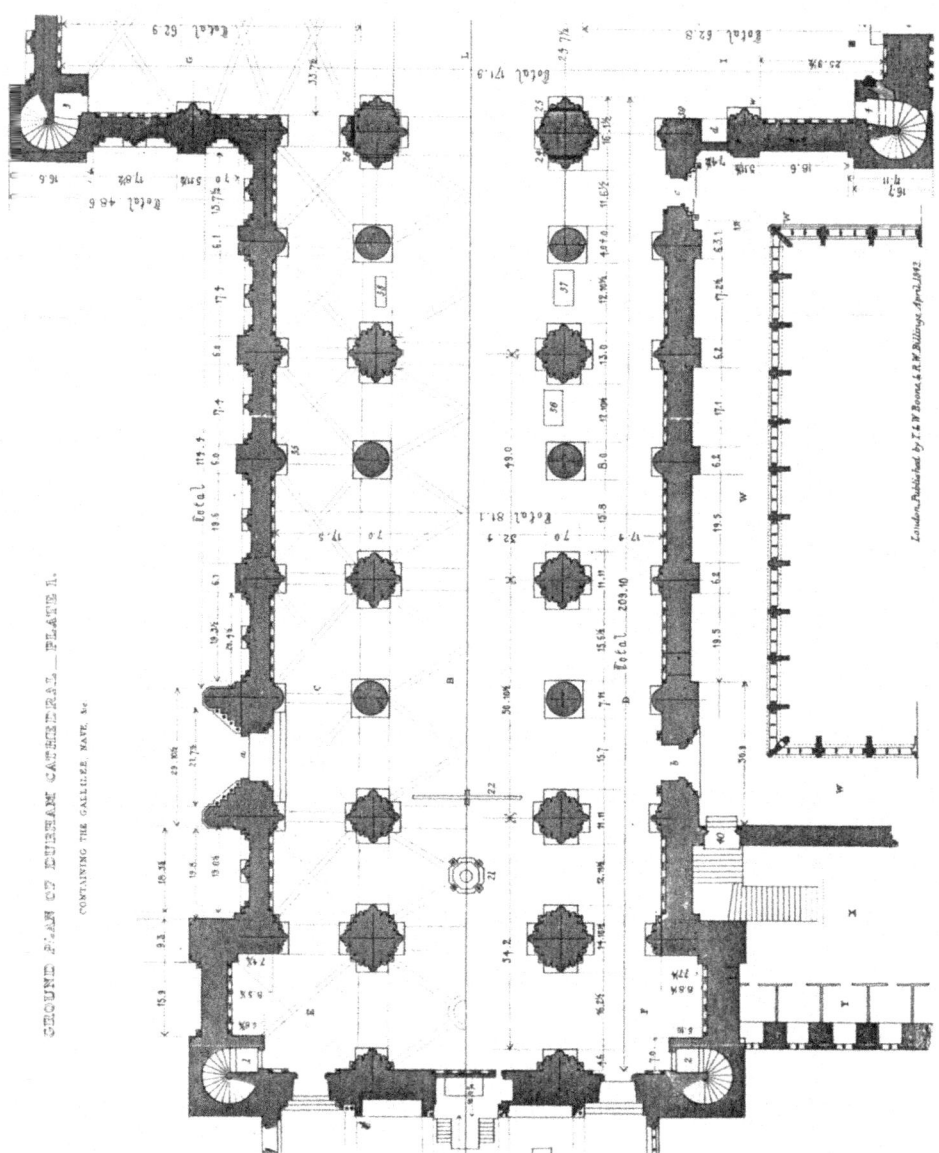

Fig. 23 Part-plan of Durham Cathedral, after Billings.

not at the third pier but at the second, marking the interim buttressing of the eastern arm. Since there seems to be no evidence of work actually being interrupted at this point, it may be reasonable to suppose that, by the time the second bay was built, the foundations of the third pier would already have been laid, thereby fixing that pier's position at exactly the same spacing as the previous bay. Whether the difference in the next three bays and the bay after that was part of the original design or the result of a change being made, it was surely deliberate and the possible implications of this will be discussed below and in the conclusion of this study.

Other building irregularities, however, are also apparent in the plan. Whilst the choir arcades are almost exactly parallel, the east transept wall is angled slightly to the south-east, the west wall slightly to the south-west, the north nave arcade and aisle are skewed to the north-west and three pillars in the nave appear to be off-set from the axis of their arcades. Nevertheless, these imperfections are slight and, because the south nave arcade appears to be at right angles to the transept arcade, the plan was aligned to both for the purposes of the investigation, with noticeable discrepancies with the structure as built being indicated on the plan. The original apses have been restored to the grid from Billings's plan.

The plan can be set out in seventeen operations starting with a single square, the first three involving all the Platonic figures once again. The first four steps are duplicated either side of the long axis of the cathedral as at Hildesheim and Caen and secondary constructions would be required for the side apses.

The procedure again suggests a greater crossing extended out to incorporate the transepts although, like Peterborough, Durham's transepts have an arcade only on the eastern side. Although the geometric connections both within the greater crossing and from it appear exact, it needs to be noted that there is a marginal mismatch between the west inner crossing as projected and as built.

As is commonly the case, the choir is narrower than the nave, so that when grid-line (4) for the outer walls – which approximates to their mid-point in the choir – is projected into the nave, it coincides with the inner face of the nave walls. It is also between the projection of these two grid-lines that a 60° rectangle (10) defines bays 2 and 3 of the nave. For the rest of the nave, however, the exercise produced a second outer grid (11) on or near the glass-line of the aisle windows and it seems highly significant that this changeover in the two grids, along grid-line (10) and between bays 3 and 4, precisely coincides with the change in pier spacing already noted. It also recalls the way a change in geometry revealed the change in the nave at Norwich. Whether this might have been the result of a variation within the original design at Durham or a change subsequently made to it, it does seem deliberate and fully, if unexpectedly, borne out by the geometry.

The final drawing shows these and other alignments, with up to five connections converging on each point of the structure. The concentration of the square over the crossing and transepts recalls Tewkesbury and Norwich. The occurrence of 60° diagonals (3) delineating the transepts has also been seen at Winchester, Ely and later Peterborough and Hereford. The large square at the east end (8) resembles one at Hereford. The large 36° rectangle extending westwards into the nave from the east outer crossing is identical to Ely (10). The coincidence of the outer nave wall-grid with the glass-line was also found at Gloucester, Tewkesbury and subsequently Hereford. The correspondence of grid intersections with the centres of stair vices has already been encountered at Caen, Ely, Norwich and Peterborough. The long 60° diagonals extending from the transepts to the western half of the nave are common to Winchester, Gloucester, Tewkesbury and later Hereford and Peterborough.

PILGRIM CHURCHES

Contemporary with the development of Norman architecture on both sides of the English Channel, another group of churches spread throughout France and into Spain along the pilgrim roads to Santiago de Compostela, once again at the hands of the Benedictines and, in common with their Norman counterparts, they were also the result variously of Benedictine reform, refoundation or new foundation. Since this development was contemporary with the Norman and Anglo-Norman buildings tested above, it is now necessary to go back to the first half of the eleventh century for the first of this group of buildings.

Ste Foy, Conques[52]

At about the time the priory at Vignory was rebuilt in the middle decades of the eleventh century, construction began on the abbey of Ste Foy at Conques, the original apse being replaced by the present chevet around 1100. Conques was a stopping-place on the pilgrim road from Le Puy to Santiago de Compostela and, along similar roads, larger versions of the same design were soon to be raised at St Martin at Tours and St Sernin at Toulouse, both of which are included in this group of examples.

In comparison with Montier and Vignory, an unprecedented degree of architectural accomplishment is suddenly apparent at Conques, for its layout is fully aisled and cruciform, with a tower over the crossing and two at the west end. The structure is completely vaulted with barrel vaults over all main spans and quadrant vaults over galleries above the aisles; and it is also fully articulated with external buttresses related to internal structure and arcade pier shafts connecting with the transverse arches of the vaults. Nevertheless, the axis of the nave is tilted towards its north-west angle away from that of the choir, which would already have been built.

Allowing for this, the plan can be set out in twelve operations starting from a single square at the crossing, the first three moves involving each of the Platonic figures. With the choir once again narrower than the nave, the geometry produced a separate outer grid for the nave, with the two grids overlapping at the east end of the nave as at Durham. In practice, this would have been a logical measure since the nave walls were clearly not intended to be centred on the axes of the first transept piers.

Numerous other alignments appeared possible, some of which could also have been used to set out the plan, with the result that each part of the structure is connected with the rest up to four times.

St Mary, Fleury[53]

The abbey enshrining Benedict's own relics, St Mary at Fleury, or St Benoît-sur-Loire, was itself a place of pilgrimage. It has already been noted that, although it was reformed by Odo of Cluny in the tenth century, as Benedict's shrine and Cluny's antecedent it enjoyed equal status at the time. Furthermore, under Abbo its school remained one of the foremost intellectual centres and led a monastic reform of its own which reached England. Following a fire early in the eleventh century, the church was progressively rebuilt, its choir being dated between 1067 and 1108 and its nave from 1150 to 1218.[54]

The transepts, crossing and choir can be set out in eight operations starting with a golden triangle followed by 45° and 60° diagonals. Much of the layout, however, is so irregular that the choir colonnades, the south choir wall and the whole of the chevet fail to connect with the geometric scheme. Yet if the misalignment of the chevet with the choir was the result of a mistake in setting-out, such as perhaps occurred with the nave at Conques, this in itself would not invalidate any geometric scheme that might have been used beforehand in designing the layout.

Two 36° diagonals were found to meet on the east grid-line of the transepts, but without otherwise relating to any part of the structure as built. Since they also intersected with the west crossing piers, the possibility of schematic setting-out points was once again raised.

There being a hiatus of nearly half a century before the rebuilding of the nave started, perhaps it is not surprising that there is a mismatch with the earlier structure. If this is taken into account, the nave can be set out in six further operations, the first four being taken from the transepts and crossing which would already have been standing. Once again, the intersection of two 60° diagonals does not coincide with an obvious part of the structure yet, from these points, the westerly bays of the nave can be set out in a single operation.

As at Durham and Conques, the outer grid for the nave aisles is wider than that for the choir and the north aisle grid corresponds closely to the glass-line of the windows. A difference in the geometry was also noticed between the three bays adjacent to the crossing and the four bays to the west and this reveals a difference in the actual building, for it turns out that the construction was split at this very point and has resulted in differences of detail, such as the clerestorey windows, which are still visible.[55] Once again, this recalls the changes in nave construction that were revealed by the geometry at Norwich and Durham.

All in all, it may be a matter of judgment as to whether such regularity as there is in the structure is sufficient to support the claim that a correlation exists. On the other hand, similarities with Conques may support a claim, such as the occurrence of golden triangles associated with both crossings and 60° diagonals defining the transepts.

St Stephen, Nevers[56]

Though not strictly a pilgrim church in the accepted sense, St Stephen at Nevers is included for its architectural kinship with some of the churches along the pilgrim roads to Santiago. After being given to Cluny in 1068 in ruins, it was rebuilt as a priory by the 1090s and resembles Conques in being a structure fully vaulted and articulated. Yet it represents a further architectural development in that its chevet is original and the internal elevation is three-storeyed with a row of clerestorey windows beneath the springing of the high vault. This constitutes an advance, too, in comparison with churches further to the south in the Auvergne and along the roads to Santiago.[57]

Its plan can be set out in thirteen operations from a single square and a 36° rectangle as at Montier and Vignory. In common with Conques and Fleury, however, the construction can be started at the crossing and includes a golden triangle in the first three steps, which lead to a greater crossing as in contemporary Norman examples.

Turning to the chevet, this is the first example in this group for which a complete construction can be advanced. Yet a mismatch between the pentagonal geometry of the apse colonnade and the triangular geometry of the flanking chevet chapels results in severe distortion in the intervening vault compartments. This was a problem soon to be resolved, as already noted at Conques where the present chevet replaced the original around 1100.

Separate grid-lines were suggested for the outer walls of the choir and nave, corresponding perhaps to their difference in thickness, or to the different position of their glass-lines, which follow the wall-grids very closely. As already observed, this would have been a logical alignment for them, the glass being the interface between sanctified interior and temporal exterior.

St Martin, Tours[58]

An important place of pilgrimage in its own right, Tours lay along the pilgrim road from Paris to Santiago. However, the abbey Heriveus rebuilt at the turn of the millennium is thought to have been entirely rebuilt again sometime between 1063 and 1080. Even this no longer exists above ground since the medieval cathedral was demolished in the nineteenth century. Nevertheless a plan of the eleventh-century abbey has been drawn up based on one by

Jacquemin in 1719 and revised in the light of modern excavations.[59] The resulting plan represents the largest and most complex pilgrim church so far and, with a fully developed chevet of five chapels, transepts with arcades and side bays on both sides and with double apses, together with a double-aisled nave with twin towers at the west end, it clearly foreshadows St Sernin at Toulouse and Santiago itself.

The plan can be set out in fourteen moves from a single square, the first three operations involving each of the Platonic figures. Supplementary constructions are needed to set out its various apses. As at Nevers and elsewhere, a greater crossing grid is suggested, though here it incorporates not one but two adjacent bays all round it.

If the proposed chronology is correct, the chevet is the first in this group which is not only contemporary with the rest of the structure, but fully developed and displaying one consistent geometric system, the apse colonnade approximating to a rotated octagon.

Because the main crossing piers appear misaligned with the choir arcades and transept piers are misaligned in their arcades, several mismatches occur with the grid. Against this, the setting-out of the nave appears to be regular and to consist of a repetition of aisle bays as at Bernay, Jumièges, Mont St Michel, Caen and Winchester, though here comprising 60° rectangles as at St Gall, Montier, Tewkesbury and Hereford and exactly as at St Peter's Old Basilica in Rome.

Numerous additional alignments are also possible and appear to be exact, including a multiplicity of diagonals which appear to intersect with each other exactly, as in preceding Norman examples.

St Sernin, Toulouse (pls 85–90)[60]

With Toulouse lying on the pilgrim route from Arles to Santiago, Sernin's shrine gained in popularity among pilgrims at a time of increased prosperity for the chapter, which followed reforms and a reorganization of Church property around the middle of the eleventh century. As a consequence, work began on the chevet of a new basilica between 1070 and 1080 under Canon Rammond Gairard. Despite an interruption caused by the chapter and bishop falling out when Cluniac monks were installed, the chevet was almost complete by 1096, whereupon a foreman was hired for the nave, aisles and west front. By the time Rammond died in 1118, most of the construction had been laid out and the three easterly bays of the nave vaulted, together with parts of the aisles, galleries and probably the south transept. Thereafter work slowed down and was to proceed fitfully until at least the fourteenth century. The west towers were never completed.[61]

In layout the basilica follows St Martin at Tours with a chevet of five chapels, twin-apsed transepts with arcades and side bays both sides, a double-aisled nave and a porch between the base storeys of the west towers. A south door enters directly into the nave. The structure may also have followed that at Tours before its demolition and does resemble Conques in being fully vaulted with barrel vaults on transverse arches over all main spans, quadrant vaults over galleries above the inner aisles and a tower over the crossing, the piers of which were hugely enlarged in 1250. It will also be seen from the plan that the pier design in the nave was changed at the fourth bay west of the crossing.

The plan also reveals some misalignments, most noticeably the ambulatory and chevet chapels which radiate from a point slightly to the north of the main axis of the rest of the church, the south choir arcade and the east arcade of the north transept, whilst both south arcades and aisles of the nave are skewed to the south-west. For the purposes of the exercise, the plan was aligned to the north-west and south-west piers of the greater crossing and a grid was plotted from their centres. Given this one premise, the layout can be constructed in fifteen moves from a single square, using all three Platonic figures in the first three operations, with supplementary constructions needed for the apsidal chapels. Steps (1) and (2) need to be repeated either side of the main axis as at Hildesheim, Caen, Nevers and Durham. The generator of the grid once again consists of a greater crossing incorporating the inner crossing and one adjacent bay all round as with Nevers and various Norman examples, rather than two surrounding bays as at Tours.

Due to the irregularity of the building, piers are related to this grid with varying degrees of accuracy. In addition to misalignments already noted are the end bay of the north transept and the south transept facade. The enlarged crossing piers are not centred on the grid either, although the originals within them may well be.

Notwithstanding this, the inner crossing turns out to be a square overlapped by squares either side of it. The layout of the chevet (4) results from the division of a semi-circle by seven as at Vignory, for which an empirical method has already been described.

Turning to the nave, another instance of geometric harmony between the three Platonic figures was revealed and appears on the first plan of the final drawing (fig. 90a). Here a 60° rectangle, which is the extension into the nave of step (5), delineates the nave and inner aisles from the north-west and south-west piers of the greater crossing, from which the grid was initially plotted, down to the bay which is entered from the south door. This 60° rectangle contains a 36° rectangle and a square to within 99.65% accuracy (pl. 106) and is identical to that found at Hildesheim, Caen, Winchester and Norwich. Furthermore, the division between this 36° rectangle and the square exactly coincides with the change in pier design already noted between bays 4 and 5 west of the inner crossing.

On revisiting the basilica, however, it was observed that the vault and arcade design actually changes one bay to the east of this, between bays 3 and 4 and, as it happens, incorporates the three easterly bays of the nave that were recorded as being vaulted at the time of Rammond's death. Whereas the transverse arches across these bays consist of two orders, those to the west are single. The arches of the main arcade are also narrower and very stilted in comparison with those to the west and there are differences in the gallery arcades above them as well. Accordingly, and subsequent to the thesis, a re-examination of the geometry, in particular the geometric connections possible along the line between bays 3 and 4, has produced steps (9) and (10). This has resulted in outer grid-lines (10) that are slightly further apart than previously which, quite unexpectedly, has released a multiplicity of additional geometric connections (pl. 89) with up to eight diagonals converging on a single pier and different sets of diagonals intersecting over each other in space.

The apparent complexity of the result might seem to stretch credulity. Yet, as it has already been remarked for Ely, different layers of geometry can be distinguished from each other as being schemes each in their own right that are both rational and coherent. In addition to the harmonic combination of the three figures that has already been noted over the eastern half of the nave (pl. 90a), the network of squares, both normal and rotated, is comprehensive, except in the choir (pl. 90b). The aisles of both transepts and the nave end in identical 60° rectangles which are also repeated at the crossing (pl. 90c) and feature variously in Winchester, Ely, Norwich and Tours. Other 60° diagonals suggest overlapping triangles, the bases of four marking out the bay of the south door (pl. 90d) in an arrangement remarkably similar to Ely (pl. 67d). A configuration of 36° triangles comes to a point either side of this same bay (pl. 90e). The radial point presumably intended for the chevet, together with the axes of the transept arms and the entrance into the west end of the nave are similarly located by 36° diagonals that not only converge to touch these points but also connect with each other across the plan in a way that is utterly consistent (pl. 90f). This, it is argued, is not the result of arbitrary pattern-making so much as a revelation of geometric configurations that are actually present in the plan, whether intended or not. If intended, they would surely display both the complexity and order that was believed to underlie the created universe.

FRENCH GOTHIC

Chartres Cathedral (pls 91–95)[62]

Chartres has been selected because of the attention it has received on the one hand as the foremost centre of Platonist studies throughout the twelfth century under its three great chancellors – Bernard, Gilbert and Thierry – and on the other for the seminal influence the cathedral was to have on the development of Gothic architecture, its construction commencing as the twelfth century closed. No actual connection, however, has yet been discovered between any theorist in the school and a designer of the cathedral. Yet, as it has already been pointed out,[63] the twelfth century marked the culmination of Christian Platonism, not its inception: for that, it is necessary to return to the tenth century and an earlier chancellor, Fulbert.

Fulbert had been one of Gerbert's pupils before opening the school at Chartres in 990 where he went on to teach various subjects of the liberal arts as well as science and religion. In 1007 he also became the bishop of Chartres, eventually dying in 1028.[64] When the Carolingian cathedral burnt down in 1020, it was Fulbert therefore who set about replacing it. Thus in Fulbert may be found a scholar and founder of a school of Platonist studies as well as a bishop and founder of a new cathedral and, when his building was in turn destroyed by fire in 1194, the present cathedral was fitted over it. The result, however, is not clear-cut for part of the Carolingian substructure was incorporated into Fulbert's building and the bay intervals towards the west end of his basilica only align with the Gothic structure approximately.[65] Nevertheless, any connection there may be between the present cathedral and a particular system of design is more likely to be found underlying it in Fulbert's earlier layout, the disposition of which may still to a large extent be discerned in the Gothic plan once the history leading up to the present building is understood (pls 17a, b).

After the fire of 1020, Fulbert started rebuilding by erecting a colonnaded apse, probably of seven bays, around the earlier martyrium with an ambulatory and three chapels radiating from it. From the chord of this apse there extended to the west, uninterrupted by any crossing, an aisled basilica of eleven roughly equal bays with one odd bay beyond it at the end. Between these last bays may have stood a two-bay narthex. Either side of the east end of the nave, there projected two chambers in the form of *porticus*, as already encountered at St Pantaleon in Cologne. In 1134, another fire damaged the west front, after which work started on the present north tower which was positioned forward of the narthex. This was completed in 1150, with the south tower following from about 1145 to 1160. During this phase, the side aisles were extended up to the backs of the new towers and the existing west front was built between their front walls. When the fire of 1194 destroyed Fulbert's church, this west front and its towers escaped destruction, as did the crypt at the other end. Consequently it was decided to fit the new cathedral between the two, with its aisle walls, piers and chevet largely following Fulbert's plan. In order to double the width of the ambulatory, its original outer wall together with the side walls of the earlier chapels gave way to the intermediate ambulatory arcade, its piers being located over the original junction between the chapel walls and the ambulatory wall. The apses of these new chapels were built around the outer profiles of their predecessors and four new chapels were fitted in between. Apart from these modifications, the transepts are the only other additions to the earlier plan.[66]

Thus within the plan of the present cathedral may still be seen Fulbert's chevet of three chapels and his single ambulatory around an apsidal colonnade divided into seven, followed by a choir and nave of eleven bays, which explains the later Gothic crossing unusually being equal in length to two of the bays either side of it. Beyond the eleven bays, the original odd bay is preserved by two even, but shorter, bays which presumably mark the interval between Fulbert's west front and the later towers. One further qualification needs to be made. The substructure of Fulbert's west front is skewed towards the north-east, so that the end bay of the north aisle is shorter by almost 1 m. At some stage, it seems this misalignment was squared off from the north-west corner with the result that the corresponding end bay of the south aisle is now shorter than its neighbours. Surprisingly perhaps, just as this unusual building history can be detected in the present plan, so it appears to be reflected in the sequence of the geometry resulting from the test. Such irregularities as there were in the layout of Fulbert's cathedral, compounded by the subsequent difficulties apparent in placing the Gothic structure over its Romanesque antecedent, undoubtedly explain the irregularities in the Gothic plan and ultimately it must be a matter of individual judgment as to whether the proposed grid is close enough to it to be convincing. In addition to the dislocation of the chevet chapels from the radiating point of the apse, several piers would be eccentric to any regular grid, some by a wide margin, including those around the apse and the new intermediate arcade of the choir and ambulatory. Against this, the great majority of piers and buttresses, especially west of the choir, along with the alignment of the outer grid with the nave aisle windows, appear close enough to be worth considering.

If the grid is accepted as the closest common denominator of all the irregularities in the structure as it stands, then Fulbert's layout, insofar as it is reflected in the Gothic plan and leaving aside the original *porticus*, can be set out in seven moves. Its enclosing grid consists of two 60° rectangles (1) extending from the centre of the apse of the axial chapel at the east end to the presumed outer grid of Fulbert's narthex at the west end. The outline of the narthex, however, is conjectural and proved incidental to the rest of the setting-out. On the other hand, step (2) locates the grid-line coinciding with Fulbert's original, but rectified, west front. Step (4) fixes the chord of the chevet and (5) the first bay in from the original west front, thereby defining the single odd bay at the west end. With step (2) emanating from the intersection of 60° diagonals (1), other early examples are recalled, such as Cologne, Montier and Fleury, where geometric construction appears independent of building construction. Returning to step (5), this also establishes a 1 : 2 : 1 ratio between aisle and nave widths and, when overlaid by step (6), fixes all bay divisions and pier positions west of the chevet.

The original chevet chapels, if their displacement is taken into account, can be set out through a combination of two half-hexagons (7), one rotated over the other, to give a division by twelve, thereby completing the presumed layout of Fulbert's cathedral.

Unlike all the examples since Vignory, the plan cannot be generated directly from the crossing, which is presumably explained by the fact that the crossing did not exist in Fulbert's layout but appears to have been created later out of two of its bays. This recalls the results for both Montier and Vignory which were also originally laid out without crossings or transepts and, as it happens, the building of Fulbert's church intervened between the two.

For the next phase of building at Chartres (pl. 94), the position of the present west front and towers can be fixed in five moves from the pre-existing grid, the new end bays of the nave simply extending the original grid-lines (1). Finally, the Gothic transepts can also be set out by extending the existing grid

( ) and by producing 60° diagonals from it, either (6a) or (6b), whilst the outer ring of the Gothic chevet can likewise be fixed by the regular triangle from step (7).

It may be seen therefore that not only can the chevet and main body of Fulbert's cathedral be set out using only the triangle, but the expansion of the grid to form the Gothic chevet and transepts simply continues its use. Such dominance by the regular triangle is unprecedented among previous examples except for St Pantaleon which was, it may be remembered, an imperial re-foundation completed only twenty or thirty years before Fulbert commenced his rebuilding. Moreover, St Pantaleon was also laid out with two *porticus* and no crossing. As for the geometry at Chartres, between the building of Fulbert's cathedral and its Gothic successor, chancellor Thierry wrote his *Heptateuchon* in which he evidently associates the regular triangle with the Holy Trinity.[67]

In addition to those procedures singular to Chartres, the 60° diagonals (5) and (6) defining the aisle bays resemble those at St Peter in Rome, in steps (3) and (9), as well as those at Montier, St Martin at Tours, Tewkesbury and Hereford. The 60° construction for the transepts (6b) is identical to Fleury and to step (3) at Durham. The long 60° diagonals connecting the transepts and the west end (6a) were also encountered at Mont St Michel, Gloucester, Tewkesbury and Hereford and resemble others at Durham, step (13), and Peterborough, step (8), a sequence of building broadly leading up to the addition of transepts at Chartres.

o o o

Notwithstanding the proliferation of 60° connections at Chartres, however, the result hardly compares with the geometric complexity and diversity of such preceding examples as Toulouse, Durham or Ely. Yet it needs to be borne in mind that more than half a century separated the designing of Fulbert's church in 1020 from these later examples, which all date from the 1080s or a few years either side. If the Gothic elaborations of the Romanesque plan of Chartres are stripped away, a degree of architectural simplicity is restored that is comparable with other layouts contemporary with it such as Vignory and Bernay. It appears therefore that geometric connections may proliferate with the passing of time and with the increasing complexity of the architecture that went with it. This could be explained by a growing experience in operating any system of design as may have existed and by the increasing ambitiousness of the architectural programme, which resulted for example in arcaded transepts and double-aisled naves and choirs being incorporated from the outset. These in turn provide many more pier positions and therefore additional opportunities for more connections to be made. Alternatively, it is possible that greater complexity simply increases the potential for chance connections to be made. In other words, the geometric system advanced in this investigation could be inherently so versatile as to provide a correlation with plans that could not possibly have been designed by it. This possibility will be examined later [68] by applying the system to a small sample of such buildings in order to determine the presence of positive or negative evidence in support of it.

St Maclou, Rouen (pls 96–105)[69]

St Maclou has been added to the original sample of buildings because, being a late medieval building in Normandy, it was thought to be interesting to see if the same geometric system could be applied to it as to earlier Norman and Anglo-Norman examples. The subject of a published study, it has also been accurately surveyed and plotted using laser and computer technology with the result that the geometry applied to it here can be checked against the survey trigonometrically.[70]

The present building replaced a previous church which was too small and had partially collapsed. Pierre Robin, a Parisian master mason, presented a drawing to parish officials for a new church and this was constructed sometime between 1432 and 1490. Being the work therefore of a single architect, modest in scale and apparently completed in a single campaign, it offered the possibility of conclusions being drawn about its design uncompromised by any of the vagaries that are usually caused by interruption or alteration between conception and completion.[71]

One of the premises of the above-mentioned study was that any method that Robin might have employed to design the plan would best be of use if it also enabled the building to be set out on site. Accordingly, a square was put forward related to the greater crossing. When a similar square was rotated over it, the intersections coincided with the outer wall-faces of the transept, which may have been fixed by site conditions given by the earlier building. The rotated square also matched the overall width of the building and, when duplicated along the main axis, the overall length was suggested as well as the centre-points for setting out the chevet and west porch. A method was shown as to how each of these could be set out on site using a single peg in the ground, together with a cord and the ability to form right angles.[72] However, it can be seen that the pier spacing is markedly irregular, as at Ely and Durham, and the published method could only account for this if the measuring points were sometimes made axial, sometimes eccentric and sometimes to wall-faces. The actual spacing, measured to centre-points from east to west in metric are:

$$\underset{\text{choir}}{\underline{5.043 \;+\; 5.877}} \;+\; \underset{\text{transept}}{\underline{6.750}} \;+\; \underset{\text{nave}}{\underline{5.860 \;+\; 5.427 \;+\; 5.604}} \;+\; \underset{\text{porch}}{\underline{4.135}}$$

In an attempt to account for this spacing in a way that is consistent, the angles of the Platonic figures were applied to the plan as in the previous examples. In order to locate the external faces of the outside walls of the side chapels, a wall thickness of 0.442 m, which was recorded in the survey, was added to the dimensions cited.[73]

As a result, the grid for the main body of the church can be set out in eight steps, with subsidiary constructions needed for the portals and chevet. The first three steps once again employ each of the three Platonic figures. Moreover, the only sequence that could be reconstructed depended on starting from the west side of the transept and, as mentioned above, there is good reason to believe that this may have been a given condition.[74]

Turning to the chevet, the setting-out of this depends on the square and the regular triangle, also on quartering their angles (pls 99, 100).The polygonal apse and ambulatory comprise one half of a rotated octagon which is also reflected in the angles of the outermost walls of the chevet chapels. The re-entrant angles of the chapels can be set up from a point one bay west of the radiating point of the chevet by quartering 60° (11) and then repeating the angles of the rotated octagon. The distance of the outer line of the chapels from the radiating point appears determined by the regular triangle (12) in a manner that strongly resembles Chartres (7). By describing an arc through the apex of this triangle (12), one pair of outer buttresses can be located where the arc is intersected by 45° diagonals (13), which are projected from the secondary radiating point. The remaining buttresses can then be fixed from this point by drawing diagonals at quarters of 90° (14, 15, 16). Finally, the alignment of the remaining buttresses can be obtained by connecting their centres to the polygonal points of the inner choir (pl. 101).

Since verifiable dimensions exist from the survey already cited, these were used to calculate the accuracy of the setting-out advanced for the main body of the church (pls 102–104). Following the method employed for Hildesheim and St Peter's Old Basilica, trigonometry was used to calculate longitudinal distances from the lateral dimensions of the survey. The differences between these calculated values and the longitudinal survey dimensions were then expressed as a percentage. However, unlike the measurements for St Peter's Basilica, it can be seen that there is a multiplicity of dimensions to be considered for St Maclou. For example, no two sides of a rectangle are exactly the same length, although all discrepancies are marginal, and most of the steps involve pairs of rectangles, either separately (5, 6) or overlapping (3, 4, 8, 9). Consequently, all the dimensions possible for each step have been presented on the drawings, with those producing the greatest degree of accuracy being shown underlined. From this, it can be asserted that the setting-out advanced coincides with the dimensions of the building to a verifiable accuracy ranging from 100% to 99.39%. It need hardly be pointed out that, to anyone employing this system in order to draw out a plan such as this with the instruments and techniques known to have been available to medieval architects, yet without the theory to check it, the geometric constructions deployed here would have appeared to be exact.

It cannot of course be stated that this is the system that was actually used to design the layout of St Maclou but it is put forward because it does show a correlation to virtual exactitude between the geometry proposed and the structure as built. It is a correlation that is mathematically demonstrable, as is also the case with Hildesheim and St Peter's Basilica and it fully accounts for the irregular spacing of piers, such as seen at Ely, Durham and Toulouse.

The spacing of arcade piers

Repetitive modules for laying out naves have been seen at Bernay, Jumièges, Caen and Winchester, as well as Norwich and Peterborough. Yet in other examples, nave bays have proved to be unevenly spaced. Where this occurs randomly, involving individual arcade piers, this may reasonably be attributed to building error. At Ely, however, the nave piers are spaced unequally to a marked extent, which is surprising since one of the simplest procedures to get right should have been the equal spacing of piers in an arcade using a single yardstick and a repeating unit of measure. The geometric investigation, however, showed that the whole of Ely's layout can be set out using the angles of the Platonic figures, including the fixing of each different bay of the nave. As a result, the spacing of piers that seems metrologically irrational appears to be geometrically rational.

Whether Ely's piers were placed irregularly by accident or design, a change in spacing of the nave piers at Durham certainly appears to have been deliberate. Even allowing for building error, it can be seen that the nave consists of two groups of three bays each with their own spacing, followed by a different bay between the porch and towers and ending with the base storey of the towers. Whether these differences were part of the original design or the result of change, they were surely intentional, yet once again the test showed that Durham's plan can be set out according to the system proposed.

In both these examples, the application of Platonic geometry can account for the uneven spacing of their nave piers, yet it cannot be stated with certainty that the irregularity at Ely was by accident or design; nor at Durham, where it was surely deliberate, that it was a variation in original design or a change subsequently made. At Rouen, there cannot be any doubt that a wide variation in pier spacing must have been part of the intended design, yet when the same geometric system was applied, not only could the main body of the church be set out in just eight steps, it also accounted for all the different pier positions, all of which raises the unexpected possibility that at least some instances of uneven spacing may be the result of design and not of accident.

Notes

1 Further differences between the thesis and this book are that, in the thesis, the geometric constructions were generally concentrated onto single plans, whilst here they are presented as sequences of steps on separate drawings, followed by one showing all the constructions possible. Some of the sequences have also been adapted from those in the thesis where a greater coherence was found. In order

to compare the findings here with the thesis, a copy is available at the British Library under the reference number DX182512.

2 Cod. lat. Monac. 410 fols 61r–114r, Busard 520–21; also *Practical geometry* 29, 52.

3 Appendix 1.

4 Appendix 2.

5 After plan by Weyres in Horn and Born I.28.

6 See pp. 260–61.

7 After plan by H. Schäfer, undated.

8 After plan by Roggenkamp, Beseler and Roggenkamp pl. IV.

9 Beseler and Roggenkamp 21, 113.

10 Beseler and Roggenkamp 132–5; I am grateful to Hans Günter Kirklies for this advice.

11 See Gem 1–4.

12 Chevallier 81.

13 A conflation of this section with Alberti's Basilica III has been published and appears in the Bibliography under Hiscock 1994.

14 Fernie 1979 (2), also Bannister 15 fig. 18; see Appendix 4.

15 Stewart 23.

16 After plan by J. Laurent, Paris, 1950; drawing no. Mon. Hist. 31835.

17 Koppe 26 figs 26, 27.

18 After plan by J. Laurent, 1969.

19 Critchlow 100–101 fig. 71.

20 Glaber, *Vita sancti Guillelmi* XV. 710–11.

21 After plan by G. Duval 1978; drawing no. Mon. Hist. 56129.

22 Sackur II.45; Grodecki 27.

23 Williams 538.

24 Rivoira II.67; Herval 40; Grodecki 27, 31.

25 See note 21.

26 Lund 17.

27 After plan by Lanfry 1954, 10 pl. IV.

28 Williams 535; Sackur II.50–1.

29 After plan by E. Corroyer, Paris, 1875; drawing no. Mont. Hist. 7385.

30 Chevallier 115; Decaëns 9.

31 Decaëns 25.

32 After plan by J. Merlet 1956; drawing no. Bibl. Dir. Arch. 29140.

33 Haren 95; Barlow 60.

34 Reilly 50; Barlow 57–8, 61–4, 82, 186–7, 240.

35 Reilly 50; Barlow 61–2, 240–41, 244.

36 After plan by R. Paul in *Builder* 1.10.1892.

37 After plan by R. Paul in *Builder* 2.4.1892.

38 Fernie 1979 fig. 1.

39 See Morgan 14–9; Colvin 763; Fernie 1990, 229.

40 After plan by R. Paul in *Builder* 5.9.1891.

41 See also Fernie 1993, 13.

42 Fernie 1993, 120.

43 Fernie 1993, 20, 46.

44 Fernie 1993, 94–100, 138–40, 206.

45 After plan by R. Paul in *Builder* 4.4.1891.

46 Barlow 82–3; Reilly 13, 50–53, 57–8, 80–86.

47 After plan by C. Mallows in *Builder* 5.12.1891.

48 After plan by R. Paul in *Builder* 1.12.1894.
49 After plan by R. Paul in *Builder* 6.2.1892.
50 After plan by C. Hodges in *Builder* 3.6.1893.
51 See Thurlby 58.
52 Plan of Conques after Berry 1947.
53 After plan by A. Le Mort 1983.
54 Berland 10.
55 Berland 18–19.
56 Nevers, after R. Ruvrich (?), undated. A new plan has recently been produced and it is hoped that the results from testing this may follow its publication.
57 For example, Notre Dame du Port at Clermont-Ferrand and Santiago de Compostela itself.
58 After plan by C. Lelong 1970.
59 Lelong 1985.
60 Plan by Y. Boiret, after Viollet-le-Duc, undated.
61 Cazes 5–6, 12–13, 20–21.
62 After plan by Service Departemental de l'Architecture d'Eure et Loir 1986.
63 See p. 25.
64 *Hist. Litt.* VI.25, 44; Knowles 94.
65 See Stegeman 1993. I am most grateful to Charles Stegeman for kindly drawing this to my attention. With Merlet's plan now requiring modification and Branner's reconstruction being chiefly useful as a conjectural diagram of Fulbert's layout, more work is needed in bringing the eleventh- and twelfth-century structures into conjunction with each other before the exact relationship between the two plans can be stated with certainty.
66 von Simson 187; Houvet 16, 19–20, 35; Swaan 119–20.
67 Masi 33.
68 See Chapter 8.
69 After plan by Neagley 402 fig.5; I am grateful to Linda Neagley for her kind permission to summarize some of her material.
70 In order to survey the monument, a digital planimetric system was used in which internal and external grids were supplemented by secondary control stations related to individual parts of the building. Measuring points were established at each change in direction along internal and external wall-faces. Using theodolites, an Electronic Distance Measurement Instrument, steel tapes, tension handles, clamps, markers and taping pins, the measuring points were located from several stations by triangulation and their co-ordinates fixed with reference to the grids. Angles were measured to the nearest second, lengths to the nearest 0.1 mm and taken independently by separate teams. Allowable variations were limited to 0.5 mm and the mean taken. The co-ordinates were then draughted on an Apollo 4000 computer using AutoCAD for the production of drawings on a Hewlett Packard Plotter. In addition to offering virtually guaranteed accuracy, precise dimensions are retrievable from the database in a way not possible from drawings produced by hand; Neagley 402–5, 419–21.
71 Neagley 395, 397–9, 407.
72 Neagley 402–6, 412–13, 417.
73 Neagley 412n52.
74 Neagley 418.

Chapter 7

Comparative Analysis

In order to evaluate the results of the investigation, each example was analysed against the criteria previously formulated. Since these were each applied to all of the examples, the number of individual checks exceeded five hundred and they are summarized here. In addition, two further types of correlation emerged from the investigation that were not anticipated when the list of criteria was formulated. These are the suggestion of schematic design being independent of building design, which will be examined below, and the occurrence of harmony between the different geometric figures, which will be discussed separately.

Of the plans tested, all appeared to answer to the geometry proposed with varying degrees of completeness and exactitude, with the sole exception of the *Plan of St Gall* when reconstructed from its inscribed dimensions. Since its dimensions do not accord with the plan as drawn and the layout as dimensioned does not otherwise appear in the historical record, its configuration is open to interpretation and would be conjectural at best. For these reasons and in order to avoid undue repetition in the following summary, this has been set aside as an acknowledged exception, leaving the summary to deal with the remaining cases for which more conclusive information is available. The following analysis of the results adopts the sequence of criteria that is set out in Appendix 2.

General coherence

Once all possible alignments were plotted on each plan, they were examined for potential schematic coherence and completeness. A coherent scheme is possible in all cases although discrepancies between the grid and irregularities in the structure are common.

The occurrence of geometric connections not coinciding with obvious points in the structure was noted for Cologne, Montier, Hildesheim, Fleury and Fulbert's Chartres. At St Peter in Rome, nine out of sixteen constructions coincided with bay 6 east of the *bema* which likewise seemed to lack any other architectural significance. The possibility these examples raise of schematic constructions being partly independent of building construction was reinforced by the thirteen cases where inner crossings were located within a greater crossing grid – independently of transepts being aisled or not – from which it was possible to generate the rest of the plan. Similarly, it was possible to deduce in all cases which steps could be causal and which consequential, since it was always possible to set out schematic grids from one single assumption.

Where inconsistencies occurred between a grid and the building plan, or within the building plan itself, possible causes for them were considered, such as changes in building campaign. This question did not apply, however, in eight cases. The displacement of piers from the grid of St Gall is likely to be explained by the method of producing the original drawing and then tracing it onto parchment.

The grid-lines for the *porticus* at St Pantaleon, defining outer and inner wall-faces, appear inconsistent with the rest of the grid, although they do align with the axis of a pair of external pilasters and the chord of the side apse. At Vignory, the mismatch with the north aisle was unexplained. So were instances of individual piers and pillars being slightly displaced in some other examples, together with a small discrepancy with the west crossing at Durham. Miscalculation in the original setting-out would nevertheless be a possible explanation in at least some of these cases. The possible mismatch with the east crossing piers at Norwich depends on how their north–south axis ought to be defined and this perhaps needs to remain an open question.

The slight discrepancy between the grid at St Peter's Basilica and its outer colonnade and aisle wall on the north side may well have arisen from their location over earlier foundations. Adjustment to earlier foundations could also explain inconsistencies at Montier and Chartres, as could simple building error, both there and at Vignory, Bernay, Gloucester, Tewkesbury and Toulouse.

The setting-out line for Montier bore no apparent relationship to the built structure and yet it does align with a conjectured bay division of its former westwork. The geometry at Durham produced two separate wall-grids which overlap in the nave and the changeover between the two exactly corresponds to an apparently deliberate change in pier spacing. A change in geometric systems in the naves at Norwich, Fleury and Toulouse revealed actual changes in arcade design. Mismatches between choirs, crossings and naves at Conques, Fleury, Tours and Toulouse could be the result of interruptions in campaigns.

At Chartres, the setting-out of the present west front and towers from the earlier grid confirms its construction history. Similarly, there is reason to believe that the setting-out west of the transept at St Maclou arose from pre-existing site conditions. The different aisle widths at Mont St Michel and the displacement of the south transept at Winchester and Ely could have resulted from adjustments needed in planning their cloister buildings.

In assessing the importance of these inconsistencies, it needs to be borne in mind that they amount only to odd occurrences in plans that otherwise match their proposed grids very closely.

If a notional tolerance of 3% for normal building error is applied, and since a discrepancy of 0.5% to 2% is visible to the eye, a wide range of building error is evident in the sample. However, in the three examples where a dimensional check was made, the plan of St Peter in Rome can be set out within 99.95% to 98.75% accuracy, with other alignments falling within a range of 99.66% to 99.20%; Hildesheim can be set out to an accuracy of 99.58%

to 98.99%; and the plan of St Maclou can be set out within a range of accuracy between 100% and 99.39%.

All examples answer to the geometry provided the irregularities in building construction, described in Chapter 6, are taken into account. Although such discrepancies are general, they are also mostly marginal. Hildesheim, Rome, Montier, Jumièges, Caen, Hereford, Conques, Chartres and Rouen appear to support the geometry proposed without further qualification. Cologne, St Pantaleon, Bernay, Mont St Michel, Norwich, Peterborough, Gloucester, Tewkesbury, Fleury, Nevers, Tours and Toulouse required subsidiary constructions to fix some of their apses.

St Gall and Vignory correlate with the geometry except for the north aisles of both and the north transept of St Gall, as does Mont St Michel except for a north transept which has been adapted to the topography. Winchester and Ely agree except for south transepts that could have been adjusted to accommodate cloister buildings. Two of the transept piers at Ely were not independently fixed, there was a slight mismatch with two crossing piers at Norwich and Durham and, with the exception of two pairs of transept piers, Tours answers to the geometry if allowance is made for a shift in its grid between the choir and nave.

The geometric constructions display a systematic evolution through time, which is clearly demonstrated by the increasing multiplicity of geometric connections, from rudimentary early examples such as St Gall and Cologne to the complexity of Durham and Toulouse. Hildesheim, for example, is more elaborate than Cologne Cathedral or St Pantaleon, Cologne. The precise correlation found at Rome could reflect a clearer understanding of applied geometry in late antiquity, as in other branches of learning, and it would not be surprising if any transmission of this in the early middle ages were less than perfect, leading to results that were more rudimentary.

Instances where geometric connections do not coincide with obvious points in the structure are concentrated among the early examples of Cologne, Montier, Fleury and Fulbert's Chartres and do not occur later, although the instance at Montier appears to correlate with its earlier westwork.

Once the greater crossing grid appears at Bernay, it occurs in one form or another in at least twelve out of eighteen succeeding examples, such exceptions as Chartres, which originally lacked a crossing, and Rouen, which seems to have been set out from an earlier transept, being nevertheless explicable. Finally, the coincidence of intersections by different sets of diagonals is found generally among the latest examples of Norwich, Peterborough, Gloucester, Tewkesbury, Durham, Tours and Toulouse.

Applicability

It was possible to deduce a method of design, starting from a single figure, in every case, the variations and omissions previously noted being excepted. The procedure could be commenced with a square in twenty-one cases: at St Gall, Cologne, St Pantaleon[1], Hildesheim, Rome, Montier, Vignory, Bernay,

Jumièges, Mont St Michel, Caen, Winchester, Norwich, Tewkesbury, Hereford, Durham, Conques, Nevers, Tours, Toulouse and Rouen. It started with a 36° rectangle at Ely, Peterborough and Gloucester; with either a 36° rectangle or a square at Montier, Vignory, Caen, Winchester, Ely, Norwich and Nevers; with a golden triangle at Fleury; with 60° rectangles at Chartres; and with the square, or rectangles with diagonals at 36° or 60° at Rouen.

The first three operations involved all three Platonic figures in twenty-two cases at St Gall, Cologne, St Pantaleon,[2] Hildesheim, Rome, Montier, Bernay, Jumièges, Mont St Michel, Caen, Winchester, Ely, Norwich, Peterborough, Gloucester, Hereford, Durham, Conques, Fleury, Tours, Toulouse and Rouen.

In every case, it was possible to reconstruct a notional planning grid, from which secondary elements could be generated. At St Gall, the grid may be more than notional for the drawing consists only of single lines which represent walls and the axes of piers. The available dimensions for St Peter in Rome and, likewise, Hildesheim and Rouen, were converted to a grid which the setting-out procedure answers to near-exactitude. With each example, secondary elements were generated from the main outline of the layout, not the other way about.

The reconstruction accounted for the whole layout at Cologne, Hildesheim, Rome, Jumièges, Caen, Hereford, Conques and Rouen. The reconstruction was also completed for Fleury and Chartres if allowance is made for general irregularities in these buildings and at Mont St Michel except for its north transept which has clearly been adapted to the topography. Gloucester was reconstructed apart from its apses and Bernay, Norwich, Peterborough, Tewkesbury, Nevers, Tours and Toulouse except for apsidal chapels, all of which variously require an extension of the geometric system to locate them, or are too irregular to answer to any regular system, or are no longer extant. This is also partially true of St Pantaleon. The plans of St Gall, Montier, Vignory, Winchester, Ely and Durham were also set out in their entirety but for the sole exceptions noted above.

Most surprising, the geometry accounted for a general irregularity in the spacing of piers in their arcades such as at Ely, Durham, Toulouse and Rouen, suggesting that the lack of regularity might be systematic.

A single grid was all that was required to set out seventeen of the plans. A single grid also sufficed at Winchester and Ely except for the slight displacement of their south transepts. If this was the result of adjustments made to accommodate the cloister buildings, it might suggest the employment of a separate grid, although this is not borne out by St Gall.

However, practical considerations such as this could well justify the separate grids encountered for the naves at Hereford and Durham in that their choirs are respectively wider and narrower than their naves and this could also have been the case with the earlier example of Bernay. Similarly the separate grids at Conques, Fleury, Nevers and Toulouse could be explained by their nave aisle walls needing to align outside the axis of their inner transept piers or outer choir aisle walls. The adjustment in the grid at Tours appears the result of a misalignment between its choir and crossing.

Outer grid-lines coincide with external walls in all examples although generally it was not possible to identify a consistent relationship between the two, such as an alignment with the inside or outside faces of walls. Given the five different positions implicit in Lechler's method,[3] perhaps this is not surprising. However in seven examples, wall-grids do align on or near the glass-line of windows for all or part of their plans. Out of a sample of twenty-six, this may be no more than chance yet, with the exception of Fleury, Nevers and Chartres, they happen to be Norman or Anglo-Norman and include not only Jumièges, Winchester and Durham but the group of neighbouring abbeys at Gloucester, Tewkesbury and Hereford.

All geometric connections appeared to intersect either with the grid or with other possible generating points in all cases. Instances where setting-out points evidently aligned either with parts of the structure having no other architectural significance, or to extensions of schematic grids beyond the confines of the built structure, have already been referred to above. It is worthwhile emphasizing, however, that the occurrence of the greater crossing grid in twelve out of eighteen examples after Bernay was unforeseen and only revealed by the test, yet in each case it could also generate the rest of each plan and enable transepts to be chosen with double or single side bays or none at all.

Widespread similarities in geometric configuration are apparent across the sample and occur within each group as well, with all examples capable of being set out through the systematic construction of planning grids and with the large majority starting with a square, using all three Platonic figures in the first three steps and a greater crossing, where a crossing was part of the original design. In addition to this, strong correspondences were found in the geometric constructions within groups of buildings that are not as common elsewhere. Conversely, where architectural similarities may be present in buildings of different groups, these were not accompanied by similarities in geometry other than those common across the sample. Also striking were cases of unexpected similarities in the geometry of buildings of different groups which, though not necessarily showing particular similarities in their architecture, turned out to be historically connected. From the sum of detailed evidence, it may suffice to cite just a few examples here.

Tours shares general similarities with Conques and Nevers, including a greater crossing and a square as a starting-point. Toulouse also displays the general similarities of Conques, Nevers and Tours, whilst the 60° end bays to the transept aisles and the common intersection of different diagonals are also found at Tours.

Strong similarities were found within the Norman and Anglo-Norman groups. In addition to all the general similarities noted above, both Bernay and Jumièges have square inner crossings, square aisle bays, 60° bays between the inner crossing and transepts and one instance of geometric harmony. Mont St Michel also has a square inner crossing, whilst the repetition of 60° nave bays and the long diagonals between transepts and nave resemble Bernay, also the 45° construction from the transept to the centre of the main apse recalls Jumièges. Caen shares general similarities with Bernay, Jumièges and Mont St

Michel. The 36° rectangles at its west end occur at Jumièges and Mont St Michel and it has square nave aisle bays in common with Bernay and Jumièges. Jumièges, on the other hand, for all its architectural correspondence with Hildesheim has less in common with its geometric construction except, interestingly enough, that the sequences for setting them out both start unusually with constructions eccentric to the main axis which can then be duplicated on the other side of it.

Winchester, one of the first Norman cathedrals to be built in England, has much in common with examples in Normandy. In addition once again to general similarities, the 60° bay between inner crossing and transepts and the square nave aisle bays are found at Bernay. The double-bay nave subdivision, square aisle bays, square greater crossing, 60° bay between inner crossing and transepts and the 36° construction for the transepts were all encountered at Jumièges. The 60° diagonals over the crossing and transepts and the instance of apparent geometric harmony resemble Mont St Michel, whilst the square nave and aisle bays and the 60° and 36° diagonals between transepts and nave were also found at Caen.

The architectural affinity between Winchester and Ely, especially apparent when their original layouts are restored, is fully matched by their geometric similarities. These are likely to be accounted for by the fact that Ely was planned under the abbacy of the recent prior of Winchester and brother of its bishop. No such likeness is evident between the architectural layouts of Winchester and Norwich, yet there are pronounced similarities in their geometry which may equally be explained by the presence of the same bishop of Winchester during the preparations for building the cathedral at Norwich. Peterborough was selected for its regional and evolutionary relationship to Ely and Norwich and its geometry turned out to be completely bound up with the whole group. For example, there were identical methods for commencing the setting-out, as between Winchester and Norwich and between Ely and Peterborough, as well as identical constructions for transepts at Winchester, Ely and Norwich, with similar geometry at Peterborough. There were also similar constructions for fixing the centre of the apse at Ely and Peterborough, the same overlap of 36° rectangles over the crossing at Ely, Norwich and Peterborough, also similar diagonals from transepts to fix nave bays at Ely and Peterborough. A modular repetition of nave bays is found at Winchester and Norwich, with a similar repetition of 36° rectangles, each divisible by three, down the main axis at Norwich and Peterborough; square bays at the ends of nave aisles at Winchester and Ely, with an identical termination at the west end also at Norwich and Peterborough; and there were more similarities besides.

A strong architectural resemblance between Tewkesbury and Gloucester, on the other hand, may be contrasted with their geometric differences. Nevertheless, the coincidence between grid and glass-line and the common intersection of different diagonals in the nave are found in both. Hereford's starting-point with a square, its square constructions north and south over the crossing and those over the choir, together with the 60° twin aisle bays, all resemble Tewkesbury, whilst the 60° diagonals from transepts to west end are also found at Tewkesbury and Gloucester. Interestingly, Hereford also displays several similarities with Durham which it succeeded by some seventeen years.

The degree of variety found within each group may be obvious even from a visual comparison of their plans. Beyond this, to the variations between Gloucester and Tewkesbury already mentioned may be added the zonal concentration of Platonic figures over Tewkesbury's plan, which also distinguishes Toulouse from its group. Similarly, the greater crossing at Toulouse can be set out just from a square and triangle, whilst Conques and Hereford are distinguished by golden triangles over their crossings.

Turning to Tewkesbury and Mont St Michel, there appears to be no reason why they should have anything particular in common, given their different locations and strikingly different architecture, Norman though it may be. Yet the first three steps in their setting-out are very similar, with each commencing with a square inner crossing and with 60° rectangles defining Mont St Michel's outer grid and Tewkesbury's first nave bay. In addition to this, the 60° diagonals from transepts to nave are very similar, whilst the pairs of 36° rectangles at the west end are identical. An historical explanation for this could well be provided by the fact that Tewkesbury was being built at the same time as Gloucester which in turn had been planned under the abbacy of a former student at Mont St Michel. As to Gloucester, the 45° and 60° diagonals from transepts to nave and the 60° diagonals and pairs of 36° rectangles in the nave are also found in the layout of Mont St Michel.

There might be even less reason to connect the Gothic cathedral at Chartres with Montier and Vignory from up to two hundred years earlier, or with the little Ottonian abbey of St Pantaleon in Cologne. Yet it has already been noted that the Gothic cathedral largely reused the substructure of Fulbert's cathedral, which had been erected shortly after 1020 when the building at St Pantaleon was just over twenty years old. Whilst there need not be a direct connection between the two, it must be a probability that Fulbert would have known something of the Cologne building if only for its imperial connections, the abbey having been re-founded by the brother of Otto I and finished on finance provided by Otto III. Both Otto III and Fulbert, it may be recalled, also shared Gerbert as their teacher. Be this as it may, it is at least possible that the layout of both projects could have been based on a system that was current at the time. Both were laid out with *porticus* flanking the east ends of their naves and both therefore lacked crossings. Flowing from this, it was discovered that the layout of Chartres could not be produced directly from its later Gothic crossing. Yet the investigation did reveal that the plans of St Pantaleon and Chartres can be set out from either their east or their west ends and, above all, are distinguished from the rest of the sample by the prevalence of the regular triangle over the other two Platonic figures. As for Montier and Vignory, they were built either side of Chartres in time and not that far away in France. They also lacked transepts and crossings and can only be set out from their west ends. Yet these instances of correlation between original plan typology and setting-out were only revealed by the geometry and were otherwise entirely unsuspected in advance of the investigation.

Geometric harmony

Another unexpected result of the investigation was the widespread incidence of apparent harmony between the three Platonic figures. All plans from Cologne Cathedral onwards answered to more alignments than were needed to set them out, as different geometric constructions involving two or more of the Platonic figures appeared to coincide with each other. One result of this was that several different alignments appeared to converge upon the same points in a plan, such as seven meeting over Hildesheim's crossing piers, six at Toulouse, five at Durham and Hereford. In addition to this, different sets of diagonals appeared to share common intersections with each other at Norwich, Peterborough, Gloucester, Tewkesbury, Durham, Tours and Toulouse, all of them, it may be noted, being relatively late examples.

Across the whole sample the division of a given distance equally into three was a necessary or optional part of the setting-out, as seen at Rome, Cologne, Hildesheim, Norwich, Peterborough and Tewkesbury. This can be executed simply through the division of a square and is shown by Serlio at the end of his *Libro primo d'architettura* dating from 1560 (fig. 24). Taking the form of a design exercise for a doorway, it demonstrates how its width between the jambs will be one-third of the base of the encompassing square, if set out from

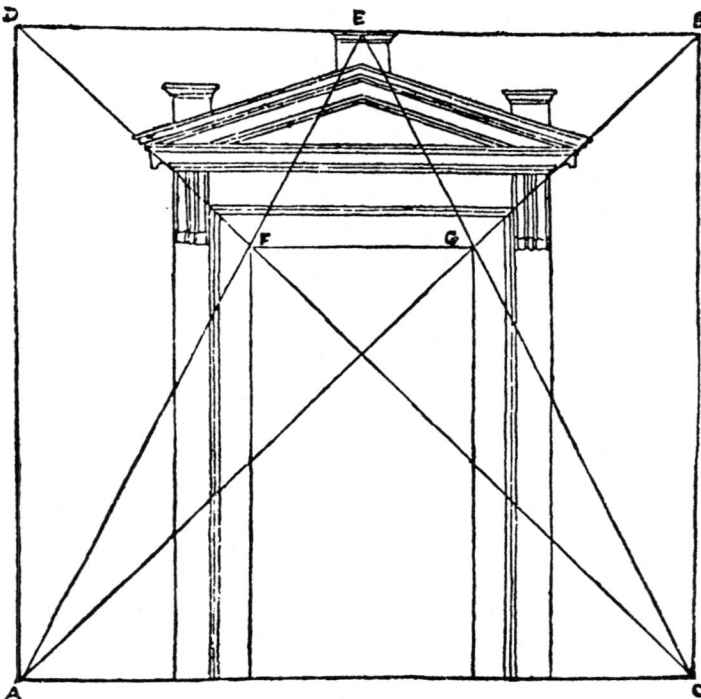

Fig. 24 Division of a length equally into three, after Serlio.

the intersection between the diagonal of the square and the diagonal of half the square. There seems to be no reason why this method should not have been known earlier in the middle ages.

In some instances, a division into three has not resulted in a similar architectural division. This either weakens the case or strengthens another – that of schematic construction and building construction being two distinct processes, such as is seen in the schematic prominence of the sixth nave bay at St Peter's Basilica and the widespread occurrence of the greater crossing grid across the sample. Just as the geometric similarities between Mont St Michel and Tewkesbury are not closely matched by their architecture, the architectural similarities of Hildesheim and Jumièges are not particularly matched by their geometry apart, that is, from the beginning of each procedure being on one side of their main axis.

In another category of geometric harmony, groups of compartments constructed from different Platonic angles appear to combine with each other to within 99.65% accuracy. They consist of a 60° rectangle containing a square and a 36° rectangle and were found at Hildesheim, Caen, Winchester, Norwich and Toulouse with a variant at Mont St Michel (pl. 106).

If a_1 = 1, then b_1 = 1 × tan 60° = 1.732

If a_2 = 1, then c = 1 × tan 36° = 0.726

b_2 = 1 + 0.726 = 1.726 = b_1 - 0.006 = 0.35%, i.e. 99.6% accuracy

A construction in which the angles of the regular triangle encompass those of the square and the pentagon in this way with seeming exactitude, would have appeared to be the most concise of all constructions to show the three Platonic figures in agreement with each other. Moreover, by superimposing the square over the 60° rectangle, such a construction could even have served as a method for arriving at the angles of the pentagon. Thus of all the examples of geometric harmony, this is arguably the most compelling in its simplicity and metaphysical import, a geometric counterpart to the numerical equation,

$$3^2 + 4^2 = 5^2$$

However, it needs to be stressed that no evidence has been encountered to suggest that this construction was either known or used. Yet for it to have been revealed by the investigation recurrently in various plans by nothing more than chance would surely be as remarkable as if it actually had been known and used by the architectural designers of the early medieval period, only to be rediscovered now. Although this will probably remain an imponderable, these different constructions are put forward because they were revealed by the investigation and do exist. Their employment would be entirely consistent with a desired expression of geometric harmony in design and their variation from exactitude is so small as to be imperceptible to the eye of someone using geometry for drawing yet lacking the theory to validate it. It may be recalled that Roriczer believed his method for constructing a pentagon was correct, yet not only is it incorrect, it is so by 4.9%, a margin he was evidently unable to detect.[4]

Conclusion

This chapter has set out to ascertain whether there is a degree of correlation between the geometric system proposed and authenticated drawings of plans of abbeys and cathedrals dating from the fourth to the fifteenth centuries.

The credibility of the results depends of course on the credibility of the evidence, including the methods used. For example, in assessing studies based on measurements taken from a particular building, it is reasonable to ask how the measurements may be verified. Similarly, in validating applications of geometry, how may their accuracy be judged? Ultimately where independent proof is lacking, the persuasiveness of the evidence must be a matter of individual judgment.

In each example investigated here, a schematic grid has been generated as distinct from the plan of the structure as built. This has resulted in variations between the two that are generally visible and can therefore facilitate a judgment being reached as to the degree of correlation present. Regarding accuracy, one numerical check of geometric harmony has shown it to be so close to exactitude as to be imperceptible to the eye. As regards the plans themselves, these were selected as originating in measured surveys against which the geometry was checked at the beginning, middle and end of the sample. As a result, St Peter's Basilica was found to fall within 99.95% to 98.75% accuracy over nearly 130 m, Hildesheim was accurate within a range of 99.58% and 98.99%, whilst Rouen also showed measurement and geometry matching each other virtually to exactitude.

As for other drawings used in the investigation, if any were to be found to be inaccurate, there is an even chance that more accurate drawings might reveal an even closer fit with the geometry proposed. All the same, the hypothetical instance of a plan being invalidated through inaccuracy would raise a question as to how the geometric system proposed might have happened to fit it in the first place. This in turn raises the question of the system itself being so versatile as to answer to plans not even designed by it, a possibility which will be discussed in the next chapter.

The geometric complexity of the results, however, may be thought surprising to say the least, although in the context of the time it could be argued that it might have been of advantage for a given system to be capable of as many harmonic connections as possible. Even so, it might still be considered that even the basic schemes for setting-out are too elaborate to be tenable, especially at such an early date. Yet the complexity is apparent mainly in the cumulative result. If each procedure is developed step by step, as shown here, then the operation is comparatively simple and hardly beyond such ingenuity as might be thought appropriate for framing a house of God. To this, however, might be added a further reservation as to how such a system might have been translated into a layout on site. Although it may be presumed that what was translated to site was the grid itself rather than the geometry that supposedly generated it, implementation might be more problematical for a grid consisting of the incommensurate proportions of geometric figures than for one generated numerically in the first place, a possibility which will also be discussed shortly.[5]

In the end, perhaps it is fair to conclude that whether this may have been a system that was actually used, or whether it is the result of a set of random coincidences, either would be equally remarkable. Whatever may be the case, the exercise conducted here at least shows that the plans tested are capable of the degree of geometric complexity demonstrated and that these geometric proportions are present in the buildings, which again may be thought remarkable in itself. It may also be fair to argue that offsetting any methodological objections are the size and breadth of the sample, the internal consistencies of the results within and between groups of buildings, the evolution of the system revealed through time, the unanticipated internal evidence suggesting the use of schematic design as distinct from constructional design, the equally unforeseen relationships between buildings not obviously connected with each other but which were only revealed through the geometry and, finally, the instances of geometric harmony.

Notes

1 Subsequent to the thesis.
2 Subsequent to the thesis.
3 See p. 198.
4 See p. 193.
5 See pp. 278–85.

Chapter 8

Counter Examples

Versatility and chance

The high degree of correlation revealed in the previous chapter between the system of Platonic geometry that has been proposed and plans of buildings from the middle ages might raise the question as to whether the system might be so versatile that layouts not designed in this way could still answer to it by chance.

Without proof that even the medieval examples investigated here were so designed, this must remain a theoretical possibility for all layouts. Each plan, embodying as it does the potential for numerous intersections within a supposed planning grid, provides many opportunities for connections to be made between them. Furthermore, unlike piers which, according to Villard de Honnecourt, could be related axially to such a grid, longitudinal wall-grids may be located anywhere within the ample thickness of their walls, thereby increasing the statistical possibility of a correlation. Moreover, given the angles employed in the test, namely 45°, 30° and 60° for the square and triangle, together with 18°, 36°, 54° and 72° for the pentagon, every point in a layout has twenty-eight possibilities of a connection being made with any other point. Given also the symmetrical arrangement of plans about their longitudinal axis, the number of points so connected will then be doubled.

So as to put the possibility of undue versatility to the test, the choice of counter examples has been based on the assumption that any medieval method of geometric design would no longer have been known or used for nineteenth-century iron-framed structures designed for secular use. Yet, in consisting of structural grids of repetitive bays divided into major and minor spans, even sometimes incorporating transepts and a crossing, such buildings are otherwise analogous to medieval abbeys and cathedrals. Accordingly, this sample consisted of plans of the Great Exhibition Building and Alexandra Palace, together with Smithfield Market which is illustrated here. To begin with, Truro Cathedral was included because, being a Gothic Revival design, its layout was presumably meant to resemble that of a medieval cathedral.

The graphic demonstration of negative evidence, however, is problematic. Whilst such connections as exist among this sample can be shown in the same manner as for the medieval layouts, the lack of more alignments can only be demonstrated by an absence of more lines. This may leave open to doubt whether additional connections could nevertheless be made, which is a doubt that ultimately may only be removed by independent attempts to make them.

Truro Cathedral

This was designed in 1880 by John Pearson and completed by his son to the original design in 1910. Geometric connections were found to be seriously incomplete, with some alignments occurring only singly, not in pairs, whilst several of the alignments only connected with separate parts of the grid which themselves were not connected. Because of this and the general incompleteness of the results, there was no possibility of setting out the plan beyond a number of individual compartments which remained unconnected with the others.

The Great Exhibition Building, London

The design of the 'Crystal Palace', which was erected in Regent's Park in 1851, was produced by the master-gardener Paxton in such a way as to take advantage of techniques of pre-fabrication. This relies upon optimum variety reduction and accordingly the layout consisted exclusively of a 24-foot square module repeated singly, doubly or in triplicate. It is for this reason that the plan answered comprehensively to the square.

As for the regular triangle and pentagon, three approximations to the former were apparent and one to the latter but these were all functions of the square module being repeated. For example, a rectangle of 4 : 7 units has a diagonal of 59.38°, one of 7 : 12 units 59.4°, and 11 : 19 units 59.83°. Against the 54° diagonal of a pentagon, a rectangle of 8 : 11 units has a diagonal of 53.96°.[1] Although these are close approximations, they occurred with the automatic repetitiveness of the basic module without beginning to offer any coherent system for setting out the plan beyond the repetition of that unit.

The Great Hall, Alexandra Palace, London

The structure that was ruined in the fire of 1980 was erected in 1875 to the design of J. Johnson. The Great Hall consisted of a nave of fifteen bays with double aisles either side. Wrought iron arches over the nave and lattice girders across the aisles were each supported on separate cast iron columns, resulting in columns standing in pairs down each side of the nave. The dimensions used in the test were provided by Peter Smith and were derived from a Greater London Council survey of about 1973.

The duplicate grid-lines and groups of columns served to increase the possibility of geometric connections being made. However, various diagonals at 45° were a function once again of the dimensions used for the grid, for example square bays of twenty-five feet which, as with the Crystal Palace, can hardly be claimed as expressing Plato's cosmology. Several other alignments involved angles of the regular triangle and pentagon, yet many failed to connect; other parts of the layout also remained unconnected and it was impossible to set out the plan from this either systematically or otherwise.

Thus, although the geometric method as proposed was sufficiently versatile for various unintended connections to be made, it could be seen that those alignments were insufficiently complete or co-ordinated in comparison with the medieval examples to enable the whole layout to be set out either from a single operation or in any other way.

Smithfield Market, London (pl. 107)[2]

This was built in 1866 by Horace Jones, who was the city surveyor and also the designer of Billingsgate and Leadenhall Markets. It is bisected north–south by Grand Avenue and east–west by Buyers' Walk. Three avenues run parallel to Grand Avenue either side of it. The blocks between these avenues contain the butchers' premises with their iron frames for hanging carcases. Offices and changing rooms are in large cabins elevated above them on more iron columns.

The total structure is organized less rationally than might be expected, falling into five different systems which are only partly co-ordinated with each other or not at all.

1   Grand Avenue is roofed with trusses supported on columns at every bay.

2   The roof trusses over Buyers' Walk are supported at alternate bays. Either side of them runs an aisle-like structure with a high-level lean-to roof. The size of its bays not only differs from those of Buyers' Walk, its structure is supported every third bay.

3   Three parallel roofs run from east to west between these aisles and the long elevations. The width of each roof truss equals two bays of Grand Avenue, at the junction with which the structure is terminated on square columns placed back-to-back with the round columns carrying the Grand Avenue roof. The parallel roofs are supported on columns longitudinally at every third bay of the aisle structure. This spacing, however, only approximates to the positions of the side avenues which are determined by the module of the external masonry elevations which is different again.

4   The structure that supports the raised offices is independent of the structure carrying the roofs.

5   The meat-hanging frames are improvised in among the grids of the elevated offices and the aisles along Buyers' Walk and also serve to demarcate the side avenues. Sometimes they align with one grid or another, or sometimes they follow a localized module of their own.

The result is a multiplicity of grids and column positions offering considerable potential for geometrical connections to be found. For the purposes of the test, grid intersections were accepted where marked by columns or by beams meeting external walls, though not where different grids passed over each other at unconnected levels. The test was conducted on a dye-line print of the 1 : 100 survey drawing and a reduced photocopy was then marked up for reproduction here.

It is immediately apparent that numerous geometric connections are possible and they include a small amount of repetition, such as the 36° diagonals over some of the bays of Buyers' Walk and near the south-east corner, the latter overlapping with two bays of 60° diagonals. There is also a number of small square bays in the meat-hanging grid either side of the avenues south of Buyers' Walk. It may be concluded therefore that the geometric system that is put forward in this study is sufficiently versatile to answer to structures that would not have been designed by it. Yet the connections are generally random, including single diagonals over incomplete rectangles or over quadrilaterals with one side out of square or, as with Truro Cathedral, with other diagonals connecting different grids that are otherwise unrelated to each other. As a result, the alignments are unsystematic and incapable of providing a method for setting out the plan. On the contrary, despite the mass of alignments shown, the main structural grids of Grand Avenue, Buyers' Walk and the parallel roofs over the rest of the market remain entirely unaccounted for by the test.

Conclusion

Whilst the geometric system is versatile enough to permit unintended connections, there is a complete absence of any overall pattern in these examples in comparison with, say, Ely Cathedral or St Sernin, Toulouse. It may be reasonable to ask, therefore, if the system is not present in plans that are unlikely to have employed Platonic geometry, why is it so abundantly present in plans that historically had good reason to employ it?

It is hardly likely to be by chance that the system only fits medieval plans and not post-medieval plans. Even if the system did fit medieval plans by chance because of an intrinsic versatility, random coincidences would produce random connections, as in the case of Smithfield, without any governing pattern necessarily being apparent. Yet many similarities have been demonstrated across the whole medieval sample that provide a complete or near-complete design method in every case and include a square or a 36° rectangle as a starting-point followed by the remaining Platonic figures, as well as the frequent recurrence of the greater crossing as a generator and many other detailed similarities noted within known architectural groups. Mere chance is also unlikely to produce so many examples where up to seven alignments converge on a single point in a plan with apparent exactitude or where intersections of different diagonals coincide with each other in space. Even variable wall-grids in relation to wall thickness could be the result of an adaptible system such as that demonstrated by Lechler, several for example aligning on or near the glass-line. Finally, is it likely that chance born of an over-versatile system would accidentally produce a method for setting out the plan of St Peter's Basilica in just eight operations to a minimum calculated accuracy of 99.11% over distances up to 129 m, or Hildesheim to a minimum of 98.99% or St Maclou to an accuracy of 99.39%?

It cannot be denied, however, that the system is sufficiently versatile to permit the schematic coherence revealed in the medieval sample. Yet, as it has already been argued, such versatility in a supposed method of design could well have been regarded as an advantage early in the middle ages for the very reason that it did increase the number of harmonic connections that could be made.

To conclude, it may be useful to identify the technical difference between the medieval and nineteenth-century examples that might explain why the system fits one and not the other. The reason why the later examples show the system to be insufficiently versatile to account for their layouts could be that the regularity of their planning grids results from the dictates of structural prefabrication and it could be the variability of medieval structures that provides the potential for such a system to permit connections, whether intended or not. Truro Cathedral, however, which is sufficiently irregular to provide a similar opportunity, appears to refute this. The explanation therefore could well turn on whether or not all medieval irregularities were accidental or whether some might actually have been intentional. Many irregularities noted, such as skewed walls and arcades and misaligned piers, must undoubtedly be the result of building error. Yet, for all the difficulties discussed in setting out complex layouts without modern surveying techniques, one of the simplest procedures to get right would have been the equal spacing of arcade piers using a single yardstick. However, such projects as Ely, Durham and especially St Maclou, which appear so accomplished in every other respect, display significant divergences in the spacing of their piers that seem at once irrational metrologically yet rational geometrically. If their spacing did vary as a function of the geometry, this could explain why so many connections are possible in medieval structures but not Truro, which is also irregular, nor in other structures which are merely mechanically regular. Surprising though this suggestion may be, the proposed system is able to account for these structures as built in all their irregularity.

Notes

1   See pp. 280 fig. 25c, 281.
2   After plan by Sterling 1986. The description that follows is the result of a site inspection that was made prior to the modernization of the market, which has now been carried out by the Corporation of London, the market's owner.

PART FOUR

Conclusions

Chapter 9

Findings, Conclusions and Implementation

The starting-point of this study lay in two alternative contentions; either that there is only evidence for geometry being used by masons as a practical procedure, or that geometry was used in architectural design in expression of universal beliefs. This raised two questions. Firstly, would the use of the geometry of the square, the regular triangle and the regular pentagon in the planning of medieval abbeys and cathedrals be consistent with the known historical context, particularly with regard to the beliefs held by the Church and the working methods used by the masons? Secondly, is there any correlation between the geometry proposed and authenticated plans of medieval abbeys and cathedrals? As a supplement to this second question, can it be answered in a way that takes account of various methodological objections that have been raised?

The purpose of this chapter, therefore, will be to summarize the sequence of findings from the earlier parts of the study and to draw from these the main conclusions. For any theory of design to be tenable, however, it must be capable of implementation. Accordingly, this chapter will conclude by showing how the system of Platonic geometry proposed here could have been translated from tracing-house to building site. By way of a postscript, Chapter 10 will explore further questions that would flow from an assumption that this system of design was actually used. For example, why should there be a lack of proof of its use in the historical record? What sources could there have been for such a system? And what may its subsequent history have been in relation to the known facts?

Summary of findings

An examination of the history of tenth-century Europe shows that a widespread resurgence in monastic life formed an important part of the cultural revival that took place under the Ottonian dynasty. This was accompanied by a revival in learning in the monastic schools which comprised the study not only of scripture but of the liberal arts as well which presented a largely Platonic view of the created universe. The monastic revival was also accompanied by reform, rebuilding and new building, involving individuals who were themselves educated, often known to each other and active at the highest levels of Church and State.

The Platonic thought inherited by tenth-century scholars had been transmitted by early Christian and non-Christian writers and posited a divine Creator bringing into being cosmos out of chaos in which harmony was maintained by the constituent parts of creation being formed in proportion to each other and to the whole. This divine order was to be apprehended partly through the study of the liberal arts culminating in the *quadrivium* of arithmetic, music, geometry and astronomy. The content of these writings reached the Latin middle ages indirectly from the Greek Fathers and directly from the Latin encyclopedists and became accepted by the Latin Church in the form of Christian Platonism principally through the influence of Augustine.

The exposition of these texts would generally have been made to novitiates within the cloister, for whom the three-part division of Christian philosophy was as rationally organized as were the subjects of the liberal arts. Foremost among these were arithmetic in signifying the divine order and geometry in exemplifying abstract essence. Geometry provided the basis for the practice of architecture which in turn commonly served as a metaphor for the divine creation. Just as Noah's Ark stands as a biblical model of salvation, so the octagonal shrine stands as an architectural model in which number, geometry, liturgical function and inaugural dedication come together in signifying salvation architecturally. Given such a correlation between metaphysical belief and architectural form in a case where the use of architectural geometry is self-evident, it would be consistent for geometry to be similarly deployed in the layouts of other religious buildings such as cruciform churches where its use is not necessarily so self-evident. Considering the pervasiveness of the first three figurate numbers in the foundation of the Christian Platonist universe and their habitual expression in terms of geometry, it is argued here that the historical context of the tenth century does justify the choice of the triangle, square and pentagon for testing against the plans of abbeys and cathedrals.

The monastic revival of the tenth century was seen to produce a second wave of larger and more complex building from around the middle of the century in which clerical founders were described either as architects, or as operating as architects, in imparting certain aspects of design to the masons.[1] In these historical personalities may possibly be seen both the scholar-theologian and the architectural programmer combined at the very time when contemporary writing was stressing the belief that God had created the world according to measure, number and weight.[2] Whilst several ninth- and tenth-century abbeys can be interpreted numerologically, Aachen, St Emmeram and the New Minster at Winchester actually carry contemporary indications that they were intentionally designed in this way.[3] Although this falls short of proving that geometry was also employed symbolically in architecture, Ramsey Abbey was said to have been made cruciform in conscious expression of the cross of salvation[4] and the design of both Aachen and St Bénigne was based on the octagon at a time when geometric figures were used didactically in text-books and expressively in manuscript illumination, sometimes under the direction of the same churchmen who were building abbeys, such as Ethelwold and William of Volpiano.[5]

As for the evidence of medieval architectural practice, not only does this point to working methods that were geometric, but the *Plan of St Gall* and the *Sketchbook* of Villard de Honnecourt actually portray planning grids of squares and other geometric proportions. Arguments that geometry, in the form of quadrature, was only used as a practical procedure devoid of symbolic intent seem to overlook, on the one hand, the dearth of documentary evidence for quadrature in the planning of complete layouts and the plentiful evidence, on the other, that it was deployed in the construction of architectural elements and details after the groundplan had been given. These arguments also overlook the Platonic dimension of quadrature, resulting as it does in modules and details that are proportionally related to each other and to the whole. Moreover, besides quadrature, Villard displays a routine familiarity with all the figures of Platonic geometry, whether or not he understood their symbolic import, and this is in noted contrast to the evident novelty to him of a Cistercian plan that consists only of squares. Whereas there is nothing in the documentary record to indicate that Platonic geometry could not have been used, the architectural record confirms that it was for, in addition to the undisputed employment of the square and the regular triangle in architectural design, structures from the Mausoleum of Theodoric in the sixth century to the Chapter House of Lincoln Cathedral in the thirteenth prove that architects also knew how to construct the pentagon even though their method may have been empirical. It is clear, however, that the translation of a drawn layout to site layout presented several opportunities for inaccuracy to occur and it is evident both from known working practices and from the built results that precision was rare. In order, therefore, to recover any schematic design, if one existed, it is necessary to determine what might have been meant, as distinct from what was built.

For the purposes of the investigation itself, every care was taken to secure the greatest accuracy for the drawings, in both their selection and their reproduction, and objective criteria were formulated for the investigation to satisfy. These were devised to establish whether the geometric system proposed here could provide a complete design method within the known competence of medieval architects and in a way that revealed both variety and consistency within groups of buildings generically related.

Excepting certain details in some of the layouts, the application of Platonic geometry accounted for the plans and satisfied the criteria in twenty-six examples, that is, in every case for which reliable drawings were available. Mismatches noted between the conjectured grids and the built results were usually explainable by likely errors in setting out the building or by other practical considerations. In the case of four examples an isolated inconsistency in the layout was left unexplained. Against this, a complete setting-out sequence was otherwise possible in each case and the application of the system displayed a clear evolution through time with demonstrable similarities between known architectural groups being balanced by a degree of individuality. Furthermore, the investigation revealed correspondences that had not been anticipated. These included similarities in the geometry of buildings not thought to be related but which turned out to have particular historical or architectural connections; the recurrence of similar schematic grids independent of the built structure; and instances of apparent harmony between the geometric figures, including one in which angles of all three Platonic figures meet in agreement with apparent exactitude.[6] In anticipation of a possible objection to the drawn evidence, namely the absence of dimensional verification, such verification has been provided in three cases, which were found to answer to the system to near-exactitude.[7] On the other hand, any drawings that might be more accurate than those used might just as easily reveal an even closer correlation with the geometry. Against a second possible objection as to the apparent complexity of the geometry as demonstrated, the basic operations needed for setting out each grid are simple, especially in the way they progress step by step. Furthermore, the capacity of the system to permit numerous harmonic connections could in any case have been thought desirable.

Finally, the possibility that the foregoing results were achieved because the proposed system may be unduly versatile was also put to the test against four analogous examples from the nineteenth century. Whilst various random geometric connections proved possible among them, no coherent pattern was revealed in any one case, still less a complete design method, in contrast to all the medieval examples. One possible explanation for this in the case of iron-framed structures is that they are mechanically regular whereas it could be the existence of variation in their medieval counterparts that allows connections to occur. The fact that this did not hold true for Truro Cathedral, despite equivalent irregularities in its layout, raised the surprising possibility that some of the variations in medieval structures could be the result of design, not accident. The irregular pier spacing in Durham's nave and at St Maclou were clearly intended and both answer to the geometric system proposed.

Main conclusions

In answer to the first question posed by this study, as to whether the use of a system of Platonic geometry in architectural design would be consistent with the known historical context, this does appear to be the case. The teaching of Christian Platonism resulted in meaning habitually being attached to numbers and geometric figures, with the first three figurate numbers implicitly acknowledged as lying at the foundation of the created universe. The monastic revival throughout Ottonian Europe provided the opportunity for widespread building and rebuilding directed by abbots and bishops who were not only educated but were frequently regarded at the time as architects in relation to their projects. At the same time, number and geometry were being used in expression of metaphysical beliefs in plays, literature, manuscript illumination, religious metalwork, frescoes, reliefs and the liturgy. With evidence that number was also used expressively in the layout of religious architecture, it would not only be consistent for geometry to have been used in this way as well, but also desirable in order to maintain the integrity of the Platonist scheme. Both the octagonal shrine and the cruciform church suggest that it was. Beside this therefore, it seems reasonable to assert that, alongside other systems including designing *ad quadratum*, the figures of Platonic geometry could also have been employed in laying out monastic and cathedral churches. This would be entirely within the known competence of medieval architects as attested by both drawn and built evidence and there is no evidence that it could not have been used. On the contrary, the documentary and architectural record show that all three of the Platonic figures were used in architectural design.

In answer to the second question, as to whether a correlation exists between a system of Platonic geometry and plans of early medieval abbeys and cathedrals, a high degree of correlation is evident in the plans investigated. Beyond a simple correlation, moreover, once allowance is made for apparent anomalies and errors in setting out some of the buildings, a procedure has been demonstrated for designing the layout of each building and the application has been shown to evolve through time across the sample as well as displaying similarities between buildings known to be related to each other. Though the procedure itself is simple and systematic, the end result appears complex, particularly for such an early date. Difficult though this may be to contemplate, it is equally difficult to suppose that the entire exercise is the result of chance. For it to have been caused by inaccuracies in drawings or technique for example, various forms of error would have needed to combine with each other in such a way that exactly coincides with the outcome of applying the same system across the whole sample. The possibility of its being the result of undue versatility also appears refuted by the failure of analogous examples from the nineteenth century to show a similar correlation. Since the geometry fails to fit post-medieval plans by chance, it can hardly be by chance that it happens to fit medieval plans. Put another way, whilst the procedure did not fit those plans that would not have employed Platonic geometry in the first place, it is abundantly present in those plans that historically had every reason to use it. Given the lack of proof, however, the surest conclusion of all is that it would be as remarkable for the findings of this study to be the result of chance coincidence as it would be that architects early in the middle ages actually did design in this way. At the very least, it shows there are alternative geometric proportions present in medieval architecture to those commonly advanced in the literature.

The most compelling evidence perhaps is what the geometry reveals about the buildings themselves, for this was completely unforeseen and only became apparent as the investigation unfolded. For example, similarities in geometry led to uncovering an unsuspected historical connection between Tewkesbury and Mont St Michel. Other similarities in geometric constructions across the sample, including the prevalence of a greater crossing and the grouping of arcade bays by threes, the detailed similarities found within groups of buildings generically related and various instances where diagonals of different figures coincide with each other, may indeed point to a general design method. Yet, persuasive though this evidence may be, it is not generally visible in the architecture. Examples where it is, however, include Norwich where a change in geometry marks a change formerly visible in the nave; Durham where a change in wall-grids coincides with a change in pier spacing; Fleury where a change in geometry in the nave pointed to a change in its detailed design, not the other way around; and Toulouse where the interplay between variations in design and variations in geometry has yielded a scheme of distinct layers, each one rational and coherent in its own right. This was only fully revealed when St Sernin was re-visited and re-examined in the light of the initial investigation. Finally, the failure to set out Chartres directly from its crossing led back to the layout of Fulbert's cathedral underlying it. This placed it instead in a contemporary group of buildings characterized by St Pantaleon, Montier and Vignory, all four of which originally lacked crossings and transepts and which have to be set out either from their west ends or from both ends.

Yet one final question remains as to how a method of design, which is based on geometric proportions and therefore produces lengths that are incommensurable, could possibly be translated into a set of dimensions for setting out on site. Without a solution to this, any geometric theory, however plausible, is likely to remain the equivalent of π in the sky.

Translation to site[8]

Since any schematic design would have needed to be converted into a set of dimensions for it to be built, the value of using geometry in the first place may itself be questioned – even more so a geometric system that produces incommensurate proportions from which linear measurements cannot be directly derived. Yet St Peter's Old Basilica, Hildesheim and Rouen show how a layout can answer to such a system to near-exactitude and still yield whatever dimensions were necessary for their construction.

The simplest system for providing the necessary dimensions would be one consisting of a grid of squares such as the *Plan of St Gall* or Villard's sketch of a Cistercian church. Once a measurement is assigned to one side of one of the squares, the entire layout can be translated directly to site. Thus, were expediency the object, then designing *ad quadratum* could be expected to be the rule, but it is not. Far more common are plans where the proportions of individual bays and of whole layouts are obviously incommensurate. Akin to this, it has been shown that variations in the spacing of arcade piers, at Durham and Rouen for example, are such that they must be the result of design rather than accident. Clearly in such cases, proportions other than a simple repetitive system were being preferred despite the greater presumed difficulty in translating them into a set of dimensions. The exercise of this preference therefore seems to point to the existence of a means of making the conversion.

Although the documentary evidence shows that the designing of a plan on parchment and laying it out on site both depended on the employment of geometry, the precise connection between design and dimension remains elusive. One possibility has already been raised,[9] namely the conversion on site of a planning grid into a building plan through squaring, using pegs and cords. It might have been possible for the plan of a building to be extrapolated from the grid by resolving any incommensurable ratios inherent in the grid into the type of square schematism sometimes found in the dimensions of a building, especially when measured between walls. Thus by swinging arcs with a cord from one peg after another, squares, double squares and the sides and diagonals of squares would result and possibly wall thicknesses could be determined. For the present, however, this necessarily remains conjectural. To return therefore to the documentary evidence, Vitruvius states:

> Dimension is the taking of modules from the parts of the work

De architectura I.2.1

It has been suggested that a procedure for doing this is evident in the *Regensburg Ordinances* of 1514 with reference in Article 13 to instruction 'on how to take the extrapolation device from the base plan'.[10] However, since the device is not described, it could equally refer to the technique of taking the elevation from the plan, especially since Regensburg was the city of Roriczer who had already published a description of the procedure through the application of quadrature. Lechler, early in the sixteenth century, then went on to show how the same operation could be used for generating the profiles and proportions of architectural details from a given module. In his example, not only was the module a particular width assigned to a wall but the procedure also allowed him to position the wall in relation to the planning grid. Thus, in enabling masons to size, profile and elevate their masonry details from a single module taken from the plan, the technique of quadrature could well be the extrapolation device mentioned in the *Ordinances*. Yet there is nothing to suggest that it was also the means of translating the plan from drawing to site. The *Tirol Hüttenbuch* of 1460, for example, refers to devising 'a stone structure by means of measures *or* by the extrapolation device'.[11] This suggests that the derivation of measures was a separate process from the extrapolation device, a distinction which would be borne out by Lechler were the device to be quadrature, because he reveals that its operation depended on the groundplan already being in place. This being the case, the method of translating the design into a site layout still remains to be determined.

Such a method, however, may be alluded to in the assertion by Vitruvius that has already been encountered, when he states that:

> Proportion consists in taking a fixed module . . . both for the parts of a building and for the whole . . . .

De architectura III.1.1

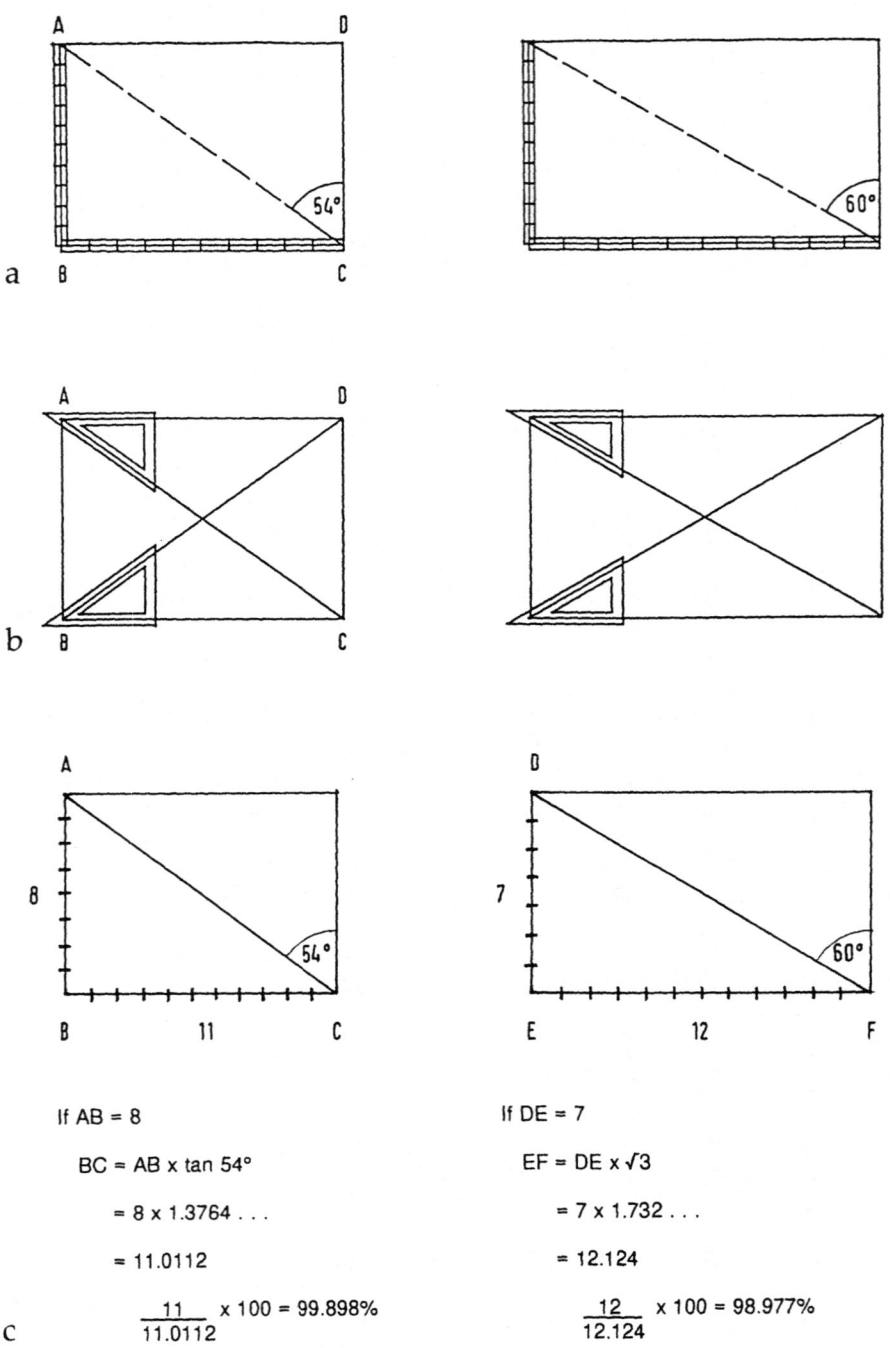

If AB = 8

   BC = AB x tan 54°

     = 8 x 1.3764 . . .

     = 11.0112

     $\dfrac{11}{11.0112}$ x 100 = 99.898%

If DE = 7

   EF = DE x √3

     = 7 x 1.732 . . .

     = 12.124

     $\dfrac{12}{12.124}$ x 100 = 98.977%

Fig. 25 Translation of layout to site, a: Enlargement by multiplication, b: By the projection of a diagonal, c: By numerical ratios.

To discover what this could mean, it may be useful to return to descriptions of medieval buildings being set out on their sites. In the tenth century, Oswald expected his masons to set out the foundations of Ramsey Abbey with straight lines, a 'threefold triangle' and compasses.[12] In the twelfth century, Gunzo's dream of the new Cluny involved Sts Peter and Paul plying ropes to trace out lines of intersecting diagonals across the site.[13] At about the same time, Gerald's dream of the king's son laying out a new church in Ireland also described making lines over the site in order to draw the plan of a building.[14] All these references clearly confirm a geometric procedure, yet the question remains as to how an architect could assign a dimension to one part of his layout and extrapolate the others when the proportions of the layout were incommensurable. Two of the most common proportions to emerge from the geometric investigation were rectangles defined by diagonals set at 60° for the triangle and 54° for the pentagon. If a dimension be given to the short side of each rectangle, representing for example a bay and therefore the distance between arcade piers, how would a medieval architect arrive at the long dimension for the width of the nave or choir, without the knowledge that their sides are in the ratio respectively of $1 : \sqrt{3}$ and $1 : \tan 54°$?

Perhaps the simplest method would be to take the rectangle from the drawing and enlarge it by a single factor using a pair of dividers (fig. 25a). The degree of magnification required, as suggested by surviving medieval drawings, might be in the region of 1 : 100, which would be laborious to repeat across the site and open to cumulative error. To overcome this, it would be possible to enlarge each side of the rectangle from the drawing by ten, marking this on rods or wooden laths. These could then be used to mark out the rectangles on site to full size by laying out the laths a further ten times along the respective sides of each rectangle. Such a process may be implied by the reference to 'latlaying' the groundwork in a fifteenth-century contract for Fotheringhay Church.[15]

Another possibility would be to reproduce the proportions of the rectangle on site by reproducing the diagonal that supposedly proportioned it on the drawing (fig. 25b). Although the architectural evidence confirms that architects knew how to draw the figures of Platonic geometry, it is not known how they constructed the angles of the pentagon, although the use of templates remains a strong possibility both in the tracing-house and on site. For example, a rectangle could be set out on the tracing-floor or in the yard and again magnified by ten. From this, a large triangle could be fabricated from laths and used in conjunction with cords for projecting the same diagonal on site, as perhaps indicated in the illustration of Gunzo's dream and in accordance with Oswald's reference to a threefold triangle.

A third possibility could be to estimate the proportion of the rectangle when compared to a square equal to its short side, since the square can be measured out on site without difficulty (fig. 25c). It turns out that a rectangle with sides 7 : 12 coincides with one defined by a 60° rectangle to 98.977%[16] accuracy and a rectangle proportioned 8 : 11 coincides with a 54° rectangle to 99.398%,[17] which margins would be imperceptible to anyone using geometry for draughting or surveying. Once these ratios were established, they could then be translated directly into dimensions.

For the investigation, these two particular ratios were arrived at with just a pair of dividers and less than a minute of experimentation. It was a procedure that did not have to rely on the pre-existence of tables of numerical ratios or any other knowledge external to the lodge. Yet for these proportions to have been regularly employed, the numerical ratios for reproducing them would have needed to be part of the knowledge of the lodge. As it happens, it has already been shown that there is historical evidence of masons actually working with ratios such as these. Among the exemplars added to Villard's *Sketchbook*, it may be recalled that there are several diagrams subdivided into certain numbers of parts (fig. 11). In addition to those that are concerned with the cutting and setting of stone is the diagram that demonstrates how to set out the angle of a spire using a triangular template in the ratio of 1 : 8.[18]

Since all the methods required are empirical, needing no more than pegs, cords, dividers and triangular set-squares, they would be well within the competence of medieval architects. Thus the investigation concludes by contending that the figures of Platonic geometry not only fit the historical context and the plans tested, but they can also provide a system that was workable. In order to summarize the complete case, it is now proposed to outline how the whole process could have been implemented from tracing-house to building site.

Case study: St Michael's Abbey, Hildesheim

Relevant material from this study is now assembled as a brief extract in order to demonstrate how a planning grid can be produced, translated to site and converted into a dimensioned building plan in four stages in a manner supported by medieval evidence. For the supporting data, see Appendix 3.

Stage 1: Designing the grid

The first three steps of the procedure for Hildesheim have been selected because they are generated by each of the Platonic figures (pl. 27).

Step (1) consists of the 45° diagonals of a square defining the east crossing and therefore the transept lengths and main arcades.
Step (2) employs the 36° diagonals of the pentagon to fix the centre-line of the side apse and axial pier terminating each aisle.
Step (3) uses the 60° sides of the triangle to define the transept arcade and the aisle wall, approximating to its inner face.

The square and the sides of the triangle can be described with compasses. The sides of the triangle and diagonals of the pentagon can be produced either from templates or from numerical ratios. A template would have been required for the inscription of the equilateral and other triangles at Vignory (pl. 15), whilst knowledge of constructing the pentagram is attested by Villard's *Sketchbook* (fig. 16) and the north transept window at Amiens.

The resultant grid was tested against a set of dimensions independently provided. These were averaged and converted to a dimensioned planning grid (pl. 32).

The diagonal that was posited for each step of the geometric setting-out, together with the rectangle it defines, was extracted from the plan. Each rectangle is shown with measurements derived from the building. A second lateral measure was then calculated from the longitudinal dimension by trigonometry using $\sqrt{3}$ for the triangle and tangent 36° and 54° for the pentagon. This mathematically correct value is shown below the measured dimension and the difference between the two expressed as a percentage.

Step (1) was taken to result in a square of the dimensions averaged.
Step (2), using the diagonal of the pentagon, is accurate to 99.58%.
Step (3), using the side of the triangle, is accurate to 99.21%.

The overall range of accuracy was found to lie between 99.58% and 98.99%. Margins such as these would have been imperceptible to anyone using geometry for drawing in the middle ages yet lacking the theory to validate it.

Stage 2: Assigning the measure

A particular measure could have been selected as a module and assigned to any part of the grid, such as the side of the square in step (1). The dimensions of the grid approximate very closely in whole numbers to the royal foot of 32.48 cm proposed by Roggenkamp, although a different unit is advanced for the abbey.

For step (1), square bays of 30 royal feet would measure 974.4 cm instead of 964.625 cm, that is, within 98.99%.
For step (2), 40 feet measures 1299.2 cm instead of 1322.125 cm, which is within 98.27%.
For step (3), 51 feet comes to 1656.48 cm as against 1657.565 cm, which is accurate to 99.93%.
Finally, 63 feet extends to the mid-point of the transept wall, measuring 2046.24 cm against 2047.935 cm, which is 99.92% accurate.

Stage 3: Laying out on site

A procedure is referred to in two twelfth-century descriptions of dreams, of 'holding surveyor's cords and . . . measuring the length and width' and 'after the fashion of surveyors, he marked the turf making lines on all sides over the surface of the earth, visibly drawing the plan of a building'.[19]

For Hildesheim, any unit of measure could be applied directly for setting out step (1), being a square. Steps (2) and (3), however, being rectangles generated by the sides of the regular triangle and the diagonal of the pentagon, have lengths that are incommensurable from which linear measurements cannot be directly derived. However, by taking these two rectangles as representing a nave, for instance, or a single bay, and assigning a dimension to the shorter side, AB, the following methods can determine the length of the longer side, BC (fig. 25).

Enlargement by multiplication The simplest method is to take the rectangle from its supposed drawing and enlarge it by multiplication using dividers. The scale of medieval plans suggests a degree of magnification in the region of 100. The sides of the rectangle can be enlarged first by ten in the masons' yard and marked on wooden laths. These could then be used to mark out the rectangle to full size by laying them out ten times along their respective lines on site. Thus the short side AB on the drawing would become AB x 10 on its lath and (AB × 10) × 10 on site. This could well be implied by the reference to 'latlaying' the groundwork in the fifteenth-century contract for Fotheringhay mentioned above.

Projection of diagonal   A second possibility fixes each rectangle on site by reproducing the diagonal that proportioned it on the drawing. Thus the rectangle is set out on the tracing-floor or in the yard, magnified again by ten. A large triangle is made out of laths and used for projecting the diagonal AC by cord across the site from DAB until it strikes BC. This appears supported by 'the threefold triangle' mentioned in the setting-out of Ramsey Abbey and with the laying out of ropes diagonally across the site for Cluny (pl. 16).[20]

Enlargement by proportion The third method reproduces the proportion of each rectangle by using numerical ratios. A rectangle with sides 7 : 12 coincides with one defined by 60° diagonals to 98.98%, while one proportioned 8 : 11 coincides to 99.9% with a rectangle having 36° diagonals. It would be a simple matter to convert these ratios into dimensions. That masons actually worked with ratios such as these is borne out by leaves added to the *Sketchbook* of Villard, in particular fol. 20v which shows how to set the angle of a spire using a template calibrated 1 : 8 (fig. 11), as already mentioned.

Stage 4: Setting out the structure

Any of the foregoing methods would result in a planning grid being laid out to full-size on site. To convert it into the plan of the structure to be built, piers, walls and architectural details can be set out as follows.

Piers can be located at grid intersections, according once again to the *Plan of St Gall* and Villard's *Sketchbook* (pl. 1, fig. 17).[21]

Walls can be set out from the grid as later demonstrated by Lechler's *Unterweisung* which shows a square divided 3 × 3.[22] This equates with the thickness of a choir wall and shows how this can be centred on the grid, or aligned along its inner or outer faces, or off-set by a third or two-thirds.

Since an architect had to know the thickness of a wall given its height,[23] a dimension can be assigned to Lechler's wall. From this, the lower diagram uses quadrature to produce the details, which Lechler states can be done provided the masons have the groundplan and dimensions.[24] Thus, not only does quadrature establish the module, it positions a wall to its grid and profiles and elevates the details as well.

To summarize, this case study has set out to demonstrate that a schematic design based on geometric proportion could be translated from tracing-house to building site and into a dimensioned building plan complete with its architectural details within the known working methods of medieval masons.

Notes

1 See pp. 158–65.
2 See pp. 141–5.
3 See pp. 146–52.
4 See p. 162.
5 See pp. 156–7, 166.
6 See pp. 257–61.
7 See pp. 213–15, 217, 249.
8 See Hiscock 1996 for a fuller account of the connection between design and dimension.
9 Refer back to Norwich.
10 *Tirol Hüttenbuch* cols 207–8, in Shelby 1977, 48; Frankl 1960, 139.
11 *Tirol Hüttenbuch* col. 203, in Shelby 1976, 211–12.
12 *Vita sancti Oswaldi* IV in Harvey 107.
13 See pl. 16.
14 Gerald, *De rebus a se gestis*, in Butler 89.
15 Knoop and Jones 1937, 30.
16 $EF = DE \times \sqrt{3}$ $= 7 \times 1.732...$ $= 12.124$

   $(12 \div 12.124) \times 100$ $= 98.977\%$

17 $BC = BA \times \tan 54°$ $= 8 \times 1.376...$ $= 11.011$

   $(11 \div 11.011) \times 100$ $= 99.898\%$

18 Villard, fols 20 and 20v.
19 Hildebert, PL159 857–94; Gerald, II.12.
20 See above, notes 13, 14.
21 See also Villard fol.15.
22 Lechler, fol. 42v, also fol. 44.
23 *Regensburg Ordinances*, article 18.6, 1514, in Frankl 1960, 140–41.
24 Lechler, fol. 43

Chapter 10

Inferences and Implications

The question of proof

One conclusion that cannot be asserted here, however, is that the geometry as proposed was actually employed to design the layouts of the buildings investigated. Whilst supporting evidence to this effect may be sufficient to be persuasive, it is largely circumstantial and falls short of conclusive proof. It may be of interest therefore to consider why there appears to be a lack of proof for a practice that would have been so widespread.

It is possible that proof of the practice may exist but has yet to be discovered. Until all medieval texts have been edited, published and studied, this will remain the case. Another explanation is that proof might once have existed but has not survived. A third possibility is that it was simply not disclosed. It has been observed for instance that different methods of construction apparent in remains of ninth– and tenth-century architecture were not recorded in contemporary documents because they were of no interest to chroniclers.[1] As an extension of this, given the textual evidence for secrecy both in the schools and in the lodges, at the very least there would have been little incentive to publicize and it could even be argued that it would have been against tradition to do so.

Alternatively, such information may have been not so much withheld as simply taken for granted. It has been pointed out, for example, that such was the pervasiveness of Platonist thought early in the middle ages, its existence would have been no more remarkable at the time than the air people breathed and, to detect evidence of the habitual, it is sometimes necessary to read between the lines of texts and interpret their apparent implications.[2] A similar argument would apply to lodge practice, the more so when its oral tradition of craft teaching is fully recognized.

Possible sources

Vitruvius

Existence of copies of the treatise *De architectura* by Vitruvius, dating back probably to the eighth century, with over fifty surviving from the eleventh century onwards, must place this text as a possible source, especially when the importance that Vitruvius gives to geometry and proportion is taken into account. According to him, geometry provides many aids for architecture and proportion results from taking a fixed module for the parts and the whole.[3] His examples are simple and generally involve squares, with plans of temples 1 : 2, basilicas 1 : 2 or 1 : 3 and domestic atria 3 : 5, 2 : 3 and the side and diagonal of a square.[4] If his text can be interpreted as supporting medieval instances of designing *ad quadratum*, it might be possible to see it as a source for such plans as St Gall and to some extent St Michael at Hildesheim. Not only do both consist largely of squares, one manuscript of Vitruvius was found in the library of St Gall during the middle ages and another bears the signature of Hildesheim's first abbot.[5] However, it is difficult to see how later plans, in which the square is no more prevalent than the other two Platonic figures, can have been derived solely from this treatise.

Greeks

With Christian Platonism rooted in the Greek world, it might be reasonable to suppose there might be a Greek origin for a method of architectural design in the West. In addition to Haghia Sophia in Constantinople, the Byzantine archetypes of the inscribed octagon and the cross-in-square clearly show the importance of architectural geometry and so a corresponding method might be expected to have been employed in the layout of Byzantine basilicas as well.

Given this possibility, any such tradition of design could have been brought to the West by some of the many Greeks who were to be found there in and around the tenth century. Greek monks were common in Rome, even sharing a monastery with followers of the Rule of St Benedict.[6] Religious communities of Greeks were recorded in Lorraine, as mentioned in Chapter 1, and it was to his school there that Bruno attracted Greek scholars, having apparently been taught by Greeks himself.[7] On the occasion of Otto II's marriage to Theophanou in 972, the Byzantine princess brought a large retinue of Greeks with her to Germany. In 1017 Greeks were to build the basilica of St Bartholomew at Paderborn and from the latter part of the tenth century were also to be found at St Bénigne in Dijon, in Burgundy in general and, interestingly enough, at Gorze.[8]

Gorze and Cluny

Whatever influence the Greeks at Gorze may have had, it has been shown that Gorze itself wielded considerable influence in the monastic reforms of the tenth century. Moreover, many of those directly associated with the architectural projects that resulted, such as Anstaeus, Adalbero, Heribert, Ethelwold, Hugh and William, either studied at Gorze or came into contact with its teaching.

The influence of Cluny, with its various reforms superseding those of Gorze, can hardly be discounted either, although no particular evidence pointing to it as a source has been encountered apart from general architectural similarities between its houses.

There is nothing to suggest, however, that any of the monastic reforms might have invented a method of design. On the contrary, this would seem to run counter to the practice of an age that valued not innovation so much as maintaining or restoring tradition, notwithstanding advances being made in constructional design. Both the Gorze and Cluny reforms for example represented a return to the Rule of St Benedict and the energies of Boethius and Gerbert were directed at preserving the knowledge of antiquity so as to maintain the classical tradition of learning in the present.

Lombards

One continuous tradition in building that could have survived throughout the so-called dark ages may possibly be traced from colleges of builders in Rome to the arrival in the sixth century of Lombards in Italy.[9] Certainly their identification with building was such that *Lombardus* came to mean mason and it was Lombard masons who were called from Dijon to Normandy to erect the monastery buildings at Fécamp under William's abbacy.[10] William himself was a Lombard and so was Lanfranc who, as the first Norman archbishop of Canterbury, presided over the massive programme of Anglo-Norman church building that followed the Conquest. At the same time, Lombard masons were also active in the Rhineland as well as in their native land.

St Peter's Basilica, Rome

If a tradition of design had survived from late antiquity, then it might be found in the architecture of early Christianity and it has already been shown that Constantine had called for apprentice architects who were versed in the liberal arts. Above all, the plan of St Peter's Old Basilica has been shown to answer to the same Platonic geometry as that proposed for the medieval examples and is capable of being set out in eight operations from a single square with the minimum calculated accuracy of 98.75%, rising to 99.95%.

Just as significant may be the frequency with which monastic founders resorted to Rome for papal confirmation of privileges and other material aid in setting up their new foundations. There seems to be no reason why this should not have included advice on laying out their buildings, as already argued, especially if a particular system of design were thought propitious. Among these visitors was Bernward of Hildesheim and, although the purpose of his visit was primarily to settle a matter of jurisdiction, it was nevertheless made while he was planning his abbey; the religious bronzework he cast on his return to Hildesheim is thought to have been inspired by identifiable examples in Rome; and the geometry revealed in the test of his plan does bear similarities with St Peter's.

It is not the intention here, however, to put forward any of these possible sources necessarily as a serious proposition, for this would require further study. The purpose rather is to show that it may have been perfectly possible for a method of design, such as that proposed, to have been available at the time in question.

Continuing history of geometric design

According to the evidence presented here, the bishops and abbots of the tenth and early eleventh centuries, whose personal direction of their architectural programmes was chronicled at the time, stand as historical personalities in whom were combined both the scholar and practitioner, the reformer and rebuilder, representing a combination of ideas and action in which ideas were Christian and Platonist and action resulted in architecture which was repeatedly described in mystical terms as being without equal. Given their enthusiasm, energy and learning, it would have taken only a small group of such individuals to establish or revive a tradition of design. In either case, it would presumably have spread with the various reform movements and subsequently with the Cluniac reform, taking root across Europe and eventually becoming established practice in masons' lodges. Once incorporated, it would have been applied by masters and working masons as lodge practice without their necessarily understanding or remembering either the metaphysics or the mathematics. Roriczer, it may be recalled, published a geometric construction for the pentagon as being correct and it is not. The lodges, thus established, would have been left to evolve, with master masons becoming lay professionals and lodge practice left to develop in various ways among Europe's lodges, distinct from parallel developments in Christian philosophy and theology.[11] That this happened seems borne out by the deliberations of the congress of architects called to Milan Cathedral at the turn of the fifteenth century.[12]

At the same time, the practice of architecture and the study of philosophy appear to have diverged to a point where masons' geometry could still carry a Platonic content, whether or not intended, or understood by lay architects, while churchmen began interpreting the finished architecture quite differently. The symbolical interpretations of religious architecture by, for example, Honorius of Autun sometime before 1130 and Hugh of Lincoln around 1225, are poetic and literal, not Platonic.[13] This may be partly explained by Hugh of St Victor when he appears to imply in the 1120s that architecture was a subject fit for the theorizing of philosophers and a practice better left to the practitioners.[14] This was part of a larger movement which saw a general separation between theory and practice in all subjects of study, coinciding with the rise of the universities at the expense of the cathedral schools. It also saw, with the rediscovery of Aristotle's texts between 1130 and 1250, the pre-eminence of the school at Chartres and the study of Plato pass to Paris and the process of questioning sanctioned by Aristotle.[15] Finally, the evidence of contemporary architecture suggests a renewed interest in designing *ad quadratum*. This might explain why some studies which have tended to examine the Gothic period rather than the Romanesque, have found in favour of the use of squares rather than all three Platonic figures, as well as seeking without success the required link between theologians and architects. If Platonic geometry were gradually supplanted by designing *ad quadratum*, this might in turn be explained either by a declining influence of Platonism, or an increasing influence of Cistercian planning within and outside the Order.

Speculative though this necessarily is, it cannot be denied that number and geometric expressionism, hitherto largely confined to textbook diagrams and manuscript illumination in the cloistered surroundings of monastic libraries, progressively rose from the private page to the public surface of religious architecture in the form of geometric relief, window tracery and wall arcading for all to see. Appearing in the tympana of eleventh-century abbey portals, becoming common in the twelfth century and even more so in the thirteenth with the invention of bar tracery, this process of progressive display coincided with the growth in public shrines, such as pilgrims' churches along the roads to Santiago, the urban abbeys and cathedrals of Norman England and finally the civic cathedrals of the Île-de-France. Framing their narratives in sculpture and stained glass, alongside the *vesica piscis* and the hexagram, the trio of Platonic figures become the commonplace of Gothic architecture, taking the form of trefoils, quatrefoils and cinquefoils in continuation of the tradition of Platonic geometry, which was soon to become absorbed into popular belief (pl. 20). Although this remains to be demonstrated and is beyond the scope of this book to pursue, it is posited here in order to show that the basic proposition of this study also fits the later developments of the period as they are known.

Perhaps Alberti should have the final word. Writing some time before 1452, he clearly attaches significance not only to geometry but to the groundwork and pavement of a work:

> Being to treat of the Design of Edifices, we shall collect and transcribe into this our Work, all the most curious and useful Observations left us by the Ancients.

> . . . to treat of the Design of the Platform, it will not be inconvenient to explain those Things first whereof that Design consists. Every design . . . is composed of Lines and Angles . .

De re aedificatoria I.1, 7

Notes

1 Lehmann-Brockhaus 1935, 12.

2 White 1978, 27, 317–18.

3 Vitruvius I.1.4; III.1.1.

4 Vitruvius IV, IV.1, V.1.4.

5 Pevsner 558; Hallinger 123; see p. 118.

6 Sackur I.332.

7 *Hist. Litt.* VI.57; Dobson 145.

8 Sackur I.162, 212, 348.

9 Rivoira 108–9.

10 Conant 1959, 58; Grodecki 26–7.

11 See Frankl 1945, 58.

12 Ackerman 89–106.

13 Honorius, *De gemma animae* PL 172, 586f, in Harvey 226; *Metrical life of St Hugh*, ed. Dimock, in Harvey 239.

14 Hugh, *Didascalicon* I.4, tr.Taylor, in White 1978, 248.

15 White 1978, 246–8, 325–8; Shelby 1972, 401–7; *Practical Geometry, passim*; Knowles 82, 163, 185, 191.

Appendices

APPENDIX 1: THE GEOMETRIC INVESTIGATION:

MEASUREMENT AND ACCURACY

The question of measurement

A number of authorities have regarded it as essential that each study of a building should be based on measurements taken from it by the person making the study[1] which, on the face of it, seems incontestible as an ideal. Yet it is no guarantee in itself that these measurements will be more accurate than someone else's, particularly if that other person is more thoroughly trained and experienced as a surveyor. Indeed, much of the literature has been diverted by differences between sets of measurements for the same building,[2] the more so when its layout is as irregular as, say, Notre Dame in Paris (fig. 20). Given the complexity as well as the irregularity of such monuments, the evidence of these disputes suggests that there can be as many different sets of dimensions as there are surveys, with each new survey adding yet another set of dimensions which in turn would require another survey to check its accuracy. Without doing so, of course, it is not possible to say which, if any, is reliable. This is not to argue that the attempt should not be made, but that any expectation of absolute certainty of absolute accuracy is likely to result in chasing a chimera.

The insistence upon original surveys also seems to imply an assumption that not only will the measurements be taken accurately and recorded accurately but they will also be plotted accurately and that measured drawings enjoy the same status of documentary evidence as manuscripts. Yet for a measured drawing to be subjected to the same independent scrutiny, at the very least the original measurements would need to be available; they would need to be fully triangulated in order to be able to check the accuracy of angles and alignment; and the drawing would need to be to a large enough scale to facilitate checking to within an acceptably small margin of error. Needless to say, these conditions are rarely met. Building plans are generally published within a scale range of 1 : 100 to 1 : 200, which is far too small for accurately checking against dimensions, and the drawings are seldom supported by a full set of measurements, triangulated or not. In the foreseeable but still distant future, the application of the laser and the computer to building surveys will perhaps become general, providing objective data, readily verifiable. One such survey, of St Maclou in Rouen, has been included in this study. In the meantime, however, so long as surveying and draughting continue to be subject to human error – and difficult to verify – it is inevitable that a certain amount has to be taken on trust. This being the case, it is argued here that it is actually preferable to obtain measured drawings from independent sources, provided they are reliable. In experimental science, for instance, it would be unthinkable for the data being tested to be not only controlled by the scientist conducting the experiment but also produced by the same person. Therefore it should be the authority of the surveyor and the survey that is persuasive, rather than the originality of the survey to a particular study.

Measured surveys provide data for either graphical or metrological analysis, or sometimes both. A drawing can immediately reveal a set of geometric relationships in a plan that are simply not discernible from a table of dimensions, yet it is generally left to the eye to determine their accuracy. For those who mistrust the eye, metrological data can be precisely checked by calculation. One notable example of this relies on calculation exclusively without the use of a single drawing.[3] In addition, metrological studies often seek units of measure that may have been used and from this, simple numerical ratios can be revealed that are either linear, as between the length of a choir and the length of a nave, or planar, as between the length of a choir and its width. The appearance of repeating modules in a plan has also led to suggestions that design may sometimes have been a purely additive process. However, whilst sets of dimensions on their own may reveal irregularities in a building through variations in linear measurements, they are less likely to reveal abnormality of angle and alignment unless tied by triangulating dimensions and, as already mentioned, this is rare to find. Without triangulation, a quadrilateral with opposite sides equal will not be verifiable as a rectangle or a parallelogram until set out as a drawing from a fixed datum and in relation to surrounding dimensions. Conversely, unequal dimensions may suggest apparent irregularity in the building not necessarily present in any underlying grid that may have been used in the design. A study of Ely Cathedral already referred to[5] shows variations in the north nave aisle bays ranging between 5.22 m and 5.02 m between the fifth and tenth bays. Since the dimensions are shown to the half-shafts of the main piers and their cross-arches, it does not necessarily follow that the piers themselves are irregularly spaced since it is common for shafts and cross-arches to be set eccentrically to their piers, or for some cross-arches to be thicker than others, discrepancies which are readily visible in some cases. It is perfectly possible that these piers are regularly spaced, but to ascertain whether or not they are, it would be necessary to determine their true geometric centres. Yet given the plan area of such a large mass of masonry that may not itself be regular or symmetrical and given that any half-shaft may be set eccentrically against it, the position of each pier's geometric centre may ultimately be a matter of experiment and judgment rather than numerical calculation.[6]

Nevertheless, it is important to avoid a false dichotomy arising between graphical and metrological investigations since they are complementary to each other and possess their own advantages and disadvantages. In a drawing, for example, irregularity on a scale already noted as being common can immediately be apparent and tested with dividers and set-square. To return to the case of the arcade pier, the most that measurements can achieve is to locate the outline of the pier accurately in space. In order to locate its centre, it is necessary to relate it both to the basic outline of the pier itself and to the centres of other piers and wall-shafts. This will generate a notional planning grid with axis lines intersecting at these centre-points, as suggested by the *Plan of St Gall* and Villard's Cistercian plan (pl. 1, fig. 17). Any irregularity in spacing or alignment may then be related to that grid, yet to arrive at the grid it is necessary to determine what might have been meant, as opposed to what was built. To achieve this, a combination of logical deduction and informed judgment is likely to be required and various criteria have been formulated in this study to control this process and maintain maximum objectivity.[8]

Accuracy of drawings

There is no doubt that the drawings used should be the result of measured surveys. Given the problems encountered in the literature, it was decided to seek drawings from the architectural and surveying professions. One exception was the *Plan of St Gall* which was never built and so a half-size facsimile of the drawing was used.[9] From the same source, the plan of the ninth-century cathedral at Cologne was also adopted. The plans of the abbeys of Hildesheim and Jumièges were reproduced from the monograph on these buildings. Nine of the English examples are from lithographs of surveys commissioned by *The Builder* in its series *Cathedrals of England and Wales* 1891–4.

The remaining examples from France and Germany were generally obtained from the architect currently in charge of each building or from the Archives et Bibliothèque de la Direction du Patrimoine. The plan of St Martin at Tours was provided by the author of its reconstruction from archaeological excavations. The plan and data for St Maclou in Rouen were similarly provided by the leader of the team that surveyed it.

Plans of the dimensioned version of St Gall, St Peter's Basilica in Rome and the Crystal Palace were reconstructed especially from recorded measurements. Drawings of Alexandra Palace and Smithfield Market are the product of original surveys. In each case, the author has been cited for verification together with the date where known.

Accuracy of reproduction

Any reprographic process which uses heat or liquid will cause some movement in organic material. In order to reduce variations to the absolute minimum, photo-copying was avoided altogether. Besides marginal movement caused by the process itself, there is no guarantee that hard copy is in exactly the same plane as the copy paper. Consequently, it is liable to distortion along a single axis at any angle in space.

Instead, each hard copy was directly photographed on a large format Littlejohn Galley Process Camera to eliminate distortion during reproduction. The negative was then printed to A3 size through a De Vere Vertical Enlarger onto resin-bonded bromide paper so as to reduce movement during and after printing virtually to zero.

Accuracy of geometric test

One of the most common objections to applying geometry to drawings arises when mazes of thick lines are drawn over very small plans,[10] which can be obviated by drawing very thin lines over large plans. Accordingly, a hair-line clutch pencil was used and A3 was chosen as the drawing size, being within range of parchment sizes used in the middle ages for drawing plans.[11]

The first task was to align the plan on the drawing board, bearing in mind that only very rarely will a single alignment account for the whole plan. Naves are commonly misaligned with choirs, transepts may not be at right angles with either, north and south arcades may not be parallel with each other or aisle walls with arcades. Therefore it is necessary to settle on an alignment that accords with the majority of the layout and it usually became obvious what this was.

Because pencil work is difficult on resin-bonded paper and because trial and error can leave a mass of confusing marks on a single drawing, experimentation was done on a series of overlays. For this, American detail paper was used because it is highly transparent and relatively stable.

Since planning grids were used at least sometimes in the middle ages, it seems fair to assume that piers would be centred on grid intersections, once again as suggested by the *Plan of St Gall* and Villard. Accordingly, the exercise commenced with the main arcades by plotting likely centres of piers with the hair-line pencil. From this was derived a provisional grid, often containing several discrepancies. Account was taken of sequential construction generally commencing with the choir, then moving to the crossing, transepts and nave. Consequently, any building discrepancy in the nave, for example, is likely to be a deviation from a crossing and choir already built, caused either by simple inaccuracy in setting out the nave, or by a hiatus in the construction. Although the nave may as a result be skewed in relation to the crossing and choir, the alignment of the choir grid was extended westwards from the crossing in order to hypothesize the intended layout, with variations with the structure as built clearly marked on the drawing. Lateral grid-lines, delineating bay divisions, were then projected out from the main piers towards the aisle walls and left ready for fixing their possible longitudinal axes.

Once the notional grid was plotted thus far, its intersections were tested for possible geometric connections under optical magnification and through the use of set-squares at the angles of the Platonic figures, namely 45° for the square, 30° and 60° for the triangle, 18°, 36°, 54° and 72° for the pentagon. This is a purely mechanical procedure, requiring judgment only over the precision of apparent intersections but, given the fineness of line and the strength of magnification used, it was possible to gauge inexactitude to within less than 1%, a margin which is well able to distinguish mismatches in draughting from presumed errors in building, for which a range of ±3% appears to be normal.[12] During this process, intersections with the lateral grid-lines were marked and, where they occurred on the aisle side of main arcades and were independently confirmed by different geometric constructions, these were put forward as possible longitudinal axes for the outer walls.

All the geometric connections that resulted were then reviewed in an attempt to discover a sequence which would enable the whole layout to be set out progressively from a single base line or figure. In cases where more than one sequence was possible, which turned out to be common, one was selected that could be shown to be consistent with other sequences already encountered.

Up to this point the exercise was confined to overlays and, however much care is taken, some shift between overlay and plan, or some movement in the overlay itself is unavoidable. Therefore the results were regarded as provisional prior to transferring them to hard copies of the plan for proceeding with the investigation.

Accuracy of presentation

Each A3 print was copied the requisite number of times for the final presentation, once again by a method designed to reduce distortion to the minimum. This time, it was also important to secure a surface that would permit precise draughtsmanship that would also stand out from the tonal density of the original plan.

Accordingly, where the original print was a line drawing, it was photographed with an Agfa Gevaert Repromaster 3500 Process Camera onto an A3 Copyproof Negative. This was then fed through a CP380 Processor with copyproof Positive Matt receiver paper, which is effectively inert. Where line-work was likely to be obscured by the tonal density of the original print, this was photographed as before but with a 400-line screen in direct vacuum contact with the Copyproof Negative between the negative and the original. It was then processed as described for unscreened prints. A variation of this, which was used latterly, produced a negative from the original A3 bromide print, using a horizontal process camera, which was then contact-printed through a tint onto Mitsubishi high-speed resin-coated contact paper.

The procedure for aligning the print and plotting the grid on the overlays was then exactly repeated on each new print ready for the geometric connections to be reconstructed from the overlays. In a small minority of cases, these needed to be modified, mainly by omitting some which turned out to be inexact. A simple colour code was introduced for each of the Platonic figures using a 0.3 mm line but with the pencil markings left in place as a check on each drawing.

The operations for setting out the complete plan were then numbered in sequence with the number of each operation identifying that part of the grid which it generated. Thus each part of the grid, which is drawn in red, carries the corresponding number. Diagonals generated by the square are green, by the regular triangle purple and by the pentagon blue.

In addition to demonstrating the sequence as a step-by-step procedure, all the geometric connections revealed by the investigation, whether required in the chosen sequence or not, are shown on separate drawings as a record and reference. In three cases, as already mentioned, the geometry has been systematically checked arithmetically and margins of error calculated as a percentage.

Notes

1   E.g. Gwilt 1006, Fernie 1990, 230.
2   E.g. Hecht 87–113.
3   Kidson 1956.
4   See p. 5.
5   Fernie 1979, 3 fig. 1; see p. 194.
6   In the event, Ely's pier spacing does appear to be irregular (see pp. 226–8) yet it took the geometric test of a drawing, not the tabulation of its dimensions, to confirm it.
7   Frankl 1945, 57; Conant 1963, 7–9; Bannister 1968, 10–22.
8   See Appendix 3.
9   Horn and Born I.76.
10   Morgan 19; Branner 1958 (2) 34.
11   See p. 199.
12   See p. 198.

APPENDIX 2: THE GEOMETRIC INVESTIGATION:

CRITERIA FOR EVALUATION

During the test, the operation of the various procedures was kept as objective and as mechanical as possible with the exercise of judgment restricted to the minimum. Where judgment was indispensable, it was governed by the following criteria, to which reference has already been made.[1]

These criteria are intended to meet further objections that have sometimes been raised when geometric theories rely on an inconsistent relationship to the structure, sometimes for example being taken to the inside of a wall, sometimes to the outside. Demonstrations of proposed systems against a single building also raise questions about their applicability to related examples and so criteria are also advanced to ascertain degrees of uniformity and variety within known architectural groups. If a degree of consistency is revealed, this may partly answer another charge, that the more lines that are drawn, the more will be proved. However, judgment about this needed to be reserved pending the test, after which the possibility of undue versatility was addressed again.[2] Other criteria are proposed and have already been touched upon, to establish whether the proposed system can provide a complete design method from a single starting point and can also be demonstrated as following the known, or likely, sequence of construction and is not, in other words, anachronistic. As well as being applicable to the investigation itself, these criteria will also be useful in evaluating the results.

General coherence

Do all possible alignments incorporate a scheme that is coherent and systematic?

Can it be deduced which lines could be causal and which consequential?

Do any inconsistencies reveal possible external causes, such as changes in building campaigns?

Do any inconsistencies fall within a tolerance of 3% that might be allowed for normal building error?

Are there any examples that do not answer to the geometric system proposed? If so, is there any possible explanation for this?

Does the application of the geometry display a systematic evolution through time?

Applicability

Can a possible method of design be deduced?
If so, can it be reconstructed from a single assumption, such as one given length?

Can the reconstruction take the form of a notional planning grid?
If so, once the main outline of the grid is established, can it generate secondary elements in the plan?
In other words, is there a workable hierarchy that can be deduced?

Does the reconstruction account for the whole layout?

Does it require more than one grid?
If so, is there a plausible explanation for this, such as a change in building campaign?

Do the outer grid-lines fall within the thickness of external walls?
If so, do they coincide with an identifiable setting-out line for locating the walls?

Do all geometric connections intersect with the grid or other possible generating points for the layout?

Is there any similarity with other buildings that are otherwise known to be related?
If so, is a degree of variety also revealed?

Some degree of inaccuracy is probably unavoidable in the original measured survey and in the drawing of that survey; in reproducing not only the drawings as hard copy but also the hard copy for testing and presentation; and finally, in the conduct of the test itself. A pertinent question therefore is whether all possible steps have been taken to ensure that the degree of inaccuracy has been reduced to a point where conclusions can be drawn on a balance of probability. If a serious doubt remains, it would then need to be asked whether it is likely that different causes of inaccuracy can have occurred randomly in such a way as to produce errors in each example, or in some examples and not others, that happen to coincide exactly with a geometric system that is otherwise uniformly demonstrated across the whole sample.

Notes

1 See p. 295.
2 Chapter 8.

APPENDIX 3: DIMENSIONS FOR ST MICHAEL, HILDESHEIM

In order to test the geometric system proposed for St Michael's Abbey in Hildesheim against the dimensions of the building, the measured survey of Roggenkamp was used on the advice of Hans Günter Kirklies, the architect presently in charge of the building, (H. Beseler and H. Roggenkamp (1954)).

Roggenkamp's measurements were initially converted to a dimensioned grid (fig. 26) and then averaged (fig. 27). The results of these calculations are presented here for verification and the averaged grid dimensions are tabulated as follows.

Grid dimensions averaged from Roggenkamp 1954

Square bays: crossings, nave and west choir

range: 944.5–988 cm
differential: 43.5 cm, or 4.4%

average: *964.625 cm*

Aisle bays

range: 689.5–698.5 cm
differential: 9 cm, or 1.29%

average: *692.94 cm*

Transept bays

range: 379.5–399.5 cm
differential: 20 cm, or 5.01%

average: *390.37 cm*

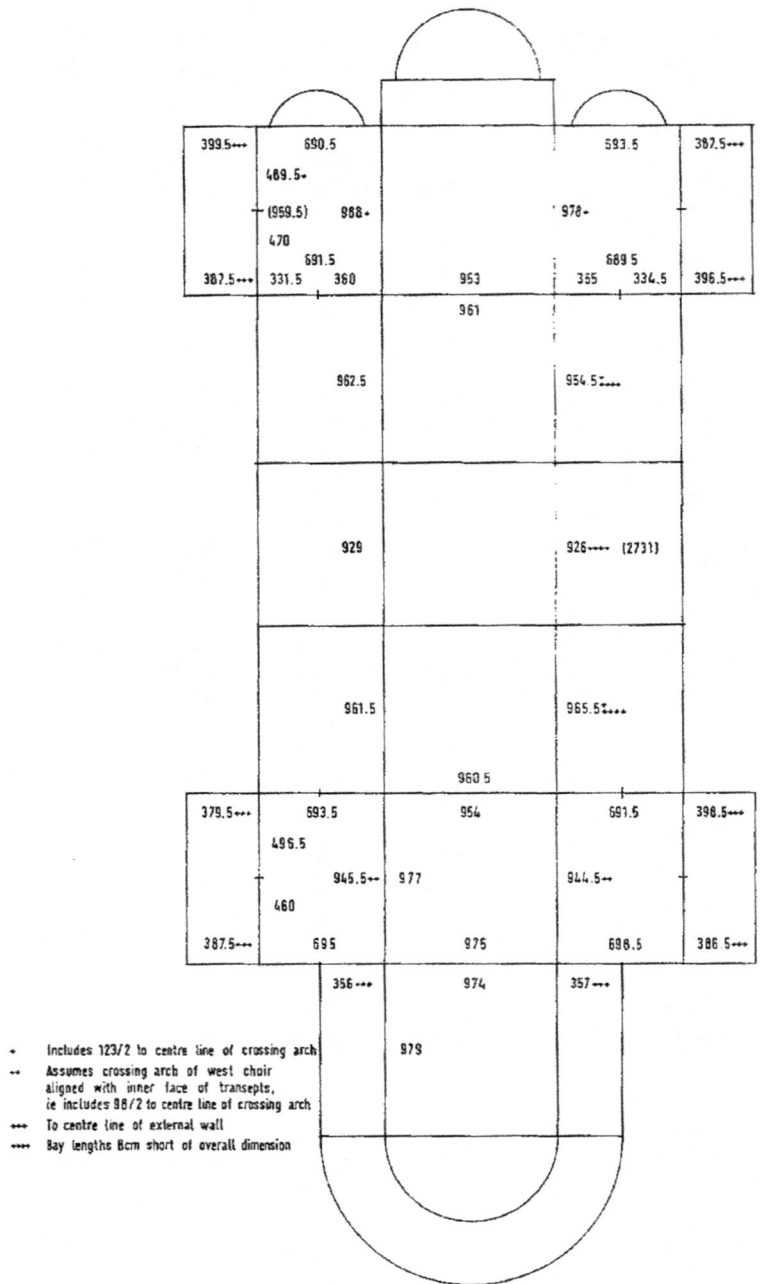

Fig. 26 St Michael, Hildesheim: grid dimensions calculated from measurements given by Roggenkamp.

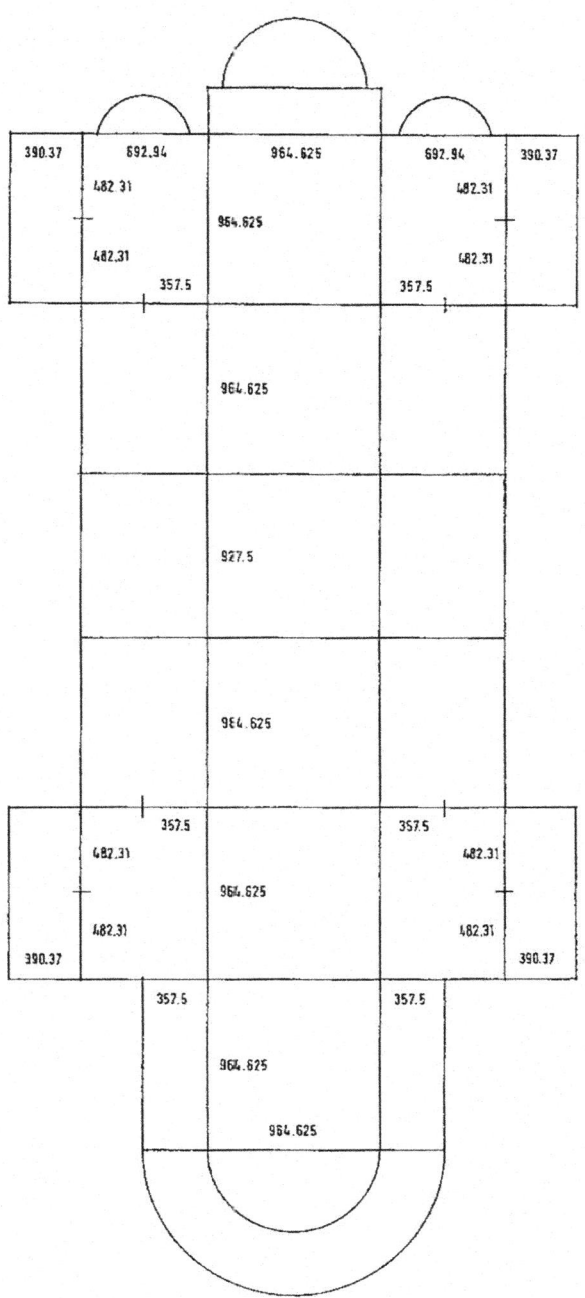

Fig. 27 St Michael, Hildesheim: grid dimensions averaged from measurements given by Roggenkamp.

Dimensions averaged from Roggenkamp, against royal foot of 32.48 cm

To test the proximity of these dimensions to a recognized unit of measure, Roggenkamp's proposal of a royal foot of 32.48 cm[1] was compared with the grid dimensions and the correlation tabulated as follows.

Step 1: crossing bay
30 royal feet   = 974.4 cm
dimension averaged from survey = 964.625 cm,   98.997%

Step 2: to side apse centre & axial pier
40 royal feet   = 1299.2 cm
dimension averaged from survey = 1322.125 cm, 98.27%

Step 3: to transept arcade & aisle wall
51 royal feet   = 1656.48 cm
dimension averaged from survey = 1657.565 cm, 99.93%

Step 9: to transept wall
63 royal feet   = 2046.24 cm
dimension averaged from survey = 2047.935 cm, 99.92%

Note

1 For the abbey, however, he proposes a local foot of a different value, see Beseler and Roggenkamp 122f; yet it can be seen here that the royal foot approximates very closely with the averaged grid dimensions.

APPENDIX 4: DIMENSIONS FOR ST PETER'S OLD BASILICA, ROME

Since the plan of St Peter's Basilica was drawn especially for the test, the dimensions from which it was plotted are presented here for verification in order that the results of the test may themselves be validated.

The provenance of the dimensions originates in an unpublished essay[1] which examines measurements from the following five sources:

1 Peruzzi, B; Sketch plan of east end (1521); Uffizi 11A.

2 Alpharanus, T; *De basilicae Vaticanae antiquissima et nova structura*, 1589; ed. Cerrati (Rome, 1914).

3 Apollonj-Ghetti, B; *Esplorazioni sotto la confessione di San Pietro in Vaticano* (Vatican, 1951).

4 Jongkees, J; *Studies on Old St.Peters*; Archaeologia Traiectina VIII (1966).

5 Bannister, T; *The Constantinian Basilica of St.Peter at Rome*; JSAH 27.1 (1968), 3–32.

From these sources, definitive dimensions were advanced in the essay referred to above and these have been accepted for this study and indicated on the following plan in round brackets (fig. 28). The dimensions shown in square brackets are those which are simply cited in the essay, without being advanced as definitive. These have been accepted for the present investigation where no other measurements have similarly been put forward. Since this present study has posited planning grids of axial lines, and on the sole assumption that those at St Peter's Basilica would have coincided with the centre-lines of colonnades and walls, the measurements proposed in the essay were converted to a set of axial dimensions for the purpose of setting up the plan and are shown unbracketed outside the plan. The column spacing east-west is derived from Bannister 15 fig. 18.

Note

1 I am most grateful to Eric Fernie for the use of his essay *Old St Peters* (1979), (2).

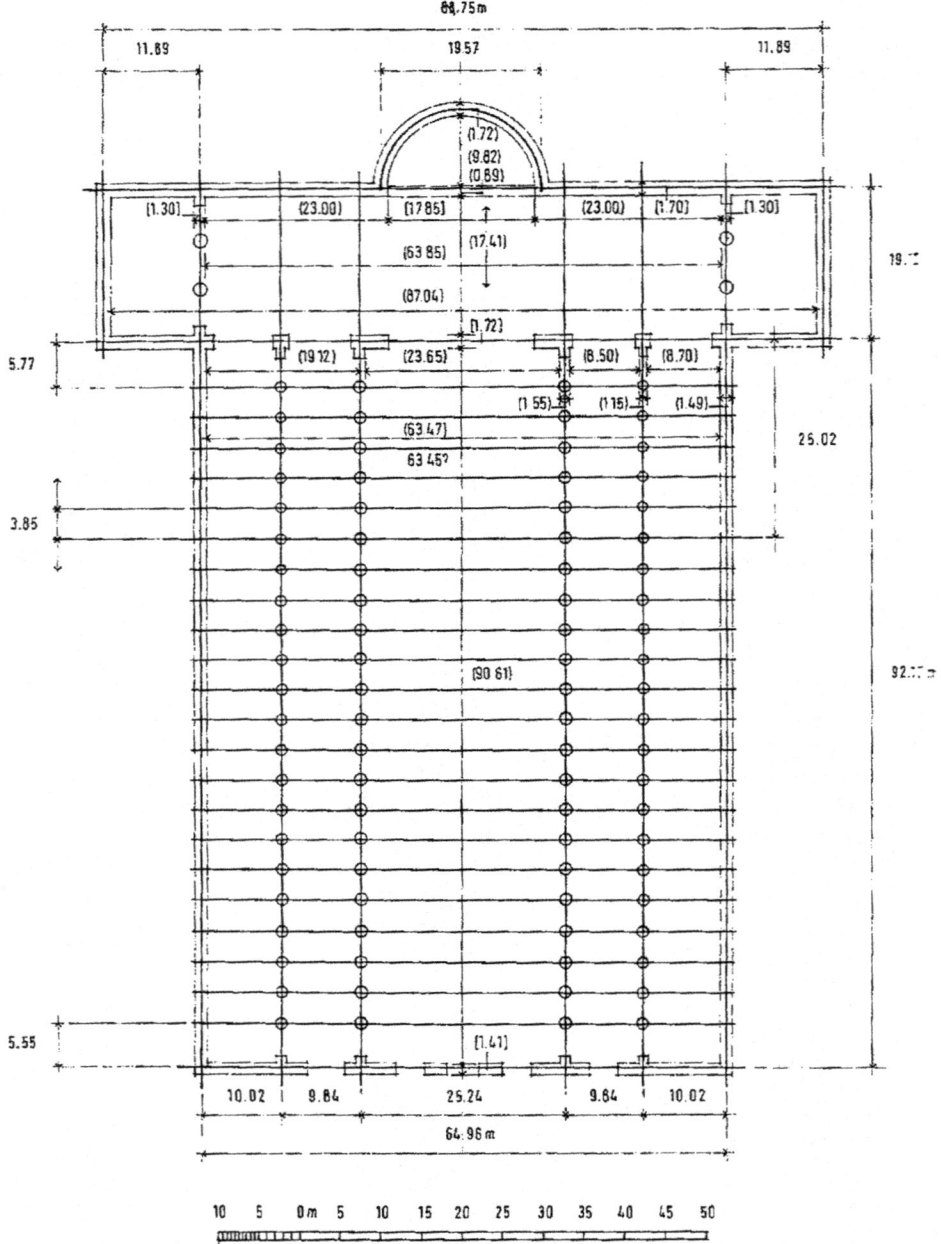

Fig. 28 St Peter, Rome: axial dimensions calculated from Fernie.

Bibliography

ACW	*Ancient Christian Writers*
ANCL	*Ante-Nicene Christian Library*
ASS	*Acta sanctorum*
FC	*Fathers of the Church*
JBAA	*Journal of the British Archaeological Association*
JSAH	*Journal of the American Society of Architectural Historians*
MGH	*Monumenta Germaniae Historica*
NPNFCC	*Nicene & Post-Nicene Fathers of the Christian Church*
OCD	*Oxford Classical Dictionary*
ODCC	*Oxford Dictionary of the Christian Church*
PL	*Patrologia Latina*

Classical, early Christian and medieval sources

Abbo, *Quaestiones grammaticales*, PL 139, 521–34.

Acta sanctorum ordinis S. Benedicti, ed. J. Mabillon (Paris, 1668–1701).

Adamnan, *De locis sanctis ex relatione Arculfi episcopi Galli*, PL 88, 779–814.

Aetius, see Diels, H., *Fragmente der Vorsokratiker, griechisch und deutsch* (Berlin, 1903), 306, 3–7.

Alberti, L., *De re aedificatoria*, in *The Ten Books of Architecture*, (Florence, 1485), tr. G. Leoni, 3rd edn (London, 1755), facsimile edn (New York, 1986).

Alcuin, *Epistolae*, in Bibliotheca Rerum Germanicarum 6, *Monumenta Alcuiniana*, ed. E. Wattenbach and E. Duemmler (Berlin, 1873).

  Versus de sanctis Eboracensis ecclesiae, MGH. Poet. lat. aev. Carol. I, tr. in West, A., *Alcuin and the Rise of the Christian Schools* (New York, 1892), 35.

Ambrose, *De fide ad Gratianum Augustum libri quinque*, PL 16, 527–698.

  Epistolarum Classis I, PL 16, 875–1220.

  Baptistery inscription, in *Sylloge Laureshamensis*.

Anglo-Saxon Chronicles, The, tr. A. Savage (London, 1982).

Annales Virdunenses, MGH. Script. IV. 7–8.

Ancient Christian Writers: The Works of the Fathers in Translation, ed. J. Quasten and J. Plumpe (Washington DC, 1946–).

Ante-Nicene Christian Library: Translations of the Writings of the Fathers down to AD 325, ed. A. Roberts and J. Donaldson (Edinburgh, 1867–72).

Aristotle, *Metaphysica*, tr. W. Ross, in *The Works of Aristotle 3*, ed. W. Ross ar
J. Smith (Oxford, 1908).

Arnold of Emmeram, *Liber II*, MGH. Script. IV. 556–74.

Ars geometriae et arithmeticae, see Boethius (1867).

Augustine, *Confessiones*, in *Saint Augustine: Confessions*, tr. V. Bourke in FC :
(1953).

> *Contra Faustum*, in *Reply to Faustus the Manichaean*, tr. R. Stothert, in *T*
> *Works of Aurelius Augustine, Bishop of Hippo*, ed. M. Dodc
> (Edinburgh, 1872).
>
> *De civitate Dei*, in *The City of God*, tr. H. Bettenson (London, 1984).
>
> *De doctrina Christiana*, tr. J. Gavigan in FC 2, 2nd edn (1950).
>
> *De musica*, in *On Music*, tr. R. Taliaferro in FC 4 (1947).
>
> *De ordine*, in *Divine Providence and the Problem of Evil, (De ordine)*, tr.]
> Russell in FC 1 (1948).
>
> *De quantitate animae*, in *St. Augustine: The Greatness of the Soul: L*
> *Quantitate Animae*, tr. J. Collerin in ACW (1950).
>
> *De sermone Domini in monte*, tr. D. Kavanagh in FC 2 (1963).
>
> *De Trinitate*, tr. S. McKenna in FC 45 (1963).
>
> *Epistolae*, tr. W. Parsons in FC 12 (1963).
>
> *In Iohannis evangelicum*, tr. J. Rettig in FC 79 (1988).

Basil, *Hexaëmeron*, in *The Treatise De Spiritu Sancto, The Nine Homilies of tl*
Hexaëmeron and the Letters of Saint Basil the Great, Archbishop of Caesare
tr. B. Jackson in NPNFCC 8 (1895).

Bede, *De tabernaculo*, in *Bede: On the Tabernacle*, tr. A. Holder (Liverpool, 1994
> *De templo*, in *Bede: On the Temple*, tr. S. Connolly (Liverpool, 1995).

Boethius, *De consolatione philosophiae*, in *The Consolation of Philosophy*, tr. \
Watts (Harmondsworth, 1969).

> *De institutione arithmetica*, see Masi, M., *Boethian Number Theory; .*
> *translation of the De Institutione Arithmetica (with Introduction and Notes*
> Studies in Classical Antiquity 6 (Amsterdam, 1983).
>
> *De institutione arithmetica libri duo, De institutione musica libri quinqu*
> *accedit geometria quae fertur Boetii*, ed. G. Friedlein (Leipzig, 1867).

Charlemagne, *Beati Caroli Magni Imperatoris Scripta sive omnium eius operum pai*
secundus: Epistolae 3, PL 98, 893–940, see Mullinger, J., *The Schools (*
Charles the Great (London, 1877), 97–9.

Chronicon abbatiae Rameseiensis, ed. W. Macray, Rolls Series 83 (1886).

Chronicon monasterii de Abingdon, ed. J. Stevenson, Rolls Series 2 (1858).

Clement, *Stromateis*, in *Stromata*, tr. W. Wilson, ANCL 4 and 12 (1867 an
1869).

Codex Theodosianus, see Mango, C., *Byzantine Architecture* (New York, 1985), 3£

Constitutions of Masonry, The, Cooke MS., BM. Add.23198, in Harvey, J., *Th*
Mediaeval Architect (London, 1972), 193, 196–7, see also Knoop, D
Jones, G. and Hamer, D., *The Two Earliest Masonic MSS* (Manchestei
1938), 75, 93, 97.

> Regius MS., BM. Reg. MS. 17.A.1, in Shelby, L., 'The "Secret" of th

Honor of Lynn White Jnr, Humana Civilitas 1 (Berkeley, CA, 1976), 207, see also Knoop, D., Jones, G. Hamer, D., (Manchester, 1938), 120.

Dominicus de Clavasio, *Practica geometriae*, ed. H. Busard, 'The Practica Geometriae of Dominicus de Clavasio', in *Archive for History of Exact Sciences* 2 (Berlin, 1965), 520–75.

Einhard, *Vita Caroli*, tr. L. Thorpe (Harmondsworth, 1969).

Elogium Boethii, MGH. Poet. lat. med. aev. V. 474–5.

Euclid, *Elementa*, see Heath, T., *The Thirteen Books of Euclid's Elements*, 2nd edn (Cambridge, 1956).

Fathers of the Church, ed. L. Schopp (New York, 1947–, Washington DC, 1962–).

Frankfurt Lodgebook, The, see Bucher, F., *Architector: The Lodge Books and Sketchbooks of Medieval Architects* (New York, 1979), 195–373.

Gerald of Wales, *De rebus a se gestis*, ed. J. Brewer, Rolls Series Giraldus Cambrensis 1 (London, 1861–), see Butler, H., *The Autobiography of Giraldus Cambrensis* (London, 1937), 89.

Gerbert, *Oeuvres de Gerbert*, ed. A. Olleris (Paris, 1867).
    Letters, see Lattin, H., *The Letters of Gerbert, with His Papal Privileges as Sylvester II*, Records of Civilization, Sources & Studies (New York, 1961).

Gervase, *Chronica Gervasii: Tractatus de combustione et reparatione Doroborniensis ecclesiae*, ed. W. Stubbs, Rolls Series 73 (London, 1879–80), see Willis, R., *The Architectural History of Canterbury Cathedral* (London, 1845), 37.

Glaber, R., *Historiarum*, PL 142, 613–98.
    Vita sancti Guillelmi abbatis Divionensis, PL 142, 697–720.

Gregory of Nyssa, *Contra Eunomium librum II*, tr. M. Day,
    De hominis opificio, in *On the Making of Man*, tr. H. Wilson,
    Ep.16: To Amphilocius, tr. H. Wilson,
    De infantibus praemature abreptis, tr. W. Moore,
    all in *Select Writings and Letters of Gregory, Bishop of Nyssa*, in NPNFCC 2nd Series 5 (1893).

Hildebert, *Vita sancti Hugonis abbas Cluniacensis*, PL 159, 857–94.

Historia dedicationis ecclesiae sancti Remigii, PL 142, 1417, see Harvey, J., *The Mediaeval Architect* (London, 1972), 56–7.

Historia monasterii Mosomensis, in MGH. Script. XIV, 600–18.

Historia I. Translationis sanctae Witburgae, A.SS. II. 604.1.

Honorius of Autun, *De gemma animae*; PL 172, 586, see Harvey, J., *The Mediaeval Architect* (London, 1972), 226.

Hroswitha, *Conversio Thaidis meretricis: Passio sanctarum virginum Fidei Spei et Karitatis*, in *The Plays of Roswitha*, tr. C. St John (London, 1923),
    also in *The Plays of Roswitha*, tr. H. Tillyard (London, 1923).

Hugh, *Didascalicon*, in *The Didascalicon of Hugh of St. Victor*, tr. J. Taylor (New York, 1991).

Iamblichus, *De vita Pythagorica*, ed. L. Deubner (Leipzig, 1937).

Irenaeus, *Adversus haereses*, tr. A. Roberts and W. Rambaut, ANCL 5 (1868).

Isidore, *Etymologiae sive origines*, ed. W. Lindsay (Oxford, 1911).

John of Metz, *Vita Iohannis abbatis Gorziensis: auctore Iohanne abbate sancti Arnulfi*, MGH. Script. IV. 335-77.

John of Ravenna, *Altera vita: ex chronico sancti Benigni Divionesis excerpta*, PL 141, 855–7.

Josephus, *Antiquitates*, in *The Complete Works of Flavius Josephus*, tr. W. Winston (London, 1876).

Lechler, L., *Unterweisung* (1516), ed. A. Reichensperger, *Vermischte Schriften über christliche Kunst* (Leipzig, 1856).

Leonis, *Epistola*, see Gerbert, *Oeuvres* 237–43.

Liber de miraculis sancti Iacobi IV, ed. P. Fita and J. Vinson (1882), see Harvey, J., *The Mediaeval Architect* (London, 1972), 34.

Liber vitae, see Birch, W., *Liber vitae: Register and Martyrology of New Minster and Hyde Abbey*, Hampshire Record Society 5 (1892), 9–10.

Life of Argerich, ed. Knoegel No.461, see Pevsner, N., 'The Term "Architect" in the Middle Ages', *Speculum* 17 (1942), 554.

Lucian, *Vitarum auctio*, in *Lucian* 2, tr. A. Harmon (London, 1915).

Macrobius, *Commentarii in Ciceronis Somnium Scipionis*, tr. W. Stahl, in *Commentary on the Dream of Scipio* (New York, 1990).

Martianus Capella, *De nuptiis Philologiae et Mercurii*, tr. W. Stahl and R. Johnson, in *Martianus Capella and the Seven Liberal Arts*, 2 vols (New York, 1991).

Metrical life of St. Hugh, bishop of Lincoln, The, ed. J. Dimock (Lincoln, 1860), see Harvey, J., *The Mediaeval Architect* (London, 1972), 239.

Miraculi sancti Bercharii, abbatum Dervensis, A.SS. II. 855.22.

Monumenta Germaniae Historica, ed. G. Pertz, (Hanover, 1826–).

Nicene and Post-Nicene Fathers of the Christian Church: A New Series, ed. H. Wace and P. Schaff (Oxford, 1800–1848).

Nicolas of Biard, *Distinctiones*, Paris, Bibl. Nat. 16490, see Mortet, V., La maîtrise d'oeuvre dans les grandes constructions du XIIIᵉ siècle et la profession d'appareilleur', *Bulletin Monumental* 67 (1906), 268.

Odo of Cluny, *Odonis abbatis Cluniacensis occupatio*, ed. A. Swoboda (Leipzig, 1900).

Origen, *In Genesim homiliae: Homilies on Genesis*, tr. R. Heine in FC 71 (1981).

Patrologiae cursus completus, Series Latina, ed. J. Migne (Paris, 1844–65).

Philippus of Opus, *Epinomis*, see Lasserre, F., *The Birth of Mathematics in the Age of Plato*, tr. H. Mortimer (London, 1964), 81–2.

Philo, *De opificio mundi*,
  De vita Mosis,
  Quaestiones et solutiones in Genesim,
  all in *The Works of Philo Judaeus*, tr. C. Yonge (London, 1854–5).

Plato, *Meno*, tr. B. Jowett, 4th edn (Oxford, 1953).
  Parmenides, tr. H. Fowler (London, 1953).
  Phaedo, tr. B. Jowett (Oxford, 1871).
  Philebus, in *The Dialogues of Plato*, tr. B. Jowett, 4th edn (Oxford, 1953).
  Republic, tr. F. Cornford, *The Republic of Plato*, (Oxford, 1941).
  Timaeus, in *Timaeus and Critias*, tr. D. Lee (Harmondsworth, 1979), also Cornford, *Plato's Cosmology*, (London, 1937).

Practical Geometry in the High Middle Ages: Artis Cuiuslibet consummatio and the Pratike de Geometrie, tr. S. Victor, American Philosophical Society (Philadelphia PA, 1979).

Proclus, *In primum Euclidis Elementorum librum commentarii*, tr. G. Morrow (Princeton NJ, 1970).

   Elementa theologica, tr. E. Dodds (Oxford, 1963).

Pseudo-Barnabas, *The Epistle of Barnabas*, tr. J. Kleist in ACW 6 (1948).

Pseudo-Dionysius, *De coelesti hierarchia*,

   De divinis nominibus,

   De ecclesiastica hierarchia,

   Epistola ad Titum,

   Mystica theologia,

   all in *The Complete Works*, tr. C. Liubheid (London, 1987).

Raynaldo, *Vita sancti Hugonis abbas Cluniacensis*, PL 159, 895–906.

Regensburg Ordinances, The, see *Tirol Hüttenbuch*, ed. J. Neuwirth (1896), also Harvey, J., *The Mediaeval Architect* (London, 1972), 149; Shelby, L., *Gothic Design Techniques* (Carbondale IL, 1977), 47–50.

Registrum primum, in *The First Register of Norwich Cathedral Priory*, ed. H. Saunders, Norfolk Record Society 11 (1939).

Richer, *Historiarum libri quatuor*, ed. G. Waitz (Hanover, 1877).

Roriczer, M., *Büchlein von der Fialen Gerechtikait* (Regensburg, 1486),

   Geometria deutsch, (Aus der geometrey) (Regensburg, c.1487),

   Wimpergbüchlein, (Regensburg, c.1488), all in Shelby, L., *Gothic Design Techniques* (Carbondale IL, 1977).

Schmuttermayer, H., *Fialenbüchlein* (Nürnberg, c.1488), see Shelby, L., *Gothic Design Techniques* (Carbondale IL, 1977).

Serlio, S., *Libro primo d'architettura* (Venice, 1560–62), see Wittkower, R., *Architectural Principles in the Age of Humanism* (London, 1988), 120.

Speusippus, *Theologumena arithmeticae*, ed. Ast (Leipzig, 1817).

Stobaeus, *Eclogarum*, ed. C. Wachsmuth (Gottingen, 1871), see Heath, T., *A History of Greek Mathematics* (Oxford, 1921), I.158.

Suger, *De administratione*,

   De consecratione, both in Panofsky, E., *Abbot Suger on the Abbey Church of St Denis and its Art Treasures* (Princeton NJ, 1946).

Sylloge Laureshamensis, Vatican Cod. Palat. 833, see Dölger, F., 'Zur Symbolik des altchristlichen Taufhauses I: Das Oktogon und die Symbolik der Achtzahl. Die Inschrift des hl. Ambrosius im Baptisterium der Theklakirche von Mailand', in *Antike und Christentum* 4.3 (Münster, 1934), 153–87.

Thorney Abbey Foundation Charter, see Hart, C., *The Early Charters of Eastern England* (Leicester, 1966), 167.

Tirol Hüttenbuch, The, ed. J. Neuwirth, in 'Die Satzungen des Regensburger Steinmetz entages nach dem Tiroler Hüttenbuche von 1460', see *Zeitschrift fur Bauwesen* 46 (1896), also Shelby, L., 'The "Secret" of the Medieval Masons', in *On Pre-Modern Technology and Science: Studies in Honor of Lynn White Jnr*, Humana Civilitas: Sources and Studies

Relating to the Middle Ages and the Renaissance 1 (Berkeley, CA, 1976), 211–12.

Villard, *Sketchbook*, Paris, Bibl. Nat. MS. fr. 19.093, see Bucher, F., *Architector: The Lodge Books and Sketchbooks of Medieval Architects* (New York, 1979).

Vita Bennonis II episcopi Osnabrugensis auctore Norberto abbate Iburgensi recognivit Henricus Bresslau, MGH. Script. sep. edn (Hanover, 1902).

Vita Evracli, auctore Reinero, MGH. Script. XX. 561.

Vita sancti Odonis archiepiscopus Cantuariensis, A. SS. V. 287.11.

Vita sancti Oswaldi archiepiscopi Eboracensis, in *Historians of the Church of York and its Archbishops 1*, ed. J. Raine, Rolls Series 71 (London, 1879).

Vitruvius, *De architectura*, in *Vitruvius on Architecture*, tr. F. Granger (London, 1931, 1934).[1]

Walter of Speyer, *Vita et passio sancti Christophori martyris*, ed. W. Harster (Munich, 1878).

Wish of Manchán of Liath, The, see Jackson, K., tr., *Celtic Miscellany*, (Harmondsworth, 1971), 280.

Modern sources

Ackerman, J., '"Ars sine Scientia nihil est": Gothic Theory of Architecture at the Cathedral of Milan', *Art Bulletin* 31 (1949), 84–111.

Andrews, F., *The Medieval Builder and His Methods* (New York, 1993).

Aubert, M., *Notre-Dame de Paris: sa place dans l'histoire de l'architecture du XIIᵉ au XIVᵉ siècle*, 2nd edn (Paris, 1929).

Baker, T., *The Normans* (London, 1966).

Ball, W., *A Short Account of the History of Mathematics* (London, 1915).

Bannister, T., 'The Constantinian Basilica of St. Peter at Rome', *JSAH* 27.1 (1968), 3–32.

Barlow, F., *The English Church 1066–1154* (London, 1979).

Barnes, C., *Villard de Honnecourt: The Artist and His Drawings: A Critical Bibliography* (Boston MA, 1982).
'Le "Probleme" Villard de Honnecourt', in Recht (1989), 209–23.

Barraclough, G., *The Origins of Modern Germany* (Oxford, 1962).
'The Monarchy and Its Resources', see Hill (1969), 67–85.

Bechmann, R, *Les racines des cathédrales: L'architecture Gothique, expression des conditions du milieu* (Paris, 1981).
Villard de Honnecourt, la pensée technique au XIIIᵉ siècle et sa communication (Paris, 1991).

Bennett, B., 'Cassiodorus', in *Dictionary of the Middle Ages* 3 (1983), 123–4.

Bergmann, K., *St. Pantaleon in Köln* (Cologne, 1976).

Berland, J.-M., *Saint-Benoît-sur-Loire*, tr. C. Davis (Paris, undated).

Bertoni, G., *Atlante Storico-Paleografico del Duomo di Modena* (Modena, 1909).

Beseler, H. and Roggenkamp, H., *Die Michaeliskirche in Hildesheim* (Berlin, 1954).

Billings, R., *Architectural Illustrations and Description of the Cathedral Church at Durham* (London, 1843).

Binding, G., 'Früh- und hochmittelalterliche Bauvermessung', see Witthöft (1986).

Birch, W., *Liber vitae: Register and Martyrology of New Minster and Hyde Abbey*, Hampshire Record Society 5 (1892).

Böckh, A., *Philolaos des Pythagoreers Lehren nebst den Bruchstücken seines Werkes* (Berlin, 1819).

Borst, L., 'Megalithic Plan Underlying Canterbury Cathedral', in *Science* 163 (Washington DC, 1969), 567–70.

Bougaud, L., *Étude historique et critique sur la mission, les actes et le culte de Saint-Bénigne apôtre de la Bourgogne, et sur l'origine des églises de Dijon, d'Autun et de Langres* (Paris, 1859).

Boyer, C., *A History of Mathematics* (New York, 1968).

Branner, R., 'A Note on Gothic Architects and Scholars', *Burlington Magazine* 99 (1957) (1), 372–5.

'Three Problems from the Villard de Honnecourt Manuscript', *Art Bulletin* 39 (1957) (2), 61–6.

'Drawings from a Thirteenth-century Architect's Shop', *JSAH* 17.4 (1958) (1), 9–22.

Review of G. Lesser: 'Gothic Cathedrals and Sacred Geometry', *JSAH* 17.1 (1958) (2), 34–5.

ed., *Chartres Cathedral*, Norton Critical Studies in Art History (New York, 1969).

Brooke, C., *Europe in the Central Middle Ages, 962–1154* (London, 1964).

Brooke, Z., *A History of Europe: From 911 to 1198*, 2nd edn (London, 1947).

Brown, P., *Augustine of Hippo* (London, 1967).

Bucher, R., 'Design in Gothic Architecture – A Preliminary Assessment', *JSAH* 27.1 (1968), 49–71.

'Medieval Architectural Design Methods 800–1560', *GESTA* 11.2 (1972), 37–51.

Architector: The Lodge Books and Sketchbooks of Medieval Architects (New York, 1979).

Bullough, D., *The Age of Charlemagne* (London, 1980).

Burkert, W., *Lore and Science in Ancient Pythagoreanism* (1962), tr. E. Minar, (Cambridge MA, 1972).

Butler, H., *The Autobiography of Giraldus Cambrensis* (London, 1937).

Butzer, P. and Lohrmann, D., eds., *Science in Western and Eastern Civilization in Carolingian Times* (Basel 1993).

Camargo, M., 'Rhetoric', see Wagner (1986), 96–124.

Cambridge History of Later Greek and Early Medieval Philosophy, ed. A. Armstrong (Cambridge, 1970).

Cantor, M., *Vorlesungen über Geschichte der Mathematik*, 2nd edn (Leipzig, 1894–1901).

Casey, R., 'Clement of Alexandria and the Beginning of Christian Platonism', *Harvard Theological Review* 13 (1925), 39–101.

Cazes, Q. and D., *Visiting Saint-Sernin's Basilica*, tr. A. Moyon (Bordeaux, 1994).

Chadwick, H. and Oulton, J., *Alexandrian Christianity* (Philadelphia PA, 1954).

Chadwick, H., 'Philo and the Beginnings of Christian Thought', see *Cambridge History* (1970), 133–92.
    Boethius: The Consolations of Music, Logic, Theology and Philosophy (Oxford, 1981).
Charpentier, L., *The Mysteries of Chartres Cathedral*, tr. R. Fraser (London, 1972).
Chasles, M., *Aperçu historique sur l'origine et le développement des méthodes en géométrie*, 2nd edn (Paris, 1875).
Chevallier, G., *Le vénérable Guillaume, abbé de Saint-Bénigne de Dijon: réformateur de l'ordre Bénédictin au XIe siècle* (Paris, 1875).
Cocke, T. and Kidson, P., *Salisbury Cathedral: Perspectives on the Architectural History* (London, 1993).
Coldstream, N., *Medieval Craftsmen: Masons and Sculptors* (London, 1991).
Colvin, H., 'Short Notice on B. Morgan: *Canonic Design in English Mediaeval Architecture*', *English Historical Review* 78 (1963), 762–4.
Conant, K., *Carolingian and Romanesque Architecture 800 to 1200* (London, 1959).
    'Medieval Academy Excavations at Cluny, IX: Systematic Dimensions in the Buildings', *Speculum* 38.1 (1963), 1–45.
    Cluny: Les églises et la maison du chef d'ordre (Mâcon, 1968) (1).
    'The After-Life of Vitruvius in the Middle Ages', *JSAH* 27.1 (1968) (2), 33–8.
    'Observations on the Practical Talents and Technology of the Medieval Benedictines', see Hunt (1971), 77–84.
Copleston, F., *A History of Philosophy* (London, 1966).
    A History of Medieval Philosophy (London, 1972).
Cornford, F., *Plato's Cosmology* (London, 1937).
    The Republic of Plato (Oxford, 1941).
Cowen, P., *Rose Windows* (London, 1979).
Critchlow, K., *Time Stands Still: New Light on Megalithic Science* (London, 1979).
Crombie, A., *Augustine to Galileo: The History of Science AD 400–1650* (London, 1952).
Crossley, P. and Fernie, E., eds., *Medieval Architecture and its Intellectual Context: Studies in Honour of Peter Kidson* (London, 1990).
Darlington, O., 'Gerbert, the Teacher', *American Historical Review* 52.3 (1947), 456–76.
Davis, M., 'The Plan of Saint-Urbain, Troyes', *AVISTA Forum* 10.1 (1997).
Decaëns, H., *Le Mont-Saint-Michel*, Travaux des mois 20 (1979).
Deutsche Literatur des Mittelalters, Die: Verfasserlexicon 1, ed. K. Ruh (Berlin, 1978–).
Dictionary of the Middle Ages, ed. J. Strayer (New York, 1983).
Diels, H., *Fragmente der Vorsokratiker, griechisch und deutsch* (Berlin, 1903).
Dobson, B., 'German History 911–1618', see Pasley (1982), 138–202.
Dölger, F., 'Zur Symbolik des altchristlichen Taufhauses I: Das Oktogon und die Symbolik der Achtzahl. Die Inschrift des hl. Ambrosius im Baptisterium der Theklakirche von Mailand', in *Antike und Christentum* 4.3 (Münster, 1934), 153–87.
Dronke, E., *Women Writers of the Middle Ages* (Cambridge, 1984).
du Colombier, P., *Les chantiers des cathédrales*, 2nd edn (Paris, 1973).

Dudden, F., *The Life and Times of St Ambrose* (Oxford, 1935).

Eichler, H., *Frühmittelalterliche Kunst* (1954).

Elkar, R. and others, eds, 'Vom rechten Mass der Dinge': Beiträge zur Wirtschafts- und Sozialgeschichte. Festschrift für Harald Witthöft zum 65. Geburtstag (St Katharinen, 1996).

Encyclopedia of Philosophy 2, ed. P. Edwards (New York, 1967).

Erdmann, C., 'The Ottonian Empire as Imperium Romanum', see Hill (1969), 96–101.

Evans, G., 'Introductions to Boethius's "Arithmetica" of the Tenth to the Fourteenth Century', *History of Science* 16 pt. 1 no. 31 (1978), 22–41.

Evans, J., *The Romanesque Architecture of the Order of Cluny* (Cambridge, 1938).
Flowering of the Middle Ages, The, (London, 1966).

Fernie, E., 'The Groundplan of Norwich Cathedral and the Square Root of Two', *JBAA* 129 (1976), 77–86.
'Historical Metrology and Architectural History', *Art History* I, (1978) (1), 383–99.
'The Proportions of the St. Gall Plan', *Art Bulletin* 60 (1978) (2), 583–9.
'Observations on the Norman Plan of Ely Cathedral, Medieval Art and Architecture at Ely Cathedral', *JBAA* (1979) (1), 1–7.
'Old St Peters', unpubl. essay (1979), (2).
'St. Anselm's Crypt, Medieval Art and Architecture at Canterbury', *JBAA* (1982), 27–38.
'The Grid System and the Design of the Norman Cathedral, Medieval Art and Architecture at Winchester', *JBAA* (1983), 13–19.
'A Beginner's Guide to the Study of Architectural Proportions and Systems of Length', see Crossley and Fernie (1990), 229–37.
An Architectural History of Norwich Cathedral (Oxford, 1993).

Fichtenau, H., *Living in the Tenth Century: Mentalities and Social Orders*, tr. P. Geary (Chicago, 1991).

Finch, R., 'Geometry in Gothic: A Study in the Application of Geometry to the Design of the Gothic Cathedrals of England', unpubl. essay, Oxford Polytechnic (1974).

Fipo, V., *La Cathédrale de Dijon*; Petites monographies des grands édifices de la France (Paris, 1928).

Focillon, H., *The Year 1000* (New York, 1971).

Fowler, D., *The Mathematics of Plato's Academy: A New Reconstruction* (Oxford, 1987).

France, J., 'Rodulfus Glaber and the Cluniacs', *Journal of Ecclesiastical History* 39.4 (1988), 497–508.

Frankl, P., 'The Secret of the Mediaeval Masons', *Art Bulletin* 28 (1945), 46–60.
The Gothic: Literary Sources and Interpretations through Eight Centuries (Princeton NJ, 1960).

Gem, R., 'Towards an Iconography of Anglo-Saxon Architecture', *Journal of Warburg and Courtauld Institutes* 46 (1983), 1–18.

Gibson, M., ed., *Boethius: His Life, Thought and Influence* (Oxford, 1981).

Gimpel, J., *The Cathedral Builders*, tr. T. Waugh (Wilton, 1983).

Godfrey, P. and Hemsoll, D., 'The Pantheon; temple or rotunda?' in *Pagan Gods and Shrines of the Roman Empire*, ed. M. Henig and A. King, Oxford University Committee for Archaeology Monograph 8 (Oxford, 1986), 195–209.

Gow, J., *A Short History of Greek Mathematics* (New York, 1923).

Grant, E., *Physical Science in the Middle Ages* (New York, 1971).

Grodecki, L., 'Guillaume de Volpiano et l'expansion Clunisienne', *Bulletin du Centre international d'études romanes* 2 (1961), 21–31.

Guthrie, K., *The Pythagorean Sourcebook and Library*, intro. and ed. D. Fideler, tr. K. Guthrie (Grand Rapids MI, 1987).

Gwilt, J., *An Encyclopaedia of Architecture: Historical, Theoretical, and Practical*, rev. W. Papworth (London, 1903).

Hallinger, K., *Gorze-Kluny: Studien zu den monastischen Bebensformen und Gegensätzen im Hochmittelalter* (Rome, 1950-51).

'The Spiritual Life of Cluny in the Early Days', see Hunt (1971), 29–55.

Hambly, M., *Drawing Instruments 1580–1980* (London, 1988).

Haren, M., *Medieval Thought: The Western Intellectual Tradition from Antiquity to the Thirteenth Century*, 2nd edn (Toronto, 1992).

Hart, C., *The Early Charters of Eastern England* (Leicester, 1966).

Harvey, J., *The Mediaeval Architect* (London, 1972).

Heath, T., *A History of Greek Mathematics* (Oxford, 1921).

The Thirteen Books of Euclid's Elements, 2nd edn (Cambridge, 1956).

Hecht, K., *Mass und Zahl in der gotischen Baukunst* (Hildesheim, 1979).

Heer, F., *The Holy Roman Empire*, tr. J. Sondheimer (London, 1968).

Herval, R., 'Un moine de l'an mille: Guillaume de Volpiano', in *L'abbaye bénédictine de Fécamp* I (Fécamp, 1959), 27–44.

Hill, B., *The Rise of the First Reich: Germany in the Tenth Century* (New York, 1969).

Hindenberg, T., *Benno II. Bischof von Osnabrück als Arkitekt* (Strasbourg, 1921).

Hiscock, N., 'The Aachen Chapel: A Model of Salvation?' in Butzer and Lohrmann (1993), 115–26.

'Metaphysical Formulae and Architectural Form: S. Peter's Old Basilica, Rome and Alberti's Basilica III', in Hocquet 11–12 (1994) (1), 265–90.

'Platonic Geometry in Plans of Medieval Abbeys and Cathedrals', PhD, Oxford Brookes University (1994) (2).

'Design and Dimensioning in Medieval Architecture', in Elkar (1996), 59–88.

Histoire Littéraire de la France 6 (Paris, 1742).

Hocquet, J.-C., ed., *Cahiers de Métrologie*, (Caen, 1994).

Holländer, H., *Early Medieval Art* (London, 1974).

Hopper, V., *Medieval Number Symbolism: Its Sources, Meaning, and Influence on Thought and Expression* (New York, 1938).

Horn, W. and Born, E., *The Plan of S. Gall: A Study of the Architecture and Economy of, and Life in a Paradigmatic Carolingian Monastery* (Berkeley CA, 1979).

Houvet, E., *Chartres Cathedral*, rev. M. Miller (Chartres, 1976).

Hubert, J., 'Les peintures murales de Vic et la tradition géometrique', *Cahiers Archéologiques* 1 (Paris, 1945).

Hunt, N., ed., *Cluniac Monasticism in the Central Middle Ages* (London, 1971).

Huntsman, J., 'Grammar', see Wagner (1986), 58–95.

Jackson, M., ed., *Engineering a Cathedral* (London, 1993).

James, J., *Chartres: The Masons who built a Legend* (London, 1982).

Jackson, K., tr., *Celtic Miscellany*, (Harmondsworth, 1971).

Junyent, E., *La Basílica del Monasterio de Santa María de Ripoll* (Ripoll, 1991).

Kidson, P., 'Systems of Measurement and Proportion in Early Medieval Architecture' 2 vols, PhD, University of London (1956).
'A Metrological Investigation', *Journal of Warburg and Courtauld Institutes* 53 (1990), 71–97.
'The Design of Reims Cathedral: Villard's Evidence Reconsidered', unpubl. paper, International Medieval Congress, Leeds (1997).

Klibansky, R., *The Continuity of the Platonic Tradition during the Middle Ages*, Supplement,
Plato's Parmenides in the Middle Ages and the Renaissance: A Chapter in the History of Platonic Studies, all in (London, 1981).

Kline, M., *Mathematical Thought from Ancient to Modern Times* (New York, 1972).

Klukas, A., 'Liturgy and Architecture: Deerhurst Priory as an Expression of the Regularis Concordia', *Viator* 15 (Berkeley CA, 1984), 81–98.

Knoop, D. and Jones, G., 'Latlaying the Groundwork', *Miscellanea Latomorum*, New Series 22 (1937), 29–31.
The Medieval Mason (Manchester, 1949).

Knoop, D., Jones, G. and Hamer, D., *The Two Earliest Masonic MSS* (Manchester, 1938).

Knowles, D., *The Evolution of Medieval Thought* (London, 1962).

Koppe, B., *Die frühromanische Empcrenbasilika in Montier-en-Der* (Saarbrücken, 1990).

Krautheimer, R., 'Introduction to an "Iconography of Medieval Architecture"', in *Studies in Early Christian, Medieval and Renaissance Art* (London, 1971), 115–50.

Kren, C., 'Astronomy', see Wagner (1986), 218–47.

Lanfry, G., *L'Abbaye de Jumièges: plans et documents* (Rouen, 1954).

Lasserre, F., *The Birth of Mathematics in the Age of Plato*, tr. H. Mortimer (London, 1964).

Lattin, H., *The Letters of Gerbert, with His Papal Privileges as Sylvester II*, Records of Civilization, Sources & Studies (New York, 1961).

Leclercq, J., 'Influence and noninfluence of Dionysius in the Western Middle Ages', in Pseudo-Dionysius, *The Complete Works*, W. C. Liubheid (London, 1987).

Leff, G., *Medieval Thought from Saint Augustine to Ockham* (Harmondsworth, 1958).

Lehmann-Brockhaus, O., *Die Kunst des 10. Jahrhunderts im Lichte der Schriftquellen*, (Strasbourg, 1935).
Schriftquellen zur Kunstgeschichte des 11. und 12. Jahrhunderts für Deutschland, Lothringen und Italien, (Berlin, 1938).

Lelong, C., 'Remarques sur la Basilique Saint-Martin de Tours au début du XIe siècle', *Bulletin Monumental* 143.2 (1985), 144–50.

Lesser, G., *Gothic Cathedrals and Sacred Geometry*, 3 vols (London, 1957, 1964).

Lethaby, W., *Medieval Art: From the Peace of the Church to the Eve of the Renaissance 312-1350*, rev. D. Talbot Rice (London, 1949).

Liebeschütz, H., 'Western Christian Thought from Boethius to Anselm', see *Cambridge History* (1970), 535–639.

Lund, F., *Ad Quadratum* (London, 1921).

MacDonald, W., *The Architecture of the Roman Empire I: An Introductory Study* (London, 1982).

Malone, C., 'Les fouilles de St. Bénigne de Dijon', *Bulletin Monumental* 138.3 (1980), 253–91.

    'Liturgical Uses of the "Eastwork" of St. Bénigne in Dijon', unpubl. paper, International Congress on Medieval Studies, Western Michigan University (1996).

Mango, C., *Byzantine Architecture* (New York, 1985).

Marlowe, J., *The Golden Age of Alexandria* (London, 1971).

Masi, M., *Boethian Number Theory; A translation of the De Institutione Arithmetica (with Introduction & Notes)*, Studies in Classical Antiquity 6 (Amsterdam, 1983).

    'Arithmetic', see Wagner (1986), 147–68.

McInerny, R., 'Beyond the Liberal Arts', see Wagner (1986), 248–72.

Merlet, R., *La Cathédrale de Chartres* (Paris, 1925).

Michell, J., *The View Over Atlantis* (London, 1975).

    City of Revelation (London, 1973).

Moessel, E., *Die Proportion in Antike und Mittelalter* (Munich, 1926).

    Unformen des Raumes als Grundlagen der Formgestaltung (Munich, 1931).

Morgan, B., *Canonic Design in English Mediaeval Architecture: The Origins and Nature of Systematic Architectural Design in England, 1215–1515* (Liverpool, 1961).

Mortet, V., La maîtrise d'oeuvre dans les grandes constructions du XIIIe siècle et la profession d'appareilleur', *Bulletin Monumental* 70.2 (1906), 263–70.

Mullinger, J., *The Schools of Charles the Great* (London, 1877).

Murray, S., *Notre Dame, Cathedral of Amiens: The Power of Change in Gothic* (Cambridge, 1996).

Murray, S. and Addiss, J., 'Plan and Space at Amiens Cathedral: With a New Plan Drawn by James Addiss', *JSAH* 49.1 (1990), 44–66.

Neagley, L., 'Elegant Simplicity: The Late Gothic Plan Design of St.-Maclou in Rouen', *Art Bulletin* 74.3 (1992), 395–422.

Ohlgren, T., *Anglo-Saxon Textual Illustration* (Kalamazoo MI, 1992).

Olleris, A., *La Vie de Gerbert* (Clermont-Ferrand, 1867).

Osborn, E., 'Clement of Alexandria', see *Encyclopedia of Philosophy* (1967), 122–3.

Oursel, R., *Living Architecture: Romanesque* (London, 1967).

Oxford Classical Dictionary, ed. N. Hammond, 2nd edn (Oxford, 1970).

Oxford Dictionary of the Christian Church, ed. F. Cross and E. Livingstone, 2nd edn (London 1953).

Oxford History of the Classical World, ed. J. Boardman (London, 1986).

Panofsky, E., *Abbot Suger on the Abbey Church of St Denis and its Art Treasures* (Princeton NJ, 1946).

Gothic Architecture and Scholasticism (New York, 1957).

Panofsky, E. and Saxl, F., *Dürer's 'Melencolia. I'* (Leipzig, 1923).

Parker, R., 'Greek Religion', see *Oxford History* (1986), 254–74.

Pasley, M., ed. *Germany: A Companion to German Studies*, 2nd edn (London, 1982).

Patch, H., *The Tradition of Boethius: a Study of His Importance in Medieval Culture* (New York, 1935).

Pedoe, D., *Geometry and the Liberal Arts* (Harmondsworth, 1976).

Pevsner, N., 'The Term "Architect" in the Middle Ages', *Speculum* 17 (1942), 549–62.

Pingree, D., 'Boethius' Geometry and Astronomy', see Gibson (1981), 155–66.

Recht, R., ed., *Bâtisseurs des cathédrales Gothiques* (Strasbourg, 1989).

Reilly, L., *An Architectural History of Peterborough Cathedral* (Cambridge, 1997).

Rivoira, G., *Lombardic Architecture, Its Origin, Development and Derivatives* (London, 1910).

Rosan, L., *The Philosophy of Proclus: The Final Phase of Ancient Thought* (New York, 1949).

Rosenau, H., *Design in Medieval Architecture* (London, 1934).

Sackur, E., *Die Cluniacenser in ihrer kirchlichen und allgemeingeschichtlichen Wirksamkeit, bis zur Mitte des elften Jahrhunderts* (Halle, 1892-4).

Salzman, L., *Building in England down to 1540: A Documentary History* (Oxford, 1952).

Sanderson, W., 'The Painter and Patrons of the Late Carolingian Frescoes at Trier', unpubl. paper given at Courtauld Institute, University of London (1996).

Schramm, P., 'Otto III and the Roman Church According to the Donation Document of January 1001', see Hill (1969), 133–45.

Shelby, L., 'The Role of Medieval Masons in Medieval English Buildings', *Speculum* 39 (1964), 387–403.

'Mediaeval Masons' Tools II; Compass and Square', *Technology and Culture* 6.2 (1965), 236–48.

'The Education of Medieval English Master Masons', *Mediaeval Studies* 32 (1970), 1–26.

'Mediaeval Masons' Templates', *JSAH* 30.2 (1971), 140–54.

'The Geometrical Knowledge of Mediaeval Master Masons', *Speculum* 47 (1972), 395–421.

'The "Secret" of the Medieval Masons', in *On Pre-Modern Technology and Science: Studies in Honor of Lynn White Jnr*, Humana Civilitas: Sources and Studies Relating to the Middle Ages and the Renaissance 1 (Berkeley, CA, 1976), 201–19.

Gothic Design Techniques (Carbondale IL, 1977).

Shortell, E., 'Design of the East End of the Collegiate Church of St. Quentin', unpubl. paper, International Medieval Congress, Leeds (1998).

Smith, D., *History of Mathematics* (New York, 1958).

Southern, R., *The Making of the Middle Ages* (London, 1967).

Stanley, W., *Mathematical Drawing and Measuring Instruments* (London, 1888).

Stegeman, C., *Les cryptes de la cathédrale de Chartres*, Société Archéologique d'Eure et Loir (Chartres, 1993).

Stewart, C., *Early Christian, Byzantine and Romanesque Architecture* (London, 1954).

Stump, E., 'Dialectic', see Wagner (1986), 125–46.

Swaan, W., *The Gothic Cathedral* (London, 1969).

Thacker, A., 'Aethelwold and Abingdon', see Yorke (1997), 43–64.

Thorndike, L., *A History of Magic and Experimental Science* (New York, 1923–34).

Thurlby, M., 'The Romanesque high vaults of Durham', see M. Jackson (1993), 43–63.

Tollington, R., *Clement of Alexandria: A Study in Christian Liberalism* 1 (London, 1914).

Ullman, B., 'Geometry in the Mediaeval Quadrivium', *Studi di bibliografia e di storia in onore di Tammaro de Marinis* IV (Verona, 1964), 263–85.

Ullmann, W., 'Imperial Hegemony', see Hill (1969), 102–18.

von Simson, O., *The Gothic Cathedral: Origins of Gothic Architecture and the Medieval Concept of Order*, 2nd edn (London, 1962).

Vregille, B. de, 'Aldebald the Scribe of Cluny and the Bible of Abbot William of Dijon', in Hunt (1971), 85–97.

Wagner, D., *The Seven Liberal Arts in the Middle Ages* (Bloomington IN, 1986).

West, A., *Alcuin and the Rise of the Christian Schools* (New York, 1892).

White, A., 'Boethius in the Medieval Quadrivium', in Gibson (1981), 162–205.

White, L., *Medieval Religion and Technology: Collected Essays* (Berkeley CA, 1978).

Williams, W., 'William of Dijon: A Monastic Reformer of the Early XIth Century', *Downside Review* 52 (New Series 33) (1934).

Willis, R., *The Architectural History of Canterbury Cathedral* (London, 1845).

Wilson, C., *The Gothic Cathedral: The Architecture of the Great Church 1130–1530* (London, 1992).

Witthöft, H., and others, eds, *Die Historische Metrologie in den Wissenschaften* (St Katharinen, 1986).

Wittkower, R., *Architectural Principles in the Age of Humanism* (London, 1988).

Wu, N., 'Uncovering the Hidden Codes: The Geometry of the East End of Reinms Cathedral', PhD, Columbia University (1996).

Yorke, B., ed., *Bishop Aethelwold: His Career and Influence* (Woodbridge, 1997).

Note

1. Reference is also made in the text to part-translations produced especially for this study by R. Burgess, dated 1989.

Index

Plates

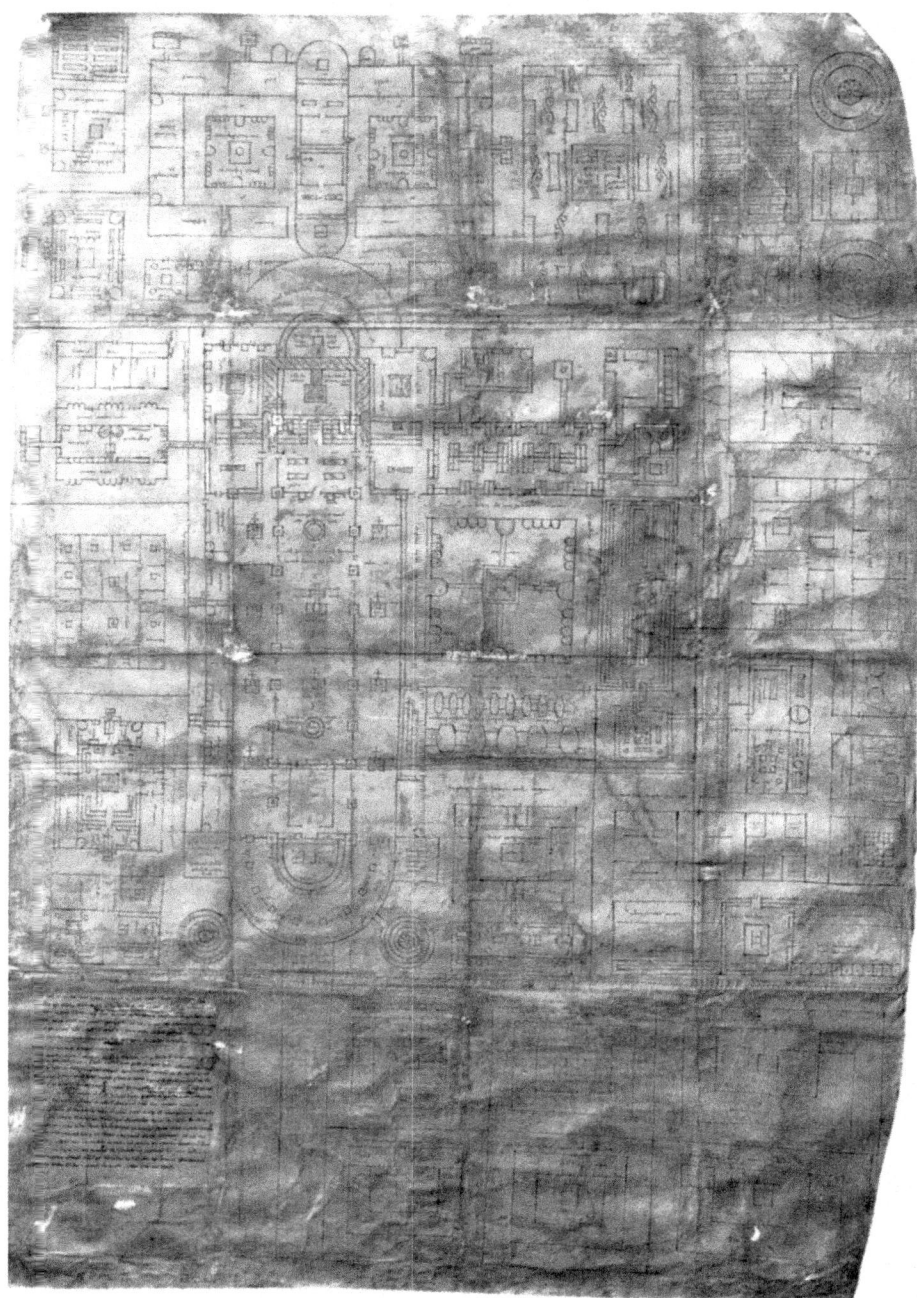

Plate 1: Plan of St Gall (St Gall MS. 1092).

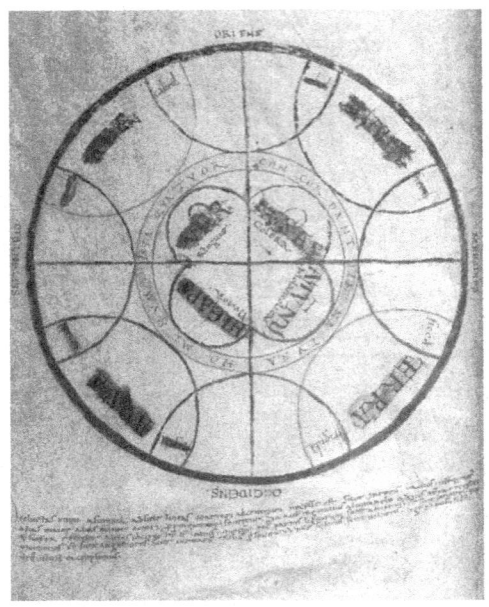

Plate 2: Division of the World, Macrobius, *Somnium Scipionis* (Oxford, Bodley MS. Auct. T. 2.27, fol. 12v).

Plate 3: Christ in Majesty, *The Vivian Bible* (Paris, Bibl. Nat. MS. lat. 1. fol. 330b).

Plate 4: Canon Table, *Eadui Codex*.

Plate 5: The Divine Architect, *Codex Vindobonensis*.

Plate 6: Otto III, *Aachen Gospels*.

Plate 7: Ascension, Ethelwold's *Benedictional* (BM. Add. MS. 49598 fol. 64b).

Plate 8: Emperor enthroned, *Registrum Gregorii*.

Plate 9: The last judgment, west portal, Ste Foy, Conques.

Plate 10: Interior, Sts Peter and Paul, Montier-en-Der.

Plate 11: Exterior, St Cyriakus, Gernrode.

Plate 12: Lanfranc architector, *Relatio translationis corporis sancti Geminiani* (Cod. 0.II.ii).

Plate 13: King and architect; *Vitae Offarum*.

Plate 14: Golden triangle and St Donato, Murano, after Moessel.

Plate 15 a: Regular triangles, pier frieze, St Stephen, Vignory.

Plate 15 b: Golden and 45° isosceles triangles, St Stephen, Vignory.

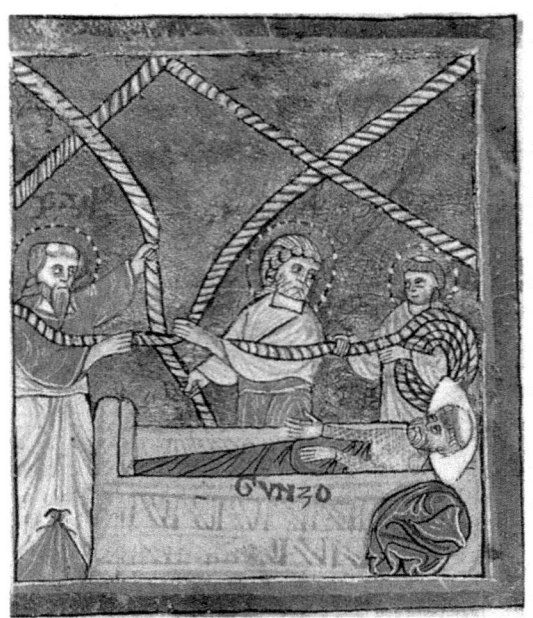

Plate 16: Gunzo's Dream, XIIc (Paris, Bibl. Nat. MS. 17716).

Plate 17: Pentagon, *Frankfurt Lodgebook*, after Bucher.

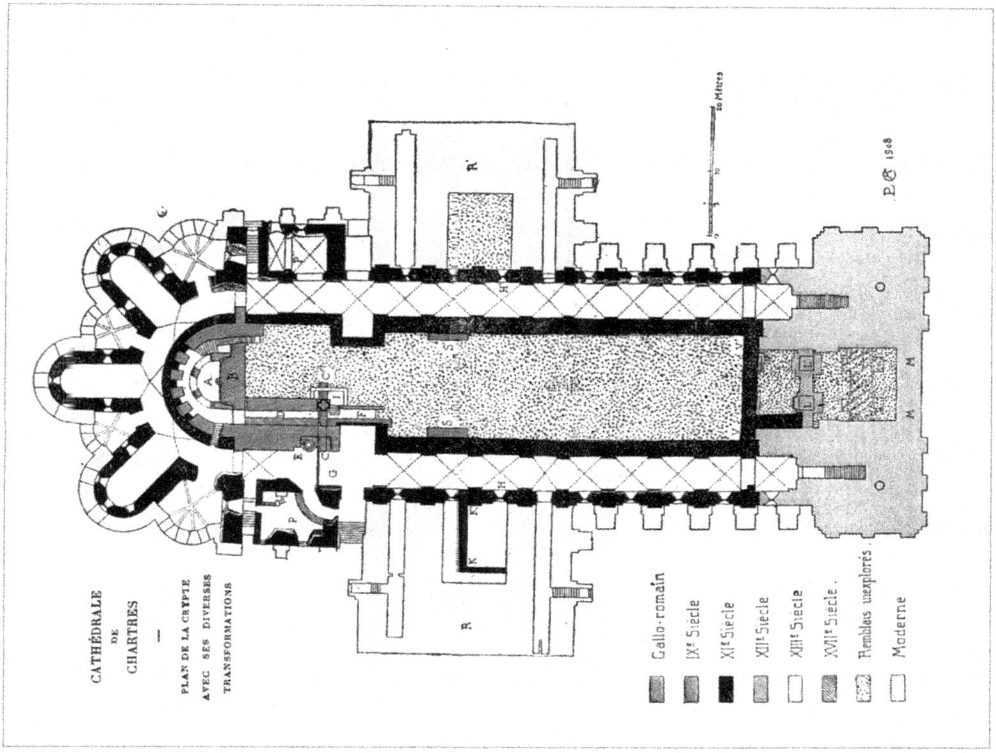

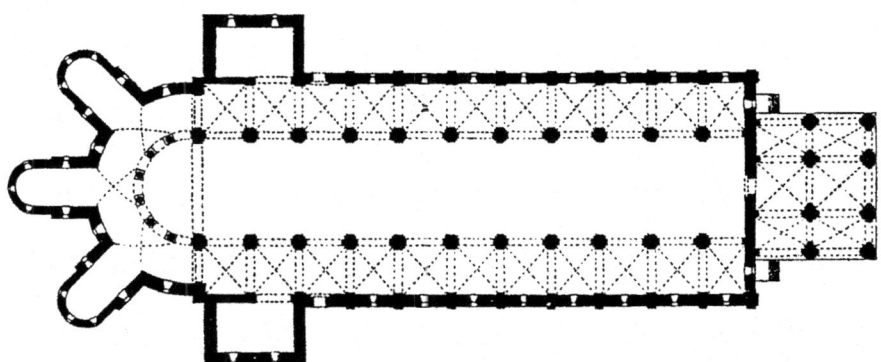

Plate 18, bottom: Plan, around 1100, Chartres Cathedral, after Branner.
Plate 19, top: Plan of crypt, Chartres Cathedral, after Merlet.

Plate 20: Trefoil, quatrefoils and cinquefoil, Lichfield Cathedral.

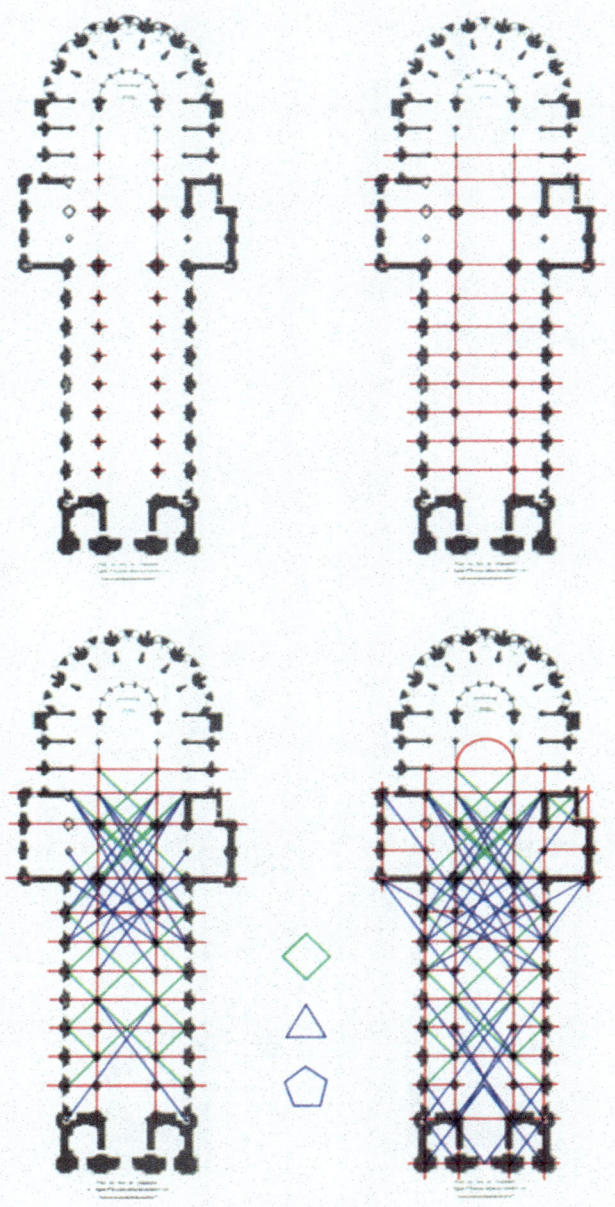

Plate 21: Geometric test: example of procedure, St Stephen, Caen, after Merlet.

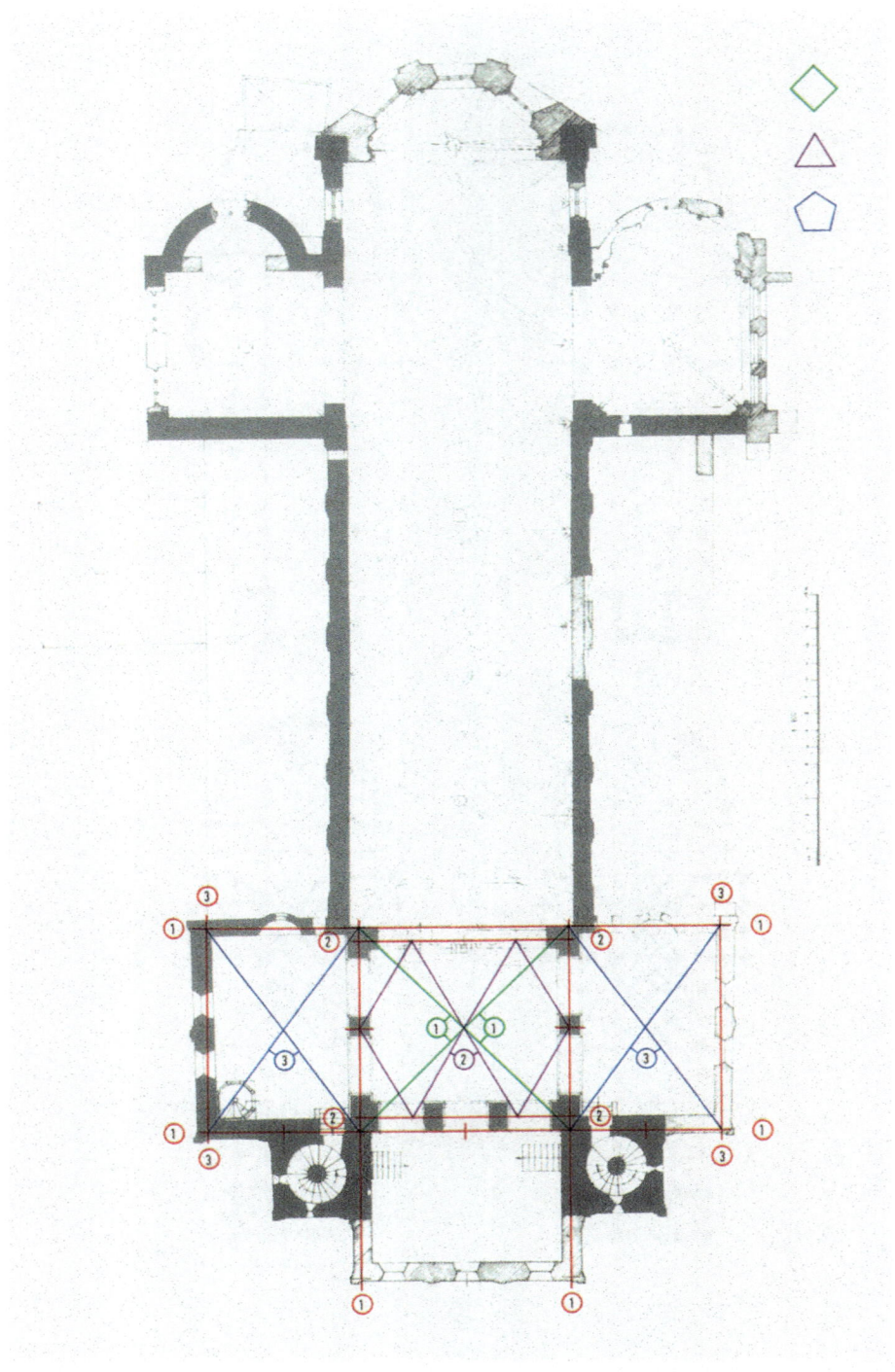

Plate 22: St Pantaleon, Cologne, after Schäfer: setting-out, steps 1-3.

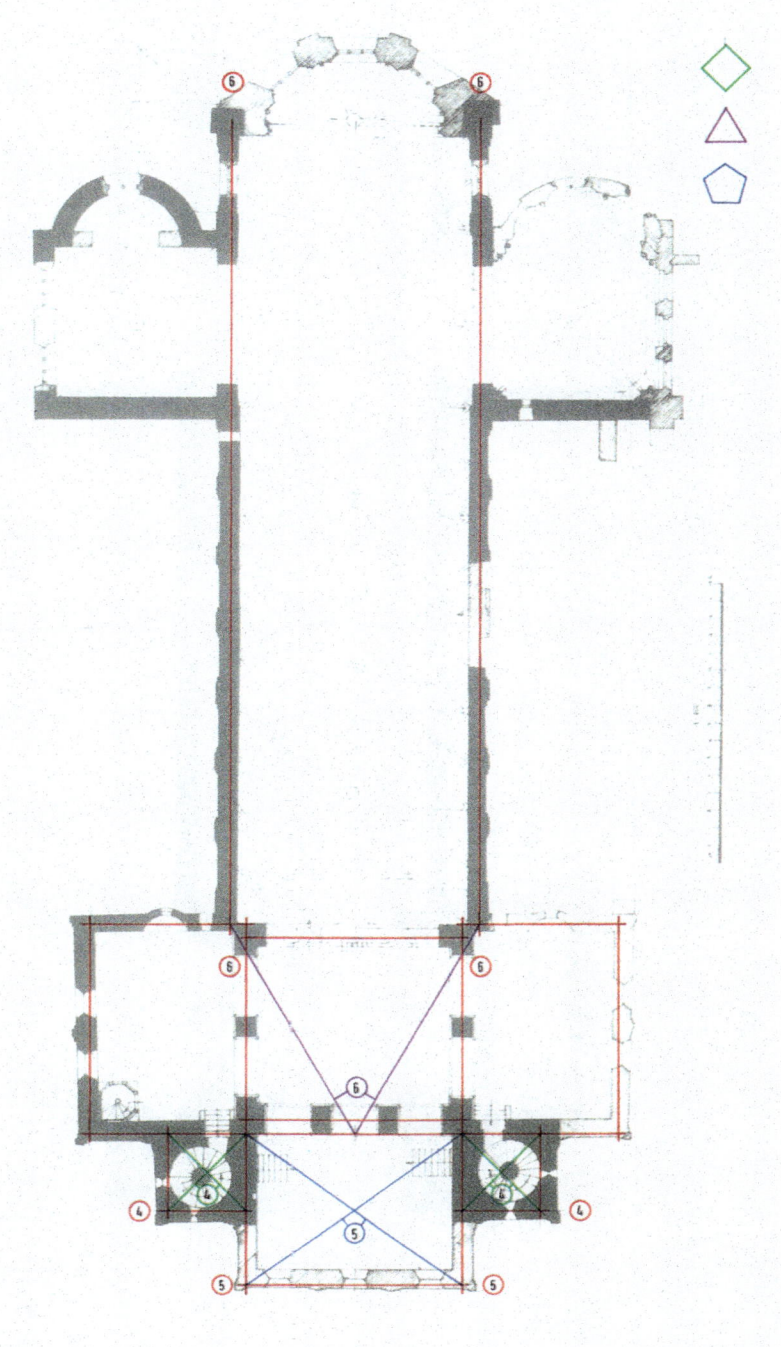

Plate 23: St Pantaleon, Cologne: setting-out, steps 4-6.

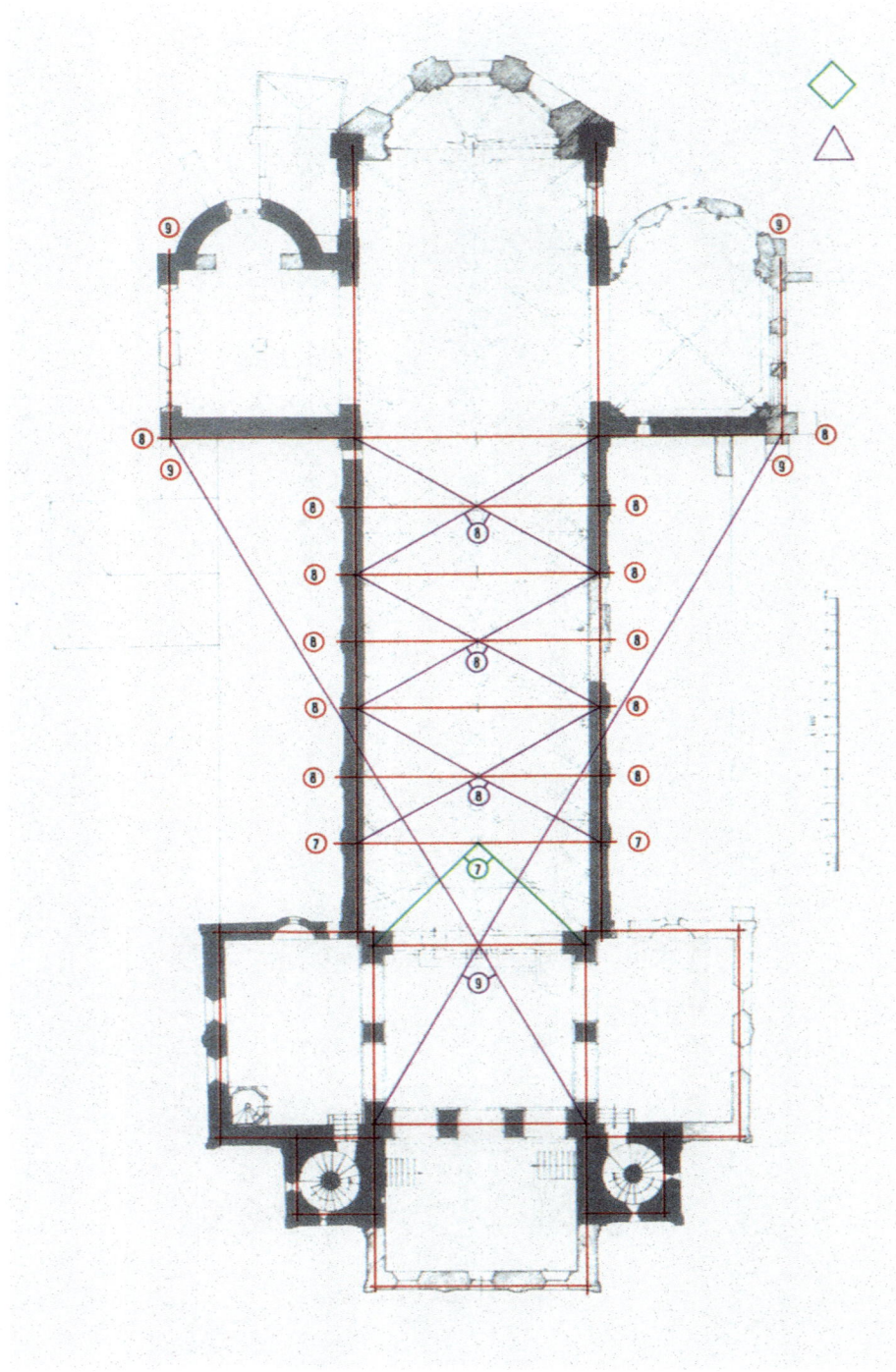

Plate 24: St Pantaleon, Cologne: setting-out, steps 7-9.

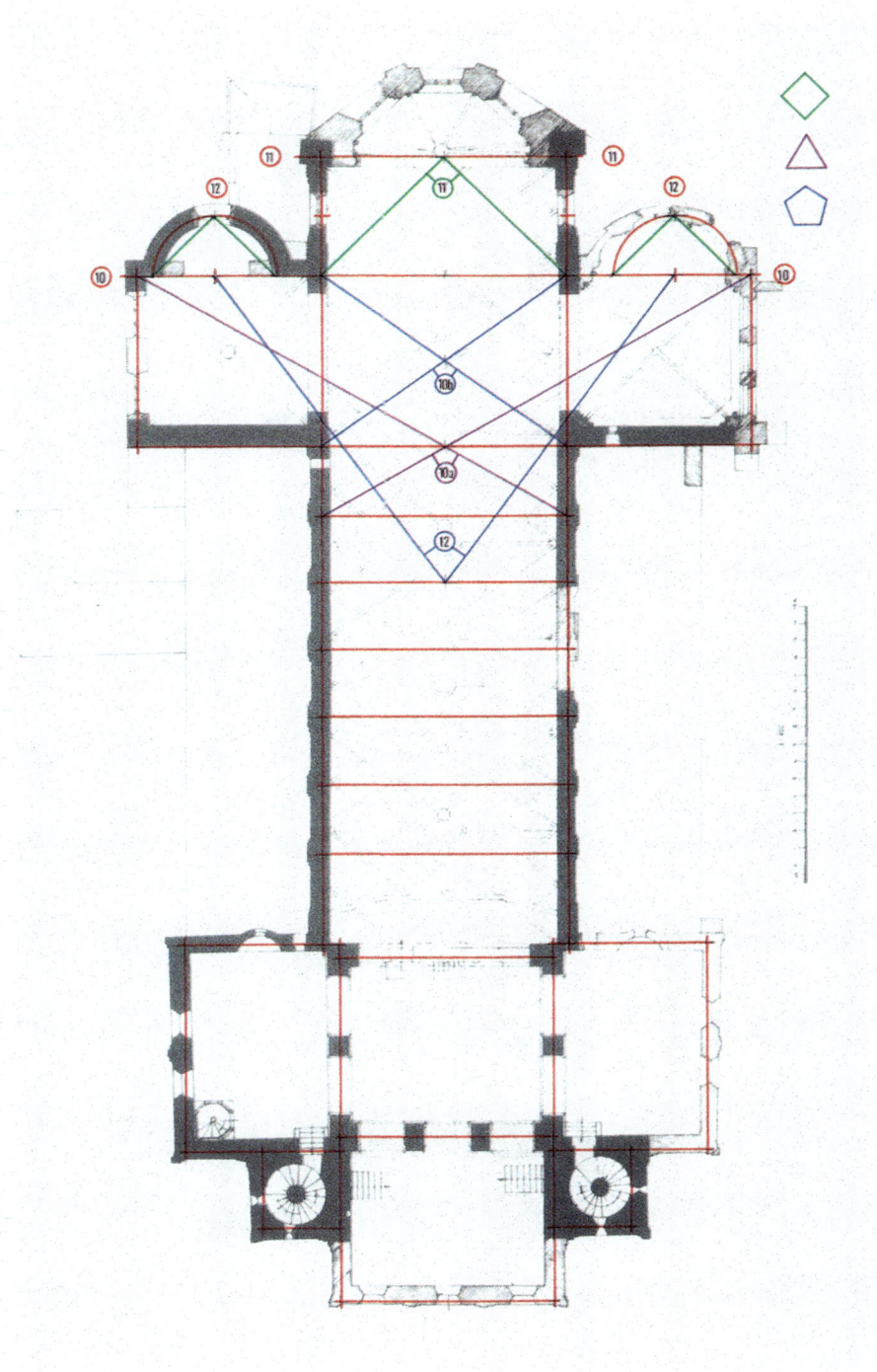

Plate 25: St Pantaleon, Cologne: setting-out, steps 10-12.

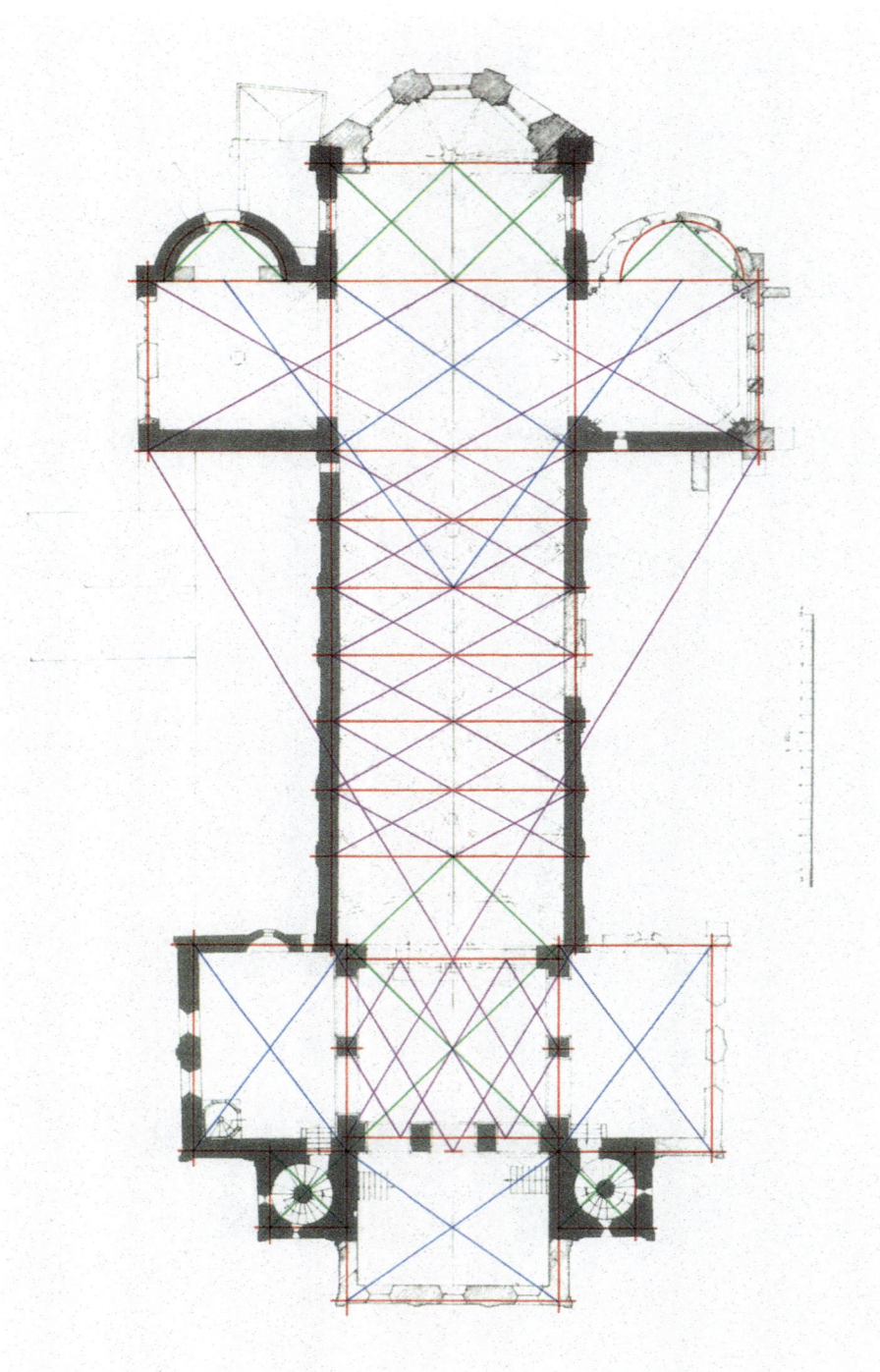

Plate 26: St Pantaleon, Cologne: all alignments.

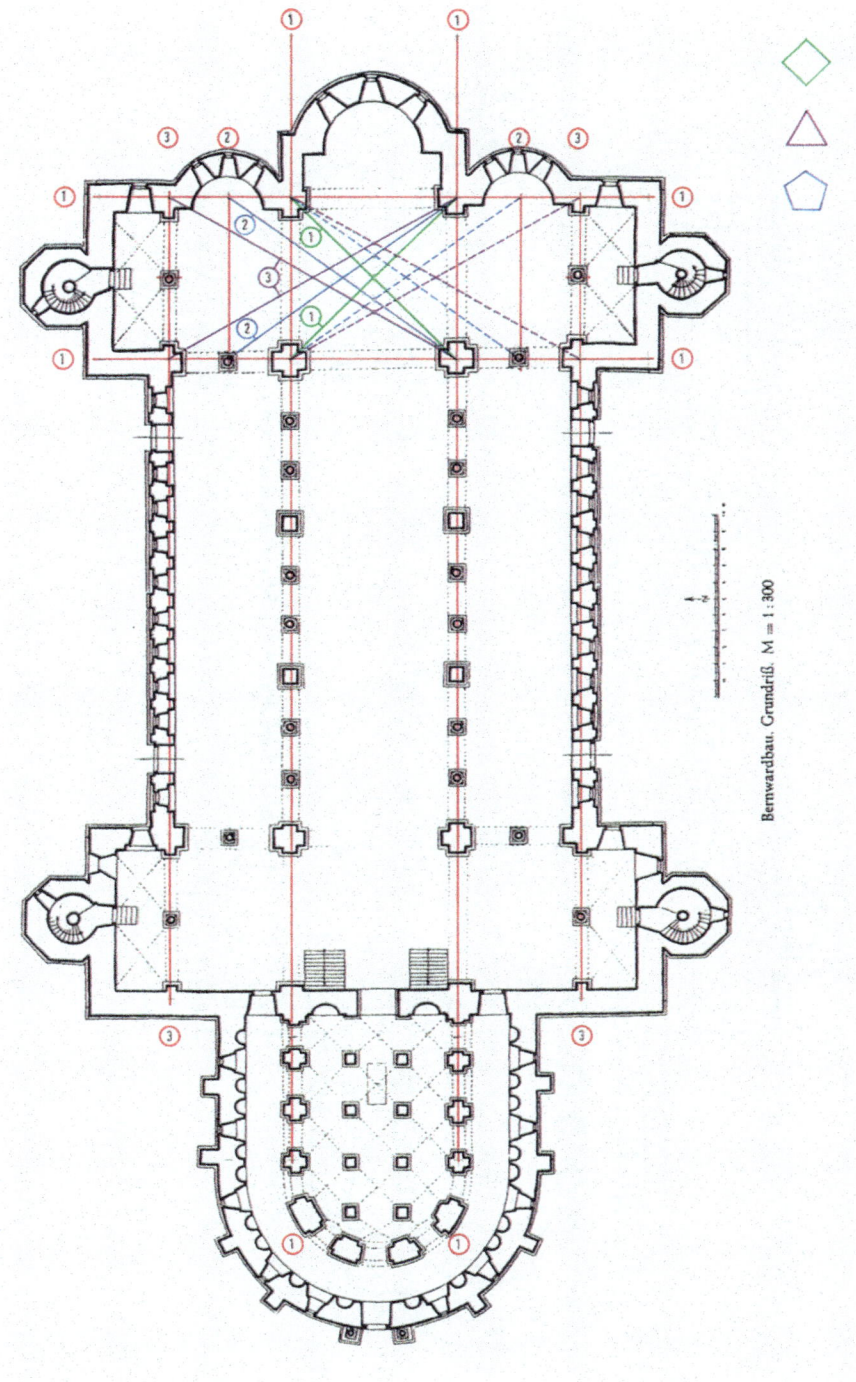

Plate 27: St Michael, Hildesheim, after Beseler & Roggenkamp: setting-out, steps 1-3.

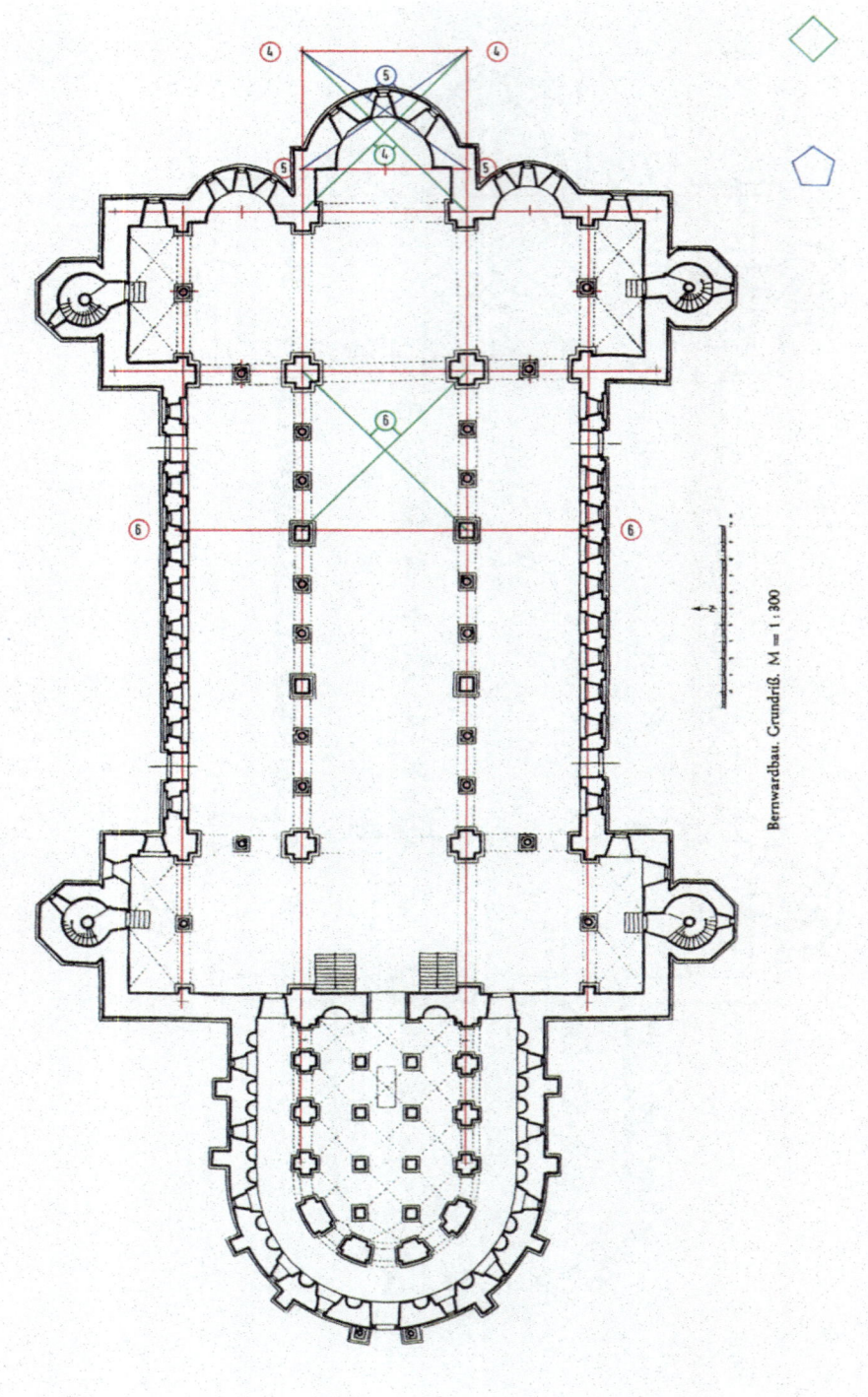

Bernwardbau. Grundriß. M = 1:300

Plate 28: St Michael, Hildesheim: setting-out, steps 4-6.

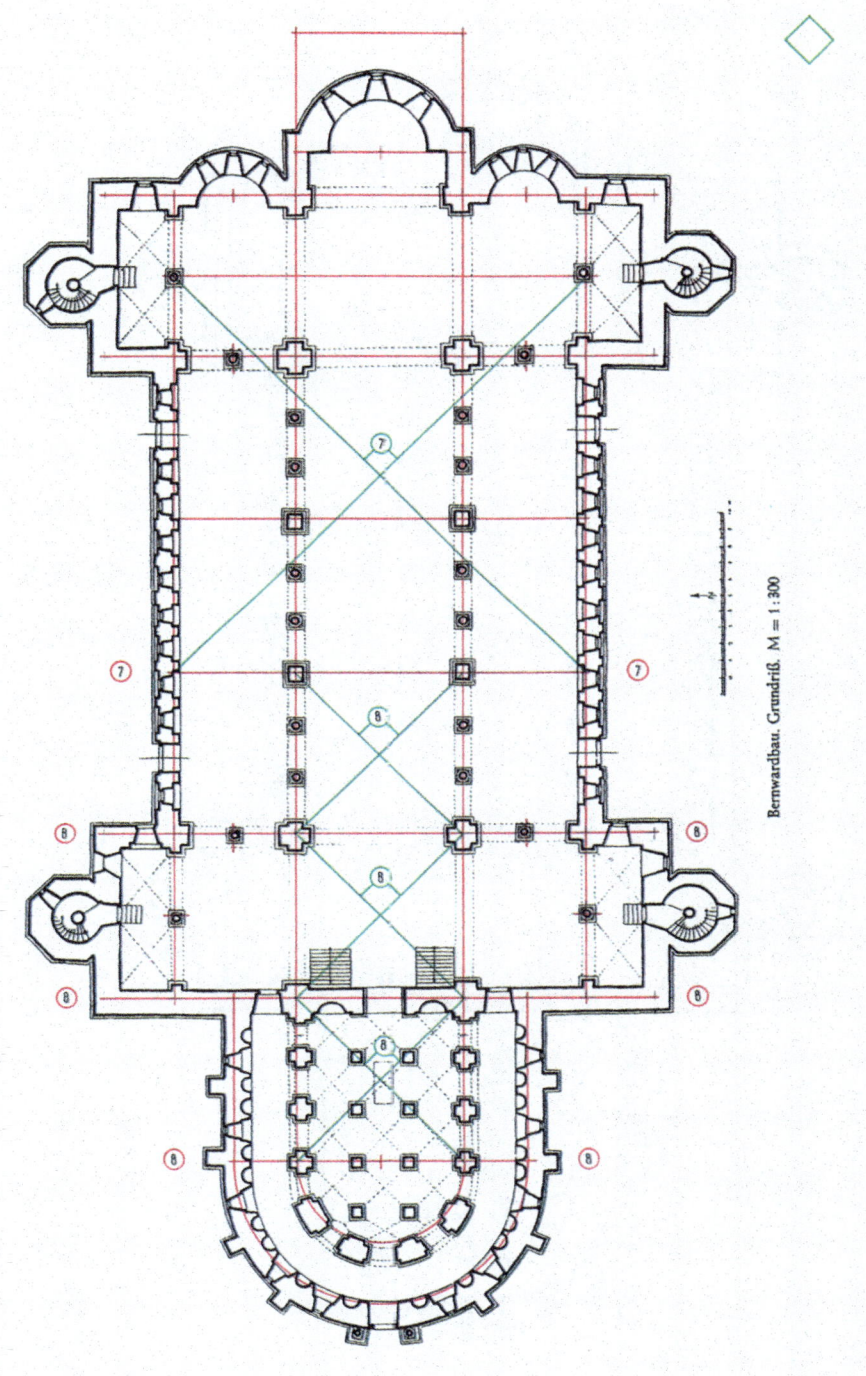

Bernwardbau. Grundriß. M = 1:300

Plate 29: St Michael, Hildesheim: setting-out, steps 7, 8.

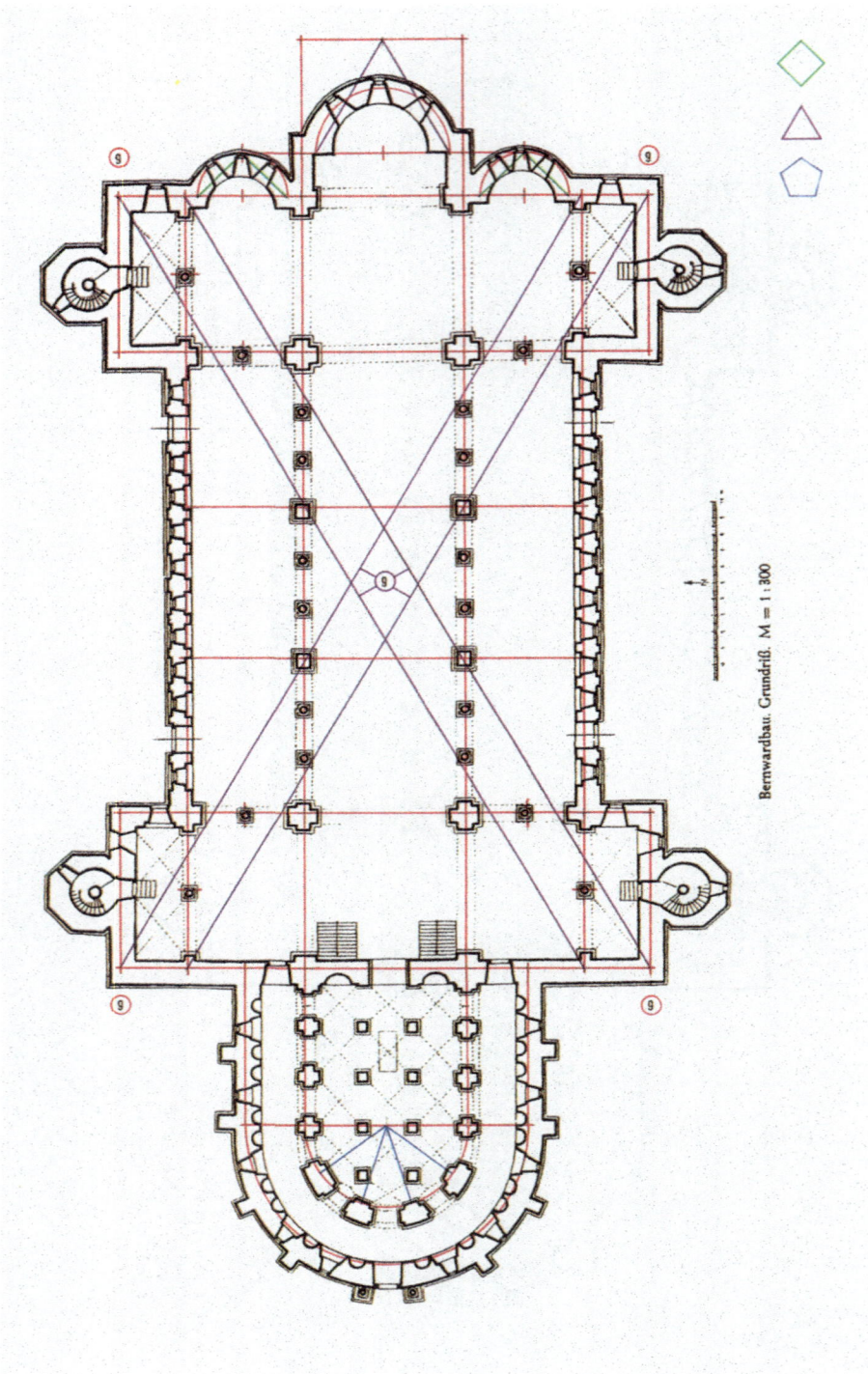

Bernwardbau. Grundriß. M = 1:300

Plate 30: St Michael, Hildesheim: setting-out, step 9.

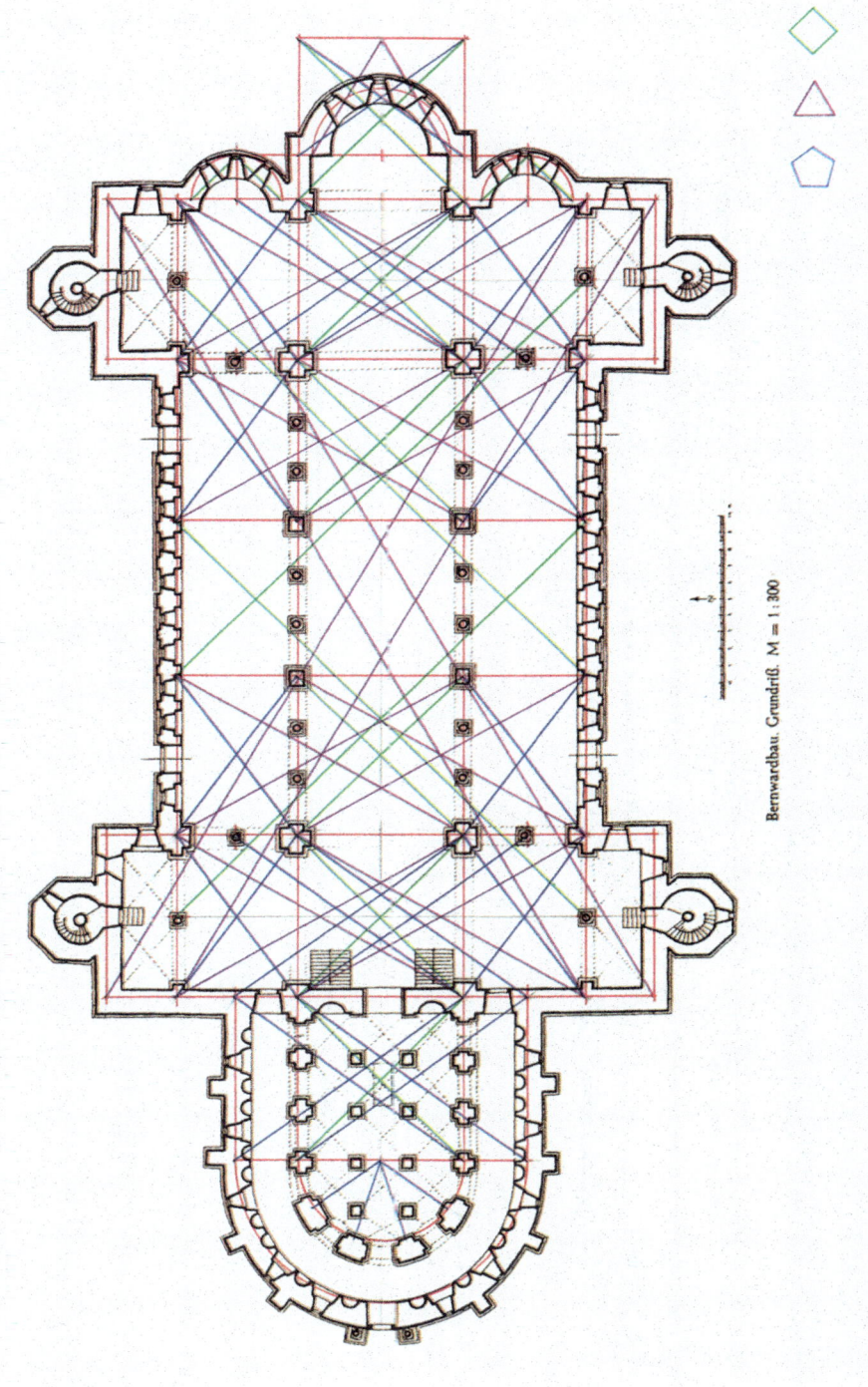

Bernwardbau. Grundriß. M = 1:300

Plate 31: St Michael, Hildesheim: all alignments.

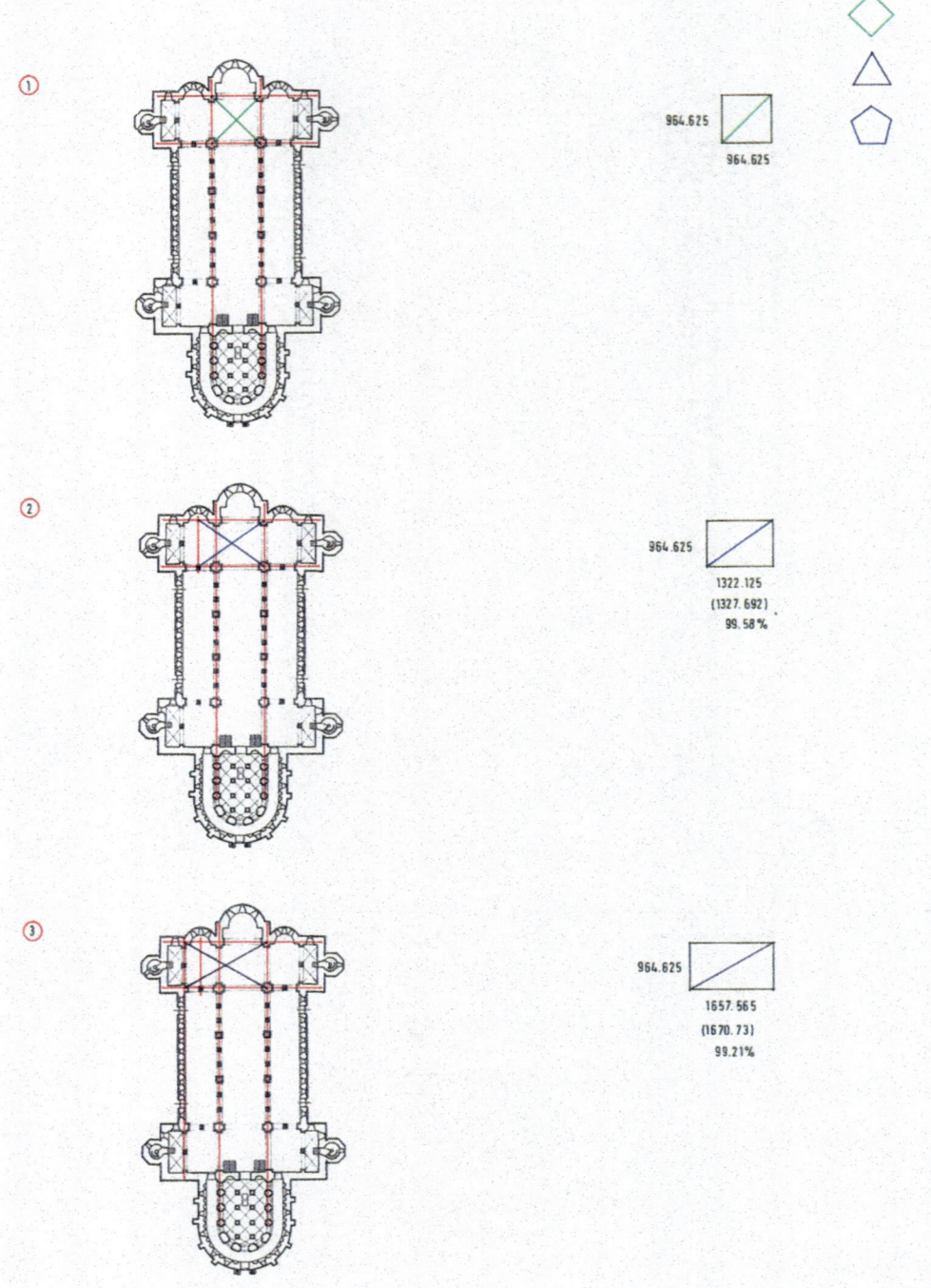

Plate 32: St Michael, Hildesheim: mathematical test, steps 1-3.

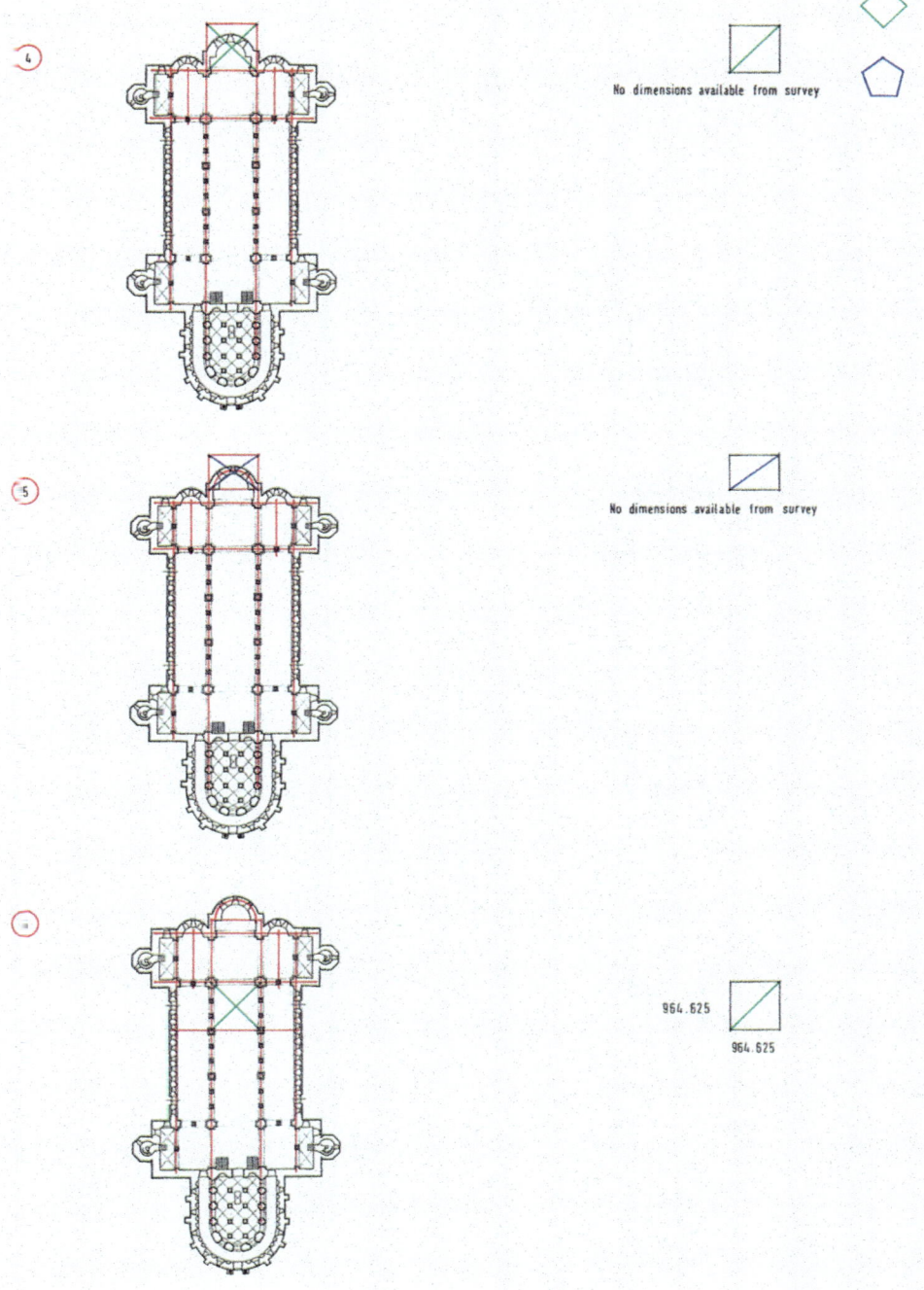

Plate 33: St Michael, Hildesheim: mathematical test, steps 4-6.

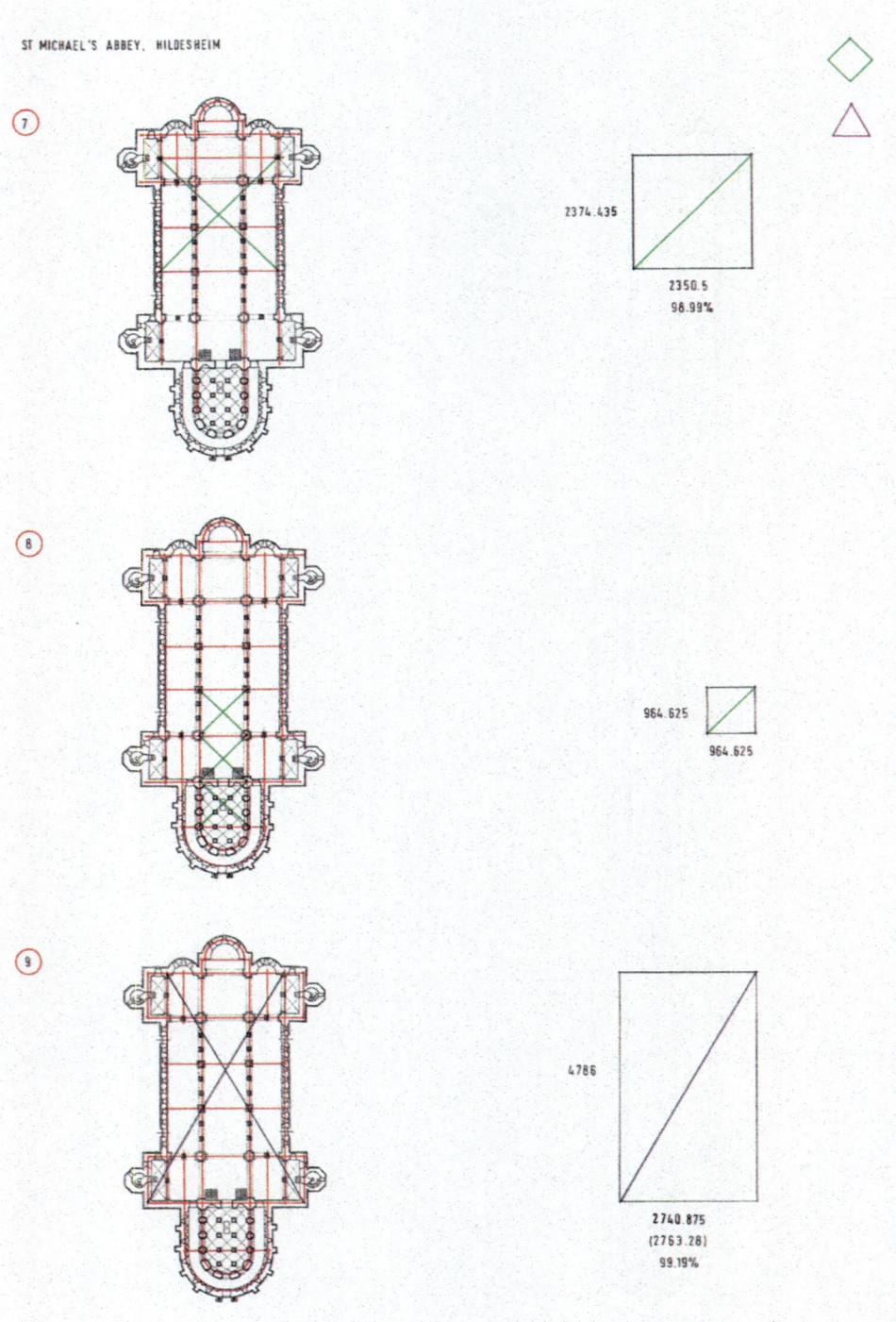

Plate 34: St Michael, Hildesheim: mathematical test, steps 7-9.

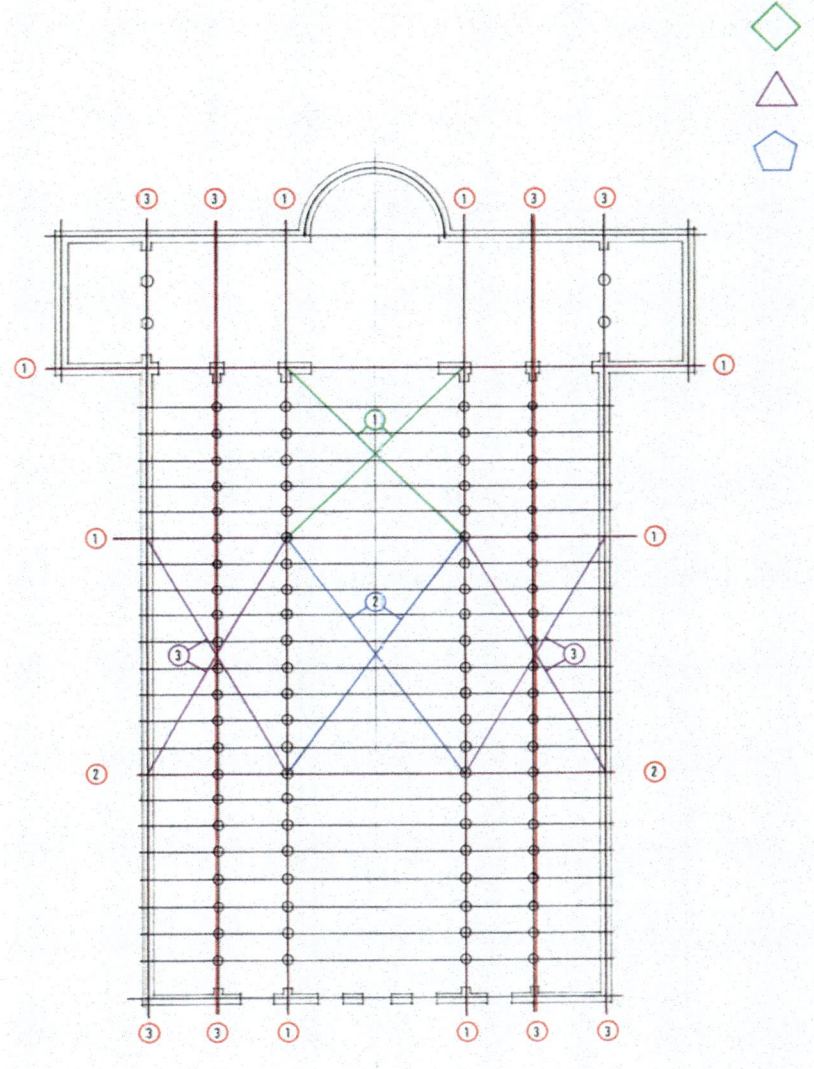

Plate 35: St Peter, Rome, after Fernie: setting-out, steps 1-3.

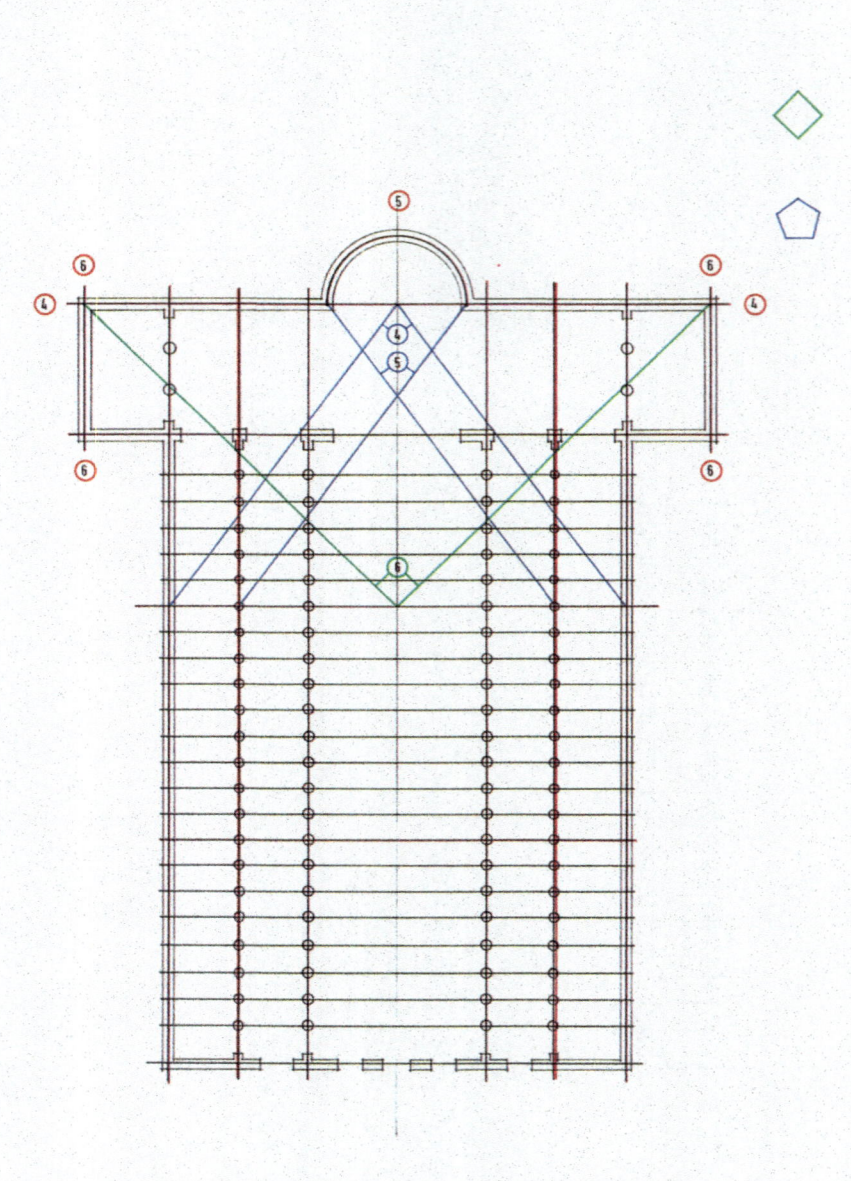

Plate 36: St Peter, Rome: setting-out, steps 4-6.

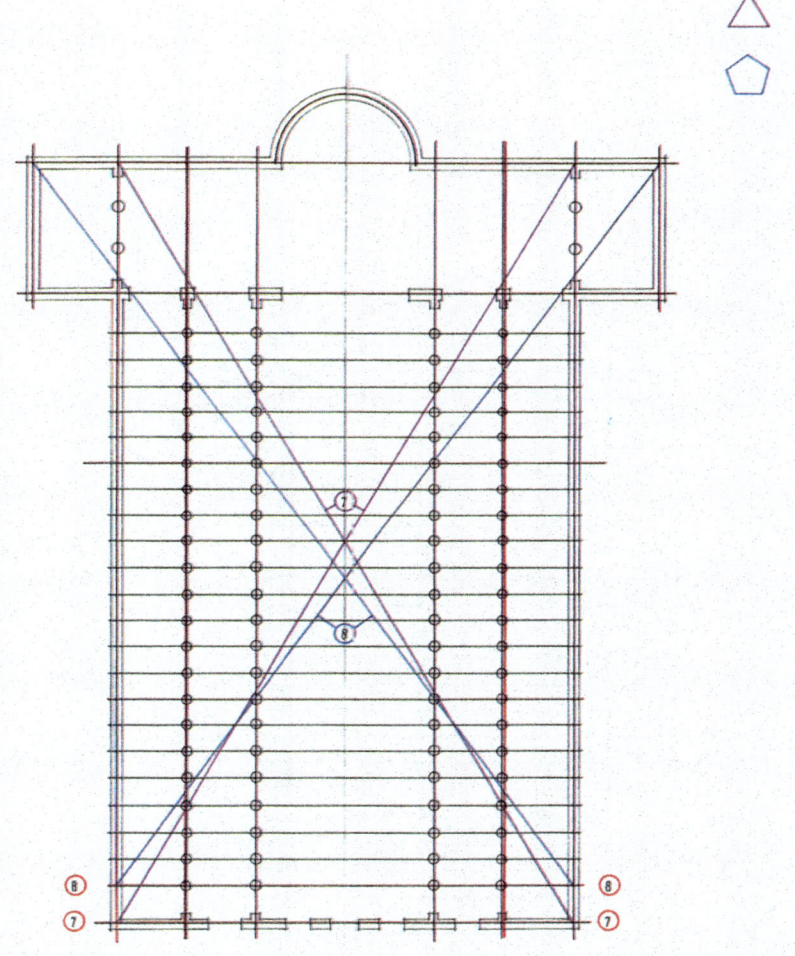

Plate 37: St Peter, Rome: setting-out, steps 7, 8.

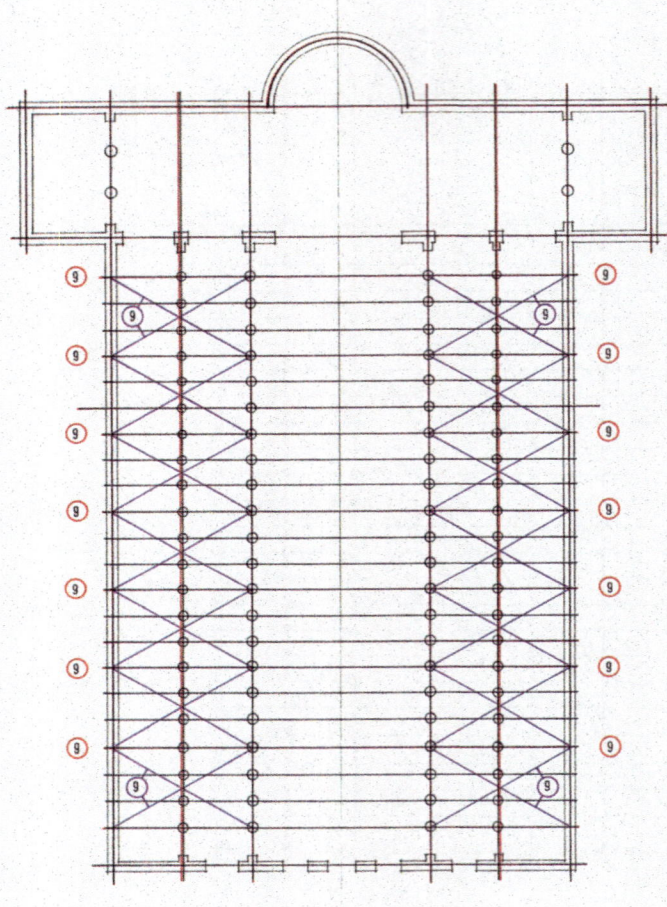

Plate 38: St Peter, Rome: setting-out, step 9.

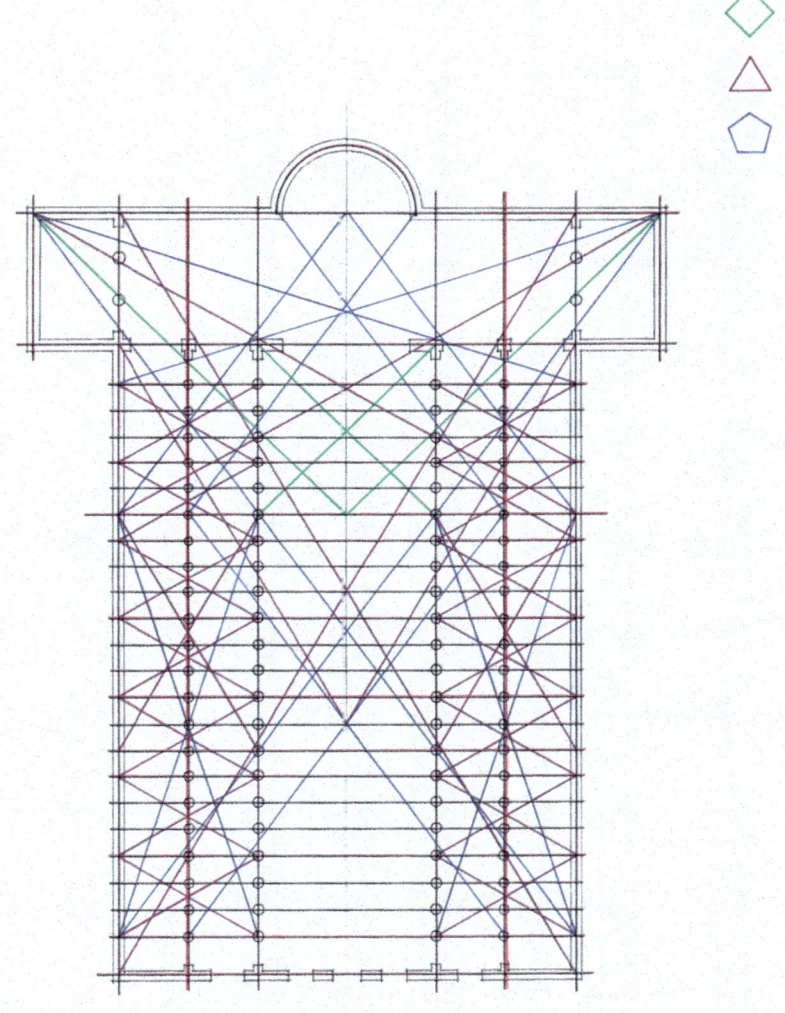

Plate 39: St Peter, Rome: all alignments.

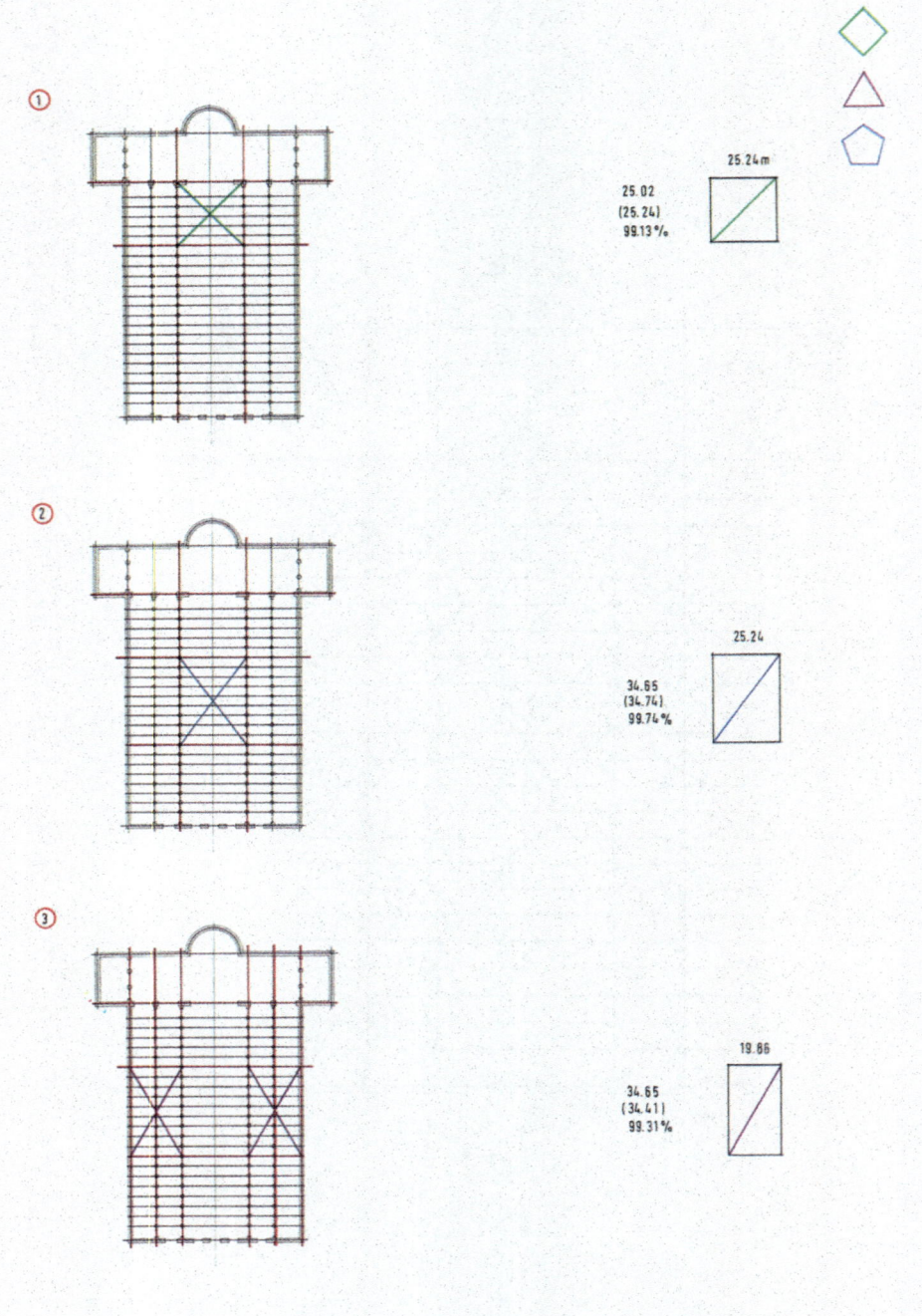

Plate 40: St Peter, Rome: mathematical proof, steps 1-3.

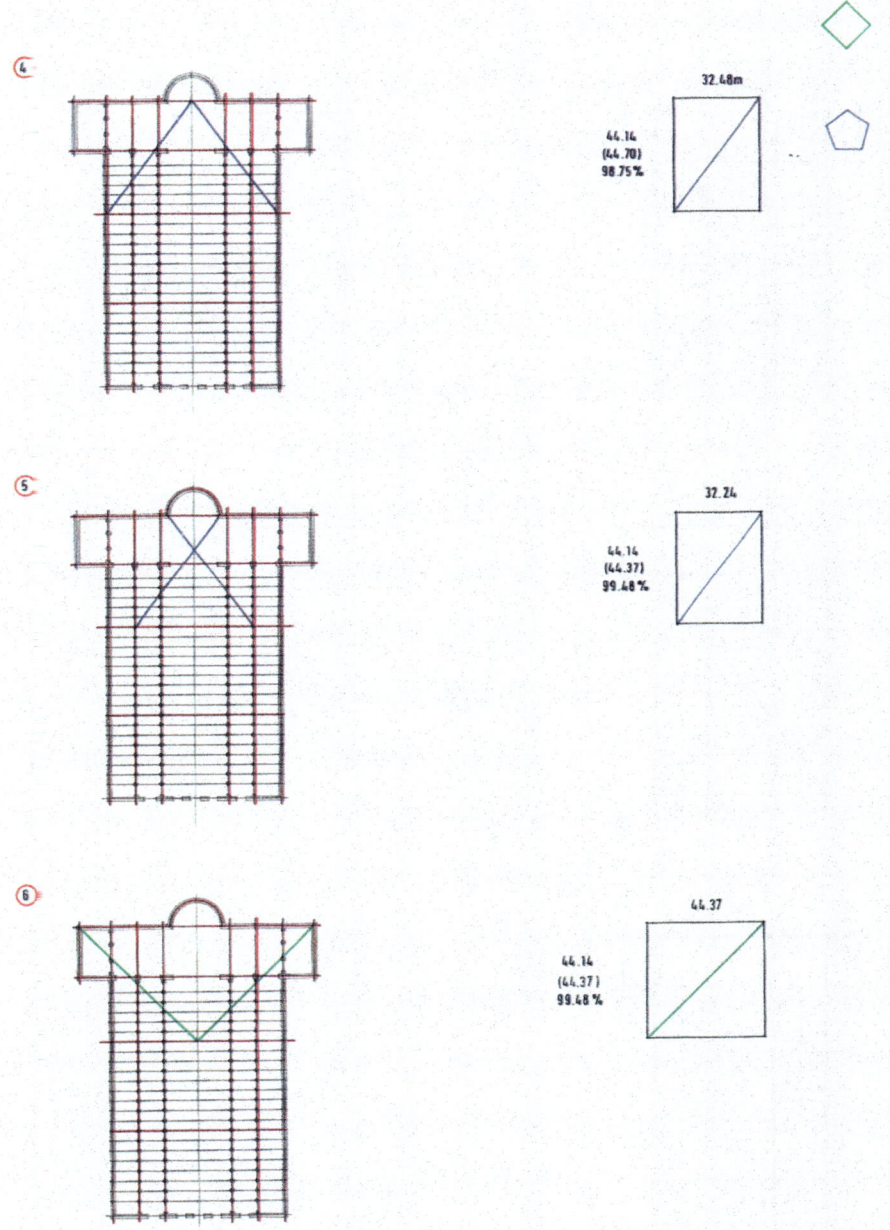

Plate 41: St Peter, Rome: mathematical proof, steps 4-6.

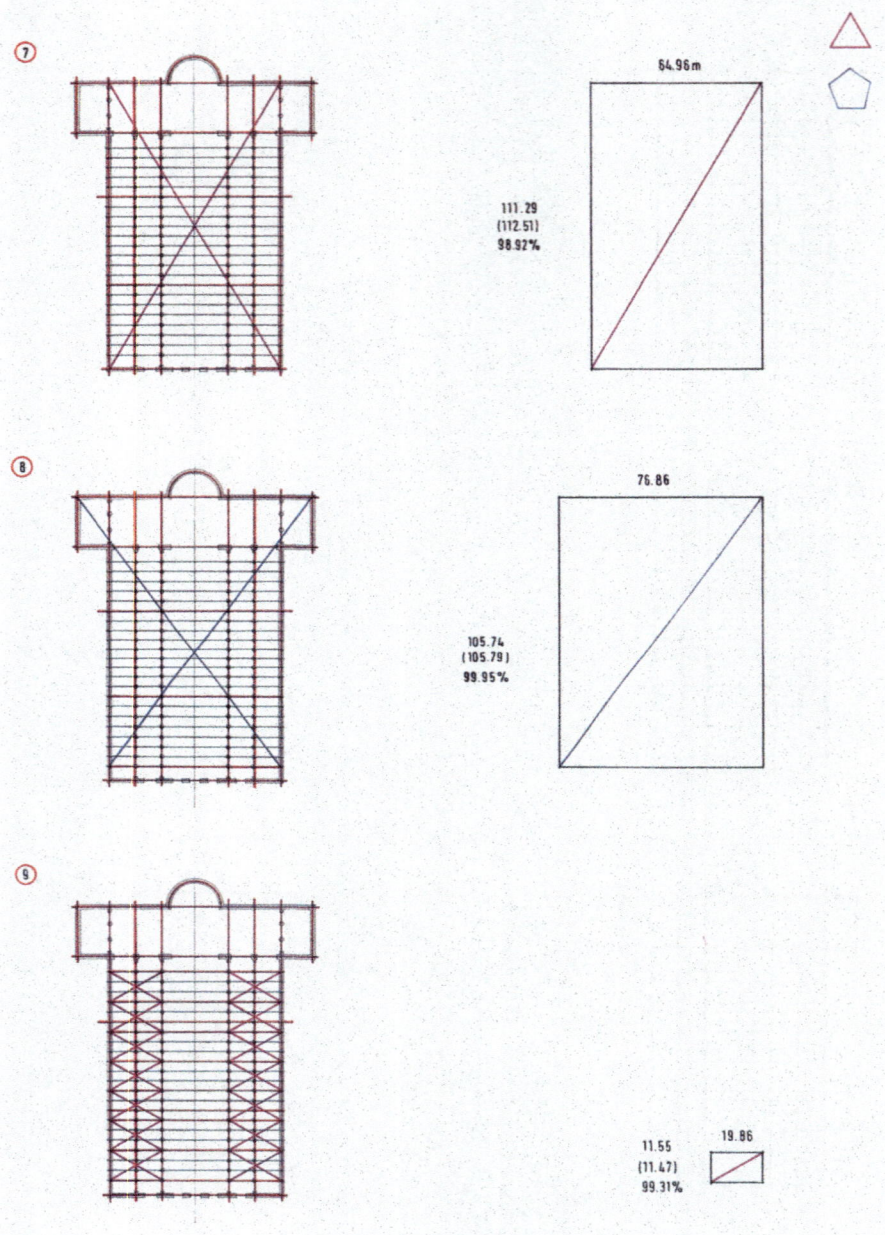

Plate 42: St Peter, Rome: mathematical proof, steps 7-9.

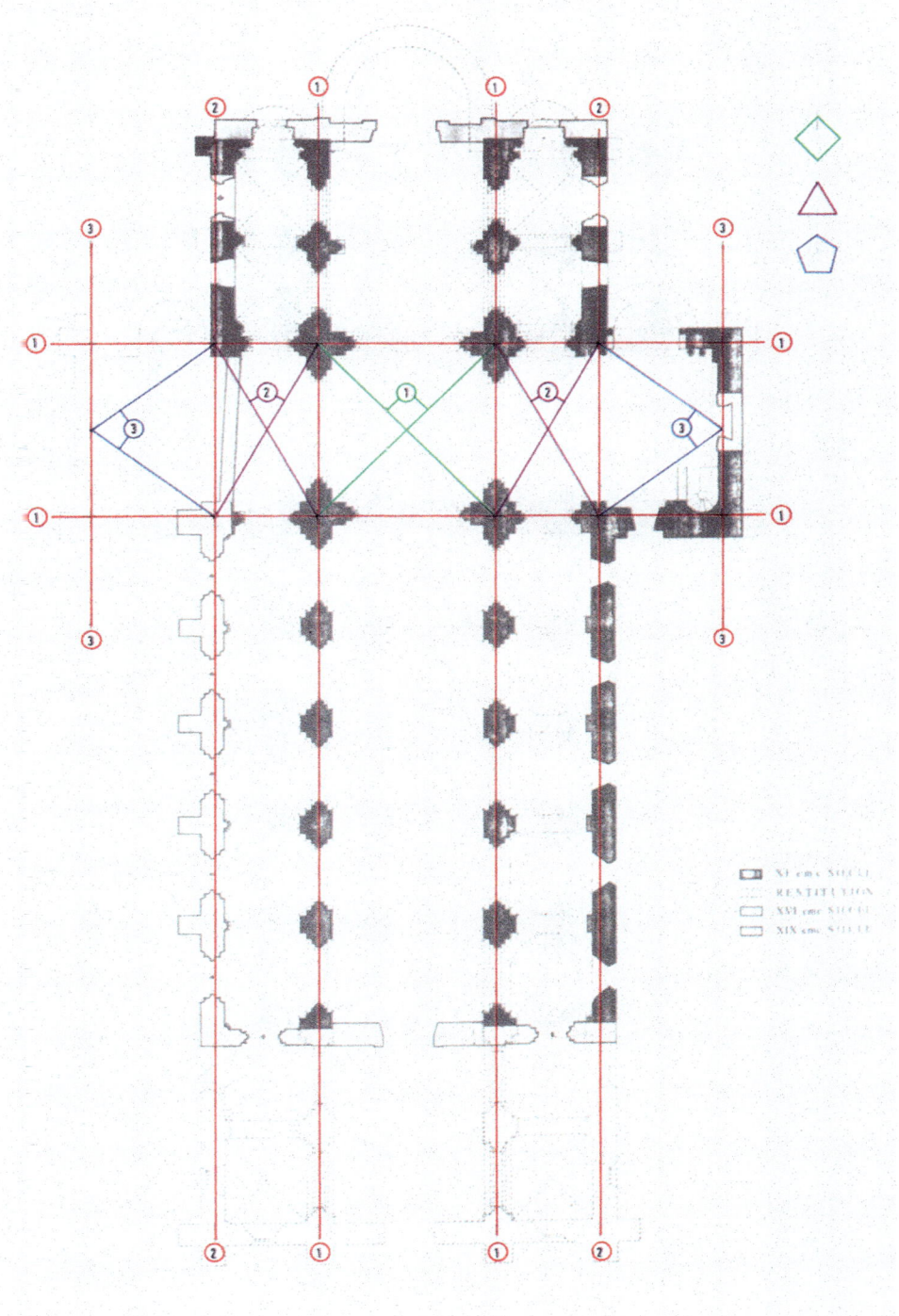

Plate 43: Bernay Abbey, after Duval: setting-out, steps 1-3.

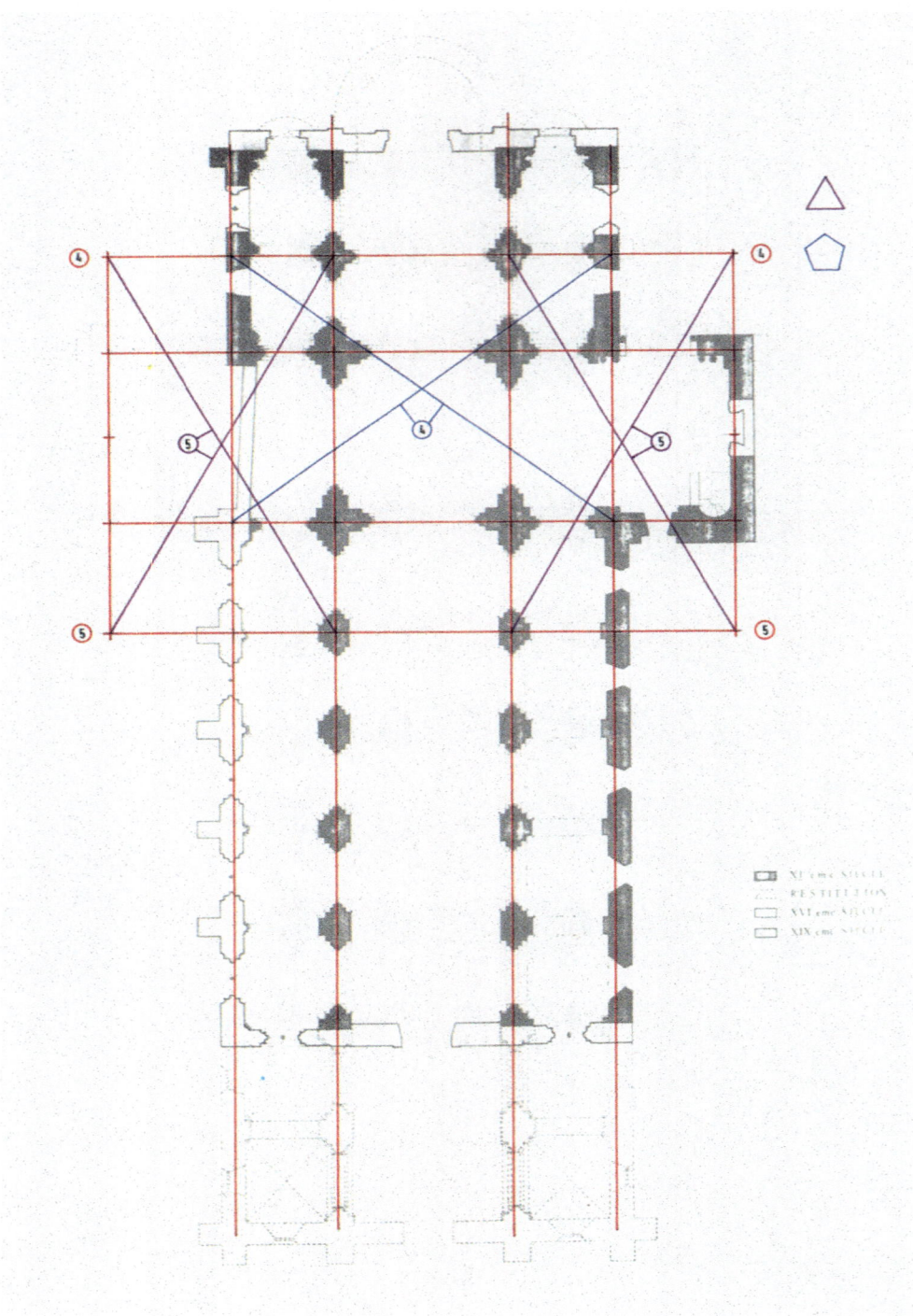

Plate 44: Bernay Abbey: setting-out, steps 4, 5.

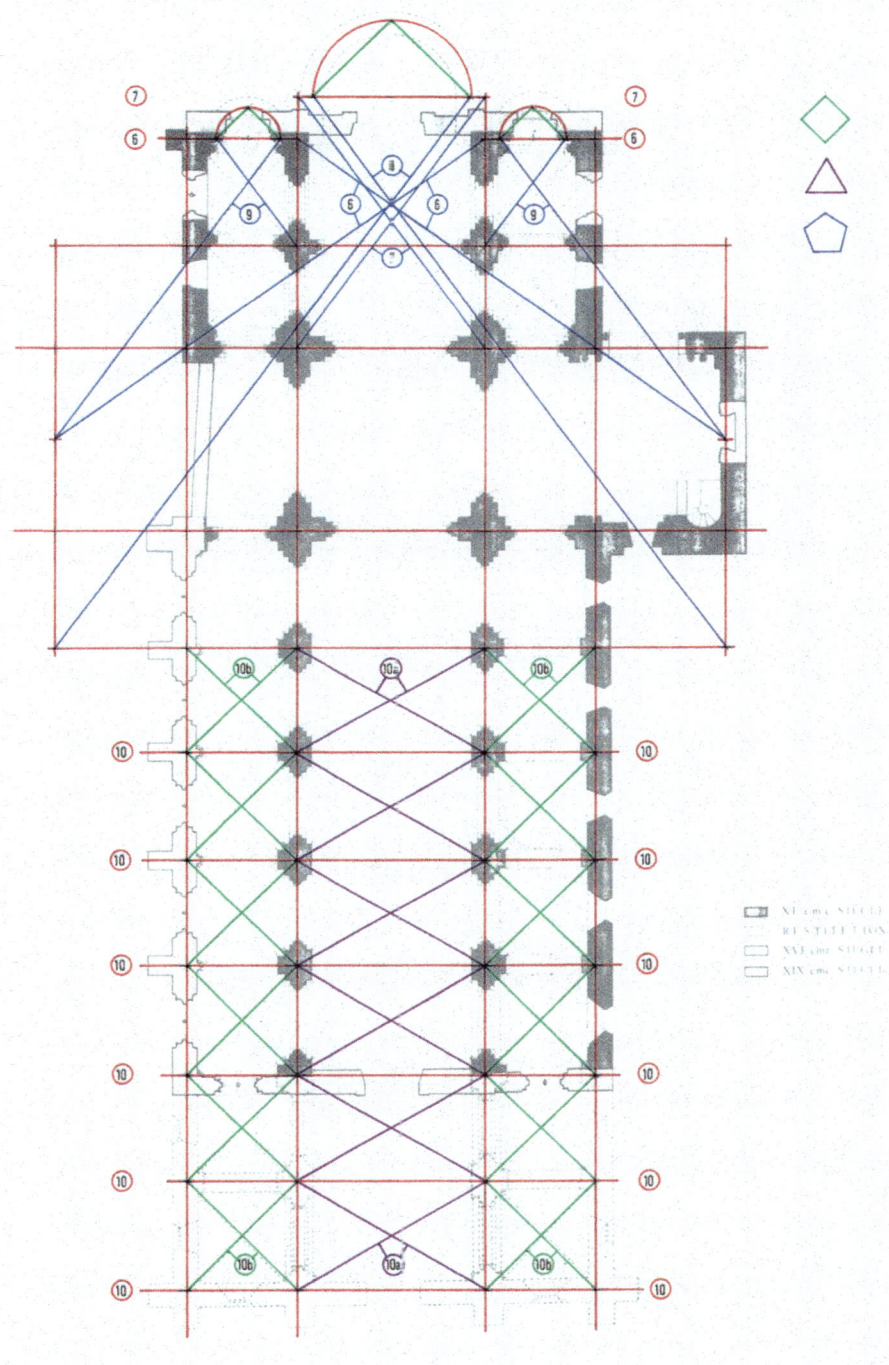

Plate 45: Bernay Abbey: setting-out, steps 6-10.

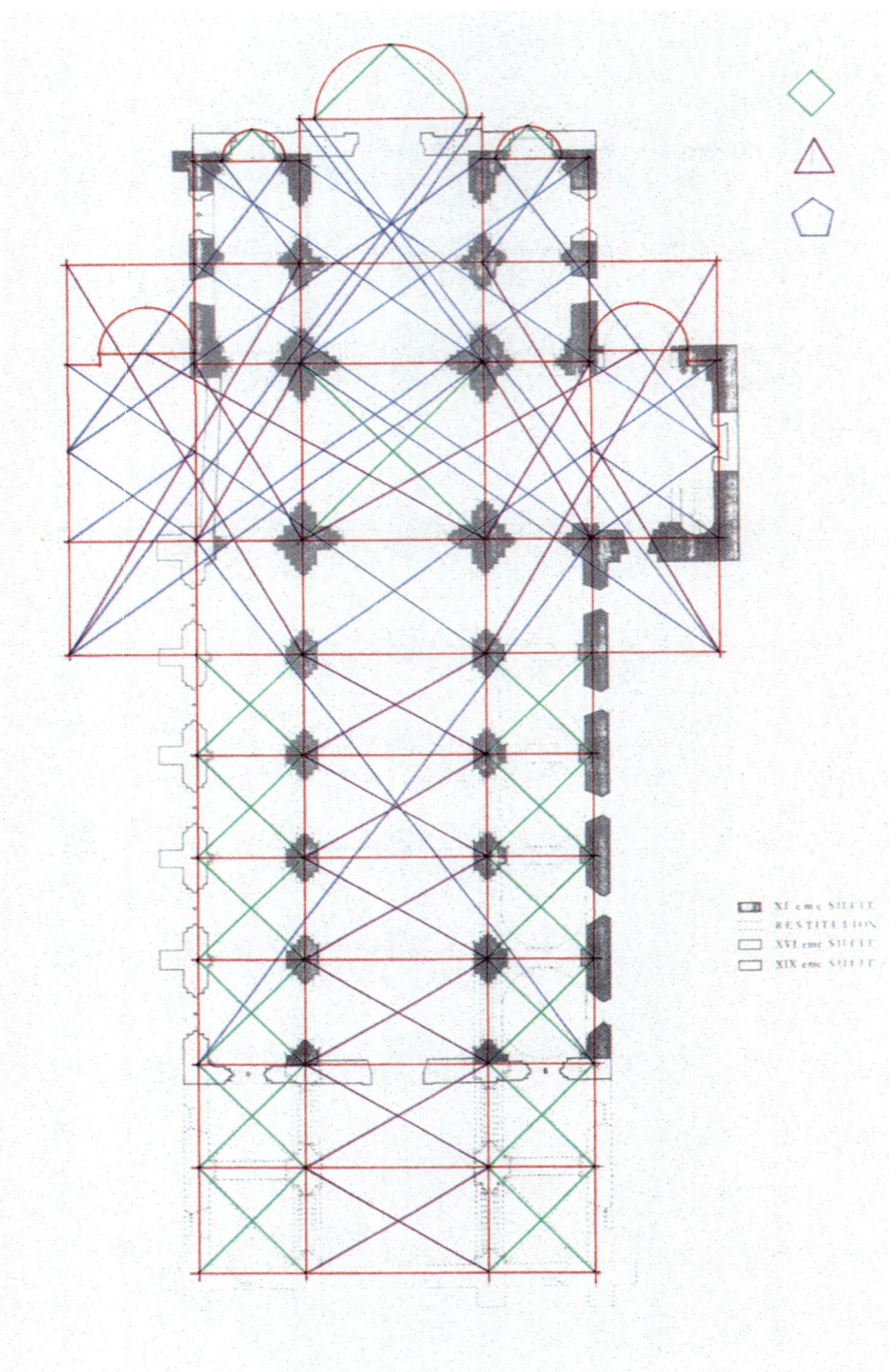

Plate 46: Bernay Abbey: all alignments.

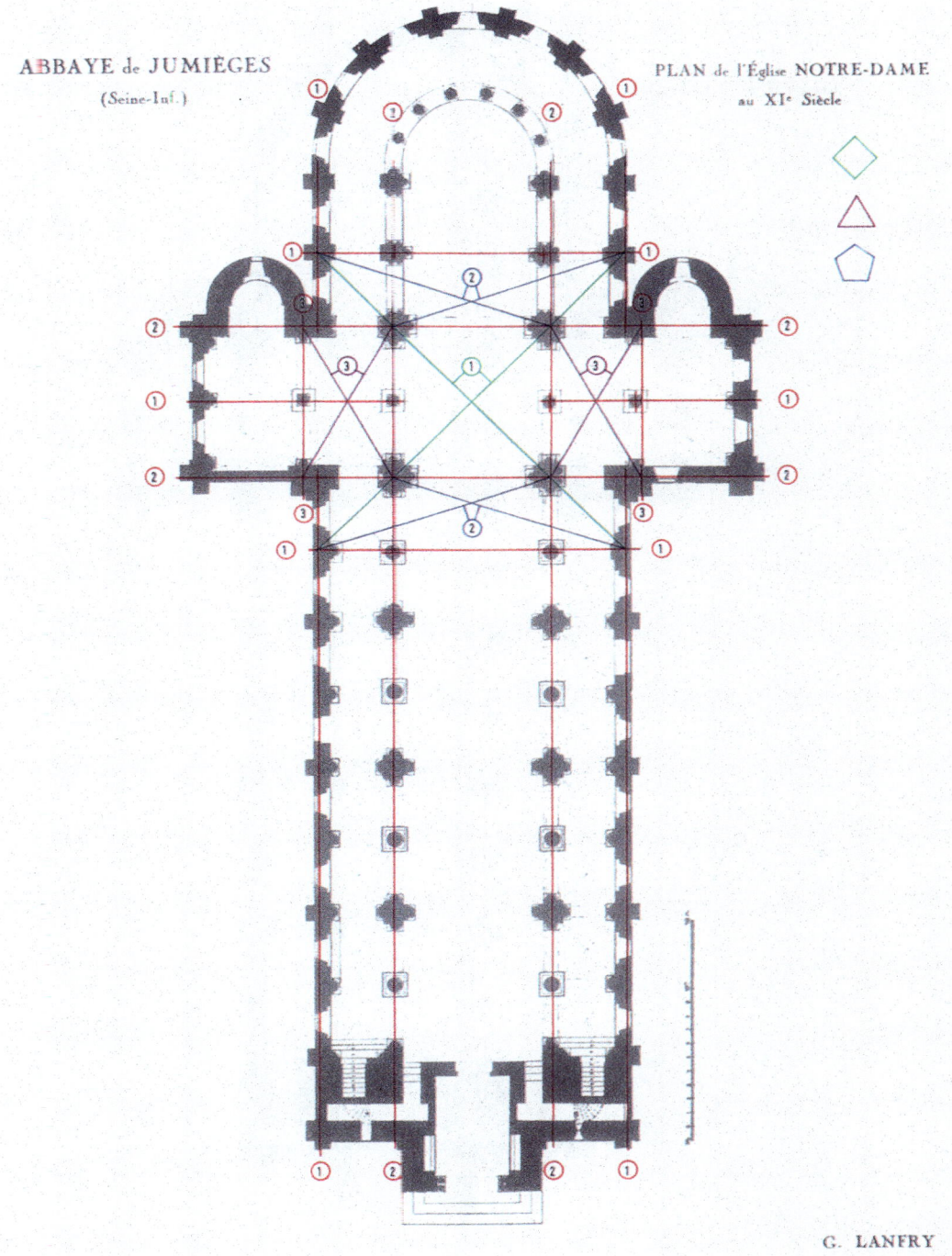

ABBAYE de JUMIÈGES
(Seine-Inf.)

PLAN de l'Église NOTRE-DAME
au XIᵉ Siècle

G. LANFRY

Plate 47: Jumièges Abbey, after Lanfry: setting-out, steps 1-3.

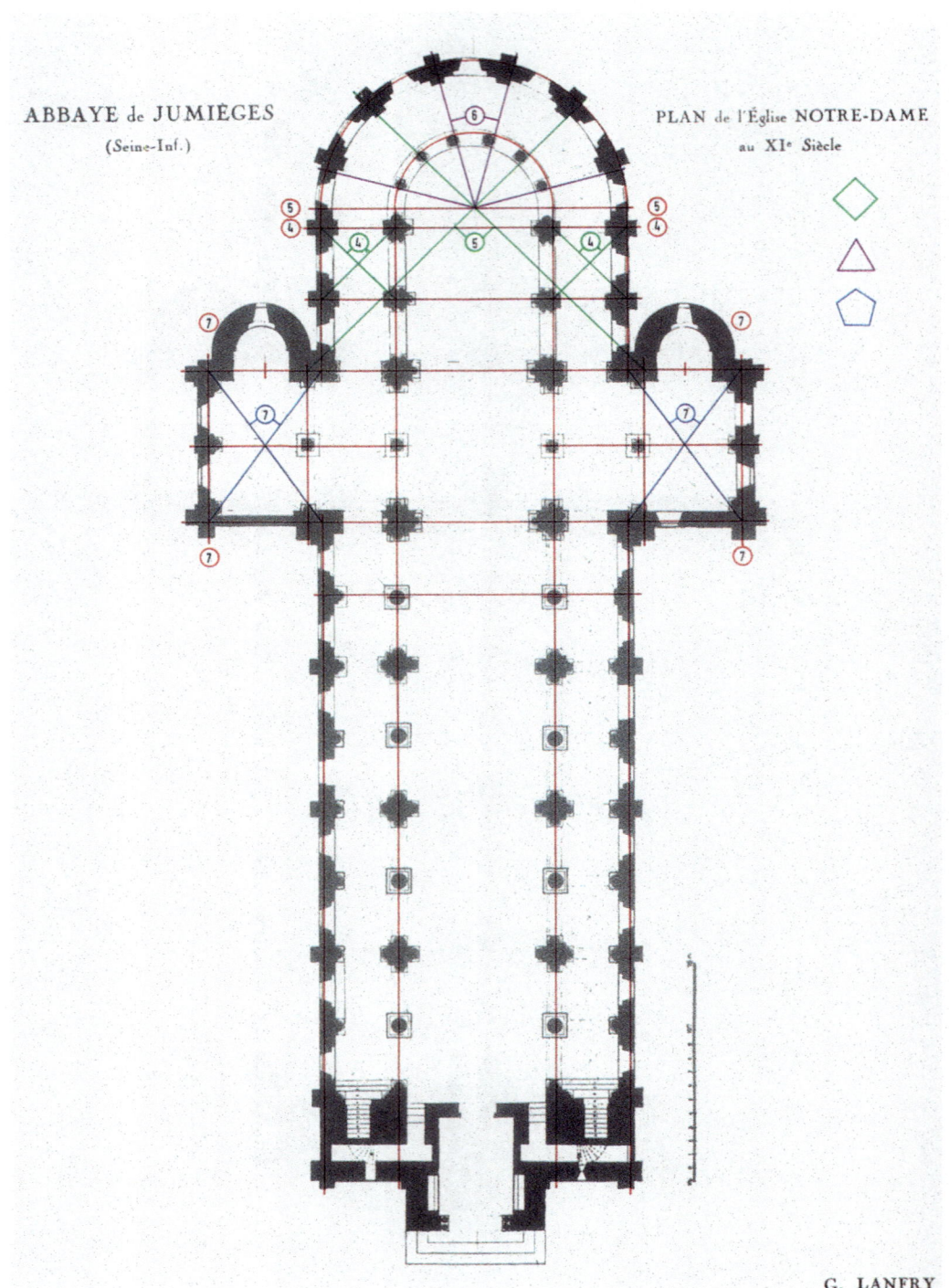

ABBAYE de JUMIÈGES
(Seine-Inf.)

PLAN de l'Église NOTRE-DAME
au XIᵉ Siècle

G. LANFRY

Plate 48: Jumièges Abbey: setting-out, steps 4-7.

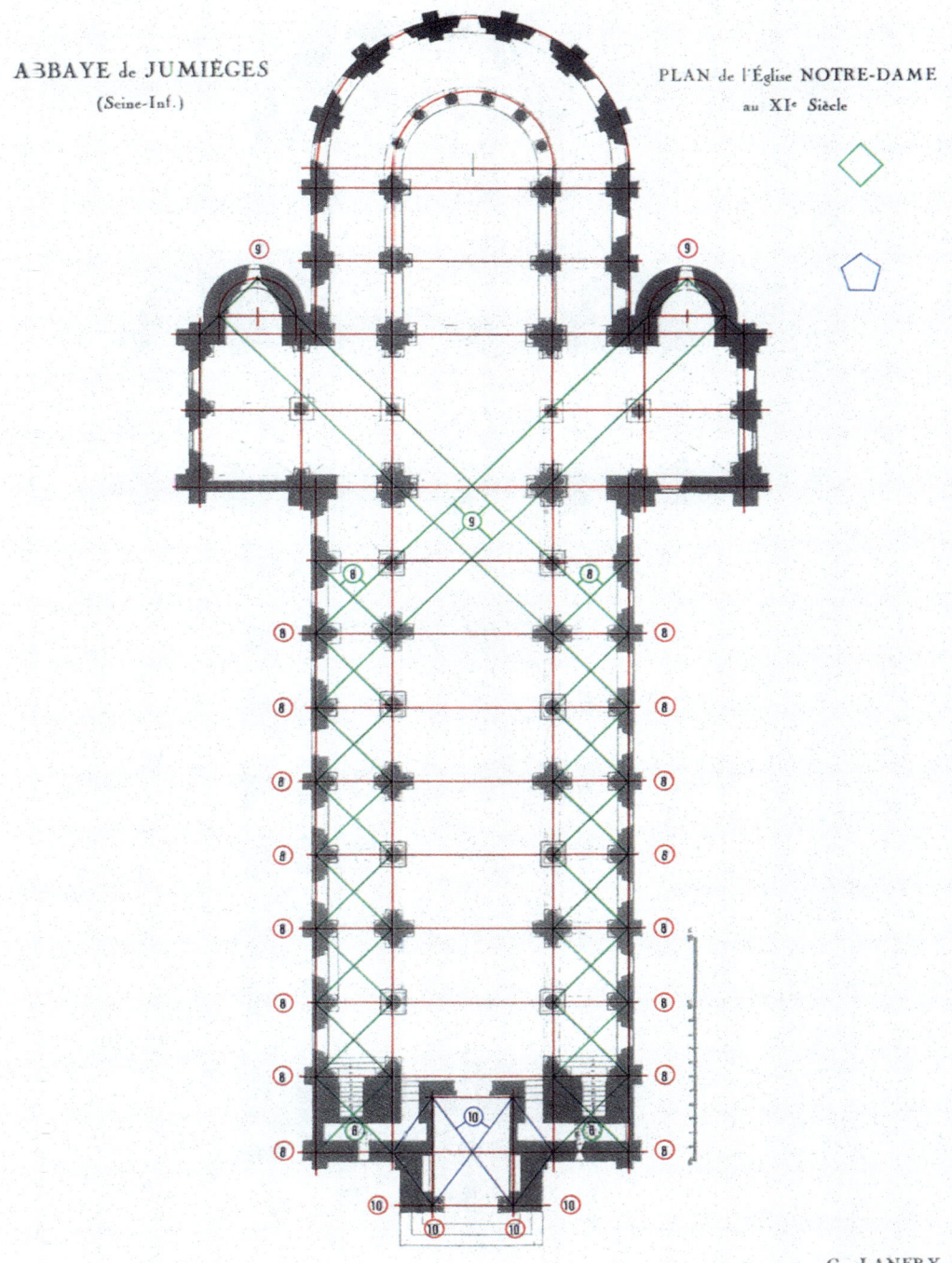

ABBAYE de JUMIÈGES
(Seine-Inf.)

PLAN de l'Église NOTRE-DAME
au XIᵉ Siècle

G. LANFRY

Plate 49: Jumièges Abbey: setting-out, steps 8-10.

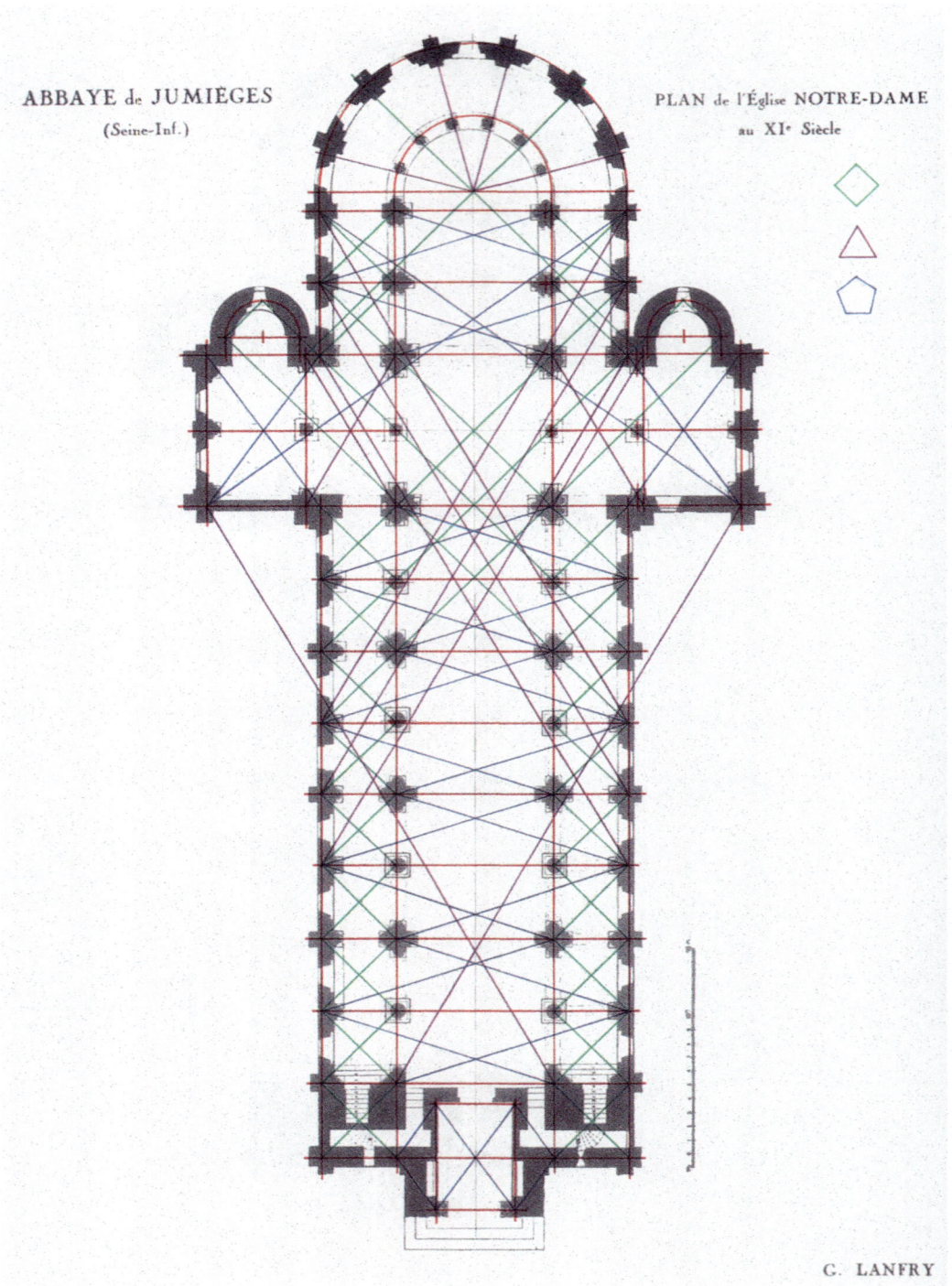

ABBAYE de JUMIÈGES
(Seine-Inf.)

PLAN de l'Église NOTRE-DAME
au XIe Siècle

G. LANFRY

Plate 50: Jumièges Abbey: all alignments.

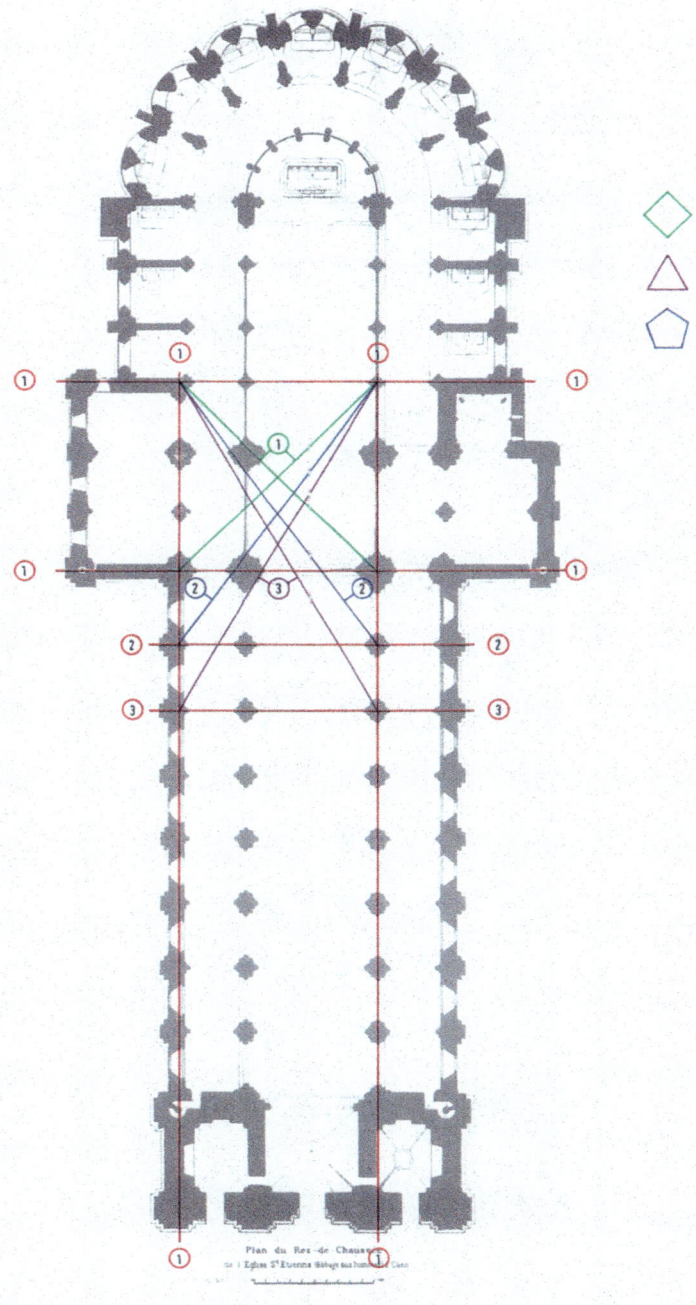

Plate 51: St Stephen, Caen, after Merlet: setting-out, steps 1-3.

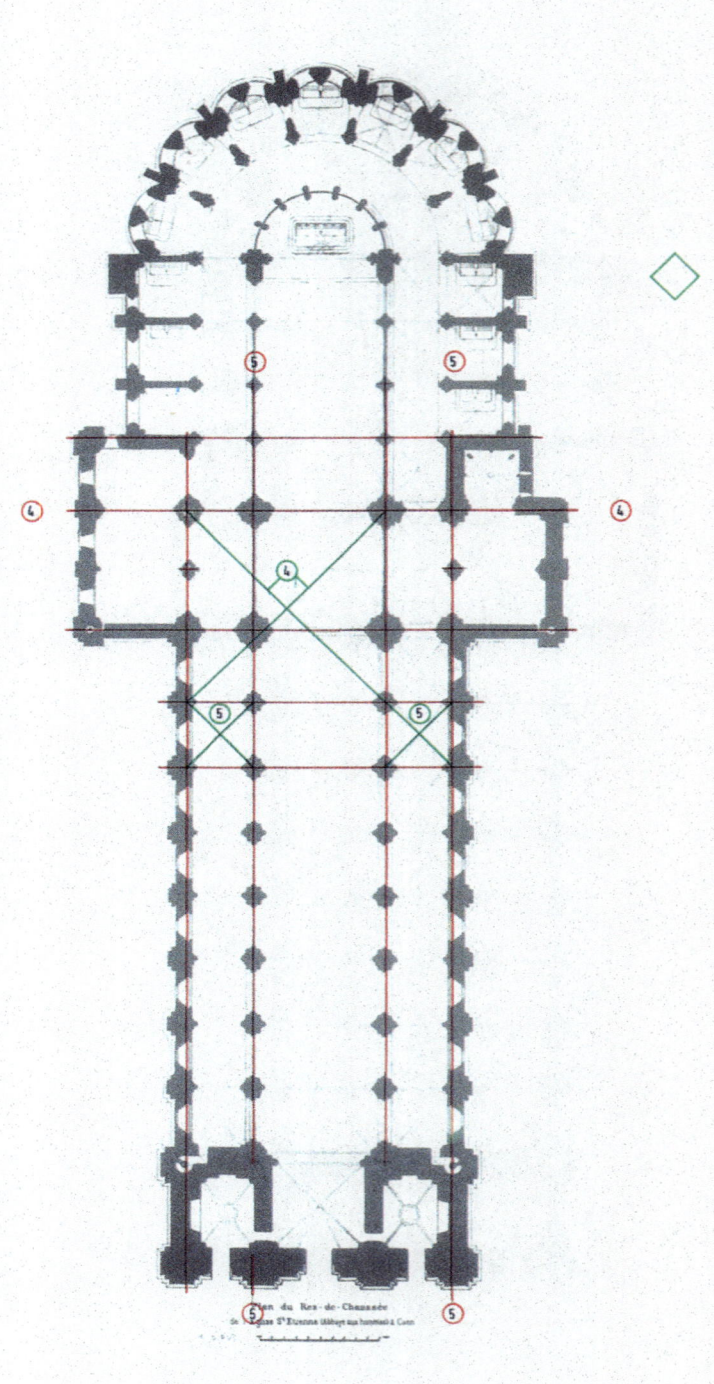

Plate 52: St Stephen, Caen: setting-out, steps 4, 5.

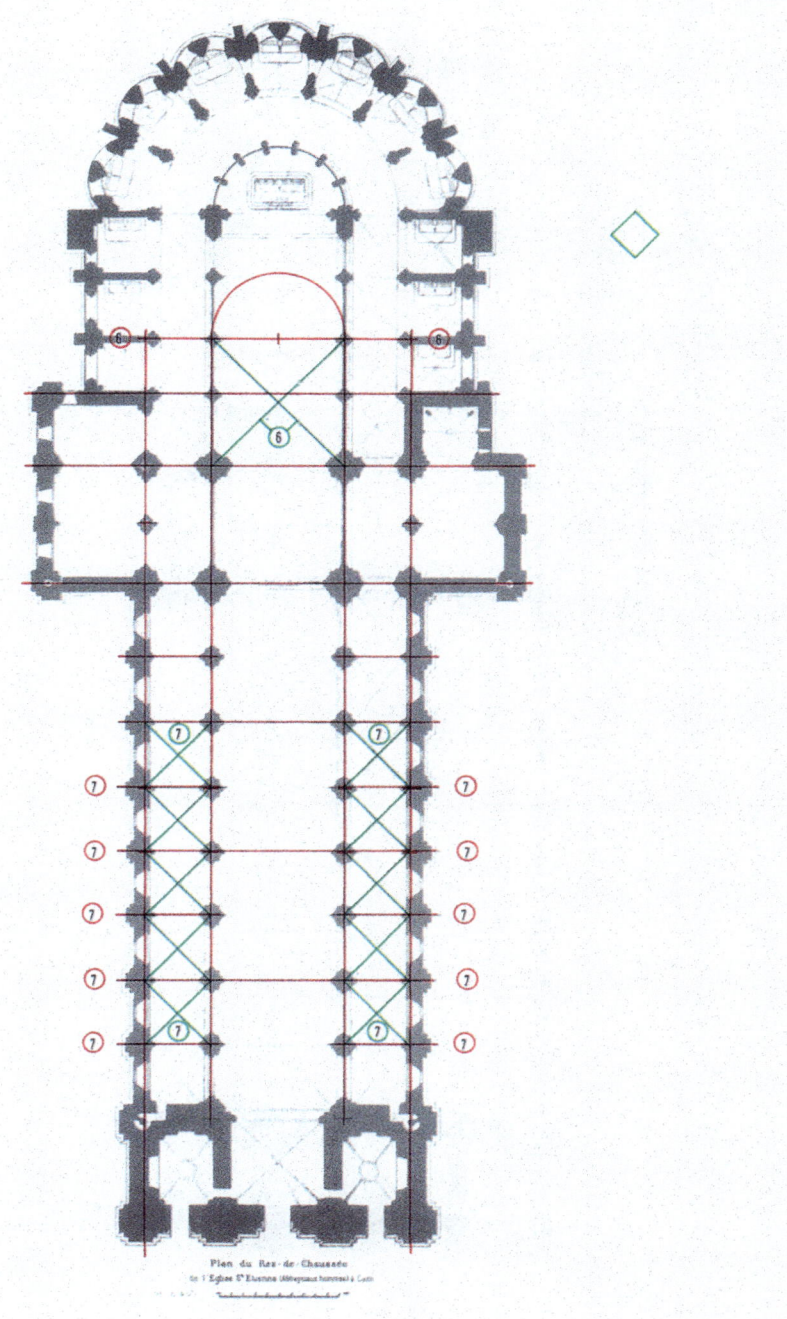

Plate 53: St Stephen, Caen: setting-out, steps 6, 7.

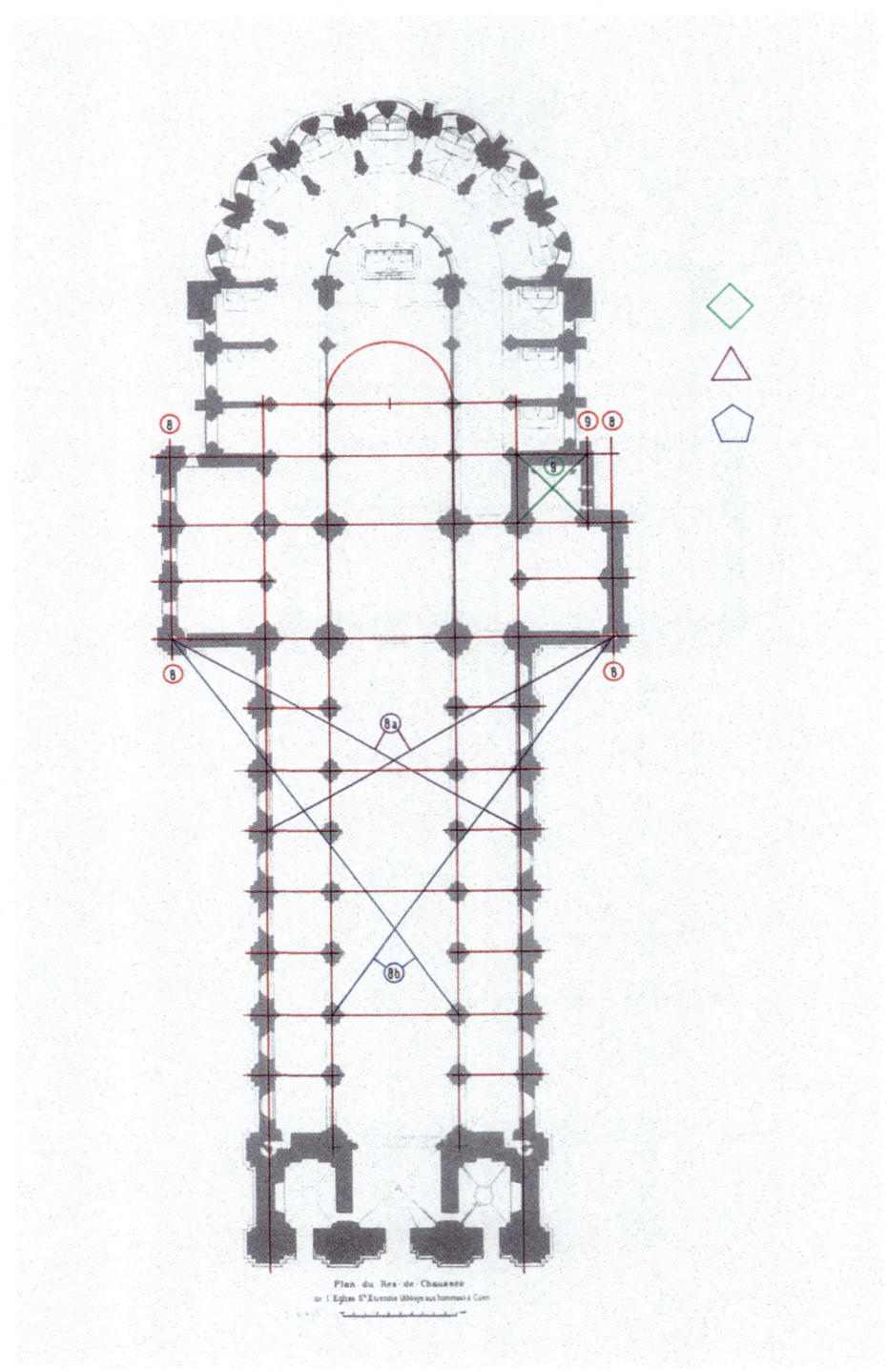

Plate 54: St Stephen, Caen: setting-out, steps 8, 9.

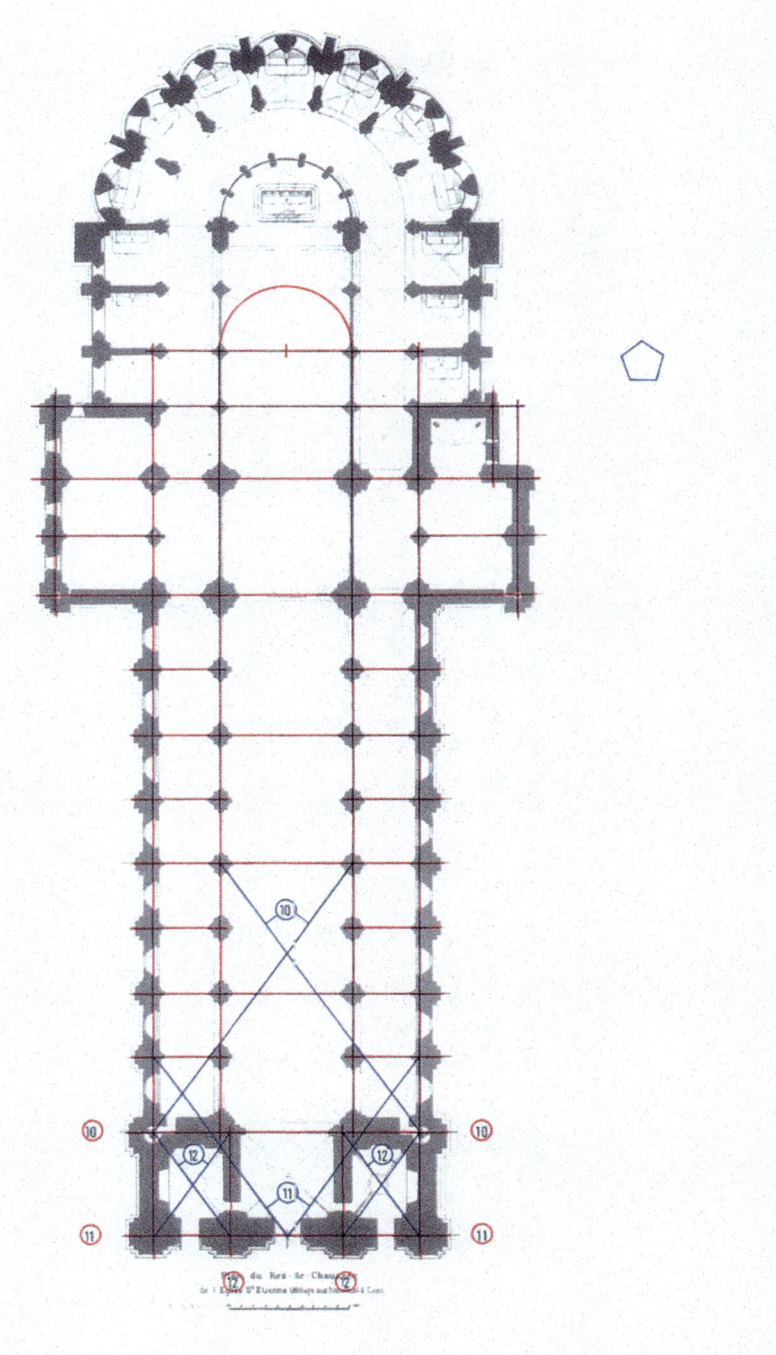

Plate 55: St Stephen, Caen: setting-out steps 10-12.

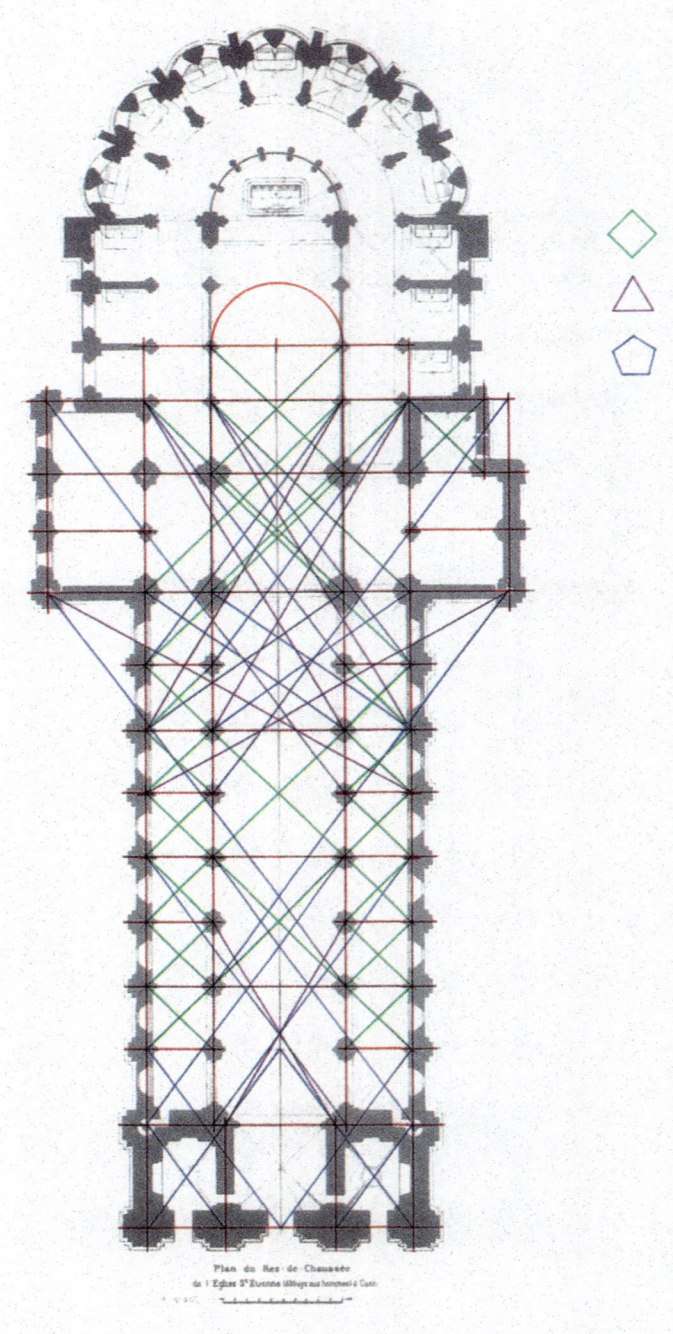

Plate 56: St Stephen, Caen: all alignments.

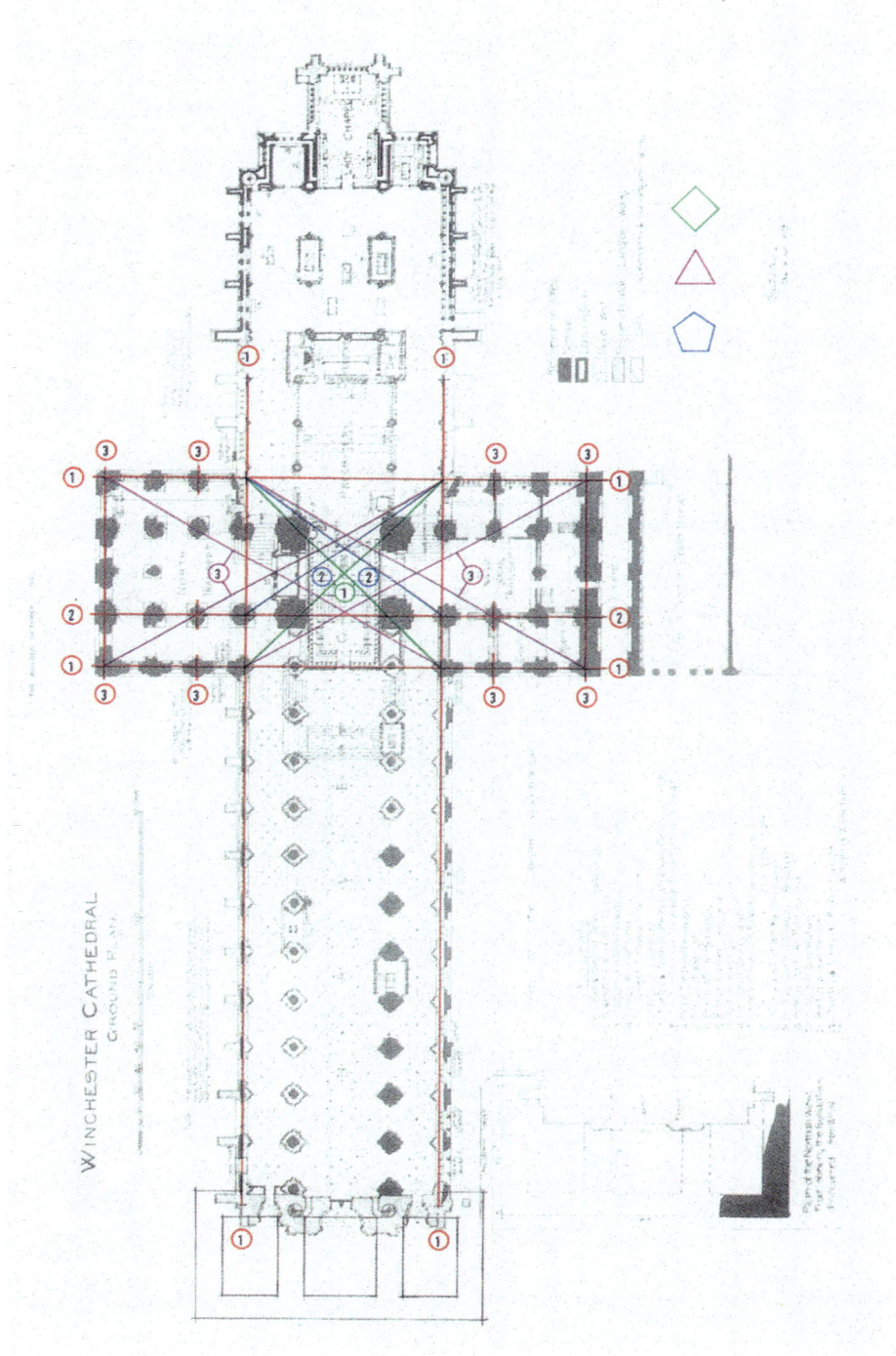

Plate 57: Winchester Cathedral, after Paul: setting-out, steps 1-3.

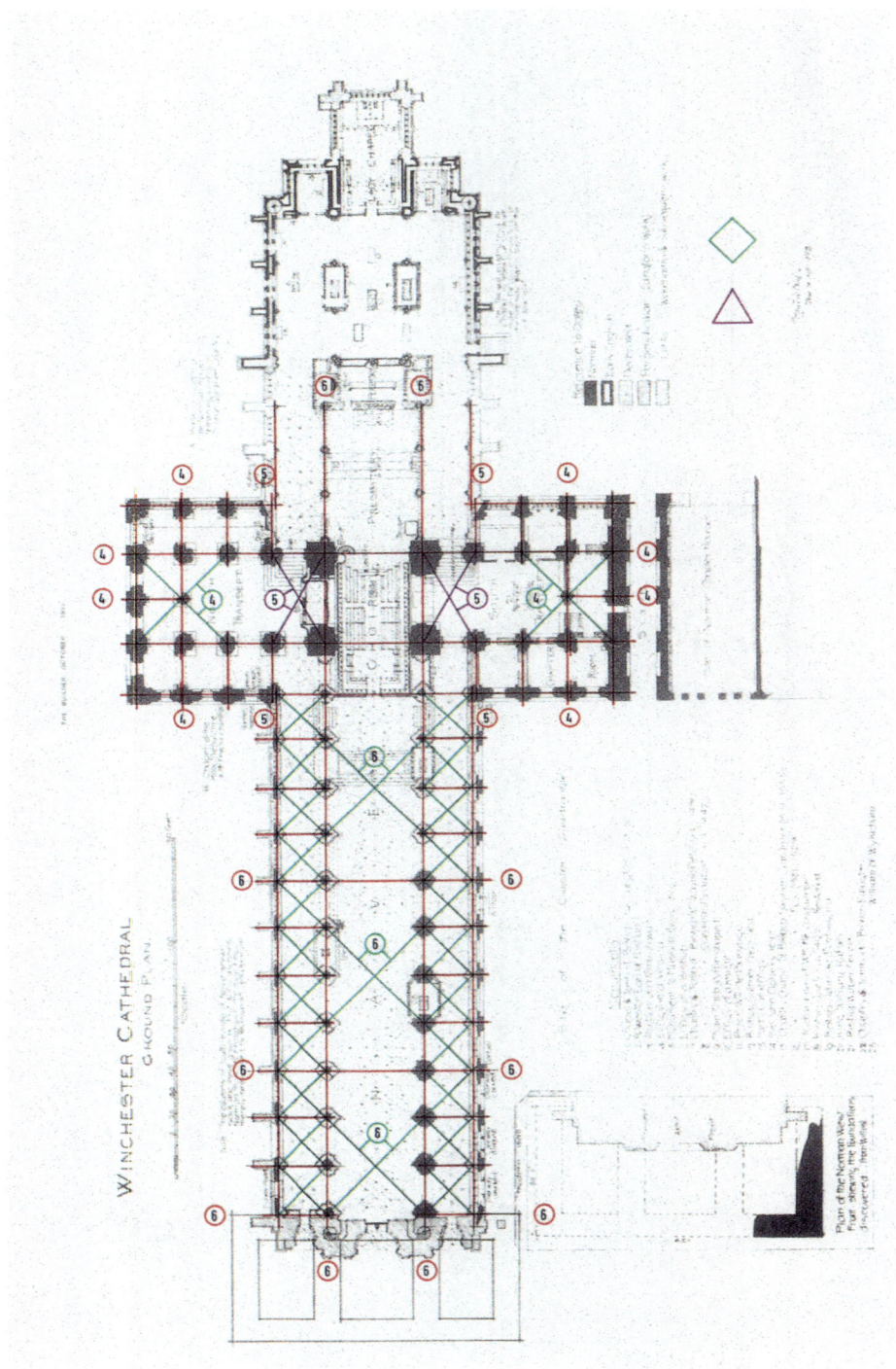

Plate 58: Winchester Cathedral: setting-out, steps 4-6.

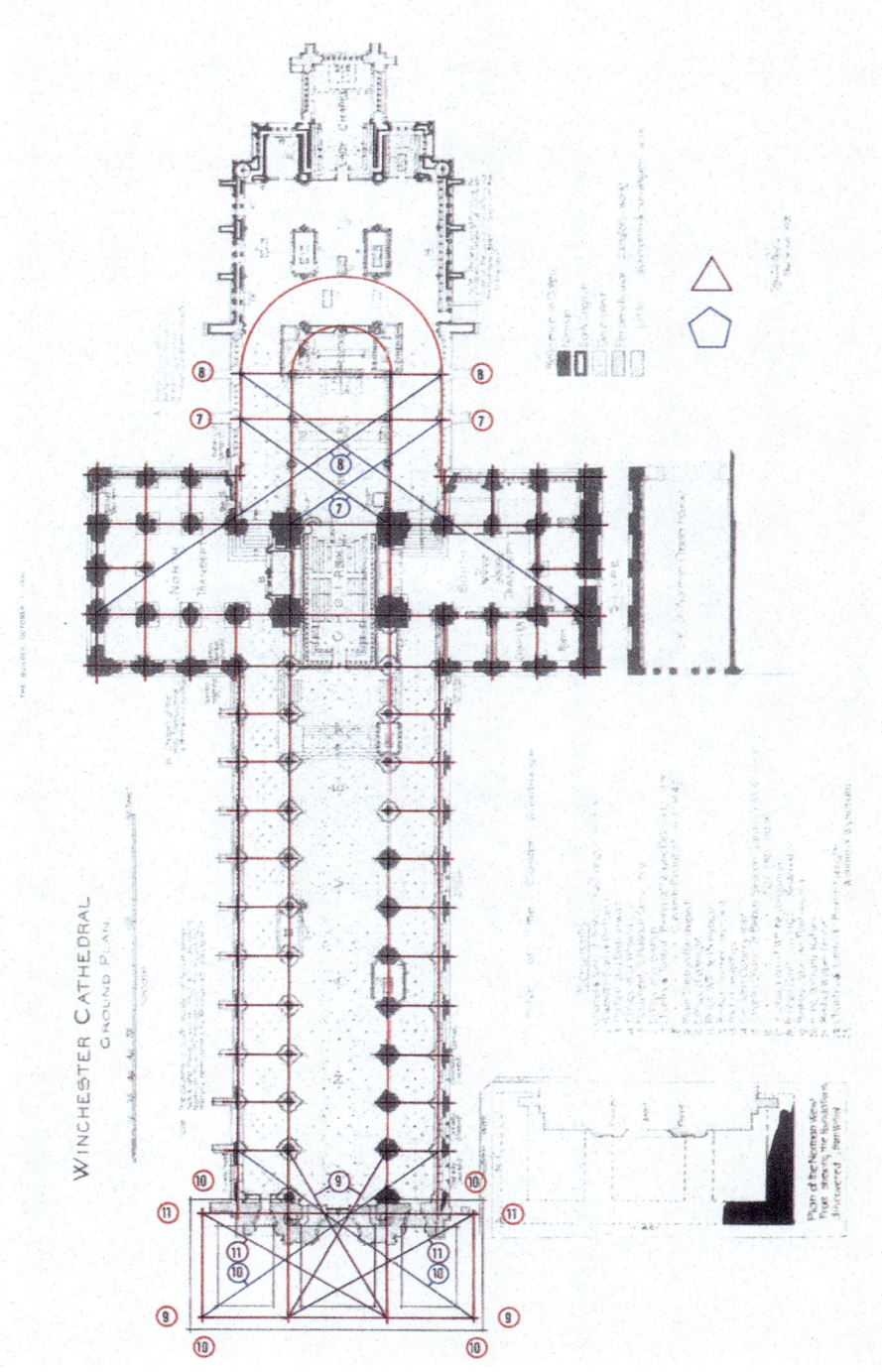

Plate 59: Winchester Cathedral: setting-out, steps 7-11.

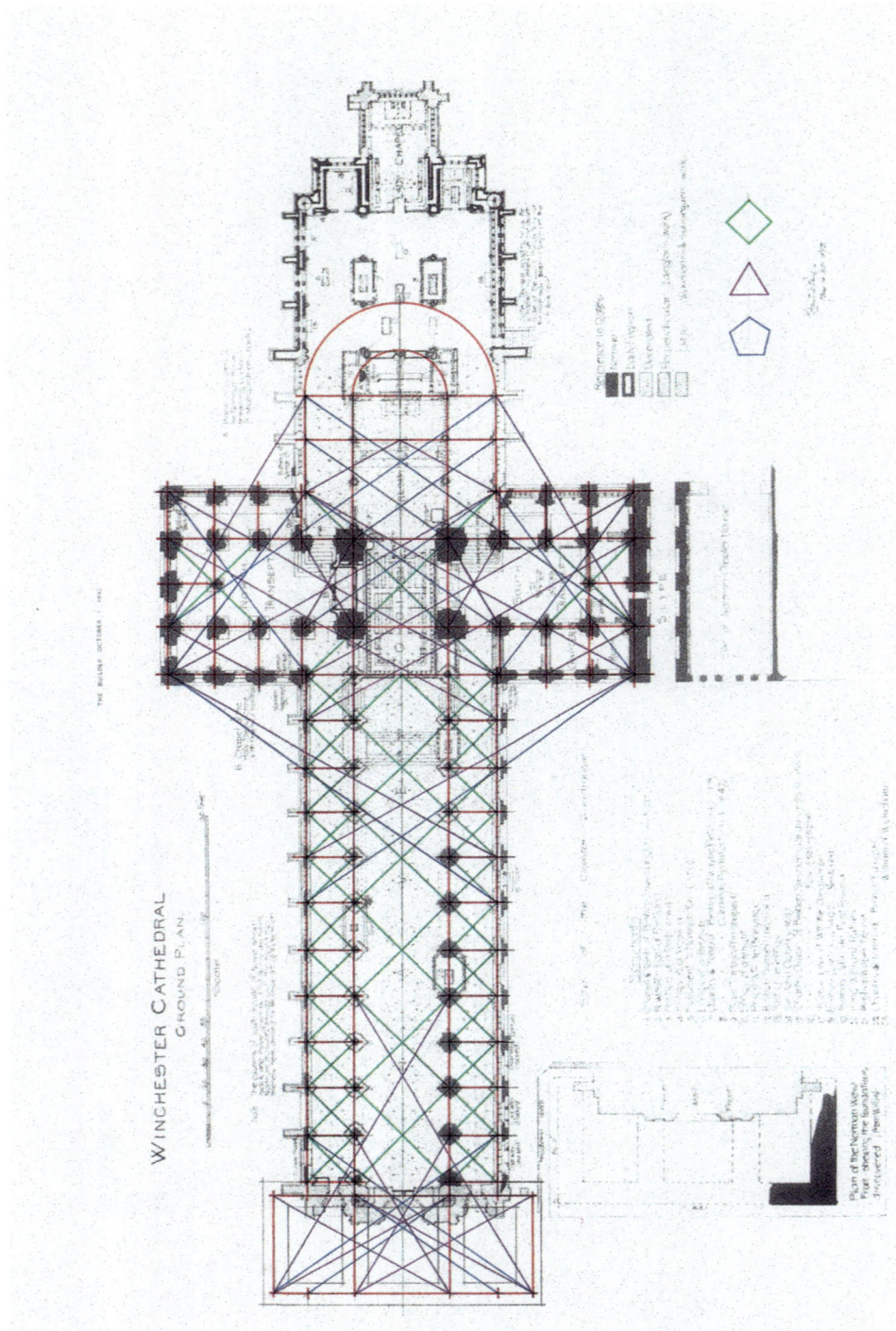

Plate 60: Winchester Cathedral: all alignments.

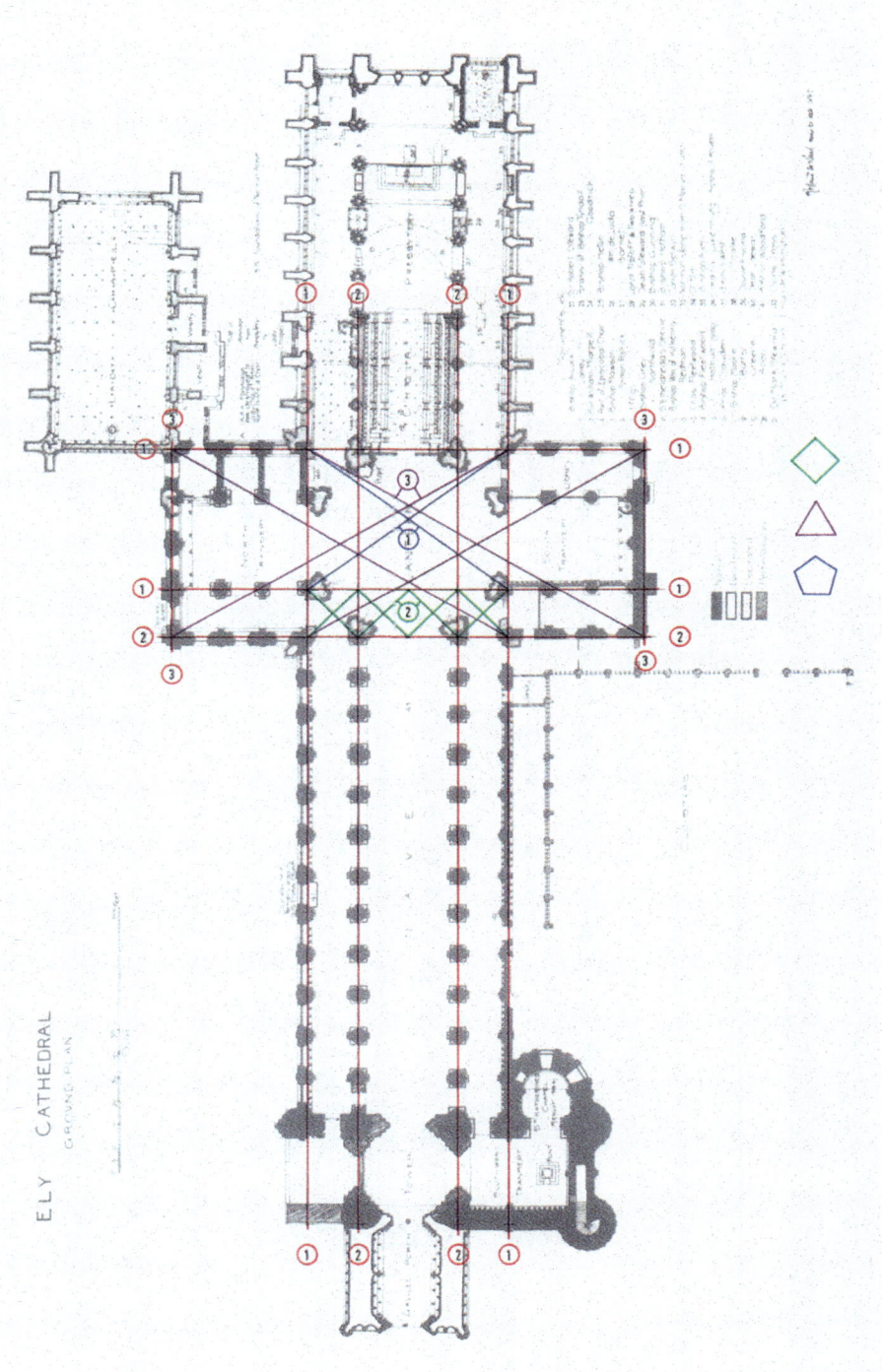

Plate 61: Ely Cathedral, after Paul: setting-out, steps 1-3.

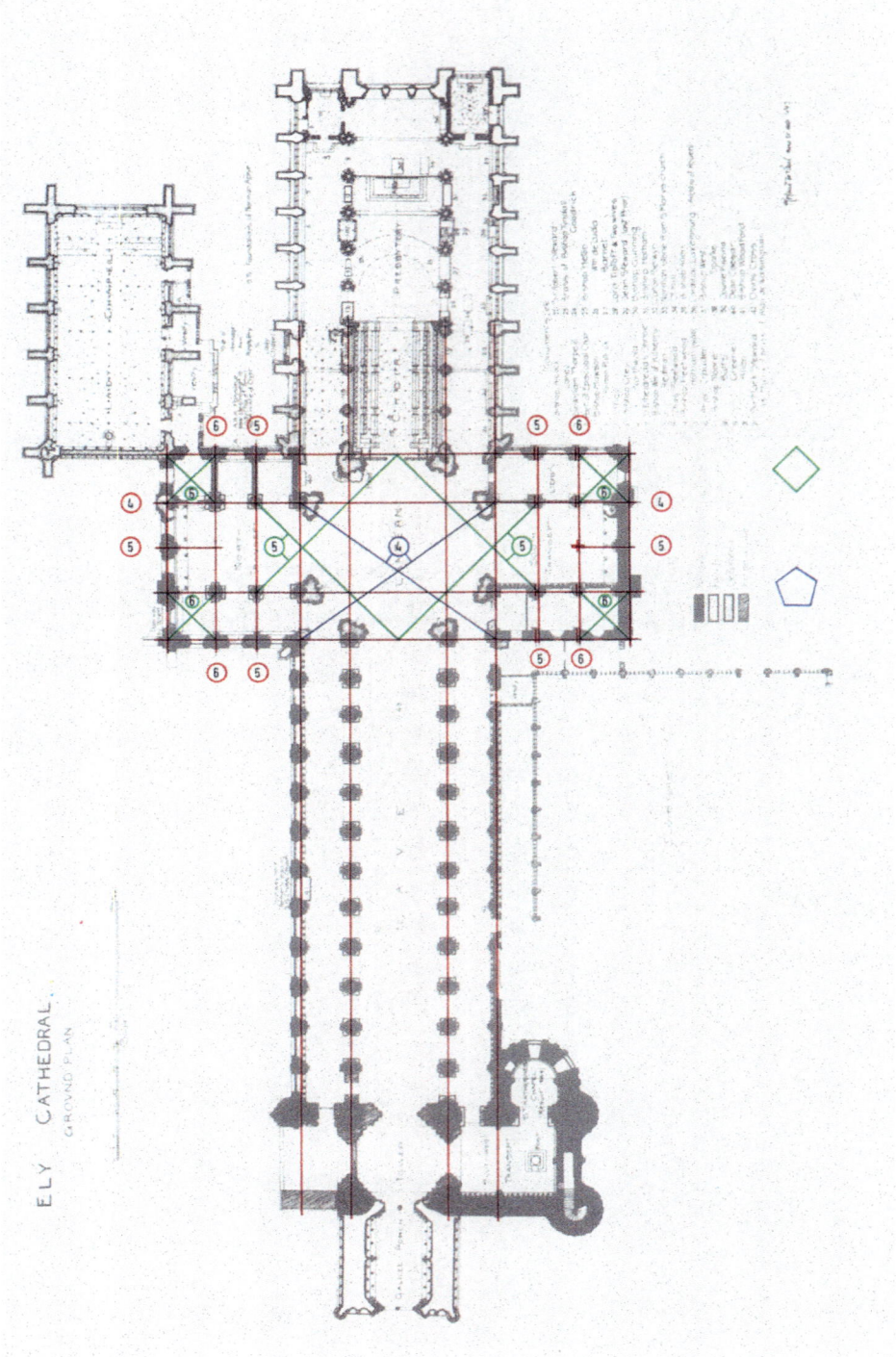

Plate 62: Ely Cathedral: setting-out, steps 4-6.

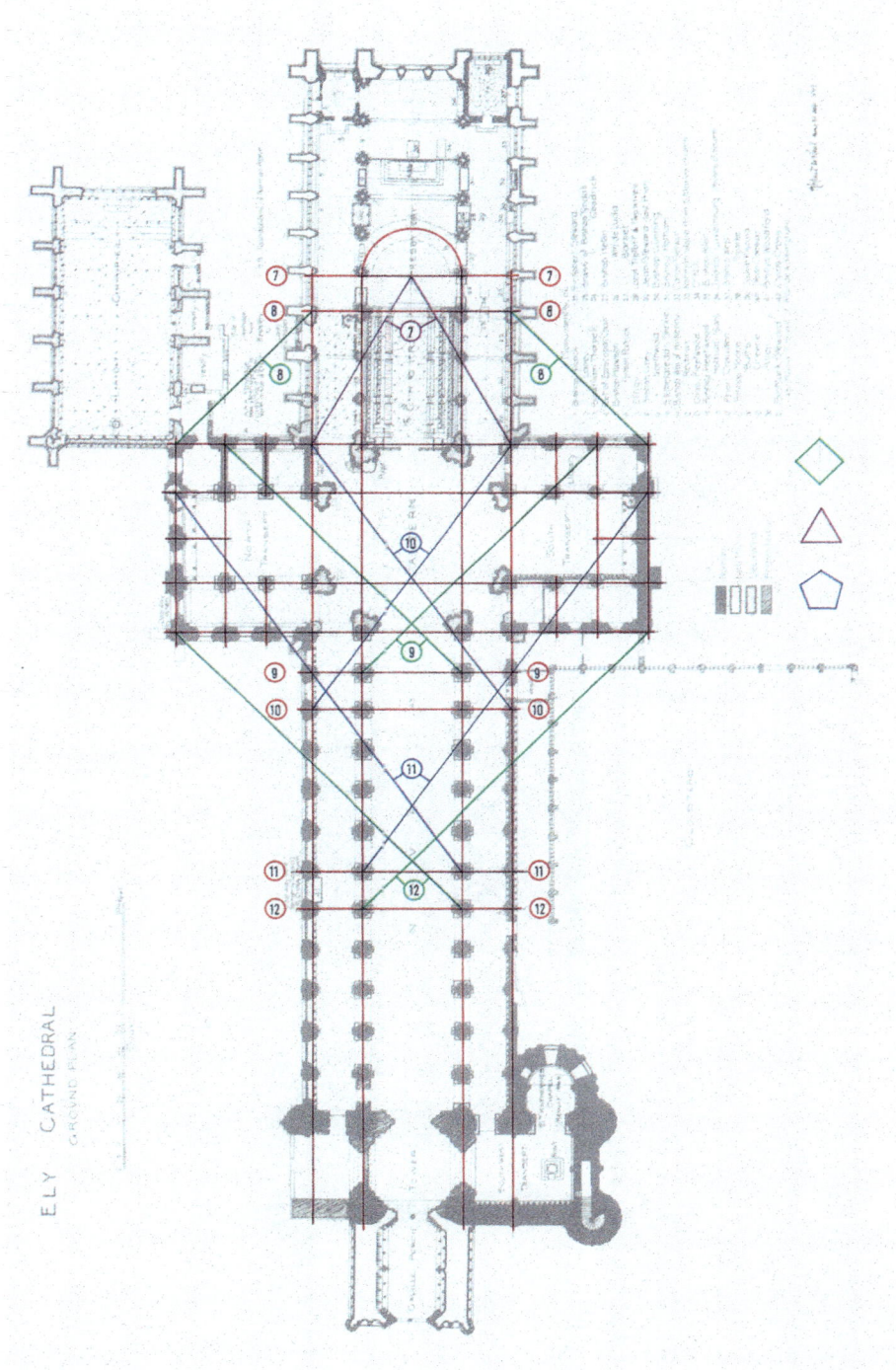

Plate 63: Ely Cathedral: setting-out. steps 7-12.

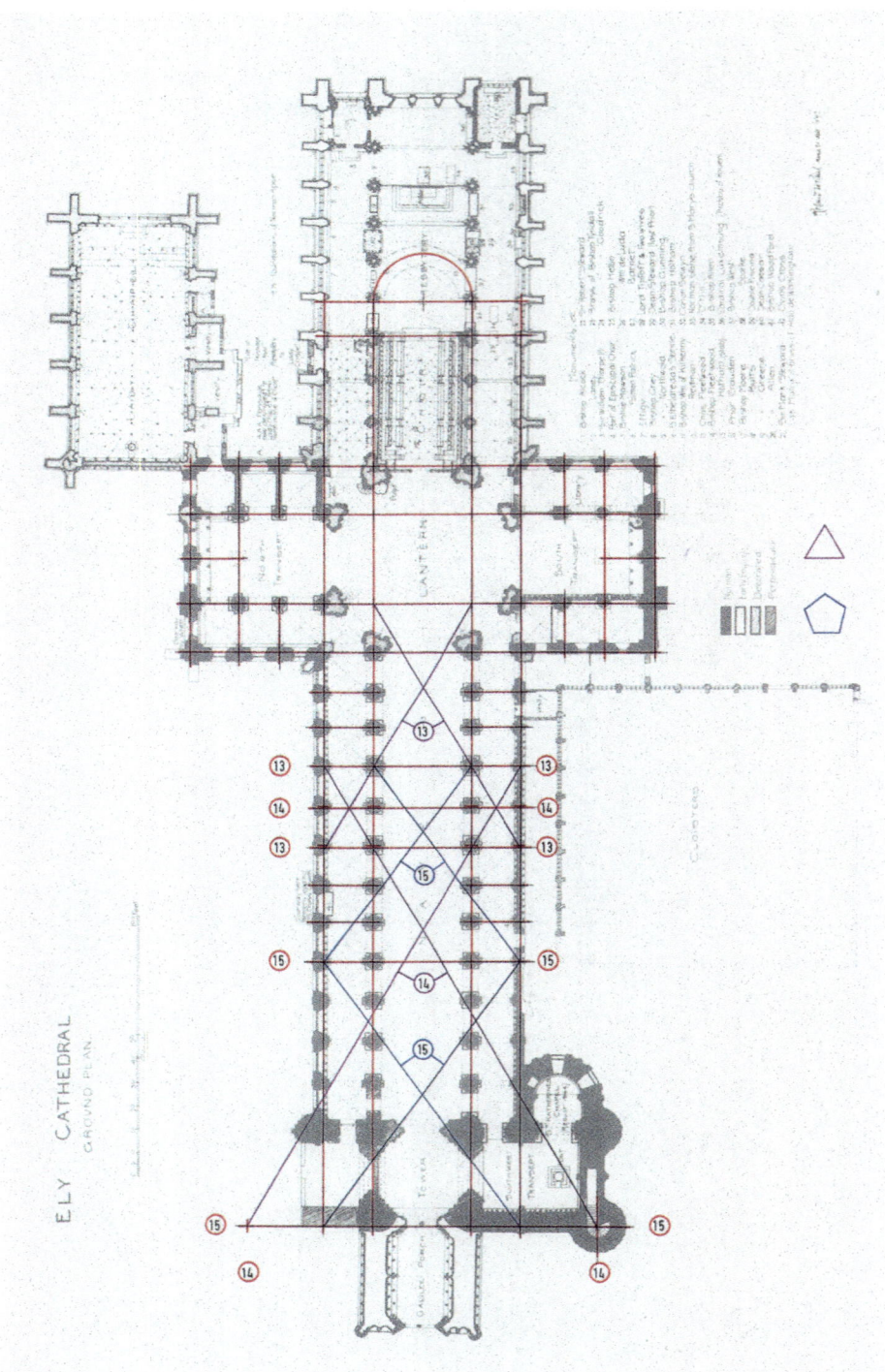

Plate 64: Ely Cathedral: setting-out, steps 13-15.

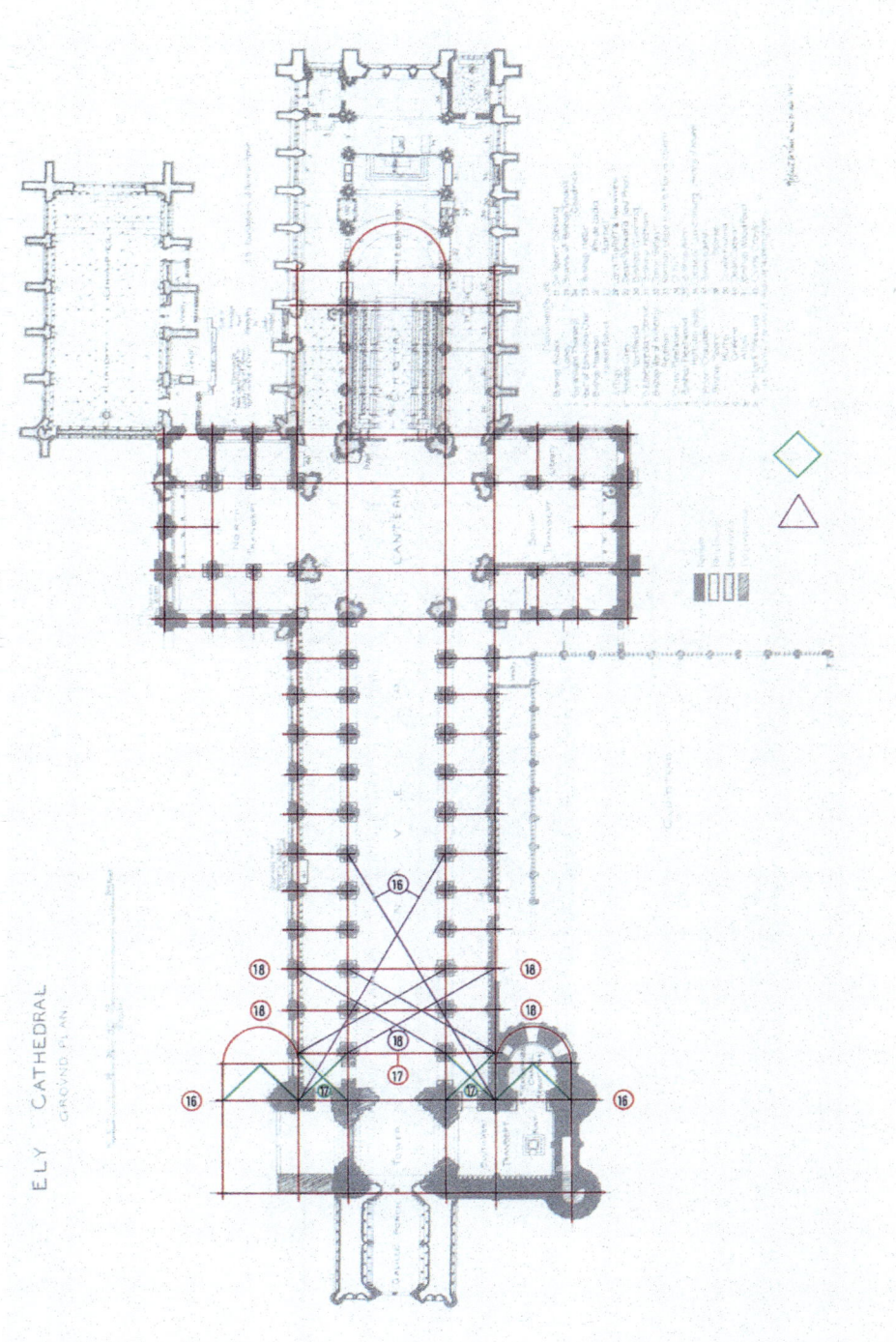

Plate 65: Ely Cathedral: setting-out, steps 16-18.

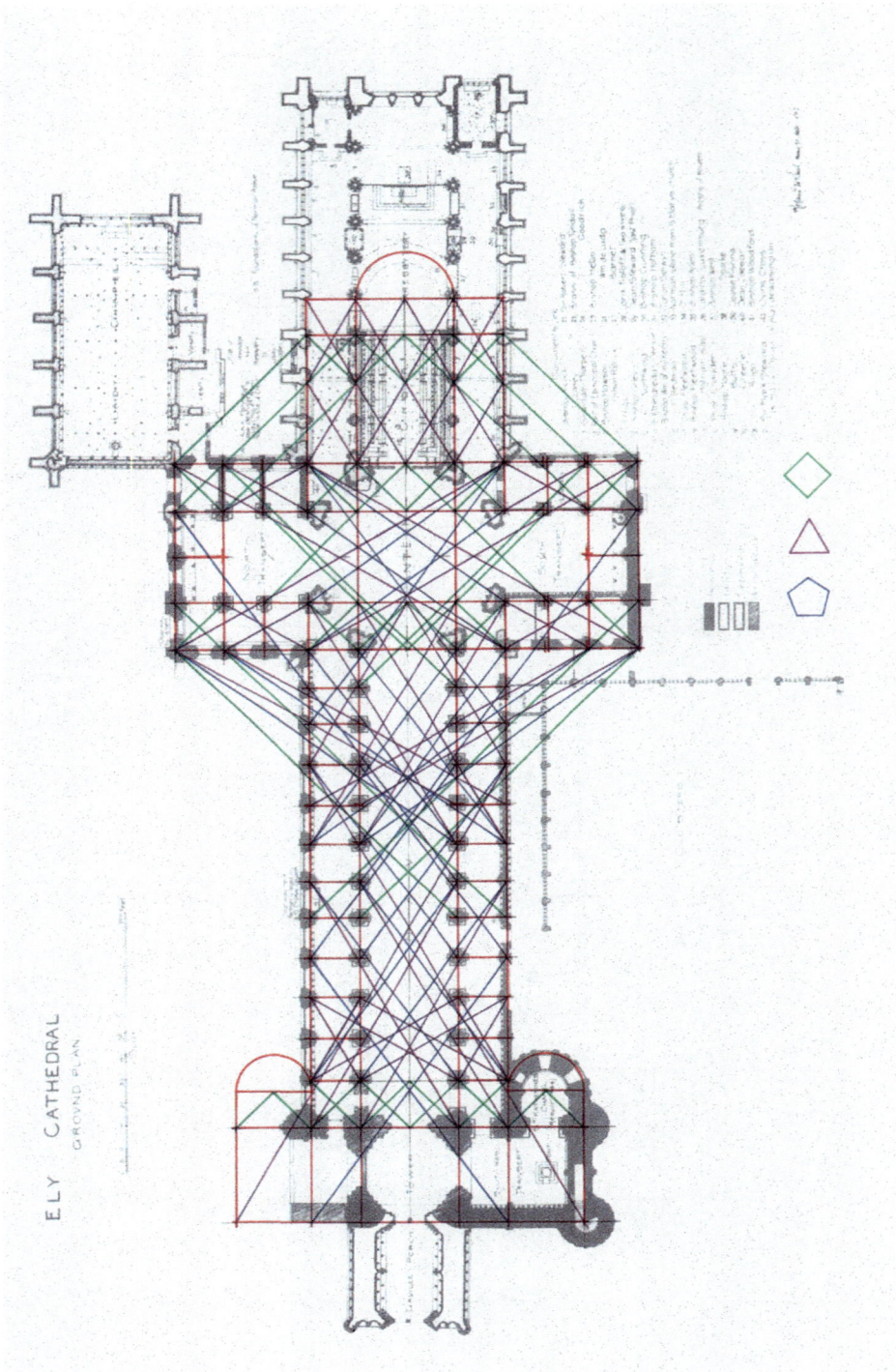

Plate 66: Ely Cathedral: all alignments.

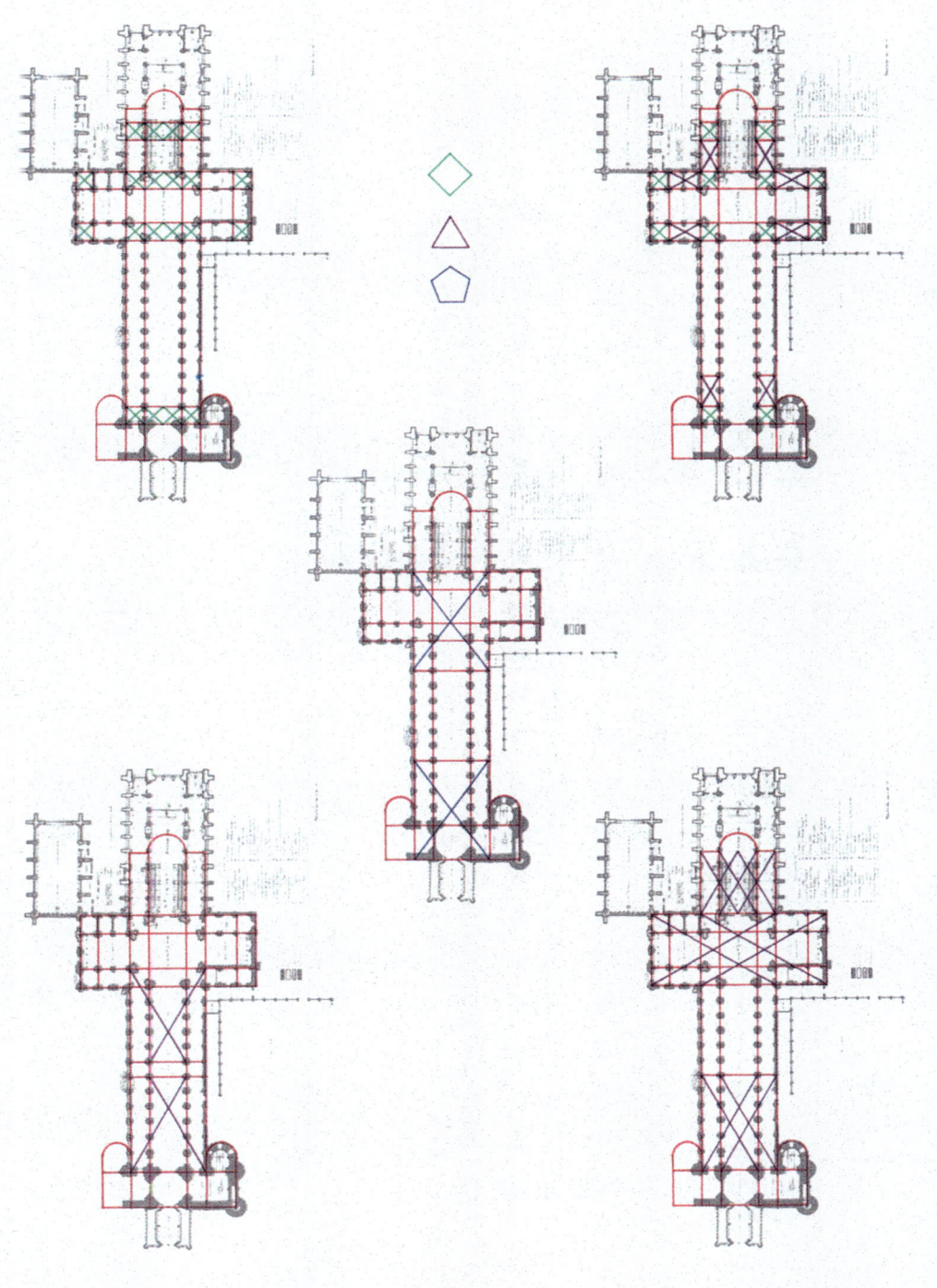

Plate 67: Ely Cathedral: analysis of alignments.

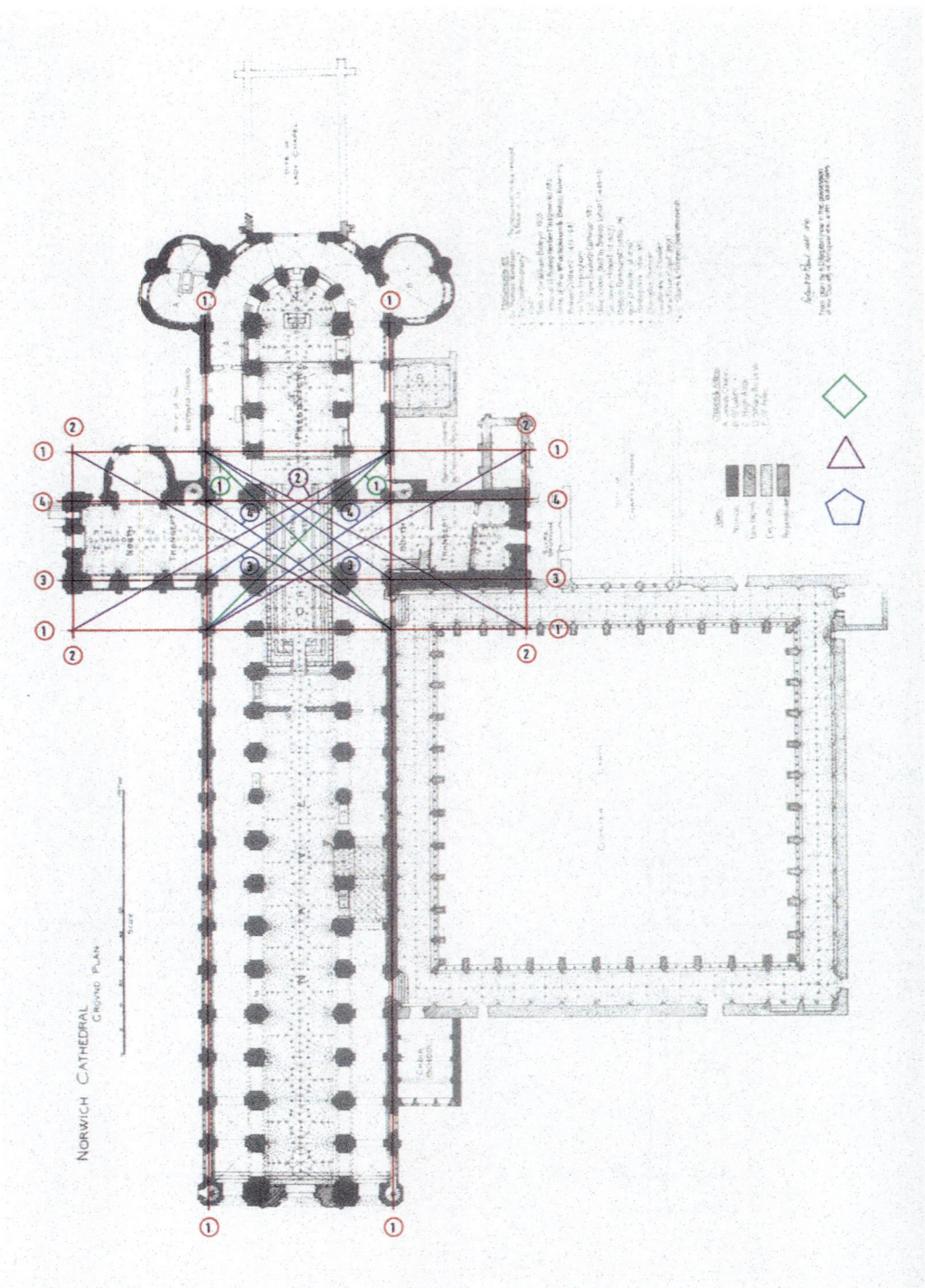

Plate 68: Norwich Cathedral, after Paul: setting-out, steps 1-4.

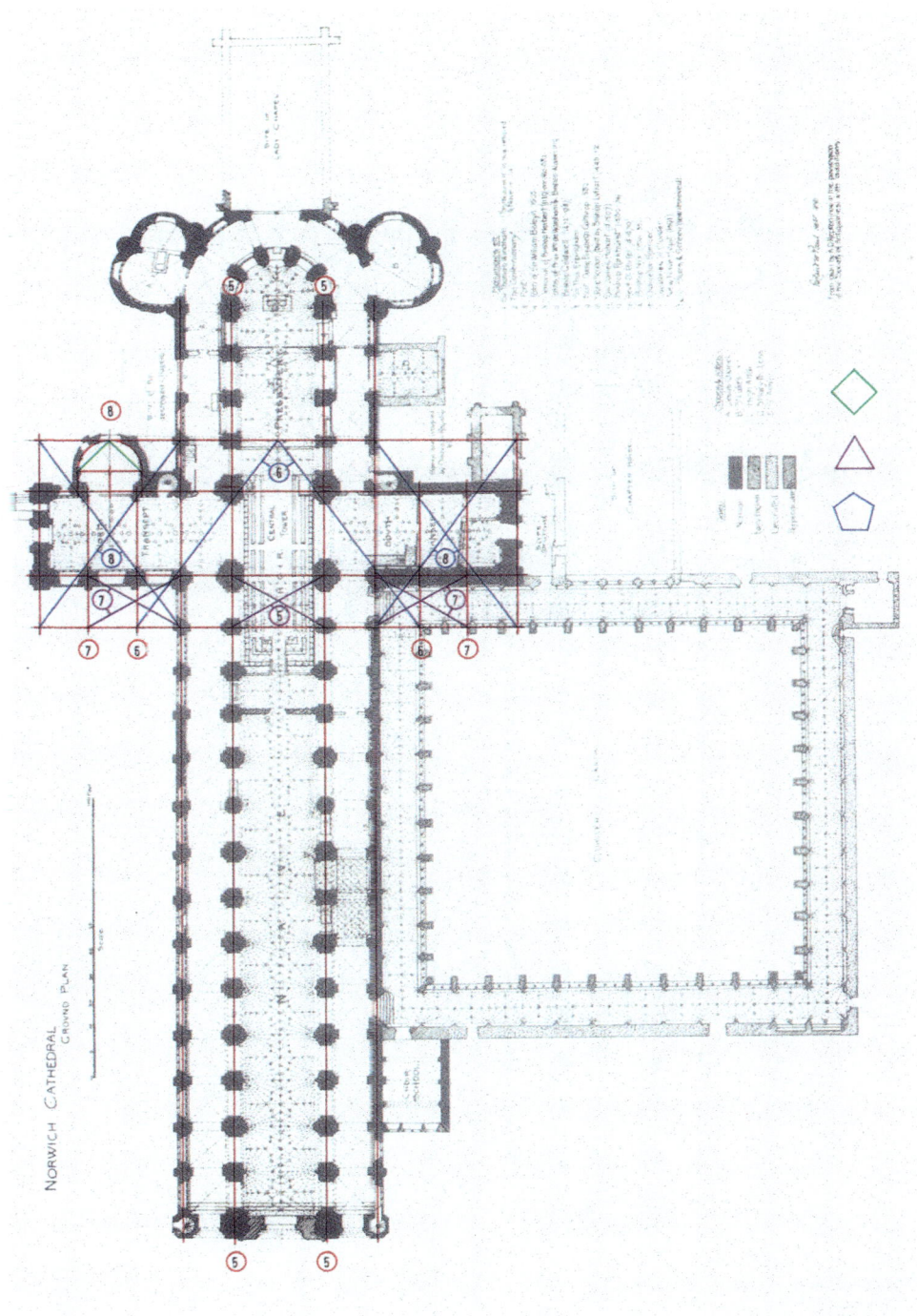

Plate 69: Norwich Cathedral: setting-out, steps 5-8.

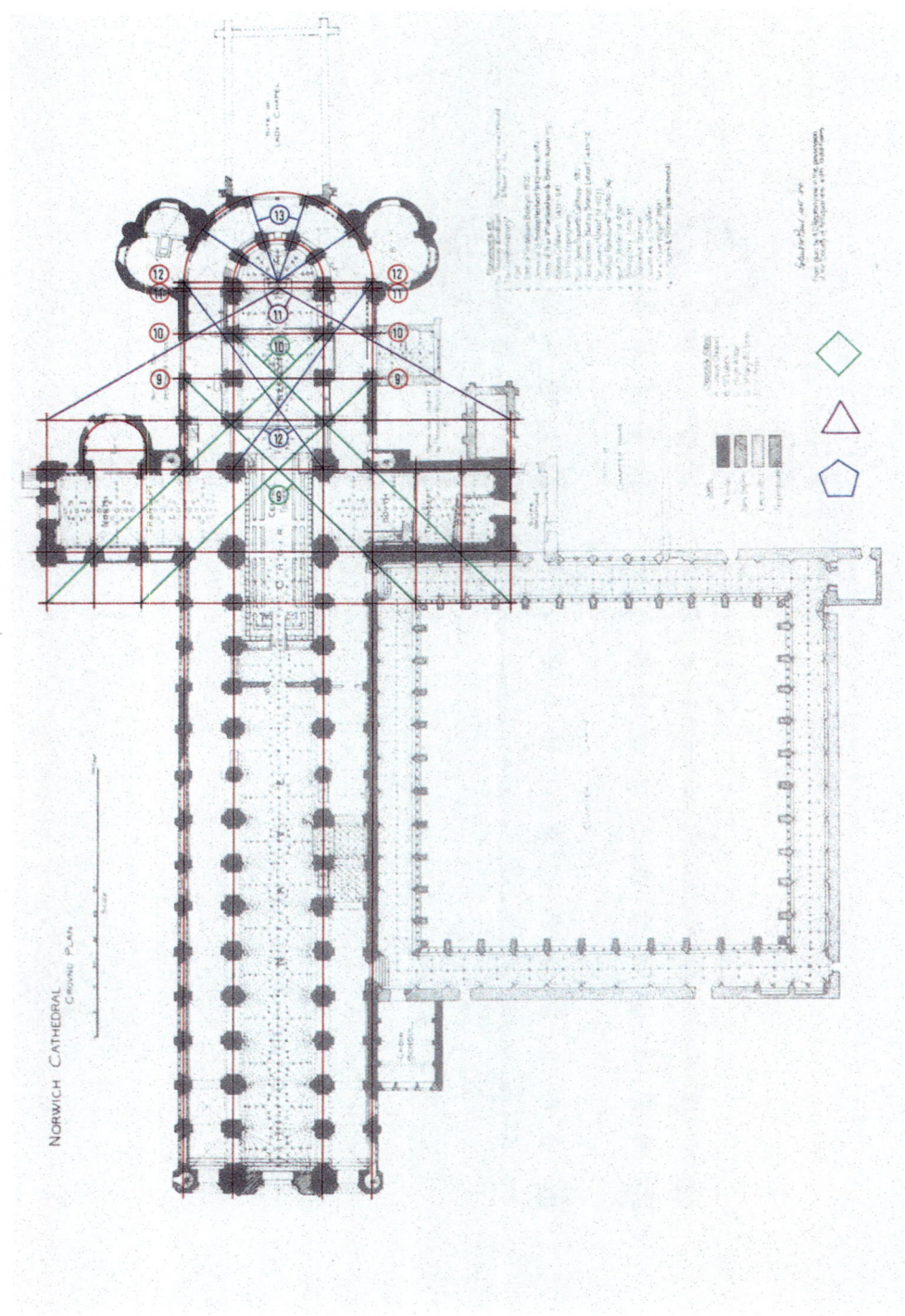

Plate 70: Norwich Cathedral: setting-out, steps 9-13.

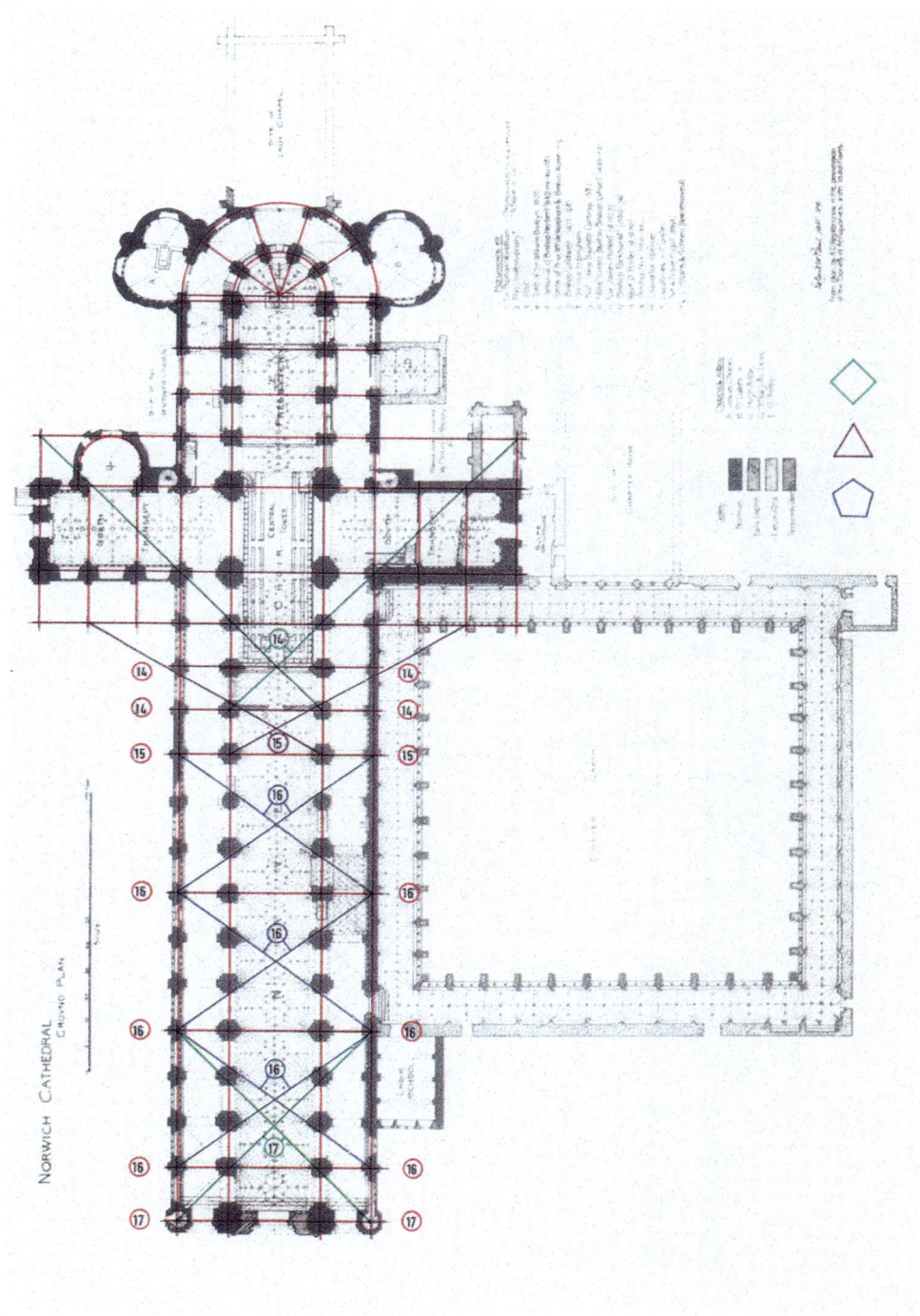

Plate 71: Norwich Cathedral: setting-out, steps 14-17.

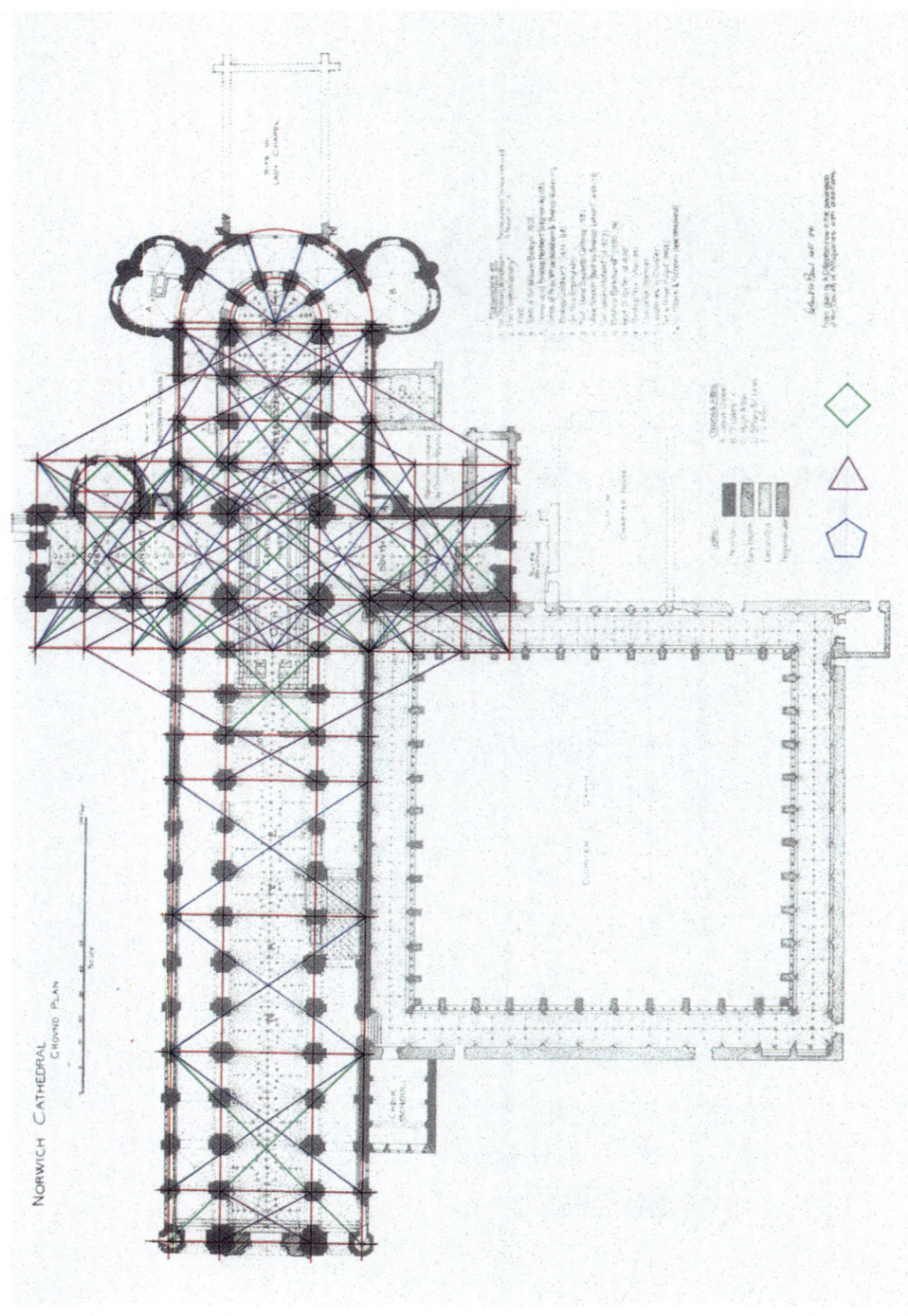

Plate 72: Norwich Cathedral: all alignments.

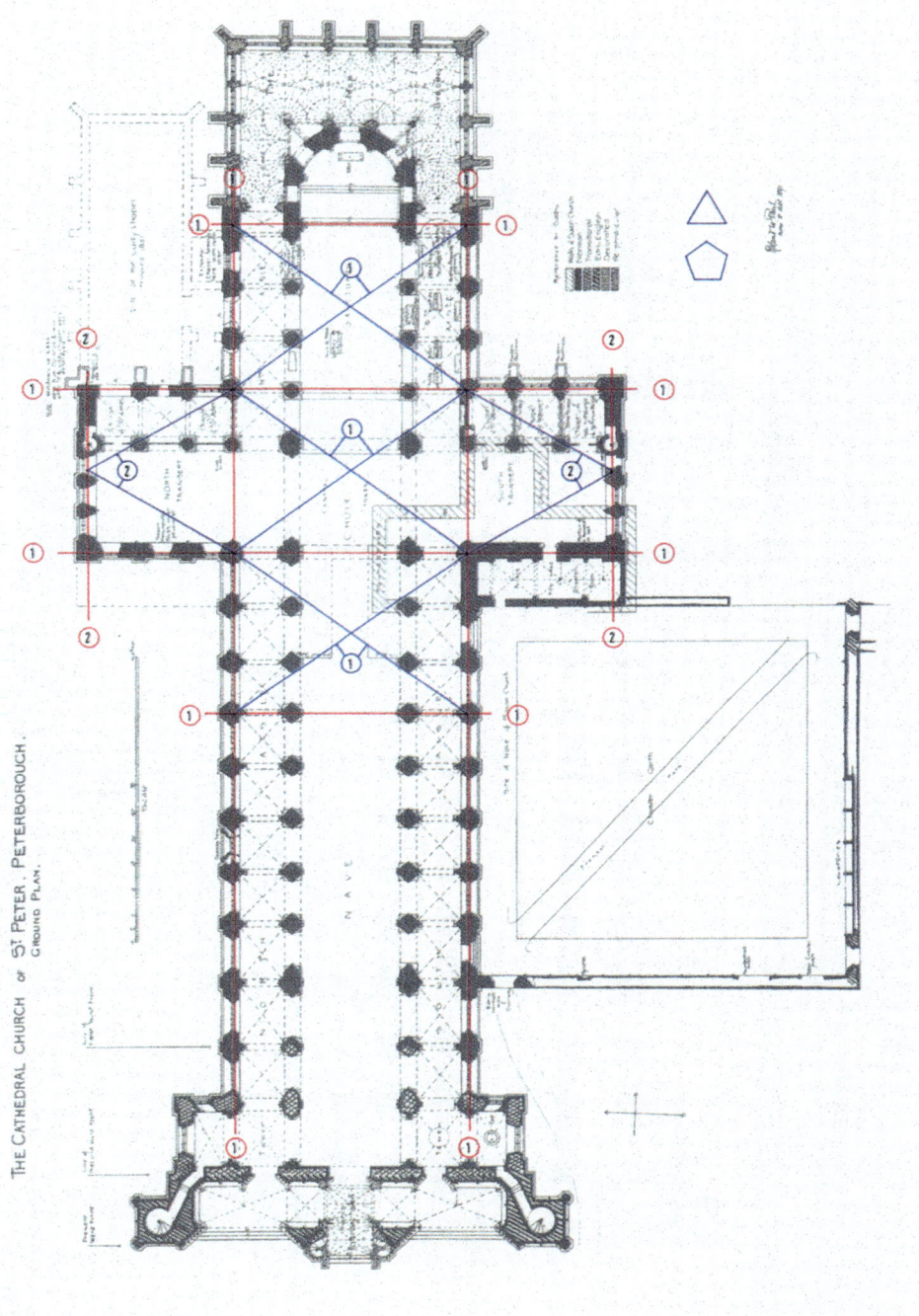

Plate 73: Peterborough Cathedral, after Paul: setting-out, steps 1-2.

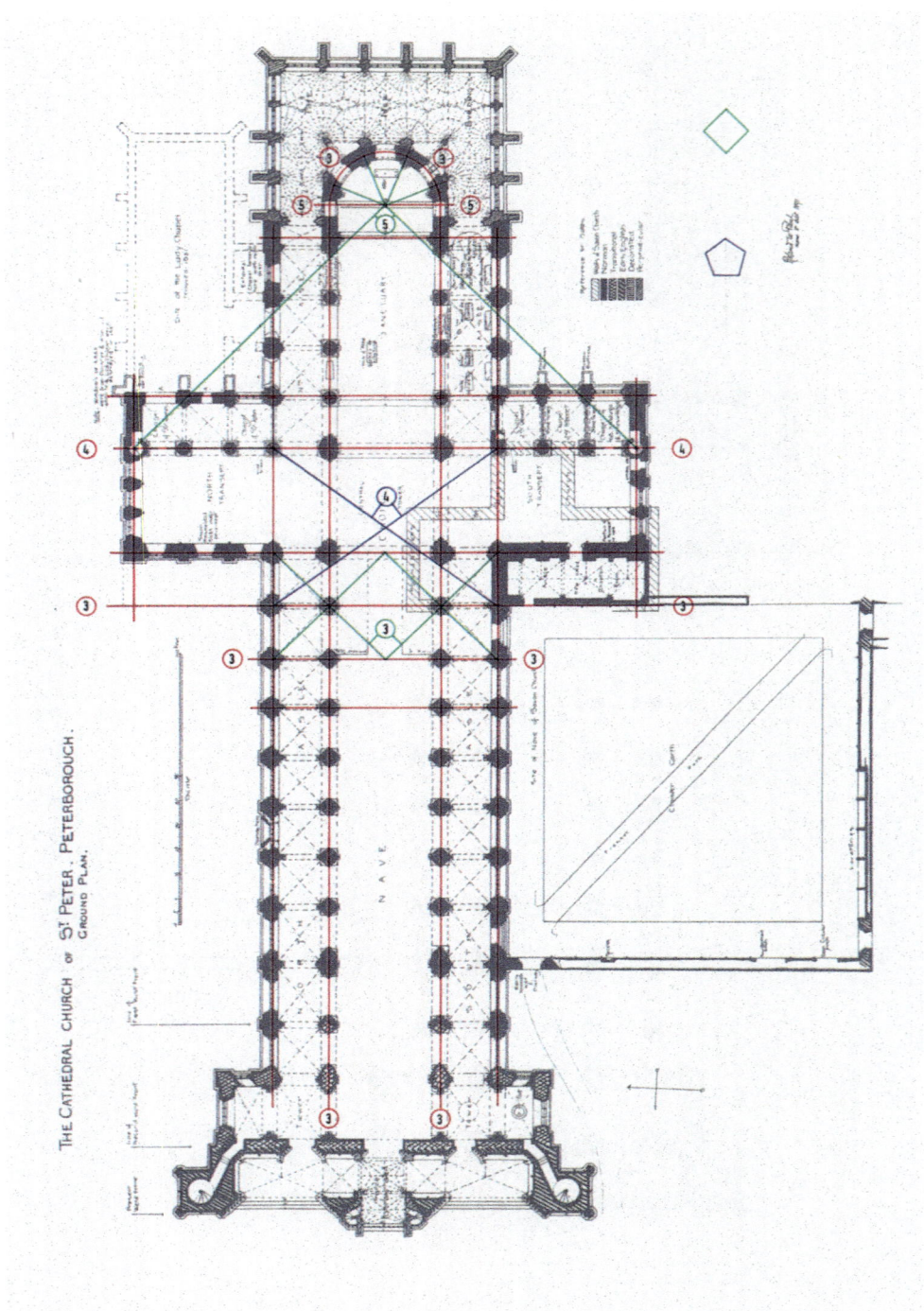

Plate 74: Peterborough Cathedral: setting-out, steps 3-5.

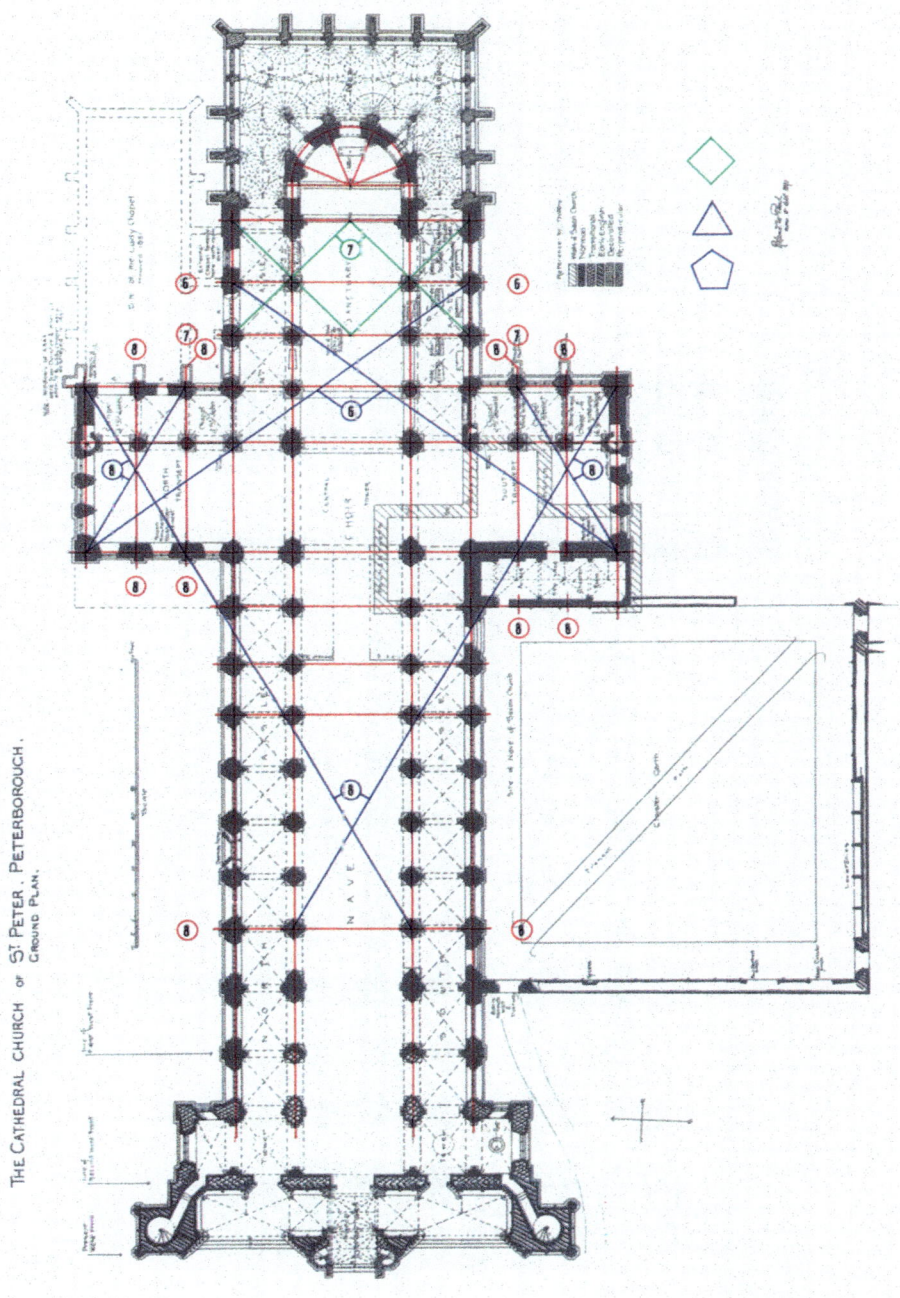

Plate 75: Peterborough Cathedral: setting-out, steps 6-8.

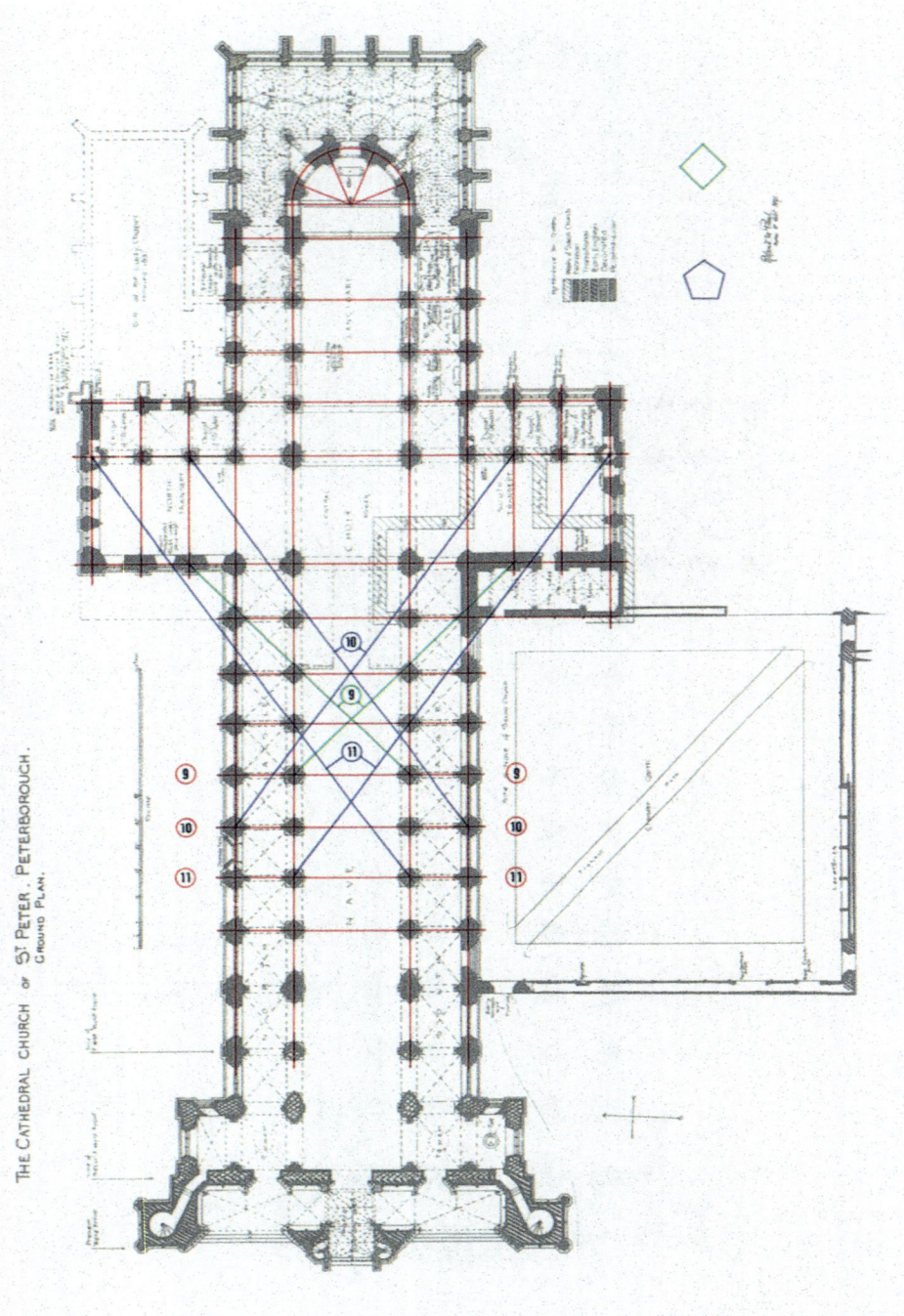

Plate 76: Peterborough Cathedral: setting-out, steps 9-11.

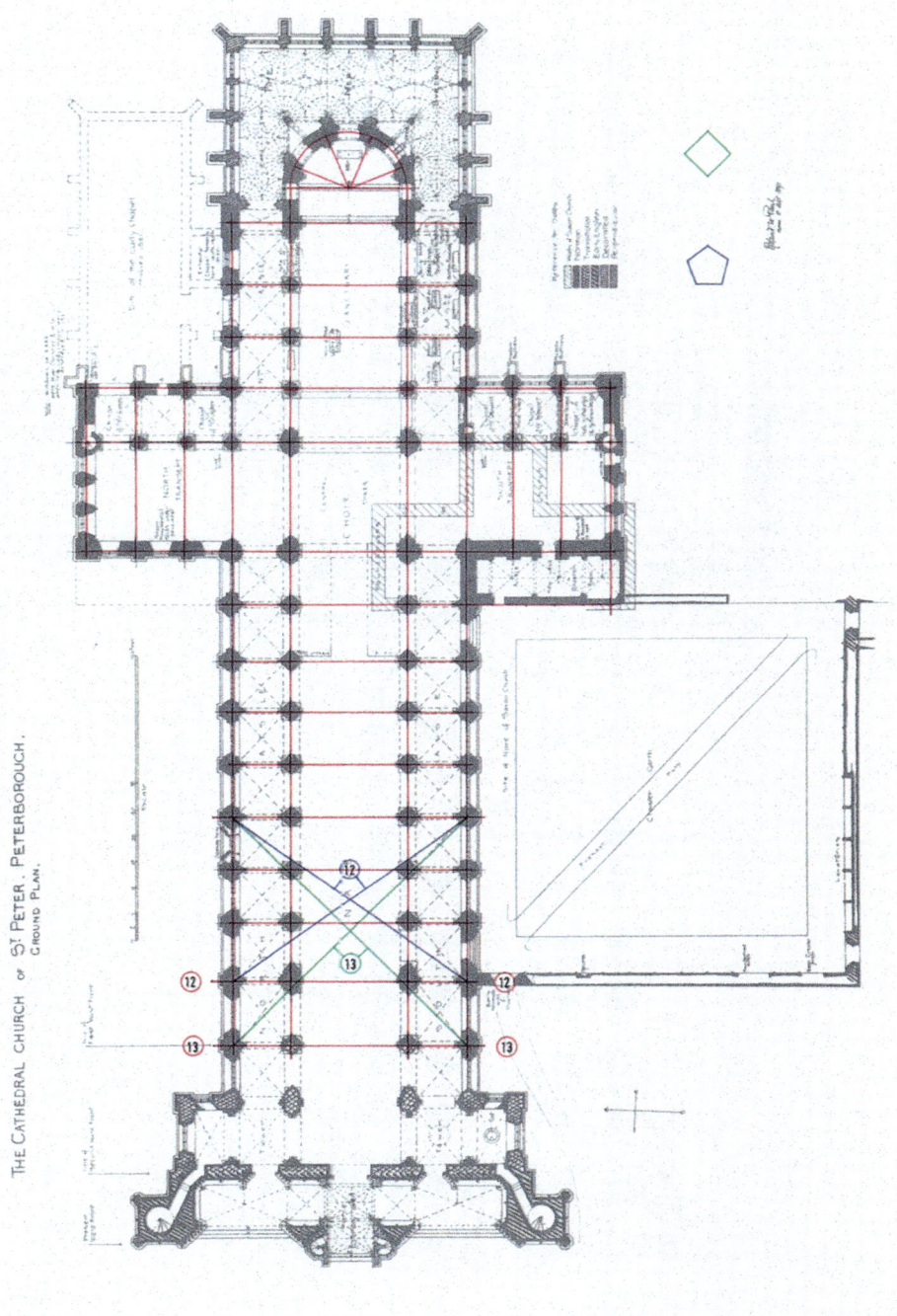

Plate 77: Peterborough Cathedral: setting-out, steps 12, 13.

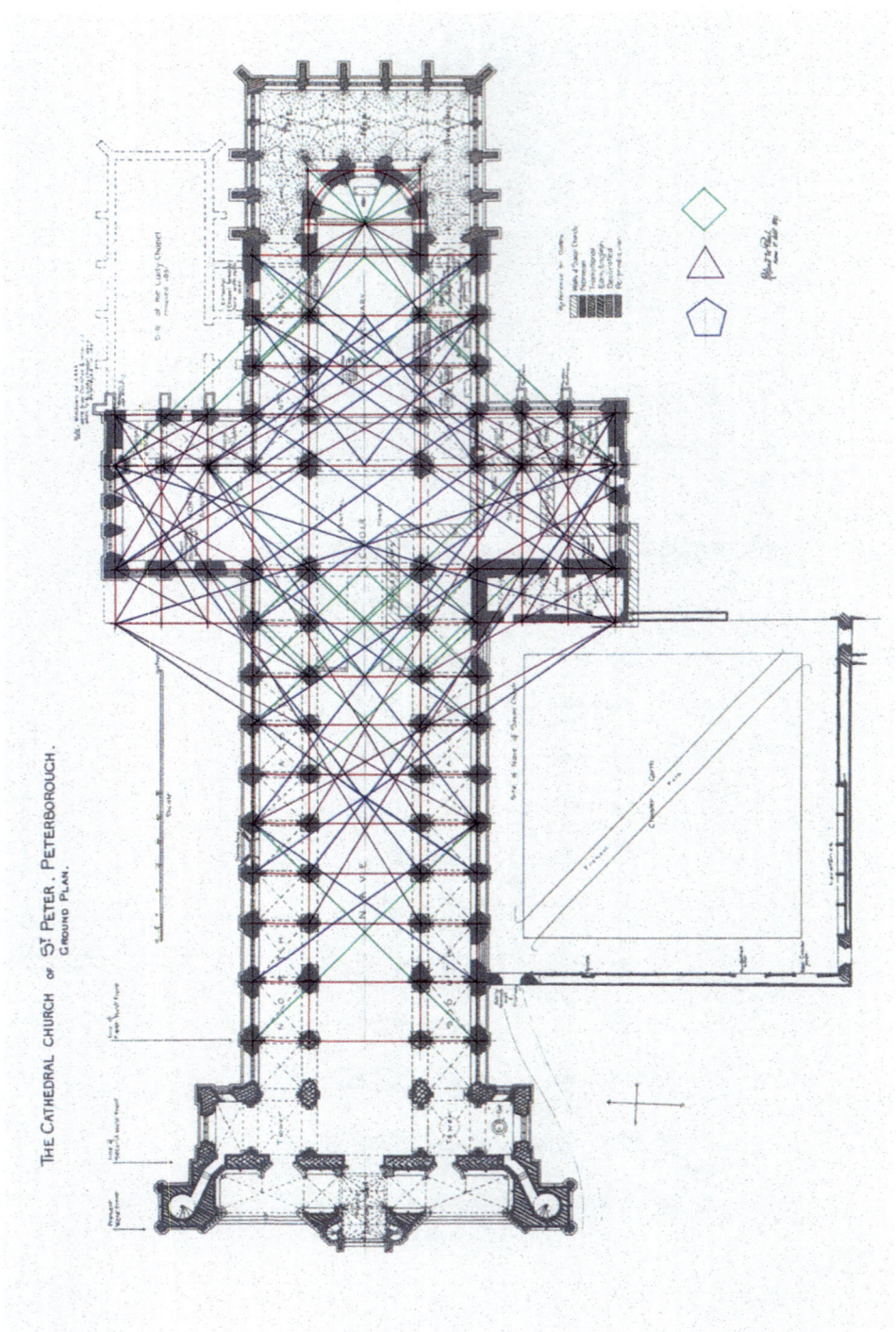

Plate 78: Peterborough Cathedral: all alignments.

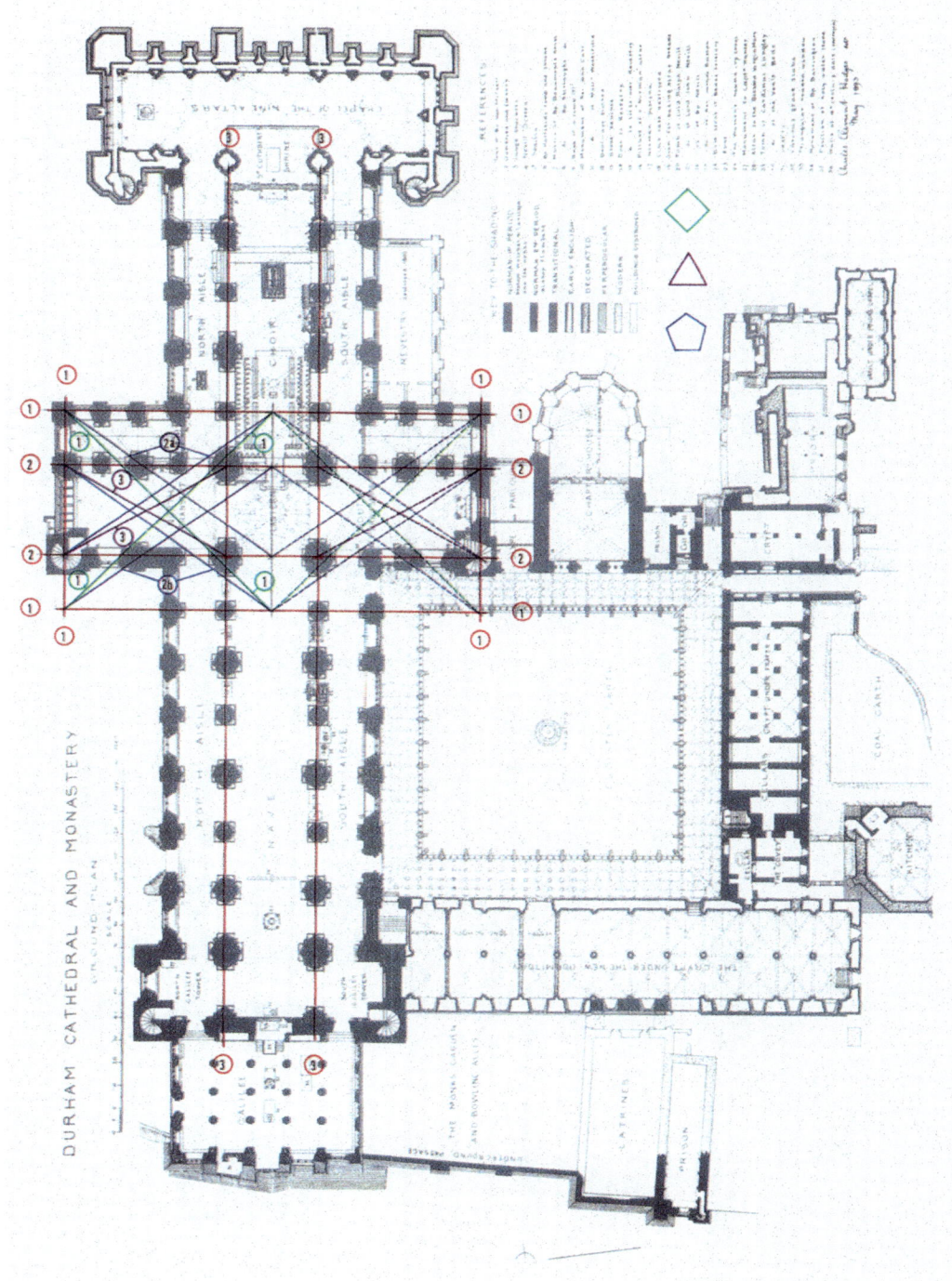

Plate 79: Durham Cathedral, after Hodges: setting-out, steps 1-3.

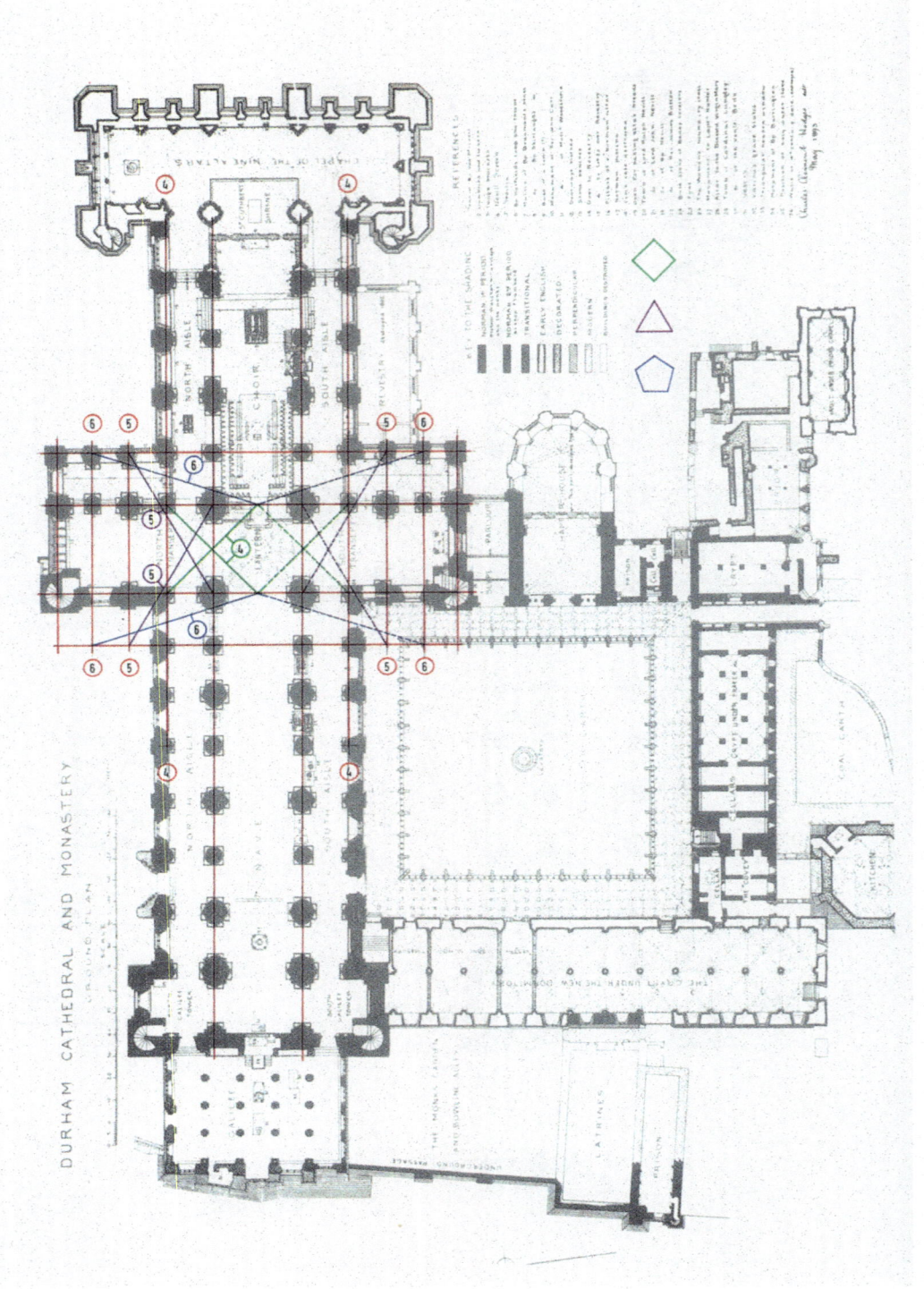

Plate 80: Durham Cathedral: setting-out, steps 4-6.

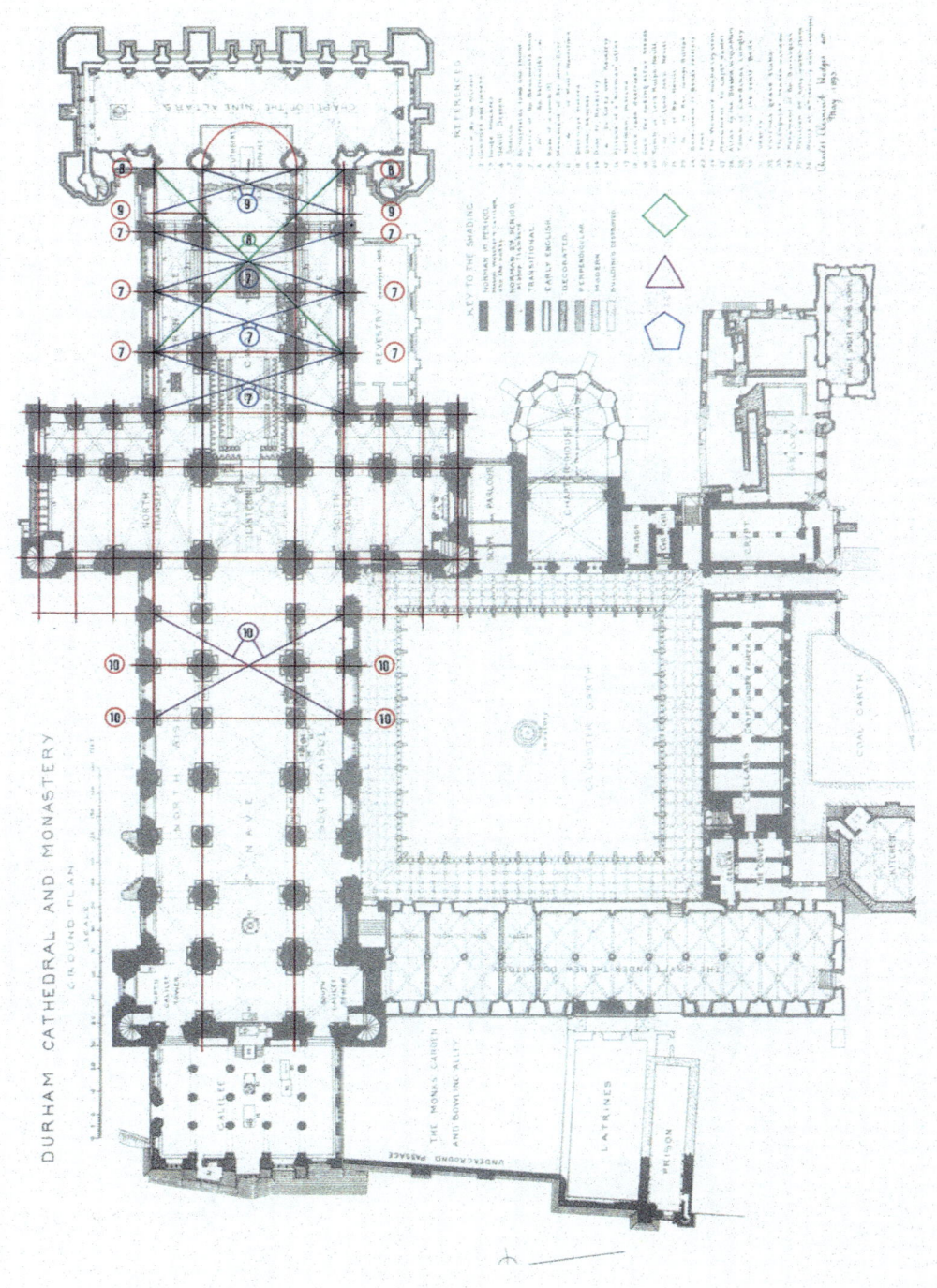

Plate 81: Durham Cathedral: setting-out, steps 7-10.

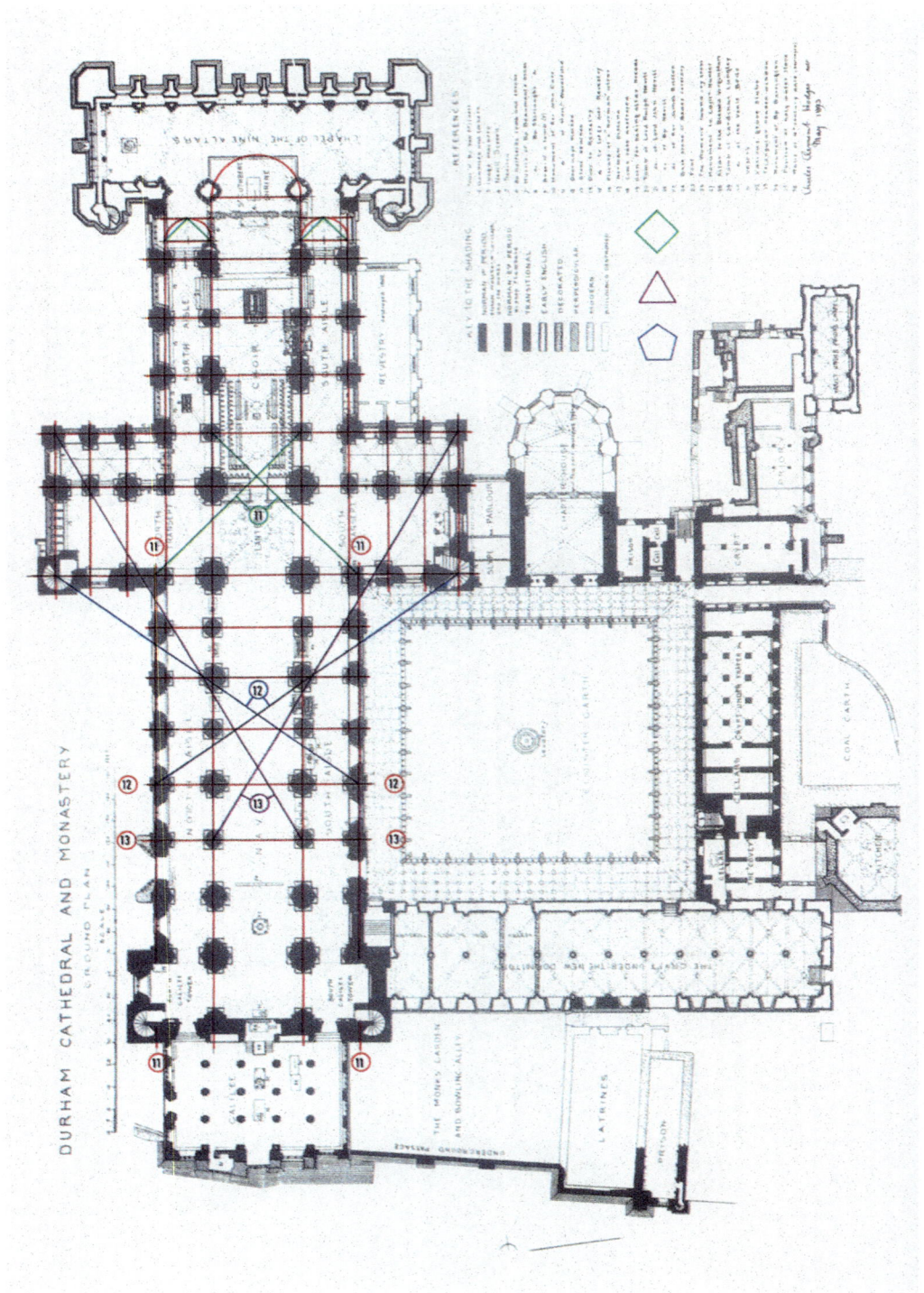

Plate 82: Durham Cathedral: setting-out, steps 11-13.

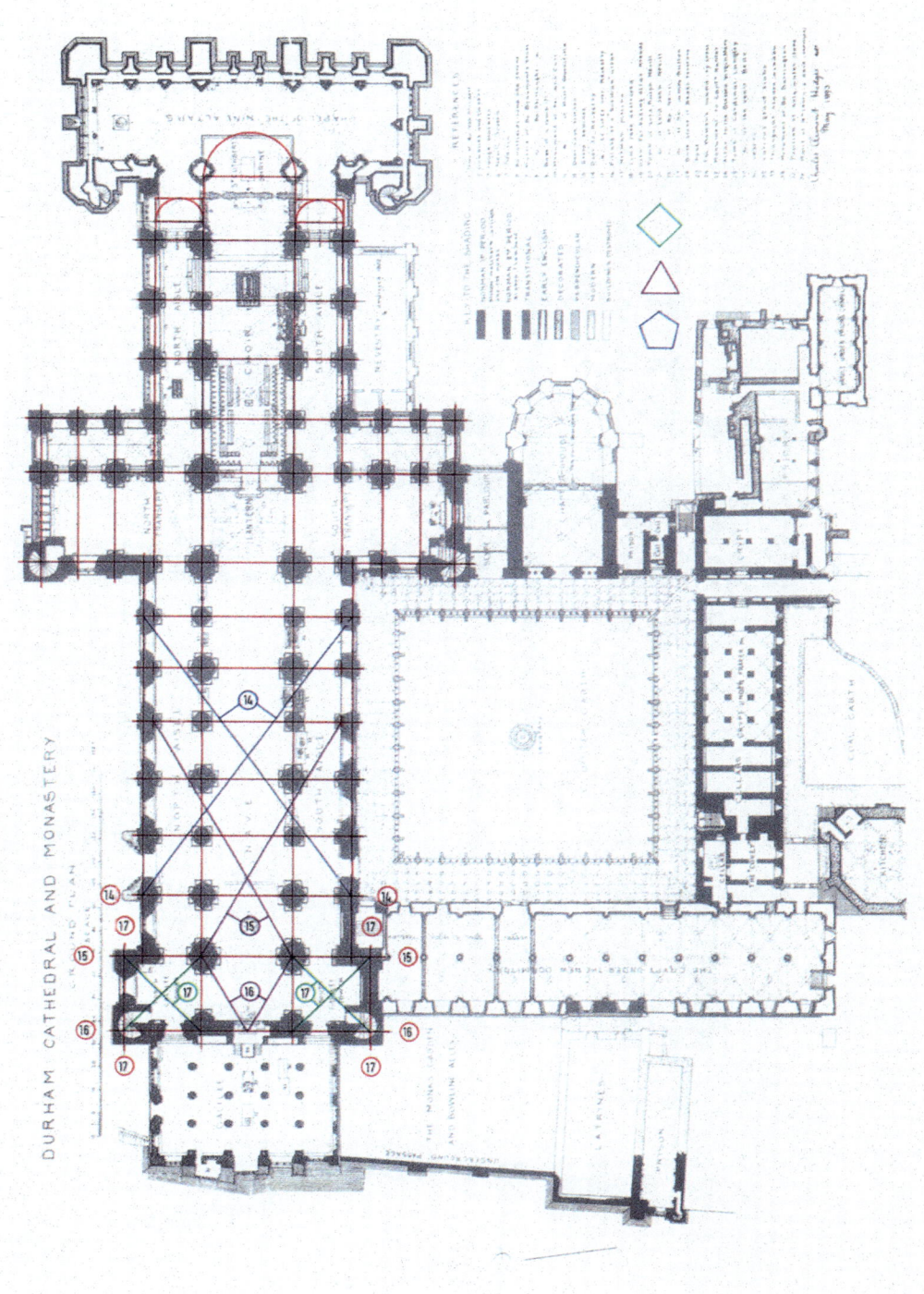

Plate 83: Durham Cathedral: setting-out, steps 14-17.

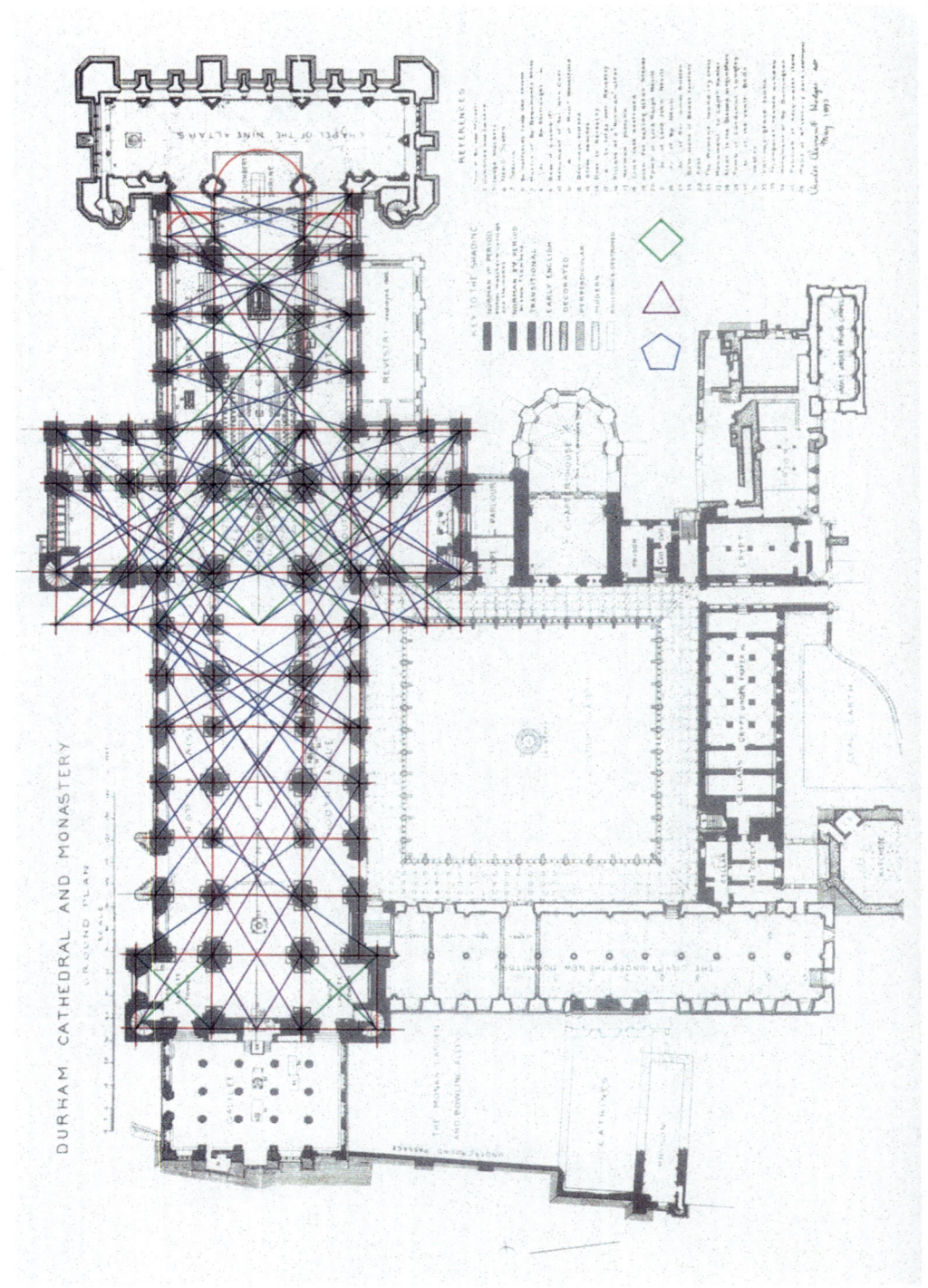

Plate 84: Durham Cathedral: all alignments.

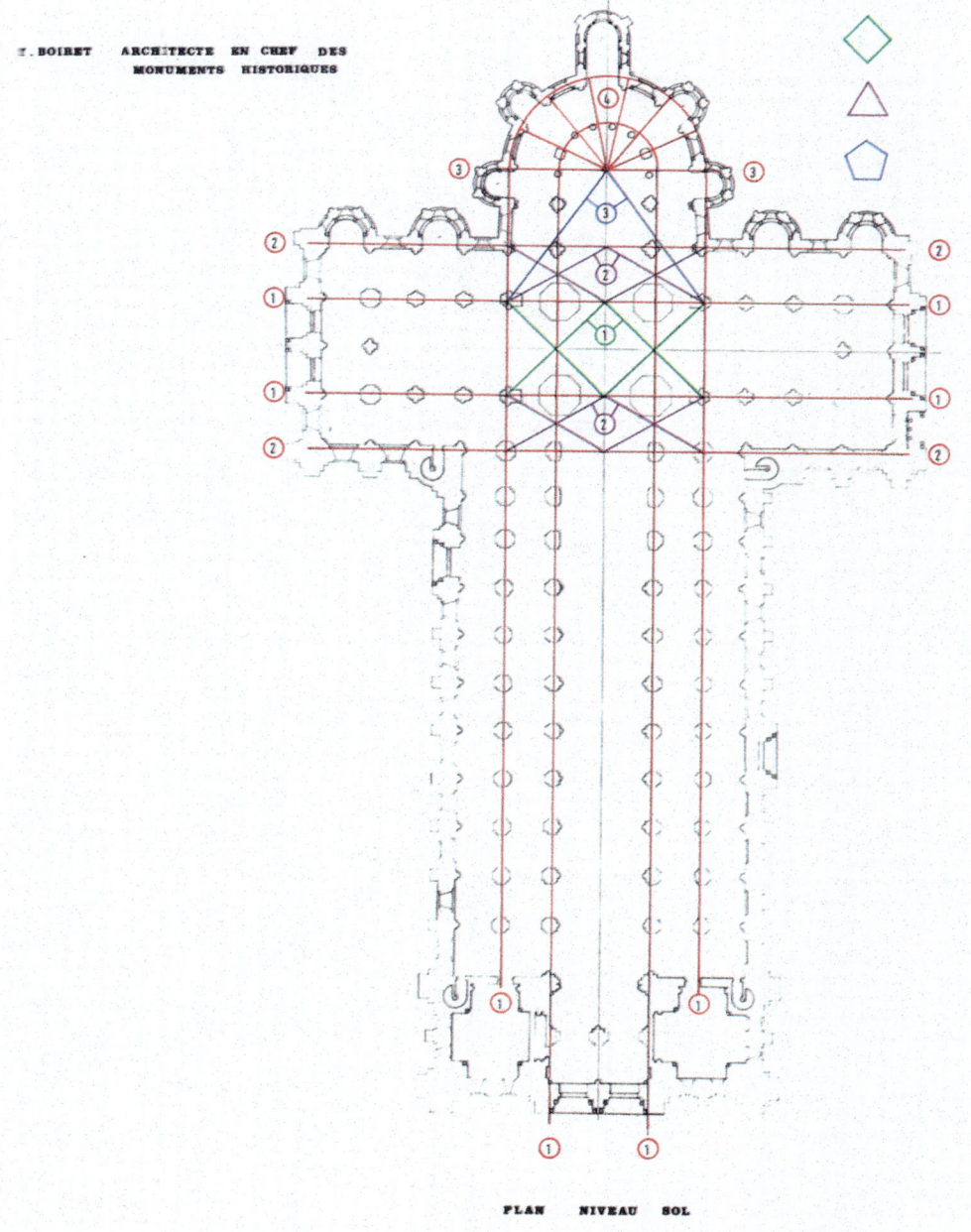

PLAN   NIVEAU   SOL

Plate 85: St Sernin, Toulouse, after Viollet-le-Duc and Boiret: setting-out, steps 1-4.

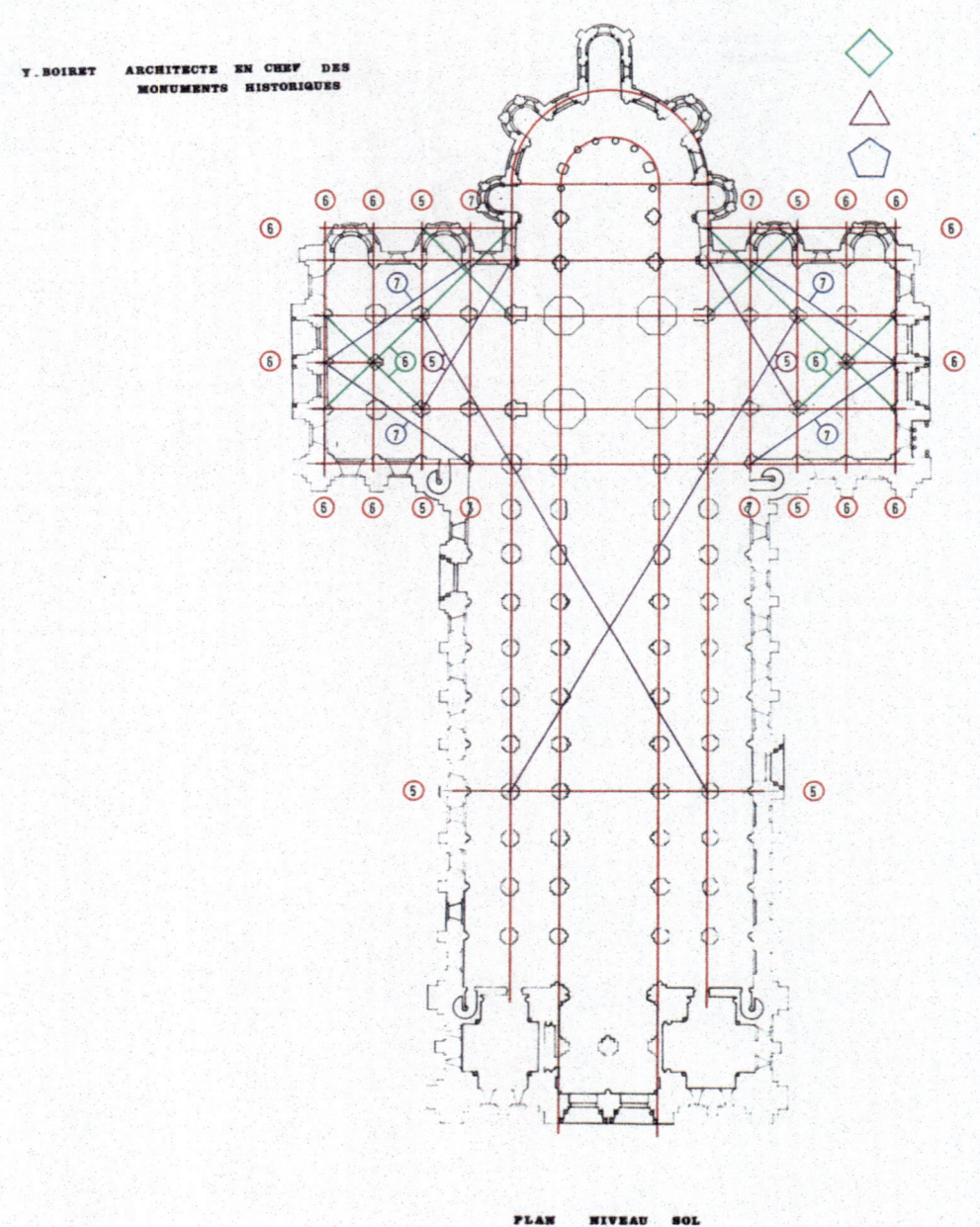

PLAN NIVEAU SOL

Plate 86: St Sernin, Toulouse: setting-out, steps 5-7.

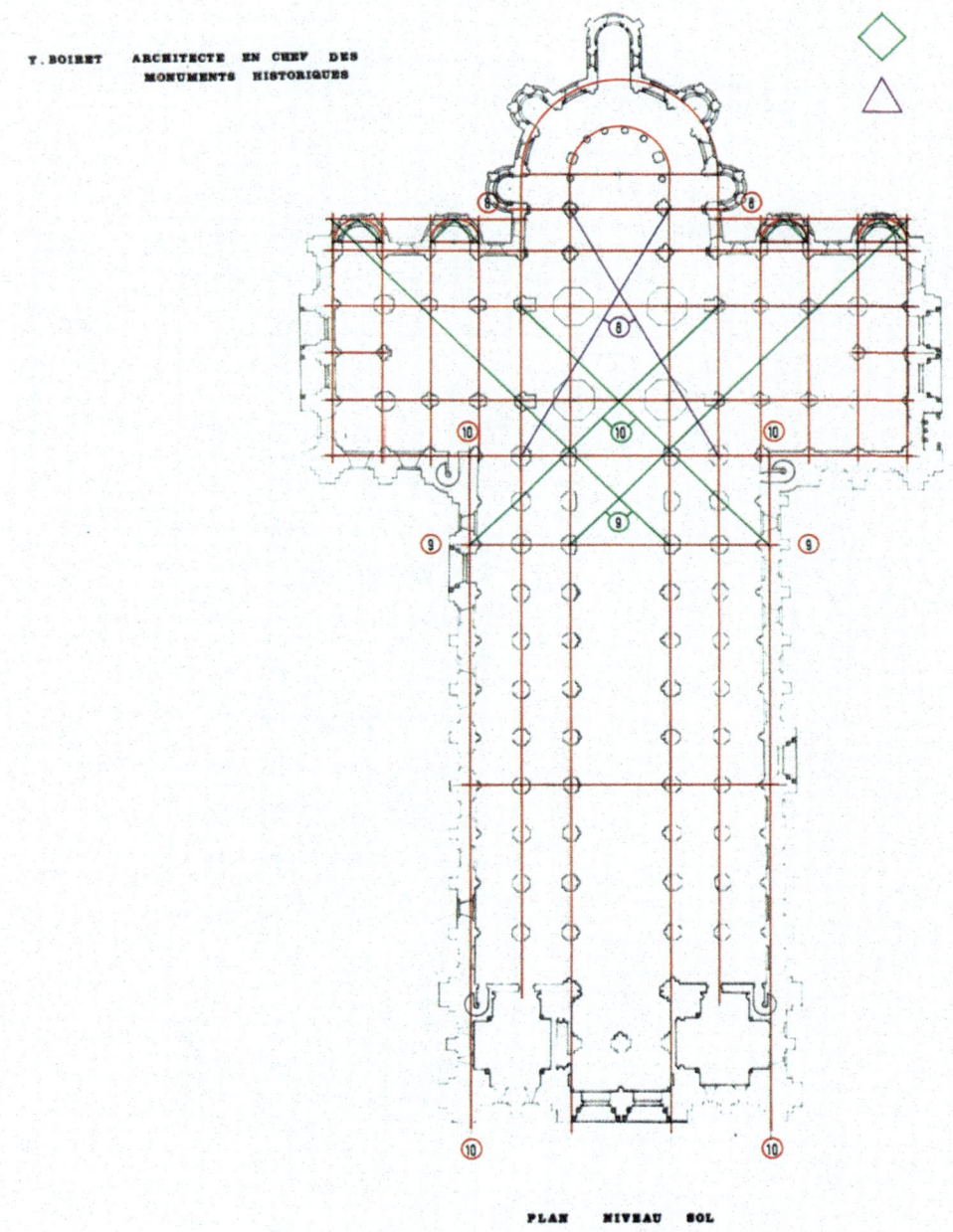

PLAN   NIVEAU   SOL

Plate 87: St Sernin, Toulouse: setting-out, steps 8-10.

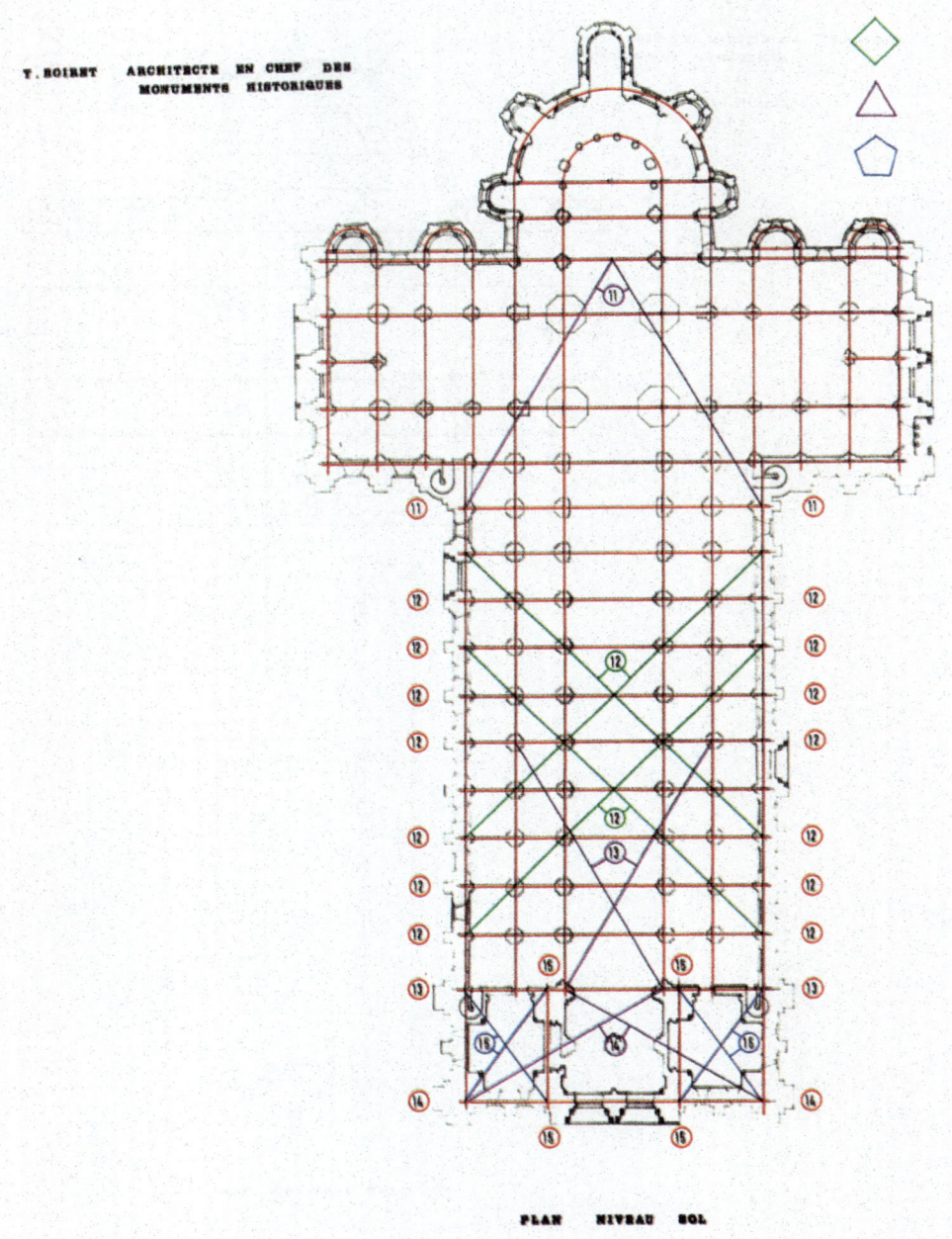

Plate 88: St Sernin, Toulouse: setting-out, steps 11-15.

Plate 89: St Sernin, Toulouse: all alignments.

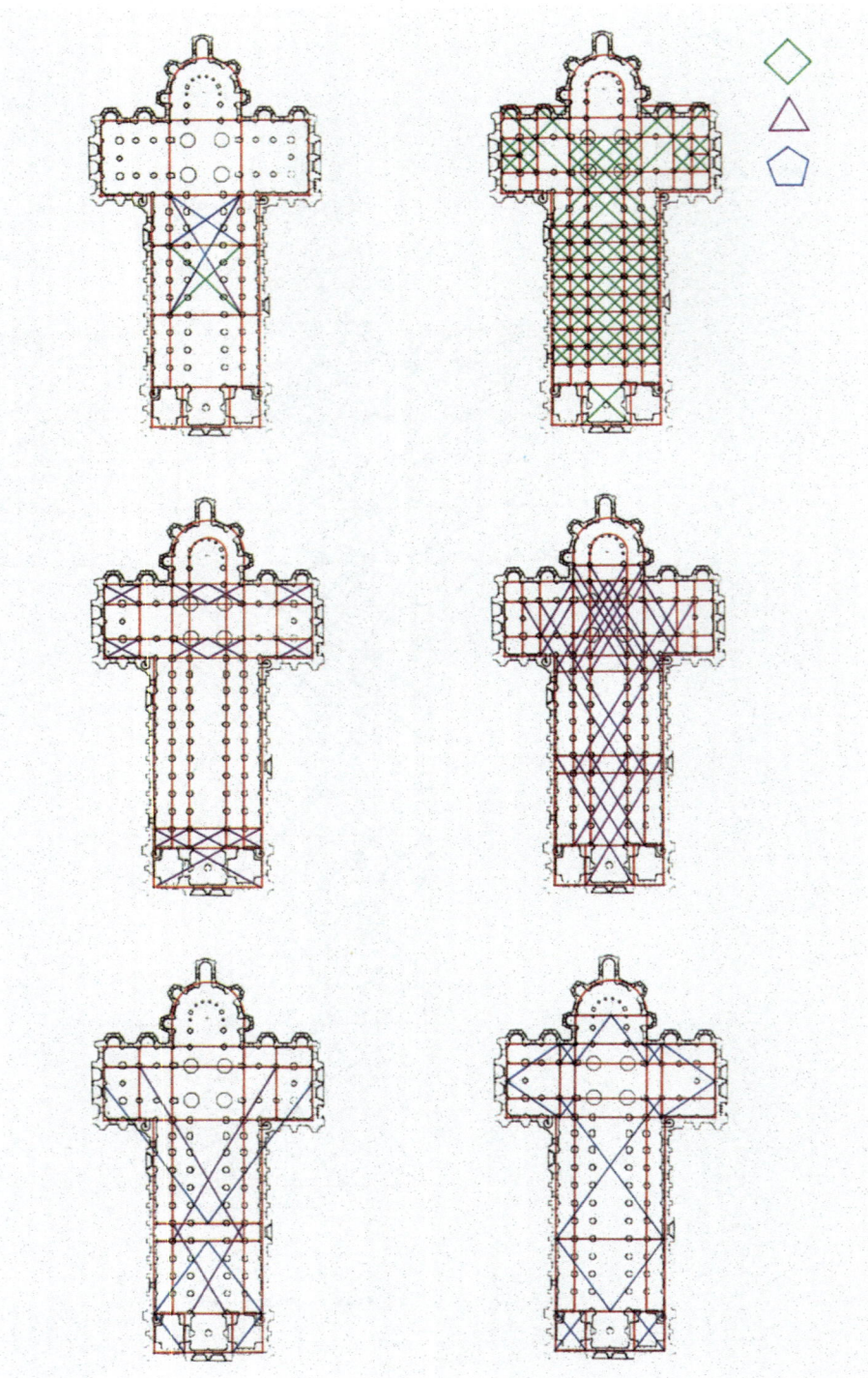

Plate 90: St Sernin, Toulouse: analysis of alignments.

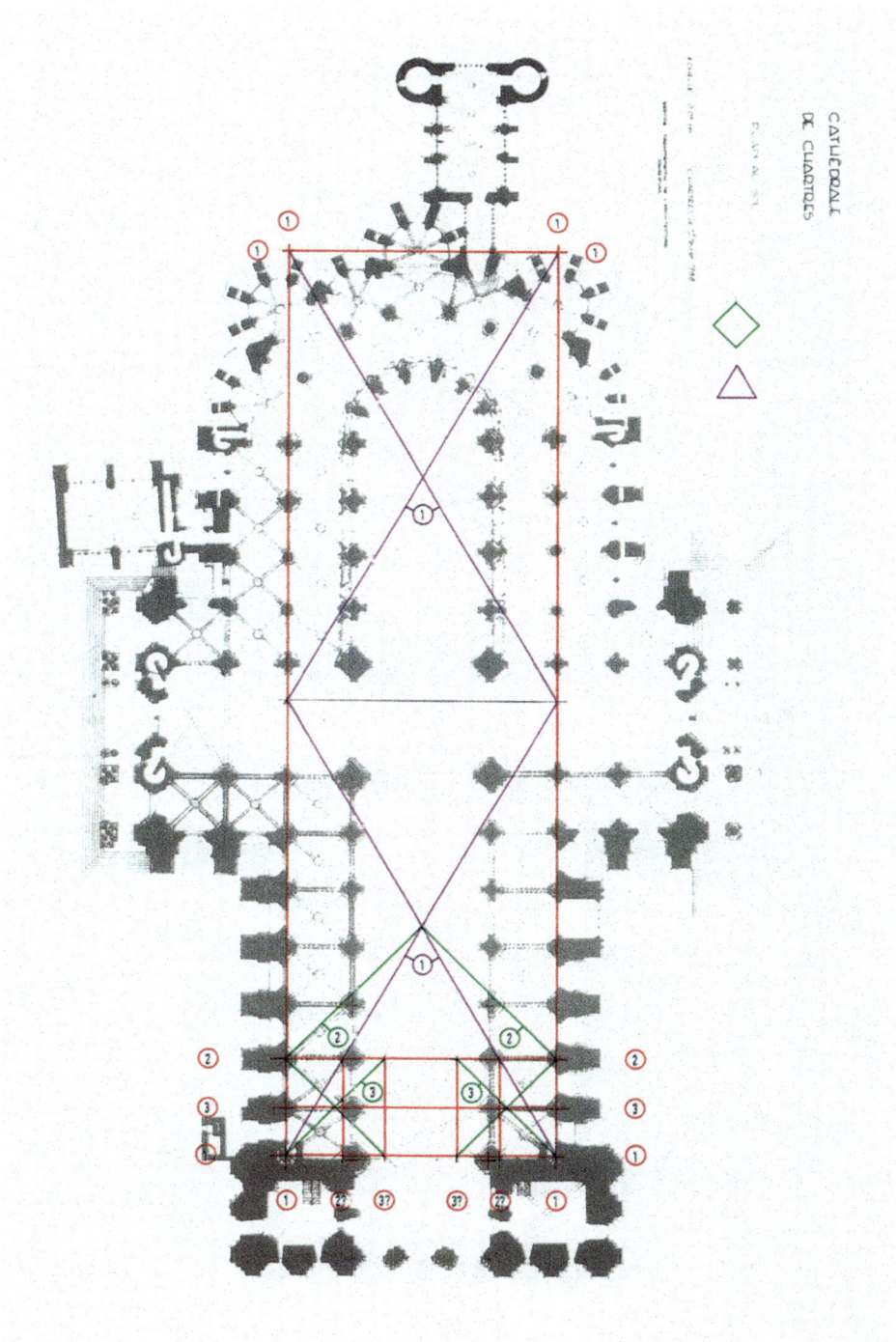

Plate 91: Chartres Cathedral, Fulbert's layout, after Serv. Dept. Arch. d'Eure–et–Loir:
setting-out, steps 1-3.

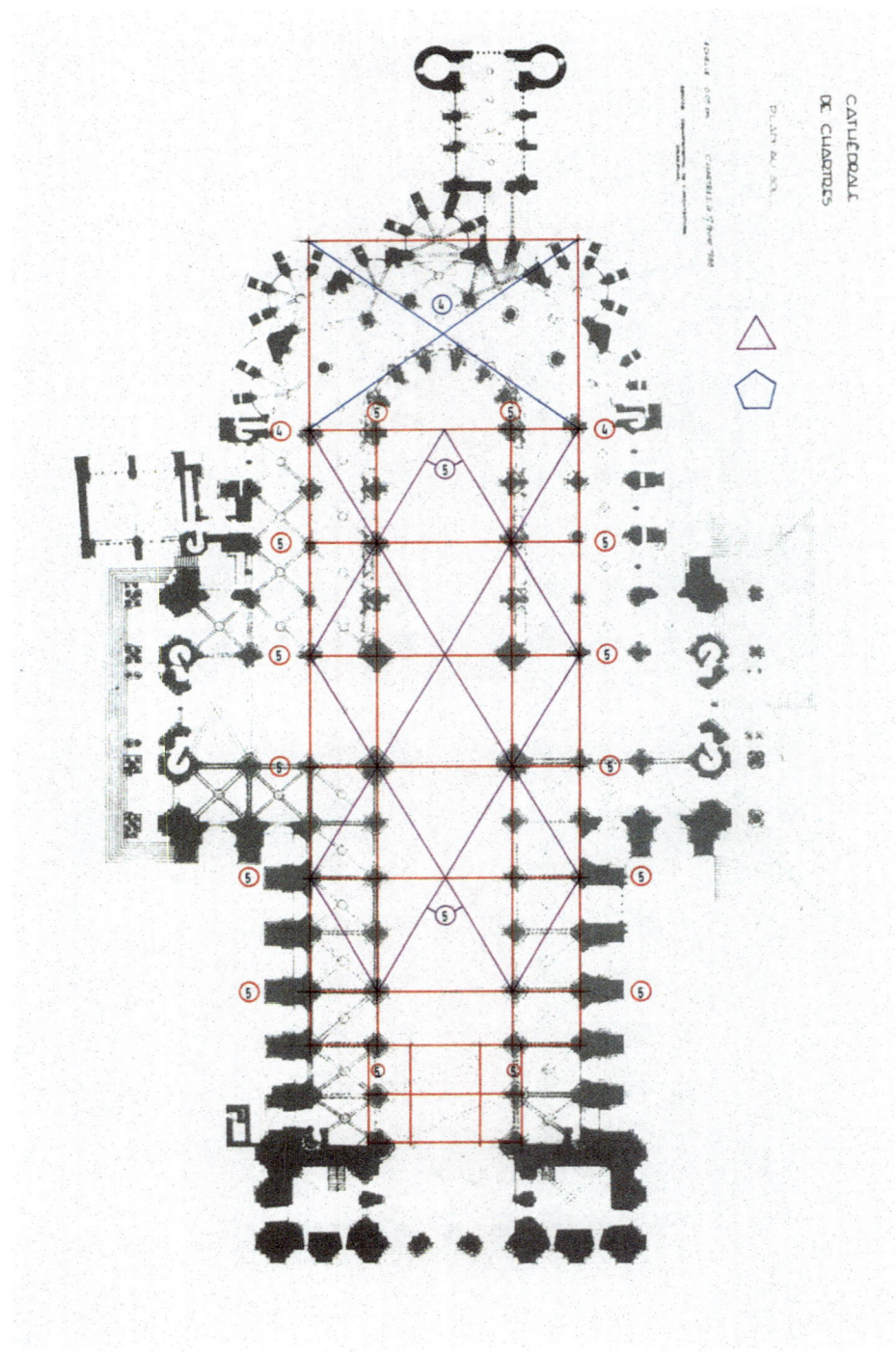

Plate 92: Chartres Cathedral, Fulbert's layout: setting-out, steps 4, 5.

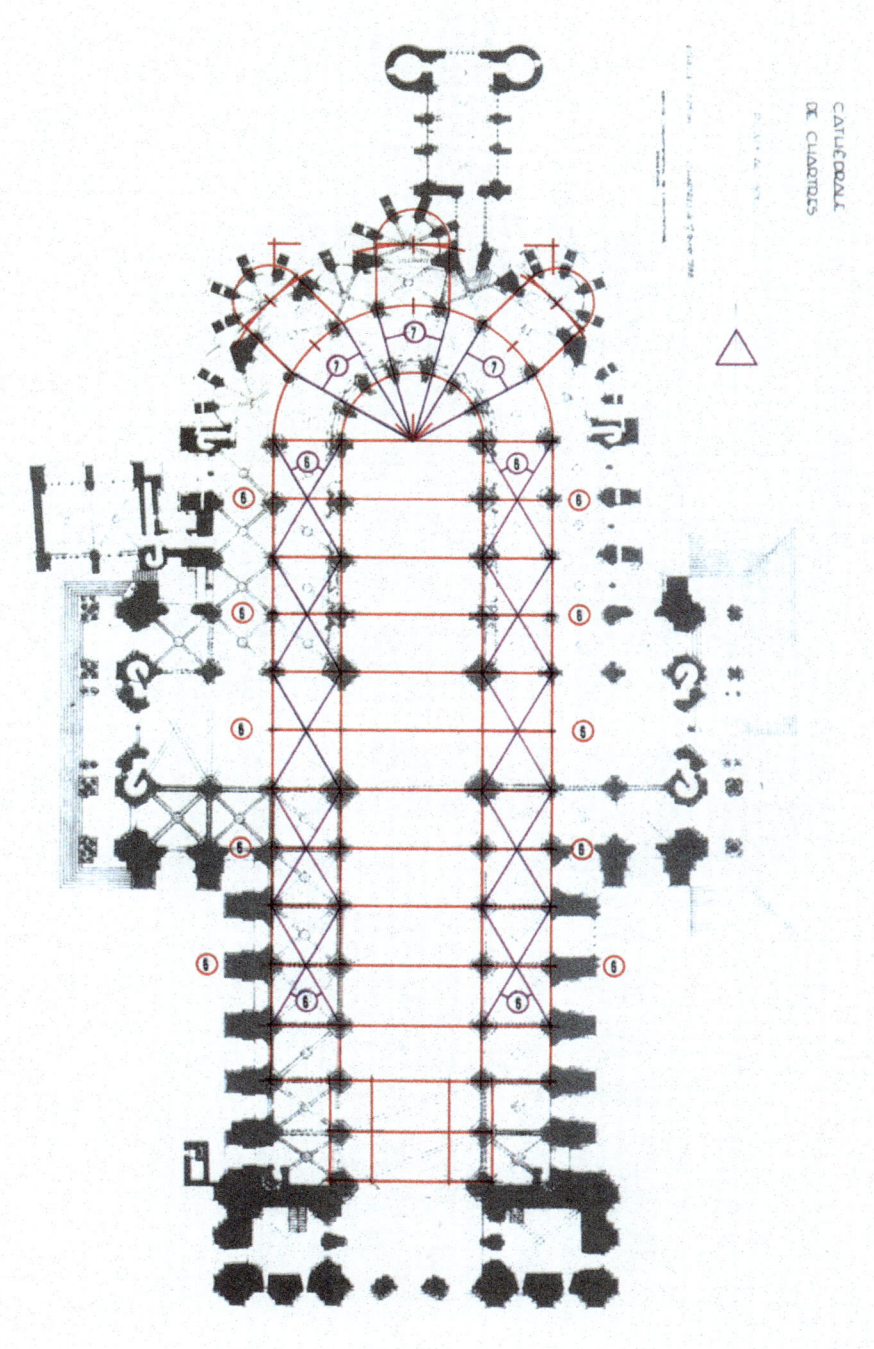

Plate 93: Chartres Cathedral, Fulbert's layout: setting-out, steps 6, 7.

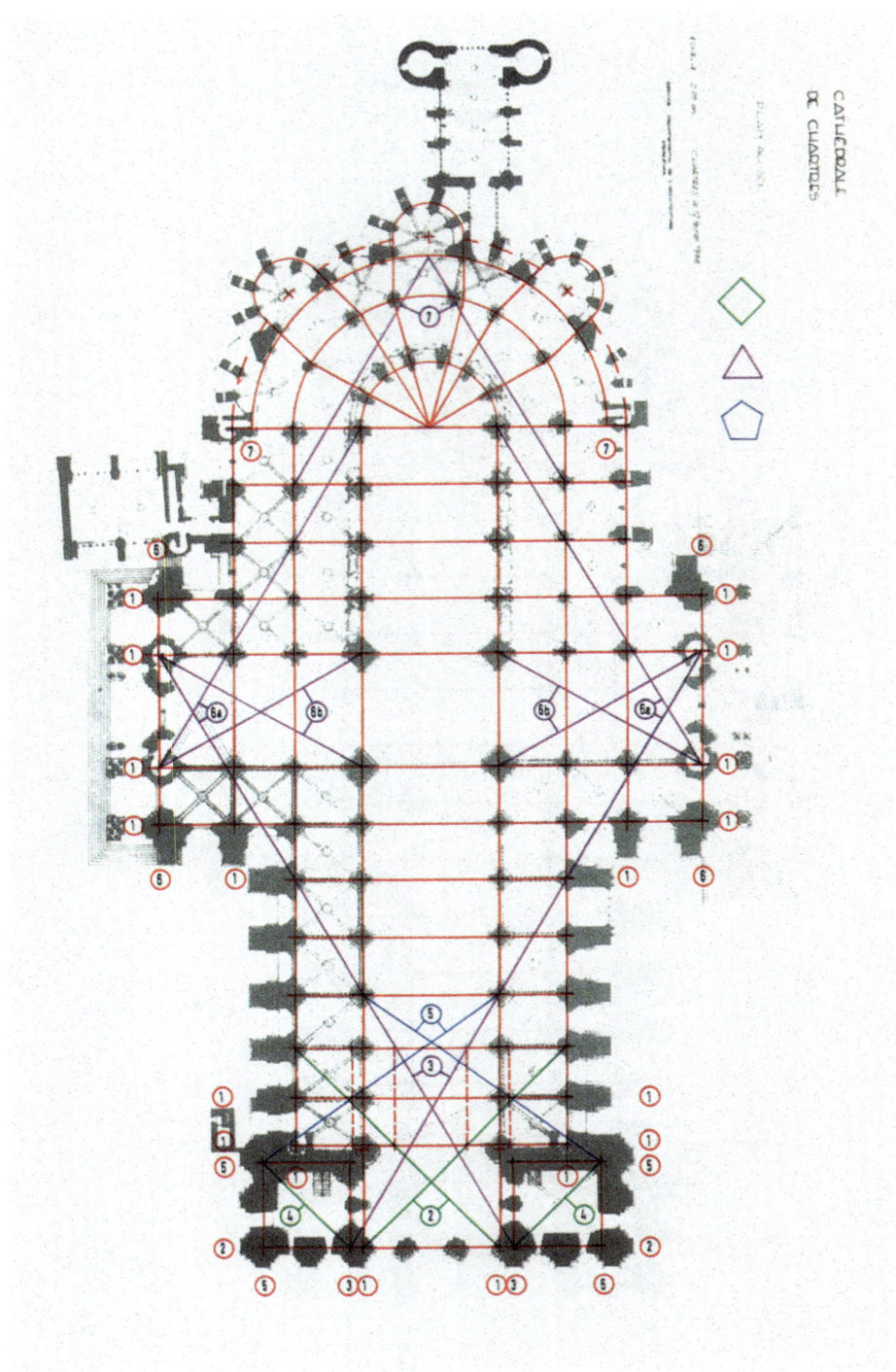

Plate 94: Chartres Cathedral, Gothic layout: setting-out, steps 1-7.

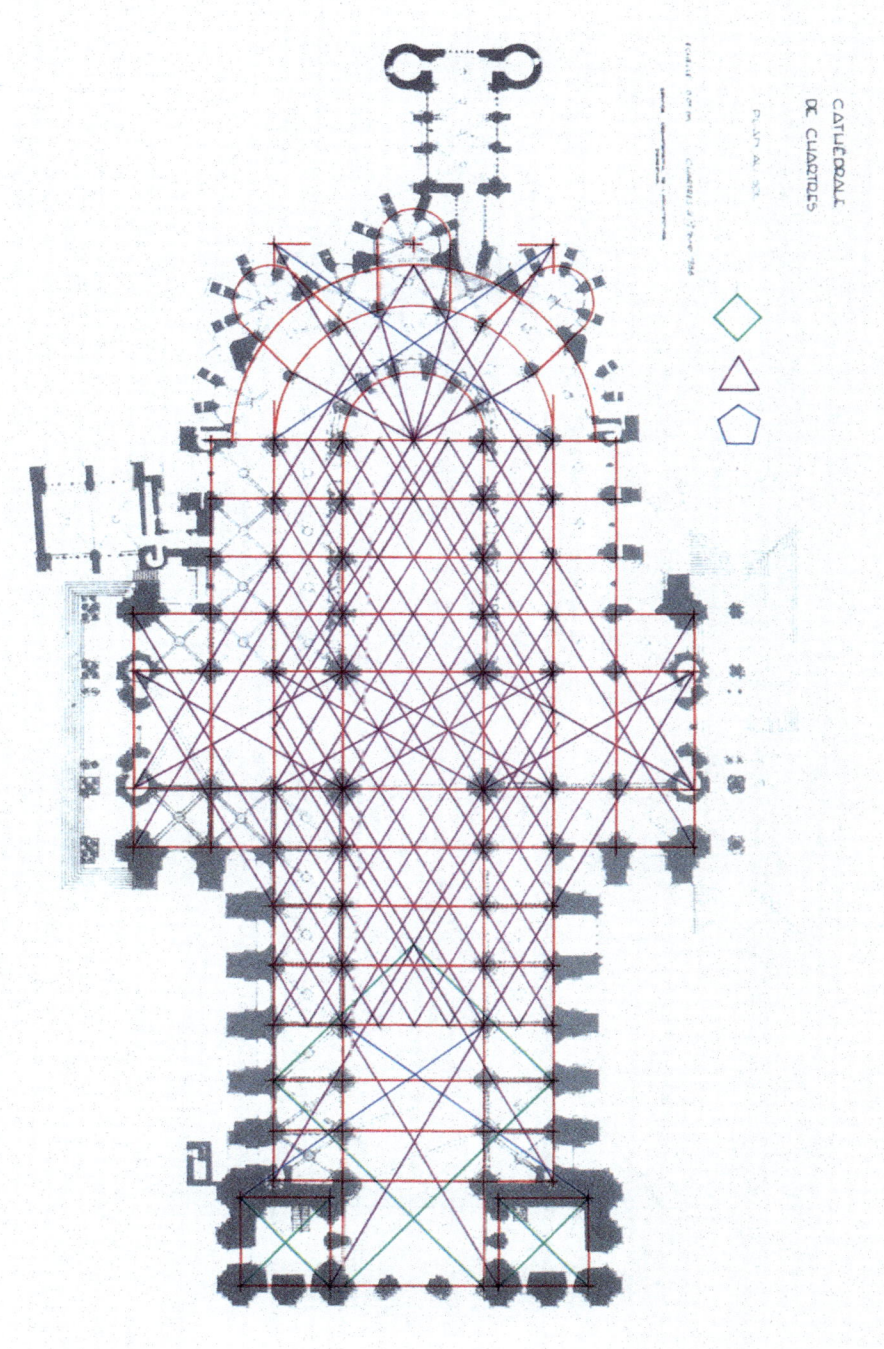

Plate 95: Chartres Cathedral: all alignments.

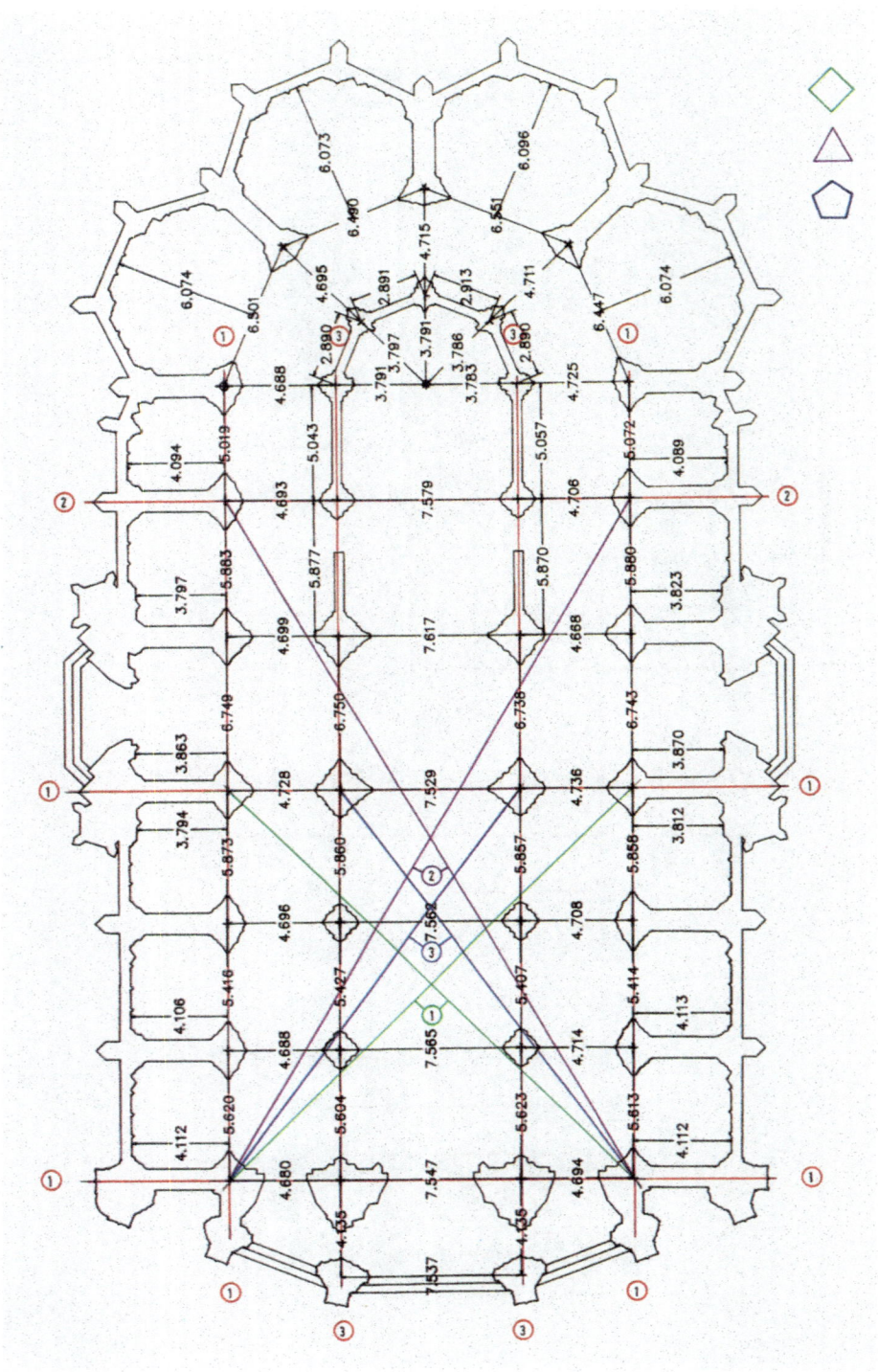

Plate 96: St Maclou, Rouen, after Neagley: setting-out, steps 1-3.

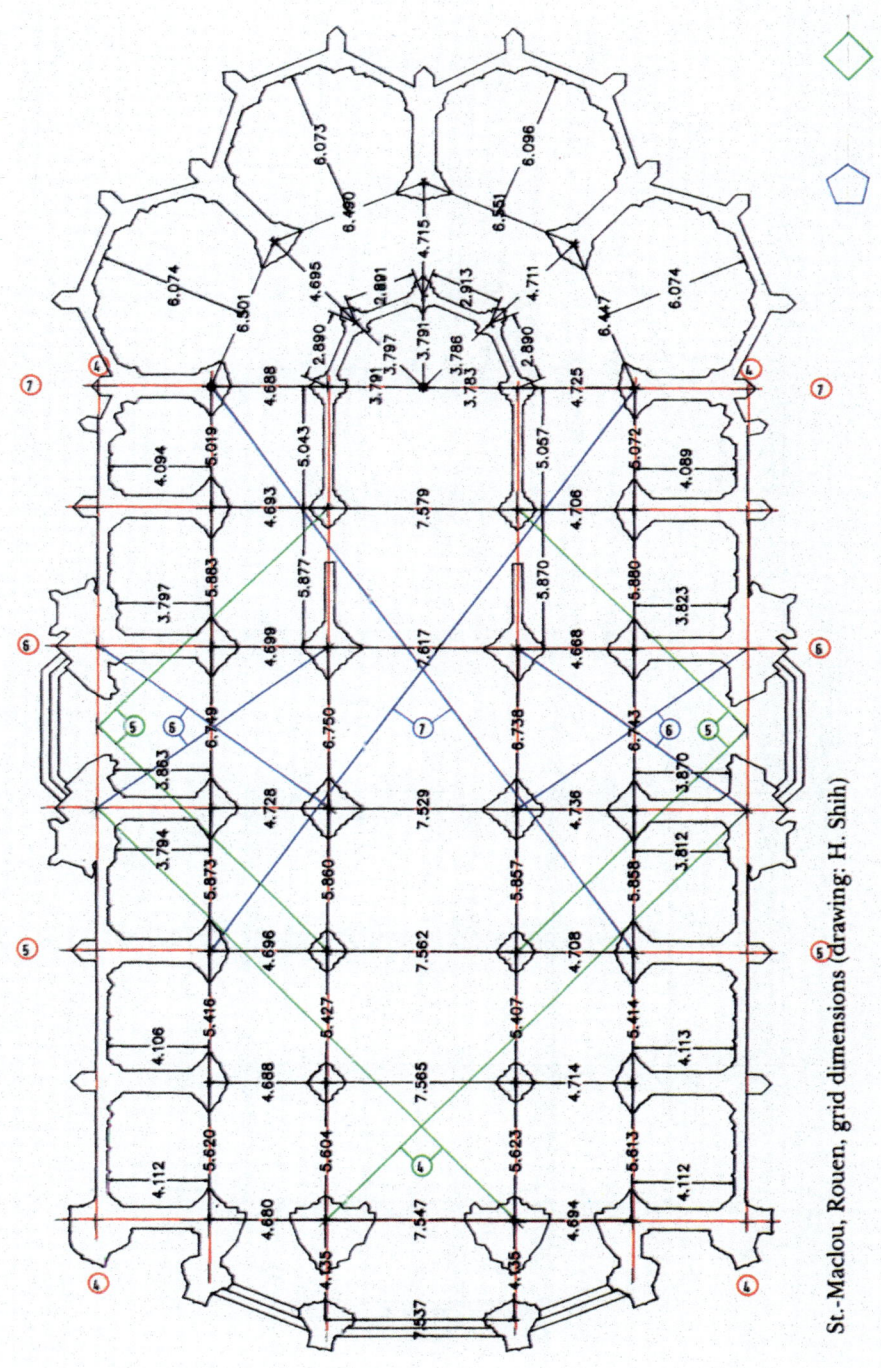

St.-Maclou, Rouen, grid dimensions (drawing: H. Shih)

Plate 97: St Maclou, Rouen: setting-out, steps 4-7.

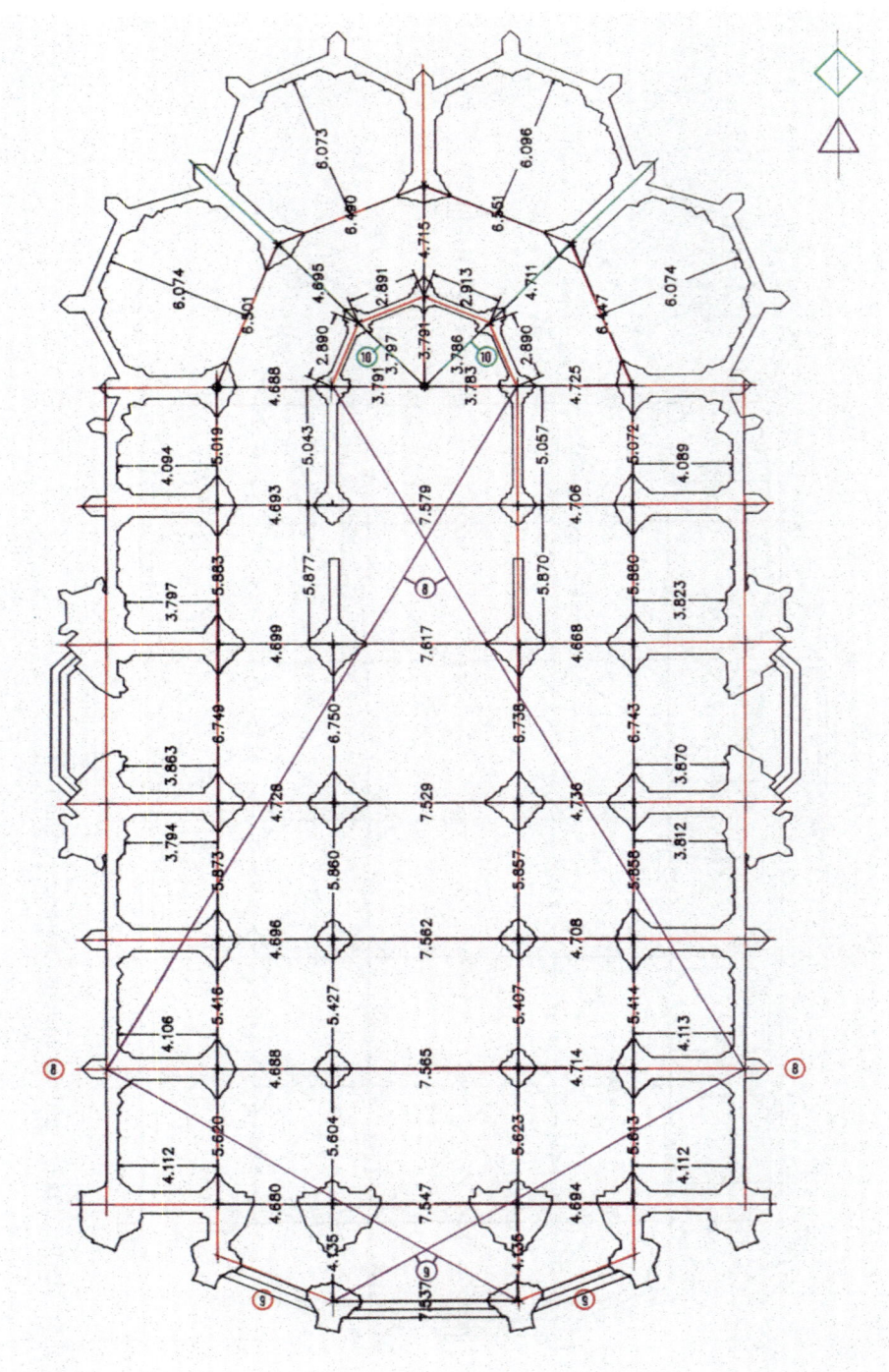

Plate 98: St Maclou, Rouen: setting-out, steps 8-10.

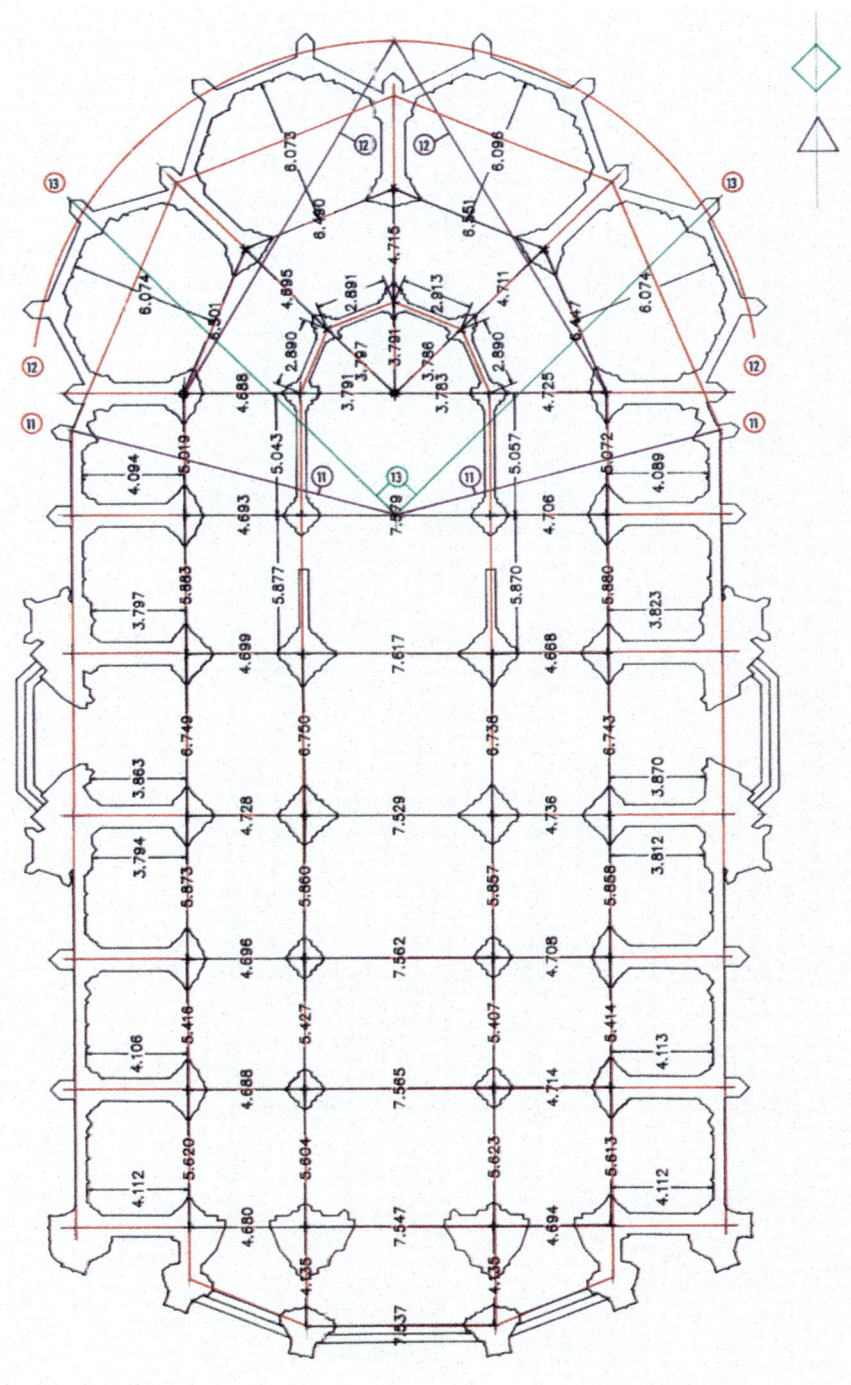

Plate 99: St Maclou, Rouen: setting-out, steps 11-13.

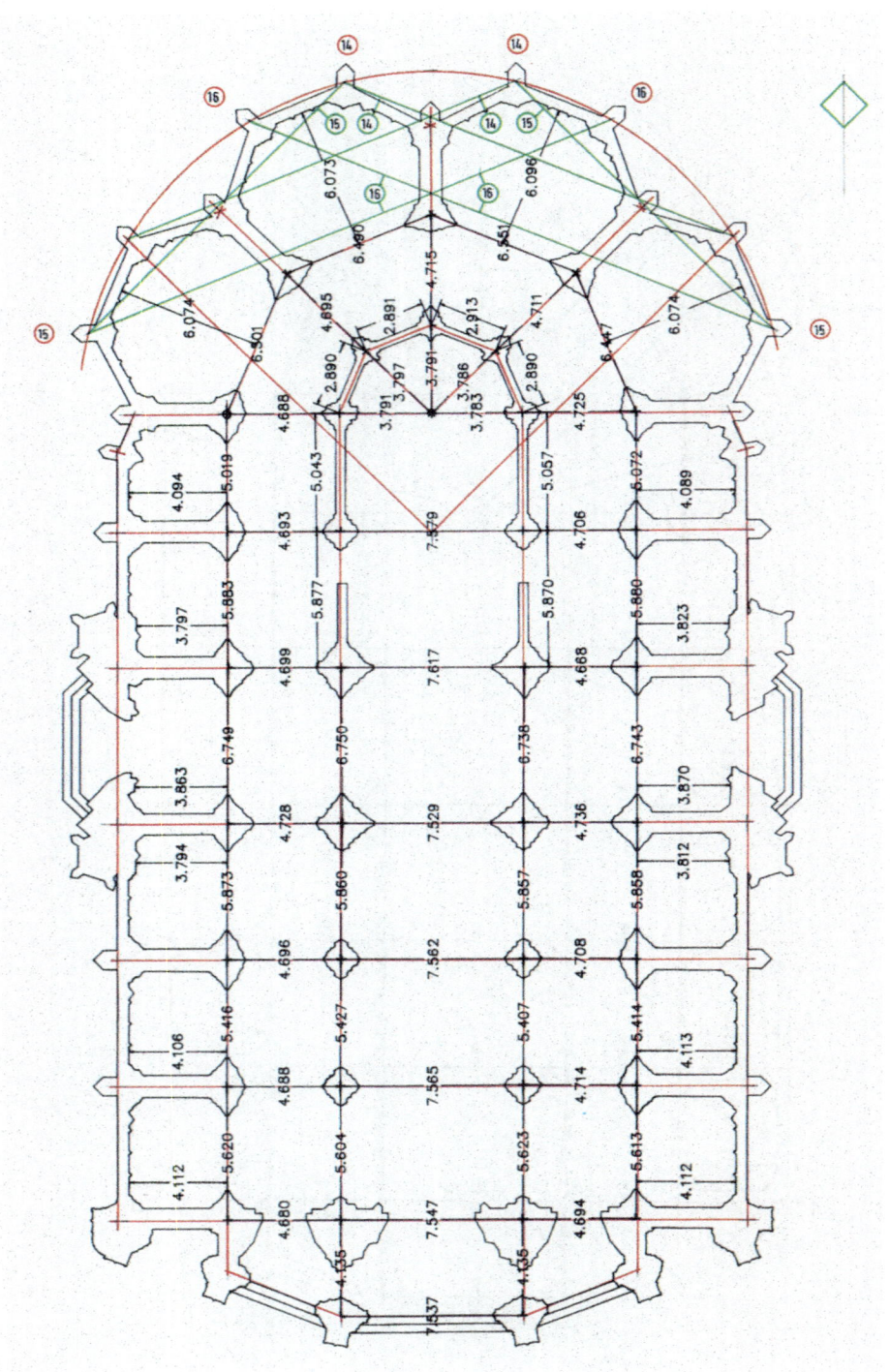

Plate 100: St Maclou, Rouen: setting-out, steps 14-16.

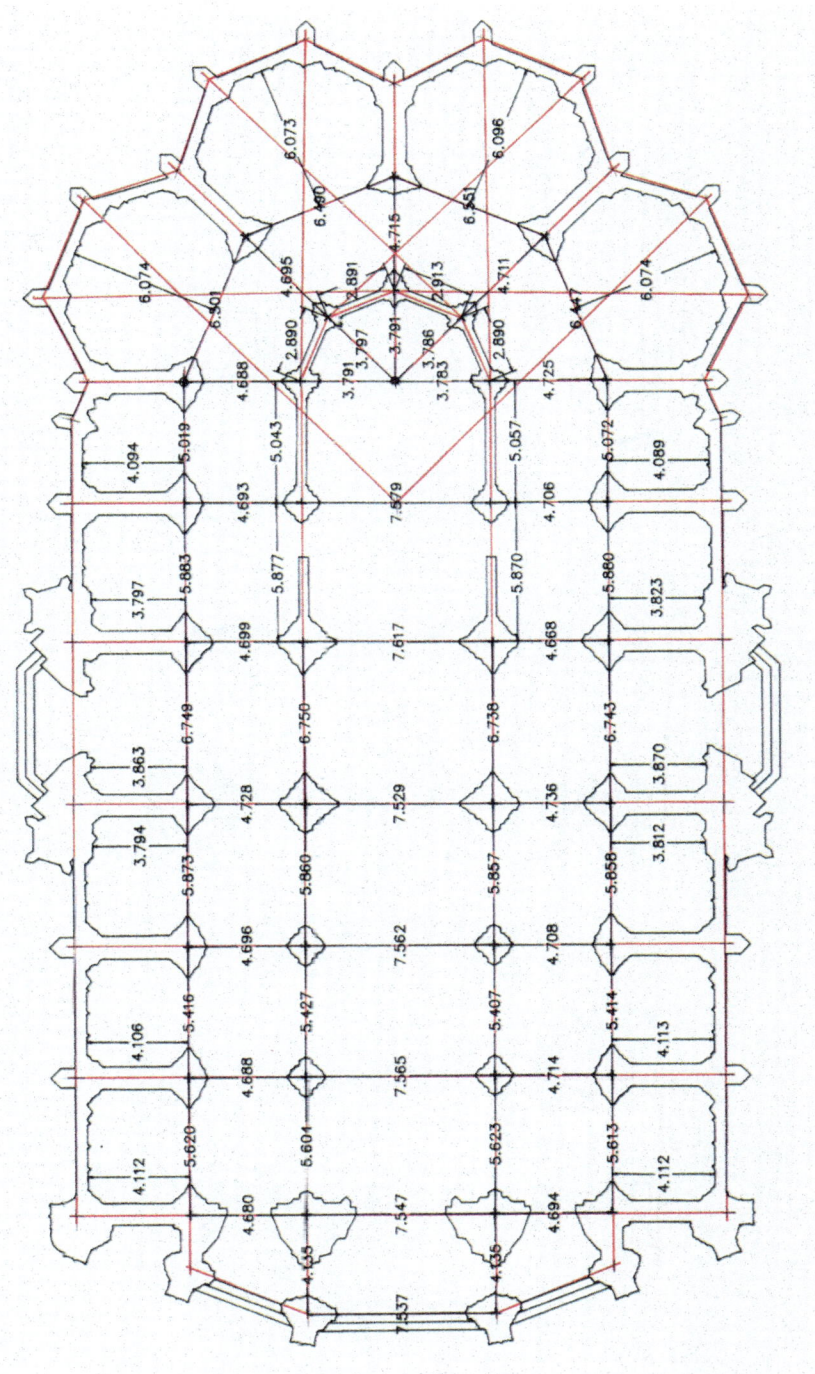

Plate 101: St Maclou, Rouen: setting-out, final.

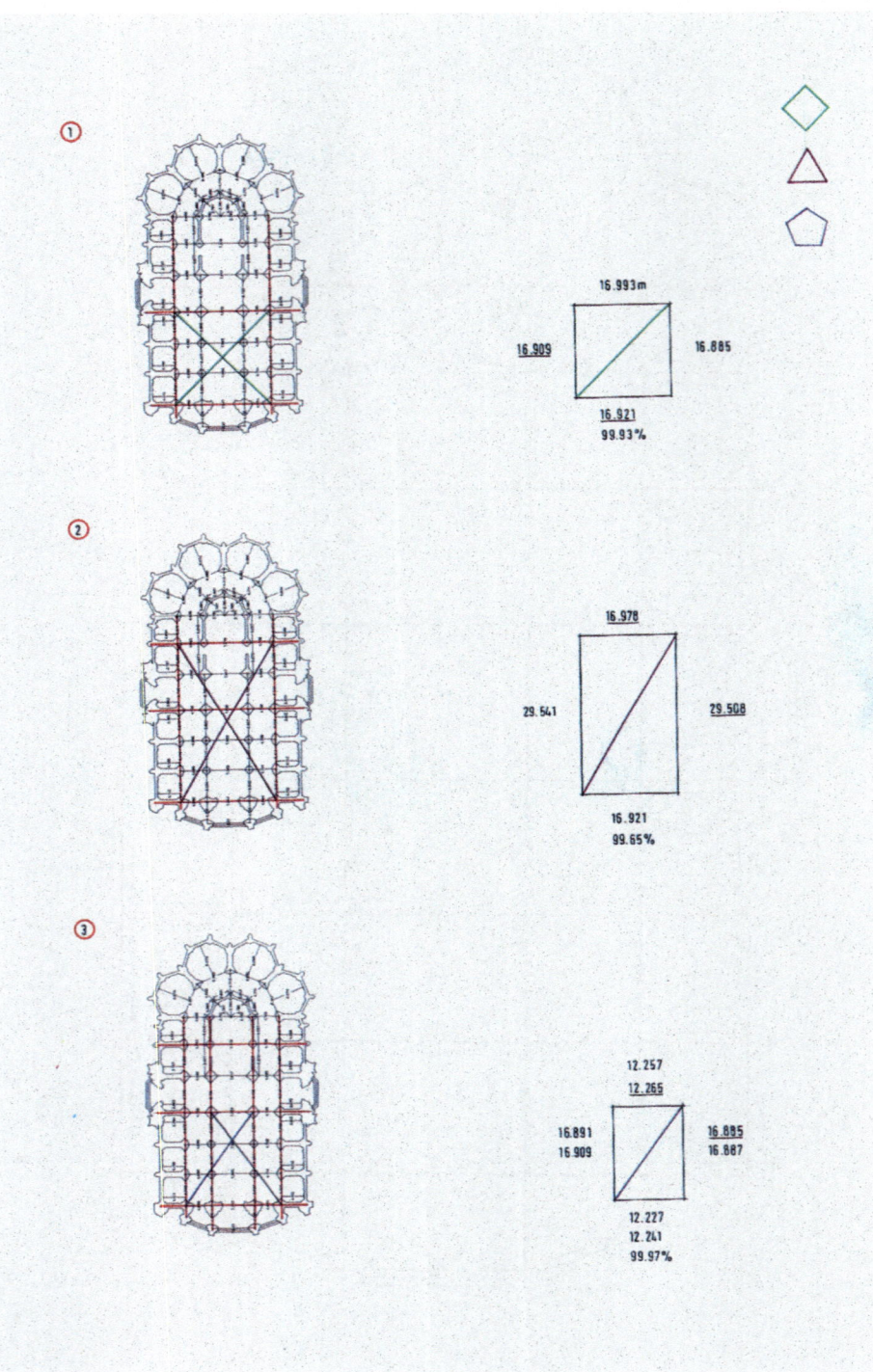

Plate 102: St Maclou, Rouen: mathematical proof, steps 1-3.

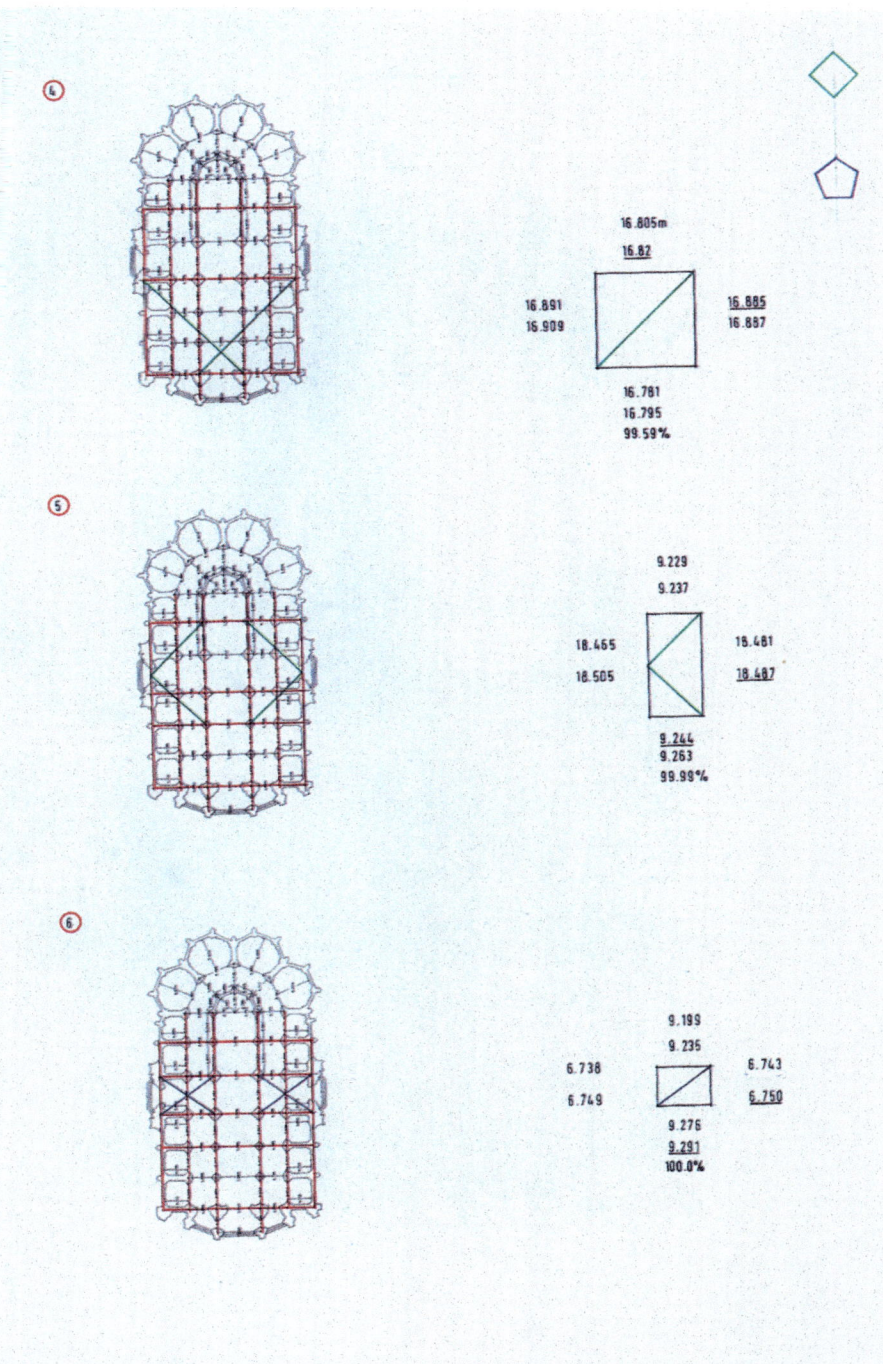

Plate 103: St Maclou, Rouen: mathematical proof, steps 4-6.

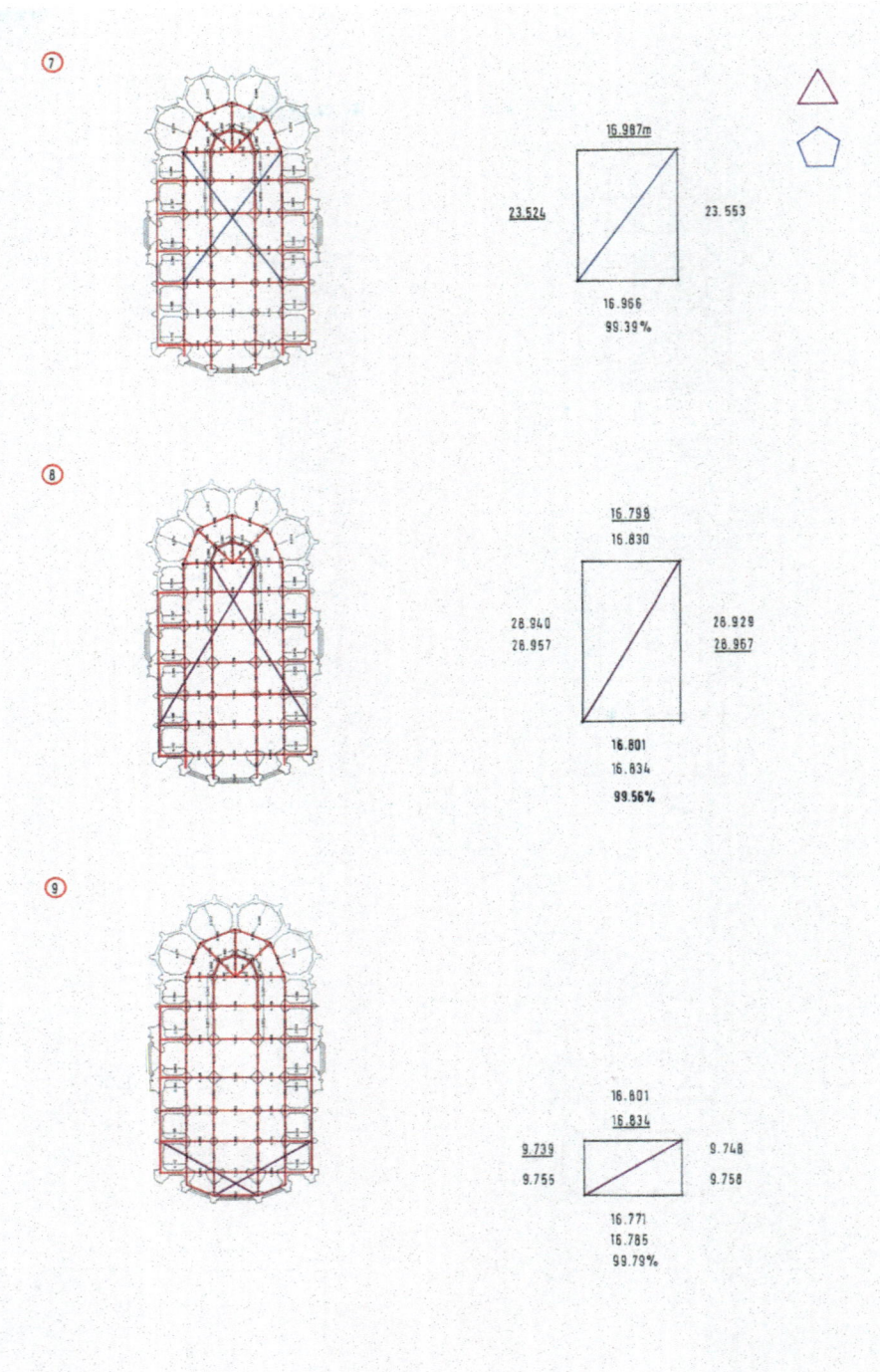

Plate 104: St Maclou, Rouen: mathematical proof, steps 7-9.

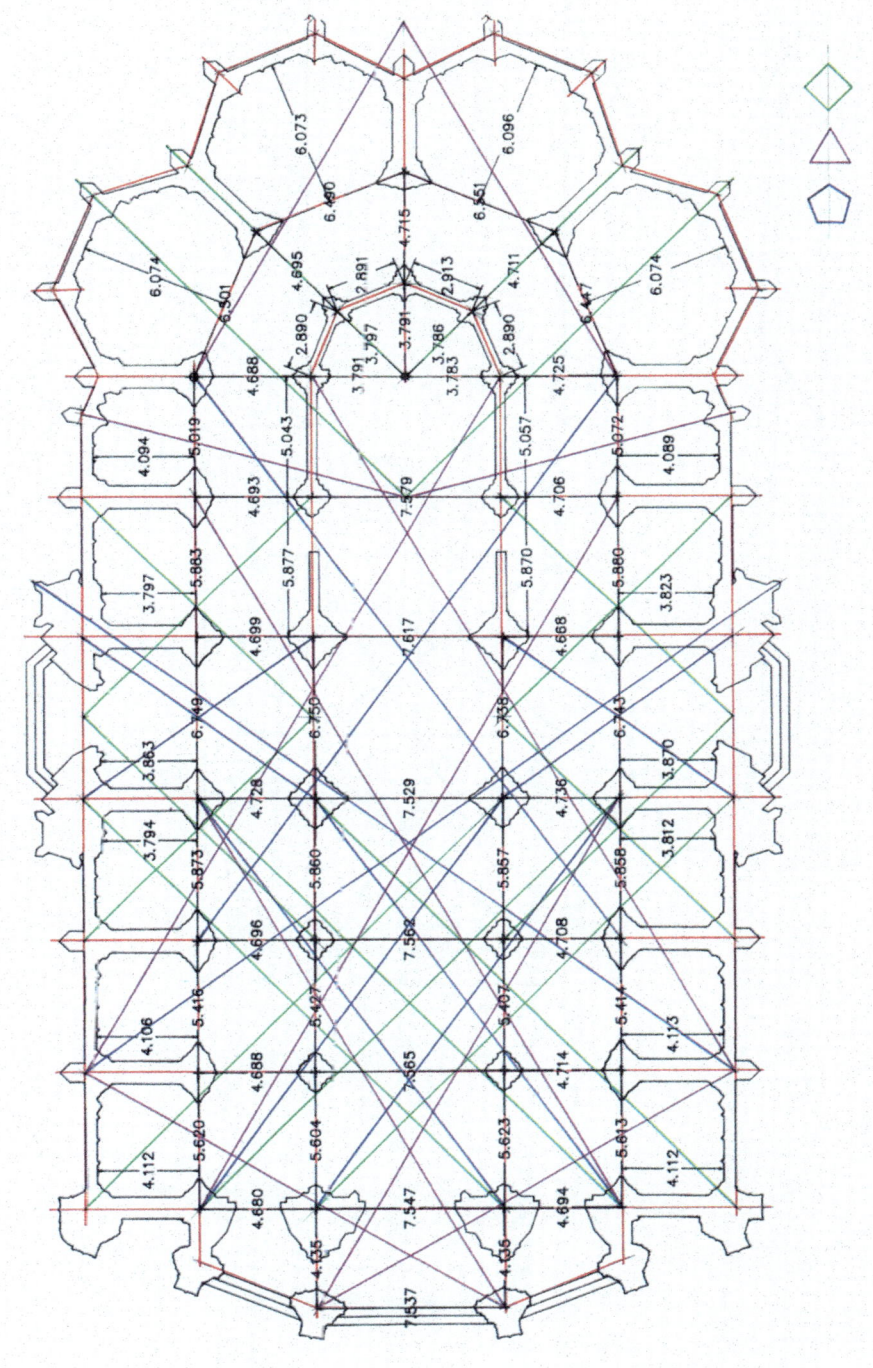

Plate 105: St Maclou, Rouen: all alignments.

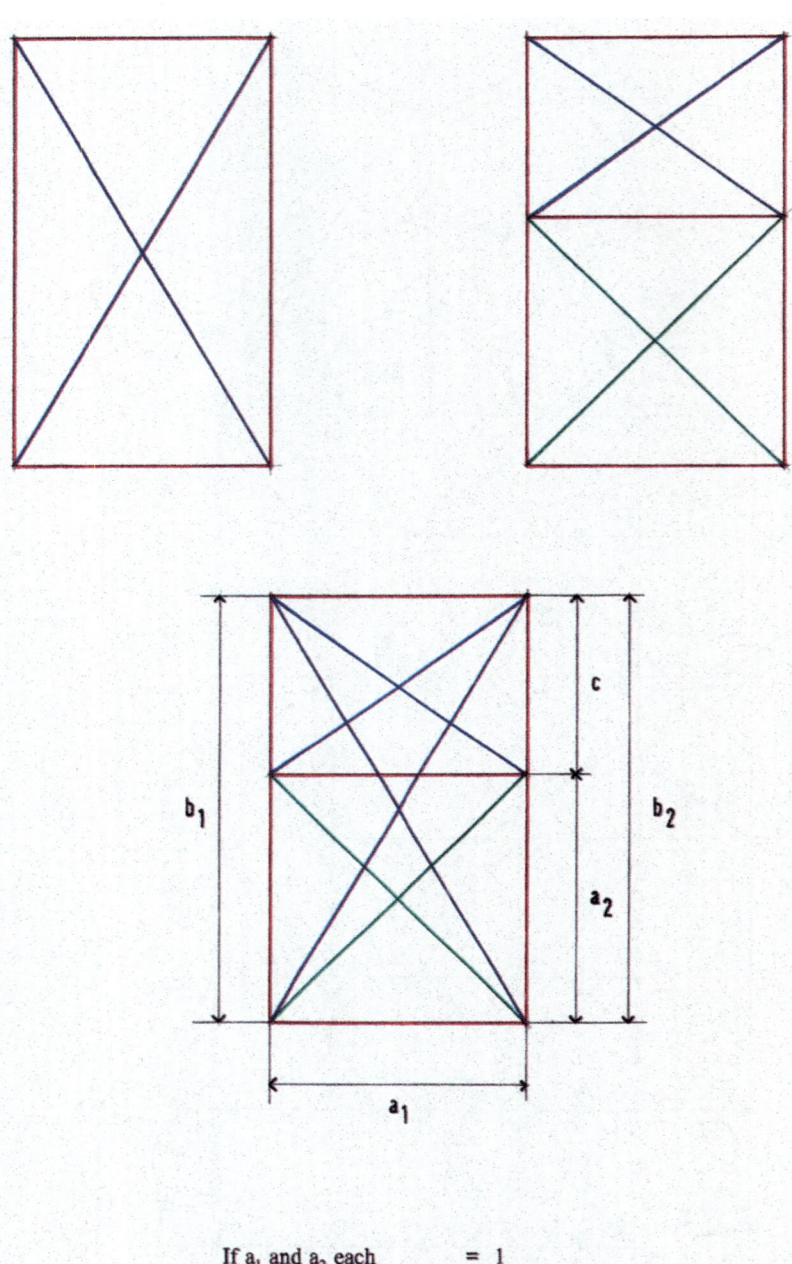

If a_1 and a_2 each   = 1
b_1 = $1 \times \sqrt{3}$ = 1.732
c = $1 \times \tan 36°$ = 0.726
b_2 = $1 + 0.726$ = 1.726

1.726 : 1.732   = 99.65%

Plate 106: 60° rectangle containing square and 36° rectangle.

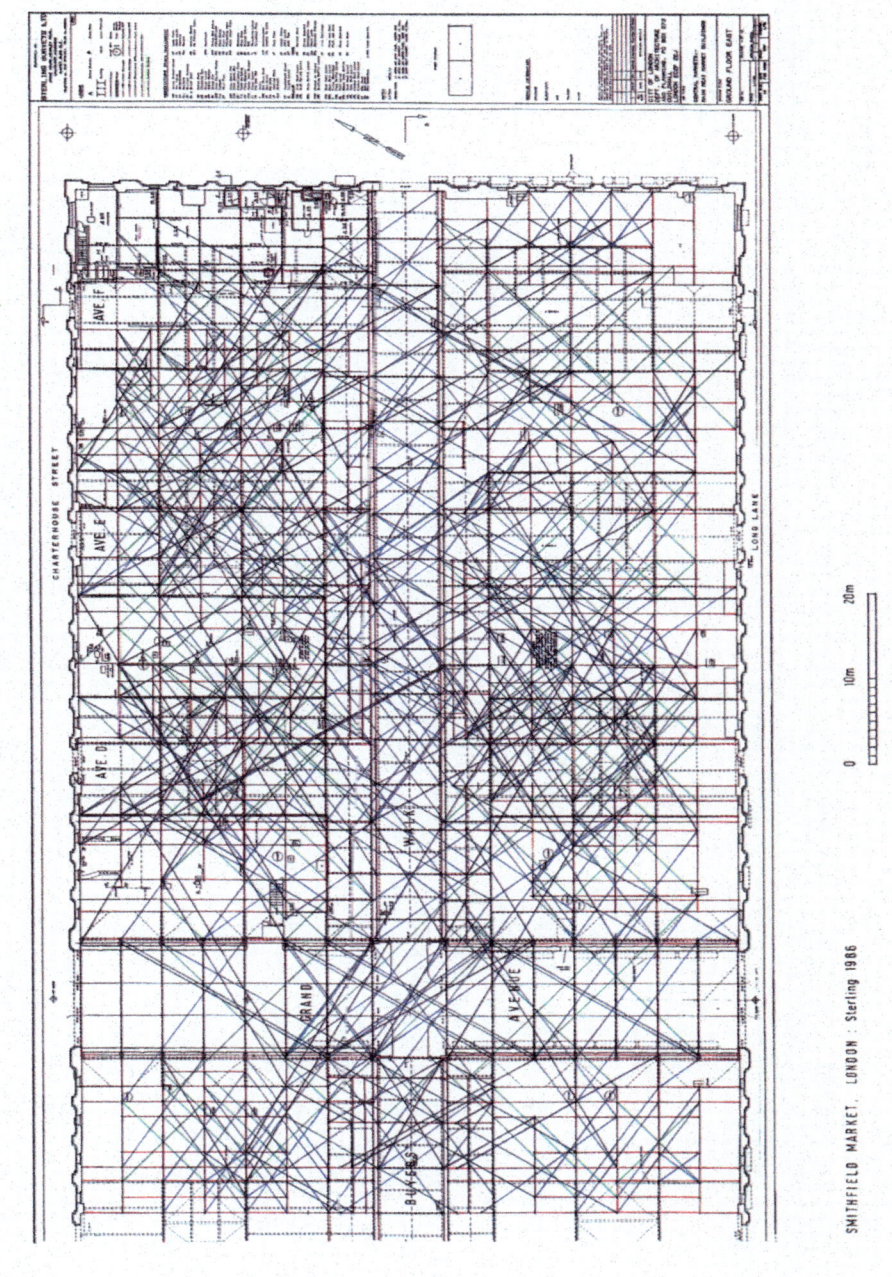

Plate 107: Smithfield Market, London, part plan after Sterling: attempted alignments.

Corrigenda

Unrevised plans were inadvertently printed on pages 302 (fig. 26), 303 (fig. 27) and 306 (fig. 28). The correct plans, incorporating the revisions, are now printed on the following three pages. These, together with the corrections listed below, will be included in any subsequent printing. The publishers regret these errors.

p. 8   line 5: omit reference to fig. 14
       fig. 1b should read 1c; fig. 1c should read 1d; fig. 1d should read 1e.
p. 177 omit reference to fig. 14.
p. 215 line 14 from bottom: 99.5% should read 99.95%.
       line 13 from bottom: (6) should read (9).
p 228 line 15 from bottom: (18) should read (15).
p 230 line 9: omit reference to Bernay.
p 233 line 8: should read . . . (4) at Ely and at Norwich.
p 246 line 19 from bottom: omit reference to Hildesheim.
p 285 note 16: UV = UT × √3 should read EF = DE × √3.
p 289 line 10 from bottom: 99.11% should read 98.75%; 99.93% should read 99.95%.
p. 291 pl. 18 should read pl. 20.
p. 301 bottom line: 388.75 cm should read 390.37 cm.